The Corning Museum of Glass
Catalog Series

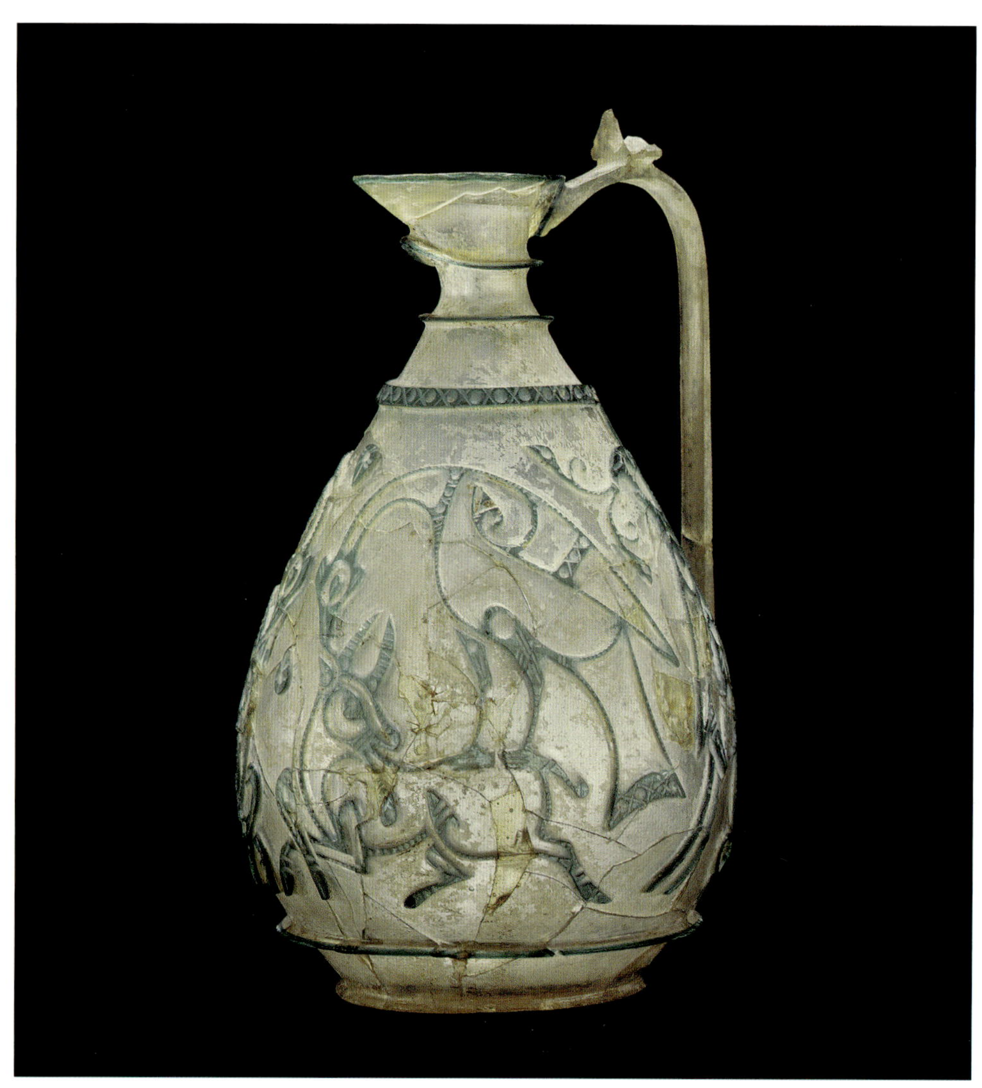

522. *The Corning Ewer, blown, cased; relief-cut, drilled; handle applied. Western Asia or Egypt, about 1000. H. 16 cm, D. (max.) 9.3 cm (85.1.1). Acquired with funds from the Clara S. Peck Endowment.*

Islamic Glass

in The Corning Museum of Glass

Volume One

Objects with Scratch-Engraved and Wheel-Cut Ornament

DAVID WHITEHOUSE

THE CORNING MUSEUM OF GLASS
CORNING, NEW YORK

In association with Hudson Hills Press, Manchester and New York

EDITOR: Richard W. Price
DESIGN AND TYPOGRAPHY: Jacolyn S. Saunders
PHOTOGRAPHY: Nicholas L. Williams, Andrew M. Fortune,
Allison S. Lavine, and Martin J. Pierce
DRAWINGS: Kim Kelley Wagner and Jill Thomas-Clark
PROOFREADER: Mary B. Chervenak
REFERENCE LIBRARIAN: Gail P. Bardhan
REGISTRARS: Warren L. Bunn II, Brandy L. Harold,
Christy L. Cook, and Melissa J. White

Published by The Corning Museum of Glass
in association with Hudson Hills Press LLC
3556 Main Street, Manchester, Vermont 05254

Publisher and Executive Director: Leslie Pell van Breen
Founding Publisher: Paul Anbinder

Distributed in the United States, its territories and possessions, and Canada by National Book Network Inc. Distributed outside North America by Antique Collectors' Club Ltd.

ISBN13: 978-0-87290-175-9 (Museum)
978-1-55595-355-3 (Trade)
Library of Congress Control Number 2009922841

Contents

Foreword

This is the first volume of a projected three-part series devoted to the early Islamic glass in The Corning Museum of Glass. The second and third volumes are intended to describe the Museum's undecorated, pressed, mold-blown, stained, and gilded and enameled objects. The present volume contains descriptions of 595 objects and fragments made (with two possible exceptions, **585** and **586**) in the Islamic world between the eighth and 11th centuries A.D.

The Museum's collection of scratch-engraved and wheel-cut early Islamic glass is both rich and varied. Its strength is derived from several sources. Between 1950 and 1979, the Museum steadily acquired objects in the marketplace, and on a modest scale it continues to do so. In 1953, for example, it acquired 91 small Roman and Islamic vessels from Maurice Nahman of Cairo, Egypt, which (it is reasonable to suppose) were probably found in Egypt; 27 of these objects appear in this volume. The Museum's holdings of early Islamic glass were enriched in a spectacular manner by a series of acquisitions from the collection of Ray Winfield Smith, beginning in 1959. Mr. Smith was deeply interested in the early history of glass, and he was an avid collector of potentially informative fragments as well as display pieces (Anon. 1982). The Museum's decision to acquire literally hundreds of Smith's fragments in addition to many of his "museum-quality" objects preserved a remarkable collection of study material. These holdings were expanded in 1976 when Carl Berkowitz and Derek Content donated further fragments from the Smith Collection. A total of 394 pieces from the collection (including two objects [**494** and **523**] and 79 fragments of cameo glass) are published here, the majority for the first time. Smith's interest in early glass extended to working with Edward V. Sayre of the Brookhaven National Laboratory in a pioneering project to determine the chemical composition of selected objects by spectrographic analysis (Smith 1964).

Another outstanding acquisition consisted of the collection of more than 2,400 glass drinking vessels formed by Jerome Strauss (Perrot 1978). The Museum acquired the entire collection through gifts and a bequest from Mr. Strauss, and gifts from The Ruth Bryan Strauss Memorial Foundation. This volume includes 46 objects from the Strauss Collection.

The scope of the collection, and in particular the large number of fragments, provides an opportunity to try to isolate different styles of ornament. This opportunity is addressed in the Discussion on pages 329–331.

DAVID WHITEHOUSE
Executive Director

ACKNOWLEDGMENTS

Like the Museum's catalogs of Roman and Sasanian glass, this volume includes observations by numerous colleagues, past and present. In particular, it incorporates results of research by former Corning curators Axel von Saldern and Sidney M. Goldstein, and by Robert H. Brill, the Museum's research scientist emeritus. I also wish to acknowledge the assistance of other friends and colleagues who contributed to the text through conversation, correspondence, and publications. They include: Stefano Carboni, who generously provided translations of the Arabic inscriptions on some of the objects published here; Kjeld von Folsach, Copenhagen; Jens Kröger, Berlin; and the late Ralph Pinder-Wilson, London.

INTRODUCTION

By the first century B.C., glassworkers in the Mediterranean region were experienced in finishing some of their products by cutting, grinding, and polishing, just as lapidaries finished objects of precious and semiprecious stone (Weinberg 1992, p. 105, no. 62, etc.). Within the next hundred years, glass cutting became one of the most popular techniques of finishing fine glassware in the Roman Empire (*Glass of the Caesars* 1987, pp. 180–181). We know very little about the tools used for this purpose, although information about the working of semiprecious stones (preserved, for example, in Book 36 of Pliny's *Natural History*) probably applies equally to the coldworking of glass; indeed, it is not unlikely that the same craftsmen worked in both materials. By the late second or early third century, Roman finishing shops were also producing glass with cut and polished decoration, and details scratched in the surface with a pointed tool (Whitehouse 1997, pp. 222 and 237–246, nos. 401–417). In the fourth century, some glasses were decorated by scratch engraving alone (*Glass of the Caesars* 1987, pp. 184–185 and 226–230, nos. 126–128).

Wheel cutting, which was practiced extensively not only by the Romans but also by their contemporaries, the Sasanians, in Iran and Iraq, declined in the Mediterranean region after the fourth or fifth century, and scratch engraving disappeared. Cutting, however, continued in Western Asia, although it is not yet clear how much cut glass was made in the late Sasanian and very early Islamic periods (Whitehouse 2005, pp. 41–57). Nevertheless, by the eighth to ninth centuries, both cutting and scratch engraving were once again parts of the repertoire of glassworkers in the central Islamic lands.

1. The Contents of the Catalog

Almost all of the cut and engraved objects in this catalog range in date between the eighth and 11th centuries. They are divided into three sections, labeled A–C, on the basis of technique. Section A describes 44 objects that were decorated by scratching the design with a hand-held tool mounted with a chip of diamond or some other very hard mineral, such as topaz or corundum; section B contains 447 monochrome objects or fragments of objects with coldworked decoration, usually cut and polished on the wheel, but sometimes accompanied by filing; and section C presents 94 pieces of cameo glass. Sections B and C are subdivided in terms of decoration or finishing techniques. In all three sections, and within each subdivision, open forms are described before closed forms, in the following order: dishes, bowls, cups, beakers, goblets, jars, bottles, pitchers, ewers, and indeterminate. Within each form, the ornament is presented as follows: humans, animals, birds, palmettes and half-palmettes, other vegetal motifs, inscriptions, and indeterminate.

The categories are:

A. Objects with scratch-engraved ornament (**1**–**44**).
B. Monochrome objects with wheel-cut ornament (**45**–**491**).
   1. Facet-cut objects (**45**–**117**).
   2. Objects decorated with disks and related motifs (**118**–**141**).
   3. Linear-cut objects (**142**–**249**).
   4. Slant-cut objects (**250**–**295**).
   5. Relief-cut objects (**296**–**488**).
   6. Objects decorated by molding and cutting (**489**–**491**).
C. Cameo glass (**492**–**585**).
   1. Linear- and/or slant-cut objects (**494**–**521**).
   2. Relief-cut objects (**522**–**585**).

Three appendixes describe the Corning Hedwig beaker (**586**), an unusual polychrome fragment of uncertain date (**587**), and fragments of carved rock crystal (**588**–**595**), one of which (**590**) may have come from a ewer similar to the celebrated ewers described by

Lamm (1929–30, pp. 191–194, pls. 65.4–67.1–4 and 67.7) and many others, and reviewed most recently in *Art of the Islamic and Indian Worlds* 2008 (pp. 62–71, lot 50).

2. Catalog Entries

Each entry contains as much as is known of the following information:

1. Catalog number and name.
2. Date, find-place, previous collections, and accession number.
3. Dimensions.
4. Description.
5. Condition.
6. Comment.
7. Bibliography.

1. *Catalog number and name.* Catalog numbers are arbitrary. Names are either generic (e.g., bowl) or the names by which the specific objects are known (e.g., the Corning Ewer).

2. *Date, find-place, previous collections, and accession number. Date:* Unless otherwise stated, all dates are A.D. Only 19 of the objects (**7**, **12**, **53**, **75**, **85**, **88**, **96**, **99**, **123**, **144**, **176**, **192**, **212**, **226**, **234**, **361**, **380**, **456**, and **529**) come from well-documented archeological contexts, and the dates in this catalog, therefore, are suggested mainly on the basis of comparisons with similar objects that were recovered by archeologists in association with other, datable material. *Find-place:* In most cases, places where objects are reported to have been found or acquired are prefaced by the phrase "said to have been found at/acquired in." Place names appear without qualification only when the information is independently corroborated; in such cases, further details are given in the "Comment." *Previous collections:* This is a list of all known previous owners (other than dealers), in chronological order. *Accession number:* The Museum's three-part accession numbers record, first, the year in which the object was acquired; second, the area of the collection to which it was assigned (area 1 comprises all ancient and Islamic glass); and finally, the cumulative number of objects acquired in that area during the year.

3. *Dimensions.* All dimensions are in centimeters (cm). The following abbreviations are used: D. (diameter), Dim. (dimension), est. (estimated), ext. (exterior), H. (height), int. (interior), L. (length), Max. (maximum), Min. (minimum), Th. (thickness: a single dimension describes a relatively consistent thickness; otherwise, the thickness is given as a range—e.g., 0.4–0.5 cm; in descriptions of relief-cut glass and cameo glass, TTh. [total thickness] refers to the combined thickness of the wall and the ornament), and W. (width). In the descriptions of relief-cut objects, the thicknesses of the wall (or floor) and the ornament are also recorded separately.

4. *Description.* Descriptions proceed from the top of the object to the bottom. The glass is described as transparent, translucent, or opaque. The colors are described, arbitrarily, as very light, light, dark, or very dark. The term "colorless" is reserved for glass that is assumed (or known) to have been intentionally decolorized.

5. *Condition.* Objects that are essentially without damage are described as "intact"; objects that have been damaged and repaired without loss are described as "complete." The condition of other damaged objects, as well as the appearance and extent of weathering, is briefly stated.

The description of some objects from the Smith Collection notes the presence of a small circular perforation. These perforations, it is believed, were made by Mr. Smith in order to conduct chemical analyses of the glass.

The phrase "flood mud" occasionally appears in catalog entries. It refers to deposits of brown silt that are found on a number of objects in the collection. The silt was deposited on and immediately after June 23, 1972, when, in the aftermath of Tropical Storm Agnes, a flood devastated Corning, New York; at the Museum, the water rose to a level of more than 1.5 meters (five feet) above the floor (Martin 1977). In the months following this catastrophe, the great majority of the flooded objects were cleaned, but a few still retain traces of silt.

6. *Comment.* This may include additional information on the technique, subject matter, and history of the object, and a discussion of comparable material. It is intended to provide the reader with information about more detailed studies of related objects.

7. *Bibliography.* The entries are confined to publications of the object in question. Publications that describe parallels and related material are cited in the "Comment."

Catalog

A

Objects with Scratch-Engraved Ornament

The simplest kind of early Islamic engraving on glass consisted of scratching the surface with a pointed tool (Carboni 2001, pp. 76–81; Kröger 2005). In recent centuries, glass engravers have tended to use tools mounted with diamond chips (Matcham and Dreiser 1997, p. 120), but other minerals with a hardness in excess of 7 on the Mohs scale (e.g., topaz and corundum) serve equally well (Brill 2001, p. 31). On early Islamic scratch-engraved glass, the entire surface may be covered with decoration that, on open forms, is frequently divided into concentric bands or radial panels. Sometimes the background is hatched, as sometimes is the ornament itself. The quality of the engraving ranges from the relatively skillful execution of a complex design laid out with care (e.g., **2**) to the perfunctory completion of a simple pattern (e.g., **6**).

Kröger (2005, pp. 142–143) listed the range of shapes that occur with scratch-engraved ornament: they include dishes and bowls, cylindrical cups, bottles, a jar, and a pitcher. At Corning, the collection comprises dishes or bowls, a deep bowl, cylindrical cups, and bottles. Kröger noted that the most widespread form appears to be the cylindrical cup, and, at Corning, 28 of the 44 specimens (64 percent) are cylindrical cups.

Kröger also stated that the colors of most scratch-engraved glasses are dark, especially deep blue, which he estimated to account for nearly 80 percent of all known examples. The collection at Corning (33 of the 44 specimens—75 percent—are deep blue) is, therefore, typical. Other colors represented at Corning are translucent mid- to deep brown (1 fragment) and five pale to light transparent colors: brown (3); blue, purple, and yellowish green (2 each); and green (1).

Early Islamic scratch-engraved glass has a wide distribution, extending from Egypt (e.g., **7** and **12**: Scanlon and Pinder-Wilson 2001, pp. 82–83, no. 39a and b; see also Kucharczyk 2009), through Israel and the Syro-Palestinian region (Lane 1938, p. 67, fig. 12G; Al ᶜUsh 1971; Bartl 1997, pp. 24–25, fig. 3.11; Hadad 2000; Strube 2003, p. 108, fig. 21), to Iraq (Lamm 1928, pp. 79–82, nos. 251–259) and Iran (Kröger 1995, pp. 116–119, nos. 164 and 165). Outlying finds have been reported from Mali (Insoll 1998, pp. 80–82, fig. 3, top left), Greece (Davidson 1952, p. 115, no. 748), Armenia (Dzhanpoladian and Kalantarian 1988, pl. 27.15), Kenya (Chittick 1984, p. 163, fig. 131e), and even China (An 1991, pp. 123–124).

Given this extensive distribution, it is not surprising to find that scratch-engraved glass appears to have been made in more than one place. Chemical analyses of the composition of 24 scratch-engraved fragments (Brill 2001, p. 31, summarizing analyses reported in *idem* 1999) revealed that 15 (**3**, **6**, **9**–**11**, **16**, **18**, **19**, **21**, **23**, **25**, **30**, **34**, **37**, and **38**) are natron-based glass and nine (including **1**, **2**, and **4**) were made with soda derived from plant ash. Brill suggested that the natron-based glass was probably made in Egypt (the most likely source of the natron) or the Syro-Palestinian region, while the plant-ash glasses may have been made farther east.

Although inscriptions occur (e.g., on a cylindrical cup in the David Collection, Copenhagen, 23/1987: Folsach 2001, p. 204, no. 295 = *idem* 1990, p. 140, no. 212; on a goblet in The Metropolitan Museum of Art, New York, 65.173.1: *Glass of the Sultans* 2001, pp. 165–166, no. 71; and on a cylindrical cup in the Khalili Collection (Kröger 2005, p. 155, no. 174), none of these has provided an indication of the date of an object. (**41** may contain a small part of a Kufic inscription.)

Our knowledge of the chronology of the group, therefore, is dependent on archeological discoveries. Fragments of Islamic scratch-engraved glass have been found in eighth-century (or supposedly eighth-century) deposits at two sites. At Susa, southwestern Iran, a fragment was excavated from Stratum 3, which is believed to belong to the period 700–750 (Hardy-Guilbert 1984, pp. 143–144, fig. 32.1, and pl. 6.7); and at Beth Shean, Israel, two fragments were recovered from deposits attributed to the Umayyad period, which ended in 750 (Hadad 2000, p. 63 and fig. 1.1 and .2). Scratch-engraved glass is found more frequently in ninth-century contexts at such sites as Samarra (Lamm 1928, pp. 79–82, nos. 251–259), Fusṭāṭ (Scanlon and Pinder-Wilson 2001, pp. 82–83, no. 39a and b = **7** and **12**), and Beth Shean (Hadad 2000, p. 65, with a list of additional find-places). Finds from Kom el-Dikka, Alexandria, came from deposits "dating to the ninth and 10th centuries" (Kucharczyk 2009, p. 42).

The most closely dated ninth-century finds, however, are six deep blue plates from the crypt of the Famen Temple in Shaanxi Province, China, which was sealed in 874 (An 1991, pp. 123–124, figs. 3–8; cf. Koch 1995, p. 499, fig. 41, nos. 2–4, pl. 138, and pl. 139, nos. 1 and 2; and *Gilded Dragons* 1999, pp. 158–159, no. 115). It is interesting to note that two of these objects have traces of gilding in the incised lines. Although fragments of scratch-engraved glass from archeological deposits of later periods have been reported at a number of sites (most notably Kom el-Dikka), it seems probable that these fragments were residual and that most vessels of this type were made in the eighth and ninth centuries.

The scratch-engraved objects at Corning are described in the following order:

1. Dishes or bowls (**1**–**4**).
2. Bowl (**5**).
3. Cylindrical cups (**6**–**33**).
4. Bottles (**34**–**40**).
5. Indeterminate forms (**41**–**44**).

1. Dishes or Bowls

1. Fragment of Dish or Bowl

8th to 9th century. Formerly in the Smith Collection (856). 55.1.110.
H. (surviving) 2.1 cm, D. greater than 18.6 cm.
Transparent deep blue. Blown; applied and scratch-engraved.

Fragment of dish or bowl. Floor descends very gently, then rises at center, with corresponding concavity on underside; traces of annular pontil mark (D. 2.7 cm); two (of originally three) solid cylindrical feet (H. 1.7 cm, D. 1.8 cm) applied to underside of base in form of tightly wound trails. Floor is covered with scratch-engraved ornament arranged in two

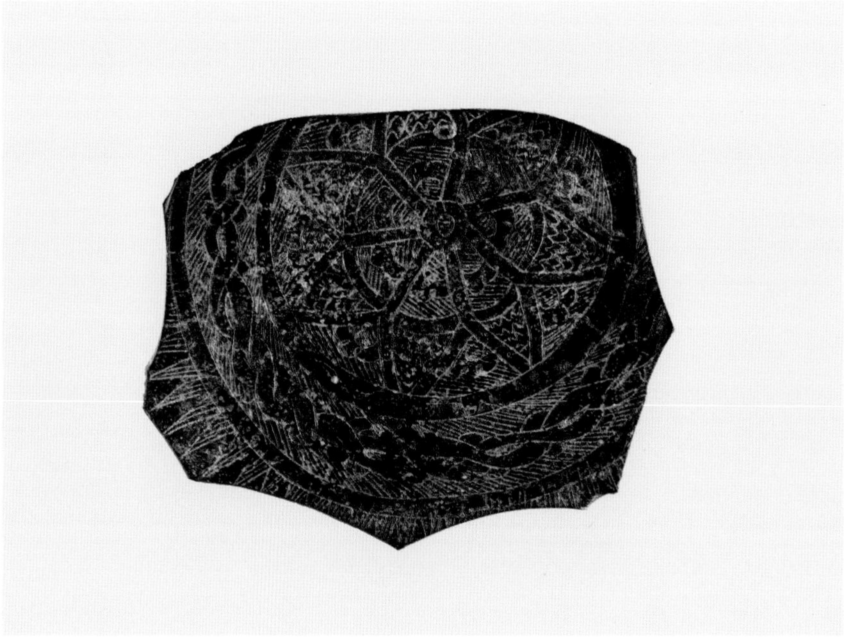

1

concentric rings around central roundel. Outer ring (W. just over 1.7 cm) contains row of contiguous transversely hatched isosceles triangles, which point toward rim, and whose bases form border line. Inner and outer rings are separated by narrow undecorated band. Inner ring (W. 2.1 cm) contains continuous two-ply cable motif enlivened with arcs, which project from some points where plies overlap, and with hatched background. Inner ring and roundel are separated by narrow undecorated band. Roundel (D. 10.2 cm) contains hollow circle at center; seven spokes radiate from this, extending to concentric circle, where they fork, each fork meeting fork from adjacent spoke at edge of roundel; each space between pairs of spokes is enlivened with bulbous arclike motif, as is each space between forks of individual spokes; triangles between converging forks are filled with rows of wavy lines; all backgrounds, except spaces between wavy lines, are hatched.

Broken on all sides. Dull and pitted, with extensive remains of pale gray, slightly iridescent weathering.

COMMENT: According to *Verres antiques* 1954, p. 51, no. 314, the fragment was acquired in Aleppo, Syria.

See **2**.

Chemical analysis revealed that the material is a soda-lime-silica glass made with plant ash (Brill 1999, v. 1, p. 96, and v. 2, p. 196, no. 6349).

BIBLIOGRAPHY: *Verres antiques* 1954, p. 51, no. 314; *Glass from the Ancient World* 1957, p. 285, no. 605.

2. Fragment of Dish or Bowl

8th to 9th century. Formerly in the Smith Collection (658). 55.1.111.
H. (surviving) 1.5 cm, D. greater than 18.2 cm.
Transparent deep blue. Blown; scratch-engraved.

Fragment of dish or bowl. Floor descends very gently, then rises at center, with corresponding concavity on underside; traces of annular(?) pontil mark. Floor is covered with scratch-engraved ornament arranged in three concentric rings around central roundel. Outermost ring (of which very little survives) contains indeterminate motifs with transverse hatching. Outermost and second rings are separated by narrow undecorated band. Second ring (W. 2.7 cm) contains band of contiguous arcs with double outline and cusps pointing outward; single deltoid leaf projects outward from each cusp, with three lobes on each side and lobe at end, axial vein, and transverse hatching on either side of vein; spaces between leaves are occupied by narrow oval motifs filled with zigzag lines; area beneath ring of arcs is hatched, except for one plain arc below each cusp. Second and innermost rings are separated by narrow undecorated band. Innermost ring contains continuous two-ply cable motif with hatched background. Innermost ring and roundel are separated by narrow undecorated band. Roundel (D. 6.8 cm) contains hollow circle at center, from which radiate eight lanceolate motifs filled with zigzags; arcs with double outlines spring from tips of lanceolate motifs, with one plain arc outside each cusp, and with

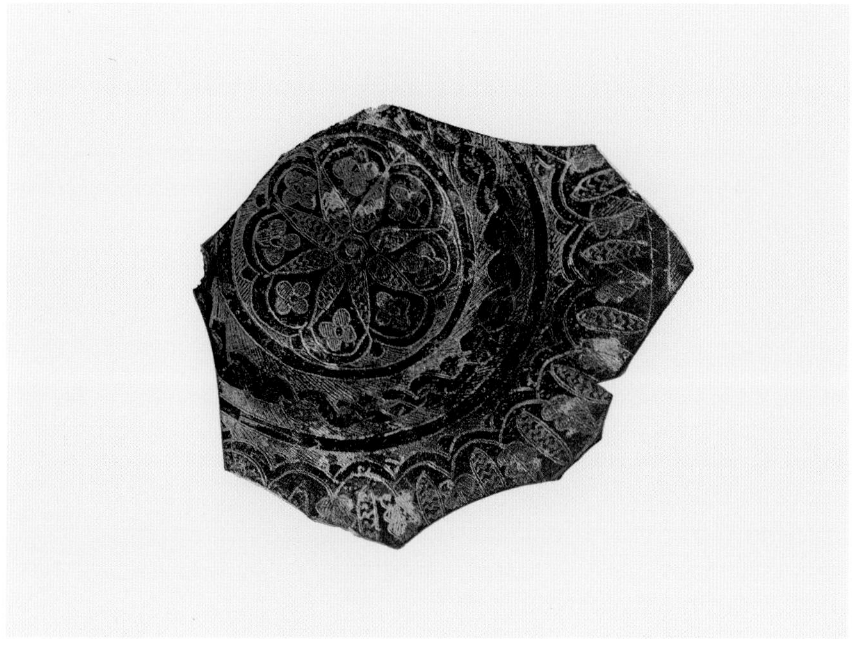

2

one hatched quatrefoil in each space enclosed by arcs; area between arcs and edge of roundel is hatched.

Broken on all sides. Dull and pitted, with extensive remains of pale gray, slightly iridescent weathering.

Comment: The rich detail of the fragment closely resembles that of the six deep blue plates from the crypt of the Famen Temple (see page 14); that of the fragmentary vessel from Nishapur in The Metropolitan Museum of Art, New York (40.170.131: *Glass of the Sultans* 2001, pp. 162–163, no. 68 = Kröger 1995, pp. 163–164, no. 164); and that of a dish or shallow bowl in the Khalili Collection (Kröger 2005, p. 150, no. 168). It also resembles the decoration of **1**. All of these objects are filled with a dense arrangement of symmetrical patterns combining concentric and radiating elements. The vessels from the Famen Temple were placed in the crypt in or before 874.

Chemical analysis revealed that the material is a soda-lime-silica glass made with plant ash (Brill 1999, v. 1, p. 96, and v. 2, p. 196, no. 6350). Analyses of **1** and the vessels in the Metropolitan Museum (*ibid.*, v. 1, p. 96, and v. 2, p. 196, nos. 6349 and 6365) showed that these, too, were made with plant ash rather than natron.

Bibliography: *Glass from the Ancient World* 1957, p. 283, no. 604.

3. Fragment of Dish or Bowl

8th to 9th century. Formerly in the Smith Collection. 51.1.143.
Max. Dim. 6.6 cm, Th. 0.25–0.3 cm.
Almost colorless, perhaps with yellowish tinge.
Blown; scratch-engraved.

Fragment from floor of dish or bowl. Bottom of wall curves down and in; floor rises slightly before curving down toward center. Interior has scratch-engraved ornament: large roundel (D. est. about 20 cm), which fills floor and contains leaves on curling stem, isolated leaves, and two elements resembling vertical strokes of Kufic letters; leaves and letters are hatched.

Broken on all sides. Extensively pitted, with light brown weathering in pits.

Comment: The fragment came from a dish or bowl with a profile resembling that of the scratch-engraved bowls from the crypt of the Famen Temple, which was sealed in 874 (Koch 1995, p. 500, nos. 2–4). The diameter of the roundel suggests that the complete vessel probably had a diameter of about 23–24 centimeters. The weathering makes it difficult to determine the true color of the glass, which nevertheless appears to be colorless or almost colorless.

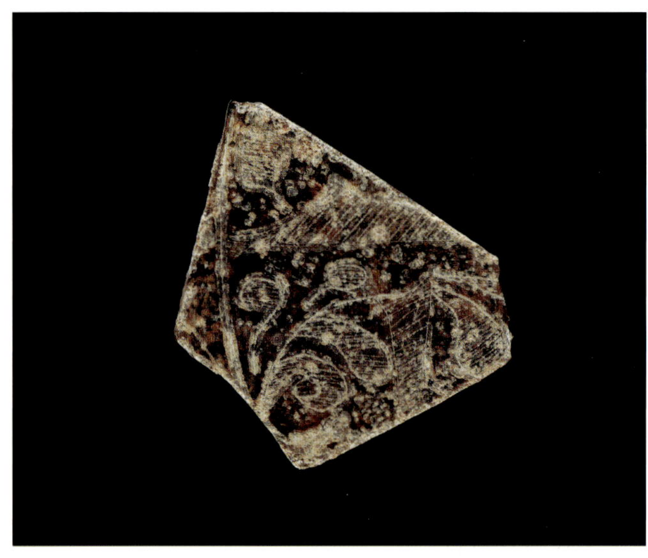

3

Chemical analysis revealed that the material is a soda-lime-silica glass made with natron (Brill 1999, v. 1, p. 95, and v. 2, p. 194, no. 6344). This suggests that the glass was made either in Egypt, the most likely source of the natron, or in the Syro-Palestinian region.

4. Fragment of Dish or Bowl

8th to 9th century. Formerly in the Smith Collection (1218-[ ]). 58.1.20.
H. (surviving) 1 cm, D. (foot-ring, est.) 6 cm.
Transparent pale yellowish green; many small bubbles. Blown; applied and scratch-engraved.

Fragmentary base of dish or bowl. Bottom of wall is straight and descends at very shallow angle; floor is almost flat; underside of base is slightly convex and has low foot-ring; large annular pontil mark (D. 2.4 cm). Floor has scratch-engraved ornament: roundel

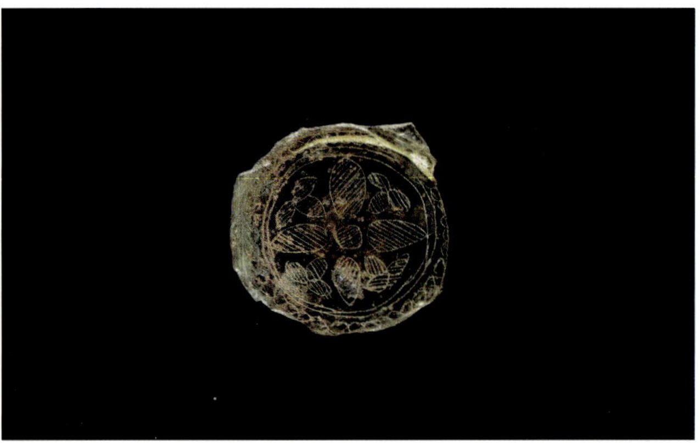

4

(D. 5.3 cm) with edge consisting of chain motif between outer and inner pairs of border lines, and center decorated with large quatrefoil with central hatched circle and four detached oval leaves, which are also hatched; between each pair of leaves, small hatched trefoil; all hatching is transverse.

Broken on all sides, with most of roundel and about one-third of foot-ring surviving. Pitted, with patches of light reddish brown weathering.

Comment: Chemical analysis revealed that the material is a soda-lime-silica glass made with plant ash (Brill 1999, v. 1, p. 95, and v. 2, p. 196, no. 6343).

2. Bowl

5. Fragment of Bowl

8th to 9th century. Formerly in the Smith Collection (1218-3). Gift of Carl Berkowitz and Derek Content. 76.1.233.
H. 3.4 cm, D. (rim, est.) about 11.5 cm.
Transparent deep blue; several small and two larger (L. 0.3 cm and 0.5 cm) bubbles. Blown; scratch-engraved.

Fragment of bowl, including approximately 15 percent of rim. Rim plain, with rounded lip; upper wall tapers, with slightly concave profile. Exterior of upper wall has two horizontal bands of simple scratch-engraved ornament. Upper band is narrow and has single border lines above and below, with one additional horizontal line with overlapping ends between upper border and rim; it contains row of isosceles triangles, bases of which are formed by lower border, and apexes of which touch upper border; both triangles and spaces between them are plain. Lower band is broader and contains series of vertical lines, each of which has, to its right, vertical row of contiguous arcs; there is no hatching.

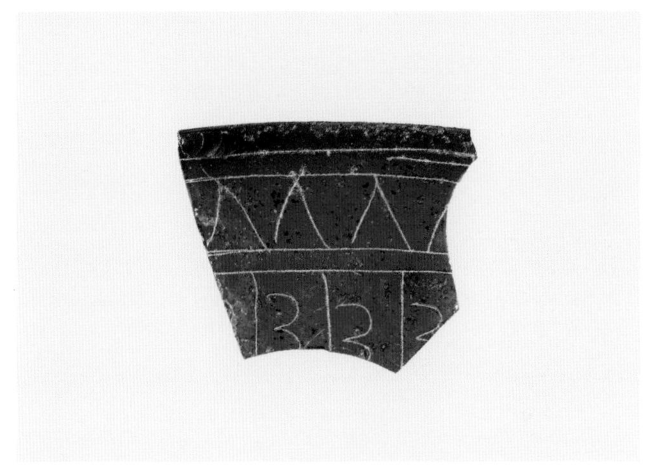

5

Shiny, with small patches of light brown weathering.

3. Cylindrical Cups

6. Cup

8th to 9th century. Formerly in the Smith Collection (900). 55.1.112.
H. 9.5–10.8 cm, D. 12.7 cm.
Transparent light blue, but appearing almost black in reflected light; few small bubbles and inclusions. Blown; scratch-engraved.

Cup with plain cylindrical rim and rounded lip. Wall slightly convex. Base plain, with pontil mark at center. Wall is decorated with continuous horizontal band of ornament, which has multiple borders at top and bottom and is divided into three large compartments and one small compartment by vertical bands of crosshatching. Each large compartment contains two vertical pairs of crosshatched triangles, with their apexes almost touching, but separated by V-shaped motifs. Spaces between triangles and upper and lower borders are filled with hatched circles.

Almost complete, but with vertical crack in wall and circular hole in base, probably made by Ray Winfield Smith in order to obtain sample for chemical analysis. Patches of light brown weathering and some iridescence.

Comment: Smith reported (in *Verres antiques* and *Glass from the Ancient World*: see below) that he acquired the object in Cairo, Egypt.

Chemical analysis revealed that the material is a soda-lime-silica glass made with natron (Brill 1999, v. 1, p. 96, and v. 2, p. 194, no. 6348). This suggests that

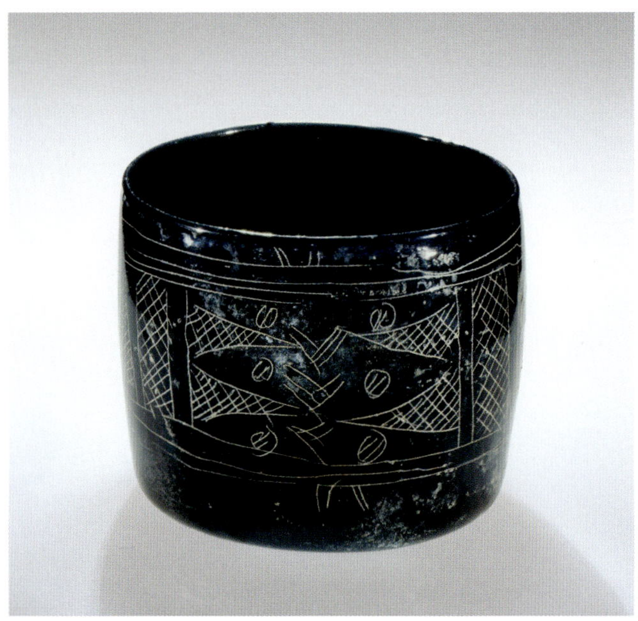

6

the glass was made either in Egypt, the most likely source of the natron, or in the Syro-Palestinian region.

Bibliography: *Verres antiques* 1954, p. 50, no. 303; *Glass from the Ancient World* 1957, p. 285, no. 606; *Glass of the Sultans* 2001, p. 163, no. 69; Kucharczyk 2009, p. 43 and p. 45, no. 21.

7. Fragments of Cup

8th to 9th century. Found during excavations at Fusṭāṭ (Old Cairo), Egypt (68.11.88). Gift of the American Research Center in Egypt. 69.1.84.
H. (surviving) 11 cm, D. (est.) about 16 cm.
Transparent light blue, with bubbles (up to 0.2 cm across) and inclusions. Blown; scratch-engraved.

Six fragments of cup with plain cylindrical rim and rounded lip. Five of these fragments join and make almost complete profile of wall, and sixth fragment is loose. Wall is nearly vertical, but it curves down and in at bottom. It is decorated with continuous horizontal band of somewhat sketchy ornament (from top to bottom): (1) 0.8–1.9 cm below rim, group of four horizontal lines; (2) band containing groups of two or three vertical lines, 1.2 cm wide; (3) group of three horizontal lines, 0.75 cm wide; (4) band of geometric ornament that, if symmetrical, consisted of lozenges with double outlines, each containing four hatched circles, and, in triangular spaces between each pair of lozenges, pair of vertical lines flanked by hatching; and (5) group of three horizontal lines, about 1.2 cm wide. Between rim and uppermost group of horizontal lines are several short vertical lines, and similar lines exist between lowest group and bottom of wall.

Surface ranges from glossy and slightly iridescent to dull with remains of off-white weathering.

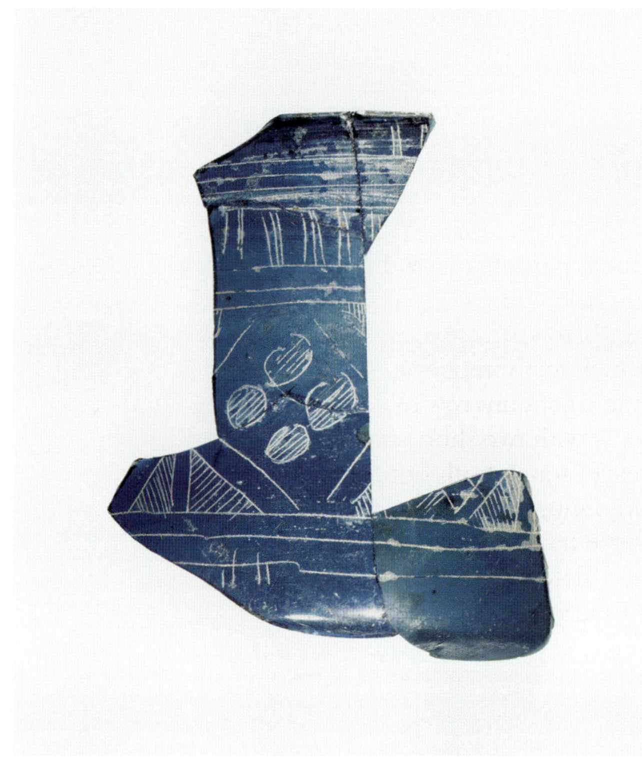

7A

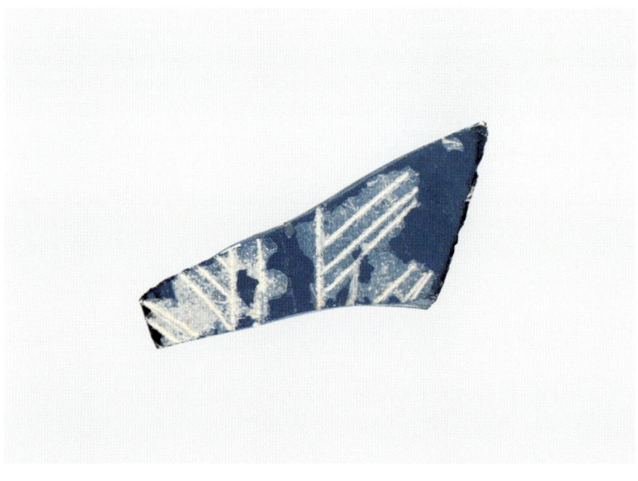

7B

Comment: The object was found during excavations directed by Prof. George T. Scanlon. The excavators (Scanlon and Pinder-Wilson 2001, p. 78, no. 36n) reported that the fragments were found in a context that contained coins of the period 800–850.

Bibliography: Scanlon and Pinder-Wilson 2001, pp. 82–83, no. 39a = Scanlon 1974, p. 84 and pl. XXXII, fig. 5b.

8. Fragments of Cup

8th to 9th century. Formerly in the Smith Collection (1113). Gift of Carl Berkowitz and Derek Content. 76.1.234.
H. (surviving) 5.9 cm, D. (upper wall, est.) about 12 cm.
Transparent light blue. Blown; scratch-engraved.

Two joining fragments from upper wall of cylindrical cup, which retain minute part of rim. Rim plain, with rounded edge; upper wall vertical. Exterior of upper wall has scratch-engraved decoration: 0.7–1.1 cm below rim, one pair of parallel horizontal lines; 1.6 cm below rim, two roughly parallel horizontal lines, which form upper border of panel. Surviving part of panel contains row of quatrefoils with long oval leaves, each with two short scratches in center; ends of upper leaves touch both border and ends of upper leaves in adjoining quatrefoils; background is filled with transverse hatching; bottom of panel is missing.

Patches of silver to gray weathering and, where this is missing, brilliant iridescence.

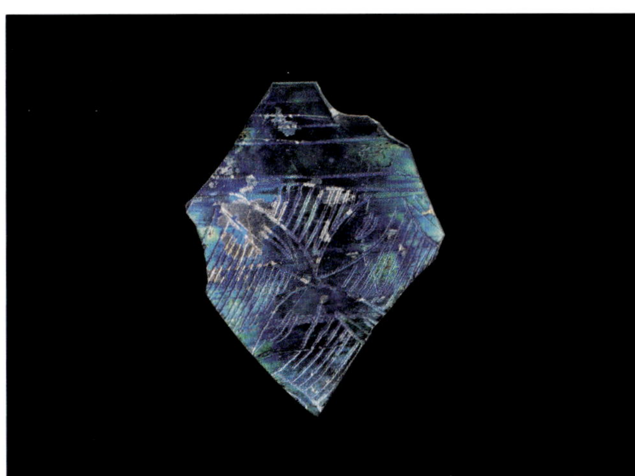

8

Comment: The quatrefoils are larger than most motifs on cups of this type.

Brill (1999, v. 1, p. 96, no. 6366) sampled the fragment, but he did not publish an analysis.

9. Fragment of Cup

8th to 9th century. 51.1.110.
H. (surviving) 7.1 cm, D. (rim, est.) 10–11 cm.
Transparent deep blue. Blown; scratch-engraved.

Fragment of cylindrical cup, with small section of rim and apparently almost complete profile. Rim plain, with rounded lip; wall vertical. Exterior has two horizontal bands of scratched ornament: upper band, just below rim, is narrow and consists of groundline from which extend groups of three short vertical lines; lower band is broad and occupies most of wall; it has pair of border lines at top, and small part of one border line survives at bottom; between borders, fragment preserves head of bird shown in profile, facing right, with hatched circular eye and hatched open beak; in front of and below bird's head are stem- and leaflike motifs, and small circles, which are also hatched.

Patches of light grayish weathering.

Comment: **25**, which is decorated with the body and leg of a bird, is of similar size and color, and it is just possible that **9** and **25** came from the same object (if this was the case, the height of the cup would have been about 10 centimeters); however, the chemical compositions of the fragments, although similar, are not identical (see below).

Zoomorphic decoration seems to be very unusual among early Islamic scratch-engraved glasses, but a fragmentary plate or bowl of yellowish brown glass decorated with two confronted birds is preserved in the al-Sabah Collection, Dār al-Āthār al-Islāmiyyah, Kuwait National Museum (LNS 56 KG: Carboni 2001, p. 81, no. 17d), and a small fragment in the Benaki Museum, Athens (39/2: Clairmont 1977, p. 76, no. 252), is decorated with a fish.

Chemical analysis revealed that the material is a soda-lime-silica glass made with natron (Brill 1999, v. 1, p. 96, and v. 2, p. 194, no. 6353). This suggests that the glass was made either in Egypt, the most likely source of the natron, or in the Syro-Palestinian region.

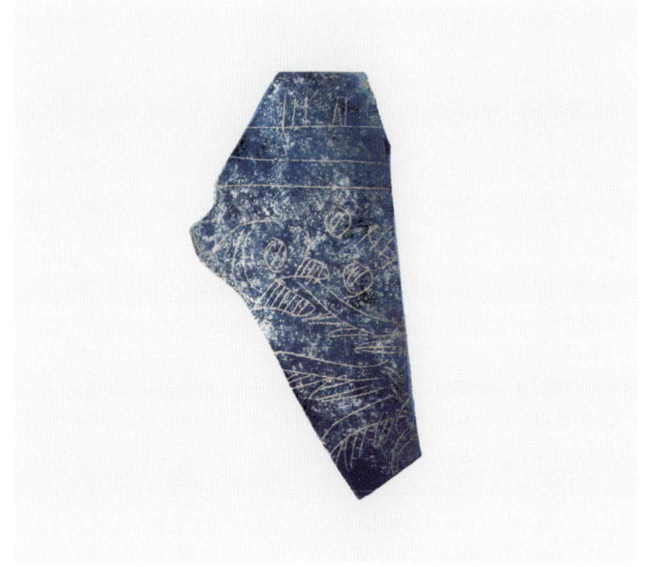

9

10. Fragment of Cup

8th to 9th century. 68.1.60.
H. (surviving) 9.4 cm, D. (est.) 10 cm.
Transparent yellowish green. Blown; scratch-engraved.

Fragment of cylindrical cup, including about 12 percent of rim. Rim plain, with rounded lip; wall almost vertical, but with slightly convex profile and curving in at bottom. Wall is decorated with one narrow band and one broad horizontal band, with pairs of horizontal lines above, between, and beneath them. Upper, narrow band appears to contain groups of vertical lines. Lower, broad band (W. 3.5 cm) contains continuous series of columns and semicircular arches, all with double outlines; each bay is divided, at center, by pair of vertical lines, which are flanked by groups of three transverse lines that create featherlike effect.

Patches of white enamellike weathering; where this is missing, surface is deeply pitted.

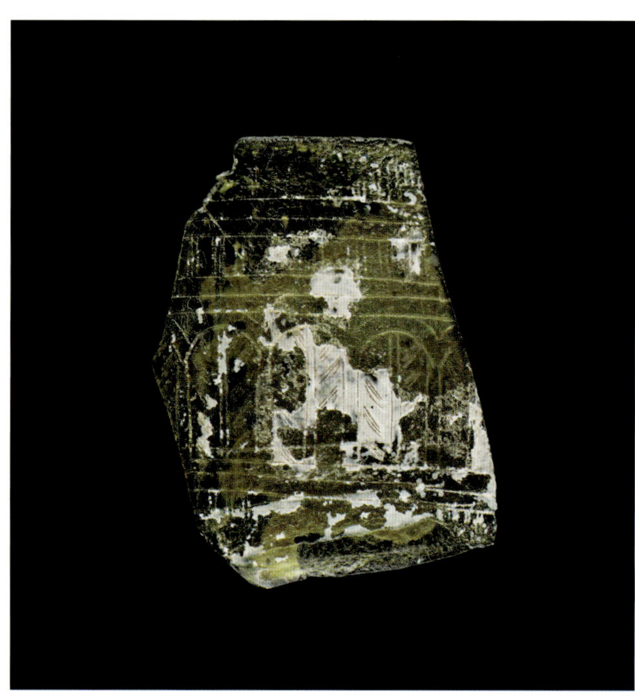

10

Comment: The condition of the surface makes the decoration difficult to discern, and it is possible (but perhaps unlikely) that additional ornament existed above the narrow band and below the broad band.

Chemical analysis revealed that the material is a soda-lime-silica glass made with natron (Brill 1999, v. 1, p. 95, and v. 2, p. 194, no. 6341). This suggests that the glass was made either in Egypt, the most likely source of the natron, or in the Syro-Palestinian region.

11. Fragment of Cup

8th to 9th century. 51.1.119.
H. (surviving) 5.3 cm, D. (wall, est.) about 10 cm.
Transparent blue. Blown; scratch-engraved.

Fragment of cylindrical cup. Wall descends vertically. Exterior has two horizontal bands of scratch-engraved ornament: (1) upper, narrow band has single border lines at top and bottom, and contains row of isosceles triangles resting on lower border and filled with transverse hatching; below this is narrow undecorated area and, below that, (2) lower, broad band, apparently divided by pairs of border lines into adjoining upright and inverted triangles; part of one upright triangle survives, containing single motif with lobed sides and wedge-shaped top, interior of which has two concentric circles; inner circle is hatched, outer circle is plain, and remainder of motif has transverse hatching; to left, small part of one inverted triangle survives; it contained some other, unidentified motif.

Broken on all sides. Surface is slightly pitted and has patches of light brownish weathering, especially in engraved lines.

Comment: Chemical analysis revealed that the material is a soda-lime-silica glass made with natron (Brill 1999, v. 1, p. 96, and v. 2, p. 195, no. 6357). This suggests that the glass was made either in Egypt, the most likely source of the natron, or in the Syro-Palestinian region.

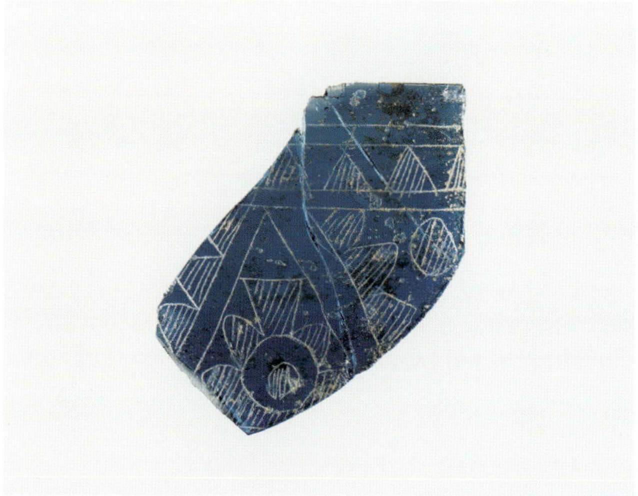

11

12. Fragment of Cup

8th to 9th century. Found during excavations at Fusṭāṭ (Old Cairo), Egypt (78.10.24). Gift of the American Research Center in Egypt. 79.1.22.

H. (surviving) 4.7 cm, D. (rim, est.) 10 cm.
Transparent yellowish brown; many very small bubbles. Blown; scratch-engraved.

Fragment of cylindrical cup, preserving small part of rim and upper wall. Rim plain, with rounded lip; wall curves down and in toward bottom. Exterior of wall has at least two horizontal bands of scratched ornament. Upper band has pair of horizontal lines at top and pair of lines dividing it from lower band. Upper (narrower) band contains uneven row of isosceles triangles, bases of which are contiguous and filled with vertical hatching; triangular spaces between each pair of hatched triangles are plain. Lower (broader) band apparently contains large isosceles triangles, sides of which are in form of long, narrow ovals with scratched outlines and plain interiors; each triangle contains one arc-shaped element with scratched outlines and plain interior; these elements have alternating upward- and downward-pointing ends. Backgrounds have transverse hatching.

Dull and pitted, with patches of slightly iridescent ivory-colored weathering.

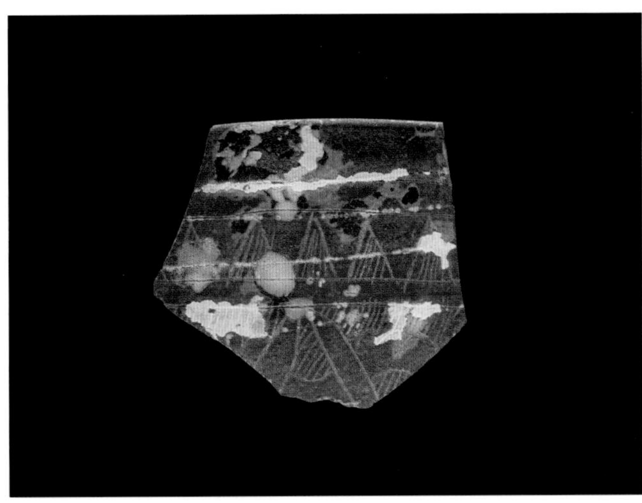

12

Comment: The object was found during excavations directed by Prof. George T. Scanlon. Scanlon and Pinder-Wilson (see below) noted that it was "found at the bottom of a pit whose undisturbed contents were principally of the 11th century but whose lower sections were of the 9th century since they included two copper coins, one of the Abu Ishaq and ʿIsa type (831–2) and the other of the Mahfuz and Salih type (802–3)." They dated the fragment to the ninth century.

Bibliography: Scanlon 1984, pp. 35–36, fig. 58; Scanlon and Pinder-Wilson 2001, p. 83, no. 39b.

13. Fragment of Cup

8th to 9th century. Formerly in the Smith Collection (1218-1). Gift of Carl Berkowitz and Derek Content. 76.1.235.
H. (surviving) 3.5 cm, D. (rim, est.) 10 cm.
Transparent deep blue. Blown; scratch-engraved.

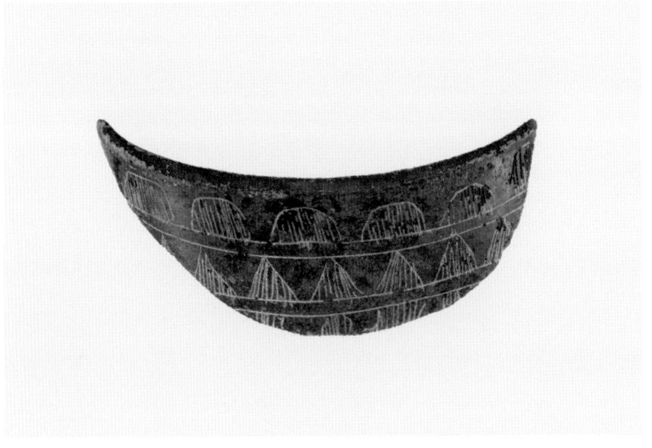

13

Fragment of cylindrical cup, including nearly 40 percent of rim. Rim plain, with rounded lip that is beveled on outside; upper wall vertical. Wall is decorated with at least three horizontal bands of ornament (from top to bottom): (1) narrow band of adjacent semicircular motifs resting on groundline; each motif is filled with vertical hatching; (2) between single border lines, narrow band of adjacent isosceles triangles, with bases resting on lower border and apexes touching upper border; triangles are filled with vertical hatching; and (3) indeterminate hatched motifs below upper border (lower part of band is missing).

Dull and pitted, with patches of gray to brown weathering.

14. Fragment of Cup

8th to 9th century. Formerly in the Smith Collection. Gift of Carl Berkowitz and Derek Content. 98.1.23.
H. (surviving) 3.4 cm, D. (rim, est.) about 10 cm.
Transparent yellowish brown. Blown; scratch-engraved.

Fragment of cylindrical cup, which includes small part of rim. Rim plain, with rounded lip; wall descends almost vertically. Exterior of wall has scratch-engraved ornament: single roughly horizontal line 1.9–2 cm below rim.

Both surfaces have numerous scratchlike fissures, which were caused by weathering.

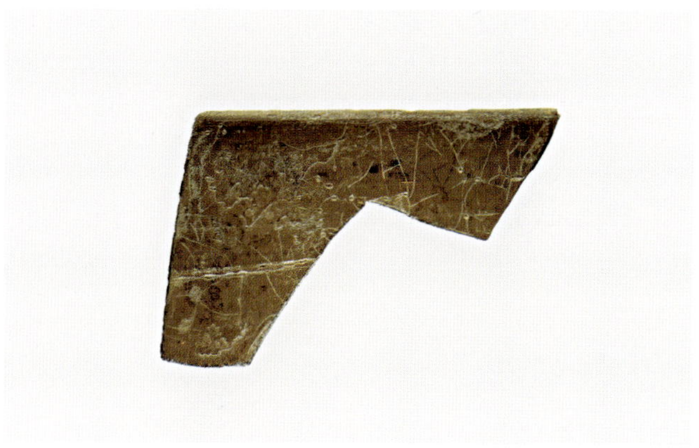

14

Comment: There is no doubt that the fissures are the result of some natural process and are not engraved.

15. Fragment of Cup

8th to 9th century. 51.1.142.
H. (surviving) 2.1 cm, D. (rim, est.) about 10 cm.
Transparent blue. Blown; scratch-engraved.

Fragment of cylindrical cup, including approximately 10 percent of rim. Rim plain, with rounded lip; upper wall vertical. Upper wall is decorated with narrow horizontal band with single border lines above and below, and one additional horizontal line between upper border and rim. Band contains row of isosceles triangles with bases formed by lower border and apexes touching upper border. Triangles are filled with transverse hatching.

Small spots of brownish weathering, especially on rim.

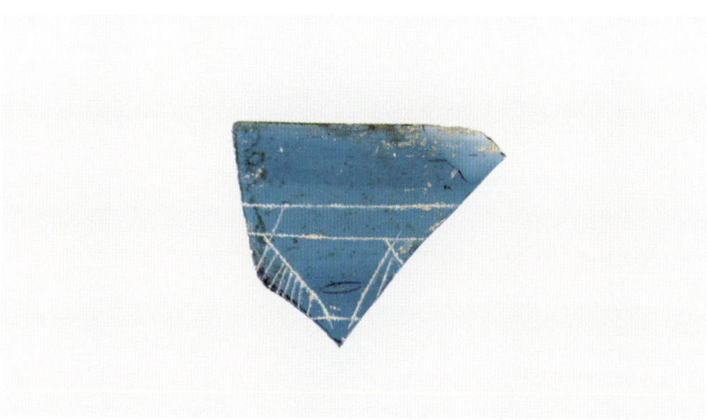

15

16. Fragment of Cup

8th to 9th century. Formerly in the Smith Collection (1218-2). Gift of Carl Berkowitz and Derek Content. 76.1.236.
H. (surviving) 4.6 cm, D. (rim, est.) 9 cm.
Transparent reddish purple. Blown; scratch-engraved.

Fragment of cylindrical cup, including 20–25 percent of rim. Rim plain, with rounded lip, which is thickened on inside; wall vertical. Wall was decorated with at least two horizontal bands of scratched ornament. Upper band is narrow and has single border lines above and below, with one additional horizontal line between upper border and rim; it contains row of adjoining isosceles triangles, bases of which are formed by lower border, and apexes of which touch upper border; they are filled with transverse hatching. Lower band is broad and has single border line at top; it is divided into panels, each of which is enclosed at sides by single border line, with plain, narrow strips between borders of adjacent panels. Parts of three panels survive (from left to right): (1) wide panel filled with straight lines that together form lattice of diamond-shaped compartments; plain compartments alternate with hatched compartments, making checkerboard pattern; (2) narrow panel with vertical chainlike-motif row of adjoining circles, three of which are filled with transverse hatching and two of which contain small circles, which are hatched; and (3) similar to (1), but with lattice composed of wavy, not straight, lines.

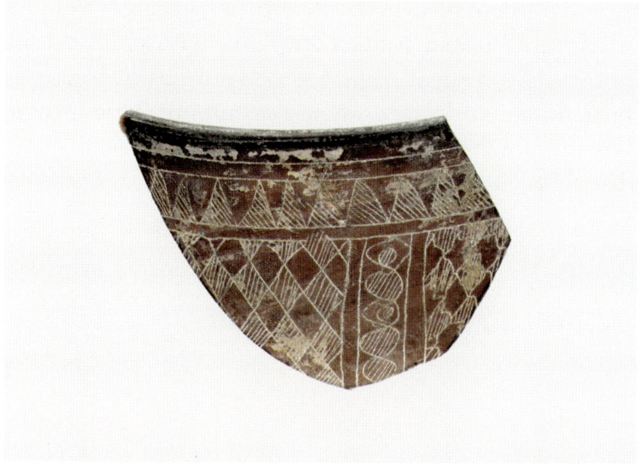

16

Dull, with patches of thin grayish weathering and hint of iridescence.

Comment: For other lattices with alternating plain and hatched compartments, see **34** and a fragmentary bottle from Kom el-Dikka, Alexandria, Egypt (Kucharczyk 2009, pp. 46–47, fig. 33).

Chemical analysis revealed that the material is a soda-lime-silica glass made with natron (Brill 1999, v. 1, p. 95, and v. 2, p. 194, no. 6368). This suggests that the glass was made either in Egypt, the most likely source of the natron, or in the Syro-Palestinian region.

17. Fragment of Cup

8th to 9th century. 51.1.117B.
H. (surviving) 4.1 cm, D. (rim, est.) about 9 cm.
Transparent very deep blue; small bubbles.
Blown; scratch-engraved.

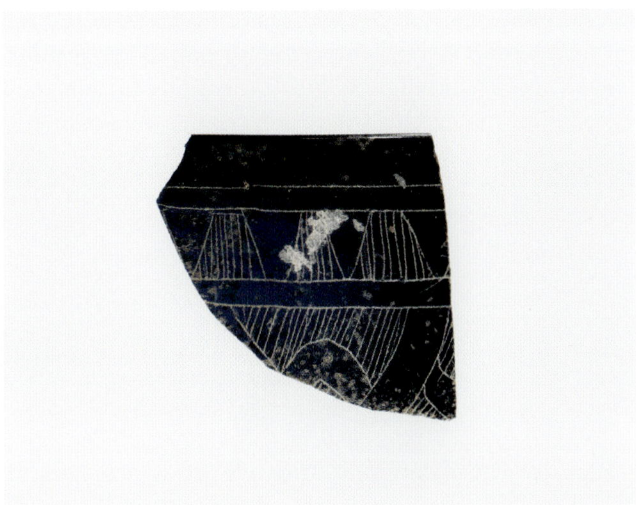

17

Fragment of cylindrical cup, preserving small part of rim and upper wall. Rim plain, with rounded lip; upper wall vertical. Exterior of wall has at least two horizontal bands of scratched ornament. Upper band has pair of horizontal lines at top and pair of lines dividing it from lower band. Upper (narrower) band contains uneven row of isosceles triangles, bases of which are contiguous and filled with vertical hatching; triangular spaces between each pair of hatched triangles are plain. Lower (broader) band apparently contains large isosceles triangles, sides of which are in form of long, narrow ovals with scratched outlines and plain interiors; each triangle contains one arc-shaped element with scratched outline and plain interior; these elements have alternating upward- and downward-pointing ends. Backgrounds have transverse hatching.

Small patches of gray to brown weathering. Abraded area on exterior may be result of removing sample for chemical analysis.

18. Fragment of Cup

8th to 9th century. 68.1.59-1.
H. (surviving) 6.6 cm, D. (rim, est.) 8 cm.
Transparent deep blue; bubbles and small stones. Blown; scratch-engraved.

Fragment of cylindrical cup, preserving small part of rim, larger part of wall, and edge of base. Rim plain, with rounded lip; wall descends vertically, then curves in at bottom. Exterior of wall has two horizontal bands of scratched ornament, each bordered by single horizontal scratched lines at top and bottom, and with two additional scratched lines: one above upper band and one below lower band. Upper (narrower) band contains row of narrow isosceles triangles, bases of which are contiguous and filled with vertical hatching; triangular spaces between each pair of hatched triangles are plain. Lower (broader) band contains two rows of contiguous arcs, of which upper row has ends pointing down and lower row has ends pointing up, defining plain area resembling twisted ribbon; backgrounds above and below this are filled with transverse hatching.

Glass has scratches, but virtually no weathering that is visible to the naked eye.

Comment: Chemical analysis revealed that the material is a soda-lime-silica glass made with natron (Brill 1999, v. 1, p. 96, and v. 2, p. 194, no. 6351, where the accession number is given as 68.1.59). This suggests that the glass was made either in Egypt, the most likely source of the natron, or in the Syro-Palestinian region.

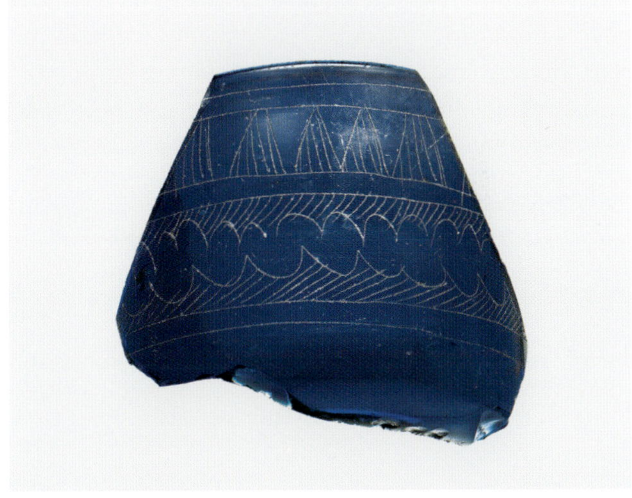

18

19. Fragment of Cup

8th to 9th century. 51.1.113.
H. (surviving) 5.3 cm, D. (rim, est.) 8 cm.
Transparent deep blue; stones and few small bubbles. Blown; scratch-engraved.

Fragment of cylindrical cup, preserving small part of rim and upper wall. Rim plain, with rounded lip;

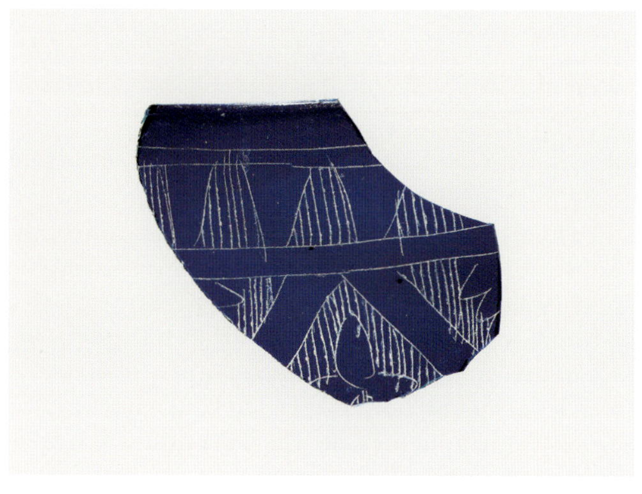

19

wall descends almost vertically, with slightly convex profile. Exterior of wall has at least two horizontal bands of scratched ornament. Upper band has pair of horizontal lines at top and pair of lines dividing it from lower band. Upper (narrower) band contains row of narrow isosceles triangles, bases of which are contiguous and filled with vertical hatching; triangular spaces between each pair of hatched triangles are plain. Lower (broader) band apparently contains large isosceles triangles, sides of which are in form of narrow stripes with scratched outlines and plain interiors; each triangle apparently contains one palmette with scratched outlines and plain interior; these elements have alternating upward- and downward-pointing tops. Backgrounds have vertical hatching.

Small patches of incipient weathering on inside; otherwise, glass is as new.

Comment: The upward-pointing palmette probably resembled the palmettes on **20** and **38**.

Chemical analysis revealed that the material is a soda-lime-silica glass made with natron (Brill 1999, v. 1, p. 96, and v. 2, p. 195, no. 6360). This suggests that the glass was made either in Egypt, the most likely source of the natron, or in the Syro-Palestinian region.

20. Fragment of Cup

8th to 9th century. Formerly in the Smith Collection (1218-7). Gift of Carl Berkowitz and Derek Content. 76.1.237.
H. (surviving) 5.1 cm, D. (rim, est.) about 8 cm.
Transparent blue; small bubbles. Blown; scratch-engraved.

Fragment of cylindrical cup, including small part of rim. Rim plain, with rounded lip; wall descends almost vertically. Exterior of wall has scratch-engraved ornament (from top to bottom): four horizontal lines, bottom two of which are close together and form upper border of broad band containing part of triangular panel; inside panel is leaf with lobed sides and open end, enlivened with hatched oval motif and hatched background; to right, and separated from it by narrow undecorated strip, corner of inverted triangle, with edge of leaf with lobed side and hatched background.

Surface almost as new.

Comment: Evidently, the principal decoration was a broad band divided into alternating upright and inverted triangles, each of which contained a palmette similar to the palmettes on **19** and **38**.

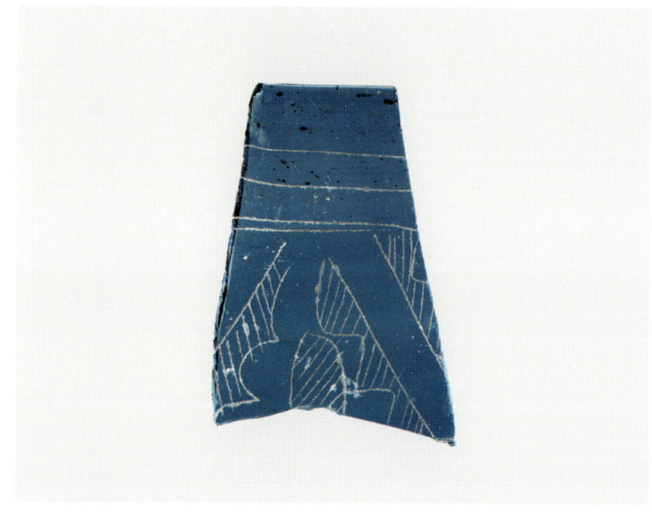

20

21. Fragment of Cup

8th to 9th century. 51.1.117A.
H. (surviving) 2.5 cm, D. (rim, est.) about 8 cm.
Transparent deep blue. Blown; scratch-engraved.

Fragment of cylindrical cup, including small part of rim. Rim plain, with rounded lip; upper wall vertical. Exterior of wall has at least one horizontal band of scratched ornament, bordered by single horizontal scratched line at top and at bottom, and with additional scratched line above it. Band contains uneven row of isosceles triangles, bases of which are contiguous and filled with vertical hatching; triangular spaces between each pair of hatched triangles are plain.

Shiny, with patches of incipient weathering.

Comment: Chemical analysis revealed that the material is a soda-lime-silica glass made with natron (Brill 1999, v. 1, p. 96, and v. 2, p. 194, no. 6356).

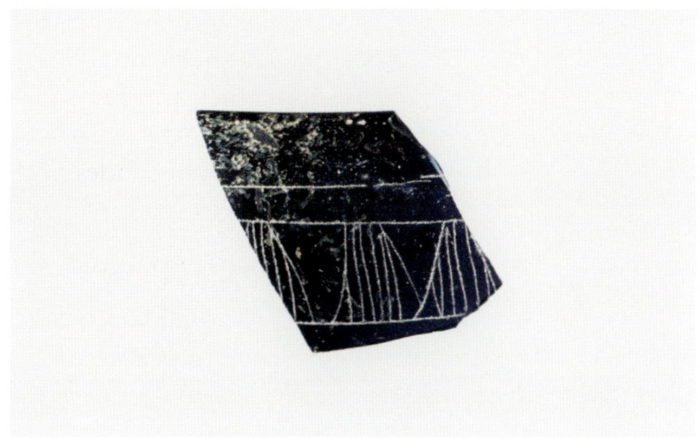

21

This suggests that the glass was made either in Egypt, the most likely source of the natron, or in the Syro-Palestinian region.

22. Fragment of Cup

8th to 9th century. Formerly in the Smith Collection (1104). Gift of Carl Berkowitz and Derek Content. 76.1.238.
Max. Dim. 5.5 cm, H. (surviving) 3.2 cm, D. (lower wall, est.) about 12 cm.
Transparent very pale green. Blown; scratch-engraved.

Three joining fragments of cylindrical cup. Lower wall descends vertically, then curves in at bottom. Fragment has parts of two presumably continuous horizontal bands of scratched ornament, each with double border line at bottom. Upper band probably has row of adjacent right-angle triangles, with vertical side on left, sloping side on right, and transverse hatching. Lower band has row of adjacent isosceles triangles with transverse hatching.

Dull, but virtually unweathered.

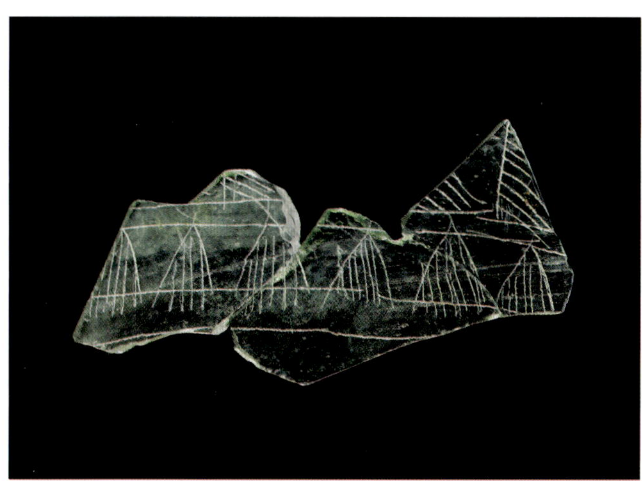

22

23. Fragment of Cup

8th to 9th century. 51.1.144.
H. (surviving) 4.5 cm, D. (wall, est.) about 11–12 cm.
Transparent pale greenish yellow. Blown; scratch-engraved.

Fragment of cylindrical cup. Wall is almost straight and probably vertical. Exterior is decorated with broad band of scratch-engraved ornament divided into panels, which are separated by narrow undecorated strip and share two parallel border lines at bottom (top is missing). Panel on left has lattice of wavy lines making overall pattern of roughly diamond-shaped motifs; panel on right is similar, but with lattice of straight lines. Below border lines at bottom is end of roughly horizontal line, perhaps part of third, incomplete border line.

Broken on all sides. Iridescent weathering.

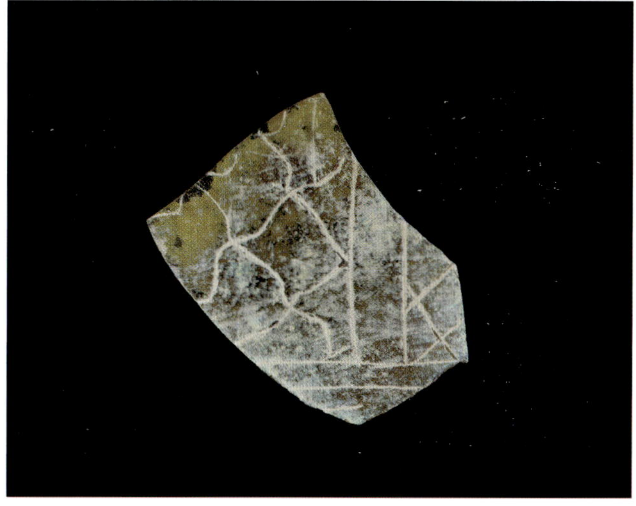

23

Comment: Panels containing lattices of straight lines, alternating with panels containing lattices of wavy lines, are also found on **16**, which is also a cylindrical cup.

Chemical analysis revealed that the material is a soda-lime-silica glass made with natron (Brill 1999, v. 1, p. 95, and v. 2, p. 194, no. 6342). This suggests that the glass was made either in Egypt, the most likely source of the natron, or in the Syro-Palestinian region.

24. Fragment of Cup

8th or 9th century. Formerly in the Strauss Collection (F12). Bequest of Jerome Strauss. 79.1.305.

H. (surviving) 6.7 cm, D. (lower wall, est.) about 11 cm.
Transparent blue; small bubbles and few very small stones. Blown; scratch-engraved.

Fragment of cylindrical cup, evidently including almost complete profile of wall from just below rim almost to base. Wall is almost straight, but has convex profile, and it curves in at bottom. Exterior of wall has three horizontal bands of scratch-engraved ornament (from top to bottom): (1) evidently just below rim, narrow band with group of short vertical lines resting on border line; (2) between pairs of border lines above and below, broad band of leaf sprays and isolated leaves, all filled with transverse hatching; and (3) evidently just above base, narrow band with border line at top, from which descends group of short vertical lines alternating with hatched semicircles.

Broken on all sides. Faint traces of weathering in scratches and broken bubbles; otherwise almost pristine. "F 12" written on interior, near lower edge, in green ink.

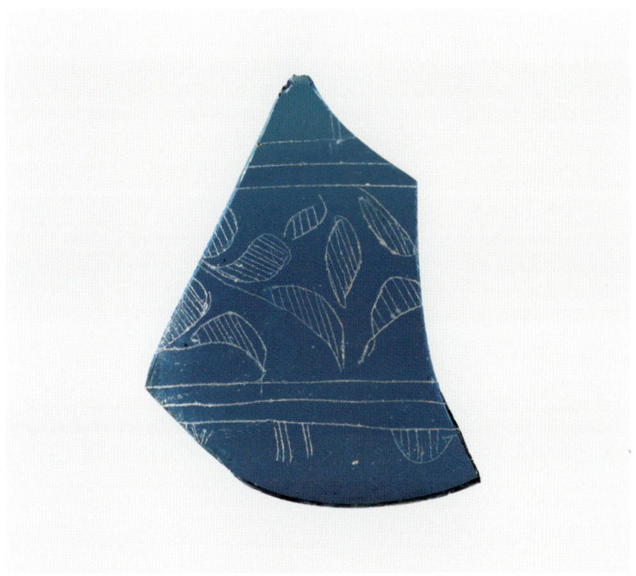

24

COMMENT: Although the fragment is very narrow at the top, the thinness of the glass suggests that it was very close (probably within a few millimeters) to the rim. It is possible that bands (1) and (3) were similar, except for the fact that (1) pointed up and (3) pointed down.

25. Fragment of Cup

8th to 9th century. 51.1.111.
H. (surviving) 6.4 cm, D. (wall, est.) about 11 cm.
Transparent deep blue. Blown; scratch-engraved.

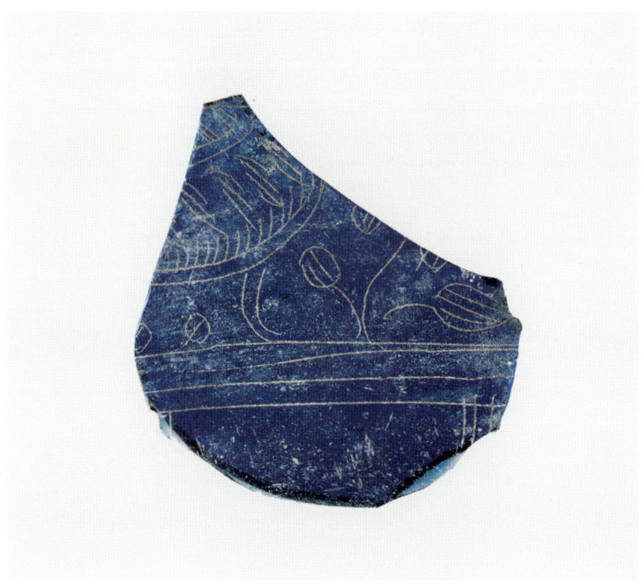

25

Fragment of cylindrical cup. Wall descends vertically and curves in at bottom. Exterior has broad band of scratch-engraved ornament with four roughly parallel horizontal border lines at bottom (upper border does not survive). Ornament consists of body, leg, and perhaps part of wing of bird standing in profile, facing right; in front of it, plant with curving stem and round or oval leaves on short stalks; below body of bird are two circular motifs; parts of bird, leaves, and circles have vertical and transverse hatching. Parts of two groups of short vertical lines project downward from bottom of border.

Broken on all sides. Dull and somewhat pitted, with patches of light grayish weathering.

COMMENT: See **9**.

Chemical analysis revealed that the material is a soda-lime-silica glass made with natron (Brill 1999, v. 1, p. 96, and v. 2, p. 194, no. 6352). This suggests that the glass was made either in Egypt, the most likely source of the natron, or in the Syro-Palestinian region.

26. Fragment of Cup

8th to 9th century. Formerly in the Smith Collection (1111). Gift of Carl Berkowitz and Derek Content. 76.1.239.
H. (surviving) 4.4 cm, D. (wall, est.) about 10 cm.
Transparent blue; two oval bubbles (larger: L. 0.55 cm) and many smaller bubbles. Blown; scratch-engraved.

Fragment of cylindrical cup. Lower wall descends vertically and curves in at bottom. Exterior has scratch-engraved ornament: broad horizontal band with single border line at bottom and three more or less parallel lines below it; surviving part of band contains geometric ornament, which is partly filled with vertical hatching and appears to contain part of diamond-shaped panel with double outline.

Broken on all sides. Dull and pitted, with patches of light gray and brownish weathering.

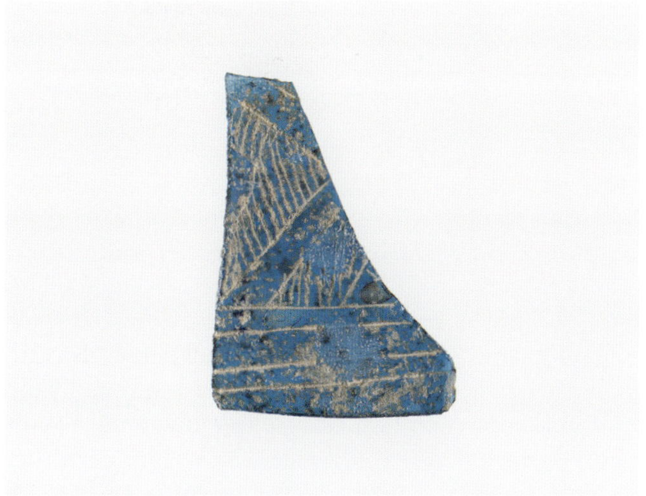

26

27. Fragment of Cup

8th to 9th century. Formerly in the Smith Collection (1218-9). Gift of Carl Berkowitz and Derek Content. 76.1.240.
Max Dim. 3.8 cm, D. (wall, est.) about 10 cm.
Transparent bluish green. Blown; scratch-engraved.

Fragment from wall of cylindrical cup. Exterior has parts of three horizontal bands of scratch-engraved

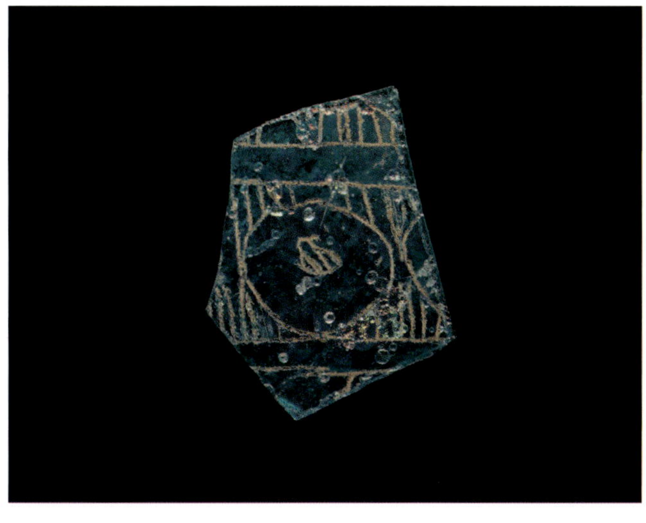

27

ornament (from top to bottom): (1) probably lower part of narrow band with single border line at bottom (top is missing) and row of hatched isosceles triangles resting on border; (2) band (W. 1.6 cm) with single border lines at top and bottom, containing circle with small hatched circle at center and small part of second circle, and with hatched background; and (3) single border line at top of band with indeterminate ornament.

Broken on all sides. Dull and pitted, with patches of iridescence.

Comment: Brill (1999, v. 1, p. 96, no. 6367) sampled the fragment, but he did not publish an analysis.

28. Fragment of Cup

8th to 9th century. Formerly in the Smith Collection (1218-8). Gift of Carl Berkowitz and Derek Content. 76.1.241.
H. (surviving) 3.3 cm, D. (wall, est.) about 9–10 cm.
Transparent blue. Blown; scratch-engraved.

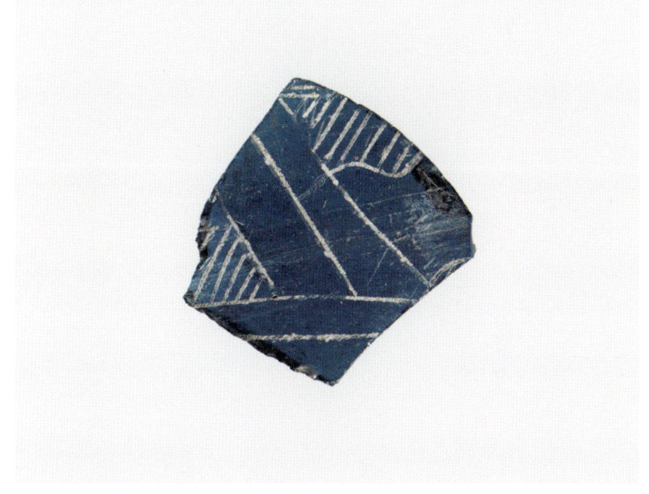

28

Fragment of cylindrical cup. Wall descends vertically. Exterior has scratch-engraved ornament: part of horizontal band with border line at bottom (?) and one roughly parallel line below that. Surviving part of band has three parallel transverse lines with, to right, two horizontal wavy lines with transverse hatching above upper line and undecorated area between them, and, to left, area of transverse hatching.

Broken on all sides. Dull, with light grayish weathering, especially in scratched lines, and hint of iridescence.

Comment: The fragment is too small to permit one to reconstruct the ornament with any degree of confidence. It is just possible, however, that the band contained contiguous, straight-sided (perhaps rhomboid) panels, which were divided horizontally by a pair of wavy lines with hatching above and below, and a plain area between them.

29. Fragment of Cup

8th to 9th century. 51.1.116.
H. (surviving) 3.9 cm, D. (wall, est.) about 9 cm.
Transparent deep blue. Blown; scratch-engraved.

Fragment of cylindrical cup. Wall descends vertically. Exterior has scratch-engraved ornament: horizontal band with single border line above and below; surviving part of band contains diamond-shaped panel with double outlines, inside which are four circles filled with vertical hatching; triangular areas between edges of diamond and border lines also have vertical hatching.

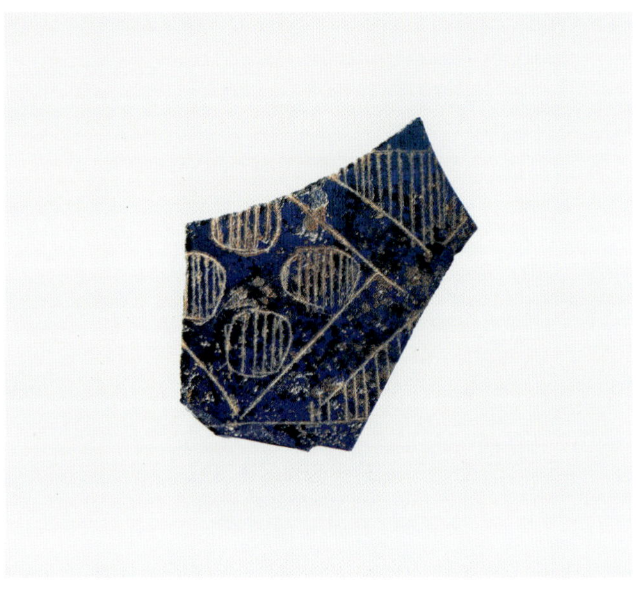

29

Broken on all sides. Small patches of light brown weathering.

Comment: The outline of the diamond-shaped panel projects upward and to right, as though a second diamond adjoined the first; perhaps all or part of the band was filled with adjoining diamond-shaped panels.

Chemical analysis revealed that the material is a soda-lime-silica glass made with natron (Brill 1999, v. 1, p. 96, and v. 2, p. 194, no. 6354). This suggests that the glass was made either in Egypt, the most likely source of the natron, or in the Syro-Palestinian region.

30. Fragment of Cup

8th to 9th century. 51.1.118B.
H. 4 cm, D. (lower wall, est.) about 8 cm.
Transparent blue. Blown; scratch-engraved.

Fragment consisting of three joining pieces of cylindrical cup. Lower wall (Th. less than 0.1 cm) descends almost vertically, but with slightly convex profile, and curves in at bottom. Exterior above curve has two horizontal bands of scratch-engraved ornament: (1) upper, broader band has single border line at bottom (top is missing), emerging from which is triangular leaf with serrated edge, enlivened with group of three short vertical lines; background on each side of leaf has transverse hatching; and (2) beneath narrow undecorated band and with single border lines at top and bottom, row of contiguous isosceles triangles with bases on lower border; these triangles have vertical hatching, and triangular spaces between them are plain; below border line at bottom, one parallel line.

Broken on all sides. Dull, with patches of grayish weathering.

Comment: For other examples of triangular leaves, but with lobed rather than serrated sides, see **38** and a bottle in the al-Sabah Collection, Dār al-Āthār al-Islāmiyyah, Kuwait National Museum (LNS 375 G: Carboni 2001, p. 76, no. 17a = *Glass of the Sultans* 2001, p. 166, no. 72 = *Islamic Art* 1994, p. 127, lot 317).

Chemical analysis revealed that the material is a soda-lime-silica glass made with natron (Brill 1999, v. 1, p. 95, and v. 2, p. 194, no. 6358, where the accession number is given as 51.1.11A). This suggests that the glass was made either in Egypt, the most likely source of the natron, or in the Syro-Palestinian region.

Dr. Robert H. Brill says that **30** and **33** were originally part of the same object.

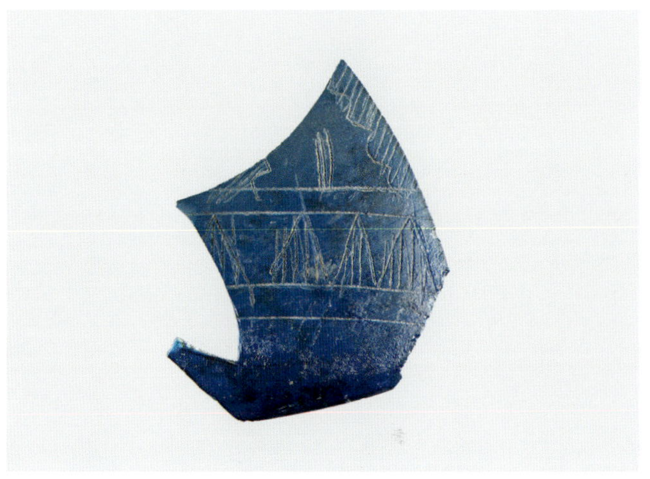

30

31. Fragment of Cup

8th to 9th century. Formerly in the Smith Collection (1106). Gift of Carl Berkowitz and Derek Content. 76.1.242.
H. (surviving) 2.4 cm, D. (edge of base, est.) about 7 cm.
Transparent blue, with small stones. Blown; scratch-engraved.

Fragment of cylindrical cup, consisting of two joining pieces. Lower wall (Th. 0.1 cm) descends vertically and curves in at bottom; edge of base plain. Exterior of lower wall has parts of two indeterminate scratch-engraved motifs.

Broken on all sides. Slightly pitted; otherwise, surface is as new.

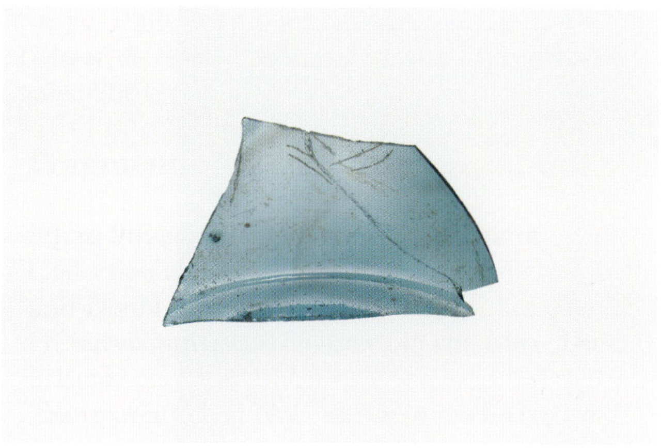

31

32. Fragment of Cup(?)

8th to 9th century. Formerly in the Smith Collection (1116). Gift of Carl Berkowitz and Derek Content. 76.1.243.
H. (surviving) 3.9 cm, D. (lower wall, est.) 10–11 cm.
Transparent deep blue; small bubbles. Blown; scratch-engraved.

Fragment of cylindrical cup(?), consisting of two joining pieces. Lower wall is straight and either vertical or tapering, and it curves in at bottom. Exterior has scratch-engraved decoration (from top to bottom): narrow horizontal band of rather uneven isosceles triangles, with bases on groundline, filled with transverse hatching; band of seven more or less parallel lines, descending from bottom of which is group of short vertical lines.

Broken on all sides. Slightly pitted, with traces of weathering, especially in scratched lines.

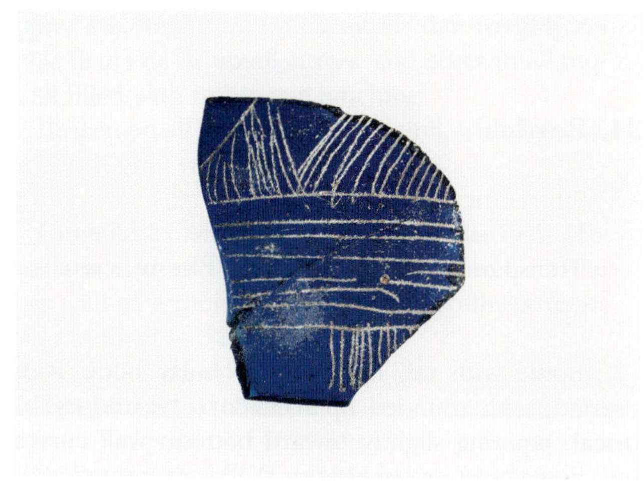

32

Comment: The fragment appears to have come from the lower wall of a cup, although it is possible that it is from near the bottom of a bowl or a pear-shaped bottle (cf. the bottle in the al-Sabah Collection, Dār al-Āthār al-Islāmiyyah, Kuwait National Museum (LNS 375 G: Carboni 2001, p. 76, no. 17a = *Glass of the Sultans* 2001, p. 166, no. 72)).

33. Fragments of Cup(?)

8th to 9th century. 51.1.118A.
Max. Dim. (a) 2.5 cm, (b) 1.4 cm.
Transparent blue. Blown; scratch-engraved.

Three small joining fragments of cylindrical cup(?). Both fragments have scratch-engraved ornament on exterior: (a) part of narrow band containing row of adjoining isosceles triangles with vertical hatching; (b) indeterminate motif with some hatching.

(a) and (b) Broken on all sides. Dull, with traces of weathering.

Comment: See **30**.

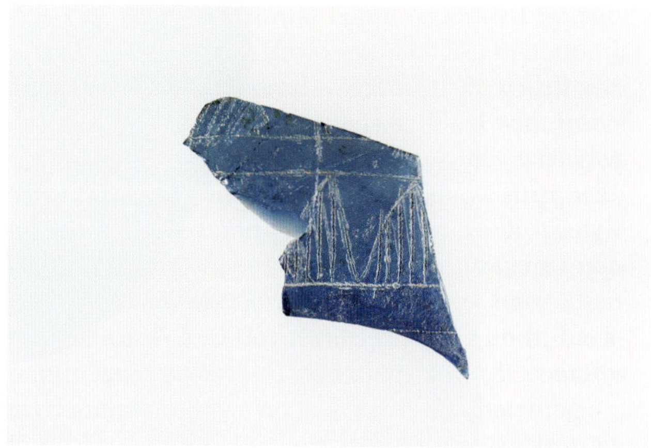

33

5. Indeterminate Forms

41. Fragment with Inscription(?)

8th to 9th century. 51.1.114.
Max. Dim. 3.6 cm, H. 3 cm, D. (est., wall) 12–13 cm.
Transparent deep blue. Blown; scratch-engraved.

Fragment. Wall is straight and perhaps descends vertically. Exterior has scratch-engraved ornament, which may include small part of Kufic inscription filled with transverse hatching, associated with small hatched circles, and indeterminate motif.

Broken on all sides. Locally pitted, especially on interior, with light brown weathering in pits and scratched lines.

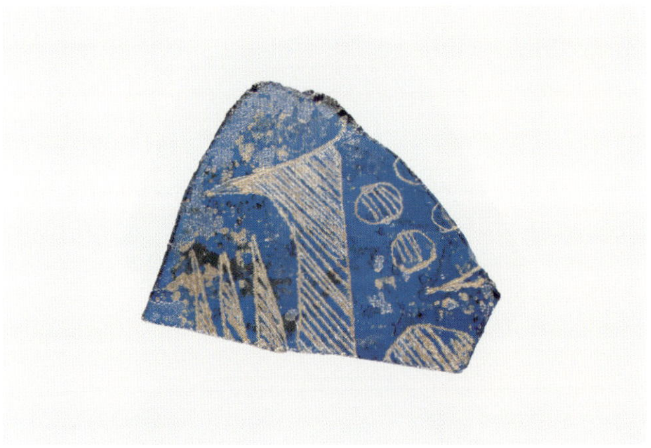

41

42. Fragment

8th to 9th century. Formerly in the Smith Collection (1115). Gift of Carl Berkowitz and Derek Content. 76.1.249.
H. (surviving) 3.1 cm, D. (lower wall, est.) about 11 cm.
Transparent deep blue. Blown; scratch-engraved.

Fragment consisting of three joining pieces that together make up about 20 percent of circumference. Lower wall (Th. 0.25–0.3 cm) descends, perhaps vertically, and curves in at bottom. Scratch-engraved ornament consists of lower part of horizontal band of indeterminate linear decoration, some of which has transverse hatching, and pair of border lines; below border, one incomplete and three complete motifs, each consisting of two groups of three short vertical lines.

No obvious weathering.

Comment: The shape, dimensions, and thickness of the fragment suggest that it came from a cylindrical cup or bowl.

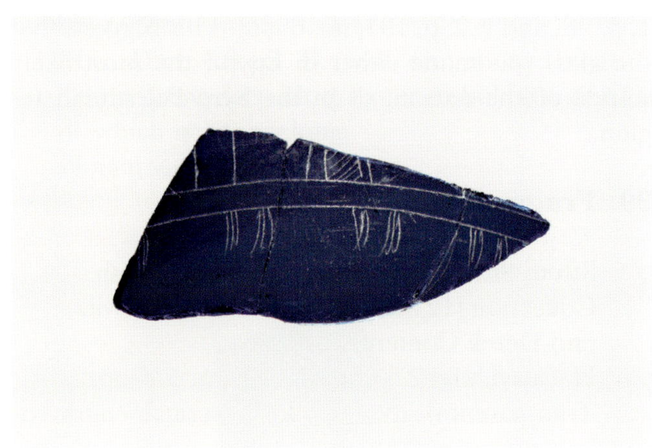

42

43. Fragment

8th to 9th century. Formerly in the Smith Collection (1118). Gift of Carl Berkowitz and Derek Content. 76.1.250.
Max. Dim. 4.3 cm.
Transparent blue; bubbles up to 0.3 cm long. Blown; scratch-engraved.

Fragment of vessel, consisting of two pieces that join. Exterior has scratch-engraved ornament: narrow band containing groups of two or three transverse stripes between upper and lower border lines; below

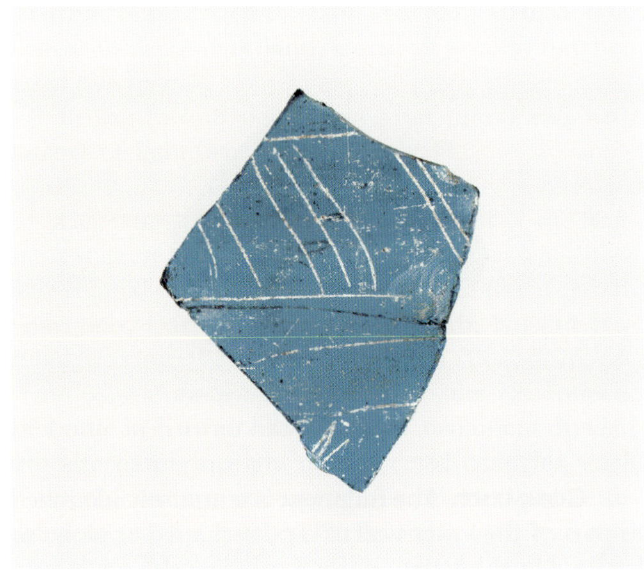

43

this, two more or less parallel lines, below which is small part of unidentified motif.

Broken on all sides. Pitted, with pale grayish weathering in pits.

COMMENT: The description supposes that the narrow band of hatching is uppermost, but this assumption cannot be verified.

44. Fragment

8th to 9th century. Formerly in the Smith Collection (1218-6). Gift of Carl Berkowitz and Derek Content. 76.1.248.
Max. Dim. 2.0 cm, Th. 0.1 cm.
Transparent purple. Blown; scratch-engraved.

Fragment from wall of vessel. Exterior has scratch-engraved ornament: two parallel lines with small part of hatched motif on one side of them, and two small circles filled with hatching on the other side.

Broken on all sides. Shiny, but with incipient weathering on interior.

COMMENT: Although the fragment is very small, its identity is not in doubt. The thinness of the wall suggests that the fragment came from a small vessel, possibly a cup.

Brill (1999, v. 1, p. 97, no. 6369) sampled the fragment, but he did not publish an analysis.

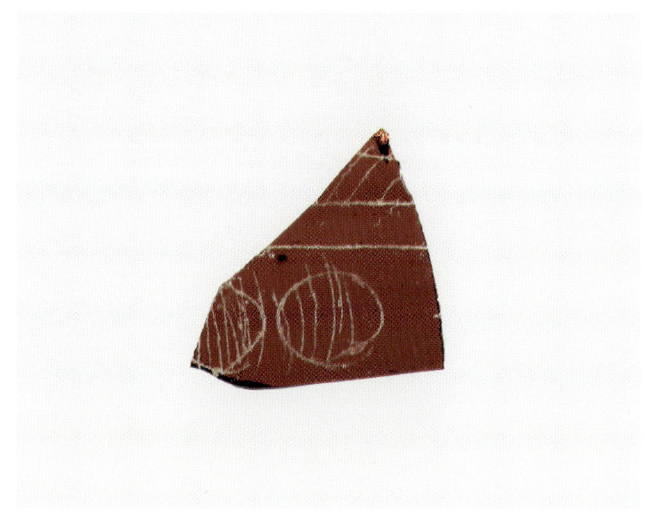

44

B

Monochrome Objects with Wheel-Cut Ornament

Some of the best-known glass made in the Sasanian Empire (224–651) consisted of monochrome thick-walled vessels decorated with patterns of hollow facets made by cutting, grinding, and polishing. The ornament varied from overall "honeycomb" patterns of shallow facets to friezes of facets combined with linear motifs. Despite uncertainty about the detailed chronology of Sasanian cut glass, it is thought that faceted objects were made throughout the period between the third and seventh centuries (*Splendeur des Sassanides* 1993, pp. 110–111; pp. 257–258, nos. 105–107; and pp. 260–264, nos. 109–113; Whitehouse 2005, pp. 41–57). Thus, while cutting on the wheel was abandoned in the Roman world after the fourth century (*Glass of the Caesars* 1987, pp. 183–185), facet cutting survived in Western Asia. Indeed, its occurrence on early Islamic objects points to continuity until about the end of the millennium.

A second variety of early Islamic cut glass with Sasanian antecedents is decorated with raised disks and bosses (*Splendeur des Sassanides* 1993, p. 111 and p. 265, no. 114; Whitehouse 2005, pp. 45–48, nos. 50–52, 54, and 55). In both the Sasanian and the early Islamic periods, objects with raised or countersunk disks appear to be much less common than facet-cut glasses.

Other types of wheel cutting were introduced after the Sasanian period and flourished in the Islamic world between the ninth and 11th centuries. Indeed, during these centuries, glass cutters produced a wide variety of objects, which include some of the finest achievements of Islamic glassworking. The wheel-cut glass of the ᶜAbbāsids and their successors has been divided into several styles, in the simplest of which the ornament was delineated by incised lines. This linear-cut decoration came to be used by glassmakers all over Western Asia, in Egypt, and perhaps farther west. A second type of ornament consists of what Ettinghausen (1952) termed the "beveled" style, in which outlines are cut on a slant and there is often no distinct second plane forming the background. The beveled or, in Kröger's (1995, p. 161) terminology, "slant-cut" style was employed by craftsmen in many media, including rock crystal, stucco, and wood. It, too, enjoyed widespread popularity.

A third style consists of relief cutting, in which the entire background is removed, leaving the ornament in relief. Numerous examples of relief-cut glass have been found in northern Iran, and scholars often associate the style with the medieval city of Nishapur, which enjoyed wealth and stability under the quasi-autonomous Sāmānid dynasty (874–1001). It is highly unlikely, however, that Nishapur was the only place of production (if, indeed, relief-cut glass was made there at all: see page 176), and other producers probably existed both elsewhere in Western Asia and in Egypt.

In addition to their occurrence on monochrome (usually colorless) objects, linear cutting, slant cutting, and especially relief cutting were used to decorate cameo glasses with one or two colored overlays (see pages 281–328).

In the following pages, the monochrome cut glass is divided into six groups. In some cases, especially in groups 3 and 4, the assignment of an object to one or another group is somewhat arbitrary because the object displays a combination of two or more types of ornament. In such cases, the object is described on the basis of the most prominent parts of the ornament.

1. Facet-cut objects (**45**–**117**).
2. Objects decorated with disks and related motifs (**118**–**141**).
3. Linear-cut objects (**142**–**249**).
4. Slant-cut objects (**250**–**296**).
5. Relief-cut objects (**297**–**489**).
6. Objects decorated by molding and cutting (**490**–**492**).

Facet-Cut Objects

While it seems clear that the tradition of making facet-cut glass continued without a break in Iran and Iraq after the Muslim conquest, at present we cannot identify with confidence any object that was made in the seventh or eighth century. However, numerous vessels attributed to the period between the ninth and 11th centuries on the basis of their form and, rarely, their archeological contexts are decorated with hollow facets. **45–117** are objects that are universally believed to be post-Sasanian, although their dates within the early Islamic period are, in most cases, uncertain.

The 72 facet-cut objects are described in the following order:

1. Dish (**45**).
2. Bowl (**46**).
3. Cylindrical cups (**47**–**51**).
4. Truncated conical beakers (**52**–**54**).
5. Bottles (**55**–**86**).
6. Small bottles (**87**–**102**).
7. Small bottles, "molar flasks" (**103**–**112**).
8. Pitcher (**113**).
9. Ewers (**114** and **115**).
10. Indeterminate (**116** and **117**).

1. Dish

45. Miniature Dish

Perhaps 9th to 10th century. Formerly in the Smith Collection (1385). Gift of Carl Berkowitz and Derek Content. 76.1.229.
H. 1–1.3 cm, D. (rim) 4.4 cm.
Transparent light greenish blue. Blown; facet- and linear-cut.

Dish: shallow. Rim plain, with rounded lip; wall curves down and in; base plain. Wall decorated with continuous band of 24 hollow oval facets, each with height greater than width. Base has raised square panel (W. 1.7 cm) decorated with linear-cut cross.

Intact. Dull and pitted, with remains of light gray weathering.

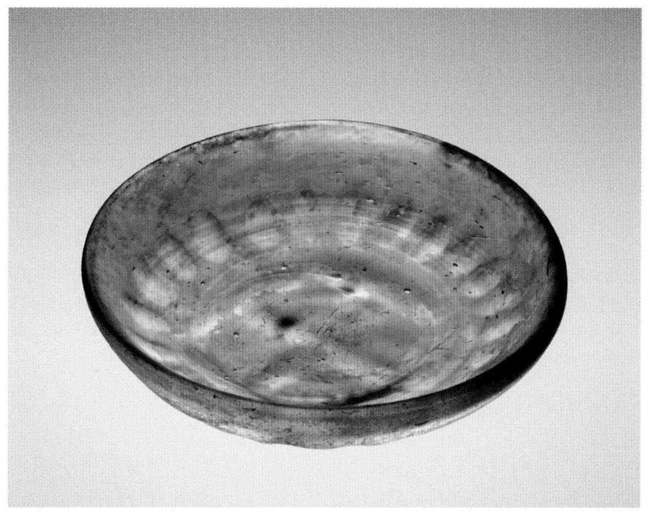

45

Comment: A larger dish, with two rows of hollow oval facets on the wall and a cross on the underside of the base, was excavated from a ninth- to 10th-century context at Fusṭāṭ; it is now at Corning (**144**).

2. Bowl

46. Bowl

9th to 10th century, possibly earlier. 62.1.3.
H. 9.3 cm, D. (rim) 10.2 cm.
Colorless. Blown; facet-cut.

Bowl: deep. Rim plain, with top ground flat and with bevel on inside; wall (TTh. 0.8 cm) straight and tapering slightly before curving down and in toward bottom; base plain; pontil mark possibly replaced with shallow circular depression (D. 1.6 cm), which has countersunk dot at center. Decoration extends from top to bottom of wall and consists of continuous band of 12 raised "petals," which have straight sides and pointed tops, and are thicker along vertical axis than at edges; sides of adjacent petals are separated by narrow grooves; each triangular area between tops of adjacent petals and rim is facet-cut in three triangular planes.

Almost complete. Broken into many pieces, with chips missing from rim and one very small loss from wall. Repaired. Extensively pitted, with patches of iridescence.

Comment: The bowl was acquired (in Germany) from an Iranian dealer. It is possible, therefore, that the object was found in Iran. It appears to be blown, although the absence of elongated bubbles raises the possibility that it was formed by casting in a mold. The two possibilities—that it came from Iran and that it was cast—may have a bearing on the identity of the object. The nature and extent of the weathering indicate that it is of some, perhaps considerable, antiquity.

The bowl is generally regarded as being an unusual example of Islamic cut glass of the ninth to 10th or 11th centuries (cf. *Treasures in Glass* 1966, p. 25, no. 26). The quality of the glass is consistent with this opinion; many of the objects traditionally associated with Nishapur are made of visually similar colorless glass with very few bubbles. The weathering, which includes small circular or subcircular patches that have spalled, also resembles weathering commonly found on decolorized glasses of "Nishapur type." The source, too, may support the view that the object is an example of "Nishapur-type" relief-cut glass.

However, the form is atypical, and the petallike motifs (are they distant reminiscences of the lotus petals commonly found on Chinese metal and ceramic vessels?) do not belong to the repertoire of "Nishapur-type" glasses. They do, however, recall the band of "rectangular cut panels surmounted by bevel-cut triangles" that adorns a beaker in the Khalili

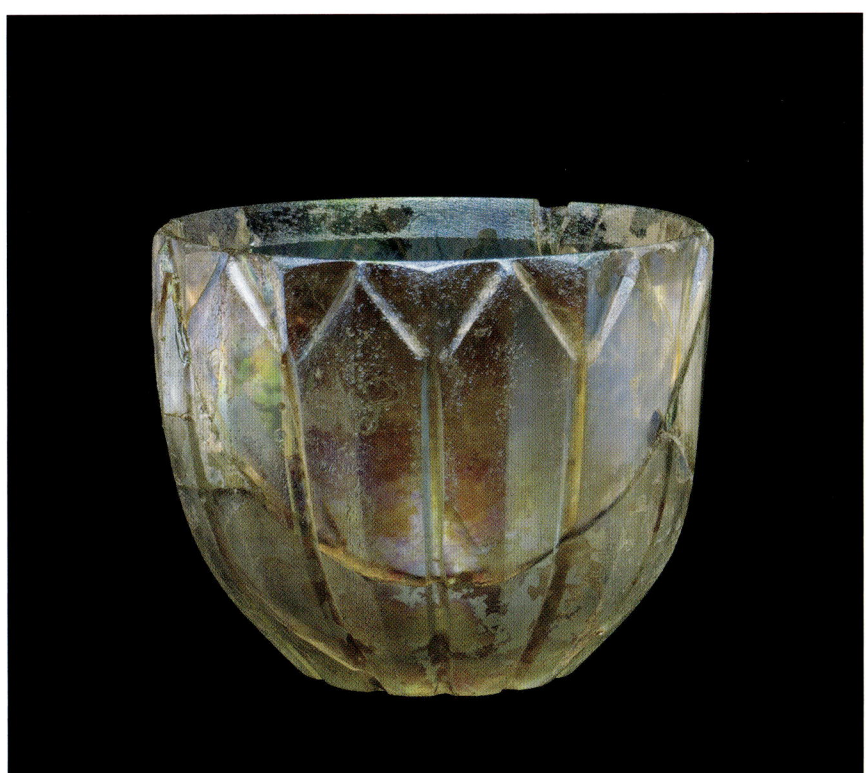

46

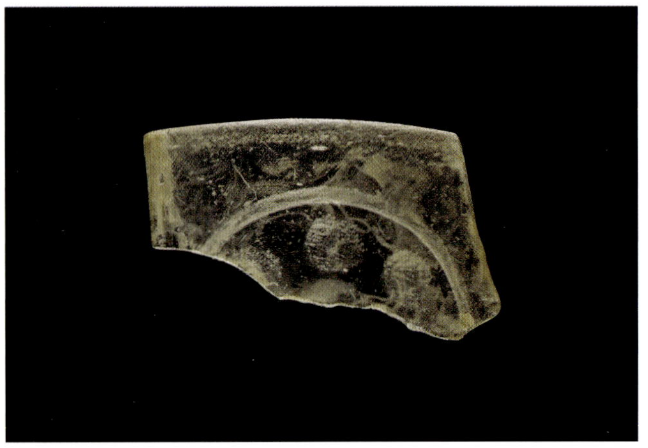

50

center, circular facet surrounded by ring of six or seven circular facets.

Broken on all sides except rim. Dull, with patches of transparent grayish weathering.

Comment: The fragment probably came from the rim and upper wall of a cup. Alternatively, it may be part of a pitcher similar to Kröger 1995, pp. 125–126 (excavated at Nishapur, northeastern Iran), which has rows of facets on the body and an isolated facet on the neck.

51. Fragment of Cup(?)

9th to 10th century. Formerly in the Smith Collection (1146). 2009.1.4.

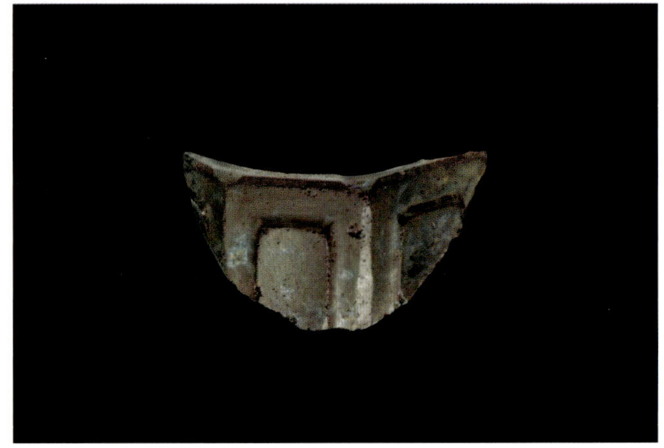

51

H. (surviving) 2.8 cm, D. (rim, est.) 5.5 cm.
Probably colorless or almost colorless. Blown; facet-cut.

Fragment of cup(?), including about 25 percent of rim. Rim plain, with flat top and narrow bevel on outside. Wall (Th. 0.4 cm) descends vertically and was cut in approximately nine continuous vertical facets, each with one raised, rectangular facet at center.

Broken on all sides except rim. Light brown, slightly iridescent weathering.

Comment: The diameter of the rim suggests that the fragment came from a cylindrical cup, although the decoration would be unusual on a cup, and it is possible, therefore, that the object was a jar or bottle.

4. Truncated Conical Beakers

52. Beaker

10th to 11th century. Formerly in the Strauss Collection (S2318). Bequest of Jerome Strauss. 79.1.52.
H. 9–9.2 cm, D. (rim) 7.5 cm, (base) 4.7 cm.
Almost colorless, with yellowish green tinge.
Blown; facet- and slant-cut.

Beaker shaped like truncated cone. Rim ground flat; wall straight and tapering; base flat; no pontil mark (but see below). Wall has both facet- and slant-cut decoration: 2.7 to 4.2 cm below rim, three continuous horizontal grooves, each with roughly V-shaped profile, in which upper side of V is four times longer than lower side; 4.9 cm below rim, fourth horizontal groove similar to those above it. On lower wall: two horizontal bands, each containing 11 contiguous hollow facets. Those in upper band are crescent-shaped, and those in lower band are subcircular, having rounded tops and bottoms but straight sides. At bottom of wall: one broad horizontal groove with same profile as other grooves, lower side of which defines foot. Underside of base has central countersunk boss (D. 2.9 cm), presumably to remove pontil mark.

Incomplete. Broken into many pieces, with small loss in bands of facets and in rim, which is chipped; restored. Dull and pitted, with translucent grayish weathering.

Comment: The arrangement of the facets, with those in the upper row directly above those in the lower row, is unusual. A fragmentary beaker, excavated at Nishapur, northeastern Iran, has bands of hexagonal facets above a single band of rectangular

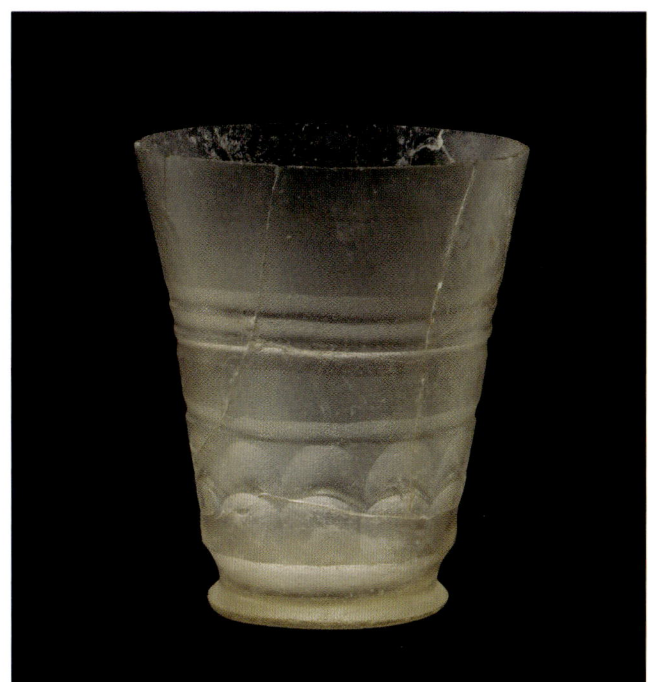

52

facets (The Metropolitan Museum of Art, New York, 48.101.264: Kröger 1995, pp. 124–125, no. 167).

53. Fragment of Beaker

9th to 10th century. Found during excavations at Fusṭāṭ (Old Cairo), Egypt (68.12.67). Gift of the American Research Center in Egypt. 69.1.95.
H. (surviving) 4.5 cm, D. (base) 4.5 cm.
Colorless. Blown; facet- and relief-cut.

Fragment of beaker. Lower wall tapers, with slightly convex profile; disk-shaped base, with splayed upper surface. Decorated on lower wall and underside of base. On wall (from top to bottom): two continuous horizontal ribs, 3.6 cm and 2.2 cm above bottom of wall; between lower rib and bottom of wall, band of 13 contiguous rectangular vertical facets. On base: at center, countersunk disk (D. 1.6 cm) containing small countersunk boss.

Incomplete. Rim, upper wall, and about 30 percent of lower wall are missing (see below). Remains of white to silvery weathering with some iridescence.

Comment: The object was found during excavations directed by Prof. George T. Scanlon. Scanlon and Pinder-Wilson (see below) note that it was "found in a pit whose contents were almost entirely of the 9th–10th century."

At first glance, it appears that a large part of the rim survives. However, although smooth, the "rim" is not parallel to the ribs, and it is more likely that, after the top of the beaker had been broken, the object was cut down to make it usable. The disk and boss project below the plane of the edge of the base, and the object is somewhat unsteady.

Bibliography: Scanlon and Pinder-Wilson 2001, p. 86, no. 41b.

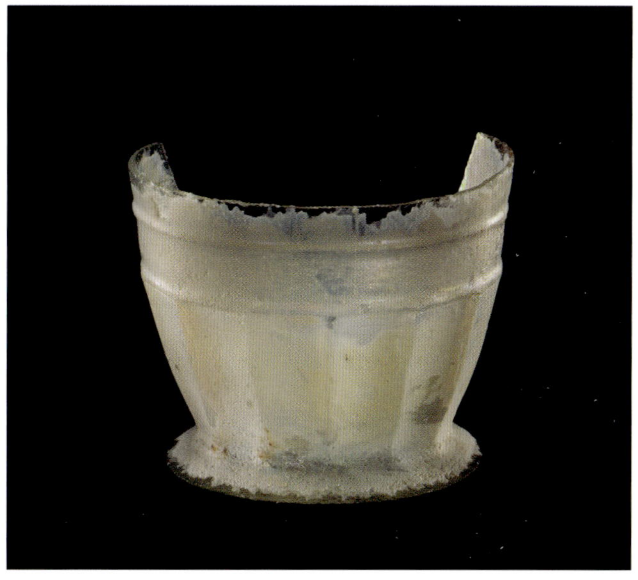

53

54. Fragment of Beaker

About 9th to 10th century. Formerly in the Smith Collection (1137). Gift of Mrs. Ray Winfield Smith. 81.1.694.
H. (surviving) 4.1 cm, D. (base) 4.6 cm.
Transparent very pale green. Blown; facet-cut.

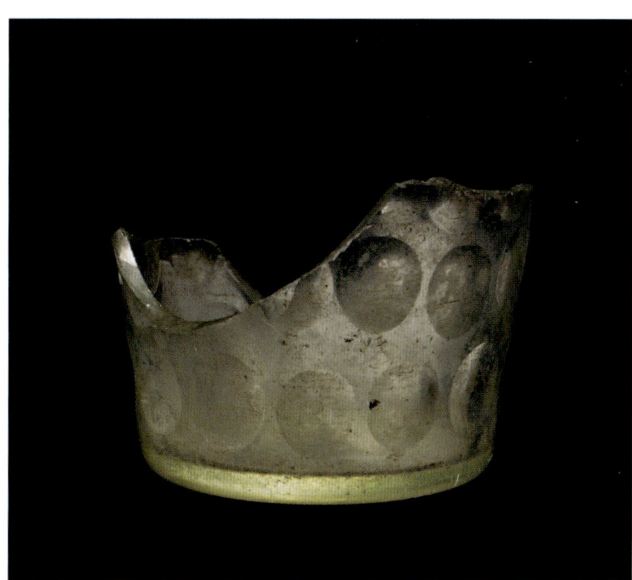

54

Fragment of beaker. Lower wall is straight; it tapers, and curves in at bottom. Base flat; pontil mark almost completely removed by grinding. Lower wall has remains of three continuous horizontal rows of hollow, roughly circular facets. Bottom row has 13 facets; number of facets in other rows cannot be determined.

Base complete, but lower wall broken on all sides. Dull, with traces of cloudy weathering.

Comment: Cf. *Hentrich Collection* 1974, p. 258, no. 403 ("probably from Iran"); and Kröger 1984, pp. 209–210, no. 184 ("Iran, said to be from Nishapur").

5. Bottles

55. Globular Bottle with Long Neck

9th to 10th century. Formerly in the Smith Collection (495). 55.1.129.
H. 21.4 cm, D. (rim) 2.2 cm, (max.) 10.6 cm.
Almost colorless, with green tinge; very many bubbles up to 2 cm long.
Blown; facet-cut.

Bottle: globular. Rim plain, with flat upper surface, except for narrow chamfer at outer edge; tall neck is cylindrical and slightly wider at bottom than at top; base narrow and slightly concave; no pontil mark.

Neck and wall have facet-cut decoration arranged in continuous horizontal bands. Those on neck contain (from top to bottom): (1) five contiguous rectangular facets, junctions of which have been cut away to make five very narrow triangular facets; (2) 13 transverse oval facets; (3) six facets shaped like rhombuses arranged to form three contiguous chevrons, with one oval facet in each triangular space above and below chevrons; (4) 16 short rectangular facets arranged to form eight contiguous chevrons; and (5) two rows of seven roughly triangular or semicircular facets. These bands of facets are separated by shallow grooves that are 0.5–0.6 cm wide. Bands of ornament on wall contain (from top to bottom): (1) 23 transverse oval facets; (2) three rows of adjacent and occasionally overlapping circular facets arranged in quincunx, with 14 facets in each row; and (3) 26 short rectangular facets arranged to form 13 contiguous chevrons. Each band of facets is framed at top by shallow groove that is 0.5–0.6 cm wide. In every case, the facets are polished, but the bands are not. Cutting exposed several large bubbles, some of which were removed by grinding and polishing.

Intact, except for chips on rim. Somewhat dull, with small patches of weathering.

Comment: The bottle was acquired in Tehran, Iran.

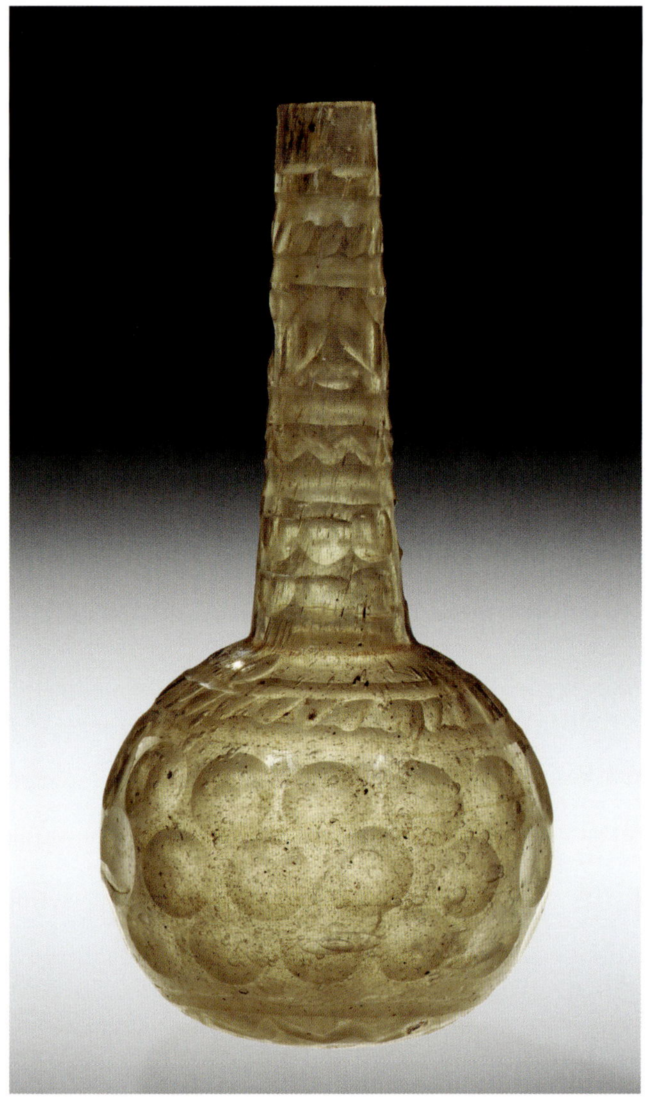

55

Bottles with the same form and similar combinations of rectangular and rhombic facets on the neck and circular facets on the wall include: *2000 Jahre persisches Glas* 1963, n.p., no. 88 (said to be from Nishapur); *Arts of Islam* 1976, pp. 137–138, nos. 122 and 125 (8287 and 8285 in the National Museum, Tehran); Fukai 1977, pl. 71 (said to be from the "Iranian highlands"); *Cohn Collection* 1980, p. 160, no. 153

(in the Los Angeles County Museum of Art); and *Khalili Collection* 2005, p. 199, nos. 236 and 237 (GLS 129 and GLS 139 in the Khalili Collection; the rim of the latter is a narrow flange); see also Bernus-Taylor 2000, p. 55, fig. 3.6.

Bibliography: *Glass of the Sultans* 2001, p. 168, no. 74.

56. Globular Bottle with Long Neck

9th to 10th century. Formerly in the Smith Collection (367). 59.1.478.
H. 19.4 cm, D. (body) 13.0 cm.
Transparent greenish blue. Blown; facet-cut.

Bottle: globular. Rim plain, with flat top; tall neck is almost cylindrical, but wider at bottom than at top; base flat. Decorated on neck, shoulder, wall, and base. Neck is cut in seven contiguous vertical facets, which extend from rim almost to bottom; shoulder has two shallow "steps"; wall is completely covered by six continuous horizontal rows of hollow circular facets, mostly arranged in quincunx; top four rows have 20 facets each, fifth row has 19 facets, and bottom row has 16 facets; junction of wall and base has one shallow "step," and base has small countersunk boss at center.

Complete, except perhaps for rim (see below). Partly covered with iridescent silver weathering; where this is missing, surface is dull and pitted. Circular hole (D. 0.6 cm) in base, off-center, may have been made by Ray Winfield Smith to obtain sample for chemical analysis.

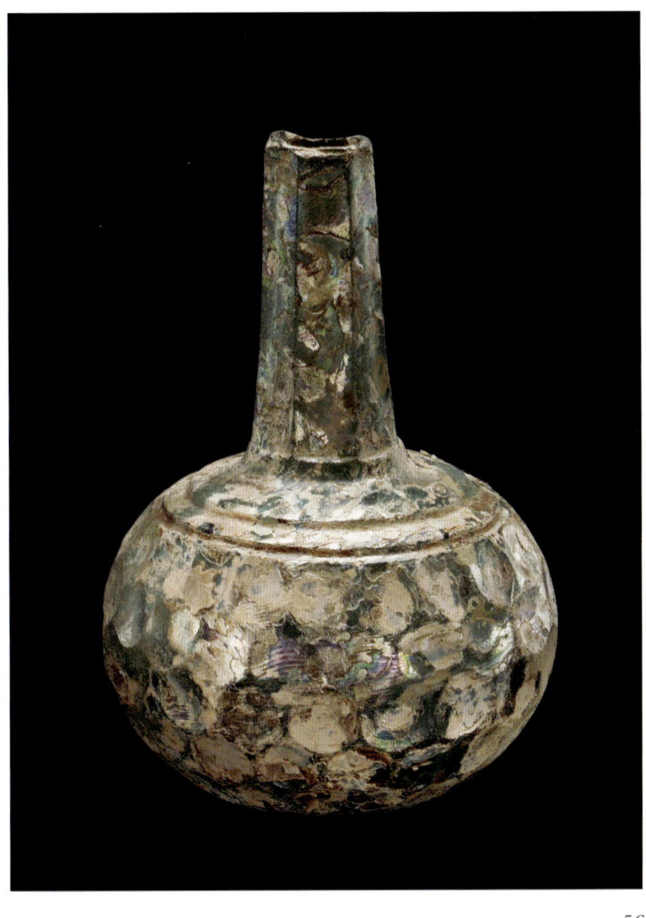

56

Comment: The rim appears to have been broken, after which the top of the neck was ground flat.
See **55**.

Bibliography: *Antikes Glas* 1951, p. 11, no. 85; *Antikes Glas* 1952–3, p. 20, no. 110; *Verres antiques* 1954, p. 53, no. 327; *Glass from the Ancient World* 1957, p. 275, no. 568; *Islamic Art* 1970, p. 45, no. 228; *Islam and the Medieval West* 1975, n.p., no. G5; Bernus-Taylor 2000, p. 55, fig. 3.6.

57. Globular Bottle with Short Neck

8th to 10th century. Formerly in the Smith Collection (897). 59.1.479.
H. 8.5 cm, D. (rim) 3.7 cm, (max.) 7 cm.
Transparent deep green; small bubbles and at least one larger bubble (L. 0.4 cm). Blown; facet-cut.

Bottle: globular. Rim has flat top and narrow chamfer on outside; neck is short and slightly wider at top than at bottom; base is plain; pontil mark is represented by small scar. Neck and wall are decorated with flat facets: on neck, upper three-quarters cut in eight contiguous vertical rectangular facets; on wall, three continuous horizontal rows of facets arranged in quincunx, with seven facets in each row; top row has horizontal oval facets, middle row has circular facets (one of which has broken bubble at surface), and bottom row has pentagonal facets; triangular spaces between some facets show no trace of cutting; two adjoining facets in bottom row have been cut back, perhaps to eliminate bubble or some other blemish. Neck and body have thick sides (0.5 cm at rim and 1.05 cm at base).

Complete, except for small chips in rim, larger chip at junction of wall and base, and circular hole (D. 0.6 cm) drilled near center of base. Exterior has extensive weathering, which has swirls of off-white, brown, and brownish green, and presents "marbled" appearance.

Comment: The overall effect of the flat facets is to give the body the appearance of a polyhedron. The object is heavy, and this raises the possibility that the glass contains lead. The hole in the base apparently was made by Ray Winfield Smith to obtain a sample of the glass for chemical analysis. At least four similar vessels have been found or acquired in Iran (see below), and it seems likely that bottles of this type were made there.

See **59** and also **58**, which was acquired in Tehran, Iran.

Bibliography: *Verres antiques* 1954, p. 50, no. 305, pl. XXV; *Glass from the Ancient World* 1957, p. 269, no. 551.

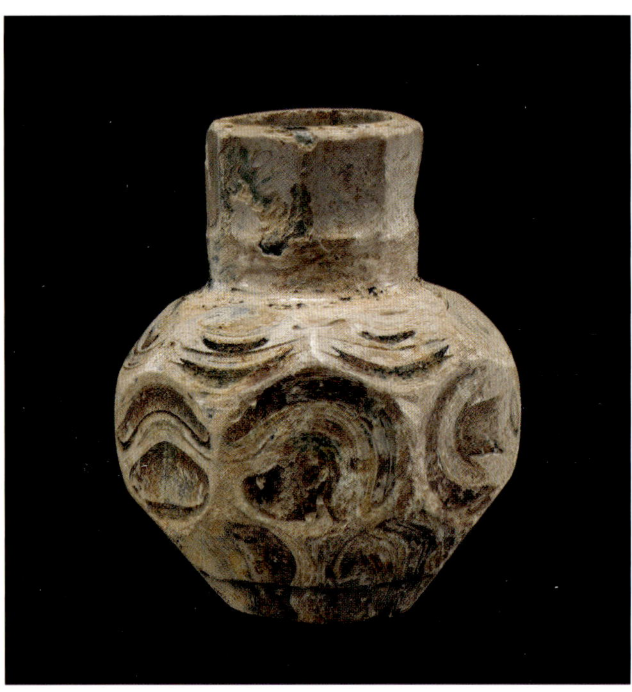

57

58. Globular Bottle with Short Neck

8th to 10th century. Formerly in the Smith Collection (498). 55.1.118.
H. 8.1 cm, D. (rim) 3.4 cm, (max.) 6.8 cm.
Almost colorless, with grayish tinge; many small bubbles. Blown; facet-cut.

Bottle: globular. Rim has flat top and narrow chamfer on outside; neck is short and slightly wider at top than at bottom; shoulder slopes, with convex profile; base is plain; pontil mark removed by grinding. Neck and wall have facet-cut decoration: on neck, upper three-quarters cut in eight contiguous vertical rectangular facets, in six cases with tall, narrow kite-shaped facet between each pair of rectangles; on shoulder, one shallow vertical step; on wall, three continuous horizontal rows of hollow facets arranged in quincunx; top row has 14 oval facets and one partial facet filling unplanned gap between two complete facets, middle row has 15 oval facets, and bottom row has 15 roughly oval facets, which are wider at top than at bottom and frequently have straight bottoms; at junction of wall and base, one very shallow vertical step. Neck and body have thick sides (0.6 cm) at rim.

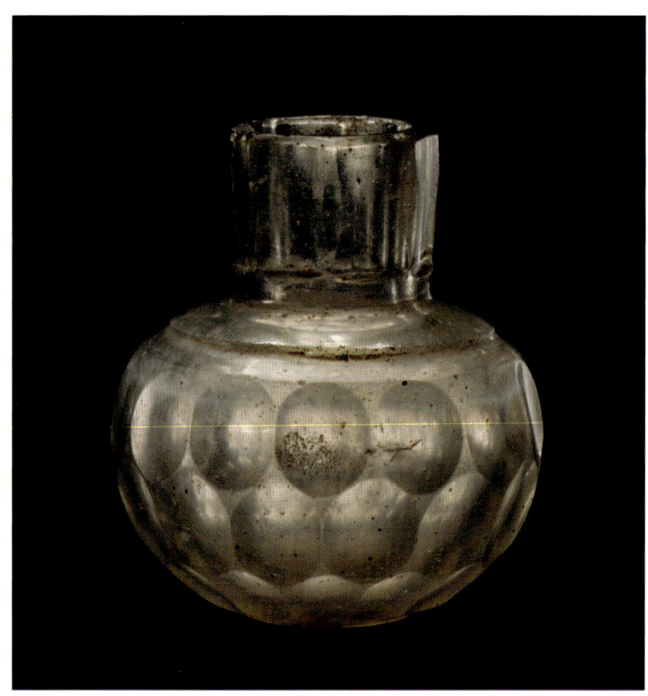

58

Complete, except for one extensive chip in rim and circular hole (D. 0.6 cm) drilled near center of base. Crack runs diagonally from chip in rim to bottom of neck. Exterior has small patches of matte off-white weathering; interior is slightly cloudy.

Comment: Ray Winfield Smith reported (in *Verres antiques*: see below) that he acquired the object in Tehran, Iran. At least three similar vessels have been found or acquired in Iran (see **59**), and it is likely that bottles of this type were made there.

The hole in the base apparently was made by Smith to obtain a sample of the glass for chemical analysis.

Bibliography: *Verres antiques* 1954, p. 50, no. 307; *Glass from the Ancient World* 1957, p. 279, no. 581.

59. Globular Bottle with Short Neck

8th to 10th century. Formerly in the collection of Steuben Glass Inc., New York, New York (AN 1618). 50.1.36.
H. 7.7 cm, D. (max.) 9 cm, (neck) 4 cm.
Colorless. Blown; facet-cut.

Bottle: globular. Rim plain, with flat top (but see below); neck short and cylindrical; shoulder slopes; wall curves down and in; base is small and flat; no trace of pontil mark (perhaps removed by grinding). Decoration consists of, on shoulder, continuous horizontal countersunk rib decorated with crosshatching; on all but lowest part of wall, four continuous rows of contiguous hollow oval facets (with heights greater than widths) arranged in quincunx; top three rows have 26 facets, and bottom row has 25 facets; at bottom of wall, shallow wheel-cut "steps," and below this, one continuous horizontal band of seven crescent-shaped cuts.

Apparently intact, except for chips in rim (but see below). Extensive matte greenish gray weathering.

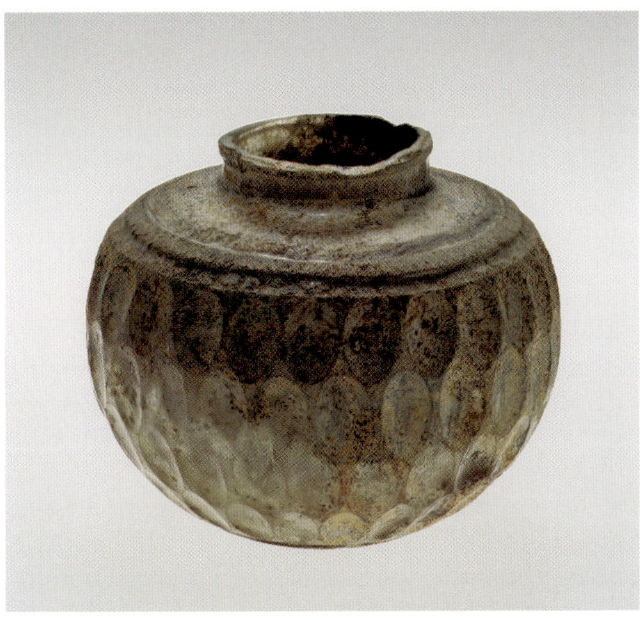

59

Comment: It is possible that the present rim is not original and that the bottle initially had a taller neck.

For globular bottles with short necks, see Lamm 1929–30, vv. 1 and 2, pp. 148–149, pl. 53, no. 4 (which has three rows of facets on the wall, but none on the neck), and pp. 149–150, pl. 53, no. 9 (with two rows of facets on the wall); *Hentrich Collection* 1974, p. 268, no. 414; Fukai 1977, pls. 79 (with three rows of small facets on the wall; said to be from the "Iranian highlands") and 80 (with two rows of facets on the wall; said to be from Gurgān, a former province in northern Iran, now part of Māzandarān Province, but hereafter referred to as Gurgān Province); *Cohn Collection* 1980, p. 161, no. 154 (bright green, with four rows of facets on the wall); Kröger 1984, pp. 215–216, no. 188 (with three rows of facets on the wall); Pinder-Wilson 1996, pp. 102–103, no. 46 (= *Islamic Works of Art* 1991, p. 192, lot 834, with seven vertical facets on the neck and three rows of contiguous facets on the wall); Kröger 1998, pp. 320–322, in the Abegg-Stiftung, Riggisberg (4.17.72); and Baker 2000, p. 219, no. F 3/74-553 (with three rows of facets on the wall; excavated at Ghubayrā, Kirman Province, Iran).

Bibliography: *Trésors fatimides* 1998, p. 187, no. 150.

60. Globular Bottle with Short Neck

8th to 10th century. Formerly in the Strauss Collection (S262). Gift of Richard C. Reedy. 79.1.273.
H. 6.3 cm, D. (rim) 2.1 cm, (max.) 5.4 cm.
Transparent light bluish green. Blown; facet-cut.

Bottle: globular. Rim has flat top and rounded profile; neck short and narrow, tapering slightly and with four horizontal ribs made by tooling; base flat, with trace of pontil scar. Shoulder has two shallow wheel-cut "steps." Wall is decorated with two continuous staggered horizontal rows of 14 contiguous oval facets (with height greater than width). Shallow wheel-cut "step" separates bottom of wall and underside of base.

Intact. Remains of ivory-colored enamellike weathering and, where this is missing, extensive pitting and trace of iridescence.

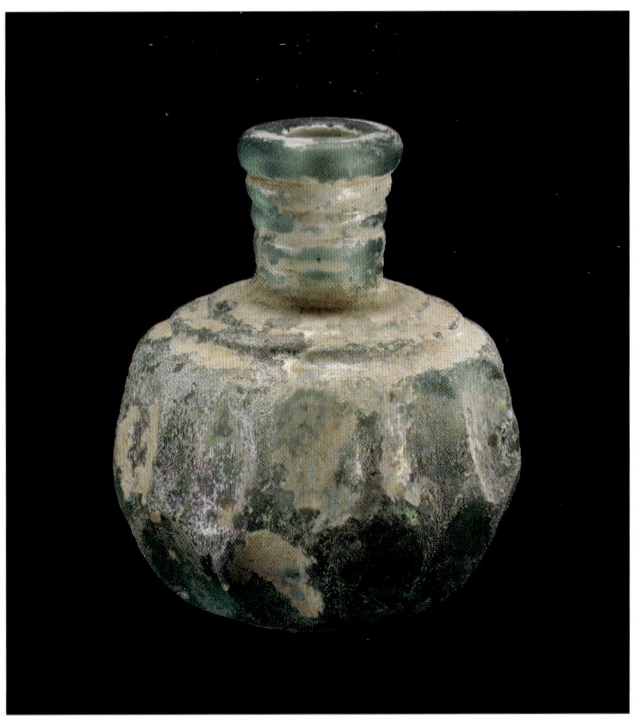

60

Comment: Small bottles with a ribbed neck are extremely common, but they seldom have wheel-cut decoration. At Fusṭāṭ, bottles with a ribbed neck are believed to have been current between about 750 and 1000 (Scanlon and Pinder-Wilson 2001, pp. 47–48, type 20).

61. Globular Bottle with Flange Rim

Probably 10th to 11th century. 54.1.107.
H. 14.9 cm, W. (rim, max.) 5.5 cm, D. (max.) 8.7 cm.
Almost colorless, with yellow tinge. Blown; facet-cut.

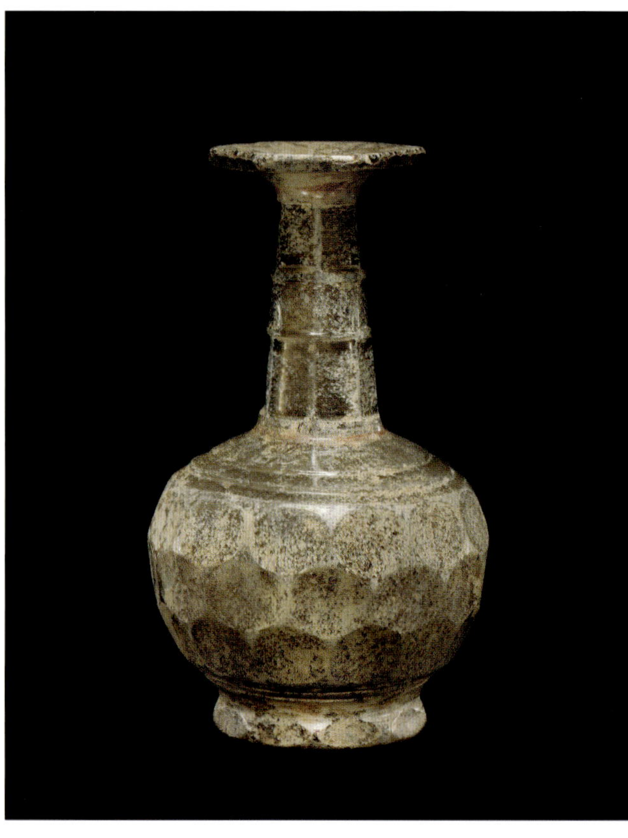

61

Bottle: globular. Rim consists of hexagonal flange, which is higher at lip than at center; neck cylindrical and wider at bottom than at top; shoulder slopes; base is disklike, with trace of pontil mark. Decorated on neck, shoulder, wall, and base. Decoration on neck consists of three bands separated by raised horizontal ribs: top band has six contiguous rectangular facets, middle band is plain, and bottom band has six larger contiguous rectangular facets. Shoulder has two shallow "steps." Wall is decorated with three continuous horizontal rows of 13 contiguous circular facets arranged in quincunx, below which are two shallow "steps." Base has nine contiguous oval facets on side and shallow countersunk boss (D. 2.4 cm) on bottom. Bottle has three horizontal bands of light red pigment: at top of neck, top of shoulder, and bottom of wall.

Intact, except for small chips on rim. Extensive patches of light gray and ivory-colored weathering and pitting.

Comment: Cf. "Recent Important Acquisitions," *JGS*, v. 5, 1963, p. 145, no. 21 (Museum für Kunsthandwerk, Frankfurt, no. H. St. 9).

Bibliography: *Guide to the Collections* 1955, p. 23, no. 15.

62. Fragment of Globular Bottle

9th to 10th century. Formerly in the Smith Collection (1123). 59.1.472.
H. (surviving) 3.1 cm, D. (base) 3.4 cm.
Transparent pale greenish yellow; bubbles.
Blown; facet-cut.

Fragment of bottle with globular body, consisting of about 30 percent of lower wall and entire base. Lower wall curves down and in; base is solid disk, slightly concave underneath; pontil mark shaped like half-moon (D. 1.1 cm). Decoration of hollow facets on wall and side of base. On wall: row of about 19 contiguous oval facets with height greater than width; below this, at bottom of wall, row of about 19 contiguous facets, which have straight sides and rounded tops and bottoms, also with height greater than width. On side of base: row of eight oval facets, some contiguous, others adjacent, and all with width greater than height; some additional grinding is visible below the facets. At highest point on wall, glass is 0.3 cm thick, and it gets thicker as it descends.

Broken on all sides. Dull and slightly pitted, with small patches of whitish weathering.

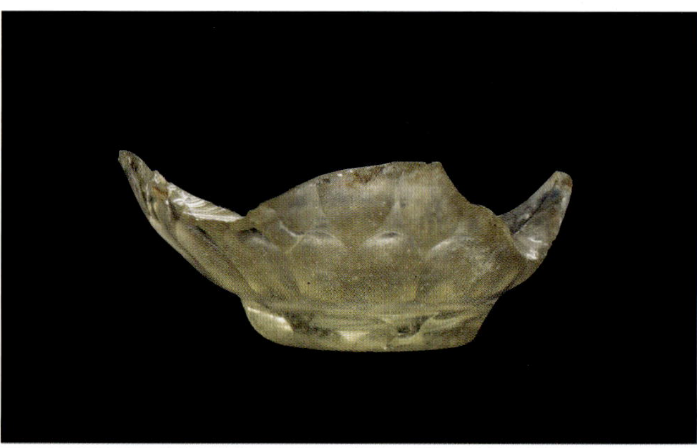

62

COMMENT: The fragment is part of a bottle with a globular body and a short or long neck. If it belonged to the variety with a short neck, it was unusually large (larger, for example, than **58**).

63. Fragment of Globular Bottle

8th to 10th century. Formerly in the Smith Collection (1221-13). 59.1.473.
H. (surviving) 2.1 cm, D. (bottom of neck, est.) about 2 cm, (bottom of fragment, est.) about 7 cm.
Transparent pale blue. Blown; facet-cut.

Fragment from shoulder of globular bottle, with vestige of neck. Shoulder is rounded and has broad frieze consisting of shallow channel decorated with two complete and two fragmentary facets; each complete facet is 2 cm wide and 1.7 cm high, and it has curved top and straight bottom.

Broken on all sides. Bottom edge is horizontal and coincides with bottom of channel, but this appears to be fortuitous. Patches of transparent pale grayish weathering.

COMMENT: If all the facets were of equal size and the band was continuous, the complete shoulder probably had nine facets.

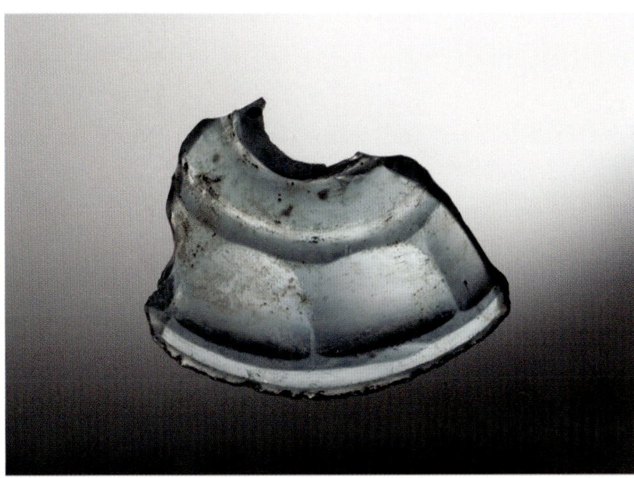

63

64. Fragment of Globular Bottle(?)

9th to 10th century. Found during excavations at Fusṭāṭ (Old Cairo), Egypt (80.10.53). Gift of the American Research Center in Egypt. 81.1.48.
H. about 5.8 cm, D. (max., est.) 8–9 cm.
Almost colorless, with yellowish brown tinge; few small bubbles. Blown; facet-cut.

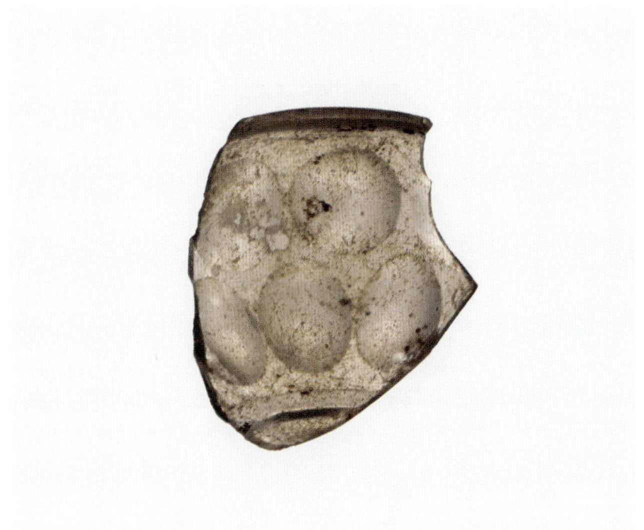

64

Fragment of bottle(?) with globular body. Shoulder slopes and wall (Th. 0.25–0.4 cm) descends in smooth convex curve. Shoulder is plain and has sloping profile interrupted by shallow "step" (D. about 4 cm). Wall is decorated with two horizontal rows of hollow facets. Upper row consists of almost contiguous circular facets, and lower row has contiguous row of oval facets with height greater than width; facets of lower row are below spaces between facets of upper row. Below facets, wall is plain, except for shallow "step" (D. 4–5 cm).

Broken on all sides. Dull and pitted, with semitransparent brownish gray weathering.

COMMENT: The fragment was found during excavations directed by Prof. George T. Scanlon. It is probably part of the wall of a bottle with a globular body and a cylindrical neck, which was either long and relatively narrow (cf. **55**) or short and relatively wide (cf. **57**). The only alternative explanation is that the vessel was an almost globular bowl. The number of facets on the fragment suggests that, when the object was complete, each row contained 16 or 17 facets.

BIBLIOGRAPHY: Pinder-Wilson and Scanlon 1987, p. 67, no. 15, fig. 15; Scanlon and Pinder-Wilson 2001, p. 91, no. 41q.

65. Fragment of Globular Bottle(?)

10th to 11th century. Formerly in the Smith Collection (1221-35). Gift of Carl Berkowitz and Derek Content. 76.1.298.
Max. Dim. 4.4 cm, D. (max., est.) about 10 cm.
Almost colorless, with yellowish tinge. Blown; facet- and linear-cut.

Fragment from wall (Th. 0.15 cm) of bottle(?) with globular body. Surviving decoration consists of parts of two horizontal bands: (1) row of contiguous circular facets (D. 1 cm), each with countersunk dot at center, and (2) separated by single groove, row of vertical oval motifs containing transverse hatching and other elements; between oval motifs, one circular facet with countersunk dot and one oval facet. Cuts were not polished.

Two fragments, which join. Broken on all sides. Dull and pitted, with light brownish weathering, especially in cuts.

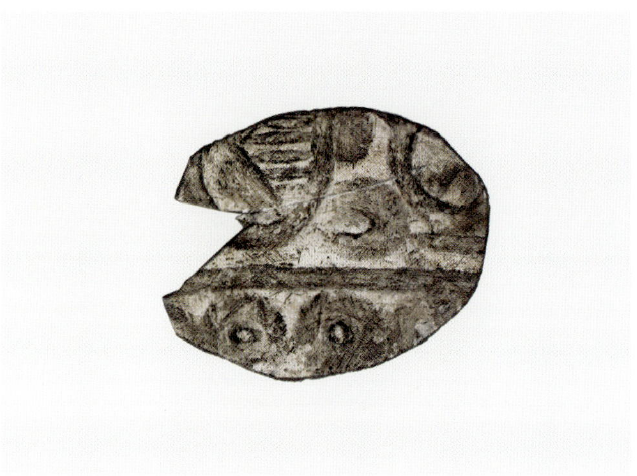

65

66. Cylindrical Bottle

10th to 11th century; painted decoration later.
58.1.39.
H. 28 cm, D. (rim) 9.9 cm, (max.) 18.3 cm.
Almost colorless, with yellowish tinge. Blown (body perhaps blown in dip mold); facet- and linear-cut, painted and gilded.

Bottle with roughly cylindrical body. It has flange rim with rounded edge, cylindrical neck, and sloping shoulder, also with rounded edge; wall is straight, and it tapers slightly toward bottom; base is plain; pontil mark. Rim, neck, shoulder, and wall have wheel-cut, painted, and gilded ornament, and underside of base was also finished by cutting. Wheel-cut ornament consists of, on neck: four continuous horizontal bands separated by ribs (from top to bottom): (1) nine contiguous square or squarish facets, (2 and 3) plain, and (4) eight contiguous square or squarish facets; on shoulder: three small concentric "steps" and, at edge, continuous row of hollow oval facets; on wall: horizontal groove at top, countersunk rib at midpoint, and horizontal groove above row of hollow oval facets at bottom; on underside of base: concentric groove (D. 6.4 cm) and ground depression at center, which would have removed most of pontil mark if one existed.

Exterior of rim, neck, shoulder, and wall seems to have been completely covered with painting and gilding, but this is mostly lost, and only traces of gilding and red paint or enamel survive. On outside of rim: possibly rosettes and at least one cruciform motif. On neck (from top to bottom): (1) one quatrefoil on each facet, (2 and 3) illegible, and (4) one rosette with eight petals on each facet. On shoulder, between steps and row of facets: part of ornament appears to be medallion flanked by crosses formées and possibly by nimbed figures; on facets: illegible. On wall: (1) above countersunk rib, according to Axel von Saldern, who described the object in 1959, "wheel-rosettes, pairs of sphinxes facing each other, medallions with human figures and arabesques" (record on file at the Museum); (2) below rib, again according to Saldern, "four(?) wheel-rosettes, alternating with four pairs (?) of human figures."

Incomplete. Broken into many pieces, with losses in edge of shoulder and wall. Dull, with traces of weathering. Most of painting and gilding is illegible.

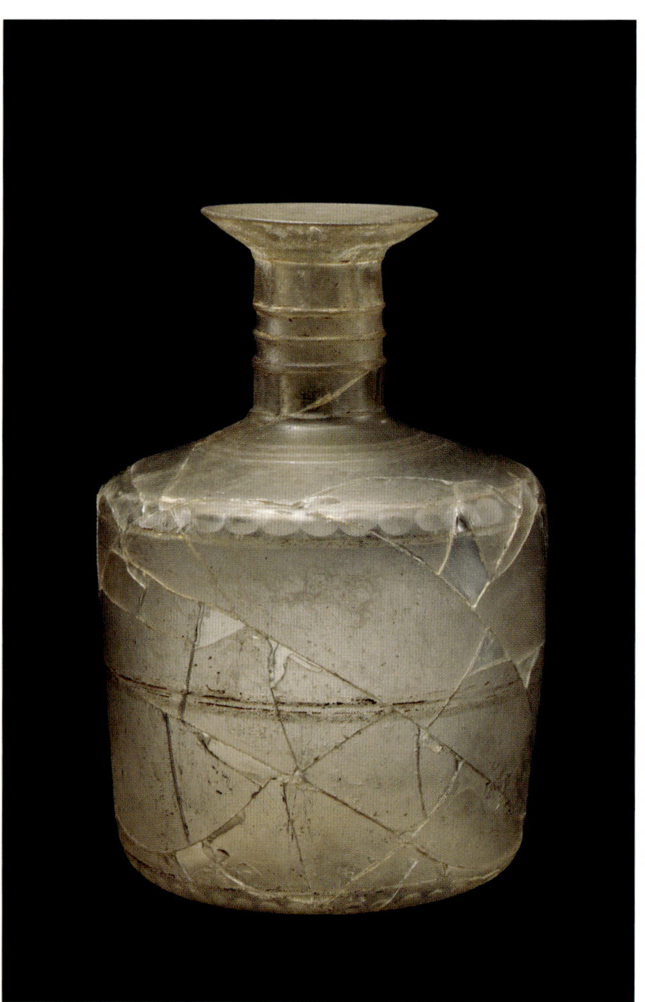

66

Comment: Evidently, the painted and gilded decoration has deteriorated dramatically since the object was described by Saldern; perhaps it was a victim of the Corning flood of 1972 (see page 10). The painting and gilding appear to be later—perhaps considerably later—in date than the vessel itself, and the presence of crosses may suggest that the added decoration was Christian.

67. Cylindrical Bottle

10th to 11th century. 53.1.8.
H. 27.3 cm, D. (rim) 7.8 cm, (max.) 15.5 cm.
Opaque turquoise blue; bubbles and white inclusions. Blown; facet- and linear-cut.

Bottle with roughly cylindrical body. It has flange rim with rounded edge, truncated conical neck, and shallow, sloping shoulder, which also has rounded edge; wall is straight and tapers toward bottom. Base is plain.

Neck, shoulder, and wall have wheel-cut ornament. Decoration on neck consists of five continuous horizontal bands separated by grooves. Bands contain following motifs (from top to bottom): (1) six square facets, (2) eight four-pointed stars linked by eight short horizontal cuts, (3) four shallow V-shaped elements alternating with four inverted Vs, (4) as (2), and (5) as (1), but with 10 square facets. Decoration on shoulder consists of, around bottom of neck, three concentric grooves, and, at junction with wall, one continuous band of oval facets between single horizontal groove near edge of shoulder and identical groove near top of wall. Wall itself has pair of continuous horizontal grooves above midpoint and continuous band of oval facets below groove, at junction with base.

Incomplete. Broken, with small losses, and restored. Matte and pitted, with patches of light brown weathering, especially in cuts.

Comment: The object is said to have come from Gurgān Province, northern Iran. A slightly smaller, almost colorless bottle with a different pattern of facets on the neck, but an almost identical pattern on the shoulder and wall, was excavated at Nishapur, also in northeastern Iran; it is now in The Metropolitan Museum of Art, New York (48.101.10: Kröger 1995, pp. 126–127, no. 171). Another bottle of almost colorless glass, with the same form as and decoration similar to that on **67**, was discovered during restoration of the stupa of the Dule Temple (Dulesi) in Ji Xian, Tianjin, China, in 1983. The bottle was one of 169 objects concealed in the stupa, apparently in 1058 (An 1991,

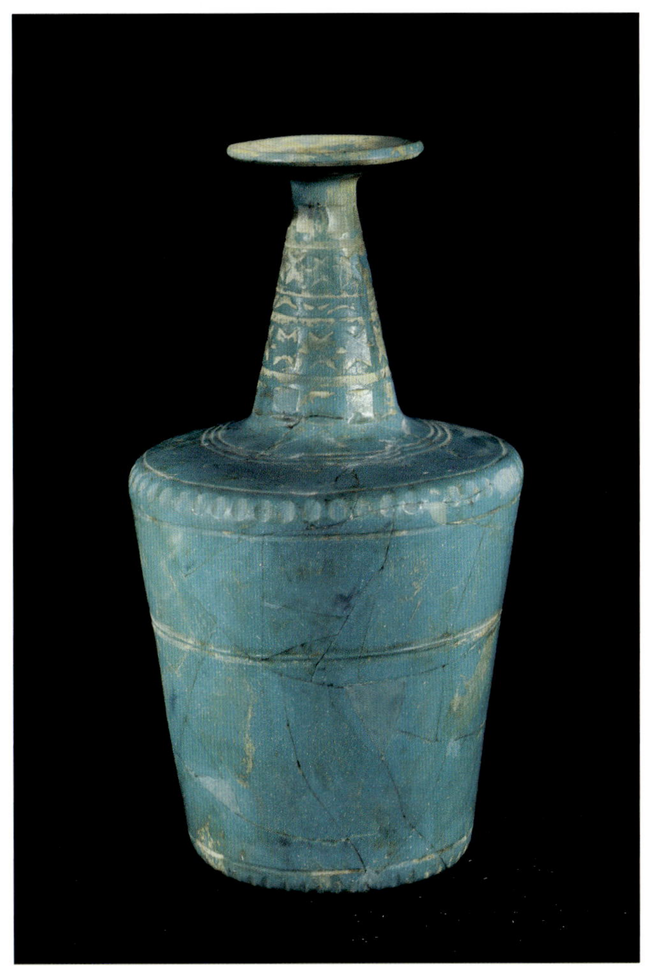

67

p. 134). For an 11th-century silver bottle of the same form, see *Afghanistan* 2002, p. 169, no. 139.

Early Islamic vessels made from opaque turquoise-colored glass are unusual. Other examples include 69.1.32 and 71.1.23; a perfume bottle in The Metropolitan Museum of Art (10.130.2649: Jenkins 1986, p. 23, no. 21); and two pitchers, one in the Gemeentemuseum in The Hague, the Netherlands (OG 01-1930), and the other in The British Museum, London (OA 1945.10-17.260: Pinder-Wilson 1991, 1999, and 2004, p. 128, fig. 160). Opaque turquoise blue glass was also used in the manufacture of Egyptian "coin weights" between 975 and 1229 (Kolbas 1983, p. 96).

Chemical analysis revealed that the material is a soda-lime-silica glass made with plant ash (Brill 1999, v. 1, p. 101, and v. 2, p. 205, no. 3099).

Bibliography: *Guide to the Collections* 1955, p. 18, no. 11; *idem* 1958, p. 26, no. 21; *idem* 1965, p. 27, no. 27; *Persian Glass* 1972, p. 13, no. 18; *Guide to the Collections* 1974, p. 26, no. 27; *Islam and the Medieval West* 1975, n.p., no. G9; Yoshimizu 1992, v. 1, pp. 102 and 292, no. 207; *Glass of the Sultans* 2001, pp. 169–170, no. 75.

68. Base of Cylindrical Bottle

Perhaps 9th to 10th century. Formerly in the Smith Collection (1148). Gift of Mrs. Ray Winfield Smith. 81.1.699.
H. (surviving) 2.3 cm, D. (base) 2.4 cm.
Transparent pale yellowish green. Blown; facet- and linear-cut.

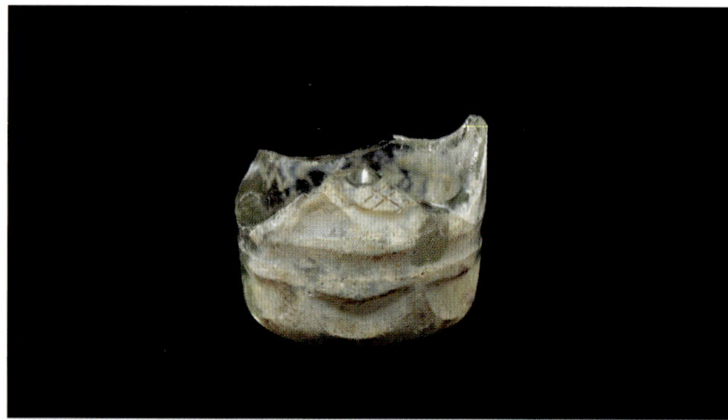

68

Base of cylindrical bottle. Lower wall (Th. 0.2 cm) vertical, but curving in at bottom; base flat; pontil mark. Decorated with indeterminate motifs above continuous horizontal groove; between groove and bottom of wall, band of seven hollow oval facets, each with length greater than height.

Part of lower wall and entire base survive. Partly covered with pale grayish enamellike weathering.

69. Fragment of Cylindrical Bottle

9th to 11th century. Formerly in the Strauss Collection (S1508). Gift of The Ruth Bryan Strauss Memorial Foundation. 79.1.206.
H. 4.1 cm, D. 3.3 cm.
Colorless. Blown; facet-cut.

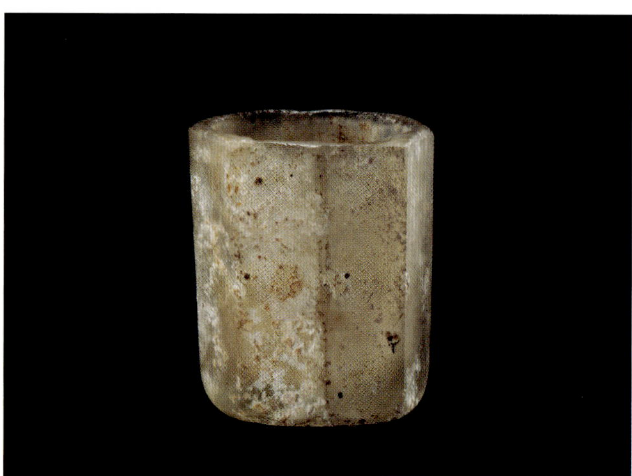

69

Fragment of bottle: cylindrical. Lower wall vertical; base flat; pontil mark. Wall cut and polished in eight contiguous vertical facets, which extend from top of fragment to bottom of wall.

Incomplete. Lower wall and base survive. Small patches of opaque white to yellowish weathering.

70. Biconical Bottle

About 9th to 10th century. Formerly in the collection of Maurice Nahman, Cairo, Egypt. 53.1.32.
H. (surviving) 6.8 cm, D. (max.) 5.8 cm.
Transparent light greenish blue. Blown; facet-cut.

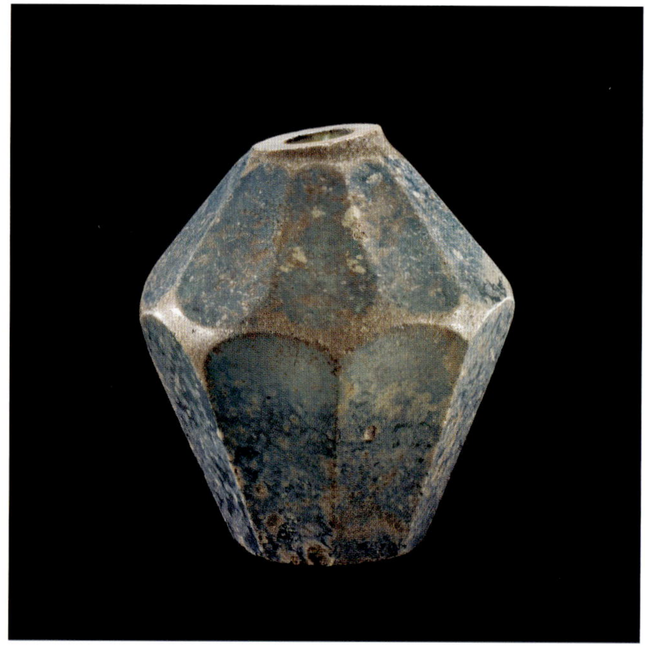

70

Bottle: biconical. Upper wall is straight, flaring to greatest diameter 4.0 cm above bottom; lower wall is also straight, but tapering; base plain; trace of pontil mark. Upper wall is divided into 10 contiguous vertical facets, which are flat; lower wall has eight similar facets; small triangular areas at tops of junctions of facets in upper wall, and irregular areas at junction of upper and lower wall, have no trace of cutting.

Incomplete. Rim and neck missing; top of wall ground flat to conceal loss. Light grayish blue weathering mottled with grayish brown, some of which is missing, especially at junction of upper and lower wall, and edge of base.

Comment: When complete, the bottle probably had a tapering cylindrical neck with eight vertical facets.

Cf. a bottle found at Susa in Khuzistan, Iran (Lamm 1931, p. 366, pl. 78.6); a bottle formerly in the Smith Collection (*Glass from the Ancient World* 1957, p. 283, no. 600); a bottle in the Museum für Islamische Kunst, Berlin (I.49/63: Kröger 1984, pp. 193–194, no. 172); a bottle in the al-Sabah Collection, Dār al-Āthār al-Islāmiyyah, Kuwait National Museum (LNS 293 G: Carboni 2001, p. 133, no. 2.37, reputedly from Afghanistan); and a bottle in the Khalili Collection (GLS 145: *Khalili Collection* 2005, p. 161, no. 188).

Cf. **71**.

71. Biconical Bottle

About 9th to 10th century. Formerly in the collection of Maurice Nahman, Cairo, Egypt. 53.1.31.
H. (surviving) 6.2 cm, D. (max.) 5.5 cm.
Almost colorless, with yellowish green tinge; many small bubbles. Blown; facet-cut.

Bottle: biconical. Upper wall is straight, flaring to greatest diameter 3.7 cm above bottom; lower wall is also straight, but tapering; base plain; trace of pontil mark (D. about 0.9 cm). Upper wall is divided into eight contiguous vertical facets, which are flat; lower wall has eight similar facets, each pair of which meet below midpoint of facet in upper wall.

Incomplete. Rim and neck missing; top of wall grozed and ground to conceal loss; small chips in ground area and edge of base. Very little weathering, but wall and edge of base are extensively scratched.

Comment: See **70**.

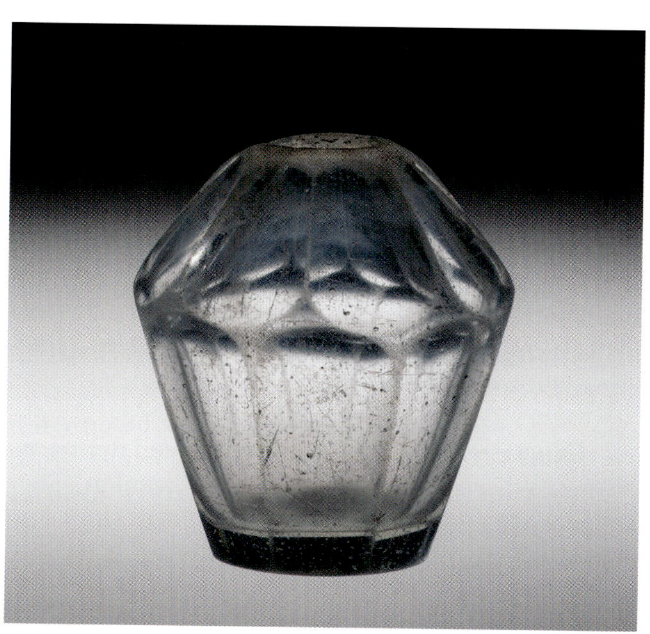

71

72. Bottle

Probably 9th to 11th century. Formerly in the collection of Maurice Nahman, Cairo, Egypt. 53.1.90.
H. 12.9 cm, W. (rim) 2.2 cm, (max., shoulder) 2.7 cm.
Almost colorless, with yellowish tinge; bubbly. Blown; facet-cut.

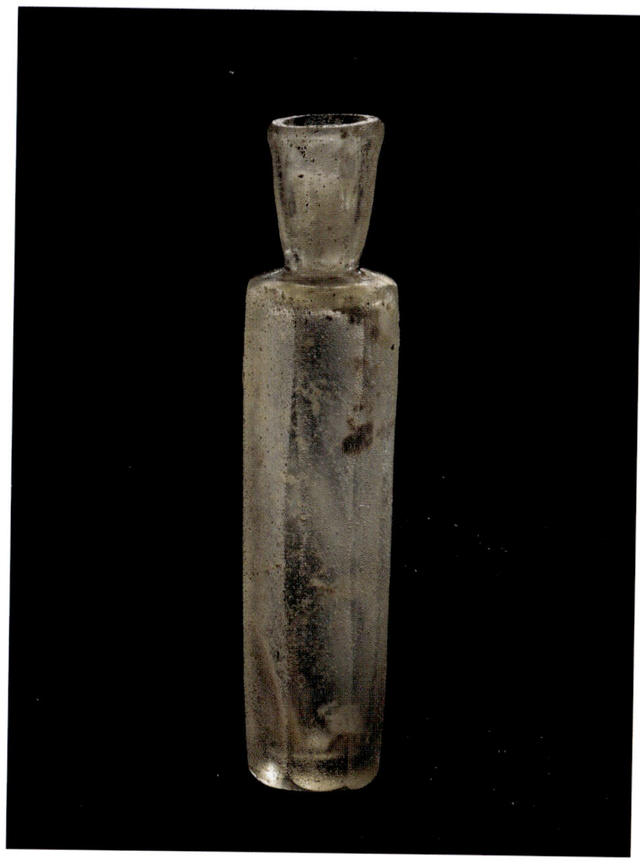

72

Bottle. Rim plain, with flat top; neck cylindrical, but narrower at bottom than at top; shoulder flat, with rounded edge; wall vertical; base flat; pontil mark. Facet-cut on neck and wall. On neck: six adjacent facets extending from rim almost to shoulder; each tapers at top, below which sides are roughly parallel and bottom is rounded. On wall: extending from top to bottom, seven adjoining or almost adjoining vertical facets. Rim and base finished by grinding.

Intact. Coldworked surfaces are dull and pitted. Patches of weathering on interior.

Comment: Presumably the bottle was found in Egypt. The shape of the facets on the neck is unusual. Similar small bottles, with six or seven vertical facets running from the top to the bottom of the wall, have been reported from both Egypt and Asia. Examples

Fragment of bottle. Rim in form of flange with rounded lip, slightly distorted; neck shaped like truncated cone, wider at bottom than at top. Neck is decorated with two continuous horizontal bands of facets. Upper band consists of five rectangular facets, and lower band has three pairs of rhomboids; in each pair, outer vertical sides are at higher level than inner vertical sides. Beneath upper band are three small semicircular facets, and two similar facets survive beneath lower band.

Rim broken and repaired, with two triangular losses. Dull and faintly iridescent.

COMMENT: The fragment is probably part of a bottle with a form similar to that of **67**.

77. Fragments from Rim and Neck of Bottle

9th to 10th century. 57.1.6b.
H. (surviving) 5.5 cm, D. (rim) 4.1 cm.
Colorless. Blown; facet-cut.

Three fragments composing most of rim and neck of bottle. Rim plain, with rounded lip. Neck is shaped like truncated cone that is narrower at bottom than at top; it is decorated with raised collar (H. 2.9 cm) bearing seven vertical facets, each somewhat rounded at top and bottom, outlined in relief.

Dull and pitted, with slightly iridescent dark and light gray weathering. Inside of neck has horizontal black line and other black marks.

COMMENT: The fragments probably came from a bottle with a bell-shaped body, similar to **370** and **371**.

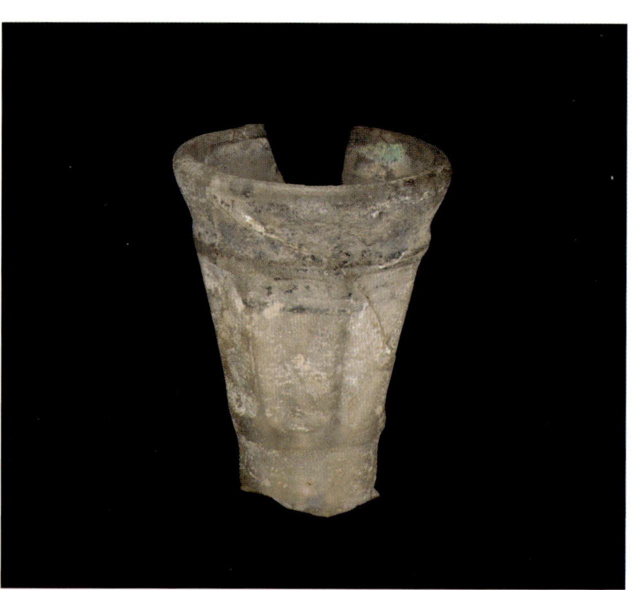

77

78. Rim and Neck of Bottle

10th to 11th century. 55.1.41.
Max. Dim. 15.5 cm, D. (rim) 2.2 cm.
Colorless or almost colorless; small bubbles.
Blown; facet-cut.

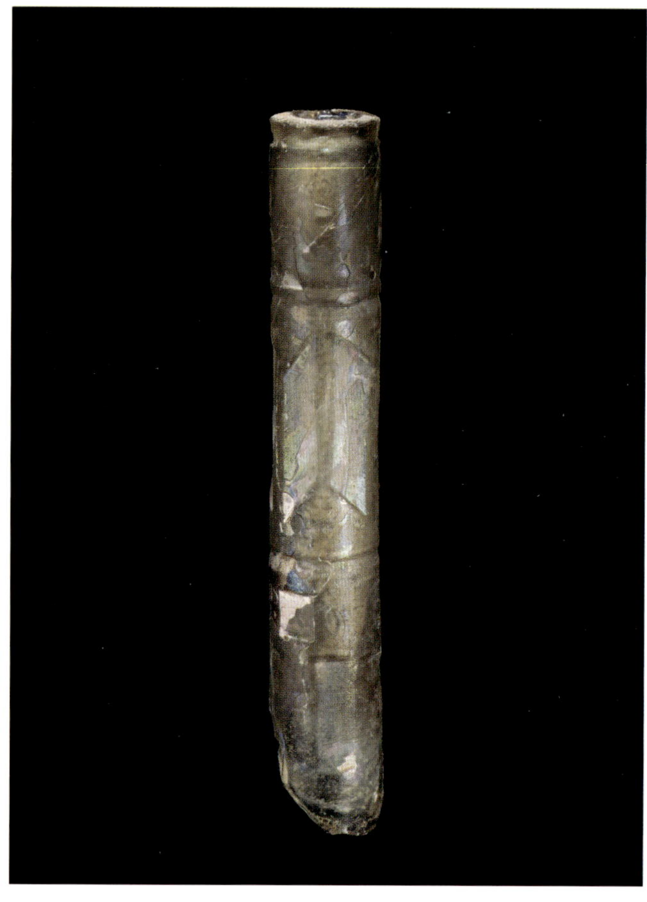

78

Rim and neck of bottle: narrow, cylindrical. Rim plain, with top ground flat; neck descends vertically. Neck is divided into three bands by shallow horizontal groove, 0.2 cm wide and with bottom 0.5 cm below rim; countersunk horizontal rib, 0.2 cm wide and with bottom 3.6 cm below lip; and horizontal groove, 0.3 cm wide and 9.5 cm below lip. Bands are treated as follows (from top to bottom): (1) is plain; (2) has three pairs of shallow rhomboids, which are markedly taller than they are wide; in each pair, outer vertical sides are at higher level than inner vertical sides, creating triangular space between their tops, which is occupied by shallow triangle; similar shallow triangle occupies triangular space between bottoms of each pair of rhomboids; and (3) row of four small rectangles, which are taller than they are wide, above row of four larger rectangles, which are markedly taller than they are wide, and, in gap between two rectangles, triangle with apex pointing down above triangle with apex pointing up. Hint of shoulder survives at bottom of fragment, and this shows that neck had only three bands.

Almost all of neck survives; small part missing at bottom. Exterior is pitted and has extensive remains of iridescent weathering; interior has both weathering and accretions.

Comment: Narrow cylindrical necks with plain rims and bands of shallow faceted decoration are typically found on bottles with globular bodies. The ornament on the bodies includes not only hollow facets but also linear- and slant-cut motifs (see **266**).

79. Rim and Neck of Bottle

10th to 11th century. Formerly in the Smith Collection (512). Gift of Carl Berkowitz and Derek Content. 76.1.220.
H. (surviving) 14.2 cm, D. (rim) 1.9 cm.
Colorless or almost colorless. Blown; facet-cut.

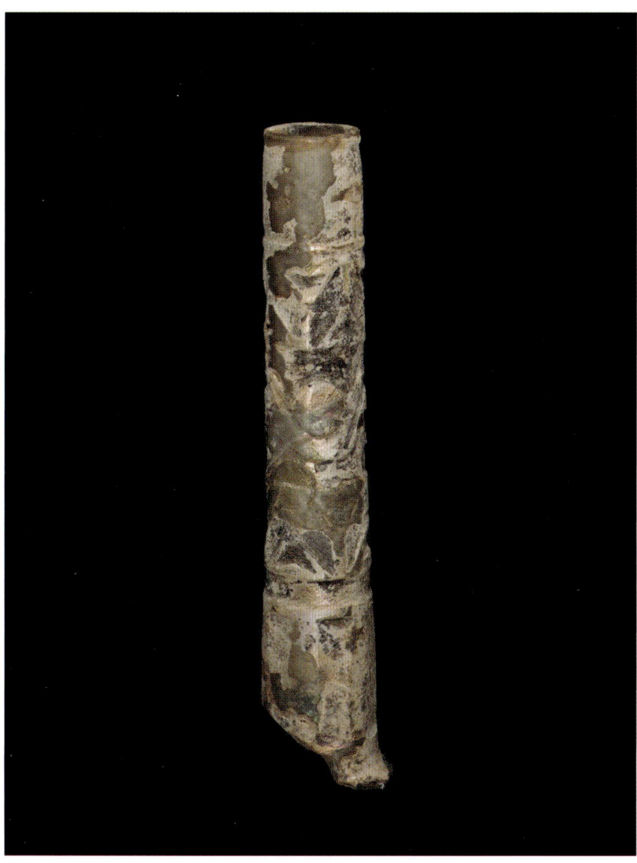

79

Rim and neck of bottle: tall, cylindrical. Rim plain, with flat top finished by grinding; side straight and very slightly splayed; top of shoulder slopes. Decoration consists of five continuous horizontal bands separated by countersunk ribs (from top to bottom): (1) plain; (2) with eight facets shaped like parallelograms arranged in chevrons and with roughly triangular facet in space above and below each chevron; (3) difficult to determine, but apparently with zigzag or similar pattern with roughly triangular facets above and below; (4) similar to (2); and (5) with six tall rectangular facets.

Rim is chipped, but intact; neck is almost complete; only very small part of shoulder survives. Mostly covered with enamellike silvery gray weathering speckled with brown.

Comment: In size, shape, and decoration, this neck is similar to that of **266**, which is said to be from Gurgān Province, northern Iran.

Bibliography: *Verres antiques* 1954, p. 52, no. 320.

80. Rim and Neck of Bottle

10th to 11th century. 55.1.42.
Max. Dim. 13.6 cm, H. (neck) 12.9 cm, D. (rim) 2 cm.
Colorless or almost colorless. Blown; facet-cut.

Rim and neck of bottle: narrow, cylindrical, and slightly wider at bottom than at top. Rim plain, with top ground flat; neck descends almost vertically; top of shoulder curves out and down. Neck is divided into

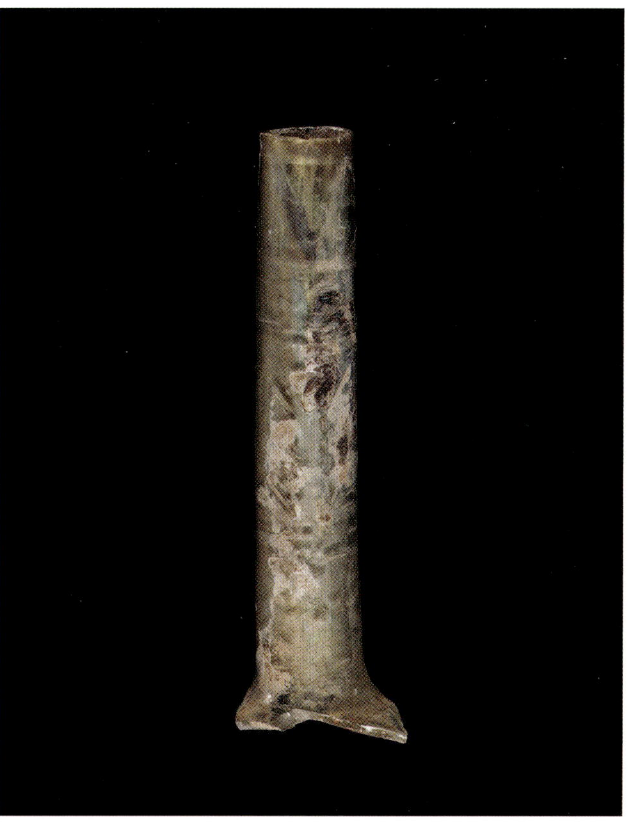

80

four bands by shallow horizontal grooves, each about 0.25 cm wide, bottoms of which are 0.5 cm, 2.8 cm, 4.7 cm, and 8.9 cm below rim. Bands are treated as follows (from top to bottom): (1) is plain; (2) has five shallow rectangular facets, which are taller than they are wide; (3) has three pairs of shallow rhomboids, which are markedly taller than they are wide; in each pair, outer vertical sides are at higher level than inner vertical sides, creating triangular space between their tops, which is occupied by shallow triangle; similar shallow triangle occupies triangular space between bottoms of each pair of rhomboids; and (4) has six shallow facets, which are almost rectangular but splay at top, and which are markedly taller than they are wide. Bottom of neck has narrow band of very lightly incised lines.

All of neck and very small part of upper shoulder survive. Exterior is pitted and has extensive patches of iridescent to matte dark brown weathering; interior has both weathering and accretions.

Comment: For parallels, see **78**.

81. Neck of Bottle

9th to 10th century. Formerly in the Smith Collection (1131). Gift of Mrs. Ray Winfield Smith. 81.1.692.
H. 6 cm, D. (rim) 7.1 cm.
Almost colorless, with greenish yellow tinge; small bubbles and one elongated bubble in neck. Blown; facet-cut.

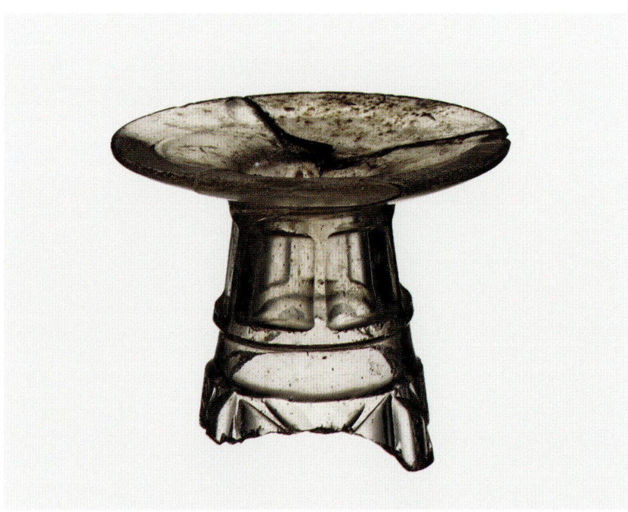

81

Neck of bottle, including entire rim and uppermost register, and small part of next register. Rim tapers sharply, with rounded edge and outermost part of upper surface ground flat and polished; neck wider at bottom than at top, and cut in horizontal registers, two of which survive. Uppermost register has continuous band of six vertical facets, each almost touching its neighbors. Next register has continuous band of four pairs of shallow rhomboids, which are taller than they are wide; in each pair, outer vertical sides are at higher level than inner vertical sides, creating triangular space between their tops, which is occupied by V-shaped cut; just below this, one small triangular facet.

Rim broken and repaired, with small losses. Surface varies from almost pristine to dull and pitted, with pale yellowish weathering in pits.

Comment: The fragment is from a bottle with a flange rim, cylindrical neck, and cylindrical body, similar in shape to **67** and many others, which include a bottle in the David Collection, Copenhagen (10/1963: *Glass of the Sultans* 2001, pp. 191–192, no. 96), and two bottles from Nishapur, now in The Metropolitan Museum of Art, New York (Kröger 1995, pp. 126–128, nos. 171–173, 48.101.10 and 40.170.61).

82. Fragment from Neck of Bottle

About 10th to 11th century. Formerly in the Smith Collection (1144). Gift of Mrs. Ray Winfield Smith. 81.1.698.
H. (surviving) 6.3 cm, D. (at bottom of neck) about 3.6 cm.
Almost colorless, with brownish tinge. Blown; facet-cut.

Fragment from neck of bottle, with small part of shoulder; rim and top of neck are missing. Side of

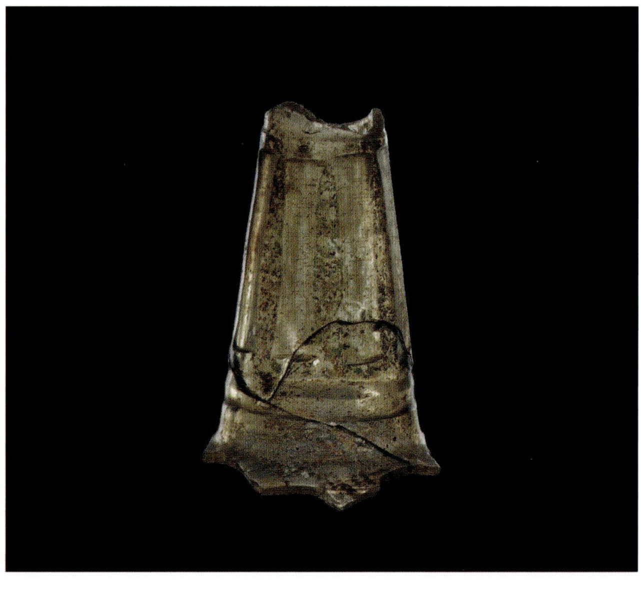

82

neck (Th. 0.2 cm) is straight and flares toward bottom. Decorated with horizontal band of seven tall rectangular facets, several with slightly concave sides; above them, at least one continuous horizontal groove; below them, near bottom of neck, two horizontal grooves.

Patches of slightly iridescent pale yellowish pink weathering.

Comment: The fragment is probably part of a bottle with a form similar to that of **67**.

83. Fragment from Neck of Bottle

10th to 11th century. Formerly in the Smith Collection (1136). Gift of Carl Berkowitz and Derek Content. 76.1.210.
H. (surviving) 5.4 cm.
Transparent very pale yellowish green. Blown; linear- and facet-cut.

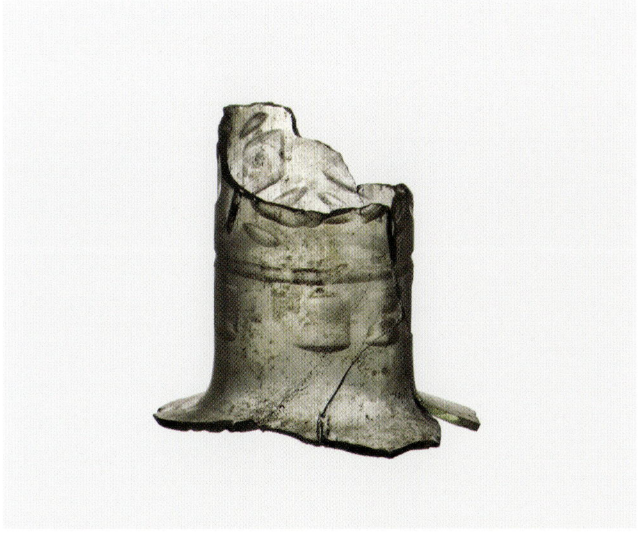

83

Fragment from lower neck of bottle. Neck is straight, and it splays slightly before merging with shoulder. Decoration consisted of several registers of facets: approximately half of penultimate register and all of lowest register survive. Penultimate register had three(?) pairs of lozenge-shaped facets with one short transverse oval facet above and below each lozenge. Lowest register has, below continuous horizontal linear-cut border, row of five more or less square facets.

Broken on all sides; repaired. Dull, with traces of transparent grayish weathering.

Comment: The fragment is probably part of a bottle with a form similar to that of **67**.

84. Fragment from Neck of Bottle

About 10th to 11th century. Formerly in the Smith Collection. Gift of Carl Berkowitz and Derek Content. 76.1.226.
H. (surviving) 5.2 cm, D. (at lower horizontal groove, est.) about 4 cm.
Almost colorless, with brownish tinge. Blown; facet-cut.

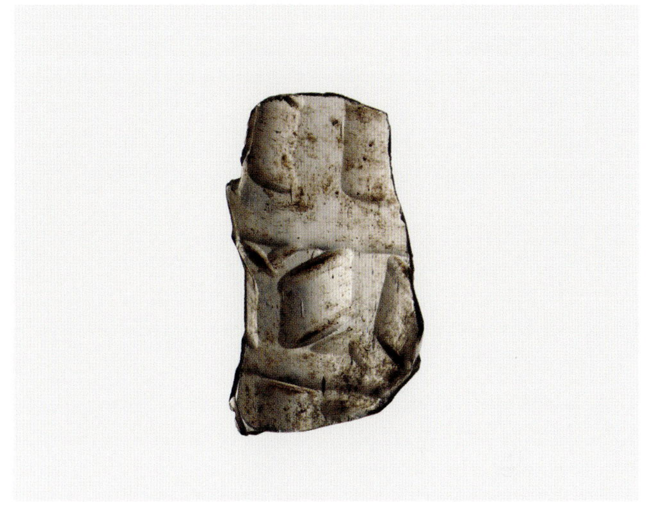

84

Fragment from neck of bottle. Side is straight and flares slightly toward bottom. Decorated with parts of three horizontal bands of facet-cut ornament separated by grooves (from top to bottom): (1) contiguous rectilinear facets, (2) pairs of adjacent facets shaped like parallelograms and arranged in chevrons, and (3) adjacent rectangular facets with height greater than width.

Broken on all sides. Speckled with brown weathering or stain.

Comment: When the lower groove is held in a horizontal plane, the fragment is seen to be part of a neck that was wider at the bottom than at the top. Its shape and its estimated diameter near the bottom indicate that the fragment probably came from a bottle resembling **67**.

85. Fragment of Bottle

10th to 11th century. Found during excavations at Fusṭāṭ (Old Cairo), Egypt (78.9.25). Gift of the American Research Center in Egypt. 79.1.17.
H. (surviving) 6 cm, D. (rim) 2.8 cm.
Almost colorless, apparently with green tinge. Blown; facet-cut.

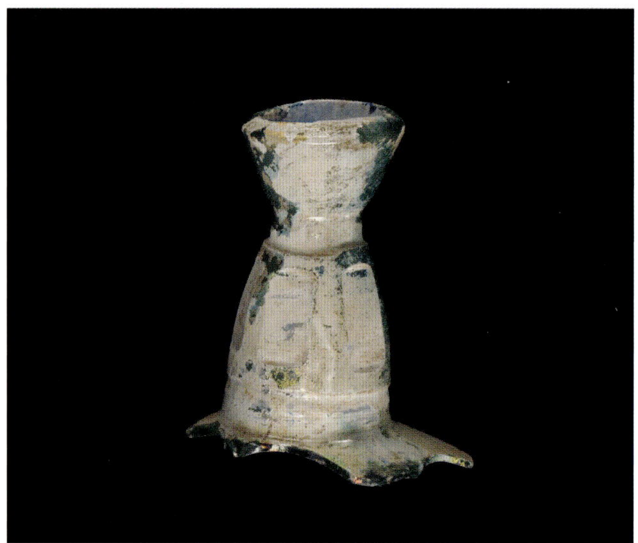

85

Fragment of bottle, consisting of entire rim and neck, and small part of shoulder. Rim plain and tapering, with bevel on outside of lip; neck shaped like truncated cone, wider at bottom than at top, with slightly concave profile; shoulder curves out and down. Facet-cut decoration on neck: continuous horizontal grooves near top and bottom, creating raised collar, which is decorated with six rectangular vertical facets.

Exterior has patches of opaque cream to pale green enamellike weathering; elsewhere, surfaces have greenish iridescent weathering.

Comment: The fragment was found, during excavations directed by Prof. George T. Scanlon, in a deposit of *sibakh* (decomposed organic materials) "above architectural traces datable to the 11th century."

The object differs from other bottles with facet-cut necks: the rim is shaped like a funnel rather than a horizontal flange, the neck is relatively short, and the thickness of the shoulder (0.1 cm) suggests that the body of the vessel was probably undecorated.

Bibliography: Scanlon and Pinder-Wilson 2001, p. 90, no. 41o.

86. Fragment of Bottle

9th to 10th century. Formerly in the Smith Collection (1142). Gift of Mrs. Ray Winfield Smith. 81.1.695.
H. (surviving) 5.9 cm, D. (rim, est.) about 4 cm.
Transparent pale yellowish green. Blown; facet-cut.

Fragment of bottle, including small part of rim. Rim plain, with top flattened by grinding and polishing; neck shaped like truncated cone that is narrower at bottom than at top. It is decorated with two horizontal bands of facets separated by two carelessly executed horizontal grooves. Upper band had about six roughly rectangular vertical facets. Lower band definitely had six roughly rectangular vertical facets.

Broken on all sides except rim. Patches of pale gray weathering and brown encrustation.

Comment: See **77**.

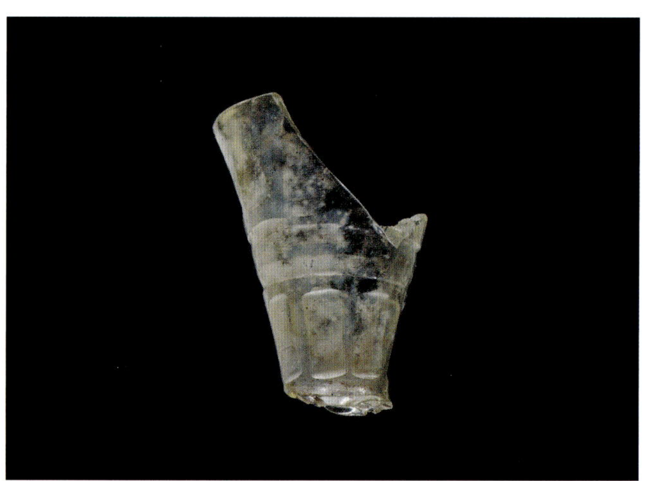

86

6. Small Bottles

87. Small Bottle

9th to 11th century or later. Formerly in the collection of Maurice Nahman, Cairo, Egypt. 53.1.99.
H. 7.4 cm, W. (rim) 1.5–1.7 cm, (base) 2.1 cm.
Almost colorless, with yellowish green tinge.
Blown; facet-cut.

Bottle: body has hexagonal cross section. Rim plain, with top ground flat; neck cylindrical, wider at top than at bottom; shoulder flat; wall vertical; base plain; no pontil mark (but see below). Neck is decorated with six contiguous vertical facets, somewhat irregular, which extend from rim almost to junction with shoulder. Wall is cut in six contiguous vertical facets, which extend from top, where they are slightly rounded, to bottom.

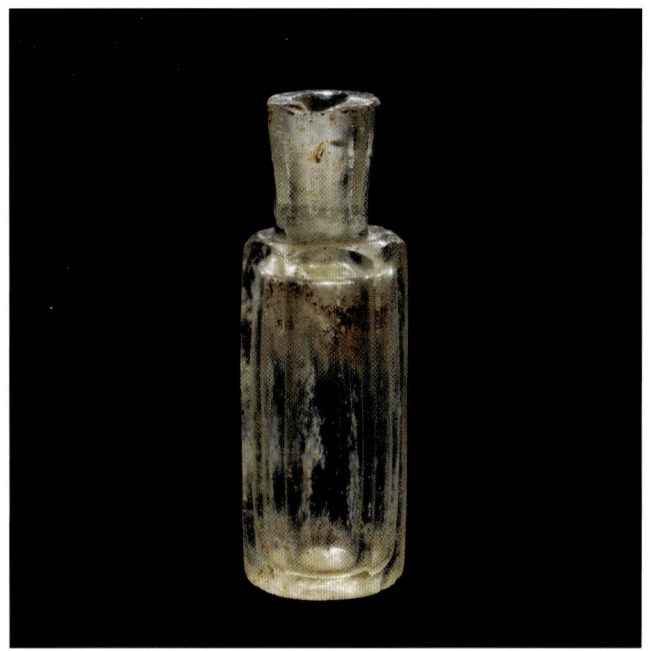

87

Intact, except for chips in rim. Patches of light brown weathering, especially on interior.

Comment: The base has been ground almost flat, but a slight indentation may be the remains of a pontil mark.

Cf. **73** and **88**.

88. Small Bottle

9th to 10th century. Found during excavations at Fusṭāṭ (Old Cairo), Egypt (68.12.27). Gift of the American Research Center in Egypt. 69.1.41.
H. 7.3 cm, W. (rim) 1.3 cm, (body) 1.7 cm.
Almost colorless, with yellowish tinge. Blown (probably mold-blown); facet-cut.

Bottle: body has hexagonal cross section. Rim plain, with slight bevel on outside; neck tapers; shoulder flat, with rounded edge; wall vertical; base flat; no pontil mark. Both neck and wall are cut in six contiguous vertical facets.

Intact. Extensive remains of mottled charcoal gray to silvery weathering.

Comment: The bottle was found during excavations directed by Prof. George T. Scanlon. Scanlon and Pinder-Wilson (see below) reported that it was recovered from "the undisturbed fill of a very deep and wide pit which provided a dating range of 800–950."

Cf. **73** and **87**.

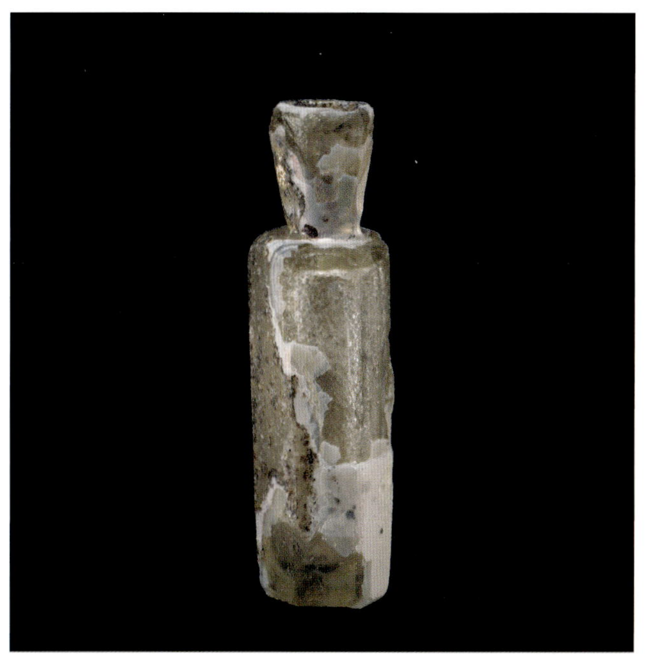

88

Bibliography: Scanlon and Pinder-Wilson 2001, pp. 87–88, no. 41e.

89. Small Bottle

9th to 10th century. Formerly in the Smith Collection (1419). 59.1.484.
H. 7 cm, D. (rim) 1.9 cm, W. (max.) 3.6 cm.
Almost colorless, with greenish tinge. Blown (perhaps in dip mold); facet- and relief-cut.

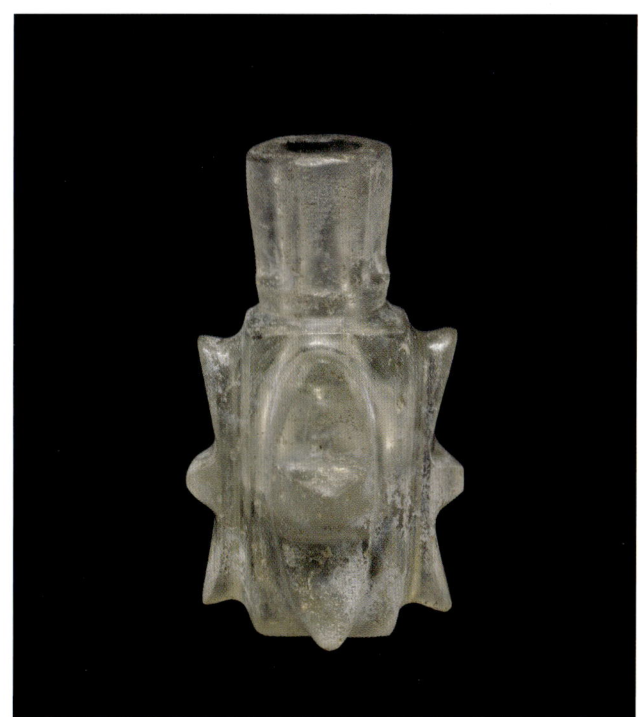

89

Bottle. Rim plain, with top ground flat; neck cylindrical; shoulder is narrow and slopes; body has vertical wall and square cross section; underside of base ground flat. Decorated on neck and wall. On neck: six contiguous vertical facets, which extend from rim almost to shoulder. On wall: each side has one raised oval motif with pointed ends, which extends almost from top almost to bottom; its vertical profile is concave, and it has prominent pyramidal boss at midpoint.

Intact. Patches of semitransparent pale gray weathering.

COMMENT: The bottle closely resembles a common variety of "molar flask," on which the raised oval motifs on the sides of the body extend below the base (in some cases, the ovals are at the angles). See **103**.

90. Small Bottle

9th to 11th century. Formerly in the collections of Maurice Nahman, Cairo, Egypt, and Ray Winfield Smith (839). 59.1.483.
H. 6.85 cm, W. (rim) 1.8 cm, (max.) 2.8 cm.
Probably colorless. Blown (body perhaps blown in dip mold); facet-cut.

Bottle with cuboid body. Rim plain, with top ground flat; neck tapers; shoulder almost flat; wall vertical; base shaped like truncated pyramid, with slightly concave underside; no pontil mark. Facet-cut decoration on neck and wall. On neck: six contiguous facets extending from top to bottom. On each side of wall: in relief, one horizontal lozenge-shaped motif, with concave surface extending for entire width of side and touching its neighbors; above this, wall tapers from shoulder, and below it, wall splays to bottom.

Complete, except for chips on shoulder and larger chip on base. Patches of opaque pale brown enamel-like weathering.

COMMENT: The object was collected in Cairo and so was probably found in Egypt.

BIBLIOGRAPHY: *Nahman Collection* 1953, n.p., lot 91; *Verres antiques* 1954, p. 46, no. 274; *Glass from the Ancient World* 1957, p. 281, no. 593.

91. Small Bottle

8th to 9th century. Formerly in the Smith Collection (1514). Gift of Carl Berkowitz and Derek Content. 76.1.198.
H. (surviving) 5.3 cm, W. (max.) 2.8 cm.
Colorless. Blown (probably mold-blown); perhaps ground; facet-cut.

Bottle with egg-shaped body. Lower neck cylindrical; shoulder rounded; wall curves down, out, and in; base rounded. Facet-cut decoration consists of continuous horizontal groove at junction of shoulder and wall; just below this, three equidistant raised triangles with apexes pointing down; on lower wall, in gaps between triangles, three equidistant raised tear-shaped motifs that are pointed at top and rounded at bottom, extending below base to serve as feet.

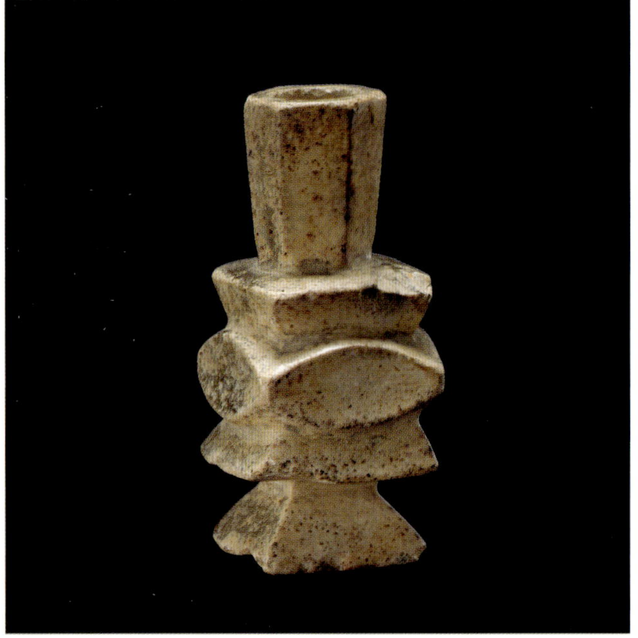

90

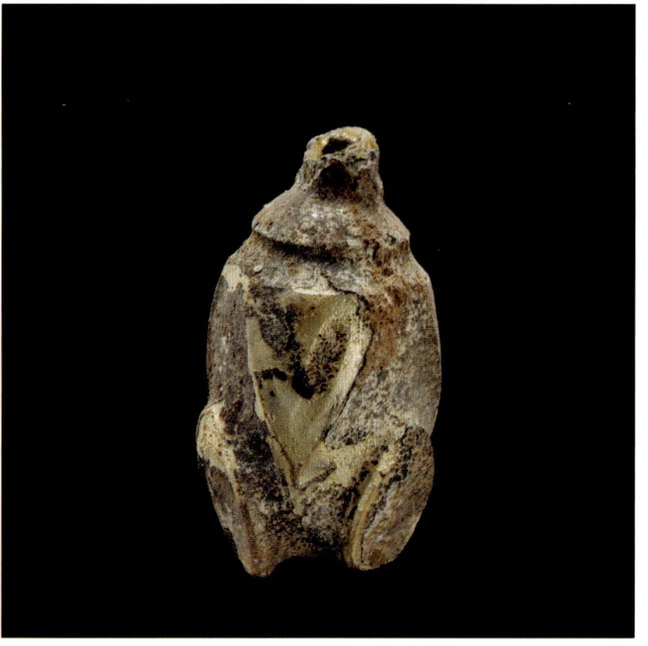

91

Incomplete. Rim and upper neck are missing. Thick opaque grayish weathering, with deep pits; some weathering is missing from wall, one triangle, and one tear-shaped motif.

Comment: The object has one fairly close parallel from an archeological context: an egg-shaped bottle with three lyre-shaped cuts at the top and three raised oval motifs at the bottom, which extend below the base and serve as feet. The bottle was found during excavations at Sīrāf, southern Iran, in context B.H2.368, which consists of material deposited and redeposited at the beginning of the ninth century.

92. Small Bottle

9th to 10th century. Found during excavations at Fusṭāṭ (Old Cairo), Egypt (68.11.40). Gift of the American Research Center in Egypt. 69.1.73.
H. 4.6 cm, D. (body) 2.1 cm.
Colorless. Blown (probably blown in dip mold); facet-cut.

Bottle with cylindrical body. Neck cylindrical at bottom; shoulder flat, with rounded edge; wall vertical; base plain and slightly splayed; no pontil mark. Wall is completely covered with decoration: at top, continuous horizontal band of six contiguous square facets; below, and with single horizontal groove at top and bottom, frieze of four hollow facets shaped like inverted Vs with, in spaces between them, small upright (above) or inverted (below) Vs.

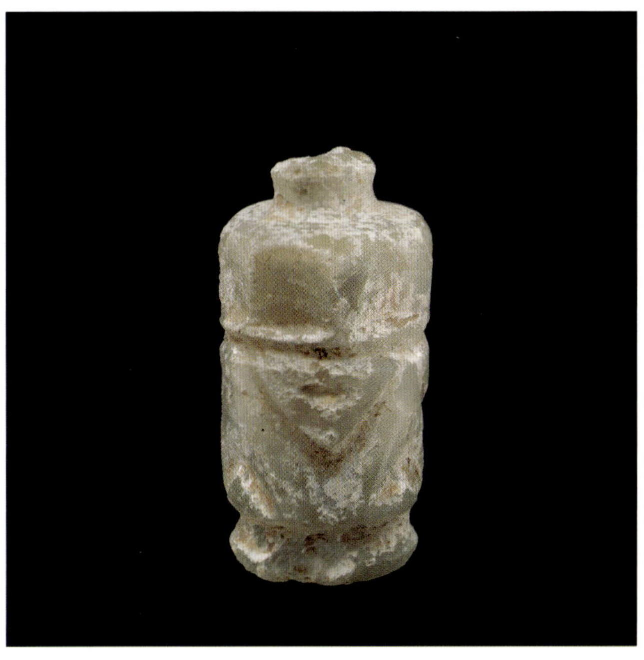

92

Incomplete. Entire rim and most of neck are missing; foot is chipped. Abraded and pitted; remains of off-white enamellike weathering.

Comment: The object was found during excavations directed by Prof. George T. Scanlon.

Bibliography: Scanlon and Pinder-Wilson 2001, p. 96, no. 42k.

93. Small Bottle

9th to 10th century. Formerly in the Smith Collection (493-5). Gift of Carl Berkowitz and Derek Content. 76.1.187.
H. (surviving) 4.1 cm, W. (body) 2.3 cm.
Almost colorless, with yellowish tinge. Blown (probably mold-blown); facet-cut.

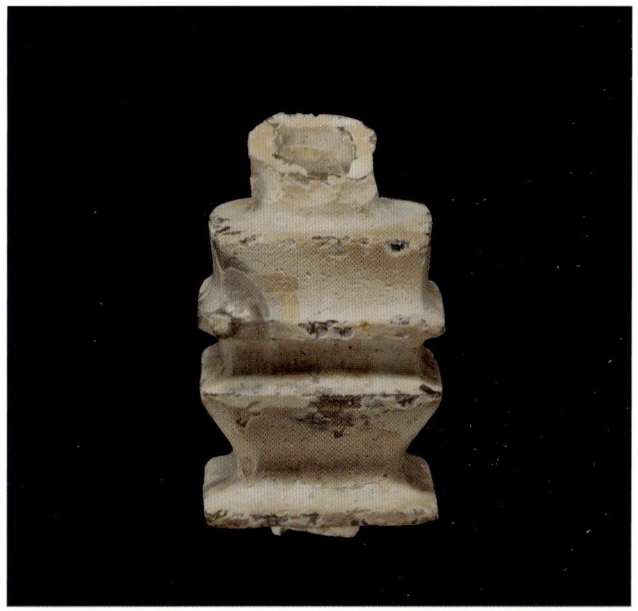

93

Bottle with body in form of rectangular parallelepiped. Lower neck is cut in six contiguous square facets; shoulder is flat; upper wall descends vertically, with continuous horizontal rib just below midpoint; upper surface of rib slopes down to edge; face is vertical, and lower surface is horizontal; lower wall tapers, then flares near bottom, which is similar to rib in upper wall but extends farther inward; top of foot has circular cross section.

Incomplete. Rim, upper neck, and foot are missing. Mostly covered with matte opaque off-white to pale brown weathering.

Bibliography: *Verres antiques* 1954, p. 54, no. 334 (part of group).

94. Small Bottle

10th century. Found during excavations at Fusṭāṭ (Old Cairo), Egypt (80.10.44). Gift of the American Research Center in Egypt. 81.1.30.
L. 4.1 cm, D. 2.7 cm.
Colorless. Blown; cut.

Bottle: cylindrical. Bottle preserves shoulder and upper half of body. Wall is decorated with upper and lower registers of triangular facets, apexes of which meet at midpoint, and which are separated by lozenges; each triangle has pair of short horizontal grooves.

Incomplete. Neck and lower body missing. Extensively weathered.

Comment: The bottle was found, during excavations directed by Prof. George T. Scanlon, in area CIV-11a[1], in a deposit of "sibakh to west of wall."

Cf. **99**.

Bibliography: Scanlon and Pinder-Wilson 2001, p. 94, no. 42g.

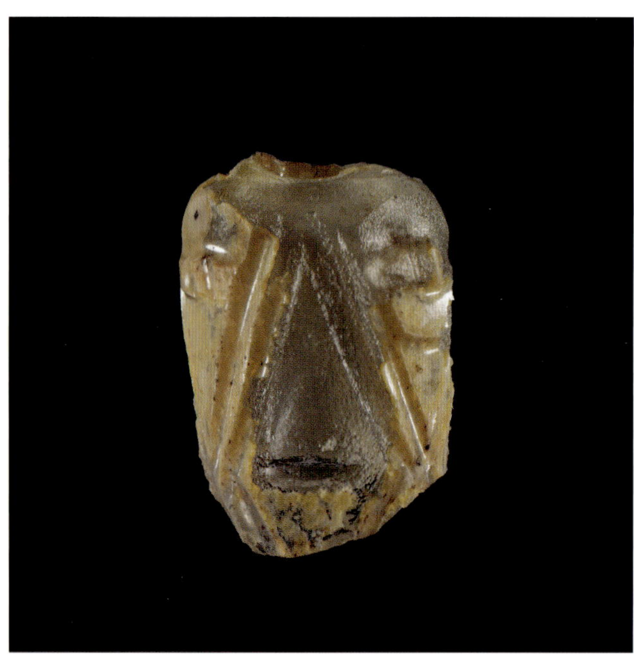

94

95. Small Bottle

Perhaps 9th to 12th century. Formerly in the Smith Collection (235). Gift of Carl Berkowitz and Derek Content. 76.1.61.
H. 3.7 cm, D. (rim) 0.9 cm, (max.) 1.4 cm.
Transparent deep bluish green. Blown; facet- and linear-cut.

Bottle with cylindrical body. Rim plain, with top ground and polished; short, tapering neck; rounded shoulder; vertical wall, which tapers at bottom; and solid conical foot, with bottom ground and polished. Wheel-cut decoration on wall: four adjoining V-shaped facets (two upright and two inverted); each triangular area at open end of V has one horizontal cut.

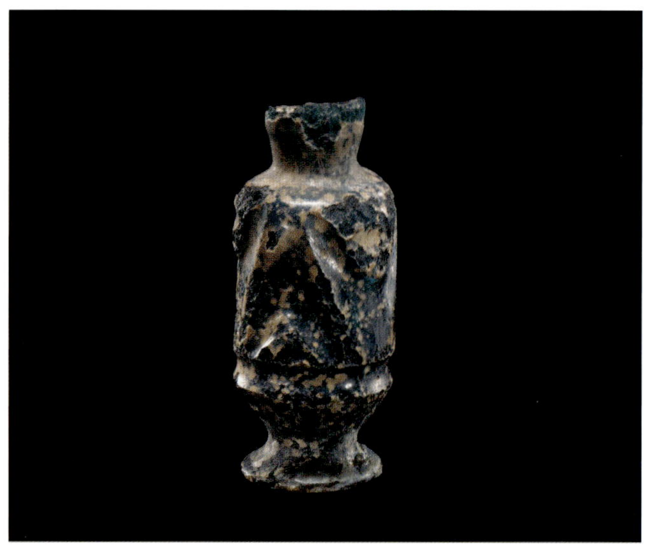

95

Incomplete. Broken, with losses from rim and neck. Pitted and abraded, with mottled tan-colored weathering.

Comment: Cf. **98** and Clairmont 1977, pp. 90–91, no. 300 (in the Benaki Museum, Athens), which have almost identical ornament.

96. Small Bottle

Perhaps about 10th century. Found during excavations at Fusṭāṭ (Old Cairo), Egypt (80.9.28). Gift of the American Research Center in Egypt. 81.1.46.
H. 3.3 cm, D. (rim) 1 cm.
Transparent pale greenish blue. Blown; facet-cut.

Bottle with cylindrical body. Rim plain, with upper surface ground flat; neck tapers; shoulder rounded; wall straight, with slight taper, which becomes more acute at bottom; foot shaped like shallow truncated cone; base flat; no pontil mark. Facet-cut decoration on neck and wall. On neck: six or seven contiguous vertical facets, which are rounded at top and bottom. On upper wall: row of five contiguous semicircular facets. On lower wall: row of five contiguous inverted triangular facets, which are rounded at bottom.

Approximately one-third of rim and neck is missing. Surfaces appear to be pristine.

Comment: The object was found, during excavations directed by Prof. George T. Scanlon, in a context attributed to the 10th century.

Bibliography: Pinder-Wilson and Scanlon 1987, p. 67, no. 14, fig. 14; Scanlon and Pinder-Wilson 2001, p. 94, no. 42f.

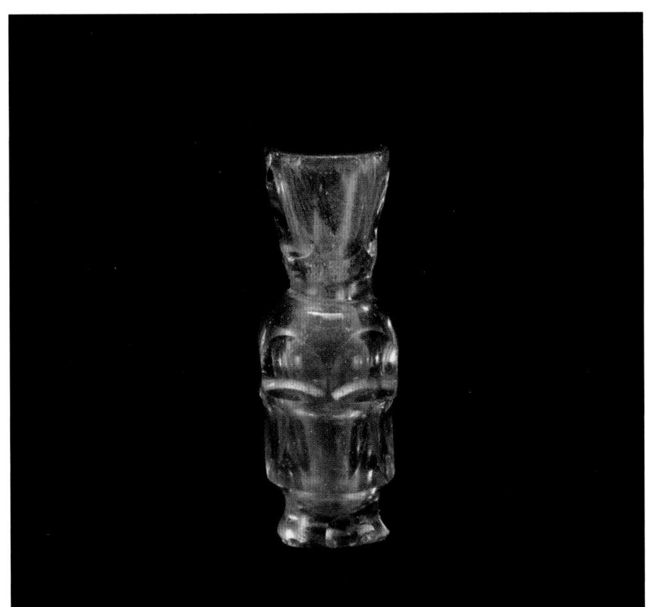

96

97. Small Bottle

9th to 10th century. Found during excavations at Fusṭāṭ (Old Cairo), Egypt (68.12.26). Gift of the American Research Center in Egypt. 69.1.87.
H. (surviving) 3.1 cm, D. (body) 2.1 cm.
Colorless or almost colorless. Blown; facet-cut.

Bottle with cylindrical body. Lower neck straight and tapering slightly; shoulder rounded; wall vertical, curving in at bottom; base plain; no pontil mark. Decorated on neck and wall. On neck: approximately six contiguous vertical facets. On wall: two vertical panels, each containing two inverted crescent-shaped hollow facets, alternating with two vertical panels, each embellished with raised vertical rib.

Incomplete. Rim and part of neck are missing. Extensive remains of dark brown and light gray enamellike weathering.

Comment: The object was found during excavations directed by Prof. George T. Scanlon.

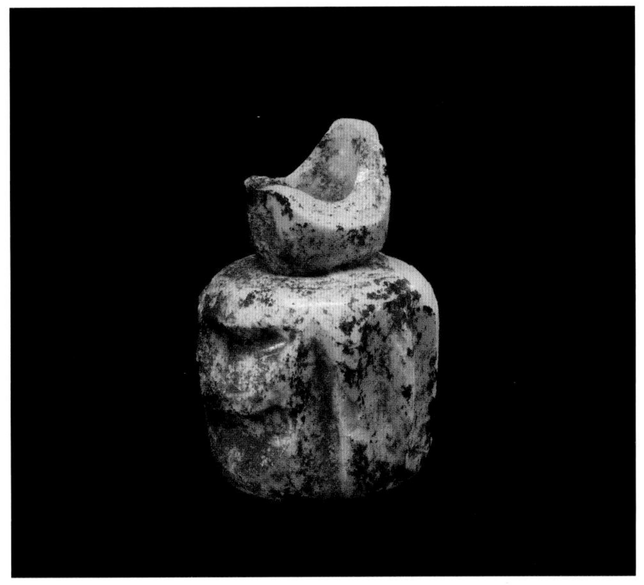

97

Bibliography: Scanlon and Pinder-Wilson 2001, p. 94, no. 42c.

98. Small Bottle

Perhaps about 10th century. Found during excavations at Fusṭāṭ (Old Cairo), Egypt (80.10.18). Gift of the American Research Center in Egypt. 81.1.31.
H. 2.9 cm, D. (rim) 1 cm.
Transparent pale greenish blue. Blown; facet- and linear-cut.

Bottle with cylindrical body. Rim plain, with upper surface ground flat; neck tapers; shoulder rounded; wall straight, with slight taper, which becomes more

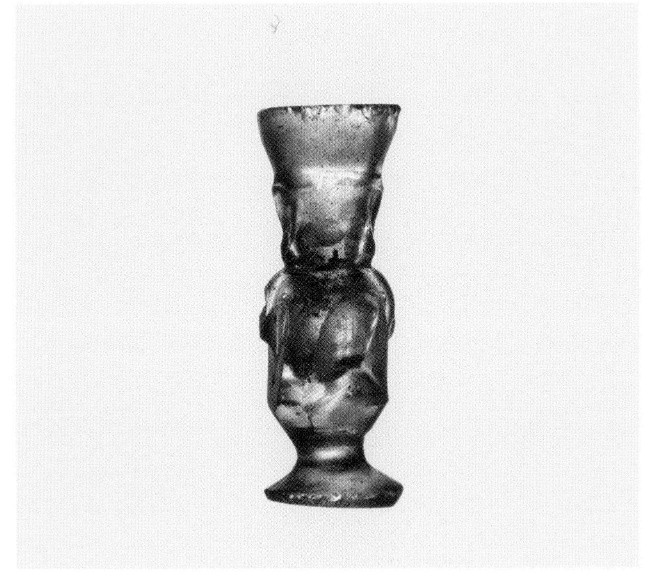

98

acute at bottom; foot shaped like shallow truncated cone; base flat; no pontil mark. Facet-cut decoration on neck and wall. On lower neck: three transverse linear cuts alternating with three oval cuts. On wall: four contiguous vertical facets; two have rounded top and raised triangle at bottom, and two are similar but inverted.

Intact. Surfaces are almost pristine.

Comment: The object was found during excavations directed by Prof. George T. Scanlon.

Cf. **96**.

Bibliography: Scanlon and Pinder-Wilson 2001, pp. 91 and 94, no. 42b.

99. Small Bottle

Perhaps 11th century. Found during excavations at Fusṭāṭ (Old Cairo), Egypt (80.9.32). Gift of the American Research Center in Egypt. 81.1.34.
H. (surviving) 2.8 cm, D. (body) 1.5 cm.
Transparent light blue. Blown (probably mold-blown); facet- and linear-cut.

Bottle with cylindrical body. Shoulder rounded; wall vertical; base flat. Decorated on wall and underside of base. Four equidistant vertical cuts run from top to bottom of wall and under base, where they meet at center; between each pair of cuts on wall, two crescent-shaped facets separated by raised area containing small oval facet.

Incomplete. Rim, almost entire neck, 50 percent of shoulder, and about 25 percent of wall are missing. No obvious weathering.

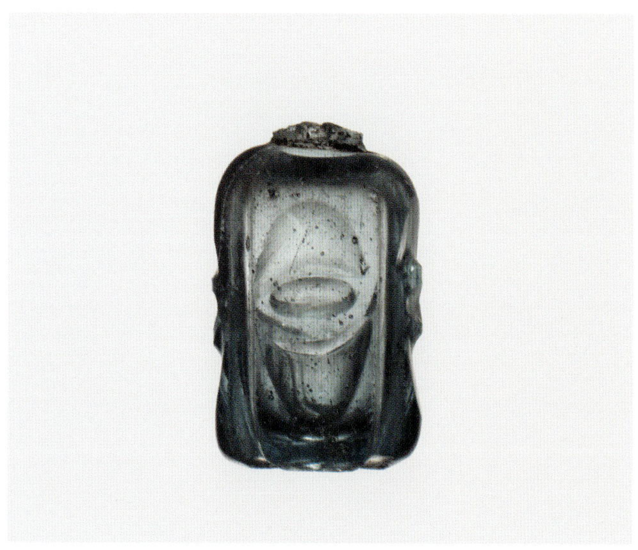

99

Comment: The bottle was found during excavations directed by Prof. George T. Scanlon. Scanlon and Pinder-Wilson (see below) reported that it was "found in the 14th level of the mound" and dated it to the 11th century.

A small bottle in the Museum für Islamische Kunst, Berlin (I.2141: Kröger 1984, p. 182, no. 161), acquired in Cairo, also has four vertical cuts on the wall, which continue under the base and meet at the center.

Bibliography: Scanlon and Pinder-Wilson 2001, p. 91, no. 42a.

100. Fragment of Small Bottle

Perhaps about 10th century. 53.1.46.
H. (surviving) 3.6 cm, W. (max.) 1.8 cm.
Almost colorless, perhaps with yellowish tinge.
Blown; facet-cut.

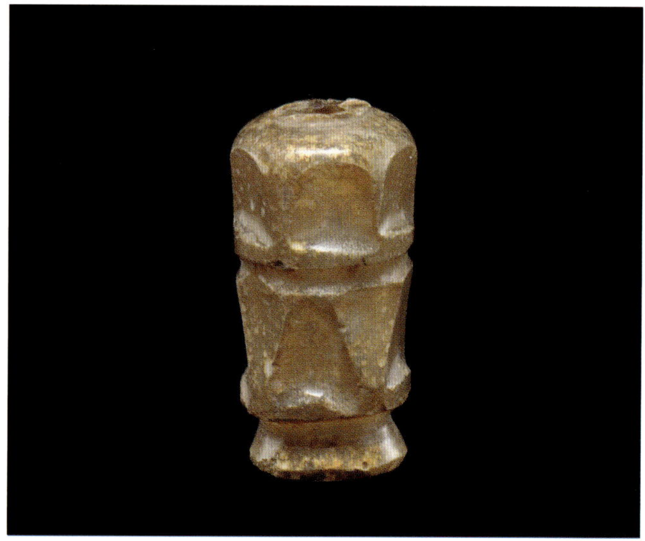

100

Fragment of bottle with cylindrical body. Bottom of neck possibly cut in six vertical facets; shoulder rounded; wall almost vertical; foot shaped like shallow truncated cone; base flat; no pontil mark. Facet-cut decoration on wall. Upper wall has row of five almost contiguous squarish facets. Lower wall has row of four inverted triangular facets, which alternate with four upright triangular facets.

Entire rim and almost entire neck are missing; body and foot are complete. Light yellowish brown weathering with iridescent highlights.

Comment: Cf. **92**, which was found during excavations at Fusṭāṭ, in a context attributed to the 10th century. For a small bottle with alternating upright and inverted triangular facets, also from Fusṭāṭ, see Scanlon and Pinder-Wilson 2001, p. 98, no. 42u.

101. Fragment of Small Bottle

About 10th century. Formerly in the Smith Collection (1220-7). 76.1.194.
H. (surviving) 3 cm, D. (body) 1.1 cm.
Colorless. Blown; facet-cut.

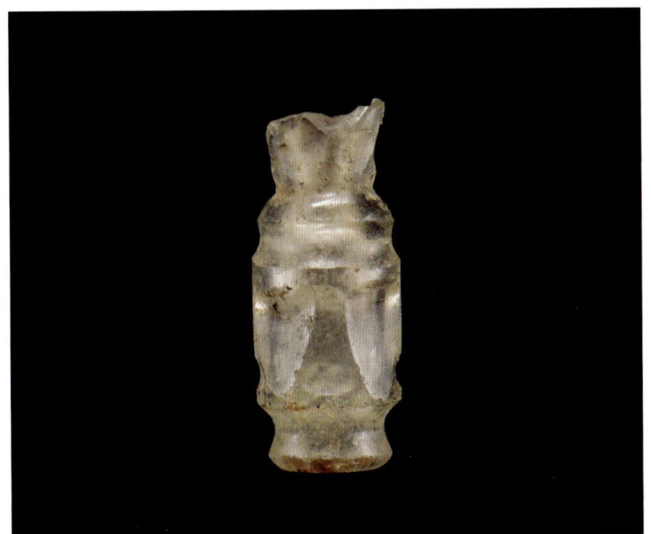

101

Fragment of bottle. Lower neck tapers; shoulder rounded; wall vertical, tapering at bottom; foot shaped like shallow cone; underside of base plain; no pontil mark. Decorated on neck and wall. On neck: remains of facets with rounded bottoms. On wall: continuous horizontal groove at top, above band of four inverted triangular facets alternating with four narrower upright facets.

Rim and large part of neck are missing; body and foot are complete. Incipient weathering, especially in facets.

Comment: For a band of upright triangular facets alternating with inverted triangular facets, see **100**.

102. Fragment of Small Bottle

9th to 11th century. Formerly in the Smith Collection (1145). Gift of Carl Berkowitz and Derek Content. 76.1.222.
H. (surviving) 2.8 cm, W. (rim) 1.7 cm.
Colorless. Blown; drilled; facet-cut.

Fragment consisting of entire rim and upper neck of miniature bottle. Rim has flat top and narrow bevel; neck has straight, tapering side cut in six contiguous vertical facets, and tubular perforation (D. 0.8 cm) made by drilling.

Apart from minute chips, surfaces are pristine.

Comment: The technique used to perforate the neck was probably identical, or at least similar, to that described by Contadini (1999, pp. 324–325).

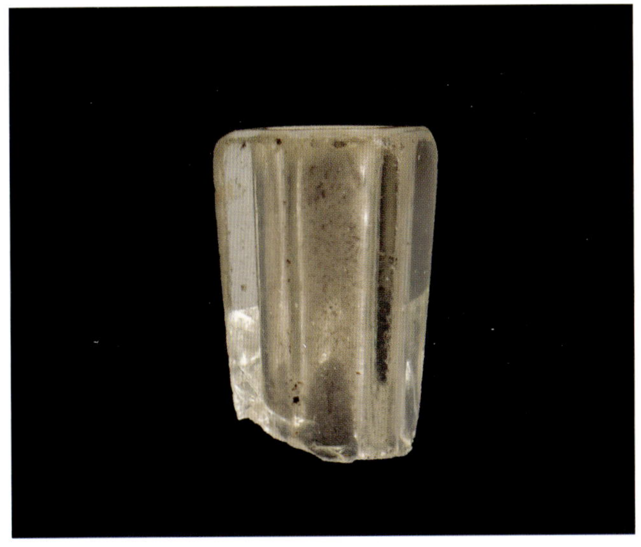

102

7. Small Bottles, "Molar Flasks"

103. Small Bottle, "Molar Flask"

9th to 11th century. 60.1.2.
H. 6.8 cm, W. (rim) 1.5 cm, (body) 1.7 cm.
Transparent light green. Blown (probably mold-blown); perhaps ground; facet-cut.

Bottle. Rim plain, with flat top; neck tapers; body has rounded shoulder, vertical sides, and square cross section; at bottom of wall, four pointed feet, one at each corner. Decorated on neck and body. On neck: upper two-thirds is cut in four equidistant vertical facets; below them is one continuous horizontal groove. Decoration on body is very similar on all four sides: at bottom, large triangular cut, which partly defines feet; at angles between each pair of sides, one narrow rhombic facet, shallow at top and bottom and deepest at widest part, which has two diamond-shaped knobs.

Intact. Somewhat dull, but with no obvious weathering.

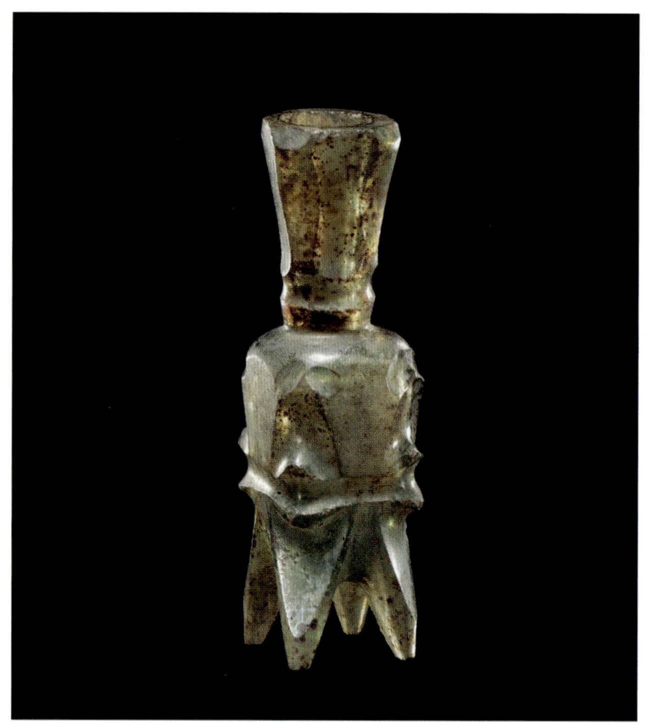

103

Comment: This is a common variety of "molar flask." Examples of bottles similar to **103** have a wide distribution, extending from Fusṭāṭ, Egypt (Scanlon and Pinder-Wilson 2001, p. 97, no. 42q), to Samarra, Iraq (Lamm 1928, p. 73, no. 217), and northern Iran, probably Rayy (Lamm 1935, pl. 37H).

Examples without known find-places include Lamm 1929–30, p. 165, pl. 61, no. 11 (in The Metropolitan Museum of Art, New York); *Hentrich Collection* 1974, p. 273, no. 419 (in the Museum Kunst Palast, Düsseldorf: 1973-78); *Cohn Collection* 1980, p. 164, no. 161 = "Recent Important Acquisitions," *JGS*, v. 4, 1962, p. 142, no. 17 (in the Los Angeles County Museum of Art); Kröger 1984, p. 176, no. 153 (in the Museum für Islamische Kunst, Berlin: I.4415); and Carboni 2001, p. 99, no. 27b = *3000 Jahre Glaskunst* 1981, p. 137, no. 607 (in the al-Sabah Collection, Dār al-Āthār al-Islāmiyyah, Kuwait National Museum: LNS 15 KG).

For other "molar flasks" with rhombic facets, see **104** and **105**.

104. Small Bottle, "Molar Flask"

9th to 10th century. Formerly in the Smith Collection (913). 55.1.115.
H. 6.1 cm, D. (rim) 1.9 cm, W. (body, max.) 2.6 cm.
Probably almost colorless, with yellowish tinge. Blown (perhaps in dip mold); facet- and relief-cut.

Bottle. Rim plain, with top ground flat; neck straight and tapering; shoulder almost flat; wall descends vertically and has square cross section; base has four small feet. Facet- and relief-cut decoration on neck, shoulder, and wall. On neck and shoulder: six contiguous vertical facets extend from rim to horizontal rib near junction with shoulder, edge of which has four long oval facets, each touching its neighbors. On wall: each angle has one narrow rhombic motif with pointed knob at midpoint, and similar projection near bottom, which terminates at base of foot. Between each pair of rhombic motifs, wall is cut in four triangular facets of different sizes. Underside of base is plain.

Complete, except for small losses from bottoms of three feet. Matte pale gray weathering.

Comment: See **103**.

Bibliography: *Verres antiques* 1954, p. 47, no. 276; *Glass from the Ancient World* 1957, p. 283, no. 595.

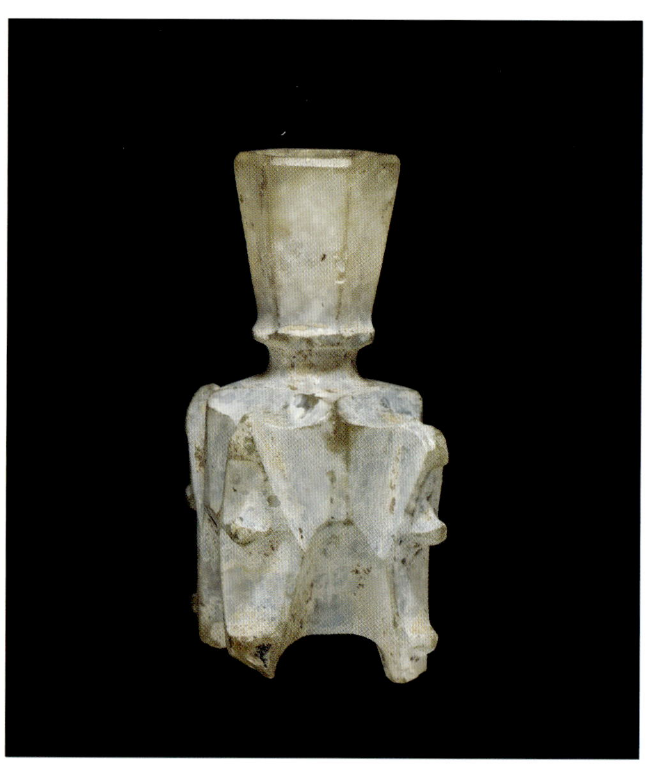

104

105. Small Bottle, "Molar Flask"

9th to 10th century. Formerly in the Smith Collection (1109). Gift of Carl Berkowitz and Derek Content. 76.1.301.
H. (surviving) 6.1 cm, D. (lower neck) 1.3 cm, W. (body) 1.8 cm.
Transparent deep green. Blown (probably mold-blown); facet-cut.

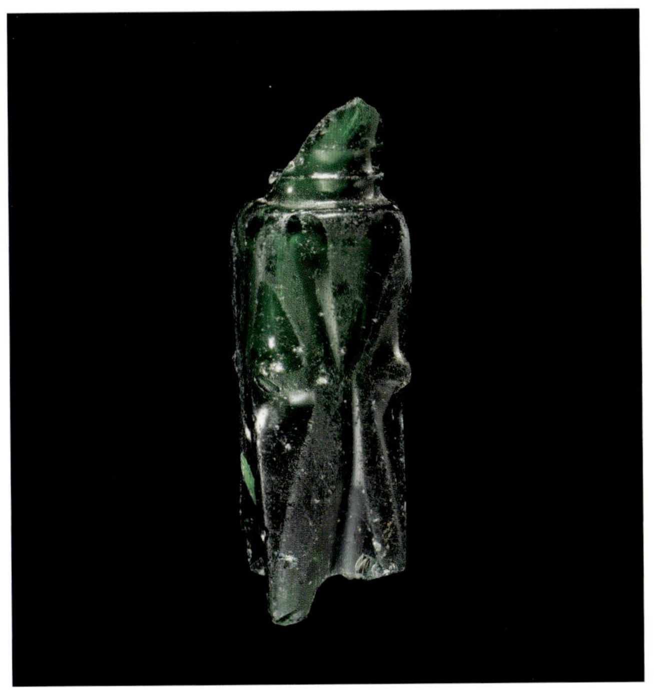

105

Bottle. Lower neck cut in vertical facets, which terminate at continuous horizontal groove near junction with shoulder; this is almost flat, with rounded edge; wall descends vertically and has square cross section; base has four small feet. Facet- and relief-cut decoration on wall, consisting of, at each angle, one narrow rhombic motif extending from shoulder to foot, with knob at midpoint. Between each pair of rhombic motifs, one V-shaped cut on upper wall and one inverted V below it.

Incomplete. Rim, most of neck, and all or part of all four feet are missing. Pitted and somewhat dull.

Comment: See **103**.

The weight of the object suggests that it may be made of lead glass.

106. Small Bottle, "Molar Flask"

9th to 10th century. Found during excavations at Fusṭāṭ (Old Cairo), Egypt (68.10.41). Gift of the American Research Center in Egypt. 69.1.61.
H. (surviving) 5.5 cm, W. (rim, max.) 1.6 cm, (body) 1.9 cm.
Almost colorless, with greenish tinge. Blown (body perhaps blown in dip mold); facet- and linear-cut.

Bottle: body has square cross section. Rim plain, with top ground flat; neck tapers; shoulder slopes toward edge; wall vertical; at each angle between sides, short foot, with horizontal pyramid-shaped projection at bottom. Decorated on neck, shoulder, and wall. On neck: six contiguous vertical facets above horizontal rib. On shoulder: four triangular facets above angles of wall, leaving square "step" just below neck. On wall: each side has horizontal groove above midpoint, with two small wedge-shaped hollow facets above and larger wedge-shaped hollow facet below it; each angle has triangular facet above groove and wedge-shaped facet below it.

Intact, except for bottoms of feet. Pitted and slightly iridescent, with remains of off-white weathering.

Comment: The object was found during excavations directed by Prof. George T. Scanlon.

For a similar bottle in the Benaki Museum, Athens (41/22), see Clairmont 1977, pp. 92–93, no. 308.

Bibliography: Scanlon and Pinder-Wilson 2001, p. 97, no. 42p.

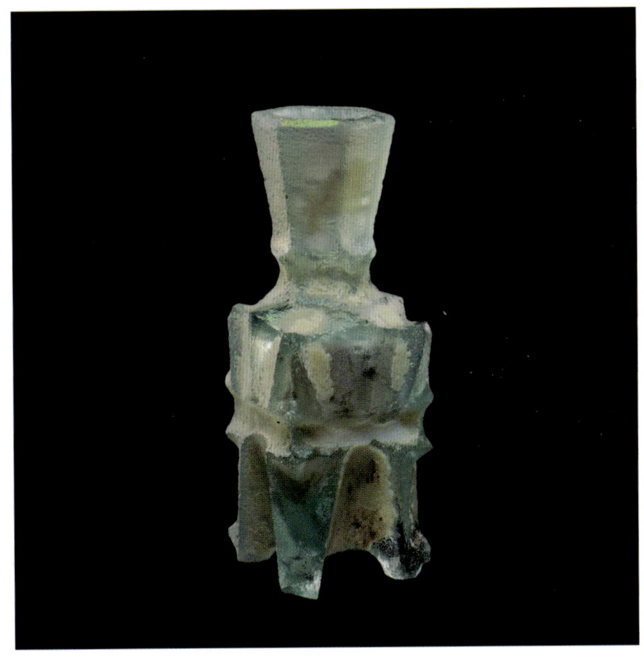

106

107. Small Bottle, "Molar Flask"

9th to 11th century. Formerly in the Feldman and Smith Collections (Smith 124). Gift of Carl Berkowitz and Derek Content. 76.1.185.
H. (surviving) 5.4 cm, W. (body) 2 cm.
Transparent bluish green. Blown (probably mold-blown); perhaps ground; facet-cut.

Bottle. Bottom of neck has circular cross section; body has narrow shoulder, vertical sides, and square cross section; at bottom of wall, four pointed feet, one at each corner. Decoration on body was probably very similar on all four sides, with horizontal groove above midpoint. On shoulder: triangular step has been removed from all four corners, leaving raised square area with angles at 45 degrees to corners. On upper wall: each side has two contiguous wedge-shaped facets, which are wider at top than at bottom. On lower wall: large wedge-shaped cut, which partly defines feet; at angles between each pair of sides, one long triangular facet, which begins just below top, ends at top of foot, and has protrusion at horizontal groove.

Incomplete. Rim, upper neck, all of two feet, and parts of other two feet are missing. Silver weathering.

Comment: For "molar flasks" with similar but kite-shaped facets, see **103–106**.

Bibliography: *Verres antiques* 1954, p. 47, no. 279.

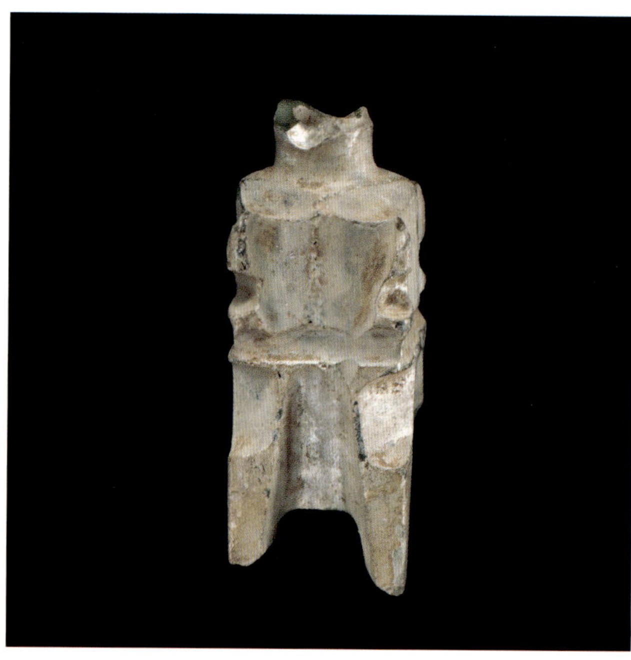

107

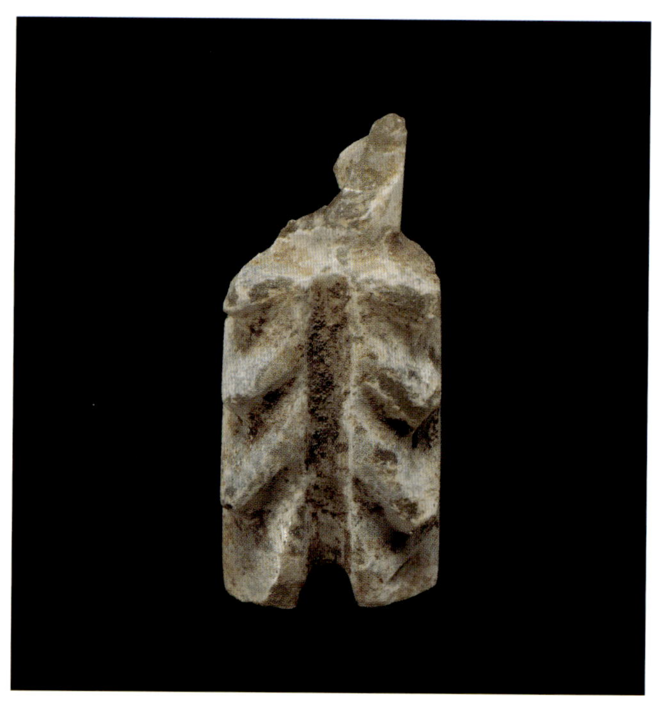

108

108. Small Bottle, "Molar Flask"

9th to 11th century. Formerly in the Smith Collection (1220-8). Gift of Carl Berkowitz and Derek Content. 76.1.195.
H. (surviving) 5.2 cm, W. (lower neck) 1.4 cm, (body) 2.3 cm.
Colorless. Blown (probably mold-blown); perhaps ground; facet-cut.

Bottle. Lower neck originally cylindrical; body tall, with slightly sloping shoulder, vertical walls, square cross section, and cavity that is egg-shaped; at bottom of wall, four short, flat feet, one at each corner. Decorated on neck and body. On lower neck: eight contiguous vertical facets; below these are two horizontal ribs. On body: each side has, at center, shallow vertical groove that runs from top to bottom; on each corner, two V-shaped facets, one above the other, at top and shallow facet extending over foot at bottom, which together create stepped effect.

Incomplete. Rim, part of neck, half of body, and two feet are missing. Opaque pale yellowish brown weathering.

Comment: The form of the interior suggests that it was not created during the process of inflation. The most likely explanation of the shape is that it was made by grinding the object with a rotating tool, perhaps akin to a bow drill (cf. Contadini 1999, p. 324, on shaping the interiors of rock crystal vessels).

The broken edges of the body (but not the neck) have been carefully ground to make a miniature dish-like container. The grinding took place before the object became weathered.

109. Small Bottle, "Molar Flask"

9th to 11th century. Formerly in the Smith Collection (1152). Gift of Carl Berkowitz and Derek Content. 76.1.190.
H. (surviving) 4.9 cm, W. (body) 2.7 cm.
Colorless. Blown (probably mold-blown); perhaps ground; facet-cut.

Bottle. Body has narrow shoulder, vertical sides, and square cross section; at bottom of wall, four pointed feet, one at each corner. Decoration on body was probably very similar on all four sides: at bottom, large triangular cut, which partly defines feet; at angles between each pair of sides, one long, triangular facet, which is deep at top and shallow at bottom, with diamond-shaped knob at top.

Incomplete. Rim, neck, half of body, and one foot are missing. Deeply pitted, with remains of pale brown weathering.

Comment: For "molar flasks" with similar but kite-shaped facets, see **105** and **112**.

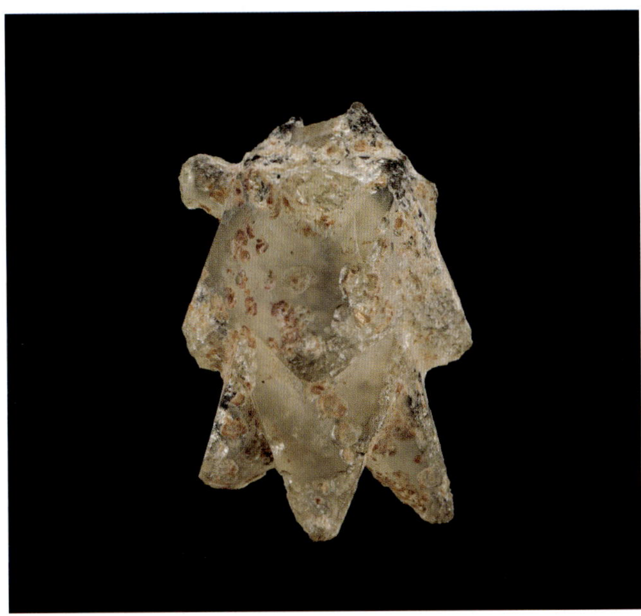

109

110. Small Bottle, "Molar Flask"

9th to 11th century. Formerly in the collection of Maurice Nahman, Cairo, Egypt. 53.1.57.
H. (surviving) 4.6 cm, W. (max.) 2 cm.
Colorless; minute bubbles. Blown (body probably blown in dip mold); facet-cut.

Bottle: body has square cross section at midpoint. Neck has circular cross section at bottom; shoulder flat; wall vertical. All four sides of body are decorated with identical rhombuses, each touching its neighbors. Rhombuses were formed by cutting away most of tops and bottoms of all four junctions of sides, leaving small triangular projections at top and bottom of body.

Incomplete. Rim, neck, and feet are missing. Dull, with incipient weathering visible under magnification.

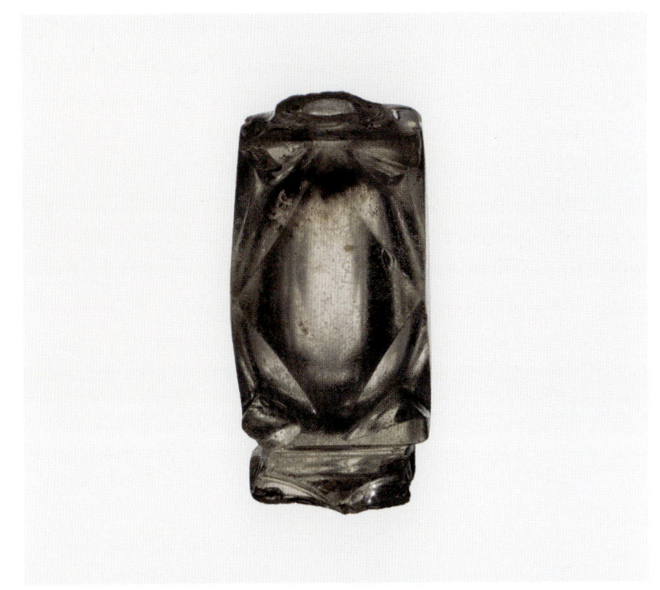

110

111. Small Bottle, "Molar Flask"

9th to 10th century. Found during excavations at Fusṭāṭ (Old Cairo), Egypt (68.11.41). Gift of the American Research Center in Egypt. 69.1.74.
H. (surviving) 4.6 cm, W. (body) 2.2 cm.
Almost colorless, with green tinge. Blown (body probably blown in dip mold); facet- and linear-cut.

Bottle: body has square cross section. Bottom of neck is cylindrical; shoulder narrow and rounded at edge; wall straight and slightly tapered; pyramid-shaped foot projects from junction of each angle of

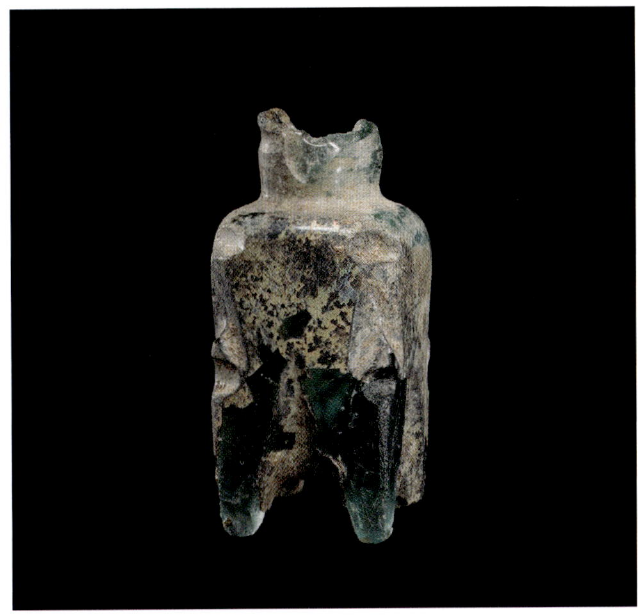

111

body. Linear-cut decoration on lower neck consists of single horizontal groove. Decoration on body is both linear- and facet-cut, and identical on all four angles: short horizontal cut at edge of shoulder and, on wall, hollow facet shaped like inverted V above hollow oval facet.

Incomplete. Rim, upper neck, and parts of all four feet are missing. Dull, with slightly iridescent charcoal gray weathering.

Comment: The bottle was found during excavations directed by Prof. George T. Scanlon.

Bibliography: Scanlon and Pinder-Wilson 2001, p. 96, no. 42m.

112. Small Bottle, "Molar Flask"

9th to 10th century. Found during excavations at Fusṭāṭ (Old Cairo), Egypt (65.4.25). Gift of the American Research Center in Egypt. 69.1.52.
H. (surviving) 4.5 cm, W. 2.1 cm.
Transparent light green. Blown (body probably blown in dip mold); facet- and linear-cut.

Bottle: body has square cross section. Shoulder is narrow, with rounded edge; wall vertical; foot projects from junction of each angle of body. Decoration on body is both linear- and facet-cut, and identical on all sides and on all four angles. Decoration on each side consists of two cuts in form of V, which meet at one horizontal cut, with long vertical cut below it. Each angle has hollow facet shaped like inverted V above short horizontal cut, which connects cuts on adjoining sides, with roughly triangular facet below it.

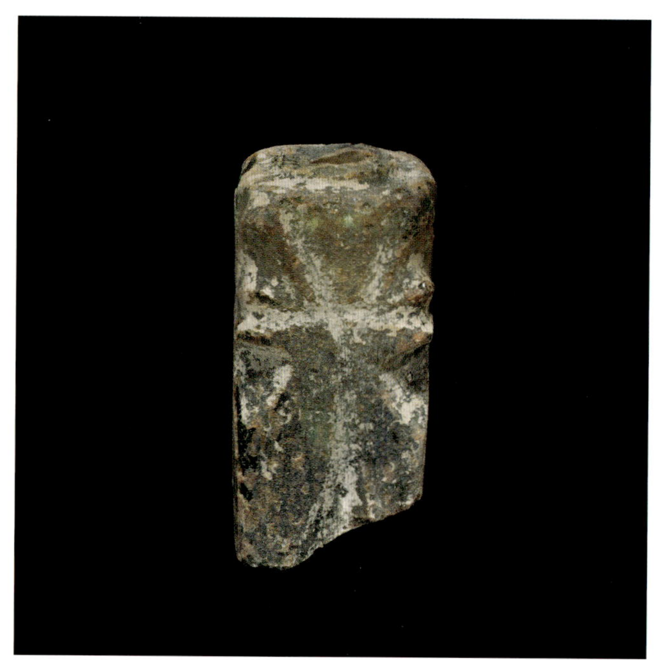

112

Incomplete. Entire rim, neck, three feet, and most of fourth foot are missing. Dull and pitted, with remains of pale grayish weathering.

Comment: The bottle was found during excavations directed by Prof. George T. Scanlon.

Bibliography: Scanlon and Pinder-Wilson 2001, p. 96, no. 42i.

8. Pitcher

113. Pitcher

9th to 10th century. Formerly in the Strauss Collection (S2522). Bequest of Jerome Strauss. 95.1.94.
OH. 14.6 cm, H. (rim) 13 cm, D. (rim) 6.7 cm, (max.) 8.7 cm.
Almost colorless, with yellowish green tinge. Blown, applied; linear- and facet-cut.

Pitcher: globular. Rim plain, with rounded lip; neck straight and tapering; base plain, with annular pontil mark (D. about 1.6 cm) partly removed by grinding; handle with circular cross section dropped onto wall at greatest diameter, drawn up and in, and attached to top of neck, with bifid thumb-rest at highest point. Decorated on neck, wall, and thumb-rest. Neck has three equidistant, linear-cut V-shaped motifs (H. 2.5 cm) descending from rim, each consisting of two Vs, one inside the other. Body is decorated with panel defined at top by double linear-cut border that is horizontal for most of vessel's circumference but descends in U-shaped curves below bottom of lower handle attachment, and at bottom by bottom of wall; panel contains four rows of hollow circular facets (D. about 1.2 cm), none of which touches its neighbors; top three rows have 15 facets, and bottom row has 14 facets. Thumb-rest has two horizontal linear cuts on each side.

Almost complete. Broken and repaired, with small losses from rim and upper wall. Dull, with remains of grayish weathering and slight iridescence.

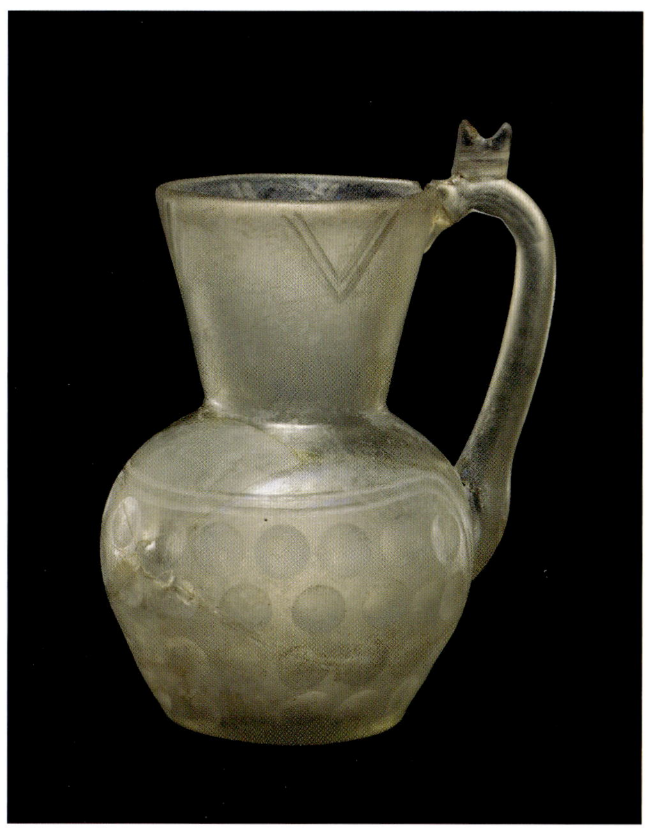

113A

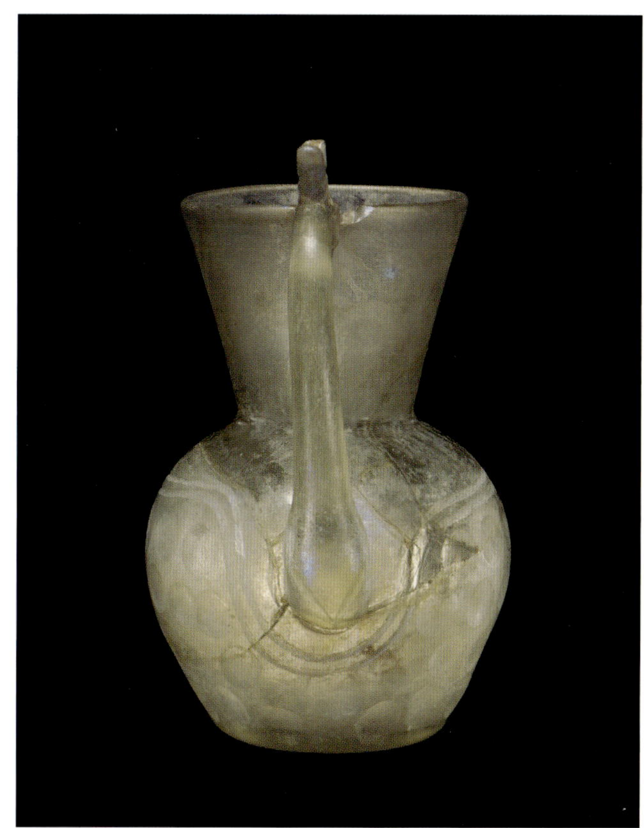

113B

Comment: The vessel is similar to a pitcher excavated at Tepe Madraseh, Nishapur, northeastern Iran, and now in the National Museum, Tehran (3955: Kröger 1995, pp. 125–126, no. 169). This is slightly smaller than **113**, but it has at least one V-shaped motif below the rim and a panel containing two rows of facets on the wall. A second ewer of the same general shape has pendent arcs instead of Vs on the neck and a panel containing four rows of facets on the wall; it is said to have come from Gurgān Province, northern Iran (Fukai 1977, p. 63 and pl. 69). A plain example is also said to be from Gurgān (*ibid.*, pl. 68). The thumb-rest of **113** closely resembles that on a conical ewer with linear-cut decoration that was "found in Persia" and is now in The British Museum, London (OA 1964.12-17.1: Pinder-Wilson 1991, 1999, and 2004, p. 117, fig. 143, left = *Masterpieces of Glass* 1968, p. 108, no. 142).

9. Ewers

114. Ewer

9th to 10th century. Formerly in the Smith Collection (944). 55.1.116.
H. (thumb-rest) 12 cm, (rim) 10.8 cm, D. (max.) 6.4 cm.
Colorless; bubbles (some large) and scale.
Blown, applied; facet-cut.

Ewer: pear-shaped. Rim everted, with rounded edge and pinched pouring lip; wall straight and flaring, then curving down and in at bottom; base is disk-shaped, with rounded edge; pontil mark partly removed by grinding. Handle with oval cross section dropped onto lower wall, drawn out and up and in, and attached to outside of rim, with pinched thumb-rest at highest point. Edge of rim thinned by grinding and polishing. Wall is decorated with hollow facets, none of which touches its neighbors: at top, row of three subcircular and oval horizontal facets above row of four horizontal oval facets; below this, occupying most of front and sides of body, panel framed at top and sides by more or less straight cuts, and containing five rows of horizontal oval facets (with, from top to bottom, six, six, seven, eight, and eight facets) and one row of 14 or 15 vertical oval facets. Handle has minor patches of grinding on one side and two irregular hollow facets at bottom.

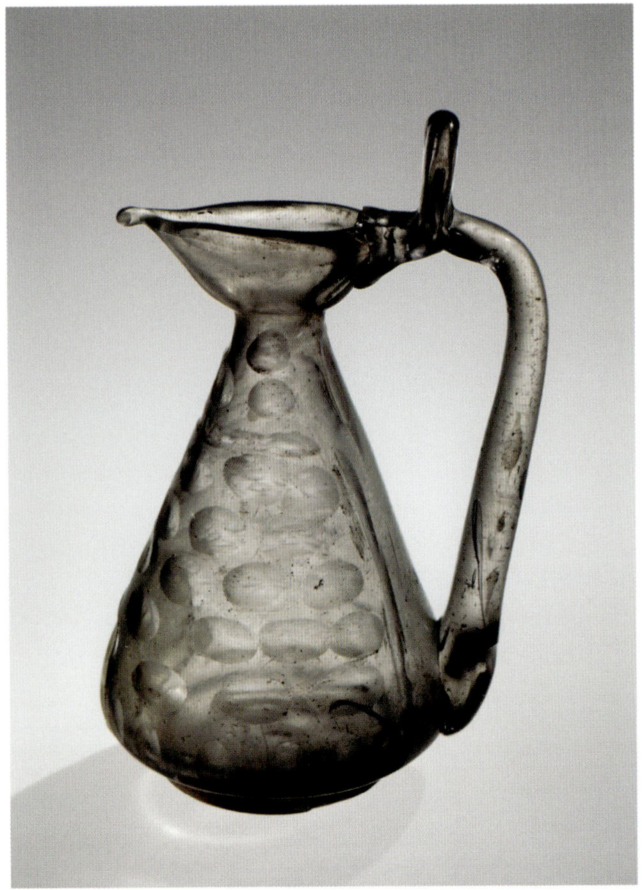

114

Incomplete. Small triangular area lost from lower wall below pouring lip, and restored; crack extends from restored area almost to handle; large chip in edge of foot. Except for stain or accretion on inside, glass is almost as new.

COMMENT: The form, which may be derived from Sasanian metalwork, has a long history. It is found in glass in pre-Islamic or very early Islamic times (cf. the ewer in the Shōsō-in Treasury at Nara, Japan, which is presumably earlier than 756: Harada and others 1965, p. iii, no. 2). Similar pear-shaped ewers include two linear-cut vessels in The British Museum, London (OA1913.11-4.1 and OA1964.12-17.1: Pinder-Wilson 1999, p. 117, fig. 143); the Corning Ewer (**523**); and a group of six rock crystal ewers, all of which were made between the ninth and the very early 11th centuries.

The perfunctory nature of the cutting may be compared, among many others, with the facet-cut ornament on a pitcher from Nishapur, Iran (Kröger 1995, pp. 125–126, no. 169).

BIBLIOGRAPHY: *Verres antiques* 1954, p. 48, no. 292; *Glass from the Ancient World* 1957, p. 273, no. 560.

115. Fragment of Ewer

9th to 10th century. Formerly in the Smith Collection (1139). Gift of Mrs. Ray Winfield Smith. 81.1.700.
H. (surviving) 4.9 cm.
Almost colorless, with yellowish tinge. Blown, applied; facet- and linear-cut.

Fragment: mouth and upper neck of ewer. Mouth has oval opening, pulled out and pinched at one end to form pouring lip; rim plain, flattened on top; opposite pouring lip, trace of handle. Upper neck has straight side and is wider at bottom than at top. One side of mouth has two short linear cuts in form of shallow V. Neck has, at top, row of four contiguous subrectangular facets that begins and ends on either side of handle.

Mouth is almost complete; only small part of neck survives. Dull and extensively pitted, with iridescent weathering.

COMMENT: See **114**.

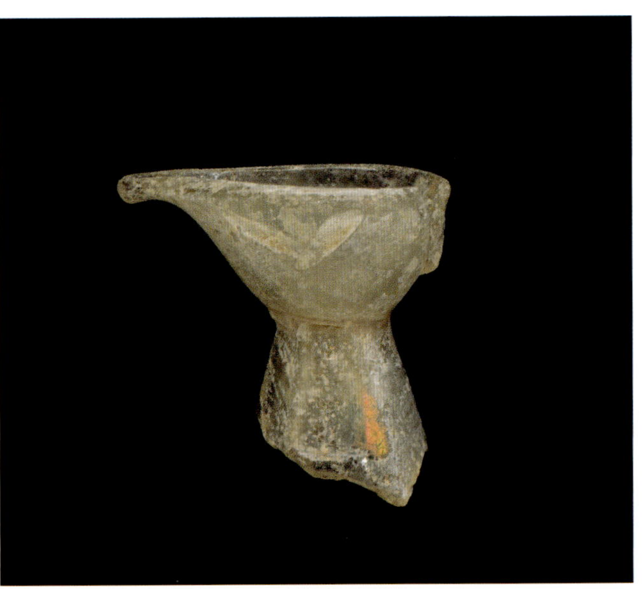

115

10. Indeterminate

116. Fragment

Date unknown; presumably not recent.
Formerly in the Smith Collection (1102).
59.1.481.
Max. Dim. 8.3 cm.
Colorless. Blown; facet- and linear-cut, and abraded.

Fragment from wall of vessel, perhaps with hemispherical body or lower body. Wall apparently curves down and in and merges with rounded base. Decoration consists of narrow linear cuts, and one circular and eight oval facets, each of which is small and hollow, and framed or partly framed by abraded band (W. 0.1–0.2 cm). Upper section of fragment has part of indeterminate hatched motif, below which are two adjacent facets (L. 2 cm) linked by one pair of short incised lines; above these lines, edges of facets are plain, but below them they are abraded. Two smaller oval facets (L. of complete example 1.1 cm) occupy part of lower wall. Bottom of wall is decorated with oval facets (L. 1.3 cm) alternating with pairs of incised lines, apparently part of a continuous band, which may have contained nine or 10 facets and pairs of lines, and which surrounded a circular or subcircular facet (D. 2 cm) at center of base.

Fragment consists of four small pieces, which join. Dull, with translucent pale gray weathering.

Comment: Under low magnification, the abrasion is seen to consist of numerous parallel scratches. Perhaps the glassworker took advantage of the curvature of the vessel to abrade the surface with a file.

The fragment is very unusual. A search of the literature failed to disclose another object decorated with hollow facets that are surrounded by narrow bands of abrasion.

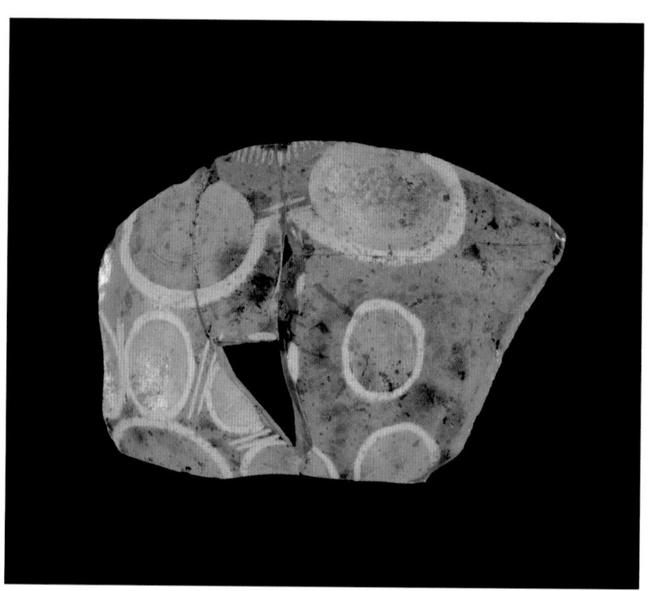

116

117. Fragment

Date unknown; possibly 18th or 19th century.
Formerly in the Smith Collection (1153).
59.1.458.
H. 4.9 cm, D. (est.) about 8 cm.
Colorless. Blown; facet-cut.

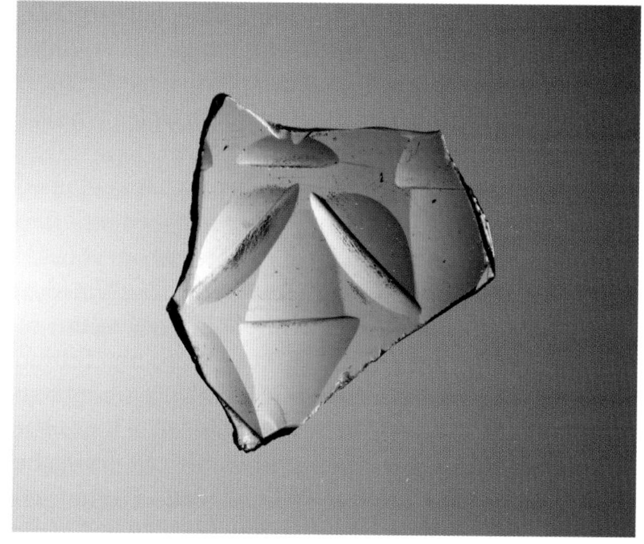

117

Fragment. Shoulder has rounded edge; wall descends vertically. Decoration on wall appears to consist of four hollow, pointed-oval facets arranged to form square panel with sides at 45 degrees to horizontal; panel contains two triangular facets with common baseline; just above panel, horizontal facet shaped like half-moon; above this, on shoulder, are bottoms of two facets, perhaps pointed ovals from another panel; fragmentary motifs on either side of panels may be pairs of triangles with common baselines; in each case, upper triangle flanks upper panel and lower triangle flanks lower panel. Possible traces of gilding in some cuts.

Broken on all sides. Dull, but without obvious weathering.

Comment: The orientation of the fragment is uncertain; the description supposes that it is from the

of the American Research Center in Egypt. 69.1.89.
(1) Max. Dim. 6.2 cm, D. (outer groove, est.) about 11 cm; (2) Max. Dim. 5.9 cm; (3) Max. Dim. 5.6 cm.
Almost colorless, with yellowish tinge. Blown; cut.

Three fragments from wall of vessel with globular body. Shoulder and upper wall curve out, down, and in. Fragment 1 has two concentric grooves at junction of wall and shoulder and, below them, parts of two contiguous countersunk disks (D. 1.7 cm); center of one survives, and this has small countersunk knob (D. 0.7 cm). Fragment 2 has parts of two identical disks and, below, part of indeterminate motif. Fragment 3 has two concentric grooves and part of one countersunk disk.

All fragments are broken on all sides. Partly covered with mottled charcoal gray to silvery weathering.

COMMENT: The fragments were found during excavations directed by Prof. George T. Scanlon. They were recovered from the filling of a cistern, the contents of which were "overwhelmingly of the 9th–10th century."

The fragments probably came from a vessel similar to a globular bowl in the Museum für Islamische Kunst, Berlin (I.2/64: Kröger 1984, p. 200, no. 179), which has three horizontal rows of contiguous countersunk disks on the wall and a rosette on the base. It is possible, however, that the fragments were part of a bottle similar to another object in Berlin (I.55/65: *ibid.*, p. 202, no. 180) or a bottle in the al-Sabah Collection, Dār al-Āthār al-Islāmiyyah, Kuwait National Museum (LNS 80 KG: Carboni 2001, p. 110, no. 2.6b).

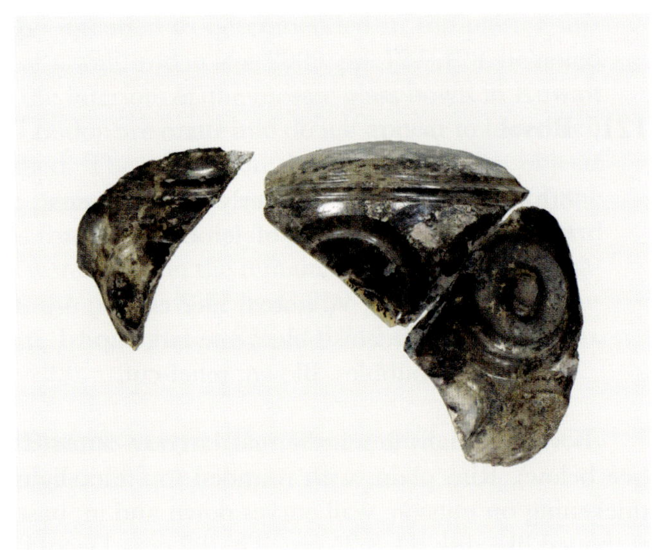
123

BIBLIOGRAPHY: Scanlon and Pinder-Wilson 2001, p. 105, no. 43h.

5. Cups

124. Cup

8th to 10th century. 70.1.7.
H. 8.8 cm, D. (rim) 10 cm.
Colorless. Blown (perhaps mold-blown); relief-cut.

Cup: cylindrical. Rim plain, with lip ground flat and shallow internal bevel; wall (TTh. 0.6 cm, Th. 0.1 cm) almost vertical, but tapering slightly; base flat. Decorated in relief on wall and underside of base. On wall: two continuous staggered horizontal rows of disks; each row has seven disks (D. 2.7 cm), which are slightly concave and have circular boss at center. At center of base: countersunk disk (D. 2.7 cm).

Incomplete. Broken and repaired. About 35 percent of rim and upper wall, including two complete bosses, restored. Pitted, with iridescent silver weathering.

COMMENT: Both the form and the decoration are well known among glass vessels from, or reputedly from, Iran. Other cylindrical cups at Corning include **47**, which has an overall pattern of drilled dots, and **159**, which has simple linear ornament. Their form may be compared with that of three objects in the al-Sabah Collection, Dār al-Āthār al-Islāmiyyah, Kuwait National Museum: LNS 430 G, decorated with half-palmettes and geometric motifs; LNS 431 G, with palmettes and half-palmettes; and LNS 328 G, with linear decoration (Carboni 2001, pp. 115 and 122, nos. 2.12a, 2.12b, and 2.23).

For examples of countersunk ring-and-dot motifs, see Kröger 1995, pp. 134–135, nos. 181–183, all from Nishapur, northeastern Iran.

BIBLIOGRAPHY: "Recent Important Acquisitions," *JGS*, v. 13, 1971, pp. 140–141, no. 30; *Persian Glass* 1972, p. 12, no. 14; Yoshimizu 1992, pp. 94 and 290, no. 189.

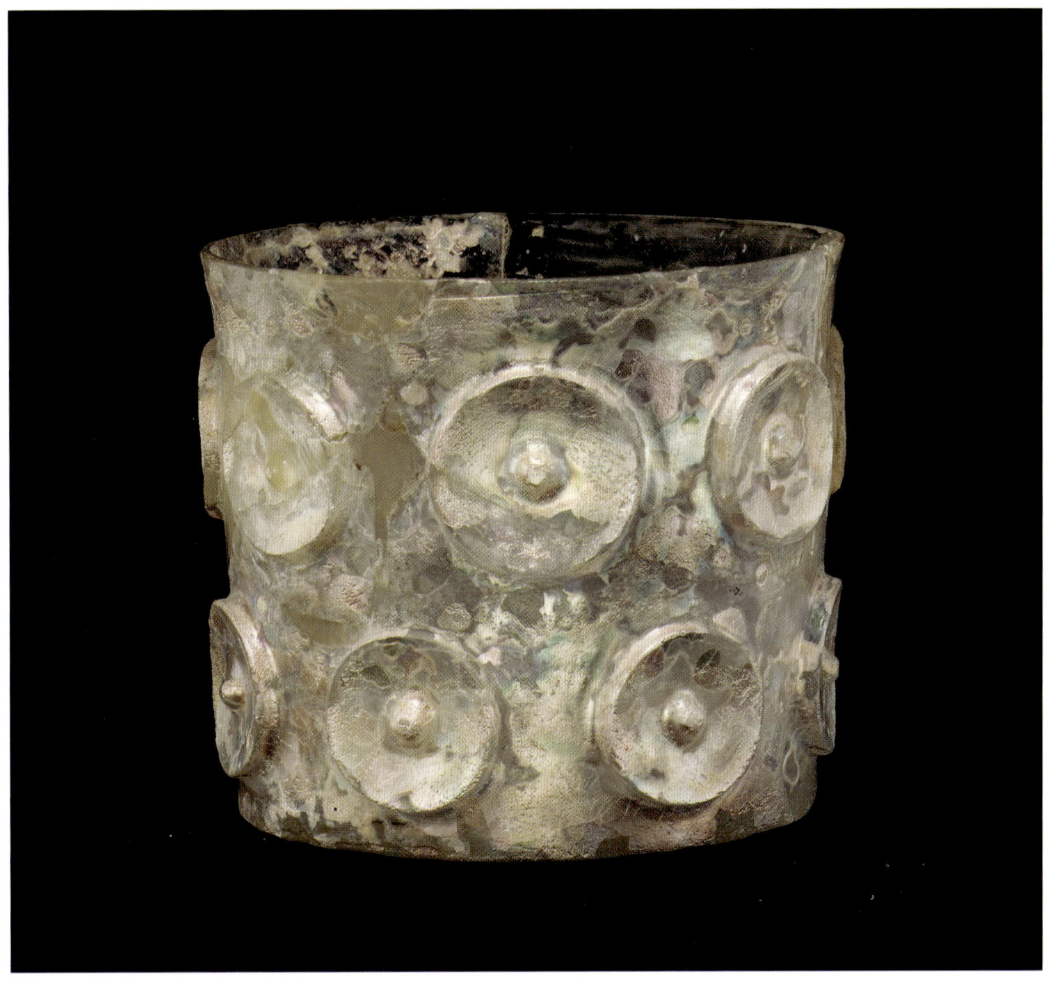

124

125. Cup

9th to 10th century. Formerly in the Strauss Collection (S2319). Bequest of Jerome Strauss. 79.1.229.
H. 8.7 cm, D. 9.5 cm.
Almost colorless, with yellowish green tinge.
Blown, probably in dip mold; cut, ground, polished.

Cup: cylindrical. Rim plain, with bevel on inside; wall vertical; base plain, with ground, but not polished, circular depression (D. 1.7 cm) at center. Decorated on wall with three continuous horizontal bands of circular motifs arranged in quincunx; each band has 11 motifs, and each motif consists of countersunk disk with countersunk knob at center.

Incomplete. Broken into many pieces, with three losses from wall and one small loss from rim; restored. Dull and pitted, with patches of iridescent silver-colored weathering.

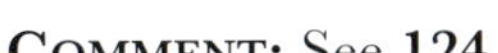

Comment: See **124**.

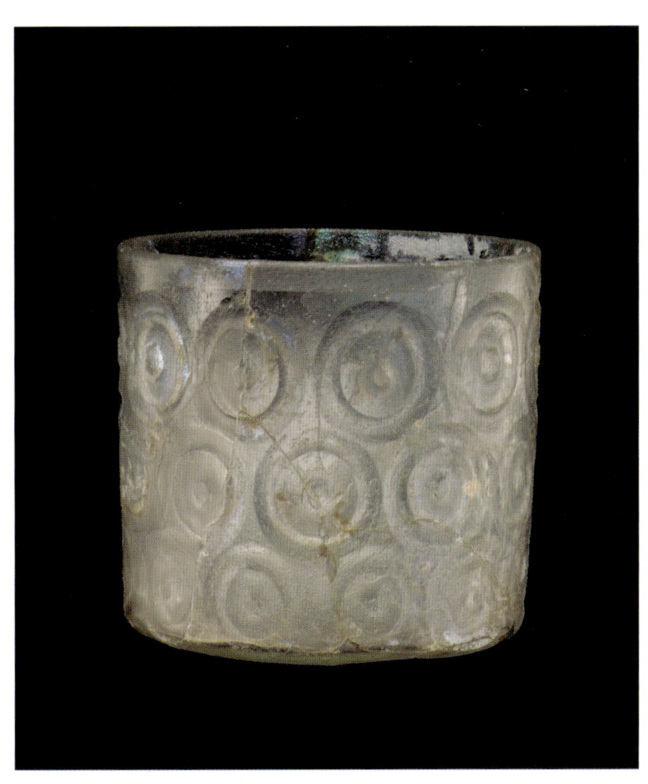

125

6. Small Jars

126. Small Jar

8th to 10th century. Formerly in the Strauss Collection (S2735). Bequest of Jerome Strauss. 79.1.268.
H. 3.7 cm, D. (rim) 3.7 cm.
Colorless or almost colorless, with green tinge.
Blown, perhaps in mold; relief-cut.

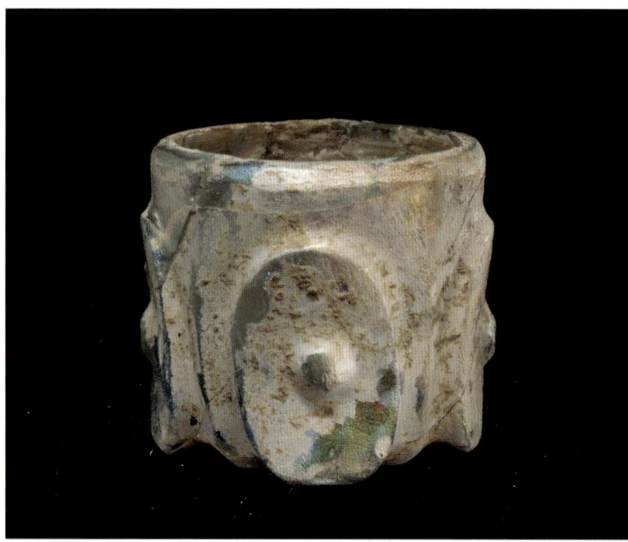

126

Jar with cylindrical mouth and four-sided wall and base. Rim plain, with flat top and narrow external bevel; wall vertical; base flat; pontil mark (W. 1.1 cm). Wall cut to form four adjoining squarish facets; each facet contains one oval boss (H. 2.7 cm, W. 2.1 cm), which is slightly concave and has circular knob at center.

Complete. Broken and repaired without loss. Slightly iridescent white to silver weathering.

Comment: Presumably, miniature jars were intended to contain small quantities of solid or glutinous substances such as cosmetic and medicinal creams and ointments. The many early Islamic miniature jars with wheel-cut ornament include Clairmont 1977, pp. 33–34, no. 100, and p. 93, no. 312 (in the Benaki Museum, Athens: 40/13 and 43/6); Kröger 1984, pp. 184–185, nos. 164 and 165 (in the Museum für Islamische Kunst, Berlin: I.6131 and I.6132); *idem* 1995, pp. 132–133, nos. 174–176, 178, and 179 (from Nishapur, northeastern Iran); and Carboni 2001, pp. 210–211, some of no. 2.6 (al-Sabah Collection, Dār al-Āthār al-Islāmiyyah, Kuwait National Museum: LNS 117 KG, 16 G, 170 G, 417 G, and 264 G). A small bottle in the same collection has six oval bosses, each with a knob at the center (*ibid.*, p. 112, no. 2.8: LNS 32 G).

127. Small Jar

9th to 11th century. Formerly in the Strauss Collection (S2708). Bequest of Jerome Strauss. 79.1.263.
H. 2.3 cm, D. (rim) 1.2 cm, (max.) 2.2 cm.
Colorless. Blown; cut.

Jar with body that expands slightly toward bottom. Rim plain, with flat top. Four flat facets extend from rim to base and occupy entire upper part of wall.

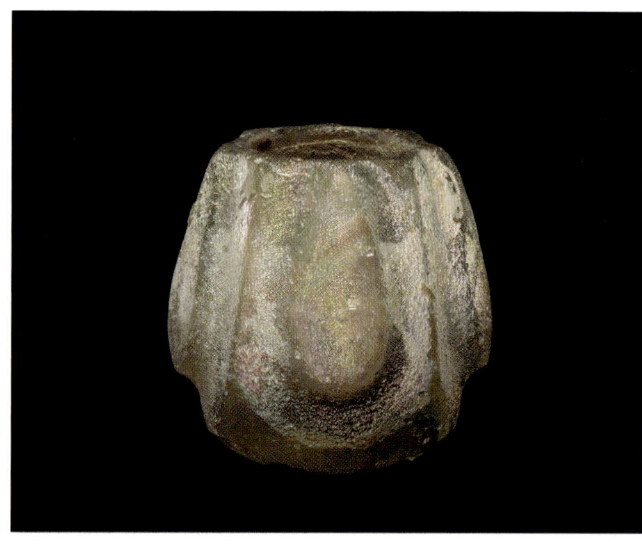

127A

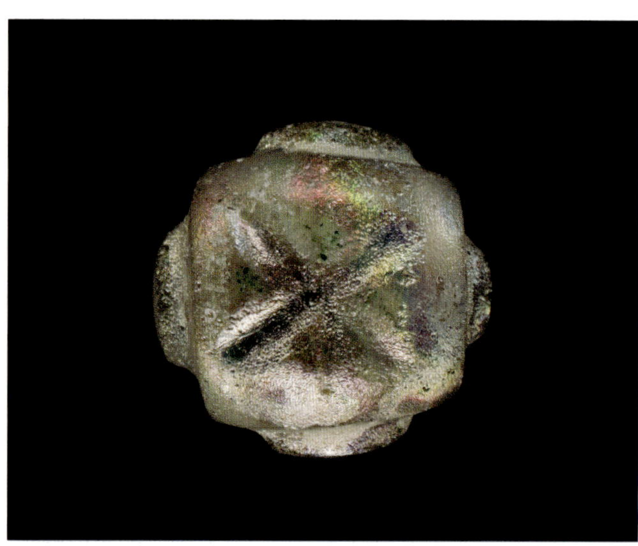

127B

Each facet has straight sides and rounded bottom, and is decorated in relief with one flat, tear-shaped boss. On underside of base, wheel-cut cruciform motif.

Intact. Pitted, with iridescent silver weathering.

Comment: Flat (as opposed to hollow) tear-shaped bosses can be seen on a bottle in the al-Sabah Collection, Dār al-Āthār al-Islāmiyyah, Kuwait National Museum (LNS 292 G: Carboni 2001, p. 94, no. 24). The treatment of the neck and shoulder of **127** recalls that of a bottle in the Museum für Islamische Kunst, Berlin, which is decorated on the wall with a frieze of countersunk oval bosses (I.2673: Kröger 1984, p. 208, no. 173). A bottle of the same form in the Museum Kunst Palast, Düsseldorf, is decorated with two rows of countersunk disks, each of which has a countersunk knob at the center (*Hentrich Collection* 1974, p. 263, no. 408).

Cf. **126**.

128. Small Jar

9th to 11th century. Gift of Farhadi & Anavian Co. 68.1.20.
H. 2.25 cm, W. (max.) 2.5 cm.
Color uncertain. Blown; relief-cut.

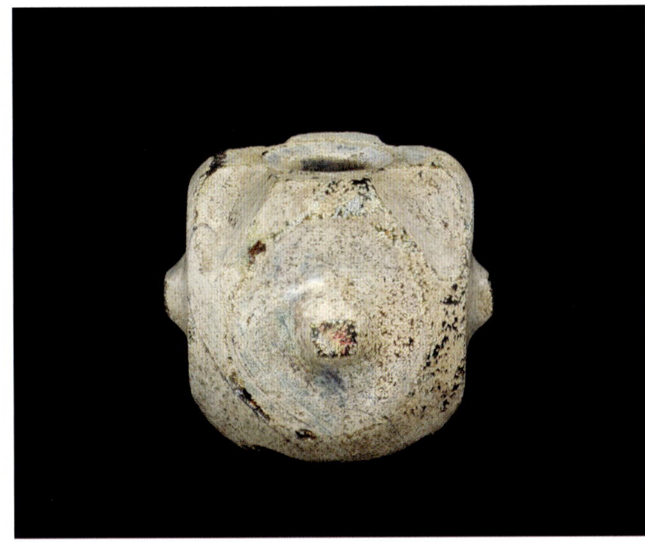

128

Jar with cylindrical mouth and four-sided wall and base. Rim plain, with flat top and narrow external bevel; shoulder flat; wall vertical, but curving in at bottom; base flat; no pontil mark. Wall cut to form four adjoining flat oval facets (H. 1.9 cm, W. 1.5 cm), each containing one small oval boss; on shoulder and upper wall, four hollow facets, one between each pair of flat facets. Underside of base has wheel-cut cruciform motif.

Intact. Opaque, slightly iridescent, greenish white weathering.

Comment: See **126**.

129. Small Jar

9th to 11th century. Formerly in the Smith Collection (1386). Gift of Carl Berkowitz and Derek Content. 76.1.197.
H. 1.9 cm, W. (max.) 2.1 cm.
Almost colorless, perhaps with yellowish tinge. Blown; relief-cut.

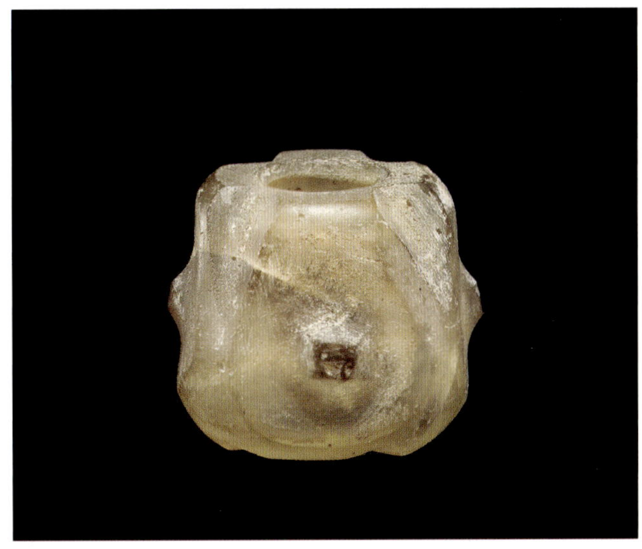

129

Jar with cylindrical mouth and four-sided wall and base. Rim plain, with top flush with shoulder, which is flat; wall vertical, but curving in at bottom; base flat; no pontil mark. Wall cut to form four adjoining flat tear-shaped facets (H. 1.6 cm, W. 1.2 cm), each containing one small oval boss; on shoulder and upper wall, four hollow facets, one between each pair of flat facets. Underside of base has wheel-cut cruciform motif.

Intact, but with crack descending from upper wall and running across base. Pitted, with grayish white weathering.

Comment: See **126**.

130. Small Jar

9th to 11th century. Formerly in the Smith Collection (1346). Gift of Carl Berkowitz and Derek Content. 76.1.196.
H. 1.7 cm, W. (max.) 1.7 cm.
Almost colorless. Blown; relief-cut.

Jar with cylindrical mouth and four-sided wall and base. Rim plain, with top flush with shoulder, which is probably flat (see "Comment"); wall vertical, but curving in at bottom; base flat; no pontil mark. Wall cut to form four adjoining flat tear-shaped facets (H. 1.3 cm, W. 1.1 cm), each truncated at top and containing one small oval boss; on shoulder and upper wall, four hollow facets, one between each pair of flat facets.

Intact. Pitted, with grayish white, slightly iridescent weathering.

Comment: The shoulder is covered by a copper alloy disk (Th. 0.1 cm) with a circular hole (D. 0.4 cm) at the center.

See **126**.

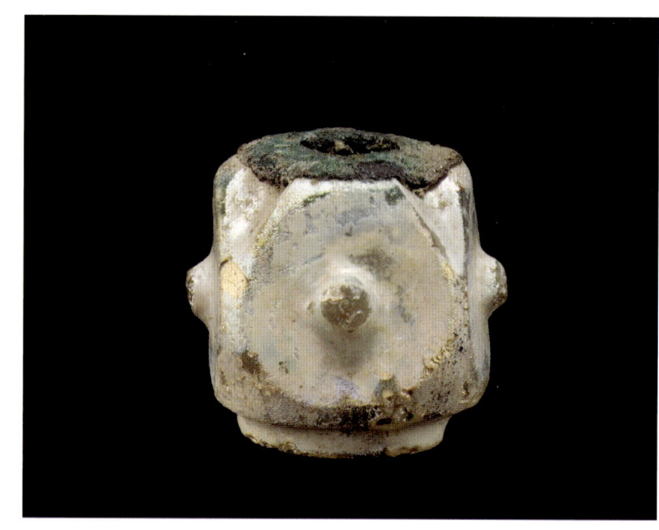

130

7. Bottles

131. Bottle with Four Disks

9th to 10th century. Formerly in the Smith Collection (1343). 59.1.432.
H. (surviving) 10.9 cm, W. (body, including disks) 10.5 cm, D. (foot) 4.4 cm.
Almost colorless, with yellowish green tinge.
Blown; relief-cut.

Bottle with polyhedral body. Lower neck cylindrical, splaying at bottom and merging with broad, sloping shoulder; wall consists of four rectangular panels (H. 5.6 cm, W. 7.4 cm) that meet at right angles, with adjacent sides farther apart at top than at bottom; beneath panels, wall tapers sharply; junctions of shoulder and each pair of panels are chamfered to create triangular surface; junctions of each pair of panels and lower wall are chamfered to create similar, but smaller, triangular surfaces; base is hollow, with splayed foot-ring, which has narrow flange just above rim and stepped profile at junction with underside; at center of base, low, circular boss.

Principal decoration cut in relief: on lower neck, continuous horizontal rib; at midpoint of shoulder, continuous horizontal flange; at center of each panel, hollow disk (D. 3.4 cm). Base and relief-cut ornament are unusually delicate and precise, and flange and disks are undercut. Additionally, each triangular surface at junctions of shoulder and panels has one hollow oval facet. Shoulder, panels, and lower wall retain faint concentric marks made by rotary cutting; surface does not appear to have been finely polished.

Incomplete. Rim and upper neck missing; more than one-third of collar missing; major losses from three disks, and minor loss from one disk; minor loss from foot; small hole in base. Dull and slightly pitted, with remains of faintly iridescent weathering, mainly on interior.

Comment: According to Ray Winfield Smith (see below), the object is "from Persia, probably found there (said to have been found in Azerbaijan)."

131 and **132** are accomplished examples of glass cutting. In both cases, a blank with a thick-walled, spherical body was carefully cut to produce a polyhedral form with ornament of considerable delicacy.

131, Smith suggested, dates from the ninth or 10th century. However, shortly after the bottle arrived at Corning, it was described as being "possibly 6th–8th century" (see below), and later, Axel von Saldern (1963, p. 16) tentatively attributed both bottles to the sixth or seventh century.

The uncertainty surrounding the date of these objects derives from the fact that, although circular bosses are a recurrent feature of Sasanian and early Islamic relief-cut glass, neither the form of the disks nor the shape of the vessels has any close parallel among the large number of Sasanian and early Islamic objects that have been published. Indeed, the only other published examples of ancient or early Islamic glass vessels made from globular blanks transformed by extensive cutting into polyhedrons appear to be four bottles: (1) in The Toledo Museum of Art (Sangiorgi 1914, p. 41, no. 137); (2) in the Carnegie Museum of Natural History, Pittsburgh (26921/1: Oliver, A. 1980, p. 140, no. 242); (3) in the Museum of Fine Arts, Boston (50.1741: Saldern 1968, pp. 17 and 94, no. 63); and (4) in the Victoria and Albert

Museum, London (Honey 1946, p. 44, pl. 14A). The bodies of the Toledo and Pittsburgh bottles are cut in two continuous horizontal rows of adjoining pentagonal facets, each of which has a simple disk-shaped boss. The bodies of the bottles in Boston and London are cut in three continuous rows of polygons—pentagons at the top and the bottom, and hexagons in the middle—each of which contains a countersunk disk. In all four cases, the junctions between the tops and sides of the pentagons in the upper or top row have been chamfered. However, their resemblance to the Corning bottles does not extend beyond the presence of polygonal panels and disks.

The Toledo bottle was originally identified as Roman, but Lamm (1929–30, p. 146, pl. 52, no. 10) subsequently claimed it for Mesopotamia or Iran about A.D. 900. W. B. Honey (1946, p. 44, pl. 14A) believed that the bottle in the Victoria and Albert Museum is "perhaps Byzantine of the 7th or 8th century" or "Byzantine or Egyptian." Saldern (1968, caption to pl. 63) suggested the following attribution for the bottle in the Museum of Fine Arts: "possibly Iraq, 6th–8th century A.D." A. Oliver (1980, p. 140, no. 242), following Saldern, dated the bottle in the Carnegie Museum to the seventh or eighth century. I am not aware of any comparable objects of rock crystal that might help us to establish the date more closely.

Saldern (1963, p. 13) likened **131** and **132** to one other object: a small bottle (H. 7.0 cm), again from the Smith Collection and now at Corning (59.1.435: Whitehouse 2005, p. 54, no. 64). The bottle has a short neck and a globular body that is decorated in relief with four bosses in the form of hollow disks, and four triangular motifs. It has one very close parallel: a bottle found in the tomb of a Buddhist monk (d. 589) at Xi'an in Shaanxi Province, China (*China: Dawn* 2004, p. 324, no. 219). However, neither the form of the vessel nor the quality of the cutting approaches that of the polyhedral bottles, which remain without close parallels.

In the absence of such parallels, the only means of establishing the date of the bottles at Corning is to seek analogies for individual features such as the disks and the horizontal ribs. As Saldern pointed out, the disks most closely resemble the disk-shaped bosses on hemispherical bowls made in the Middle East in the Sasanian period. Continuous horizontal ribs or flanges, however, are not known to have been part of the

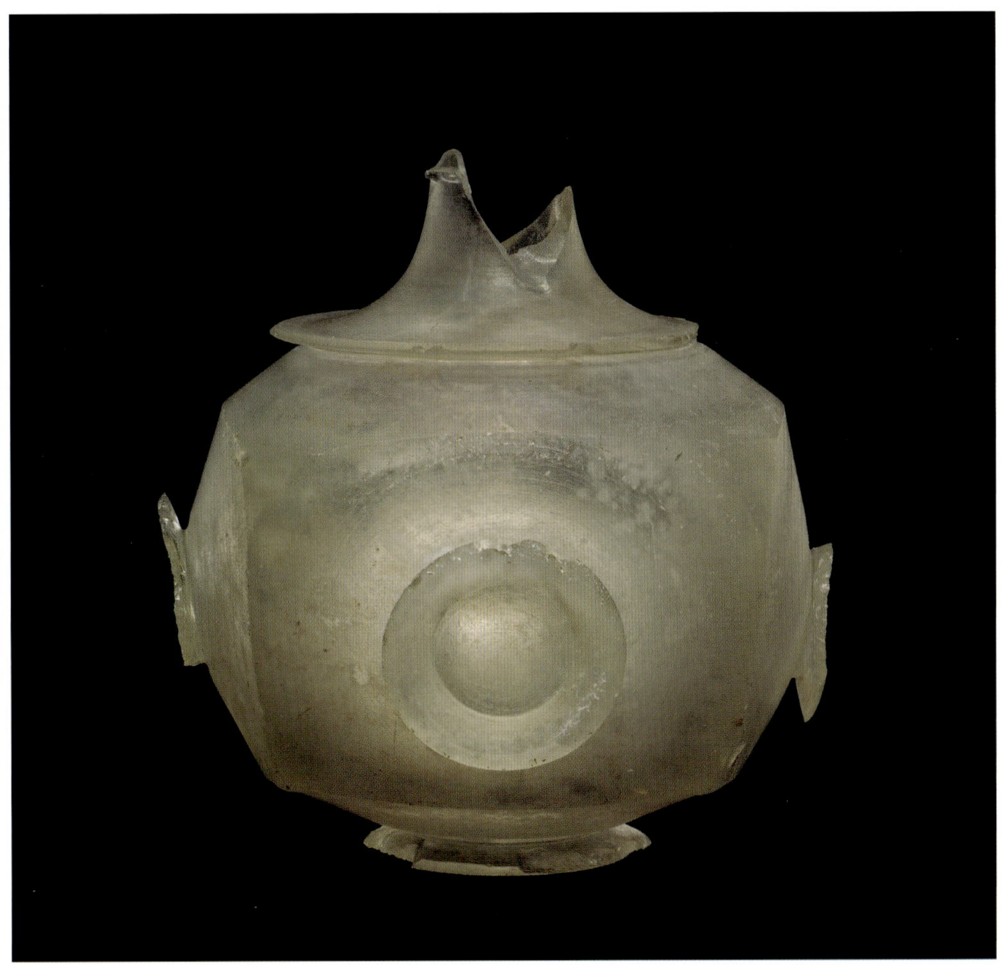

131

Sasanian glass cutter's repertoire, and their presence on the Corning bottles suggests that we should seek parallels that are later than the Sasanian period. The crispness of the profile of the rib on the shoulder of **131** recalls the raised bands that adorn the necks and form the lower borders of a well-defined group of early Islamic vessels that include the Corning Ewer, the Buckley Ewer in the Victoria and Albert Museum in London, and the six closely related rock crystal ewers in the Treasury of San Marco in Venice (two examples), the Palazzo Pitti in Florence, the cathedral at Fermo, the Louvre, and the Victoria and Albert Museum (Whitehouse 1993a, p. 54). Among these objects, one of the rock crystal ewers in the Treasury of San Marco has, at the bottom of the wall, a flange that rivals the thinness of the flange on **131**. It bears an Arabic inscription naming the Fatimid caliph al-ᶜAzīz Biʾllāh (r. 975–996) (Erdmann 1971, pp. 112–113, no. 124).

A basket-shaped bowl formerly in the Foroughi Collection, Tehran, is one of the few other Islamic relief-cut glasses that stand comparison with our bottles (*7000 Years of Iranian Art* 1964, p. 160, no. 602; Saldern 1995a, p. 235, fig. 12). Like **130**, the Foroughi bowl was found in Iran.

These observations suggest that **131** and **132** were made in the Middle East (perhaps in Iran) after, rather than during, the Sasanian period. Indeed, the crisp linear cutting, especially on the first bottle, suggests comparison with a group of relief-cut glass and rock crystal ewers that came into use in the ninth century and flourished until at least the last quarter of the 10th century. Until better, more closely dated parallels come to light, the two polyhedral bottles should be regarded, as Smith conjectured, as exceptional products of the ninth or 10th century.

BIBLIOGRAPHY: *Glass from the Ancient World* 1957, p. 267, no. 547; "Recent Important Acquisitions," *JGS*, v. 2, 1960, p. 140, no. 11; Saldern 1963, p. 13, fig. 11.

132. Bottle with Five Disks

9th to 10th century. Formerly in the Smith Collection (1515). 59.1.433.
H. (surviving) 10.3 cm, W. (body, including disks) 10.2 cm, D. (foot) 4.3 cm.
Almost colorless, with yellowish green tinge; few bubbles, mostly very small. Blown; relief-cut, ground, polished.

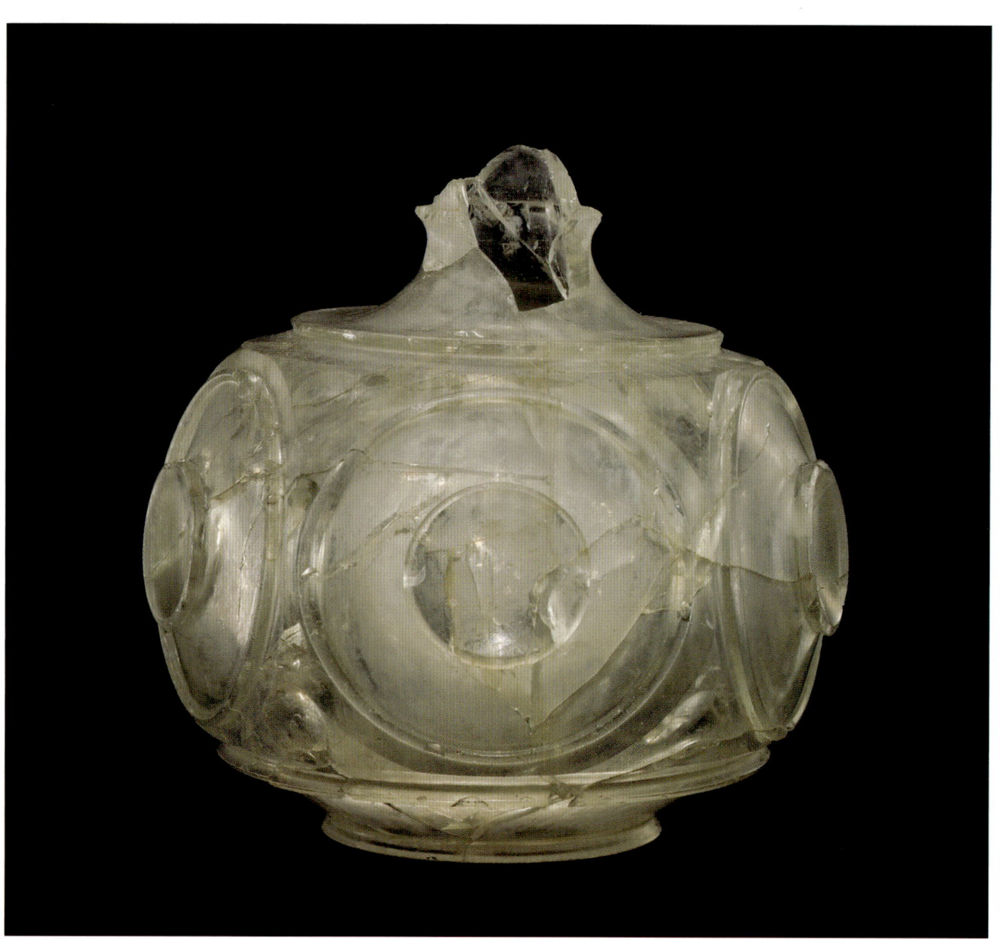

132

Bottle with polyhedral body. Lower neck cylindrical, splaying at bottom and merging with broad, sloping shoulder; wall consists of five rectangular panels (H. 5.7 cm, W. 5.9 cm) that meet with internal angles of about 108 degrees; beneath panels, wall tapers sharply; junctions of shoulder and each pair of panels are chamfered to create triangular surface; junctions of panels and lower wall are chamfered to create similar triangular surfaces; base is hollow, with splayed foot-ring, which has narrow flange just above rim and stepped profile at junction with underside; at center of base, low, circular boss.

Principal decoration cut in relief: on lower neck, continuous horizontal rib; at midpoint of shoulder, continuous horizontal flange; on each panel, raised circular rib near edge (D. 5.5 cm) and raised hollow disk (D. 2 cm) at center; on lower wall, continuous horizontal rib. Base and relief-cut ornament are carefully finished, and edges of disks are undercut. Additionally, each triangular surface at junctions of shoulder and panels has one hollow oval facet.

Incomplete. Rim and upper neck missing; approximately half of rib on neck missing; major loss from one disk, and minor loss from second disk; small hole in base; many cracks and chips in all parts. Dull and very slightly pitted.

Comment: See **131**.

Bibliography: Saldern 1963, p. 12, fig. 10.

8. Small Bottles

133. Small Bottle

8th to 9th century. Formerly in the Smith Collection (867). 55.1.117.
H. 8.4 cm, D. (rim) 2.4 cm, (max.) 6.2 cm.
Almost colorless, with grayish tinge; many small bubbles. Blown; facet-, linear-, and relief-cut.

Bottle with globular body. Rim plain, with flat top and narrow bevel at outer edge; neck straight and slightly narrower at bottom than at top; base narrow and very slightly concave; trace of pontil mark. Wheel-cut decoration on neck and wall: entire neck is cut in six contiguous vertical facets; wall has four contiguous relief-cut circular motifs (D. about 4.5 cm), each of which has boss at center and two concentric "steps"; four shallow arc-shaped linear cuts on shoulder link each circular motif to its neighbors.

Almost complete. Rim slightly chipped; concentric hole at base (drilled to obtain sample for chemical analysis). Base is worn, but object is virtually without weathering.

Comment: Ray Winfield Smith (in *Verres antiques*: see below) noted that the object may have come from Syria.

Although clearly related to wheel-cut glasses decorated with disks and knobs, **133** stands somewhat apart. While the diagnostic feature of this group is the presence of a countersunk disk with a small raised knob at the center (Carboni 2001, pp. 74–75), in this case the circular motifs are not flat, but retain the convex profile of the original wall. Similar ornament is found on a small globular jar in the Khalili Collection (GLS 603: *Khalili Collection* 2005, p. 172, no. 206).

Bibliography: *Verres antiques* 1954, p. 50, no. 306.

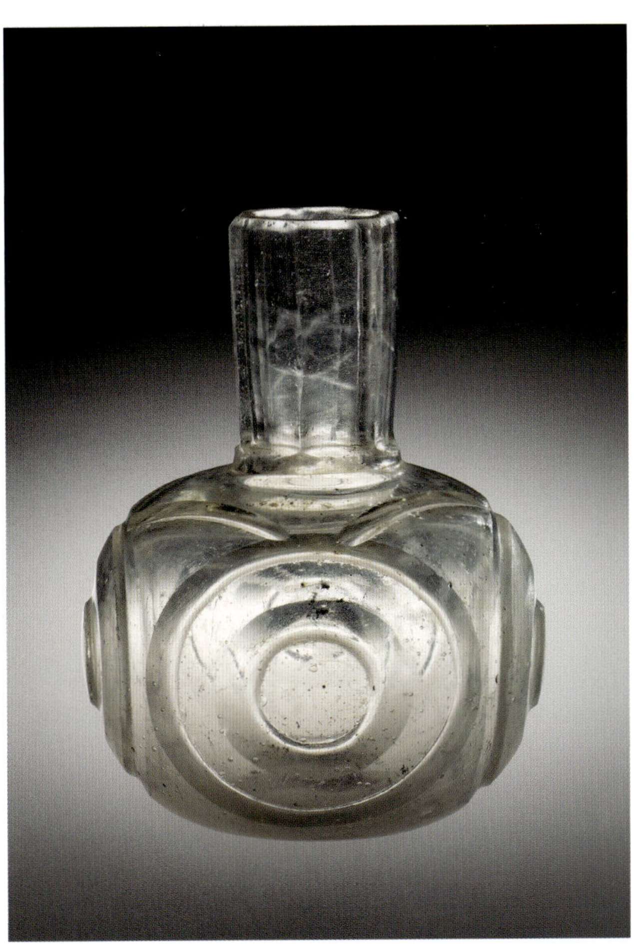

133

134. Small Bottle

9th to 10th century. 63.1.19.
H. 8.1 cm, D. (max.) 4.7 cm.
Almost colorless, with greenish yellow tinge.
Blown; cut.

Bottle: biconical, with greatest diameter above midpoint. Rim ground flat; neck tapers; base flat; no pontil mark. Wheel-cut decoration: on neck, six flat vertical facets; on body, step-shaped molding at top, below which four equidistant stepped facets extend to bottom of wall. Each facet has, at center, downward-pointing tear-shaped boss with flat surface bisected by vertical cut; boss rests on larger tear-shaped boss, truncated at bottom, also with flat surface, which rests on third, larger truncated tear-shaped boss; above largest bosses, four arc-shaped cuts, which make continuous stepped facet.

Almost complete. Broken and repaired, with very small losses along breaks. Dull and extensively pitted, with traces of iridescent weathering.

Comment: Tear-shaped bosses bisected by single vertical cuts are also found on **132** and on a small bottle in the Khalili Collection (GLS 290: *Khalili Collection* 2005, p. 164, no. 191).

Bibliography: *Glass from the Ancient World* 1991, p. 79, no. 55.

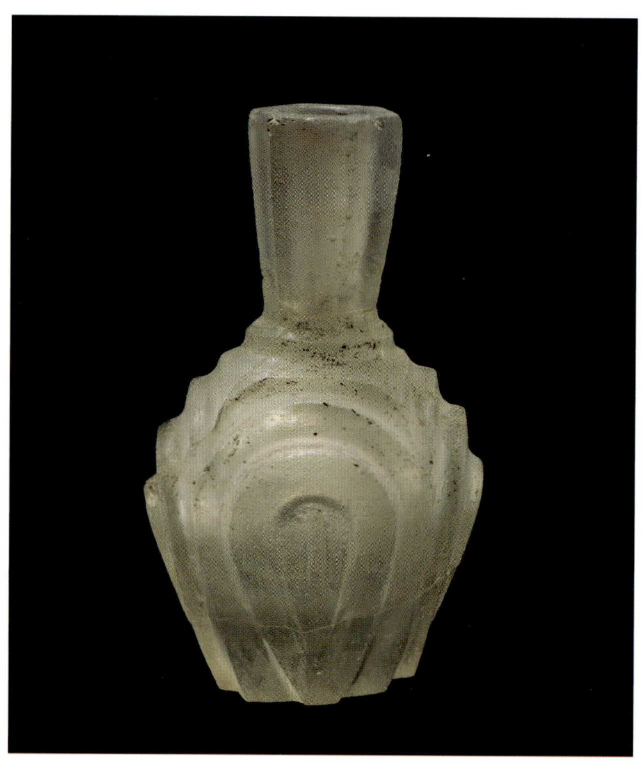

134

135. Small Bottle

8th to 9th century. 68.1.8.
H. 6.7 cm.
Almost colorless, with yellowish green tinge.
Blown; cut.

Bottle. Rim plain, with flat upper surface; neck wider at top than at bottom; shoulder almost flat; body has vertical sides and square cross section; base flat. Decorated on neck and body. On neck: six contiguous vertical facets extending from lip to junction with shoulder. On body: two opposing sides, each with raised circular disk (D. about 2.4 cm) with countersunk circular boss at center; on other two sides, raised oval motif extending from edge of shoulder to bottom of wall, with pointed ends and vertical groove extending from top to bottom. Underside of base has shallow circular depression (D. 0.8 cm), perhaps to remove pontil mark.

Chipped, but otherwise intact. Pitted, with remains of iridescent weathering.

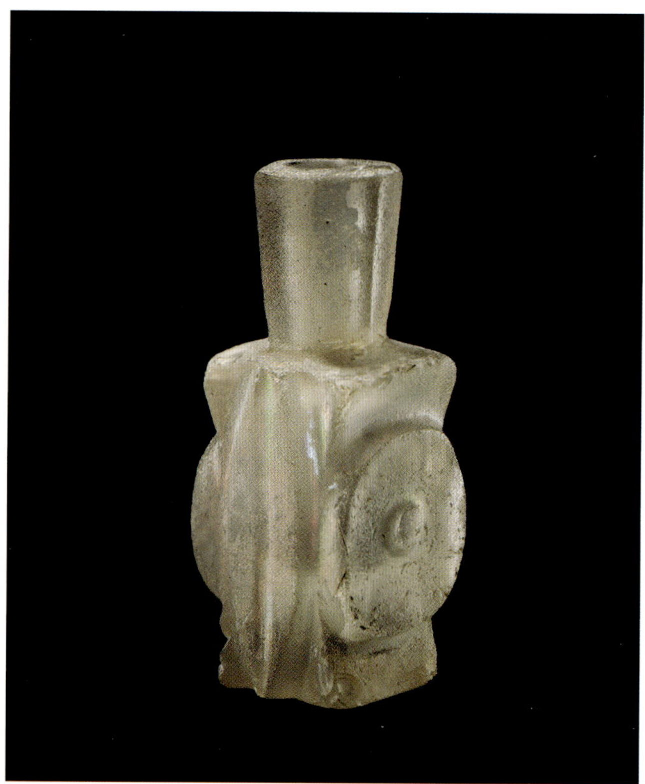

135

Comment: Tear-shaped bosses bisected by single vertical cuts are also found on **134** and on a small bottle in the Khalili Collection (GLS 290: *Khalili Collection* 2005, p. 164, no. 191).

For objects with a similar form, see Lamm 1929–30, p. 161, pl. 59, no. 19; and Carboni 2001, p. 116, no. 214 (in the al-Sabah Collection, Dār al-Āthār al-Islāmiyyah, Kuwait National Museum: LNS 163 G).

BIBLIOGRAPHY: *Islam and the Medieval West* 1975, n.p., no. G4.

136. Small Bottle

9th to 10th century. Formerly in the Smith Collection (1221-5). 59.1.485.
H. 4.5 cm, D. (max.) 4.7 cm.
Almost colorless, with grayish green tinge. Blown; cut.

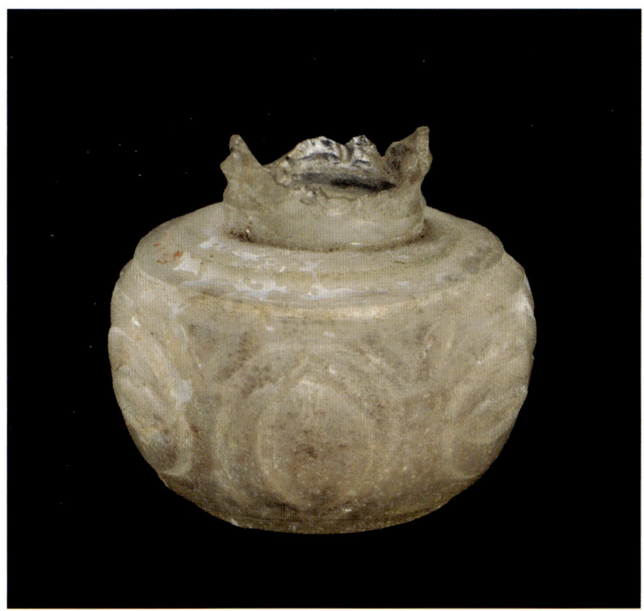

136

Bottle: roughly globular. Lower neck cylindrical; shoulder slopes; wall curves down and in; base flat. Decorated on lower neck, shoulder, and wall. On neck, one or possibly two continuous horizontal grooves, and on shoulder, two horizontal "steps." Wall has continuous band consisting of three circular bosses alternating with three oval bosses, each pair of bosses separated by linear-cut Y-shaped motif with short crossbar at top of vertical element. Each circular boss has horizontal eye-shaped motif, and each oval boss is slightly concave and plain. At bottom of wall, one horizontal "step."

Incomplete. Rim and upper neck are missing; wall has large crack, and small section of upper wall is lost. Dull, with patches of brown and white weathering.

COMMENT: The bosses are in low relief.

137. Small Bottle

Probably 8th to 10th century. Formerly in the Smith Collection (358). Gift of Mrs. Ray Winfield Smith. 81.1.696.
H. (surviving) 4 cm, D. (max.) 5.4 cm.
Colorless or almost colorless. Blown; cut.

Bottle: spheroid. Rim and almost entire neck probably missing (see "Comment"); shoulder and wall descend in smooth curve; base plain and slightly concave; no pontil mark. Wall is decorated with continuous frieze bordered at top and bottom by horizontal rib embellished with transverse cuts (at top) and vertical cuts (at bottom). Frieze is cut in seven contiguous square panels, each containing raised diamond-shaped motif with, at center, countersunk dot.

Body unbroken. Remains of shiny, brownish gray enamellike weathering; where this is missing, surface is dull and extensively pitted.

COMMENT: Presumably, when it was new, the bottle had a short cylindrical neck resembling the neck of **133**. If this is correct, after the neck had been broken, its bottom was roughly ground to make the object usable.

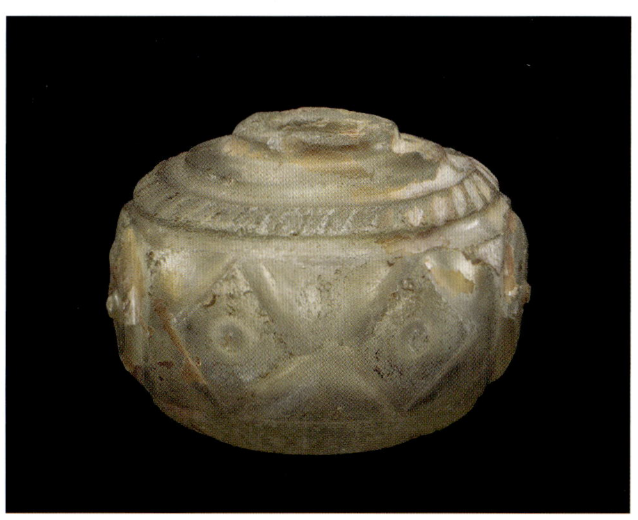

137

9. Small Bottles, "Molar Flasks"

138. Small Bottle, "Molar Flask"

9th to 11th century. Formerly in the Strauss Collection (S2046). Gift of Jerome Strauss. 77.1.12.
H. 8.8 cm, W. 2.3 cm.
Semitranslucent dark blue. Blown; facet-cut.

Bottle. Rim plain, with flat top; neck roughly cylindrical, but wider at top than at bottom; body tall, with vertical walls and square cross section; at bottom of wall, four pointed feet, one at each corner. Decorated on neck, body, and feet. On neck: four vertical rectangular facets alternating with four triangular facets, with one horizontal groove below them. At each angle of body: one elongated rhombic facet, which continues to bottom of foot; facet is deepest at widest point, where it contains prominent circular knob. On wall, between each pair of facets: two oval notches at top and deep triangular groove at bottom.

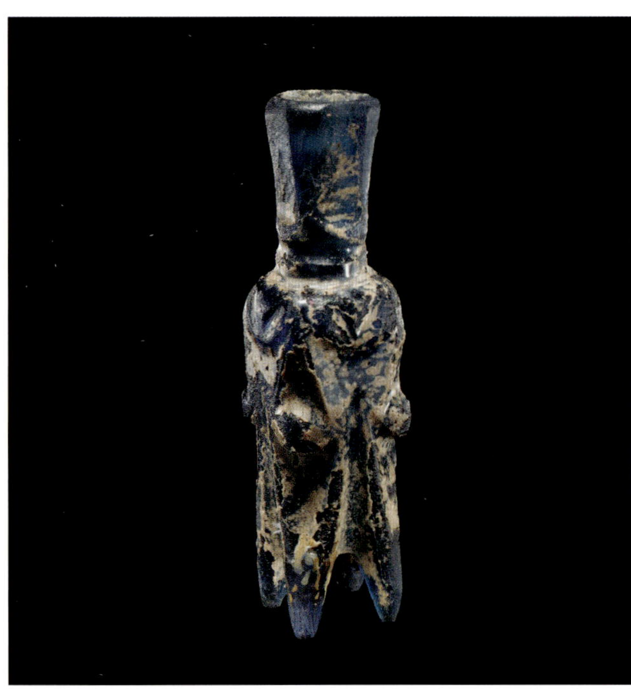

138

Intact. Much of surface is shiny, with patches of opaque buff weathering; small areas at top of neck and bottoms of feet are eroded and matte.

Comment: Elongated rhombic "shields" are among the more common decorative motifs found on "molar flasks." For another example at Corning, see **139**.

For two examples found during excavations at Fusṭāṭ, Egypt, see Scanlon and Pinder-Wilson 2001, p. 97, no. 42q (colorless with yellowish tinge), and p. 98, no. 42v (colorless with greenish tinge).

Examples without provenance include Lamm 1929–30, p. 166, pl. 61, no. 11 (blue: in The Metropolitan Museum of Art, New York); *Glass from the Ancient World* 1957, p. 283, no. 595 (yellowish); *Hentrich Collection* 1974, p. 273, no. 419 (bluish green: in the Museum Kunst Palast, Düsseldorf, P. 1973-78); Clairmont 1977, p. 93, no. 309 (colorless: in the Benaki Museum, Athens); Carboni 2001, p. 99, no. 27a, b (colorless with yellow tinge and transparent yellowish brown: in the al-Sabah Collection, Dār al-Āthār al-Islāmiyyah, Kuwait National Museum, LNS 122 G and LNS 15 KG); and *Khalili Collection* 2005, p. 156, no. 176 (in the Khalili Collection, GLS 20). Lamm 1929–30, p. 219, pl. 76, no. 30 is a similar flask made of rock crystal. For a flask with "shields" at the center of each side of the wall instead of at the angles, see Kröger 1984, pp. 183–184, no. 162 (yellowish: in the Museum für Islamische Kunst, Berlin, I.2339).

139. Small Bottle, "Molar Flask"

9th to 11th century. Formerly in the collection of Maurice Nahman, Cairo, Egypt. 53.1.60.
H. 7.8 cm, D. (rim) 1.8 cm, W. (shoulder) 2.2 cm.

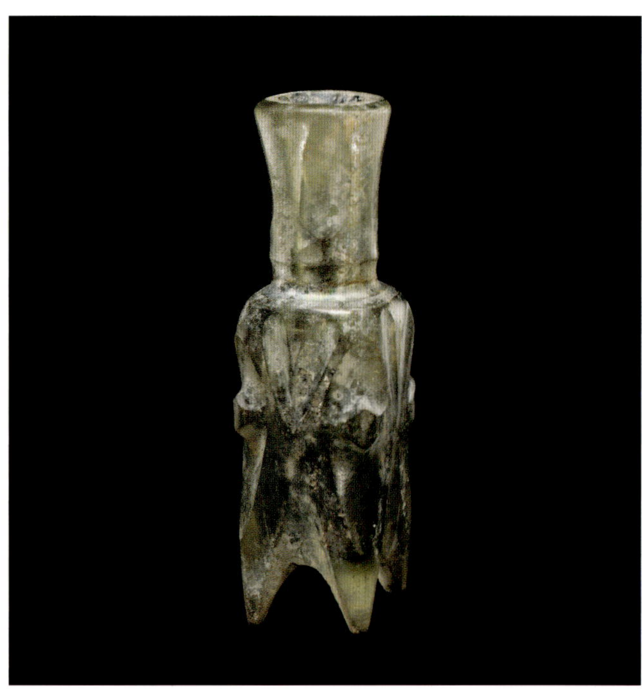

139

Transparent light green. Probably cast; drilled, cut, ground, polished.

Bottle. Rim plain, with flat top; neck roughly cylindrical, but wider at top than at bottom; shoulder narrow, with rounded edge; body tall, with vertical walls and square cross section; at bottom of wall, four short, pointed feet, one at each corner. Decorated on neck and body. On neck: four vertical oval facets, one above each side of body, and one continuous horizontal groove just above shoulder; at each angle of body: one elongated rhombic facet, which is deepest at widest point, where it contains prominent diamond-shaped boss; on wall, between each pair of facets: one V-shaped cut above one long triangular cut, which terminates between feet.

Almost intact. One foot apparently broken in antiquity and repolished. Partly dull, with patches of pale gray to tan-colored weathering; interior filled with earth.

COMMENT: See **138**.

10. Pitcher

140. Pitcher

9th to 10th century. 69.1.6.
OH. (surviving) 19.6 cm, H. (rim) 18.3 cm, D. (rim) 6.9 cm, (max.) 11.4 cm.
Colorless; many small and some larger bubbles. Blown; cut; handle applied.

Pitcher with globular body. Rim plain, with internal bevel; neck (Th. 0.45 cm) shaped like inverted and truncated cone; shoulder slopes and merges with wall, which curves smoothly down, out, and in; base plain; pontil mark probably removed and replaced by shallow circular depression (D. 2.1 cm) made by grinding. Handle attached to wall at greatest diameter, drawn up and over and in, and attached to rim and top of neck; at highest point, rectangular finial with sides parallel to sides of handle.

Decorated on neck, shoulder, wall, and handle. On neck (from top to bottom), beginning and ending at sides of handle: band of eight contiguous vertical facets (H. 4.3 cm), each containing tongue-shaped element in relief; bottoms of tongues are attached to one another; below facets, horizontal grooves, two broad and one narrow. On shoulder and part of wall: two continuous shallow "steps," which, opposite handle, are on shoulder, but curve down and out, and meet below handle attachment. On rest of wall: two horizontal rows of raised disks with countersunk knobs at centers; upper row contains six disks (D. about 2.6 cm) with rounded bosses (D. about 0.7 cm); lower row contains seven disks (D. about 2.8 cm) with rounded

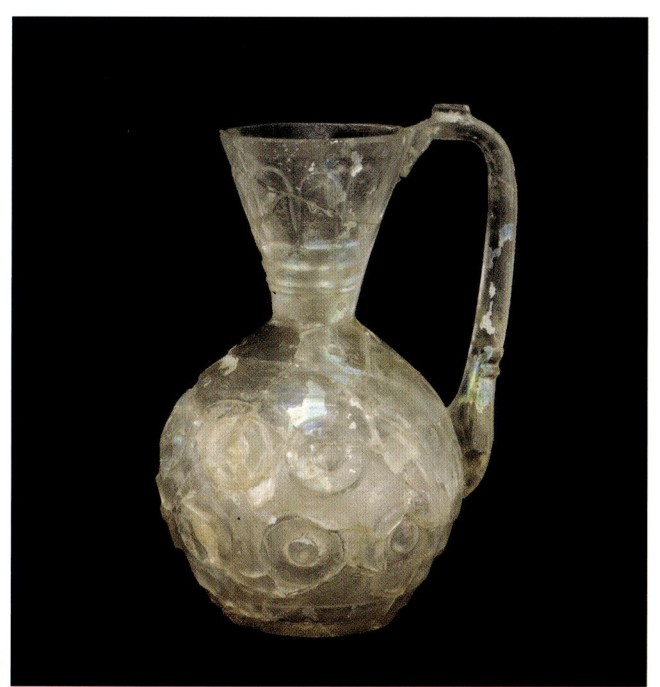

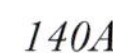

140A

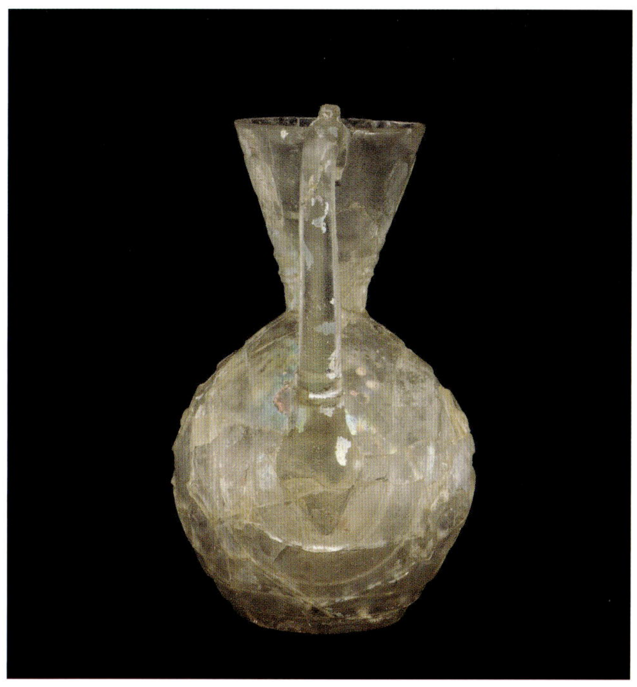

140B

2. Miniature Tray

146. Miniature Tray

Perhaps 9th to 11th century. Anonymous gift. 2009.1.20.
H. 1.2 cm, L. 5.7 cm, W. 2.8 cm.
Transparent light bluish green. Cast or pressed(?); ground, linear-cut.

Miniature tray: hexagonal, with two long sides and pointed ends. Rim is narrow, with flat top and rounded edge; wall descends in shallow curve to form cavity on interior and convex profile on exterior; tray rests on three conical feet, two near one end and one near opposite end. Bottom of rim flattened by grinding. Underside has linear decoration: three cuts make prominent Y-shaped motif with stem between pair of feet and branches between pair of feet and single foot; on each side of Y, one short cut perpendicular to stem.

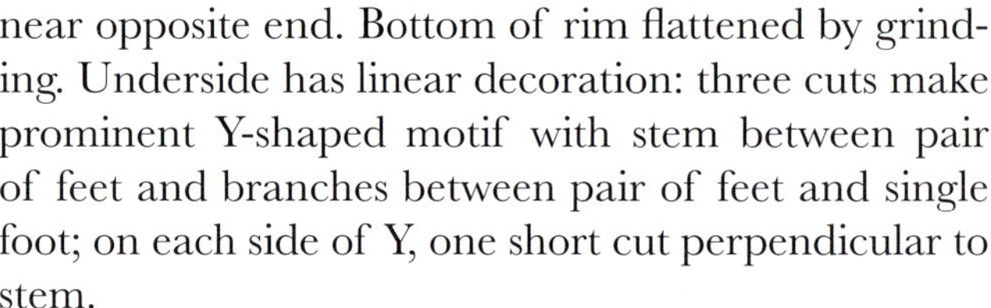

Intact. Dull and extensively pitted, with brownish weathering in pits.

Comment: The size of the object suggests that it was intended for the preparation of substances used in small quantities, such as cosmetic or medicinal compounds.

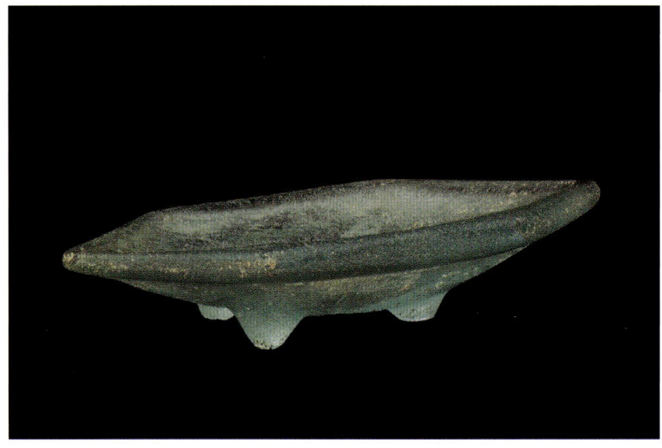

146A

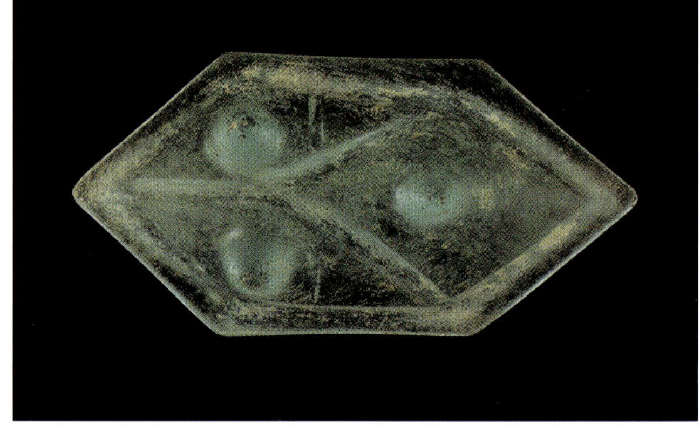

146B

3. Bowls

147. Bowl with Three Menorahs

9th to 11th century. Formerly in the Strauss Collection (S1868). Gift of Jerome Strauss. 70.1.50.
H. 5.6 cm, D. 12.8 cm.
Almost colorless, with yellowish green tinge. Blown; linear-cut.

Bowl: shallow. Rim plain and rounded; side straight and tapering, curving in at bottom; base flat. Pontil mark mostly removed by grinding. Linear-cut decoration on wall consists of menorah with seven branches and diamond-shaped motif, each repeated three times, one alternating with the other. Each menorah has stepped base consisting of two horizontal cuts, shaft composed of two vertical cuts, and candle holders consisting of two horizontal cuts surmounted

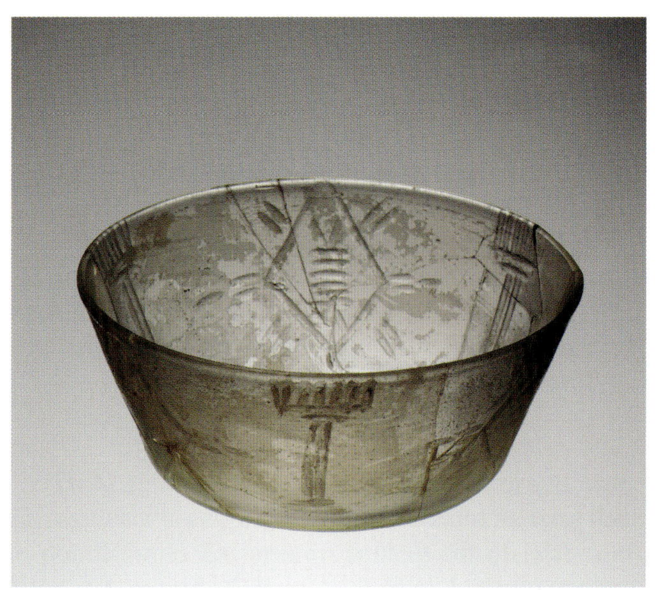

147

by seven short vertical cuts. Second diamond-shaped motif contains vertical band of (from top to bottom): V-shaped cut, four or five short horizontal cuts aligned vertically, and inverted V-shaped cut; outside, pair of short parallel cuts halfway along each side and perpendicular to it, and group of three short horizontal cuts extending from angles at sides of diamond but not top and bottom.

Broken, with two small losses from rim and wall; restored. Dull, with patches of thin brownish weathering. Evidently cleaned.

COMMENT: For a relief-cut bowl with straight, tapering sides and a flat base from Fusṭāṭ, see Scanlon and Pinder-Wilson 2001, p. 101, no. 43b (= Pinder-Wilson and Scanlon 1973, p. 26, no. 20). Presumably the menorahs indicate that the object was made for, or presented to, a Jewish patron.

BIBLIOGRAPHY: *Glass Drinking Vessels* 1955, p. 31, no. 61.

148. Bowl with Geometric Ornament

9th to 11th century. Formerly in the Strauss Collection (S2091). Bequest of Jerome Strauss. 79.1.216.
H. 7 cm, D. 14.9 cm.
Transparent pale yellowish green. Blown; linear-cut.

Bowl with plain rim, curving side, and splayed base. Rim plain; foot spreads; bottom slightly pushed in; prominent pontil mark. On side, one horizontal trail just below rim, and another just above foot. Between trails, horizontal band of linear-cut ornament; upper and lower borders composed of short stripes, sometimes touching, sometimes not; between them, pairs of vertical stripes defining 17 square panels, each containing a lozenge with two horizontal stripes; spacing of vertical stripes was not entirely successful, and one narrow panel with horizontal stripes was inserted to fill gap. Below this band, one row of oval motifs.

Incomplete. Broken into many fragments and repaired; one large and several small areas restored; wheel-cut areas have semiopaque to opaque whitish to grayish brown weathering, patches of which also remain on inside and under foot; elsewhere, most weathering apparently removed.

COMMENT: The object belongs to a large group of drinking vessels, bowls, and other forms with wheel-cut ornament of indifferent quality, composed of short, straight stripes. Although frequently attributed to Iran, the undoubted source of many vessels of this type, examples have been found all over the Middle East and the eastern Mediterranean, and the origin of **148** is not known.

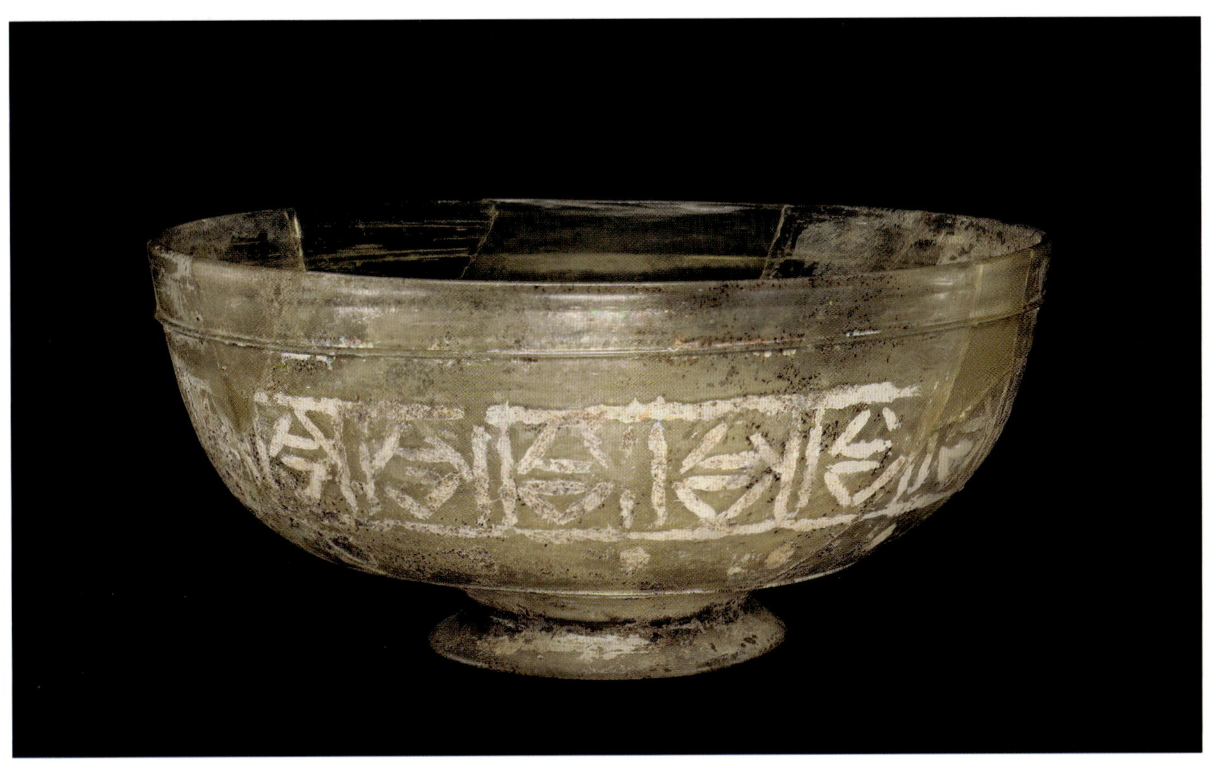

148

149. Fragment of Bowl with Fleur-de-Lis

Probably 10th to 11th century. Formerly in the Smith Collection (744). Gift of Carl Berkowitz and Derek Content. 76.1.224.
H. (surviving) 6.4 cm, D. (rim, est.) about 13 cm.
Almost colorless, with brownish tinge. Blown; linear- and slant-cut.

Fragment of bowl that was probably hemispherical, including approximately 20 percent of rim. Rim plain, with rounded lip; wall (Th. 0.2–0.3 cm) has smooth, convex profile. Decorated with large part of diamond-shaped motif (H., est., about 6 cm) with border consisting of broad linear cuts separated by band of narrow crosshatching (total W. 0.9 cm). Diamond contains quatrefoil composed of oval elements at top and bottom and volutes at sides; outlines of ovals are linear-cut, outlines of volutes are slant-cut, and centers of all four elements are crosshatched. Spaces between quatrefoil and border are occupied by short linear cuts.

Broken on all sides except rim. Scratched; remains of brownish weathering, especially in cuts.

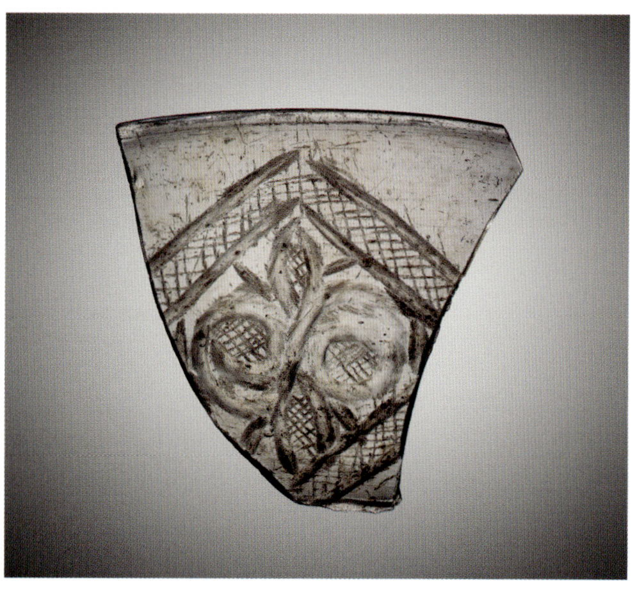

149

Comment: The quatrefoil, with or without the diamond-shaped frame, is a fairly common motif on linear- and slant-cut glass; **269**, for example, has rudimentary quatrefoils inside diamonds, and **266** has quatrefoils that lack frames. Another vessel with quatrefoils in diamond-shaped frames is a bottle in the Cohn Collection (*Cohn Collection* 1980, p. 165, no. 163). A bottle in the Museum für Islamische Kunst, Berlin (I.27/63: Kröger 1984, pp. 221–222, no. 192), has schematic leaf scrolls in diamond-shaped frames, as do three similar bottles in The British Museum, London (OA 1913.10-9.1: Pinder-Wilson 1991, 1999, and 2004, p. 118, fig. 144); The Metropolitan Museum of Art, New York (48.130: Clairmont 1972, pp. 148–149, no. 12); and (in 1997) a private collection in Japan (Fukai 1977, n.p., pl. 72).

Bibliography: *Verres antiques* 1954, p. 51, no. 310.

150. Base of Bowl

9th to 10th century. Formerly in the Smith Collection (1221-2). Gift of Carl Berkowitz and Derek Content. 76.1.270.
H. (surviving) 2.5 cm, D. (max., est.) about 6.5 cm, (base) 1.7 cm.
Almost colorless, with greenish yellow tinge. Blown; cut.

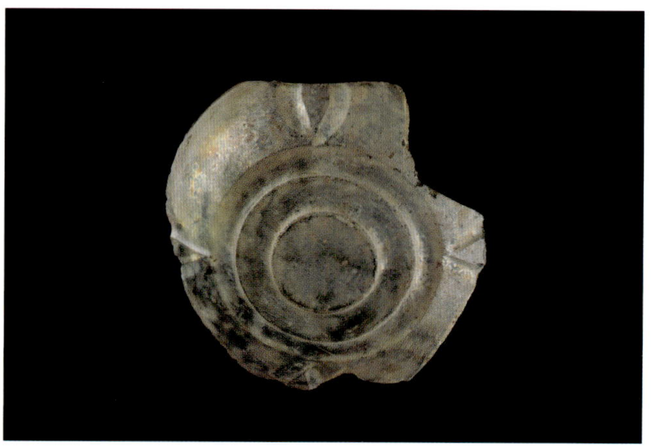

150

Small part of lower wall and complete base of bowl. Uppermost part of wall descends in steep curve to greatest diameter, 2 cm above base, below which it curves down and in. Vestige of linear-cut horizontal line, 2.3 cm above base; below this, lower parts of four equidistant oval (?) motifs with broad, linear-cut outlines. Bottom of wall is cut in two horizontal "steps" surrounding shallow, disk-shaped base.

Broken on all sides. One large area and many small patches of silvery gray iridescent weathering.

151. Fragment of Bowl

9th to 11th century. Formerly in the Smith Collection. 68.1.59-6.
H. 2.3 cm, D. (rim) 4.7 cm.
Colorless or almost colorless, perhaps with yellowish tinge. Blown; linear-cut.

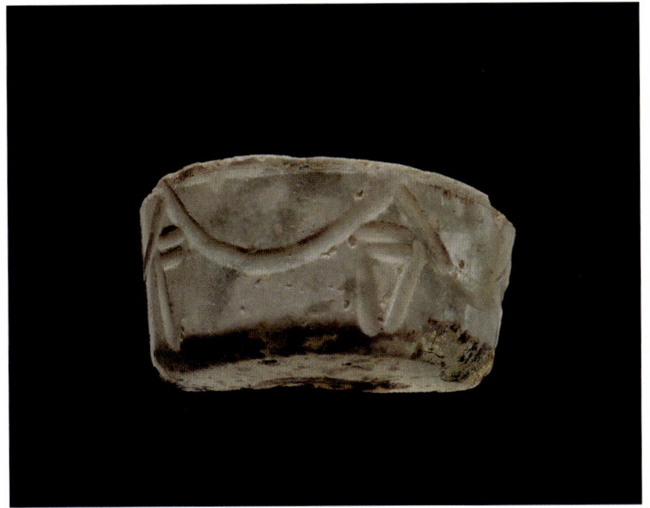

151

Fragment of miniature bowl; half of vessel survives. Rim plain, with top ground flat; wall (Th. 0.25–0.45 cm) straight and tapering, curving in at bottom; base flat; pontil mark mostly removed by grinding. Decorated on wall: descending from rim, row of contiguous shallow arcs; between each pair of arcs, one narrow isosceles triangle with apex at bottom; above each triangle, one short horizontal cut.

Chipped. Mostly covered with slightly iridescent off-white enamellike weathering.

Comment: The size of the arcs suggests that the complete vessel had five triangles.

152. Fragment of Bowl

About 9th to 11th century. Formerly in the Smith Collection (1158). 59.1.462.
H. (surviving) 1.3 cm, D. (est.) about 11 cm.
Almost colorless, with greenish tinge. Blown; linear-cut.

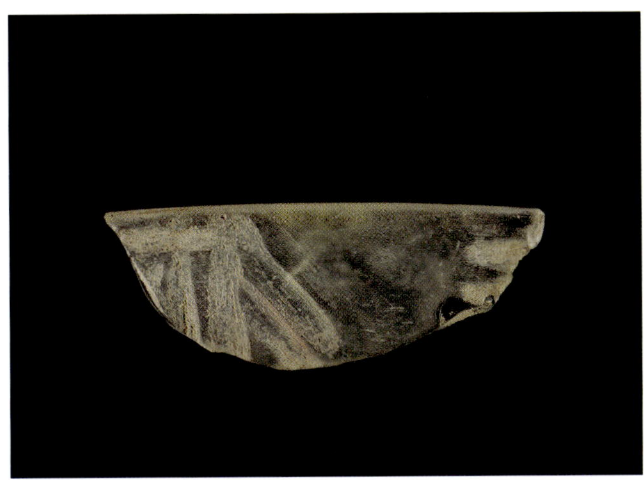

152

Fragment of bowl. Rim plain, with rounded lip; top of wall straight, with pronounced taper. Decorated just below rim with small parts of two motifs (W. of cuts 0.2–0.25 cm). On left: two vertical lines, flanked on one side by two transverse cuts and on other side by trace of presumably similar cuts. On right, parts of two horizontal cuts, one above other.

About 10 percent of rim survives; other edges broken. Dull; cuts are matte.

153. Fragment of Bowl(?) with Six-Pointed Star

About 11th century. Formerly in the Smith Collection (1150). 59.1.465.
Max. Dim. 7.7 cm.
Transparent pale yellowish green; numerous small bubbles. Blown; linear-cut.

Fragment from base of bowl (?). Lower wall curves down and in, and merges with flat base, which is narrow and thicker at center than at edge; no pontil mark. Decorated on underside of base with, at center, countersunk circular element (D. 2.3 cm) contained within six-pointed star (W. 5.2 cm) formed by 12 straight cuts.

Broken on all sides. Slightly pitted, with small patches of iridescence.

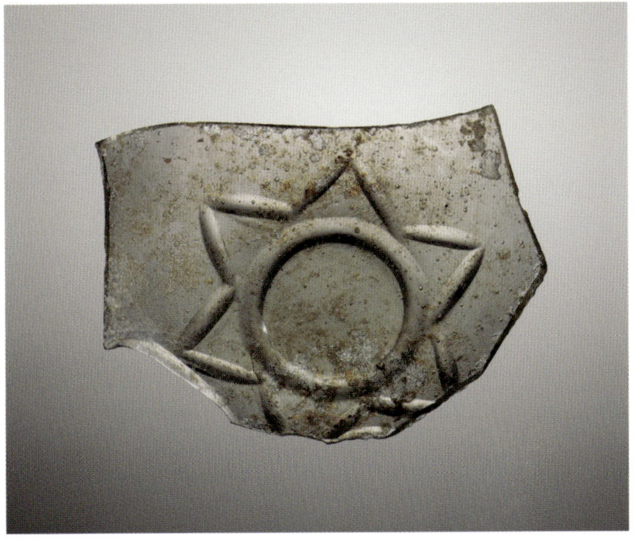

153

Comment: The fragment may be from a shallow bowl similar in form to a bowl found during excavations at Fusṭāṭ, in a context datable to the eighth or ninth century (Scanlon 1972–3, p. 126, fig. 3; Pinder-Wilson and Scanlon 1973, p. 24, no. 17; Scanlon and Pinder-Wilson 2001, pp. 83–84, no. 40a = Kubiak and Scanlon 1973, fig. 14).

154. Fragment of Bowl(?)

About 11th century. Formerly in the Smith Collection (1120). 59.1.474.
Max. Dim. 6.9 cm.
Transparent dark green; numerous small bubbles. Blown; linear-cut.

Fragment from base of bowl(?). Lower wall curves down and in, and merges with flat base, which is thicker at center than at edge; no pontil mark. Decorated with traces of linear cutting on lower wall and, at transition between wall and base, two continuous horizontal lines that, when seen from below, are concentric circles (D. about 11 cm and 10 cm respectively). Inner circle contains triangle with concave sides; surviving area between circle and side of triangle has lens-shaped element filled with four short cuts; additional short cuts exist inside triangle and on either side of lens.

Broken on all sides. No obvious weathering.

COMMENT: See **153**.

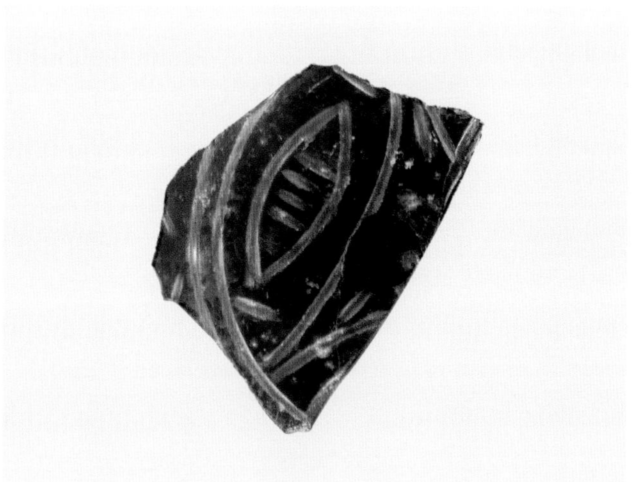

154

155. Fragment of Bowl(?)

10th to 11th century. Formerly in the Smith Collection. 68.1.59-33.
H. (surviving) 2.4 cm, D. (max., est.) about 7 cm.
Almost colorless, with greenish tinge. Blown; linear-cut.

Fragment apparently from wall (Th. 0.15–0.25 cm) of more or less hemispherical bowl with linear-cut decoration. Ornament includes parts of two horizontal grooves (W. 0.3 cm and 0.4 cm), which together make border 0.9 cm wide, and two broad, curving cuts that meet at top to form leaflike element.

Broken on all sides. Dull, with light gray and brownish weathering, and slight iridescence.

COMMENT: If the fragment is part of a hemispherical bowl, it is unusual, but cf. Scanlon and Pinder-Wilson 2001, p. 91, no. 41q, with faceted decoration, excavated at Fusṭāṭ. It is also possible that the fragment is from a bottle with a globular body.

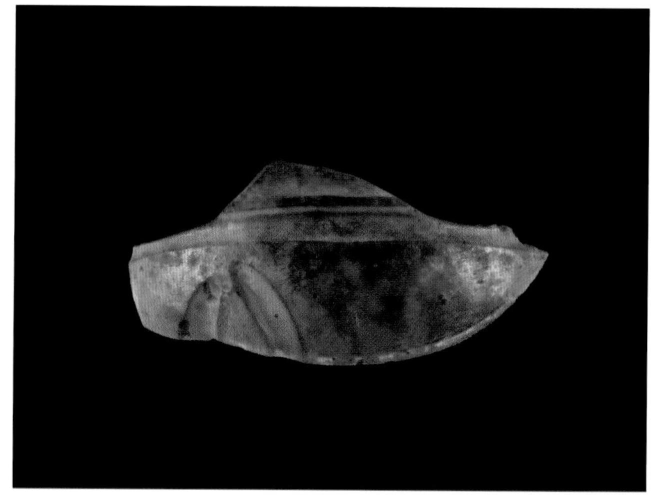

155

4. Cups

156. Cup with Handle

10th to 11th century. 76.1.20.
OH. 11.2 cm, H. (rim) 10.1 cm, D. 12.1 cm.
Almost colorless, with yellowish tinge. Blown; applied, linear-cut.

Cup. Wide, flaring mouth with beveled rim; narrow, sloping shoulder with rounded edge; wall bulges to greatest diameter near midpoint, then curves down and in; base has shallow foot-ring made by tooling; annular pontil mark (D. about 1.6 cm). Handle, with circular cross section, dropped onto wall at midpoint, drawn up and out and in, and attached to outside of rim; just below highest point, rectangular thumb-piece made from separate bit. Unpolished wheel-cut decoration on outside of mouth and wall. On mouth: band of ornament that occupies about two-thirds of circumference and is interrupted by handle, consisting of horizontal line below row of nine crescents with

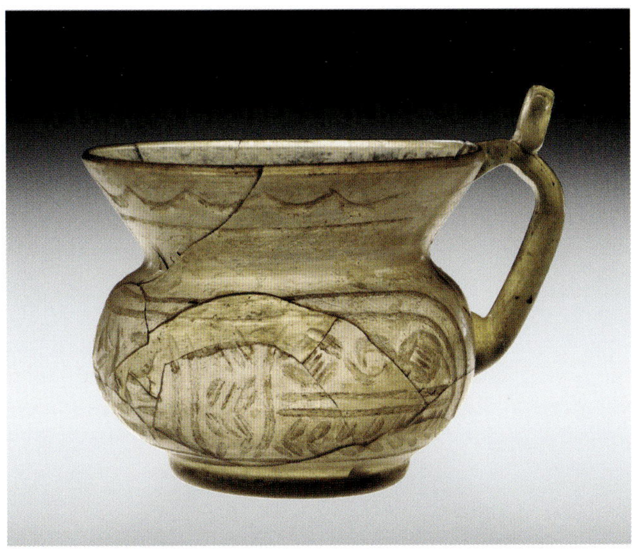

156

contiguous, upward-pointing tips. On wall: broad band of ornament that occupies more than three-quarters of circumference and is interrupted by handle, consisting of three panels of equal size bordered by two continuous horizontal lines at top and one continuous horizontal line at bottom; outer panels almost identical, each containing two registers divided by two horizontal lines, with two hatched circular motifs separated by scroll in upper register and band of chevrons in lower register; panel at center contains indeterminate motifs, possibly pseudo-epigraphic, and assorted crescents and short lines; at ends of band, upper border lines descend in S- and reversed S-shaped curves, then meet below lower attachment of handle.

Incomplete. Broken into many pieces, with three losses from wall; restored. Remains of matte grayish weathering, especially in areas of cutting.

Comment: Cf. **157**.

157. Cup with Geometric Ornament and Half-Palmettes

9th to 11th century. Formerly in the Strauss Collection (S2157). Bequest of Jerome Strauss. 79.1.172.
H. 11 cm, W. 14 cm.
Almost colorless, with greenish tinge; many bubbles. Blown; linear-cut.

Cup with squat globular body. Rim broad and flaring, with plain lip; neck straight and tapering; footring made by folding; pontil mark. Linear-cut decoration on neck and wall. On neck (from top to bottom): (1) horizontal band that stops on either side of handle; (2) two rows of contiguous arcs defining band of nine diamond-shaped panels, each with lattice motif; (3) space filler; and (4) border line. On wall: frieze that stops on either side of handle; double border lines above, two pairs of border lines separated by short horizontal and transverse strokes below; main motifs are row of four crosshatched centers, each within diamond. Marked on either side by two half-palmettes on same stem.

Incomplete. Restored from many fragments; parts of body and entire handle restored in plastic. Small areas of weathering, especially on underside of base.

Comment: For a cup with similar ornament, cf. 47.579: *Annual Report of Walters Art Gallery*, no. 41, 1973, pp. 31 and 41; and "Recent Important Acquisitions," *JGS*, v. 16, 1974, p. 127, no. 13.

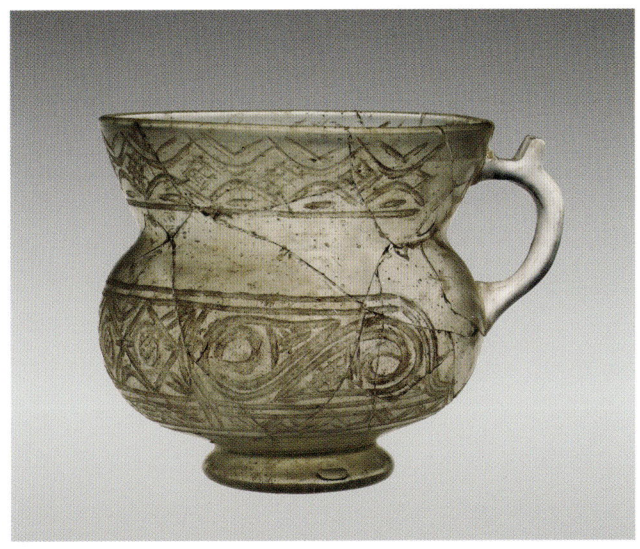

157

158. Cup with Inscription

9th to 10th century. Formerly in the Strauss Collection (S2160). Bequest of Jerome Strauss. 79.1.93.
H. 8.8 cm, D. 9.1 cm.
Almost colorless, with green tinge; very few minute bubbles. Mold-blown; linear-cut.

Cup: roughly cylindrical. Rim plain, with bevel on inside; wall straight, tapering slightly, then tapering sharply before curving down and in to bottom; base plain; no pontil mark. Wall has linear decoration (from top to bottom): 2.2–2.7 cm below lip, two continuous horizontal ribs separated by groove; at point where profile changes, one continuous horizontal groove; on lower part and at bottom of curved section, narrow vertical "step." Underside of base has one line of Kufic inscription intended to be read from the inside:

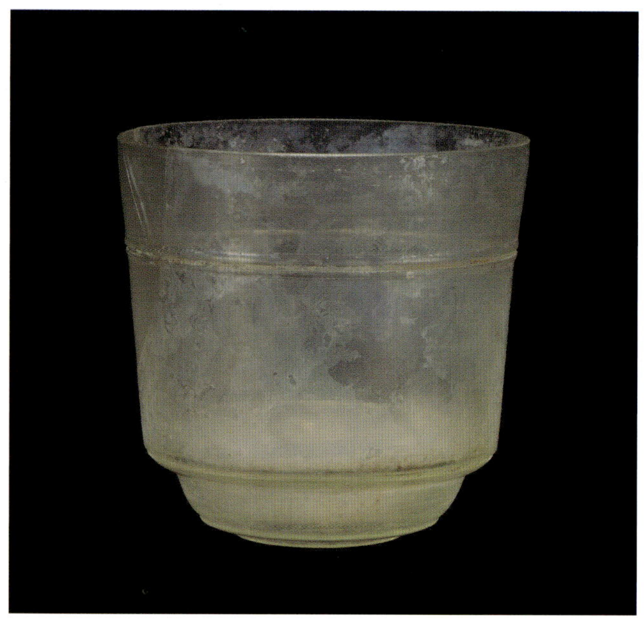

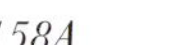

158A

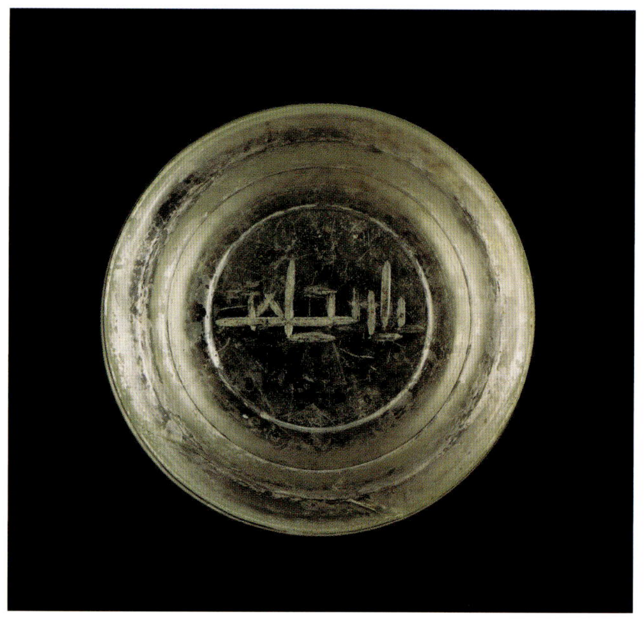

158B

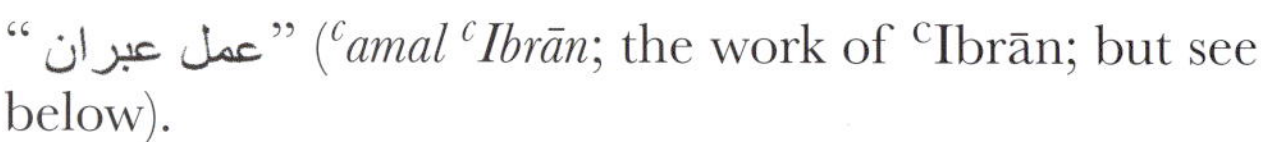

" عمل عبران " (*ʿamal ʿIbrān*; the work of ʿIbrān; but see below).

Complete. Broken into several pieces without loss, and repaired. Lightly pitted, with patches of transparent pale gray weathering.

Comment: The change of profile on the outside is echoed on the interior, and clearly the object was blown in a dip mold. Dr. Stefano Carboni points out that the reading of "ʿIbrān" is uncertain; instead of being a personal name, the word may mean "the Jew." A fragmentary beaker excavated at Nishapur also has, on the underside of the base, a signature that was intended to be read from the inside (Kröger 1995, p. 138, no. 191).

159. Cup

9th to 10th century. Found during excavations at Fusṭāṭ (Old Cairo), Egypt (68.11.8). Gift of the American Research Center in Egypt. 69.1.70.
H. 10.2 cm, D. (rim) 10.2 cm.
Almost colorless, with yellowish tinge; very bubbly. Blown; linear-cut.

Cup: cylindrical. Rim plain, with rounded, slightly thickened lip; wall vertical; base flat; roughly circular pontil mark (D. 1.6 cm). Decoration on wall consisted of linear-cut arcade, which, if symmetrical, had two diametrically opposed lozenges with double

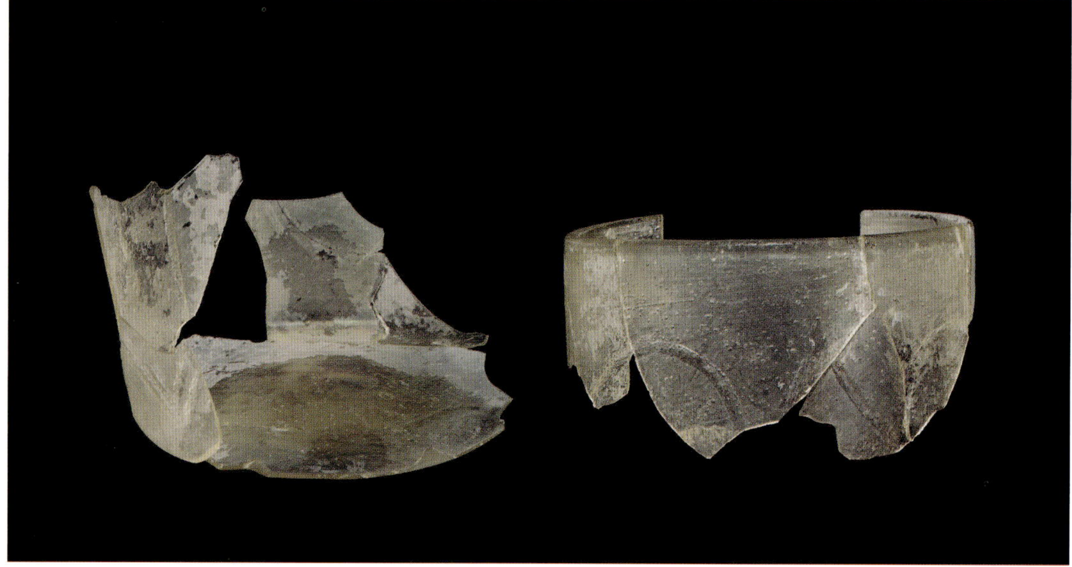

159

outlines separated by triangular arch with semicircular arch on either side of it, all with single outlines; arches terminated in pendent vertical lines with circular element at bottom, and triangular arches enclosed single vertical lines. Cuts are about 0.3 cm wide.

Incomplete. About 80 percent of rim, small parts of upper and lower wall, and almost entire base survive. Only parts of the lozenges, three semicircular arches, and one triangular arch survive. Pitted, with remains of weathering; evidently cleaned.

Comment: The object was found during excavations directed by Prof. George T. Scanlon.

At one point, the upper and lower parts of the wall join, and so, contrary to the description by Scanlon and Pinder-Wilson (see below), the height of the vessel is certain.

Bibliography: Scanlon and Pinder-Wilson 2001, pp. 84–85, no. 40c.

160. Cup

9th to 10th century. Formerly in the Strauss Collection (S2229). Bequest of Jerome Strauss. 79.1.224.
H. 8.1 cm, D. 8.3 cm.
Almost colorless, with yellowish green tinge.
Blown, probably in dip mold; linear-cut.

Cup: cylindrical. Rim plain, finished by grinding and polishing; wall vertical, uppermost 1 cm of which is beveled on inside; base flat; pontil mark removed by grinding. Wheel-cut decoration: on wall, two pairs of narrow horizontal grooves, 1.5–2 cm below rim and 1.9–2.4 cm above bottom; under base, circular depression, 1.7 cm across at center, surrounded by concentric groove (D. 3.8 cm).

Broken into many pieces, with losses in three places; restored. Surface pitted; small amount of weathering; some iridescence. Evidently cleaned.

Comment: This is a common early Islamic form. Linear-cut examples have a wide distribution in the central Islamic lands, extending from at least Fusṭāṭ, Egypt, in the west (e.g., Scanlon and Pinder-Wilson 2001, pp. 84–85, no. 40c) to Nishapur, Iran, in the east (e.g., Kröger 1995, pp. 148–149, no. 199). Other cylindrical linear-cut beakers, which lack archeological provenances, include Carboni 2001, p. 115, no. 2.12a (in the al-Sabah Collection, Dār al-Āthār al-Islāmiyyah, Kuwait National Museum, LNS 430 G); and *Arts of the Islamic World* 2008, p. 125, lot 82 (with incised signature "Abu Hurra" on underside of base).

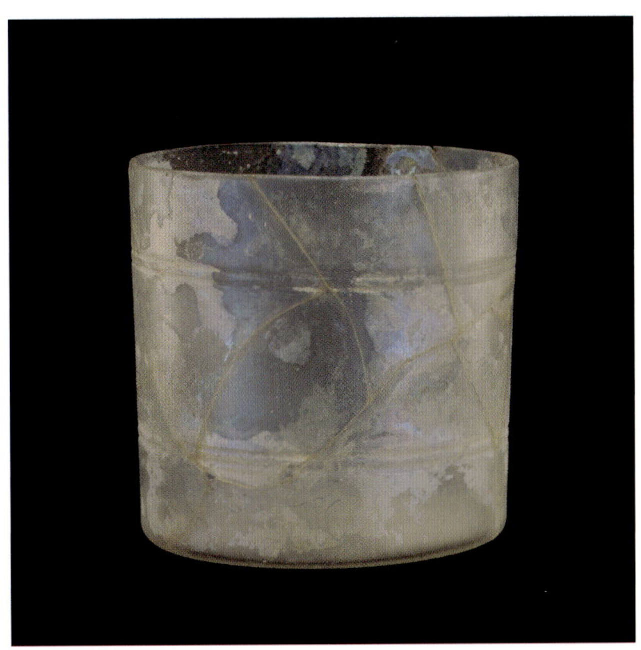

160A

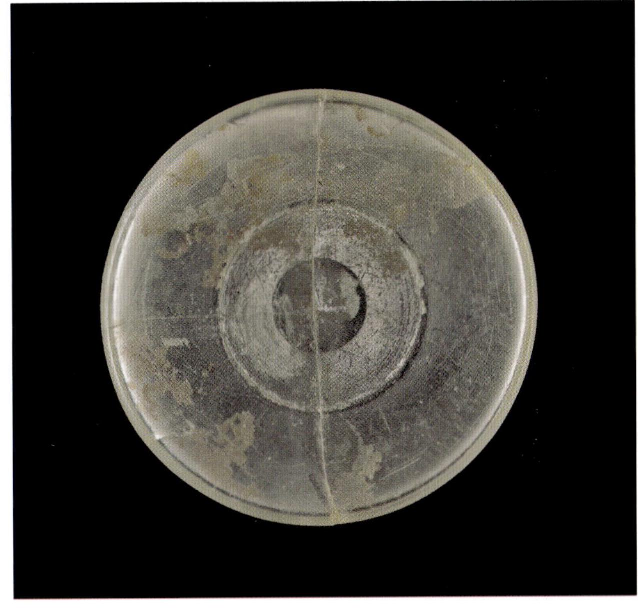

160B

161. Fragment of Cup

9th to 10th century. Formerly in the Smith Collection (1221-26). Gift of Carl Berkowitz and Derek Content. 76.1.214.
H. (surviving) 5.1 cm, D. 8 cm.
Almost colorless, with yellowish green tinge.
Blown; linear-cut.

Fragment of cylindrical cup, including about one-sixth of rim. Rim plain, with flattened top; wall vertical. Decoration apparently consists of triangle or lozenge with straight outlines and apex near rim; interior

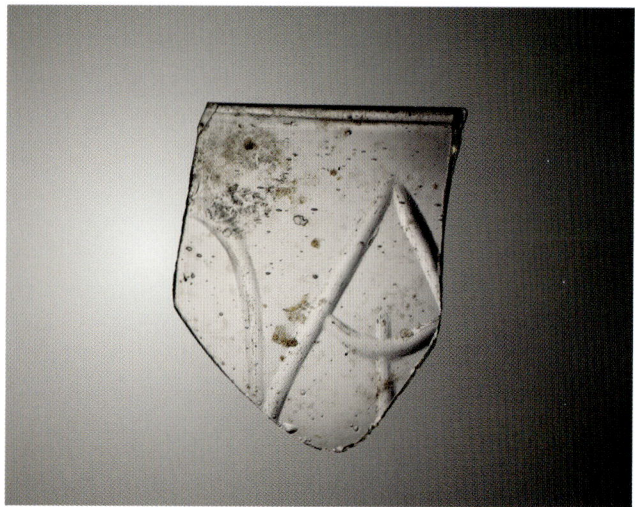

161

of motif contains one curved horizontal line intersecting with one straight vertical line; to left, part of curvilinear motif.

Broken on all sides except rim. Patches of light brown stain or weathering.

Comment: Cf. **163**.

162. Fragment of Cup

9th to 11th century. Formerly in the Smith Collection (1160). Gift of Carl Berkowitz and Derek Content. 76.1.225.
H. (surviving) 4.8 cm, D. (rim, est.) about 10 cm.
Almost colorless, with greenish yellow tinge; small bubbles. Blown; linear-cut.

Fragment of cylindrical cup, including less than one-10th of rim. Rim plain, with slightly thickened, rounded lip; wall vertical. Decorated on wall with part of indeterminate motif, of which one curved and two straight unpolished cuts survive.

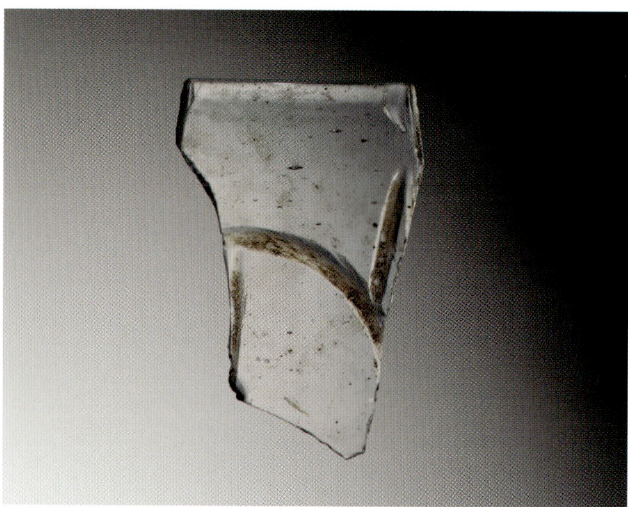

162

Broken on all sides except rim. Traces of pale gray and brown incipient weathering, especially in cuts.

163. Fragment of Cup

9th to 10th century. Formerly in the Smith Collection (555-20). Gift of Carl Berkowitz and Derek Content. 76.1.213.
H. (surviving) 4.5 cm, D. 7 cm.
Almost colorless, with yellowish green tinge. Blown; linear-cut.

Fragment of cylindrical cup, including about one-quarter of rim. Rim plain, with flattened top; wall vertical. Decoration apparently consists of lozenge with slightly concave outlines and with trace of short horizontal cut on upper part of interior; to left, part of curvilinear motif.

Broken on all sides except rim. Faint cloudiness may be incipient weathering.

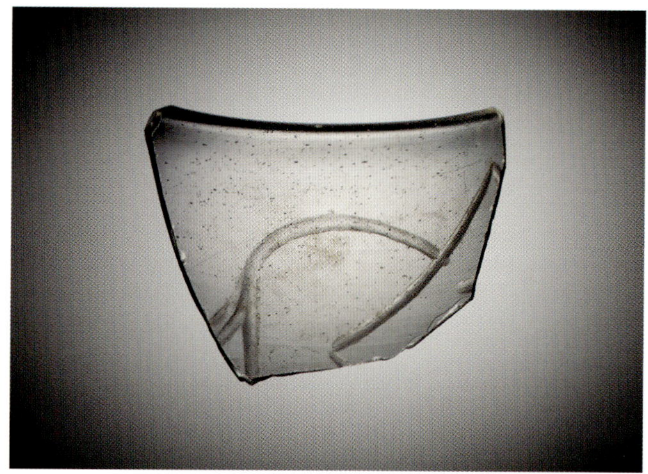

163

Comment: A cylindrical cup with linear-cut lozenges was found in the Jawsaq al-Khāqānī, the palace built by Caliph al-Muᶜtaṣim at Samarra, Iraq (Lamm 1928, p. 68, no. 185; cf. a drawing of this object published in Kröger 1995, p. 147), and another, decorated with stylized leaves and other motifs, was discovered at Nishapur, northeastern Iran (Kröger 1995, pp. 148–149, no. 199). Other examples of linear-cut cylindrical cups include vessels in the David Collection, Copenhagen (10/1966: Folsach 1990, p. 140, no. 213 = *idem* 2001, p. 204, no. 296), and the al-Sabah Collection, Dār al-Āthār al-Islāmiyyah, Kuwait National Museum (LNS 430 G: Carboni 2001, p. 115, no. 2.12a).

164. Fragment of Cup

About 10th to 11th century. Formerly in the Smith Collection. 68.1.59-15.
H. 4.5 cm, D. (rim, est.) about 5.5 cm.
Transparent light bluish green. Blown; linear-cut.

Fragment of cylindrical cup, consisting of about one-fifth of rim and small part of base. Rim plain, with rounded lip; wall (Th. 0.1–0.3 cm) vertical, curving in at bottom; base perhaps concave. Decorated with horizontal band (H. 3.1 cm) bordered at top and bottom by horizontal groove. Band contains two rows of contiguous arcs; one row descends from upper border, and other row projects upward from lower border. In each space between upper and lower rows, group of three transverse cuts.

Pitted, with patches of iridescent light brown weathering.

Comment: The size of the arcs suggests that the complete vessel had six or seven arcs, and the same number of groups of transverse cuts.

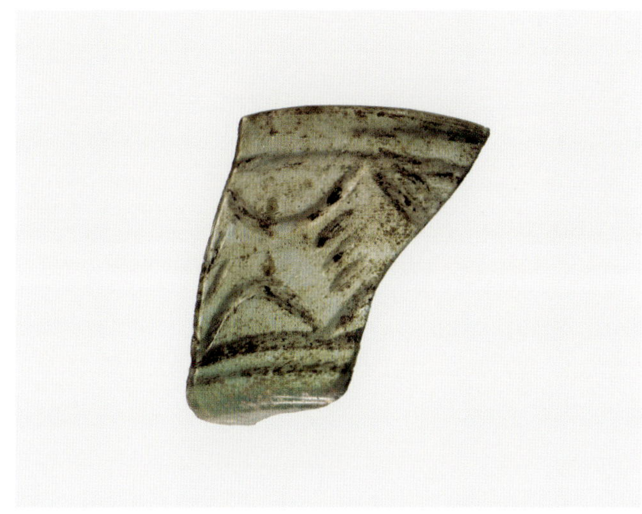

164

5. Beakers

165. Beaker with Human Figure and Bird

9th to 11th century. Formerly in the Smith Collection (955). 55.1.123.
H. 9.7 cm, D. (rim) 7 cm, (base) 4.8 cm.
Colorless; many minute bubbles. Blown; linear-cut.

Beaker shaped like truncated cone. Rim plain, with top ground flat; wall (Th. 0.1 cm) straight and tapering; base plain; pontil mark mostly removed by grinding. Wall has linear-cut decoration consisting of continuous horizontal frieze with two parallel lines forming border at top and single groundline at bottom. Frieze contains four motifs (from right to left): (1) human figure standing or squatting to front; he wears closely fitting cap with long, narrow "ears"; face is large, eyes are almond-shaped, torso is short, arms are indicated by oval elements, legs are short and perhaps bent, and feet stand on groundline; (2) almost completely missing; it cannot be identified, unless surviving part is tail of bird facing right; (3) plantlike motif with single stem, pair of leaves above midpoint, and leaf or leaf spray at top; and (4) bird standing to left, facing (1).

Incomplete. Broken, with loss of about 20 percent of rim and 15 percent of wall; restored. Extensively pitted, with traces of iridescent weathering. Hole (D. 0.5 cm) near edge of base presumably was made by Ray Winfield Smith to obtain a sample for chemical analysis.

Comment: Very few medieval Islamic glasses depict human figures. For another example, see **319**. If the second motif was indeed a bird, the ornament was symmetrical, with the human figure flanked by birds, and with the plantlike motif on the opposite side of the wall.

The presence of human figures on **165** and **319** recalls the lively combinations of painted humans, birds, animals, and vegetation found on ceramic buffwares from northeastern Iran. Buffwares are decorated

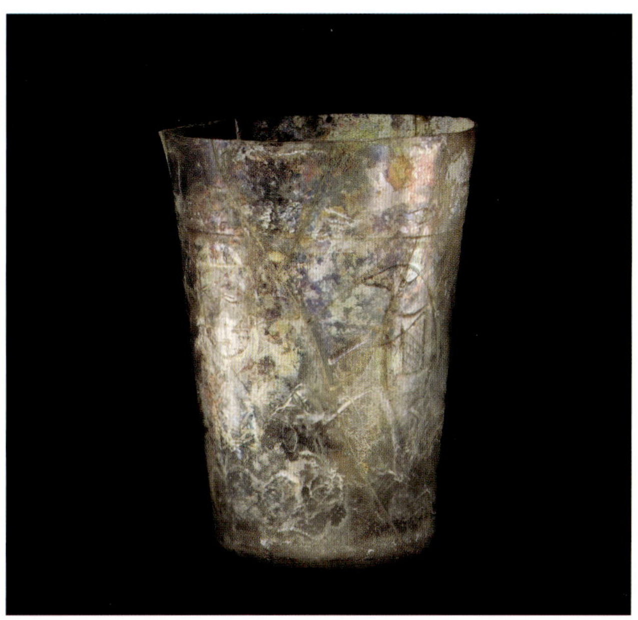

165

in black, red, yellow, and green under a transparent glaze. The largest number of finds has been recorded at Nishapur, where examples began to attract attention during the excavations of 1935–1940 (Wilkinson 1973, pp. 3–53). In addition to Nishapur, where kilns for its manufacture were discovered, buffware has been found at Merv (Mary), Turkmenistan; Afrasiyab (Old Samarqand), Uzbekistan; and elsewhere. It is believed to be of the 10th century (Watson 2004, pp. 247–251).

Bibliography: *Verres antiques* 1954, p. 54, no. 337; *Glass from the Ancient World* 1957, pp. 266–267, no. 541.

166. Beaker with Birds

10th to 11th century. Formerly in the Smith Collection (1352). 59.1.477.
H. 12.7–13.3 cm, D. (rim) 9.7 cm.
Colorless. Blown; linear-cut.

Beaker shaped like truncated cone, but somewhat lopsided. Rim plain, with top ground flat; wall straight and tapering; base plain; pontil mark (D. 1.3 cm). Small oval area (H. about 7 cm, W. 2.5 cm) in upper part and midsection of wall is flat, not curved (see below). Rather perfunctory linear-cut decoration on wall: one narrow register and one broad register separated by continuous horizontal line. Upper, narrow register begins 3.5 cm below rim; it has pair of continuous horizontal lines at top and contains two bands of short transverse cuts; cuts do not touch one another, but resemble 12 pairs of chevrons or two continuous zigzags. Lower, broad register is divided by four pairs of vertical cuts into two broad and two narrow panels (clockwise): (1) wide panel containing standing bird shown in profile, facing left; it has large, curling crest, crosshatched body, and long tail feathers; (2) narrow panel with geometric decoration that includes large U-shaped motif above smaller element shaped like letter A, but with double V-shaped crossbar; (3) wide panel containing schematic bird shown in profile, facing left; it appears to have open beak and has crosshatched breast; and (4) similar to (2). All cuts are about 0.2 cm wide.

Incomplete. Broken, with extensive losses from rim (about 50 percent) and upper wall, and smaller losses from midsection and lower part of wall (including part of bird in panel 3) and in base; restored. Dull, with remains of grayish weathering, especially in cuts.

Comment: The flattened area in the wall was probably caused by placing the vessel on its side in the annealing oven before the glass had cooled sufficiently to be fully rigid (cf. a similarly flattened area on the wall of the Portland Vase: Gudenrath and Whitehouse 1990, pp. 115–118). The lopsided shape of the beaker was probably caused at the same time.

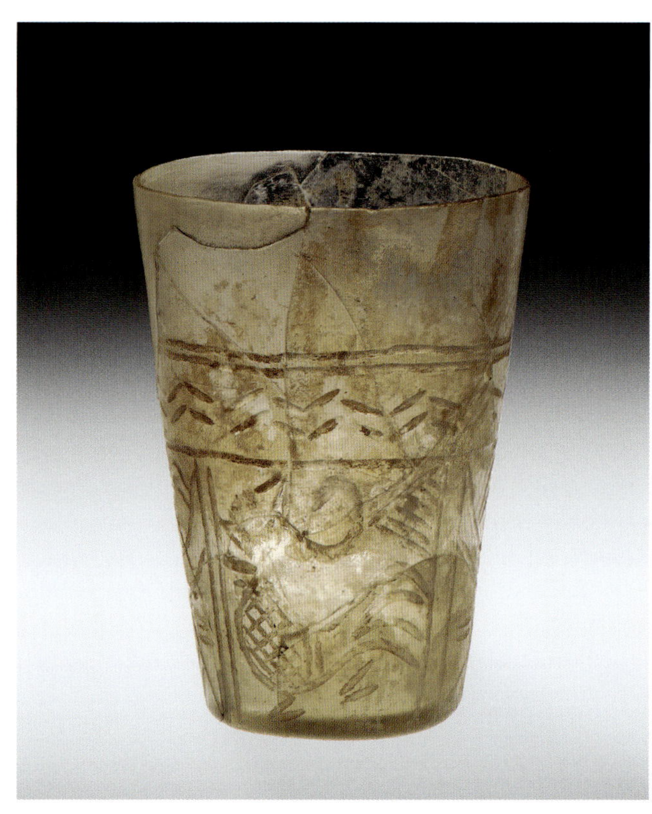

166

The linear decoration consists of broad, abraded grooves executed in a style that has little regard for precision. The two parallel lines that form the upper border, for example, are neither straight nor of even thickness. This style of cutting (which Kröger 1995, pp. 150–152, calls the "Intermediate Style") has a wide distribution in the Islamic world. It may have come into use in the ninth century, the supposed date for a fragment found at Samarra (Lamm 1928, p. 67, no. 180), and the presence of similar beakers with abraded decoration among the cullet on the Serçe Limanı shipwreck shows that the type was still in use about the year 1025 (Bass 1984, esp. fig. 5a). Numerous beakers decorated in the Intermediate Style have been found in Iran; see, for example, Kröger 1995, pp. 153–155, nos. 203–208, from Nishapur. Others are from Egypt. The latter include a complete example from Thebes, now in The British Museum, London (Lamm 1929–30, p. 152, pl. 56, no. 2), and fragments from Fusṭāṭ (*ibid.*, p. 153, nos. 5–8).

Cf. *Glass from the Ancient World* 1957, p. 267, no. 541, which is decorated with "a highly stylized frontal human figure and a bird in profile."

Bibliography: *Islam and the Medieval West* 1975, n.p., no. G3.

167. Fragment of Beaker with Bird

Late 10th to early 11th century. Formerly in the Strauss Collection (F34). 79.1.304.
Max. Dim. 7.1 cm, D. (est.) 7–8 cm.
Colorless; minute bubbles. Blown; slant- and linear-cut.

Fragment of beaker. Wall (Th. 0.1–0.2 cm) is straight and tapers. Decoration consists of part of frieze (H. 5.3 cm) with double borders at top and bottom. Frieze contains parts of two elements flanking oval motif above two inverted Vs. Outline of oval motif is slant-cut, and it surrounds smaller crosshatched oval that is pointed at top; inverted Vs are linear-cut. Element on right consists of bird standing in profile, facing left. It has slant-cut head with slant-cut beak and crest, and eye represented by countersunk dot; neck and body have linear-cut outlines, with one transverse line on neck and crosshatching on body; leg and foot consist of two cuts in form of reversed L; surviving part of tail is slant-cut. Element on left is linear-cut and indeterminate; it is not another bird. In spaces between elements and oval motif, and above bird, are several short linear- and slant-cut lines.

Broken on all sides. Little incipient weathering.

Comment: The fragment is part of a truncated conical beaker. Changes in the thickness of the wall indicate that the bottom of the fragment came from just above the base. The rather erratic character of the engraving recalls the handful of linear-cut glasses from the Serçe Limanı shipwreck, which is dated to within a decade of 1025 (Bass 1984).

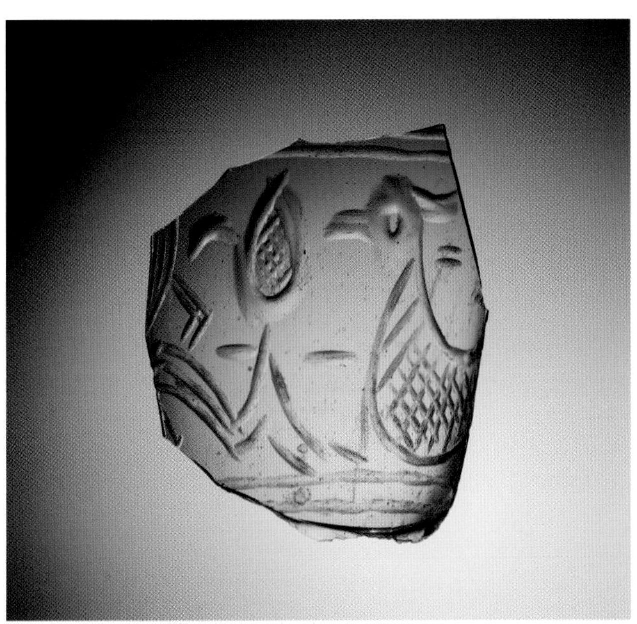

167

168. Fragment of Beaker with Bird

About 10th century. Formerly in the Smith Collection (1221-19). Gift of Carl Berkowitz and Derek Content. 76.1.228.
H. (surviving) 2.4 cm, D. (top of fragment, est.) about 6 cm.
Almost colorless, with greenish yellow tinge; small bubbles. Blown; linear-cut.

Fragment of beaker. Lower wall (Th. 0.15–0.3 cm) is straight and tapers. Decoration consists of lower part of bird and horizontal border. Bird, facing right, has outline of breast and abdomen; front of body is crosshatched; each leg and foot is indicated by two short cuts. Beneath bird, border has single horizontal groove above two horizontal rows of short V-shaped cuts that form zigzags.

Upper edge of fragment ground to form improvised rim; other edges are broken. No obvious weathering.

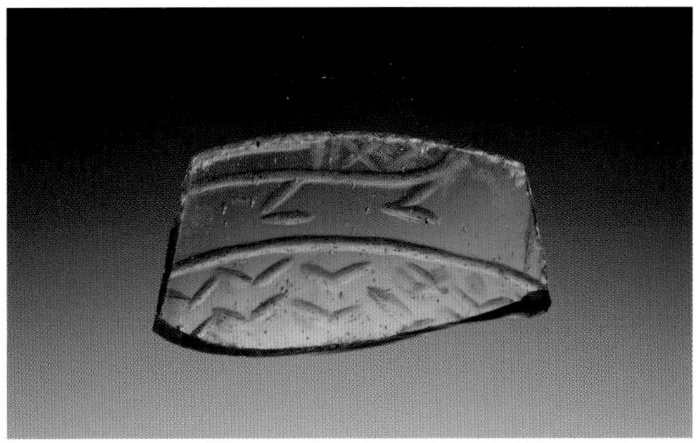

168

Comment: The size, shape, and thickness of the fragment indicate that it came from the bottom of the wall of a beaker. The ground upper edge indicates that, after the beaker had been broken, the lower part was made into a container that had a diameter of six centimeters and was probably a little more than three centimeters high.

169. Fragment of Beaker(?) with Bird

9th to 11th century. Formerly in the Smith Collection. 68.1.59-29.
H. 3 cm, D. (base, est.) about 5 cm.
Transparent very pale yellowish green. Blown; linear-cut.

Fragment of beaker(?). Lower wall (Th. 0.3 cm) straight and tapering; base (Th. 0.3–0.45 cm) plain.

174. Fragment of Beaker or Bottle with Six-Pointed Star

About 10th century. Formerly in the Smith Collection. 68.1.59-4.
H. (surviving) 2.3 cm, D. (base) 4 cm.
Colorless or almost colorless. Blown; linear-cut.

Fragment of beaker or bottle. Lower wall (Th. 0.2 cm) straight, tapering and curving in at bottom; base plain; pontil mark. Decorated on wall and underside of base. Wall has horizontal band (H. 2 cm) bordered by single grooves. It contains two horizontal rows of short contiguous arcs; arcs in upper row have ends pointing down, while ends of arcs in lower row point up. Base has two superimposed triangles that form six-pointed star.

Approximately half of base survives. Broken on all sides. Iridescent grayish silver weathering.

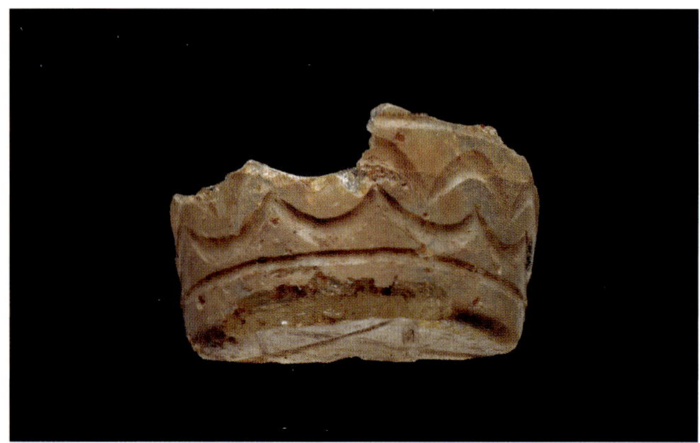

174

175. Beaker with Arcade

10th to early 11th century. 64.1.24.
H. 9.8 cm, D. 7 cm.
Colorless. Blown; linear-cut.

Beaker shaped like truncated cone. Rim plain and ground flat; wall straight and tapering; base flat; pontil mark (D. perhaps about 1.2 cm) almost completely removed by grinding. Wall is decorated with two hastily executed, continuous linear-cut friezes, which begin 2.5 cm below rim and end 0.6 cm above bottom. Upper frieze has two horizontal border lines at top. It consists of arcade of (originally) eight segmental arches supported on columns with capitals; arches are indicated by single lines, and columns and capitals by pairs of parallel lines; spandrels between arches are filled with crosshatching or V-shaped motifs. Upper and lower friezes are separated by narrow band with single borders at top and bottom; band contains pairs of transverse cuts alternating with short horizontal cuts. Lower frieze has arcade of seven arches similar to upper arcade, but with V-shaped motifs in every spandrel. Between rim and upper frieze, one short, possibly epigraphic motif.

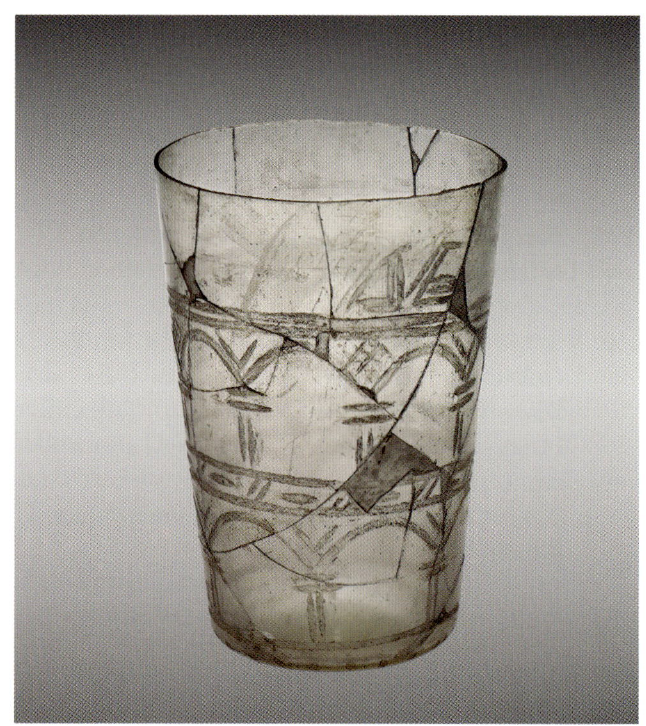

175

Incomplete. Broken into several pieces, with two losses from rim and wall; restored. Dull, with traces of yellowish weathering and some iridescence.

Comment: Linear-cut beakers of this type, found in Iran, are traditionally attributed to Nishapur (cf. Kröger 1995, pp. 153–155, nos. 203–208). However, they have a wide distribution, which includes, in the eastern Mediterranean, the Serçe Limanı shipwreck. The finds from Serçe Limanı show that the type was still in use in the early 11th century.

See **178**.

176. Fragment of Beaker with Arcade

10th century. Found during excavations at Fusṭāṭ (Old Cairo), Egypt (80.10.36). Gift of the American Research Center in Egypt. 81.1.26.
H. 4.3 cm, W. 5.2 cm.
Almost colorless, with yellowish green tinge. Blown; linear- and relief-cut.

Fragment of beaker: tapering cylinder. Fragment preserves lower portion of beaker with tapering walls and thick base. Below horizontal wheel-cut groove is band of 11 relief-cut gadroons, each with vertical groove; base has pontil mark surrounded by wheel-cut circle.

Incomplete. Upper wall missing. Thick white weathering.

Comment: The fragment was found during excavations directed by Prof. George T. Scanlon. Similar fragments from Fusṭāṭ are dated by the excavator to the ninth or 10th century, but related objects from Nishapur or Serçe Limanı would be dated to the 10th or 11th century.

Bibliography: Pinder-Wilson and Scanlon 2001, p. 99, no. 42z″.

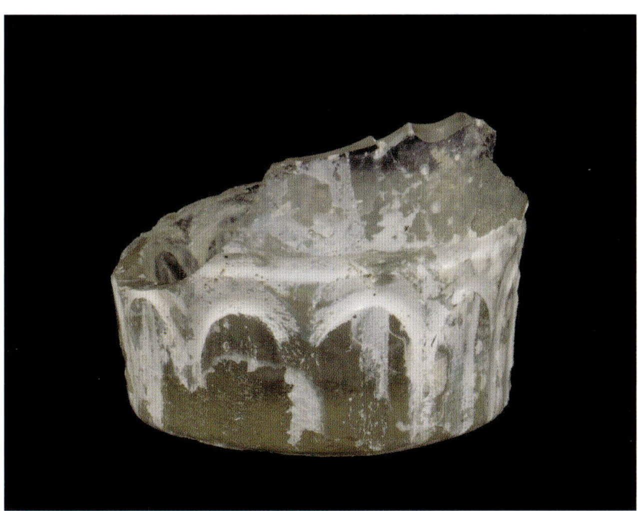

176

177. Beaker

10th to 11th century. Formerly in the Strauss Collection (S2227). Bequest of Jerome Strauss. 79.1.222.
H. 13.4 cm, D. 9.7 cm.
Transparent very pale yellowish green; few bubbles. Blown; linear-cut.

Beaker shaped like truncated cone. Rim plain; wall straight and tapering; base flat; pontil mark roughly circular (D. 1.4 cm). Wall has continuous frieze of irregular linear-cut decoration, made with shallow cuts 0.2–0.3 cm wide; it extends from about 3.6 cm below rim to about 1 cm above bottom, and it consists of one wide (upper) and one narrow (lower) register. Wide register has upper and lower borders, each consisting of two closely spaced horizontal lines; between borders, broad band of ornament divided by pairs of vertical lines into two wide panels alternating with two narrow panels; each narrow panel contains two crosses consisting of four diagonal cuts touching or almost touching at center, one above the other, and additional cuts in some spaces between arms of crosses; each wide panel contains narrow horizontal band of curved cuts arranged in wavelike pattern above two horizontal lines, below which broader band is divided into three triangular compartments by pairs of diagonal cuts, with groups of straight and comma-like cuts in each compartment. Narrow register has continuous

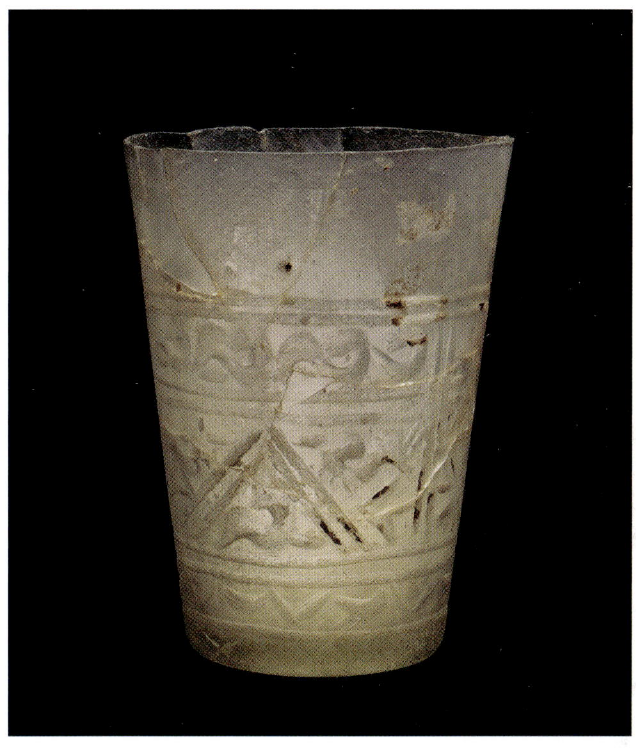

177A

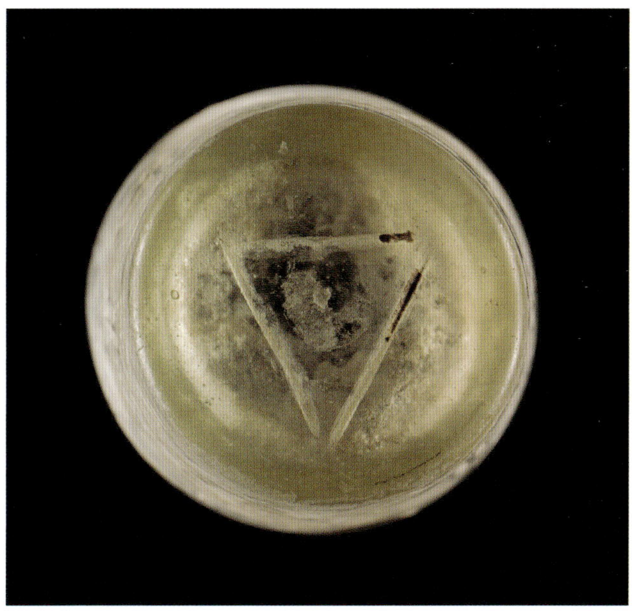

177B

band of pairs of straight cuts arranged in form of V, alternating with single crescent-shaped cuts; below this, one continuous horizontal line. On underside of base, three straight cuts arranged in triangle that encloses pontil mark, which was partly removed by polishing.

Incomplete. Broken into many pieces, with losses from rim and wall (about 10 percent of total; restored in plastic). Most of surface is dull and pitted, with remains of light tan-colored weathering in cuts.

COMMENT: The decoration was executed hastily; the layout is careless, and the cuts are of various widths and depths. Beakers with this shape and quality have been recovered in large quantities among glass reportedly found in Iran. However, they also appear among the cargo of cullet found on the shipwreck at Serçe Limanı on the coast of Turkey, opposite Rhodes. The Serçe Limanı ship sank about the year 1025, and this suggests that many beakers of this type probably date from the early 11th century (Bass 1984).

178. Beaker

10th to early 11th century. Formerly in the Strauss Collection (S1834). Gift of Jerome Strauss. 70.1.48.
H. 10.3 cm, D. (rim) 7.2 cm.
Almost colorless, with green tinge. Blown; linear-cut.

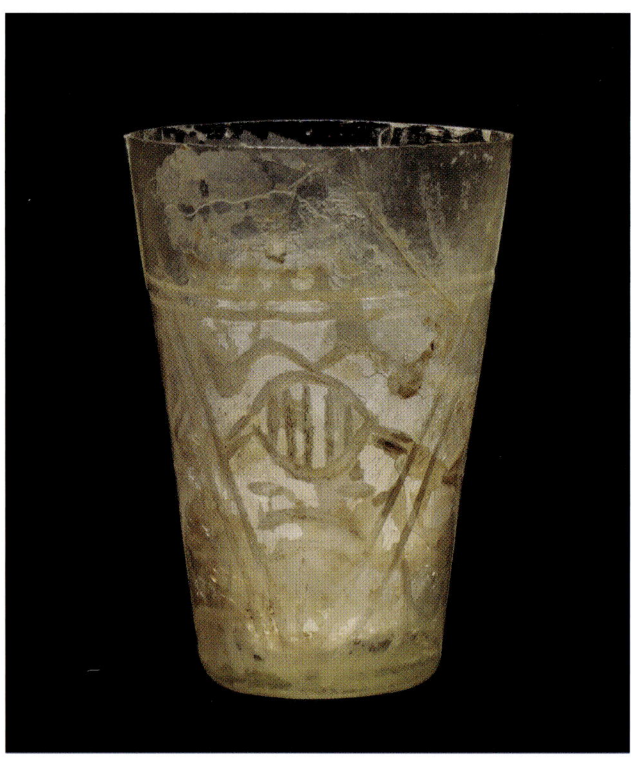

178

Beaker shaped like truncated cone. Rim plain and ground flat; wall straight and tapering; base flat; pontil mark roughly circular (D. about 1.6 cm). Wall is decorated with hastily executed, continuous linear-cut frieze, which begins 2.6 cm below rim and ends slightly above bottom; at top, two horizontal border lines. Below this, frieze is divided in two by opposed pairs of vertical lines; each half contains V-shaped panel with double outline, containing hatched oval motif and space fillers; outside each panel, abstract ornament of curving lines and pairs of short, straight stripes.

Incomplete. Broken into several pieces, with two losses from rim and upper wall; restored. Dull, with traces of yellowish weathering and some iridescence.

COMMENT: Linear-cut beakers of this type, found in Iran, are traditionally attributed to Nishapur (cf. Kröger 1995, pp. 153–155, nos. 203–208). However, they have a wide distribution, which includes, in the eastern Mediterranean, the Serçe Limanı shipwreck, and this shows that they were still in use in the early 11th century.

For the bottom of a beaker with very similar decoration on the lower wall, see Morrison 1984, p. 170, fig. 137d (excavated in a mid-ninth to early 11th-century context at Manda, Kenya).

179. Fragment of Beaker

10th to early 11th century. Formerly in the Smith Collection (1156). 59.1.464.
H. (surviving) 8.1 cm, D. (est.) 10 cm.
Almost colorless, with yellowish green tinge; many bubbles, which are elongated near rim.
Blown; linear-cut.

Fragment of beaker. Rim plain, with rounded lip; upper wall tapers, with concave profile. Decorated with rather irregular, broad linear cuts (W. 0.15–0.3 cm) and narrow incised details: two horizontal lines, 2.6–3.9 cm below lip, enclosing row of inverted V-shaped motifs with double outlines; below this, part of frieze containing two vertical oval motifs with double outlines, filled with incised crosshatching, that are separated by smaller vertical oval motif, pointed at bottom and filled with crosshatching, and other, indeterminate linear ornament.

About 20 percent of rim survives; otherwise, broken on all sides. Pitted, especially in cuts, and with patches of light grayish weathering.

COMMENT: The tapering upper wall sets this object apart from the linear-cut beakers from Nishapur, which have straight sides (Kröger 1995, pp. 153–161, nos. 203–208, 210–215, 217, and 218). The last two of these have rather careless decoration, which Kröger terms the "coarse style." The term is equally appropriate for **179**. Such beakers are common among the glass from Hama, Syria (Riis and Poulsen 1957, pp. 57, 82–87, 90, 96, and 108).

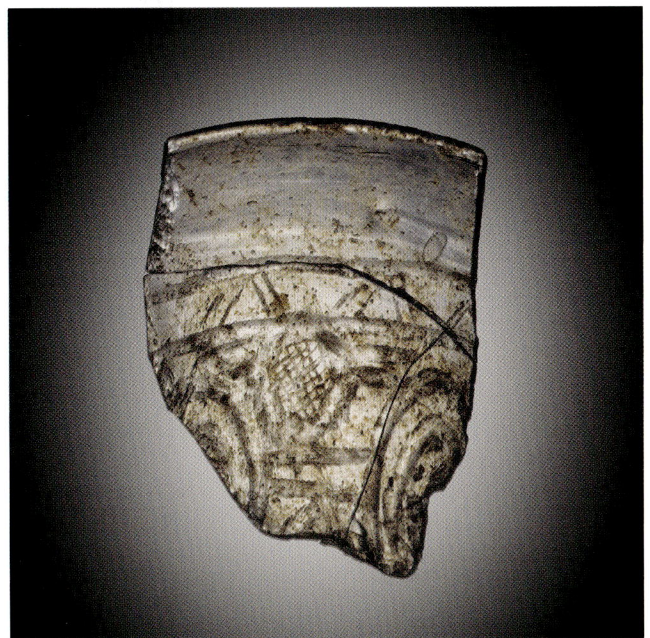

179

180. Fragment of Beaker

9th to 11th century. 2009.1.1.
H. (surviving) 5.7 cm, D. (max., est.) about 7 cm.
Almost colorless, with yellowish tinge. Blown; linear-cut.

Fragment of beaker. Wall (Th. 0.1 cm) is straight and tapering. Linear-cut decoration consists of part of frieze (W. 3.3 cm) bordered at top and bottom by pair of horizontal grooves. Surviving part of frieze has decoration with grooved outlines and incised details. It consists of two horizontal zigzags composed of adjoining oval elements, all filled with transverse hatching, which descend from upper border and point upward from lower border; in spaces between them, single crosshatched lozenges; in spaces between zigzags and borders, pairs of short vertical lines.

Broken on all sides. Dull, with remains of brown and off-white weathering.

Comment: At Corning, the fragment has been stored with the material from the American Research Center in Egypt's gift of glass from excavations at

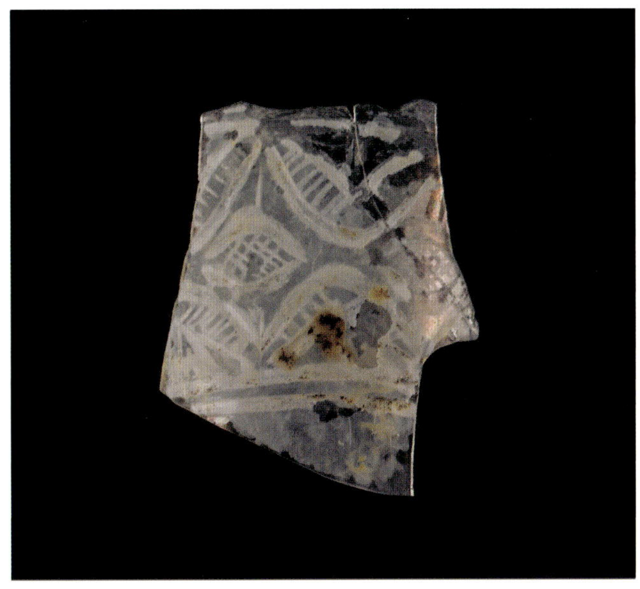

180

Fusṭāṭ. However, it has nothing that identifies it, and it does not appear in Scanlon and Pinder-Wilson 2001. We do not know, therefore, how or when the Museum acquired it.

181. Fragment of Beaker

10th to 11th century. Formerly in the Smith Collection (1221-29). Gift of Carl Berkowitz and Derek Content. 76.1.299.
H. (surviving) 4.6 cm, D. (max., est.) about 8–9 cm.
Probably almost colorless, with yellowish tinge. Blown; linear-cut.

Fragment from upper wall of beaker (Th. 0.1–0.15 cm) with straight, tapering profile. Linear-cut decoration consists of small parts of upper border and

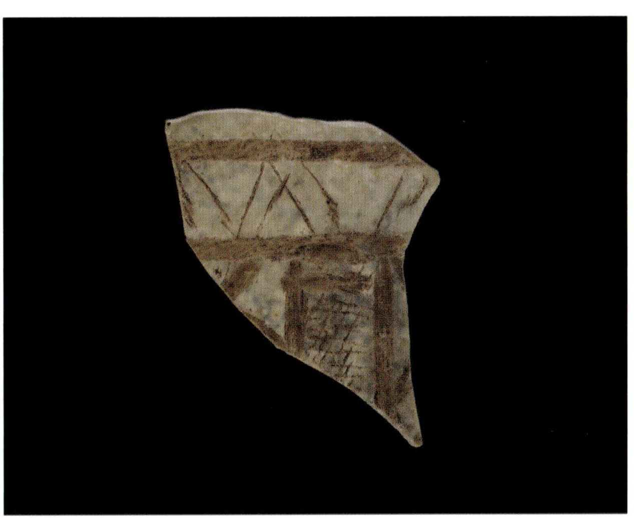

181

frieze. Upper border is defined at top and bottom by broad horizontal lines (W. 0.2 cm), between which are pairs of narrow lines forming irregular zigzag. Surviving part of frieze has vertical stripe bordered at sides and reinforced at top by broad lines (W. 0.2 cm), and filled with crosshatching. On either side of stripe, indeterminate ornament, which includes broad diagonal lines. All broad cuts are shallow and were not polished.

Broken on all sides. Dull, with patches of transparent grayish weathering and brown weathering, especially in cuts.

COMMENT: The shape and size of the fragment indicate that it was part of the upper wall of a beaker.

182. Fragment of Beaker

10th to 11th century. Formerly in the Smith Collection (1222-7). 81.1.697.
H. (surviving) 3.9 cm, D. (base) 4.5 cm.
Almost colorless, with yellowish green tinge.
Blown; linear-cut.

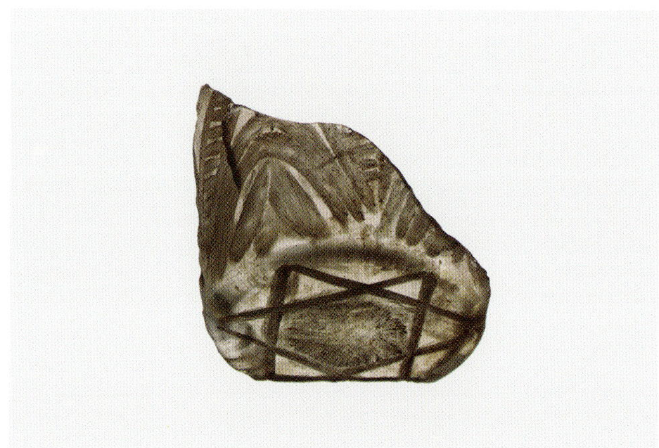

182

Fragment of beaker, consisting of small part of wall and most of base. Lower wall straight and tapering; base flat, with shallow ground depression at center, presumably to remove pontil mark. Decorated on wall and underside of base. On bottom of wall: part of one and very small parts of two other triangular motifs. Surviving motif consists of two converging narrow, pointed oval elements, each with single outline and transverse hatching, inside which are two parabolas, one inside other, containing two converging straight lines with one small cut at center. Surviving parts suggest that other two motifs may have been identical. Underside of base is covered with six-pointed star composed of two superimposed triangles. All cuts are 0.2–0.4 cm wide, and rough.

Missing part of base appears to have been removed with diamond saw, perhaps for chemical analysis. Surface dull; interiors of cuts matte.

COMMENT: In general terms, the decoration may have resembled the pattern on a linear-cut bottle in the al-Sabah Collection, Dār al-Āthār al-Islāmiyyah, Kuwait National Museum, which has a continuous band of alternating upright and inverted triangles (LNS 36 KG: Carboni 2001, p. 120, no. 2.20a).

183. Fragment of Beaker

10th to 11th century. Formerly in the Smith Collection (1221-24). Gift of Carl Berkowitz and Derek Content. 76.1.272.
H. (surviving) 3 cm, D. (est.) about 6 cm.
Almost colorless, with yellowish tinge. Blown; linear-cut.

Fragment from upper part of straight, vertical or slightly tapering wall (Th. 0.1 cm) of beaker with unpolished linear-cut decoration. Surviving ornament comprises small parts of upper border and frieze. Border consists of two horizontal cuts, 1.4 cm apart. Frieze apparently includes triangular motifs and hatching.

Broken on all sides. Dull and somewhat pitted; some light brownish weathering, especially in cuts.

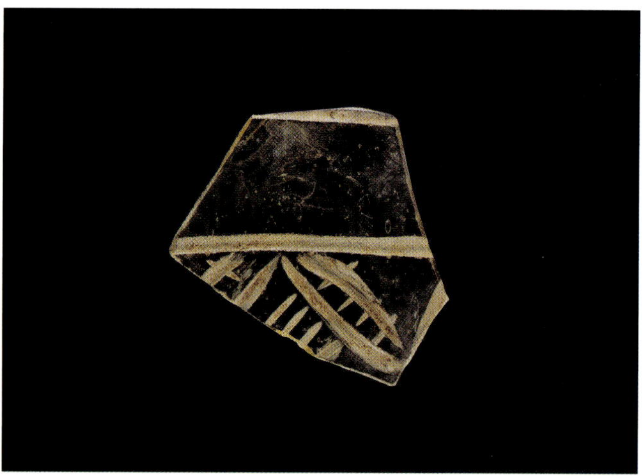

183

184. Fragment of Beaker

10th to 11th century. Formerly in the Smith Collection. 68.1.59-60.
Max. Dim. 2.8 cm, D. (est.) perhaps about 7 cm.
Almost colorless, with yellowish tinge. Blown; linear-cut.

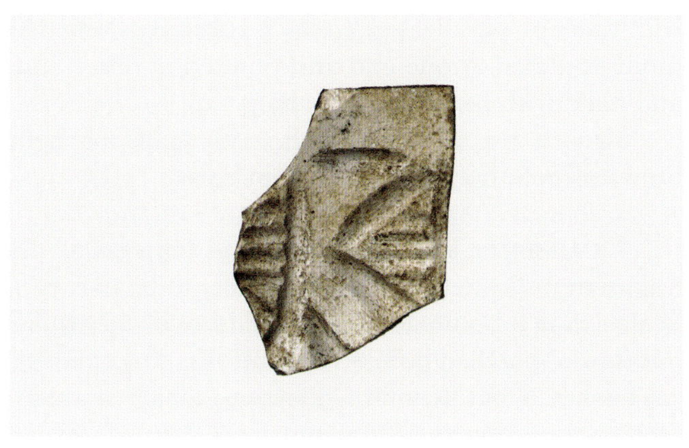

184

Fragment from rim and upper wall (Th. 0.1 cm) of beaker. Rim is plain, with ground top; wall appears to be vertical. Decorated with parts of two hatched triangular motifs, side by side; between them, at top, short horizontal cut, and, at bottom, part of transverse cut.

Broken on all sides except rim. Dull and pitted, with transparent pale grayish brown weathering.

185. Fragment of Beaker

9th to 10th century. Formerly in the Smith Collection. Gift of Carl Berkowitz and Derek Content. 76.1.271.
H. (surviving) 2.1 cm, D. (max., est.) about 4 cm.
Almost colorless, with yellowish tinge. Blown; linear-cut.

Fragment of beaker with straight, tapering wall (Th. 0.1 cm). Ornament consists of horizontal band with groove at top and at bottom. Band contains row of roughly semicircular motifs projecting downward from upper border and upward from lower border, each of which contains pair of short cuts and several incised dots; upper and lower semicircles touch one another. Spaces between each pair of semicircles are filled with crosshatching.

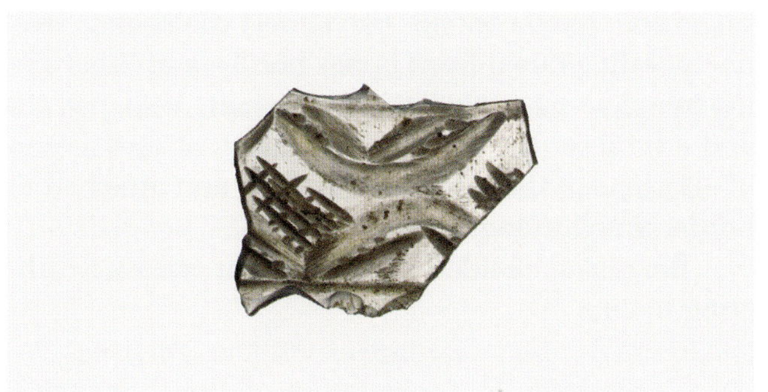

185

Broken on all sides. Cuts have pale gray, slightly iridescent weathering.

Comment: The decoration resembles the central band of ornament on a beaker excavated at Nishapur, northeastern Iran (Kröger 1995, pp. 157–158, no. 212).

186. Fragment of Beaker(?)

About 10th century. Formerly in the Smith Collection. 68.1.59-21.
H. (surviving) 4.4 cm, D. (est.) about 5–6 cm.
Almost colorless, with yellowish tinge. Blown; slant- and linear-cut.

Fragment from wall (Th. 0.1 cm) of beaker(?) with straight, perhaps tapering side. Decoration consists of two roughly parallel horizontal lines (W. 0.2 cm), presumably forming upper border of frieze. Below these, surviving part of frieze contains, on left, apex of narrow triangular panel flanked by narrow, pointed leaflike elements and containing hatched tear-shaped motif, and, on right, indeterminate curvilinear design.

Broken on all sides. Traces of iridescence.

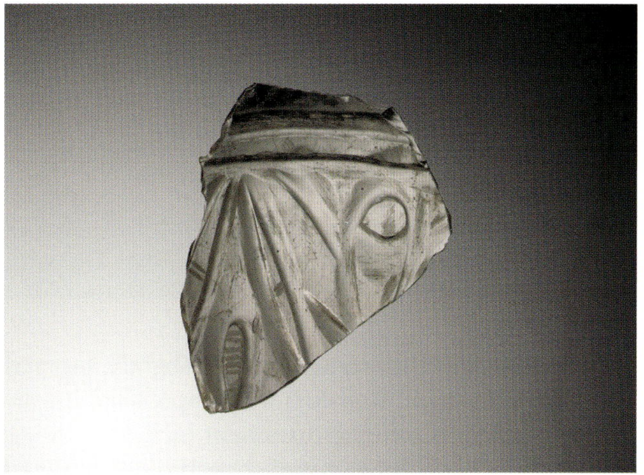

186

187. Fragment of Beaker(?)

10th to 11th century. Formerly in the Smith Collection (627-A). 76.1.273.
H. (surviving) 4.2 cm, D. (est.) about 5–6 cm.
Almost colorless, with greenish yellow tinge. Blown; linear-cut.

Fragment from straight, perhaps tapering lower wall (Th. 0.1–0.3 cm) of beaker(?) with unpolished linear-cut decoration. Ornament consists of interlaced or cable motif with hatched oval at center.

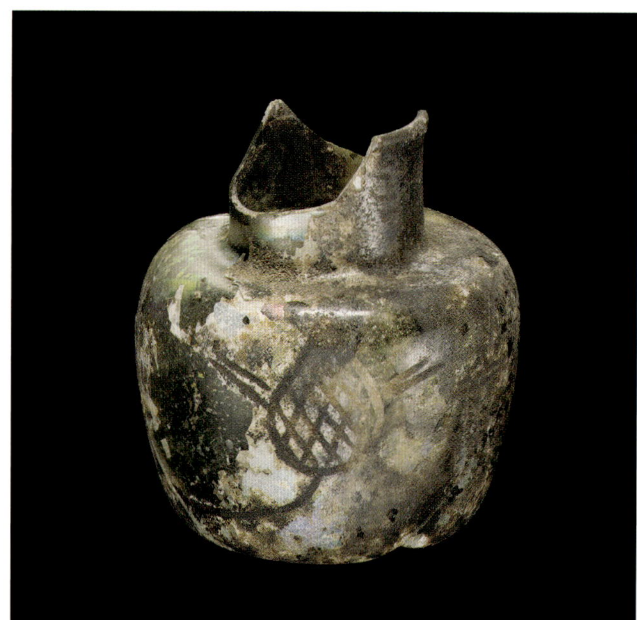

192

the underfill of an element of a domicile which was in ruins before the 10th century."

Bibliography: Scanlon and Pinder-Wilson 2001, p. 85, no. 40e.

193. Small Jar

9th to 11th century. 56.1.131.
H. 3.9 cm, D. (rim) 2.6 cm, (max., est.) 4 cm.
Colorless or almost colorless; bubbly. Blown; linear-cut.

Jar with globular body. Rim everted, with rounded lip; wall curves down, out, and in; base narrow and plain, perhaps with trace of pontil mark. Midsection of wall is decorated with continuous band of five pairs of hastily executed transverse cuts arranged to form row of V-shaped motifs; in triangular spaces inside each V and between each pair of Vs are one or two short oval cuts.

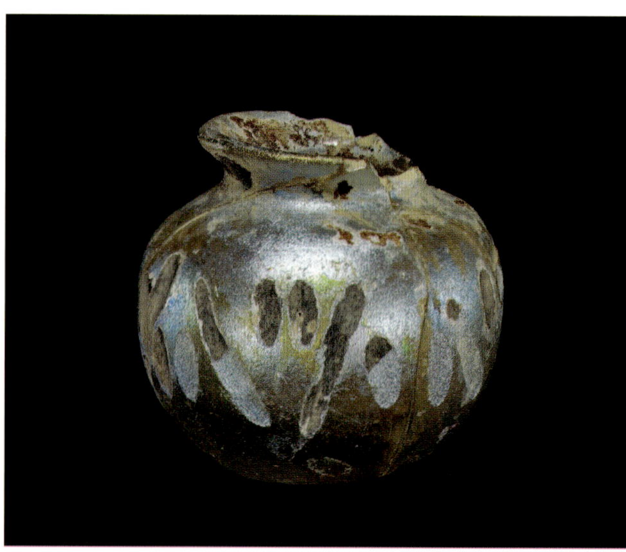

193

Incomplete. Broken and repaired; about 50 percent of rim is missing. Patches of matte dark brown weathering; where this has been lost, surface is iridescent.

Comment: Small globular jars, with or without decoration, are commonly found in archeological excavations, and they appear in numerous collections. However, the majority of these have short cylindrical necks (e.g., Kröger 1995, pp. 63–70, most of nos. 60–86). For examples with everted rims, see Auth 1976, pp. 228–229, nos. 517 and 518, and p. 232, no. 541.

194. Small Jar

9th to early 11th century. Formerly in the Strauss Collection (S1589). Gift of Jerome Strauss. 65.1.51.
H. 3 cm, D. (rim) 3.2 cm.
Semitransparent pale green. Blown; linear-cut.

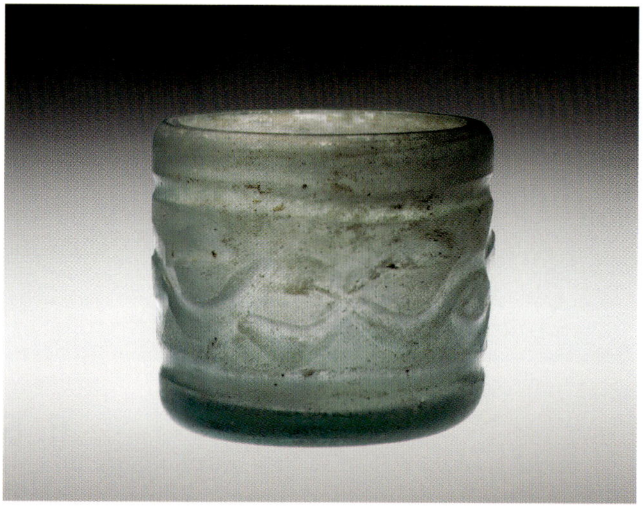

194

Jar: cylindrical. Base flat; sides straight and vertical; rim ground flat. On the side, rather irregular wheel-cut ornament consisting of continuous twisted ribbonlike motif between two horizontal lines. The ribbon consists of a wavy line with arc-shaped lines above and below.

Intact. Dull, but weathered only locally, usually in cuts.

Comment: Islamic sites such as Fusṭāṭ, Sīrāf, and Nishapur have yielded numerous small jars and bottles for ointments and cosmetic preparations (e.g., Scanlon and Pinder-Wilson 2001, pp. 50–53, nos. 22 and 23, which include 69.1.91 and 69.1.102, from Fusṭāṭ; and Kröger 1995, pp. 61–63, nos. 54–57, from Nishapur). **194** presumably was intended to contain a relatively costly substance, but something less expensive than the preparations placed in "molar flasks."

195. Small Jar

9th to 10th century. 56.1.119.
H. 2.4 cm, D. (lower wall, max.) 2.4 cm.
Almost colorless, with green tinge. Blown; linear-cut.

Jar with body shaped like lower part of pear. Rim plain (but see below); wall straight, expanding as it descends, but curving down and in at bottom; underside of base flat. Linear-cut decoration on wall: three equidistant and very similar raised tear-shaped motifs extending from rim to bottom of wall, each containing two horizontal cuts at midpoint and three vertical cuts beneath them; between each pair of tear-shaped motifs, single element consisting of vertical cut with, at top, two pairs of slanting cuts that rise as they proceed outward, and below bottom, two short horizontal cuts.

Intact, except for extensive chipping of rim. Dull and pitted, with traces of weathering and slight iridescence.

Comment: The object was acquired from the Tehran-based dealer Abbas Mazda, who maintained that it had been found at Rayy, Iran (letter dated April 23, 1956, on file at The Corning Museum of Glass).

Cf. Carboni 2001, p. 132, no. 2.36b.

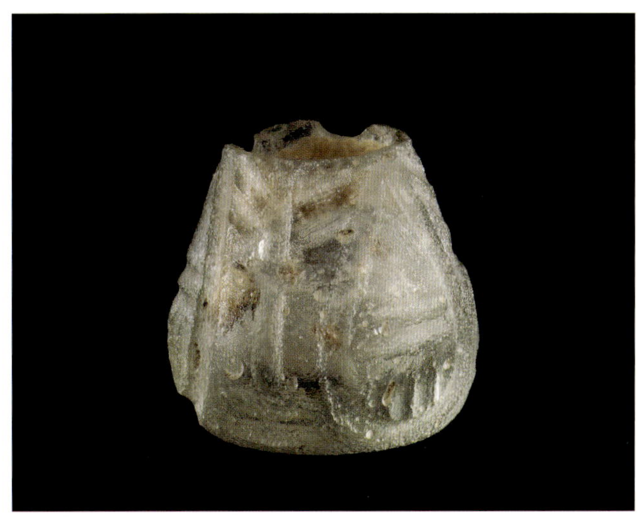

195

7. Large and Medium Bottles

196. Globular Bottle

10th to early 11th century. 59.1.582.
H. 25.5 cm, W. (rim) 5.4 cm, D. (max.) 18.1 cm.
Colorless or almost colorless. Blown; facet- and linear-cut.

Bottle with globular body. Rim is beveled on inner and outer sides of lip, and tapers; neck is wider at bottom than at top, and has straight side except at bottom, where it curves down and out; wall curves out, down, and in; base is slightly concave and has circular depression (D. 3 cm) at center; no pontil mark. Rim, neck, and wall have facet- and linear-cut ornament. On lip and outside of rim: 10 contiguous vertical facets. On neck: 11 contiguous vertical facets extending from top to bottom of straight section, below which, at bottom of curve, is one continuous band of 47 hollow circular facets bordered by groove at top and bottom. On wall: one continuous register bordered at top by pair of grooves and at bottom by single groove. Register contains 12 contiguous vertical panels, with single groove dividing each panel from its neighbors. Six panels are relatively broad and filled with crosshatching. These alternate with six narrower panels, each of which contains one vertical groove rising from apex of isosceles triangle formed by lower border of register and two pairs of short grooves; near top of vertical groove, one hollow circular facet, and at top of groove, triangular group of six hollow circular facets (one above two above three).

Incomplete. Body broken, with one large and several small losses; restored. Dull, with patches of silvery gray weathering and iridescence.

Comment: The form of the vessel, and in particular the treatment of the rim and the neck, is similar to that of a bottle, reputedly from Khorāsān Province, northeastern Iran, in the Museum für Islamische Kunst, Berlin (I.14/65: Kröger 1984, pp. 219–220, no. 191). The motif in the narrow panels is reminiscent of the more elaborate relief-cut motif on the underside of **296**, which is frequently interpreted as a stylized "tree of life" (see pages 176–178). The cross-hatched panels may be compared with the ornament on a ewer, said to be from Iran, in The British Museum, London (OA 1964.12-17.1: Pinder-Wilson 1991, 1999, and 2004, p. 117, fig. 143, left = *Masterpieces of Glass* 1968, p. 108, no. 142).

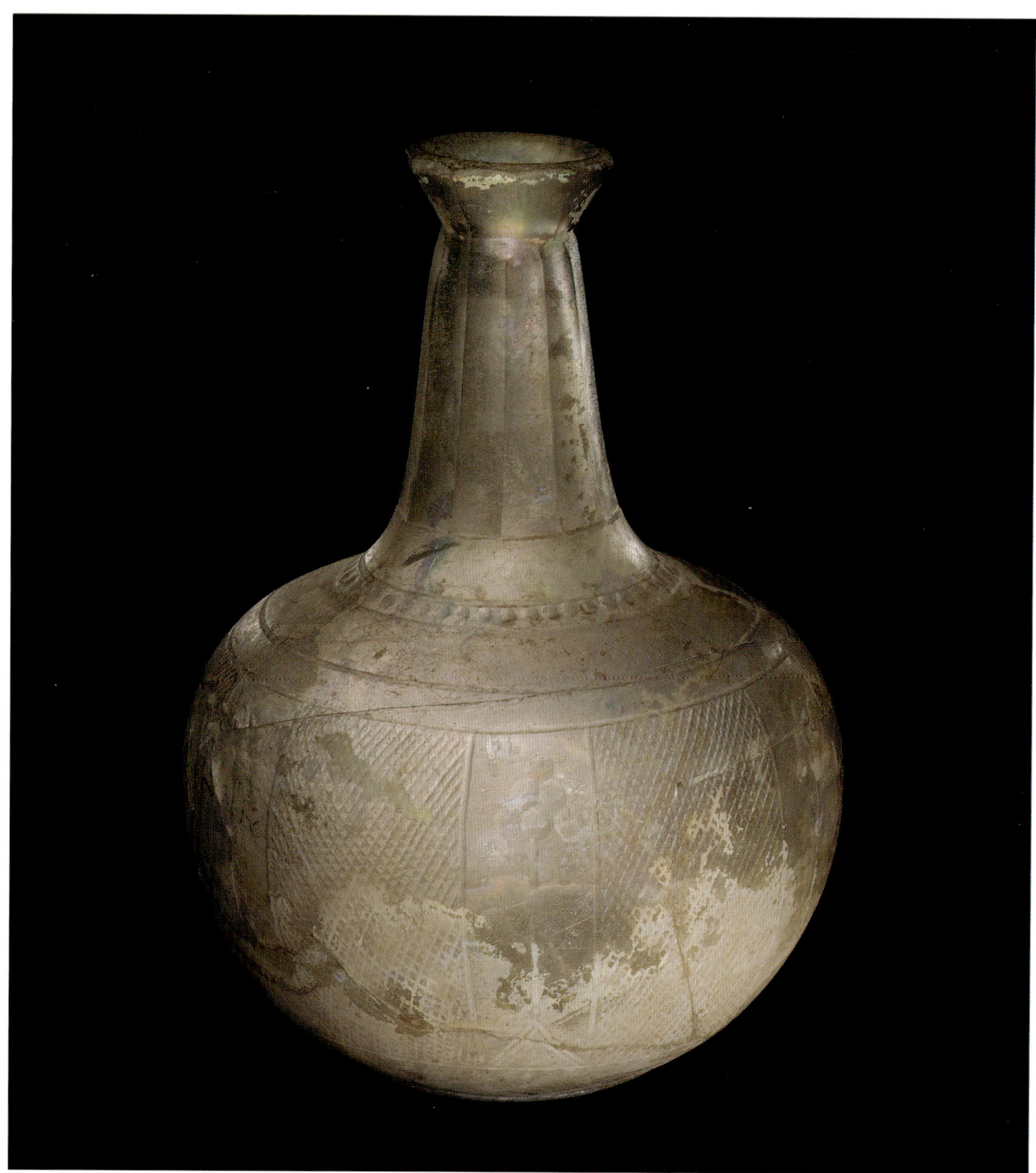

196

197. Globular Bottle

Probably 10th century. 54.1.106.
H. 23 cm, D. (rim) 2 cm, (max.) 9.5 cm, (base) 5.8 cm.
Almost colorless, with yellowish tinge; minute bubbles. Blown; facet-, linear-, and slant-cut.

Bottle with globular body. Rim plain, with flat top; neck cylindrical; wall curves out, down, and in; base has hollow foot-ring made by folding; no pontil mark. Decorated on neck and wall. On neck: four continuous horizontal bands (from top to bottom): (1) plain; (2 and 3) six narrow oval facets arranged to form row of chevrons, with one short horizontal cut in each triangle above and below chevrons; and (4) four tall rectangular facets. Above each band is one horizontal groove. On wall: continuous horizontal frieze of linear- and slant-cut ornament: two rhombuses with double outlines at top and single outlines at bottom, each containing one stylized tendril on curving stem, with short, straight cuts in background. On either side of rhombuses, wide ogival arch with double outline, in which upper lines spring from angles at sides of rhombuses and lower lines are parallel to outlines of bottoms of rhombuses. Each arch contains two stylized tendrils separated by hatched oval motif. In spandrels on either side of arches, similar tendril-like motifs with short, straight cuts in backgrounds. Frieze is bordered at top by narrow band of rudimentary chevrons and at bottom by single line.

Intact, except for minor chips in rim. Extensive pale buff to dark gray weathering; locally pitted.

COMMENT: The rhombuses and the band of chevronlike ornament on the wall are similar to decoration occupying the same positions on **269**. A closer parallel with the same form as **197**, a frieze containing two rhombuses separated by ogival arches, and numerous tendrillike motifs, which was allegedly found at Nishapur, northeastern Iran, is in the Museum für Islamische Kunst, Berlin (I.27/63: Kröger 1984, pp. 221–222, no. 192). Another bottle with the same form and very similar ornament on the body, said to have come from Sultanabad (modern Arāk) in western central Iran, is in The British Museum, London (OA 1913.10-9.1: Pinder-Wilson 1991, 1999, and 2004, p. 118, fig. 144, left = *Masterpieces of Glass* 1968, p. 109, no. 143). See also a bottle decorated with rhombuses, said to be from Gurgān Province, northern Iran, in The Metropolitan Museum of Art, New York (48.130: Clairmont 1972, pp. 148–149, no. 12).

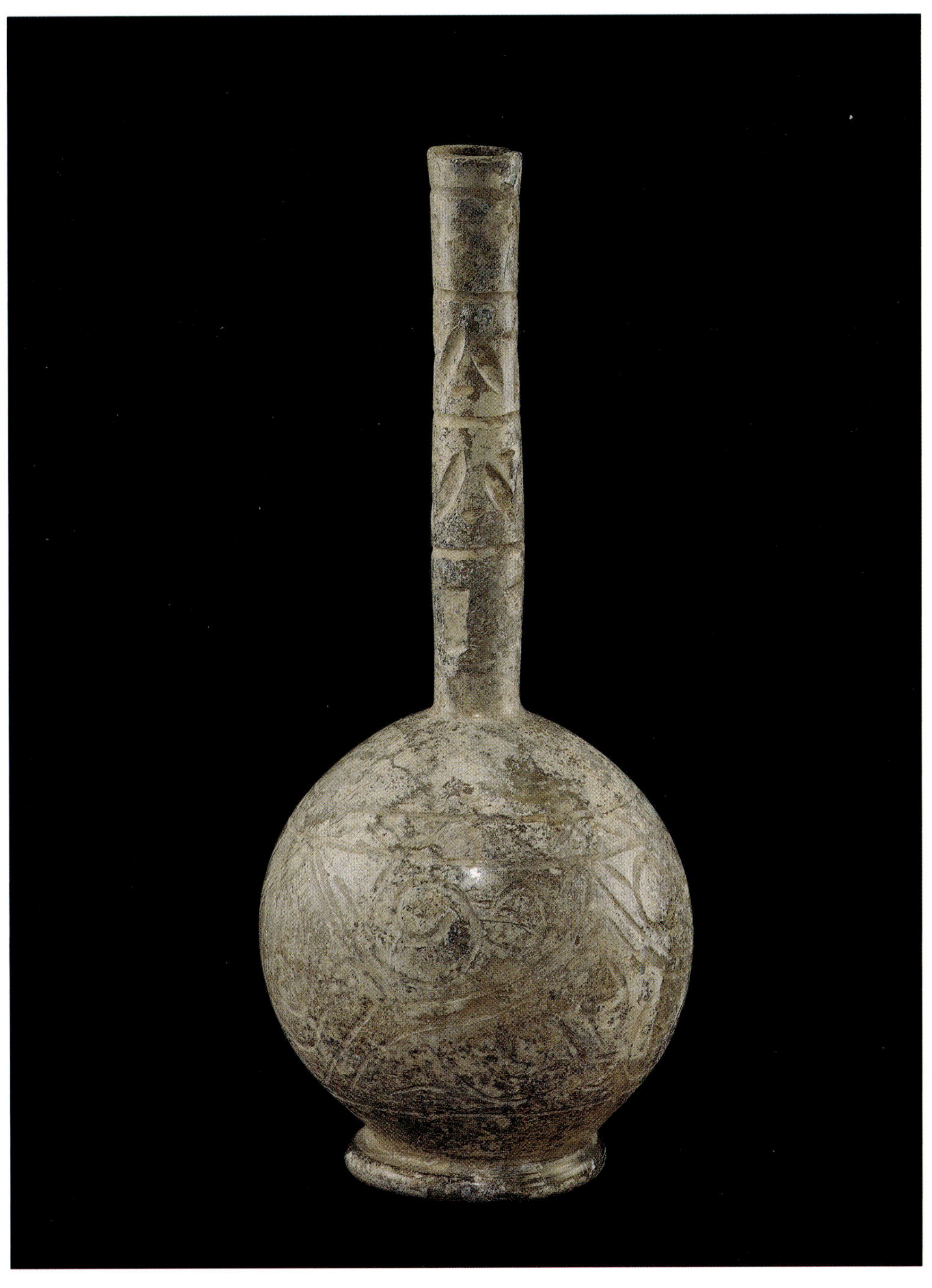

197

198. Globular Bottle

9th to 10th century. Formerly in the Smith Collection (579). 55.1.130.
H. 19.5 cm, D. (max.) 9.2 cm, (base) 6.7 cm.
Almost colorless, with greenish yellow tinge; many small and minute bubbles, and few impurities. Blown; facet- and linear-cut.

Bottle with globular body. Rim plain, with flat top; neck cylindrical; wall curves out, down, and in; base has tubular foot-ring made by folding; no pontil mark. Decorated on neck and wall. On neck: five continuous horizontal bands (from top to bottom): (1) plain, (2) row of four square facets, (3) six rhomboidal facets forming continuous band of tall, narrow chevrons, (4) row of four square facets, and (5) four tall rectangular facets; bands 1–3 are separated by continuous grooves, with additional grooves above 1 and below 3. On wall: continuous frieze framed at top and bottom by narrow bands of linear-cut chevrons with double lines, contained within grooves, and with additional groove

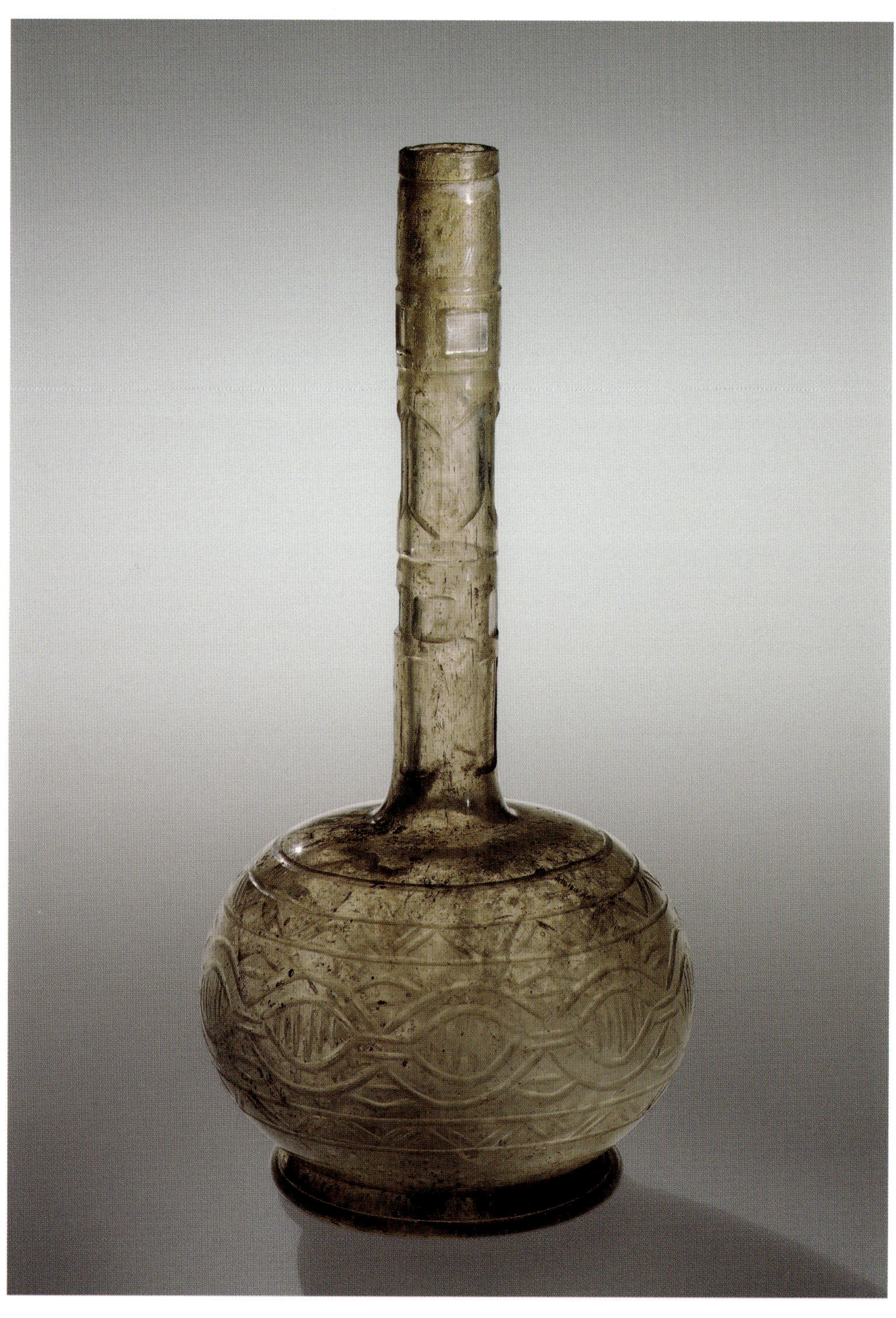

198

above upper band. Frieze contains 10 contiguous oval motifs with double outlines; each oval contains six short vertical cuts and has two horizontal cuts where it meets its neighbors; spaces above and below each junction are filled with one short horizontal cut and one longer arc-shaped cut.

Intact, except for chips in rim and circular hole (D. 0.5 cm) drilled in base (see below). Slightly weathered, with light brown accretion on interior.

COMMENT: Cf. **269**, which has an identical pattern of facets on the neck, and **197**. The form is similar to that of a bottle in the al-Sabah Collection, Dār al-Āthār al-Islāmiyyah, Kuwait National Museum (LNS 42 G: Carboni 2001, p. 132, no. 2.35).

BIBLIOGRAPHY: *Antikes Glas* 1951, p. 11, no. 80; *Antikes Glas* 1952–3, p. 20, no. 113; *Verres antiques* 1954, p. 54, no. 330; *Glass from the Ancient World* 1957, pp. 274–275, no. 570.

199. Fragment of Globular Bottle

10th to 11th century. 64.1.69.
H. (surviving) 6.4 cm, D. (max., est.) about 9 cm.
Almost colorless, with greenish tinge. Blown; linear-cut.

Fragment from wall (Th. 0.15–0.2 cm) of bottle with globular body. Decorated with three horizontal bands of ornament (described from top, assuming that motifs are repetitive): (1) with single horizontal border at bottom, and with row of oval motifs, each with poorly defined circle at center; (2) also with single horizontal border at bottom, and with upright and inverted V-shaped motifs in spaces between borders and outer circles; and (3) with pair of horizontal borders at bottom, and with band of herringbone hatching.

Broken on all sides. Dull, with light gray weathering, especially in cuts.

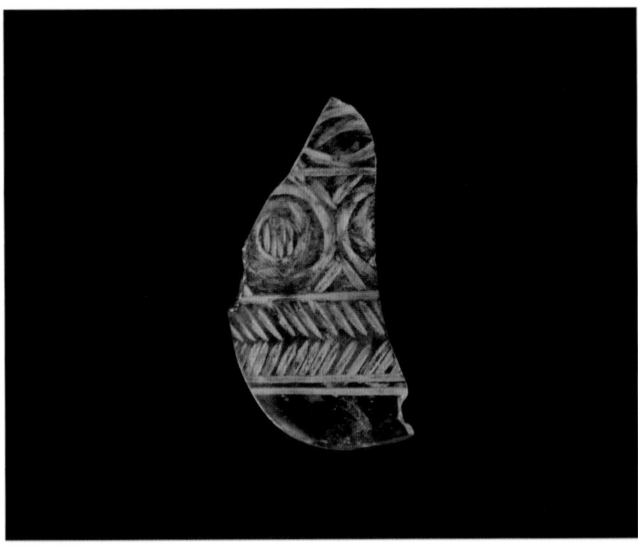

199

COMMENT: The shape of the fragment suggests that it is part of the wall of a bottle with a globular body, and its variable thickness further suggests that the orientation is as described above, with the greater thickness toward the bottom. The fragment was identified as Islamic when it entered the collection in 1964, and although parallels for the ornament are difficult to find, there seems to be no reason to revise this identification: cf., for example, the rows of contiguous circles, each with a countersunk circle at the center, on a bottle in the Cohn Collection at the Los Angeles County Museum of Art (*Cohn Collection* 1980, p. 161, no. 155).

200. Cylindrical Bottle with Bulls

10th to early 11th century. Formerly in the Smith Collection (1237). 55.1.126.
H. 25.5 cm, D. (rim) 7.6 cm, (shoulder) 13.6 cm, (base) 10.2 cm.
Transparent emerald green; small bubbles. Blown; facet- and linear-cut.

Bottle with roughly cylindrical body. Rim is broad flange with rounded lip; neck cylindrical, but wider at bottom than at top; shoulder rounded; wall tapers slightly and curves in at bottom; base plain and slightly concave; irregular pontil mark (Max. Dim. 2.1 cm).

Top of rim, neck, shoulder, and wall have rather perfunctory facet- and linear-cut ornament. Top of rim is decorated with eight pairs of short radial cuts that begin at lip. Neck has three continuous horizontal bands of facets bordered by one or two grooves. Bands contain following motifs (from top to bottom): (1) and (2) five contiguous pairs of triangular facets forming motifs shaped like bow ties, and (3) 10 rectangular facets. Decoration on shoulder consists of two continuous horizontal bands separated by groove: (1) upper band is bordered by pair of grooves at top and consists of 14 contiguous linear-cut lozenges; and (2) lower band is bordered by single groove at bottom and consists of about 33 shallow circular and oval facets. Wall is decorated with broad horizontal band bordered at bottom by one groove, which forms groundline for three linear-cut bulls with long, curving horns, walking in left profile. At bottom of wall, continuous row of about 50 small transverse oval facets.

Incomplete. Broken into many pieces, with small losses in shoulder and loss of about 30 percent of wall (object sustained further damage in the Corning flood of 1972: see page 10); restored. Dull or matte, and pitted, with patches of light brown enamellike weathering.

Comment: Ray Winfield Smith (see below) reported that the object came from Iran.

Bibliography: *Glass from the Ancient World* 1957, p. 269, no. 548; Smith 1957, p. 99.

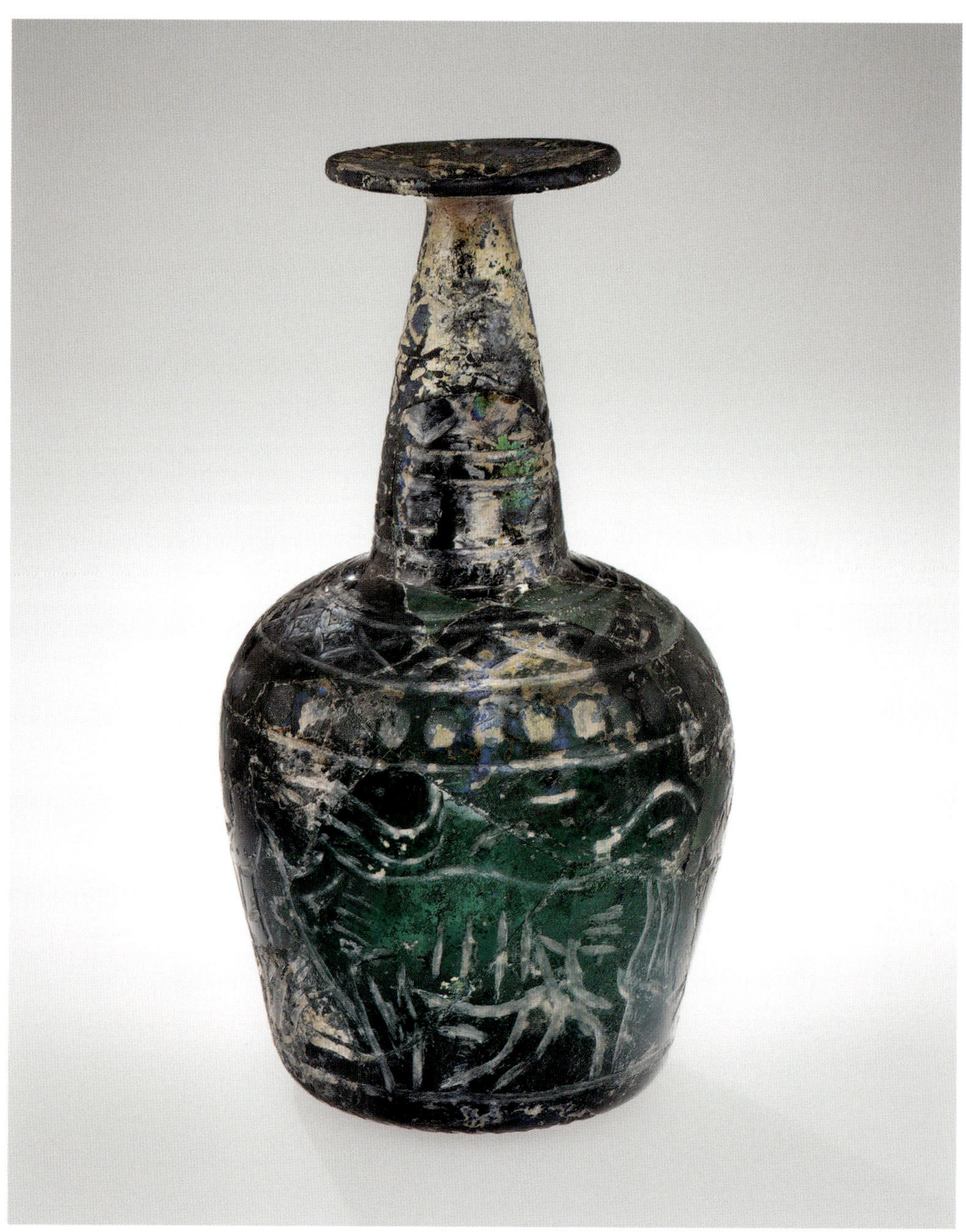

200

201. Cylindrical Bottle

9th to 10th century. Formerly in the Smith Collection (519). 55.1.124.
H. 12.7 cm, D. (rim) 5 cm, (base) 7.4 cm.
Colorless; one large bubble (L. 2.5 cm) in neck, and few small bubbles. Blown; facet- and linear-cut.

Bottle with cylindrical body. Rim in form of horizontal flange with rounded lip; neck cylindrical; shoulder slopes and has rounded edge; wall is vertical before curving in at bottom; base plain; pontil mark (D. 1 cm). Decoration on neck, shoulder, and wall. On neck: uppermost two-thirds has band containing seven vertical rows of oval facets, with three facets in each row, above one continuous groove. On shoulder: one

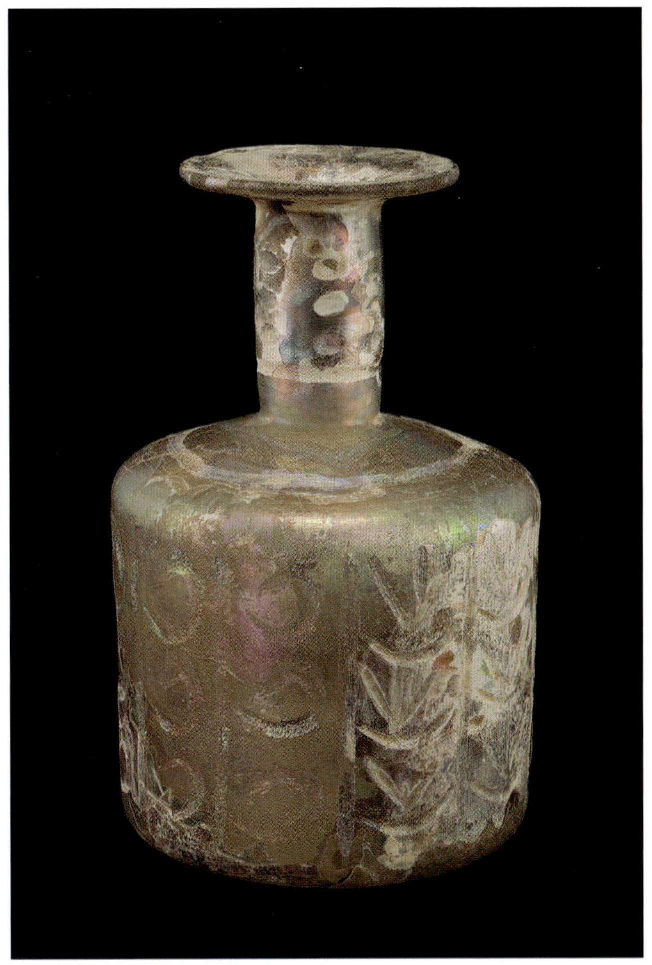

201

continuous horizontal groove. On wall: 10 vertical panels separated by single vertical lines. Each panel contains vertical row of similar linear-cut motifs (clockwise): (1–3) three hook-shaped motifs, (4 and 5) three motifs that consist of short vertical line bisecting V-shaped element above shallow horizontal crescent, (6) perhaps like (1–3), (7) uncertain, and (8–10) like (4) and (5).

Intact, except for circular hole (D. 0.6 cm) in base (see below). Dull and pitted, with light silvery gray weathering, especially in cuts, and patches of iridescence.

Comment: According to the catalog entry in *Verres antiques* (see below), the object was acquired in Iran. Ray Winfield Smith (in *Glass from the Ancient World*: see below) suggested that the geometric motifs on the wall are "stylized Cufic characters," but this seems unlikely. The hole drilled in the base was presumably made by Smith to acquire a sample for chemical analysis.

Bibliography: *Verres antiques* 1954, p. 54, no. 333; *Glass from the Ancient World* 1957, pp. 270–271, no. 557.

202. Neck of Bottle

About 11th century. 55.1.48.
Max. Dim. 15.7 cm, H. (neck) 14.8 cm, D. (rim) 2 cm.
Transparent pale yellowish green; numerous elongated bubbles and some scale. Blown; linear-cut.

Neck of bottle: narrow and cylindrical. Rim plain, with top ground flat; neck descends almost vertically, but is slightly wider near bottom than at top, and it has small constriction just above shoulder, which curves out and down. Neck has broad band of linear decoration, which was cut but not polished, and which begins 2.6 cm below rim and ends 3.8 cm above shoulder. Decoration consists of latticelike pattern of diagonal cuts, none of which join. Cuts form two pairs of roughly diamond-shaped panels, with two open triangles at top of lattice and two at bottom. Panels in upper pair are about 4.5 cm high, and those in lower pair are about 5 cm high. Upper panels are filled with four short cuts at right angles to side, which do not touch but form crosslike design and have one shorter oval cut above and one below; junctions of upper panels are marked by two short oval cuts. Lower panels are similar, but have two short oval cuts above cross and two below it. Each triangular space at top

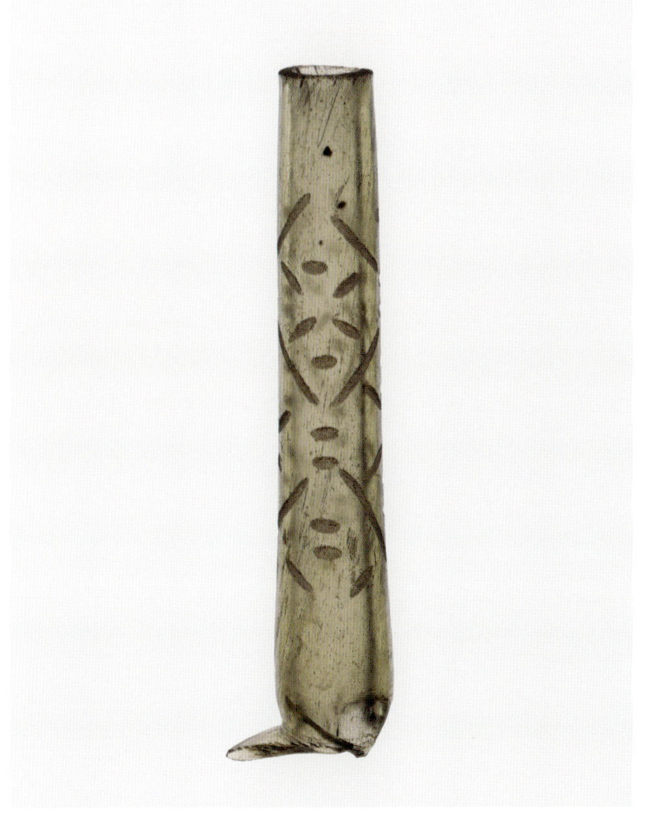

202

of decoration contains one short oval cut, while each triangular space at bottom contains two short oval cuts and two longer diagonal cuts. Constricted area at bottom of neck has narrow band of light abrasion.

Almost all of neck and very small part of upper shoulder survive. Dull and pitted, with traces of weathering in cut surfaces.

COMMENT: The object is related to the long tubular necks with faceted decoration that are commonly found on bottles with globular bodies, such as **266**. However, the replacement of more or less carefully executed facets by rather irregular, unpolished linear decoration suggests a date in the 11th century.

203. Base of Bottle

Probably 10th to 11th century. Formerly in the Smith Collection (1132). Gift of Carl Berkowitz and Derek Content. 76.1.216.
Max. Dim. 7.2 cm.
Transparent pale yellowish green; small bubbles. Blown; linear-cut.

Base of bottle: flat, thicker at center than at edge; irregular pontil mark (W. 2 cm). At center: linear-cut, unpolished, roughly equilateral triangle (L. of sides 2.9–3.2 cm). In one corner and in adjacent area outside triangle, patch of shallow abrasion, which was made before the sides of the triangle.

About two-thirds of base survives. Broken on all sides. Underside is dull.

COMMENT: The pontil mark includes a deep gouge, which interrupts one side of the triangle, presumably because the diameter of the cutting wheel prevented it from reaching the bottom. Perhaps the abrasion was an abandoned attempt to eliminate the pontil mark.

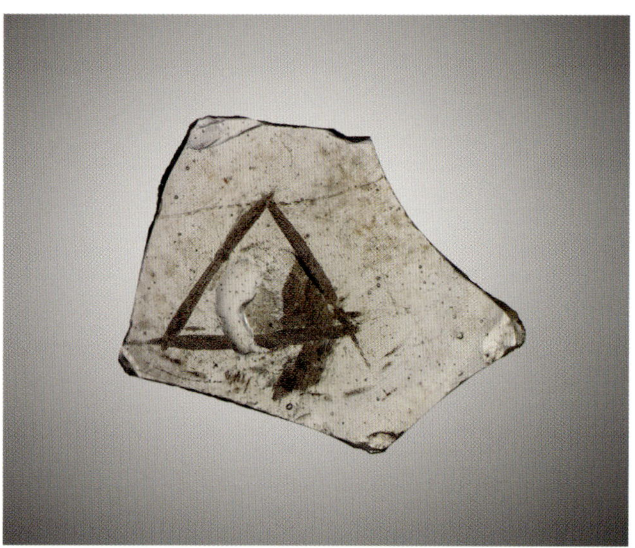

203

204. Base of Bottle

Probably 10th to 11th century. Formerly in the Smith Collection (1135). 59.1.470.
H. (surviving) 1.1 cm, D. 6.6 cm.
Transparent pale yellowish green. Blown; linear-cut.

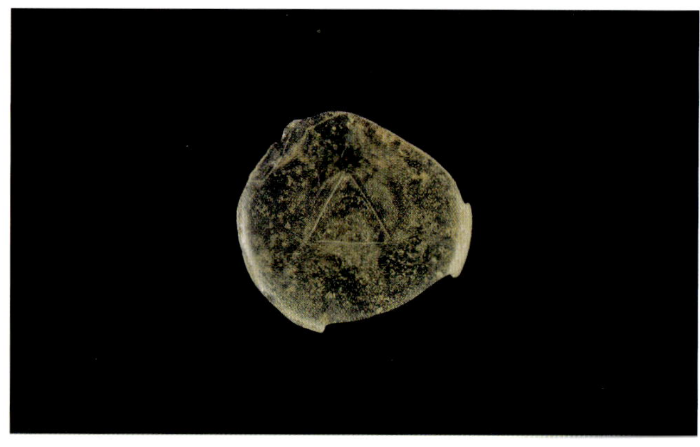

204

Base of bottle. Bottom of wall curves down and in; base flat, thicker at center than at edge; pontil mark almost completely removed by grinding. At center, linear-cut equilateral triangle (L. of sides 2.6 cm).

Broken on all sides. Dull, and speckled with light brownish gray weathering.

205. Fragment of Bottle

9th to 10th century. 51.1.125.
H. (surviving) 4.2 cm, D. (border, est.) about 14 cm.
Colorless. Blown; linear- and slant-cut.

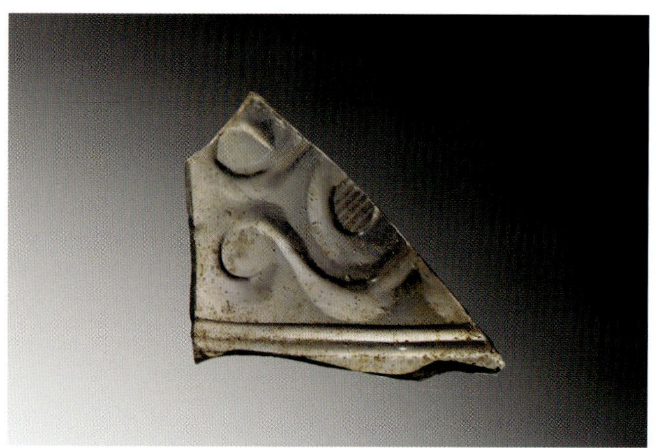

205

Fragment of bottle. Lower wall straight and tapered. Decorated with band of ornament bordered at bottom by two closely spaced horizontal grooves. Surviving decoration consists of slant-cut oval motif filled with linear-cut transverse hatching and framed above and below by slant-cut crescents that extend at either side and terminate in volutes.

Broken on all sides. Transparent, slightly iridescent weathering.

Comment: The size and shape of the fragment suggest that it came from the lower wall of a bottle that may have been similar in form to **67**.

206. Fragment of Bottle or Jar

9th to early 11th century. Formerly in the Smith Collection (1221-15). Gift of Carl Berkowitz and Derek Content. 76.1.276.
Max. Dim. 3.9 cm, D. (body, est.) about 6 cm.
Almost colorless, with yellowish green tinge.
Blown; linear-cut.

Fragment from shoulder and wall of bottle or jar, with vestige of neck. Shoulder and upper wall are rounded, below which wall begins to curve down and in. Wall has linear-cut motif, which, if it was symmetrical, consisted of circle (D. about 3 cm) containing diamond-shaped motif with hollow sides; interior of diamond was crosshatched, and each space between circle and side of diamond had one short transverse cut.

Broken on all sides. Slight weathering in cuts.

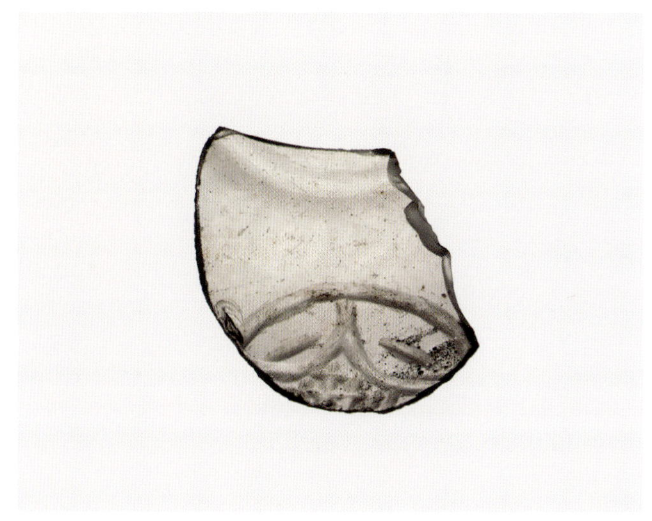

206

8. Small Bottles

207. Small Bottle

Date uncertain, perhaps 19th century. Formerly in the Smith Collection (810). 55.1.114.
H. 8.5 cm, D. (rim) 1.5 cm, W. (body) 3.6 cm and 2.7 cm (see below).
Transparent yellowish brown; apparently bubble-free. Mold-blown; facet- and linear-cut.

Bottle. Rim plain, with flat top; neck short and cylindrical; body has two broad and two narrow vertical faces; base plain; no pontil mark. Body is divided by two continuous horizontal grooves into short upper part with square horizontal cross section, taller middle part with rectangular cross section, and short lower part with square cross section. In upper part: each broad face has two deep cuts arranged to form inverted V, and each narrow face has, at bottom, raised semicircular motif with sloping flange at bottom; in middle part, each broad face consists of rectangular panel bordered on all four sides by grooves and decorated with raised pointed oval motif filled with crosshatching, narrow faces are plain, and junctions of all four faces are chamfered; in lower part, each broad face has incised cross with arms of unequal length, and each narrow face has, at top, raised semicircular motif with sloping flange at top.

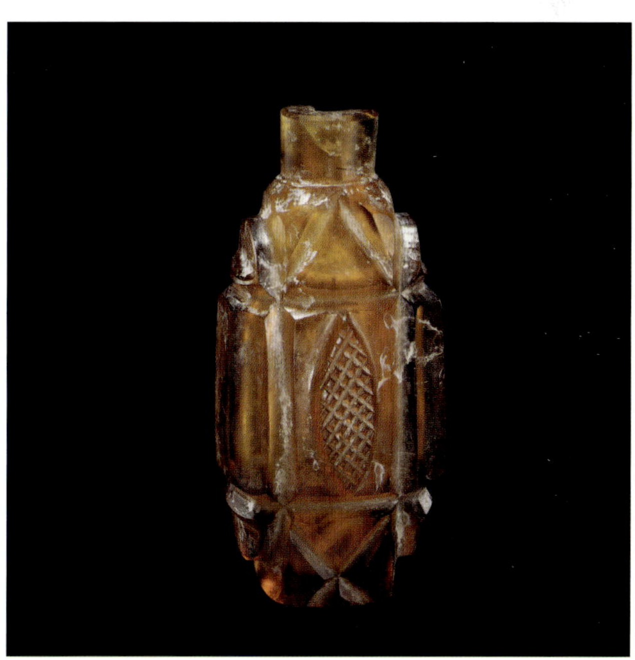

207

Body complete, but half of rim and neck are missing. Traces of pale grayish weathering and iridescence.

Comment: Ray Winfield Smith (in *Glass from the Ancient World* 1957) maintained that the object "shows considerable affinity to Islamic cut work of about the 10th century A.D.," but he added a note of caution: "Its antiquity, however, is by no means assured, and it can well be a nineteenth-century product, possibly Turkish." Neither the form nor the character of the cutting has close parallels among early Islamic cut glass, and I believe that Smith's uncertainty was amply justified.

Bibliography: *Antikes Glas* 1952–3, p. 20, no. 111; *Verres antiques* 1954, p. 48, no. 289; *Glass from the Ancient World* 1957, p. 283, no. 598.

208. Small Bottle

9th to 11th century. Formerly in the collection of Maurice Nahman, Cairo, Egypt. 53.1.40.
H. 8 cm, W. (rim) 1.6 cm.
Transparent light yellowish green. Blown (body perhaps blown in dip mold); facet- and linear-cut.

Bottle with cylindrical body. Rim plain, with top ground flat; neck roughly cylindrical, but wider at top than at bottom; shoulder rounded; wall descends vertically, then tapers at bottom; base solid and shaped like shallow truncated cone. Facet- and linear-cut decoration on neck and wall. On neck: upper two-thirds cut in five contiguous rectangular facets with heights twice their widths; below them, continuous horizontal groove. On wall: two registers separated by continuous horizontal groove. Upper register occupies one-third of wall and contains two V-shaped facets with sides separated only at top, alternating with two facets shaped like inverted U with sides separated only at bottom. Lower register occupies two-thirds of wall and contains two facets shaped like truncated isosceles triangles with two triangular "steps" adjoining base, alternating with two identical motifs, which are inverted.

Intact. No apparent weathering; interior is dirty.

Comment: The object was acquired in Cairo and probably was found there.

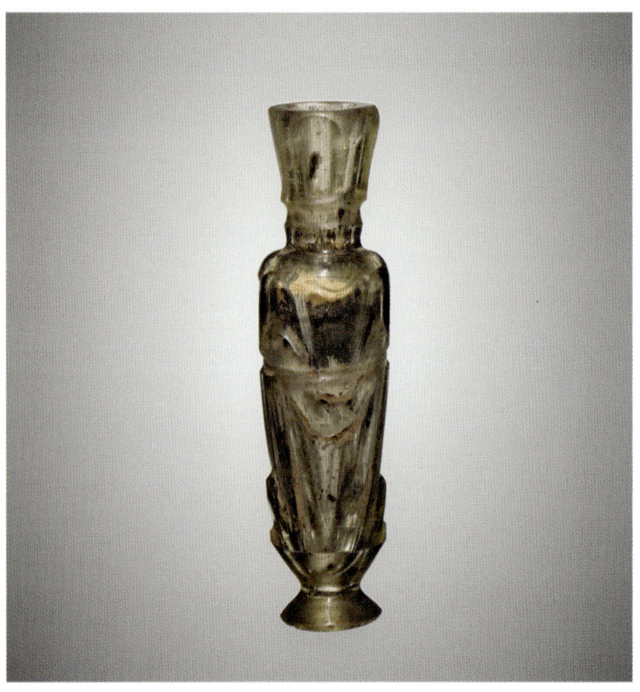

208

209. Small Bottle

Probably 10th to 11th century, but possibly later. Formerly in the collection of Maurice Nahman, Cairo, Egypt. 53.1.39.
H. 8 cm, D. (rim) 2.25 cm.
Transparent bluish green; small bubbles, and black inclusions near rim. Blown (body perhaps blown in dip mold); linear-cut.

Bottle with cylindrical body. Rim plain, with rounded lip; neck shaped like funnel; shoulder rounded; wall vertical, curving in at bottom; base flat; pontil mark. Rather perfunctory decoration on neck and

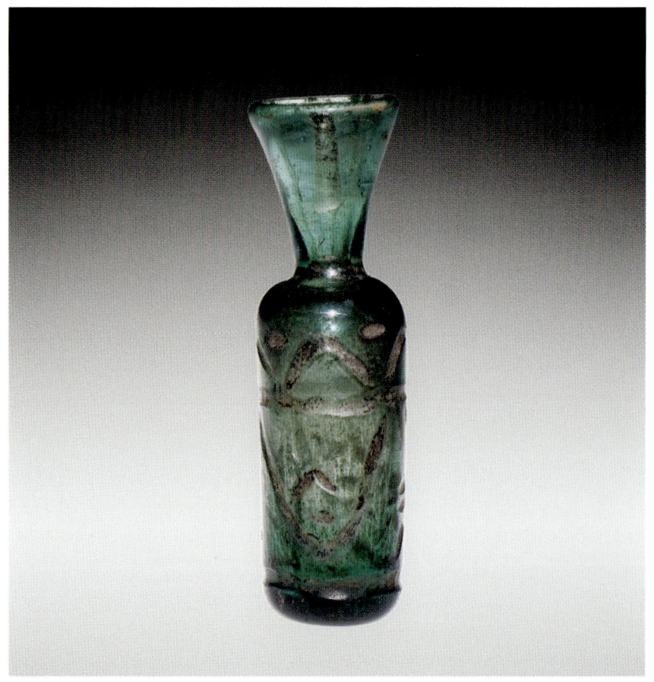

209

wall, using cuts 0.2–0.25 cm wide. On neck: three equidistant vertical cuts extending from rim two-thirds of distance to bottom. On wall: two registers, each with continuous horizontal groove at bottom. Upper register occupies one-third of wall and contains four inverted U- or V-shaped motifs, separated at top by single short oval cuts. Lower register occupies two-thirds of wall and contains three large U-shaped motifs, each of which has, inside, inverted V-shaped motif above single oval cut and, outside, inverted V-shaped motif above two oval cuts.

Complete. Crack runs from midpoint of wall to center of base. Grayish weathering in cuts, but not on unworked surface.

Comment: The object was acquired in Cairo and probably was found in Egypt.

210. Small Bottle

Probably 10th to 11th century, but possibly later. Formerly in the collection of Maurice Nahman, Cairo, Egypt. 53.1.42.
H. 7.25 cm, D. (rim) 1.9 cm.
Probably almost colorless, with greenish tinge. Blown (body perhaps blown in dip mold); facet- and linear-cut.

Bottle with cylindrical body. Rim folded in and flattened; neck shaped like funnel; shoulder rounded; wall vertical, curving in at bottom; base flat; no pontil mark. Rather perfunctory decoration on neck and wall, using cuts 0.15–0.25 cm wide. On neck: three triangular facets extending from apexes at rim to bases two-thirds of distance to bottom; below them is one continuous horizontal groove. On wall: two registers, each with continuous horizontal groove at bottom. Upper register is narrower and contains five triangular facets alternating with vertical cuts. Lower register has two inverted V-shaped motifs with curved sides; each contains two triangular cuts flanked by short transverse lines; each space between V-shaped motifs contains one triangular cut and two transverse lines.

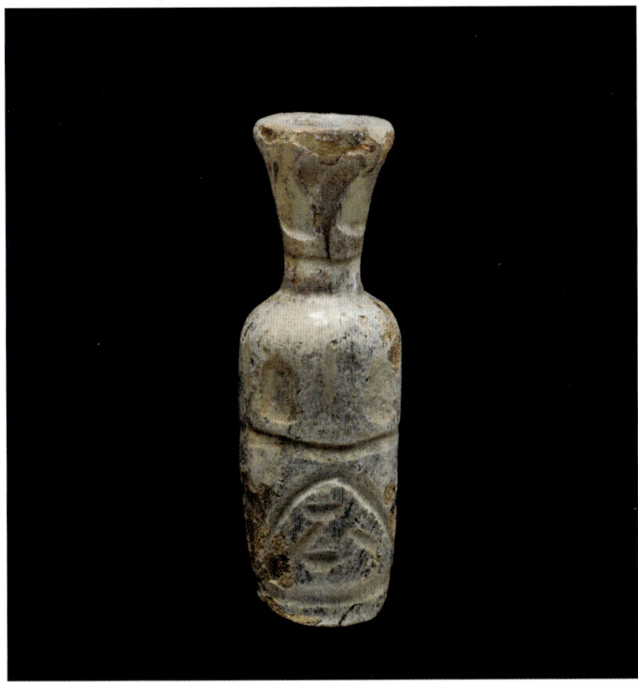

210

Intact, except for chips in rim and edge of base. Thick layer of slightly iridescent light greenish gray weathering.

Comment: The object was acquired in Cairo and probably was found in Egypt.

211. Small Bottle

10th to 11th century. Anonymous gift. 2009.1.18.
H. (surviving) 5.2 cm, D. (max.) 3.3 cm.
Almost colorless, with grayish tinge. Blown; linear-cut.

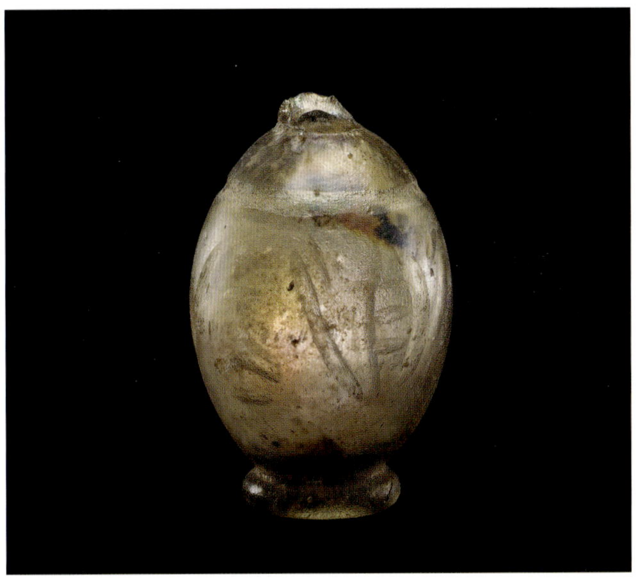

211

Bottle: egg-shaped. Bottom of neck cylindrical; wall descends in smooth convex curve; foot narrow and disk-shaped; base flat; no pontil mark. Decoration on wall consists of continuous horizontal groove about 1 cm below bottom of neck; beneath this, two opposed motifs, each consisting of V-shaped element enclosing oval filled with three short horizontal cuts; these alternate with two groups of three short horizontal cuts and one crescent-shaped cut.

Incomplete. Body and foot are intact, but rim and almost entire neck are missing. Remains of grayish iridescent weathering.

212. Small Bottle

9th to 10th century. Found during excavations at Fusṭāṭ (Old Cairo), Egypt (68.12.49). Gift of the American Research Center in Egypt. 69.1.88.
H. 4.8 cm, D. (rim) 1.3 cm, (body) 1.4 cm.
Perhaps transparent light green. Blown; facet- and linear-cut.

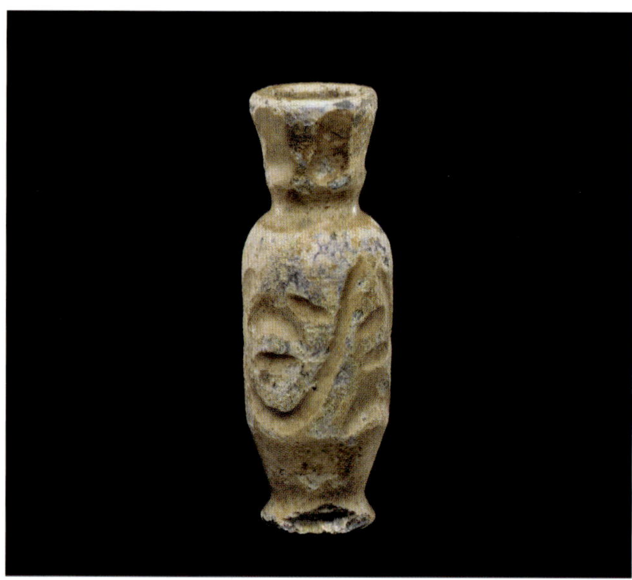

212

Bottle with cylindrical body. Rim plain, with flat top; neck tapers; shoulder rounded; wall straight, tapering at bottom; base splays slightly and is flat on underside; no pontil mark. Neck is decorated with continuous band of six hollow facets with straight sides and rounded tops and bottoms. Wall has continuous band composed of two V-shaped motifs, which touch at upper extremities; triangular spaces between Vs are filled with groups of short cuts and crescent-shaped facets.

Intact, except for chips in edge of base. Matte pale buff to light greenish weathering.

Comment: The object was found during excavations directed by Prof. George T. Scanlon. Scanlon and Pinder-Wilson (see below) report that it was discovered "in the fill of a room that was part of an enthronged [*sic*] 11th century domicile."

Bibliography: Scanlon and Pinder-Wilson 2001, p. 96, no. 421.

213. Small Bottle

9th to 11th century. Formerly in the collection of Maurice Nahman, Cairo, Egypt. 53.1.44.
H. (surviving) 4.4 cm, D. (shoulder) 2 cm.
Almost colorless, with faint greenish tinge.
Blown (body perhaps blown in dip mold); linear- and perhaps facet-cut.

Bottle with cylindrical body. Lower neck cylindrical; shoulder slopes; wall descends vertically, then tapers at bottom; base splays slightly and is solid; no pontil mark. Upper part of neck perhaps decorated with six contiguous facets. Wall has linear-cut decoration extending from continuous horizontal groove below shoulder to just above taper: three V-shaped motifs, which touch one another at top; each contains smaller V-shaped motif with triangular cut; each space between large V-shaped motifs is filled with two triangular cuts. Base ground flat.

Incomplete. Rim and upper neck are missing. Pitted, with light grayish, slightly iridescent weathering.

Comment: The object was acquired in Cairo and may have been found there.

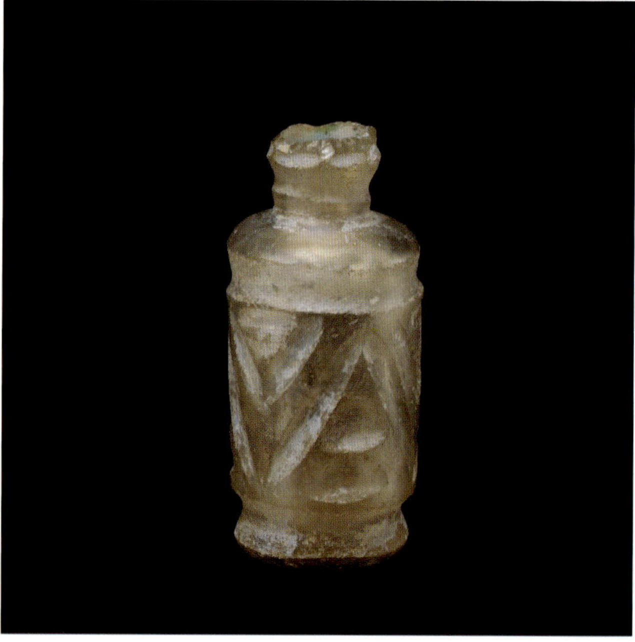

213

214. Small Bottle

9th to 11th century. 64.1.80.
H. (surviving) 4 cm, D. (max.) 2.1 cm.
Almost colorless, with greenish tinge. Blown (body perhaps blown in dip mold); facet- and linear-cut.

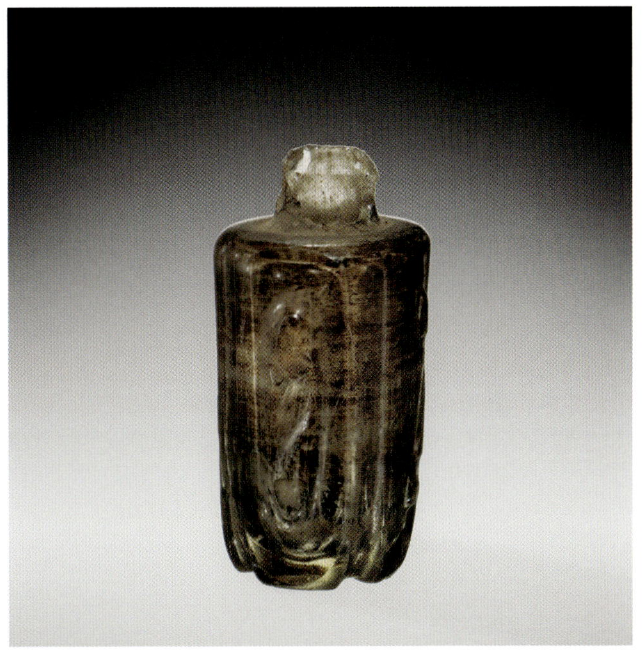

214

Bottle with cylindrical body. Lower neck cylindrical, perhaps with hollow horizontal rib; shoulder flat; wall straight, tapering very slightly; base flat; no pontil mark. Facet- and linear-cut decoration on wall and underside of base: four equidistant vertical grooves extend from top to bottom and continue under base, forming cross; grooves separate four identical panels, rounded at bottom, with flat faces; each panel has raised rectangular motif, rounded at top and bottom, containing linear-cut Z-shaped motif. Base ground and polished.

Incomplete. Rim and most of neck are missing. No obvious weathering; unidentified deposit on interior.

215. Small Bottle

Date uncertain. 56.1.120.
H. (surviving) 2.1 cm, D. (max.) 3.4 cm.
Almost colorless, with greenish tinge. Blown; linear-cut.

Bottle with body shaped like cushion. Shoulder flat, with rounded edge; wall curves down, out, and in; base plain; pontil mark (W. 1.1 cm). Shallow linear-cut decoration on wall: two almost identical motifs consisting of vertical line with short horizontal line at top and bottom; on either side, extending outward from bottom at about 45 degrees, straight line that terminates in E-shaped motif. Motifs are separated by pairs of vertical lines.

Incomplete. Rim and neck are missing. Dull and pitted, with remains of weathering on interior.

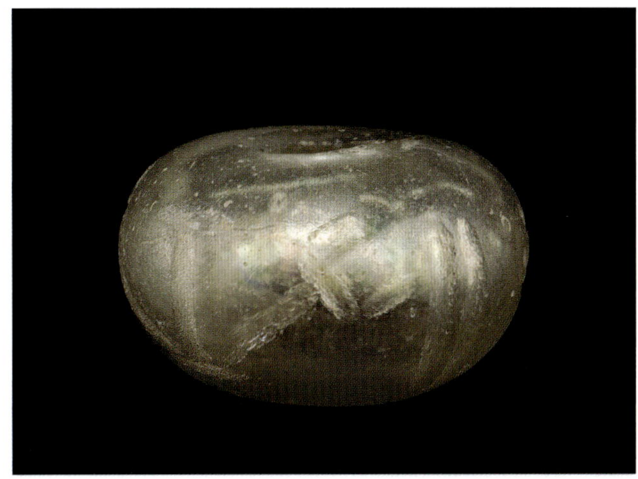

215

Comment: The date and origin of this object are uncertain.

216. Fragment of Small Bottle

About 9th to 11th century. Formerly in the Smith Collection. Gift of Carl Berkowitz and Derek Content. 76.1.279.
H. (surviving) 2.4 cm, D. (rim, est.) about 2 cm.
Transparent deep blue. Blown; facet- and linear-cut.

Fragment of small bottle. Rim plain with rounded, somewhat irregular lip; neck cylindrical; shoulder appears to slope down toward edge. Decoration on neck consists of two pairs of transverse cuts converging at top and, below them, horizontal band of roughly circular hollow facets. Cuts show no sign of polishing.

About one-quarter of rim survives; other edges broken. Surface has no obvious weathering; cuts are matte.

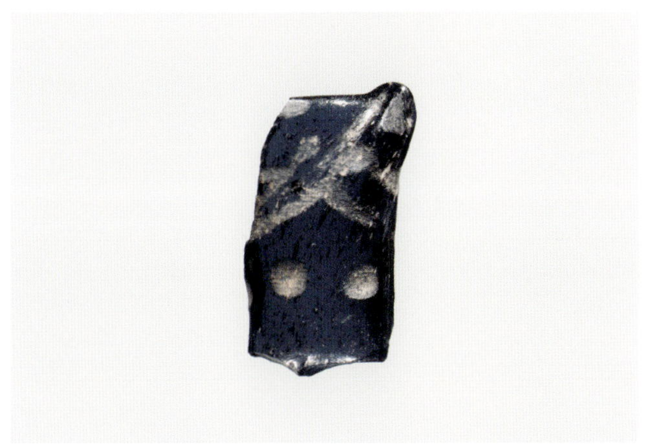

216

9. Small Bottles Shaped like Fish

217. Small Bottle Shaped like Fish

10th to 12th century. 51.1.136.
H. (surviving) 4.8 cm, W. (max.) 2 cm.
Colorless, with yellowish brown tinge. Blown (probably mold-blown); perhaps ground; linear- and facet-cut.

Bottle. Lower neck has roughly circular cross section; body has cross section resembling flattened oval, with two broad, flat sides and two narrow, rounded sides; flat sides taper slightly, while rounded sides curve out, down, and in; at bottom, two short extensions of narrow sides form bifurcated "tail." On each broad side: raised diamond-shaped panel, bisected horizontally by slant-cut lens-shaped motif containing four or five vertical cuts; above and below lens-shaped motif, one vertical line extending inward from top and bottom of diamond, defined by vertical groove. On each narrow side: vertical row of five facets shaped like crescents.

Incomplete. Rim and much of neck are missing. Specks of pale yellowish brown weathering.

Comment: Objects shaped like stylized fish were made in Egypt, and probably elsewhere, in a variety of media, including rock crystal and precious metal. Glass objects of this type, like "molar flasks," are generally believed to have been containers for perfume or some other substance used in small quantities. But

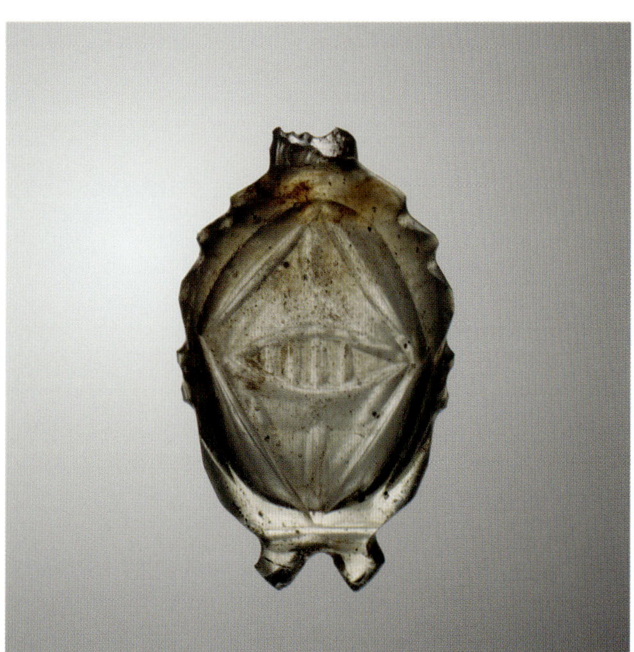

217

Carboni (2001, p. 109), noting that an example in the al-Sabah Collection, Dār al-Āthār al-Islāmiyyah, Kuwait National Museum (LNS 307 G: no. 32 on p. 109), supposedly came from a hoard of jewelry, suggested that it was an amulet, which could be "tied to a string by its tail and worn around the neck." In the case of **217**, however, the form of the tail does not lend itself to this explanation.

The numerous parallels include *Hentrich Collection* 1974, p. 271, no. 418; Clairmont 1977, p. 91, nos. 301 and 302; Hasson 1979, pp. 17 and 25, no. 27; and Carboni 2001, p. 109, no. 32, and p. 134, no. 2.40a–f.

For a similar object, see Lamm 1929–30, pl. 62, no. 23 (from Egypt).

218. Small Bottle Shaped like Fish

10th to 12th century. Formerly in the Smith Collection (489). Gift of Carl Berkowitz and Derek Content. 76.1.186.
H. (surviving) 4.8 cm, W. (max.) 2 cm.
Colorless. Blown (probably mold-blown); perhaps ground; linear- and facet-cut.

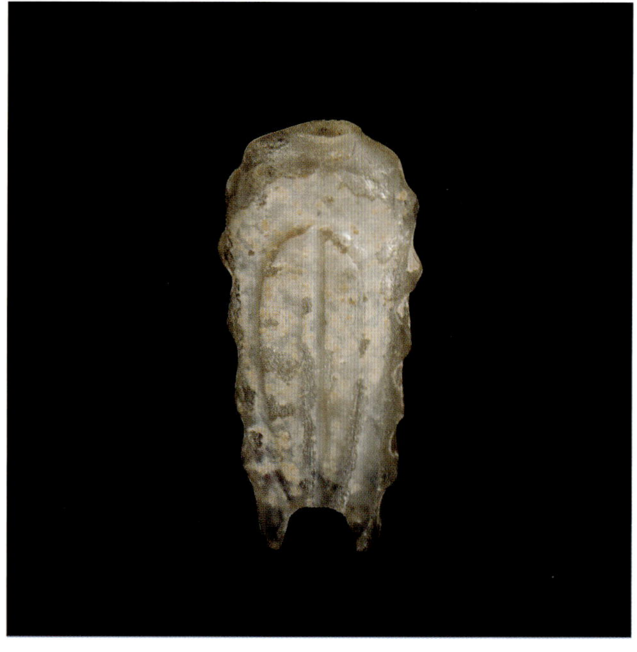

218

Bottle. Body has rectangular cross section with two broad and two narrow sides, all of which are straight and slightly tapered; at bottom, two short extensions of narrow sides form bifurcated "tail"; on underside, neatly drilled shallow hole (D. 0.25 cm). On each broad side: raised oval panel, wider at top than at bottom, bisected by vertical groove. On each narrow side: vertical row of six notchlike facets.

Incomplete. Rim and neck are missing; tips of tail are chipped. Patches of opaque pale yellowish brown weathering.

Comment: See **217**.

Bibliography: *Verres antiques* 1954, p. 47, no. 280.

10. Small Bottle, "Spearhead Flask"

219. Small Bottle, "Spearhead Flask"

About 10th century. Formerly in the collection of Maurice Nahman, Cairo, Egypt. 53.1.69.
H. 12 cm, D. (shoulder, max.) 3.8 cm.
Transparent deep blue; bubbles. Blown (perhaps in dip mold); linear-cut.

Bottle with carrot-shaped body. Rim plain, with rounded lip; neck cylindrical, but wider at top than at bottom; shoulder slopes and has rounded edge; wall tapers, with circular cross section at top and square cross section at bottom; base flat; no pontil mark. Neck and wall have broad, rather irregular linear-cut ornament. On neck: five oval or circular cuts just below rim and, under these, one continuous horizontal groove. On body (from top to bottom): (1) eight lanceolate motifs, rounded at top and pointed at bottom, each with short arc-shaped cut above and pairs of short horizontal cuts at bottom, between it and its neighbors; (2) two continuous more or less horizontal grooves; (3) on each of four sides, two or more short straight or arc-shaped cuts; and (4) also on each side, one pair of vertical cuts.

Intact. Surface appears to be deep purple and has matte grayish weathering, especially in cuts; some iridescence.

Comment: The pairs of vertical cuts at the bottom of the wall convey the impression that the vessel had four feet, like a "molar flask" such as a blue "bevel-cut" bottle reported to have come from a 10th-century context at Fusṭāṭ (Old Cairo), Egypt (Scanlon and Pinder-Wilson 2001, pp. 98–99, no. 42z).

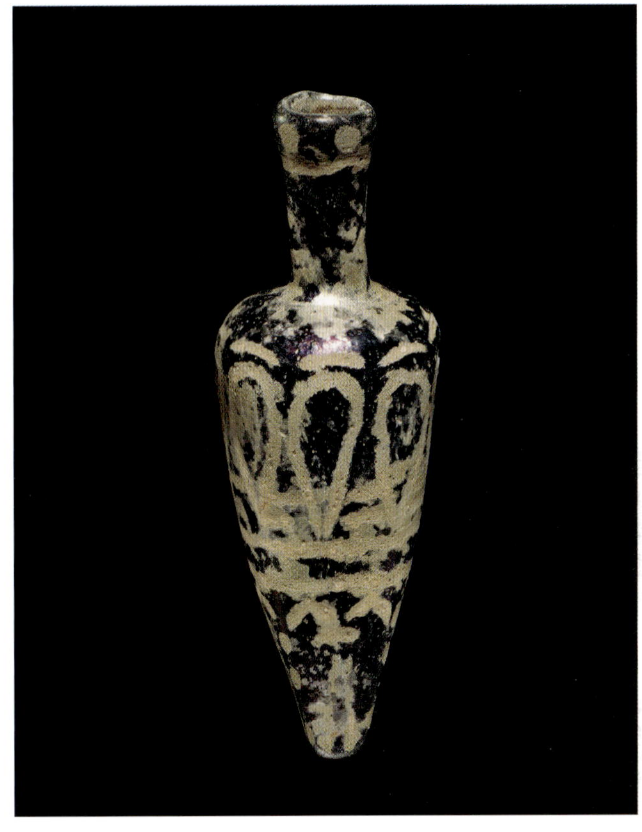

219

11. Small Bottles, "Molar Flasks"

220. Small Bottle, "Molar Flask"

9th to 10th century. Formerly in the collections of Friedrich L. von Gans and Ray Winfield Smith (Smith 287). 55.1.113.
H. 11.1 cm, D. (rim) 2 cm, (shoulder) 3.8 cm.
Translucent deep blue, appearing black in reflected light. Blown (body blown in dip mold); facet- and linear-cut.

Bottle. Rim plain, with flat top; neck cylindrical, but wider at top than at bottom; shoulder flat, with rounded edge; wall straight and tapering; horizontal cross section is circular below shoulder and square below midpoint; four small feet, one at each angle of lower wall. Decorated on rim, neck, and wall. On rim and neck: outside of rim has continuous band of five horizontal half-oval facets alternating with five small circular facets; upper neck has band of five horizontal

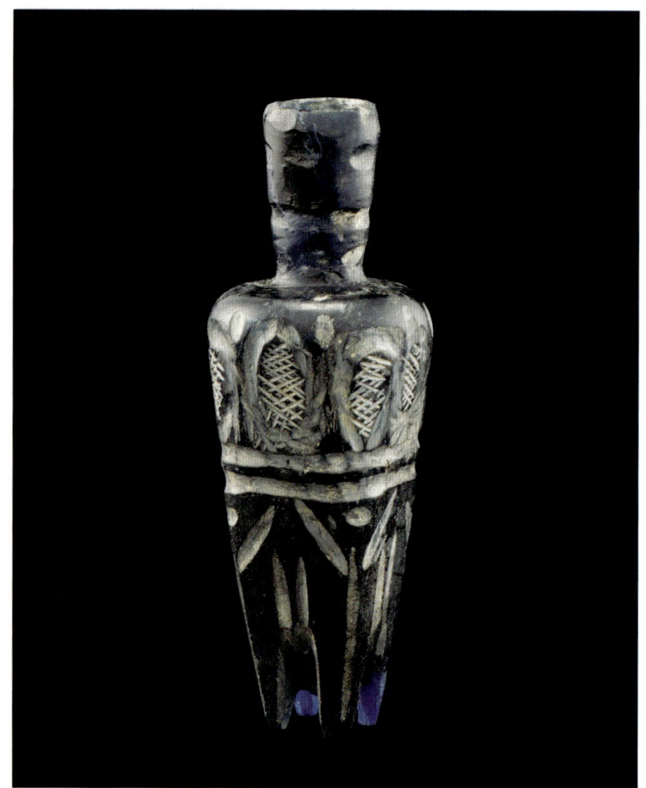

220

oval facets; midpoint of neck has uneven continuous horizontal groove; lower neck also has band of five horizontal oval facets, placed rather unevenly. On wall: two registers of unequal size separated by pair of horizontal grooves (W. of each 0.25–0.3 cm). Upper, smaller register has four upright oval motifs, pointed at one end, with tips pointing down, alternating with four upright oval motifs; all have broad outlines and are crosshatched; at edge of shoulder, between each pair of ovals, small oval facet. Lower register has pair of vertical grooves at center of each side and single vertical groove at each angle; grooves at angles fork at top and have small oval facet between branches.

Incomplete. Damaged in the Corning flood of 1972 (see page 10); part of neck and two feet restored. Somewhat dull, with pitting and light gray weathering in coldworked areas.

Comment: According to *Gans Collection* 1921 (see below), the object was found at Novorossiysk on the Black Sea coast of Russia.

The cutting, especially of the outlines of the oval motifs on the upper wall, is perfunctory.

Bibliography: *Gans Collection* 1921, p. 75, no. 225; Eisen 1927, v. 2, p. 582 and fig. 235, IV, d; Lamm 1928, p. 61; *idem* 1929–30, v. 1, p. 164, no. 5, and v. 2, pl. 61, no. 5; Anon. 1930, p. 30; *National Geographic Magazine*, April 1951, p. 544; *Verres antiques* 1954, p. 46, no. 273; *Glass from the Ancient World* 1957, pp. 280–281, no. 592; Lang 1982, p. 13; *Glass from the Ancient World* 1991, p. 78, no. 54.

221. Small Bottle, "Molar Flask"

9th to 11th century. Formerly in the collection of Maurice Nahman, Cairo, Egypt. 53.1.62.
H. 10 cm, W. (rim) 1.8 cm, (body) 2.2 cm.
Translucent deep blue. Blown (probably mold-blown); perhaps ground; facet- and linear-cut.

Bottle. Rim plain, with flat top; neck roughly cylindrical, but wider at top than at bottom; body tall, with rounded shoulder, vertical sides, and square cross section; at bottom of wall, four pointed feet, one at each corner. Decorated on neck and body. On neck: upper two-thirds has four equidistant vertical facets, below which is one continuous horizontal groove. On upper body: each side has two elongated tear-shaped cuts arranged to form V, and each corner has single triangular cut; below these, two continuous horizontal grooves. On lower body: each side has narrow triangular cut with apex at top, and each corner has triangular cut with apex at bottom.

Incomplete. Three feet have been restored in plastic. Dull and pitted, with traces of weathering in cuts.

Comment: The decoration on the body is very similar to that of **222**.

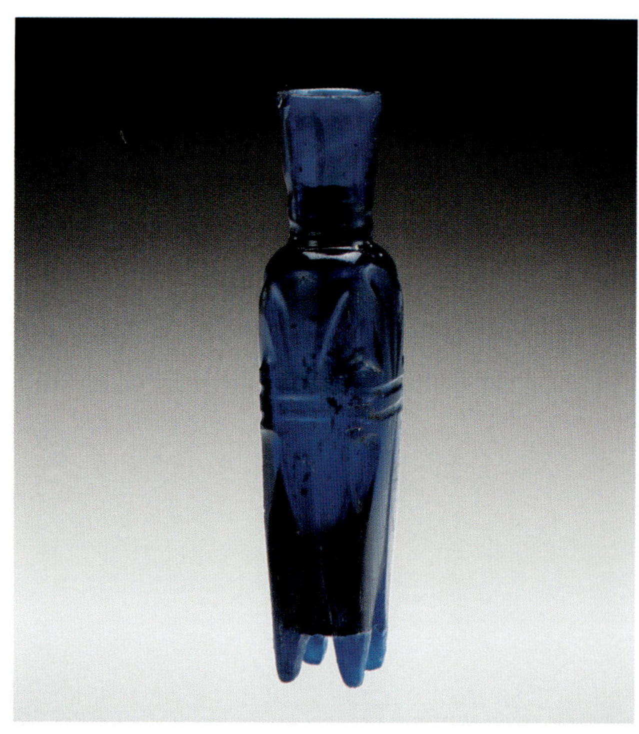

221

222. Small Bottle, "Molar Flask"

9th to 11th century. Formerly in the collection of Maurice Nahman, Cairo, Egypt. 55.1.32. H. 9.2 cm, D. (rim) 1.7 cm, W. (body) 1.8 cm. Translucent deep green. Blown (probably mold-blown); facet- and linear-cut.

Bottle. Rim plain, with flat top; neck roughly cylindrical, but wider at top than at bottom; body tall, with vertical walls and square cross section; at bottom of wall, four pointed feet, one at each corner. Decorated on neck and body. On neck: surface was removed at top and bottom to create raised band that is decorated with two linear-cut V-shaped motifs, with four roughly triangular hollow facets above and between them. On upper body: each side has two elongated tear-shaped cuts arranged to form V, and each corner has single triangular cut; below these, two continuous horizontal grooves. On lower body: each side has narrow triangular cut with apex at top, and each corner has triangular cut with apex at bottom.

Incomplete. Two feet are missing, and two are chipped at bottom. Dull, with light gray weathering in cuts.

Comment: The bottle is surprisingly heavy, and this suggests that, like some other deep green objects (e.g., **490**), the glass contains a significant quantity of lead oxide. The decoration on the body resembles that on **221**.

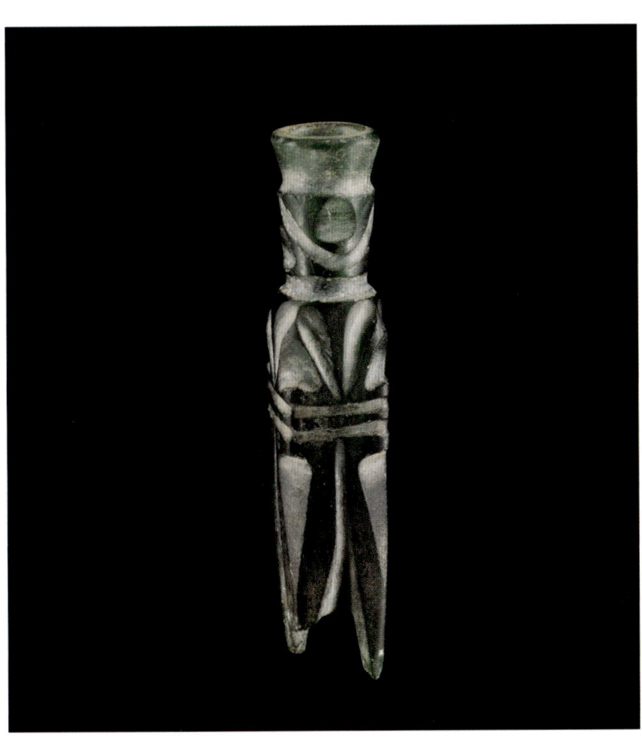

222

223. Small Bottle, "Molar Flask"

10th to 11th century. Formerly in the collection of Maurice Nahman, Cairo, Egypt. 53.1.71. H. 9.1 cm, D. (rim) 1.5 cm, (shoulder) 3.4 cm. Transparent deep blue. Blown (body blown in dip mold); linear-cut.

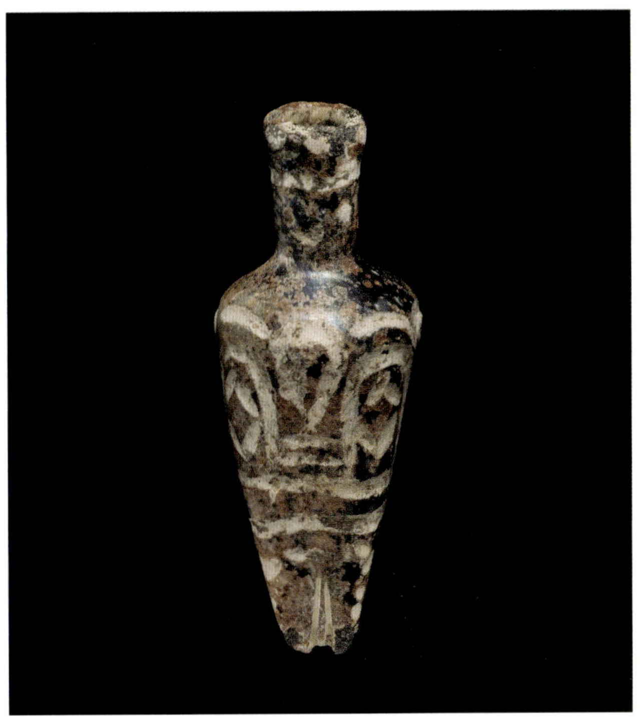

223

Bottle. Body shaped like carrot, but lower half has square cross section. Rim plain, with rounded top; neck cylindrical, but narrower at bottom than at top; shoulder slopes and has rounded edge; wall straight and tapering; base consists of four vestigial feet. Linear-cut decoration on neck and wall. On neck: band of six rather irregular circular cuts just below rim and, lower down, continuous horizontal line above band of three small circular cuts. On wall: upper and lower registers, separated by two continuous horizontal lines. Upper register is broad and contains four motifs shaped like inverted U, each containing diamond-shaped element composed of four short cuts; one short arc above each inverted U, and tear-shaped motif and two short horizontal cuts between each pair of Us. Lower register has horizontal cut, combination of cut and dots, or row of dots on each flat face, and vertical row of dots; at center of each flat face, two vertical lines, which separate each foot from its neighbors. Except for vertical lines, cutting is broad, shallow, and carelessly executed.

Complete, except for one foot. Undecorated surfaces are covered with mottled deep blue and brown enamellike weathering; interior of cuts is mostly matte and gray.

COMMENT: Perhaps the decoration has been cleaned mechanically.

This object, like **224**, belongs to a group of "molar flasks" with perfunctory linear cutting and small or vestigial feet. For a large example (H. 14 cm) found "in the disturbed fill of a sanitation sump which contained an Ayyubid dirham and a Mamluk water-bottle filter" at Fusṭāṭ, Egypt, see Scanlon and Pinder-Wilson 2001, pp. 98–99, no. 42z. Other bottles in this group include Lamm 1929–30, v. 1, p. 164, and v. 2, pl. 61, no. 5 (said to have been found at Novorossiysk on the Black Sea coast of Russia); Clairmont 1977, p. 92, no. 305 (in the Benaki Museum, Athens, 43/7); and Kröger 1984, pp. 171–172, no. 147 (in the Museum für Islamische Kunst, Berlin, I.5544).

224. Small Bottle, "Molar Flask"

10th to 11th century. Formerly in the collection of Maurice Nahman, Cairo, Egypt. 53.1.70.
H. 8.9 cm, D. (rim) 1.4 cm, (shoulder, max.) 3 cm.
Opaque light blue. Blown (body blown in dip mold); linear-cut.

Bottle. Body shaped like carrot, but lower half has square cross section. Rim plain, with rounded top; neck cylindrical, but narrower at bottom than at top; shoulder slopes and has rounded edge; wall straight and tapering; base consists of four vestigial feet. Linear-cut decoration on neck and wall. On neck: band of six rather irregular circular and oval cuts just below rim and, lower down, two more or less continuous horizontal lines. On wall: upper and lower registers of roughly equal size, separated by two continuous horizontal lines. Upper register contains four contiguous shallow U-shaped motifs with ends curling in and down, separated by A-shaped motifs without crossbar. Lower register has four contiguous V-shaped motifs, each with oval cut inside and smaller circular cut below; between each V, one or, in one case, two vertical lines, which separate each foot from its neighbors. Cutting is broad, shallow, and carelessly executed.

Virtually intact, but with losses from tips of feet. Patches of opaque yellow to light brown weathering, especially in cuts.

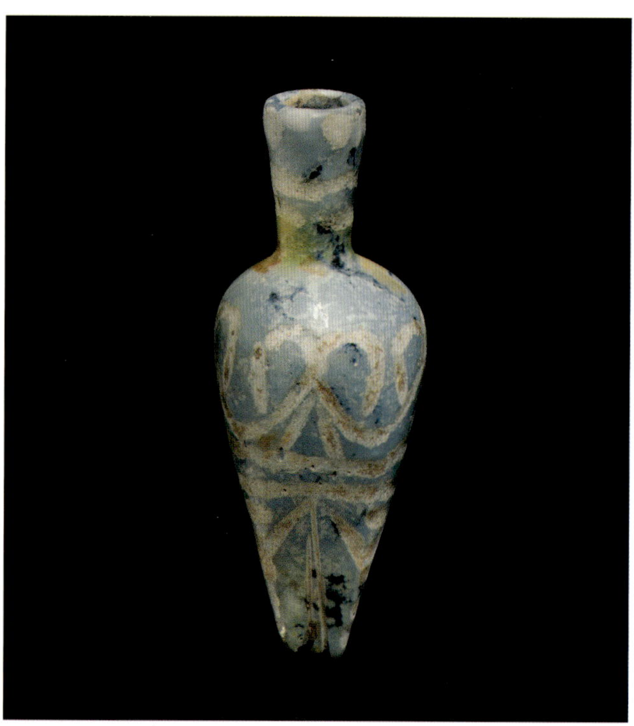

224

COMMENT: See **223**.

225. Small Bottle, "Molar Flask"

9th to 11th century. Formerly in the collection of Maurice Nahman, Cairo, Egypt. 53.1.59.
H. 7.3 cm, W. (rim) 1.6 cm, (body) 1.8 cm.
Transparent light green. Blown (probably mold-blown); probably ground; facet- and linear-cut.

Bottle. Rim plain, with flat top; neck tapers; body tall, with rounded shoulder, vertical sides, square cross section, and small egg-shaped cavity with pointed bottom; at bottom of wall, four pointed feet, one at each corner. Decorated on neck and body. On neck: upper two-thirds is cut in eight contiguous vertical facets, with four broad facets alternating with four narrow ones; beneath them is one continuous horizontal groove. Decoration on body is very similar on all four sides: at top, fanlike group of four short linear cuts, which touch at bottom; at bottom, large triangular cut, which partly defines feet; at angles between each pair of sides, one long rhombic facet, shallow at top and bottom and deepest at widest part, which has prominent diamond-shaped knob.

Incomplete. Rim is chipped, and parts of three feet, almost all of neck, and most of one foot are restored. No obvious weathering.

COMMENT: The pointed ovoid form of the interior suggests that it was not created during the process of inflation. The most likely explanation of the shape is that it was made by grinding the object with a rotating tool, perhaps akin to a bow drill (cf. Contadini

1999, p. 324, on shaping the interiors of rock crystal vessels).

For other "molar flasks" with rhombic facets, see **103–105**.

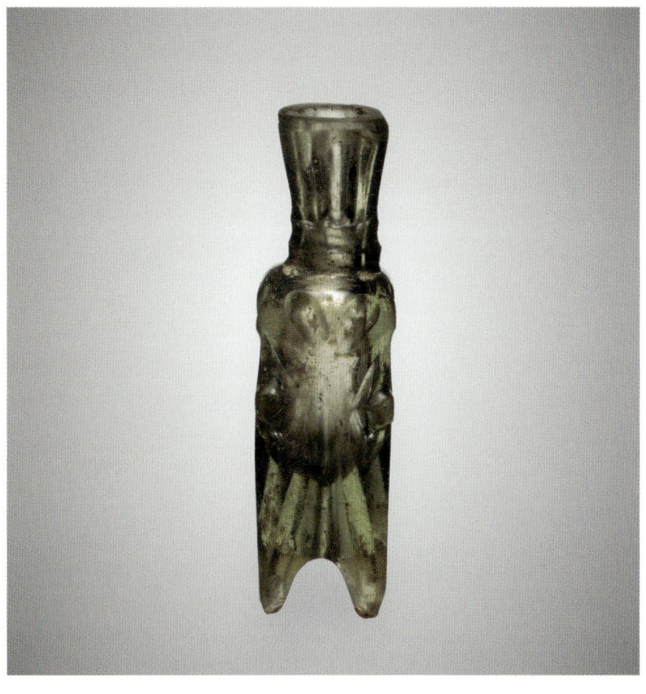

225

226. Small Bottle, "Molar Flask"

9th to 11th century. Found during excavations at Fusṭāṭ (Old Cairo), Egypt (68.11.25). Gift of the American Research Center in Egypt. 69.1.42.
H. 7.3 cm, W. (rim) 1.3 cm, (body) 1.4 cm.
Almost colorless, with yellowish green tinge. Blown (probably mold-blown); probably ground; facet- and linear-cut.

Bottle. Rim plain, with flat top; neck tapers; body tall, with rounded shoulder, vertical sides, square cross section, and small egg-shaped cavity with pointed bottom; at bottom of wall, four pyramid-shaped feet, one at each corner. Decorated on neck and body. On neck: six contiguous vertical facets. On wall: angle between each pair of sides has two hollow facets: large facet shaped like inverted V and, below it, smaller, roughly circular facet.

Intact, except for chips at bottoms of feet. Extensively pitted, with remains of opaque off-white weathering on inside of neck.

Comment: The bottle was found during excavations directed by Prof. George T. Scanlon. According to Scanlon and Pinder-Wilson (see below), it was

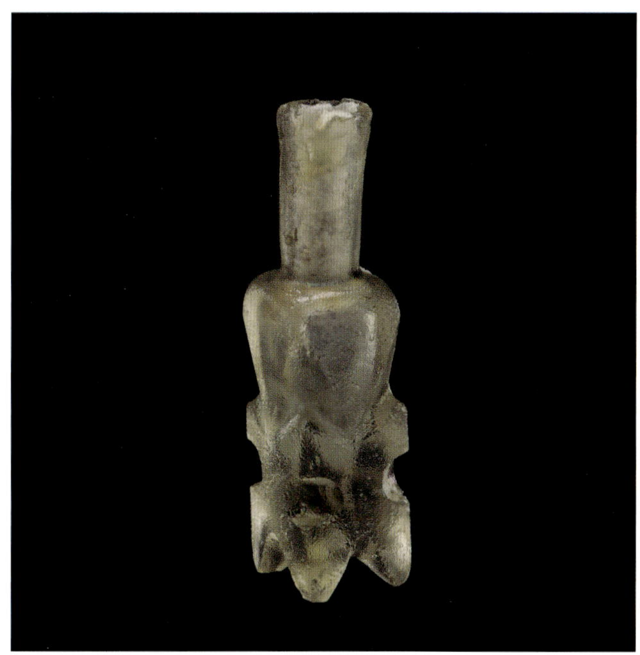

226

recovered from "a pit whose undisturbed contents . . . permit a dating to the 9th–10th century."

Bibliography: Scanlon and Pinder-Wilson 2001, p. 98, no. 42y.

227. Small Bottle, "Molar Flask"

9th to 11th century. Formerly in the collection of Maurice Nahman, Cairo, Egypt. 53.1.58.
H. 6.8 cm, W. (rim) 1.1 cm, (body) 1.9 cm.
Colorless. Blown (probably mold-blown); facet- and linear-cut.

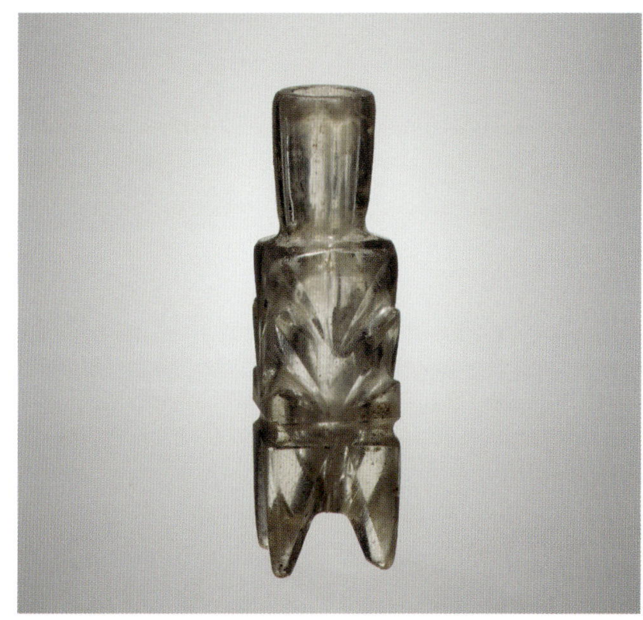

227

Bottle. Rim plain, with flat top; neck roughly cylindrical, but wider at top than at bottom; shoulder flat; body tall, with vertical walls and square cross section; at bottom of wall, four pointed feet, one at each corner. Decorated on neck and body. On neck: six contiguous vertical facets extending from rim to shoulder. On body: at each angle, two deep notches shaped like inverted Vs; on each face, shallow vertical cut between upper pair of Vs; on lower body, one continuous horizontal groove.

Almost complete. Part of one foot is missing, and other feet are chipped. Dull, but virtually unweathered.

228. Small Bottle, "Molar Flask"

9th to 11th century. Formerly in the collection of Maurice Nahman, Cairo, Egypt. 53.1.54.
H. 6 cm, W. (rim) 1.2 cm, (body) 1.5 cm.
Almost colorless, with yellowish tinge. Blown (probably mold-blown); facet- and linear-cut.

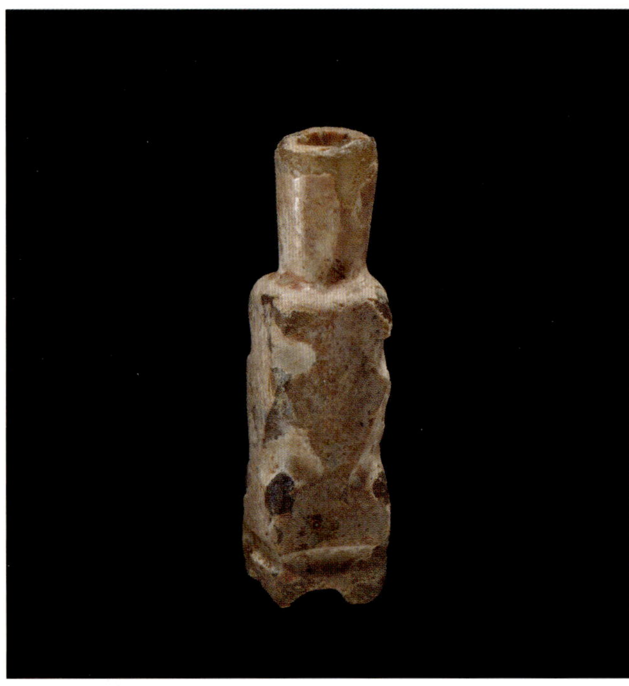

228

Bottle. Rim plain, with flat top; neck roughly cylindrical, but wider at top than at bottom; body tall, with rounded shoulder, vertical walls, and square cross section; at bottom of wall, four very short feet, one at each corner. Decorated on neck and body. On neck: six contiguous vertical facets extend from top to bottom. On body: each side is plain, except for horizontal cut at bottom; each corner has small roughly diamond-shaped facet above larger facet shaped like inverted V.

Intact. Mostly covered with opaque light brown enamellike weathering.

229. Small Bottle, "Molar Flask"

9th to 10th century. Formerly in the collection of Maurice Nahman, Cairo, Egypt. 53.1.61.
H. (surviving) 8.8 cm, D. (rim) 1.7 cm, W. (shoulder) 2.3 cm.
Transparent very pale green; small bubbles. Blown (body blown in dip mold); linear-cut.

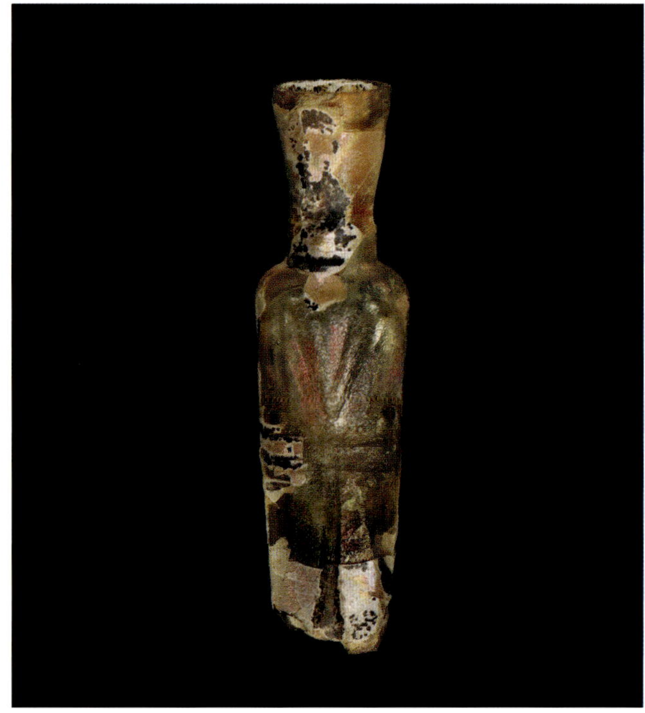

229

Bottle. Rim plain, with top ground flat; neck tapers; shoulder slopes and has rounded edge; wall straight and tapering very slightly, with square cross section; at bottom of wall, four feet, one at each corner. Decorated on neck and wall. On neck: four shallow facets (H. 1.5 cm, W. about 0.4 cm). On wall: upper and lower registers, separated by two continuous horizontal lines. Upper register is relatively narrow, with two cuts making V-shaped motif on each side and triangular cut at each angle. Lower register has one narrow cut shaped like inverted V on each side and one cut shaped like inverted isosceles triangle with rounded baseline at each angle; legs are defined by inverted Vs, which continue downward and merge at bottom of wall.

Incomplete. All four legs are entirely or almost entirely missing. Remains of matte weathering, which is pale pinkish brown on plain surfaces and dark gray in cuts.

230. Small Bottle, "Molar Flask"

9th to 11th century. Formerly in the collection of Maurice Nahman, Cairo, Egypt. 53.1.56.
H. (surviving) 7.4 cm, W. (rim) 1.7 cm, (body) 1.8 cm.
Transparent green. Blown (probably mold-blown); perhaps ground; facet- and linear-cut.

Bottle. Rim plain, with flat top; neck wider at top than at bottom; body tall, with sloping shoulder, vertical walls, cross section that is squarish with rounded angles, and cavity that is conical with rounded end; at bottom of wall, four pointed feet, one at each corner. Decorated on neck and body. On neck: upper two-thirds consists of eight contiguous vertical facets; below these are two horizontal ribs. Body is divided into two parts by continuous horizontal groove below midpoint and has similar decoration on all four sides. On upper body: each side has inverted V-shaped cuts separated by vertical row of five horizontal cuts at corners. On lower body: each side has narrow V-shaped cut separated by triangular facets at corners, each of which has notched protrusion at top.

Incomplete. All four feet are missing. Virtually unweathered.

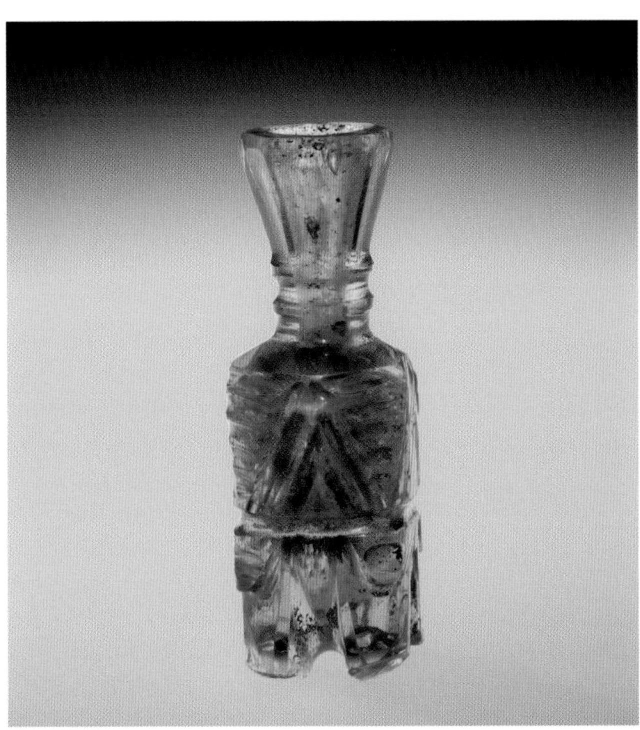

230

Comment: The shape of the interior suggests that it was not formed during the process of inflation. The most likely explanation of the shape is that it was made by grinding the object with a rotating tool, perhaps akin to a bow drill (cf. Contadini 1999, p. 324, on shaping the interiors of rock crystal vessels).

231. Small Bottle, "Molar Flask"

9th to 11th century. Formerly in the Smith Collection (1110). Gift of Carl Berkowitz and Derek Content. 76.1.189.
H. (surviving) 6.3 cm, W. (body) 1.9 cm.
Transparent light green. Blown (probably mold-blown); perhaps ground; facet- and linear-cut.

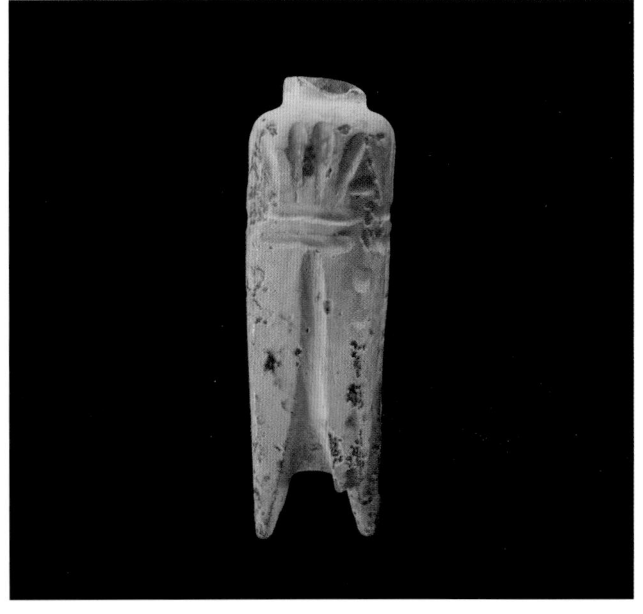

231

Bottle. Neck has circular cross section at bottom; body tall, with rounded shoulder, slightly tapering sides, and square cross section; at bottom of wall, four pointed feet, one at each corner. Decorated on body: each side has, at top, two short vertical cuts, and each corner has single triangular cut; below these, two continuous horizontal grooves. On lower body: each side has narrow triangular cut with apex at top, and each corner has two small subtriangular cuts.

Incomplete. Two feet are missing. Dull and pitted, with matte off-white to light green weathering.

232. Small Bottle, "Molar Flask"

About 9th to 11th century. Found during excavations at Fusṭāṭ (Old Cairo), Egypt (68.11.49). Gift of the American Research Center in Egypt. 69.1.106.
H. (surviving) 6 cm, W. (body) 2.1 cm.
Transparent deep green. Blown (probably mold-blown); linear-cut.

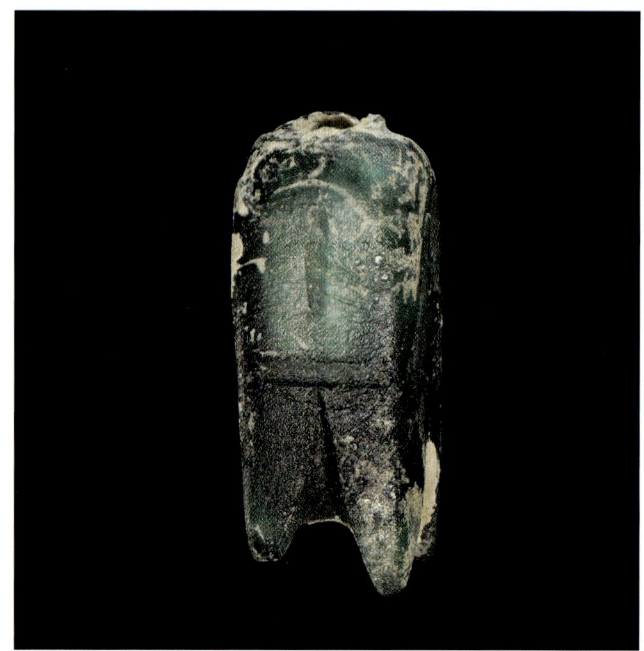

232

Bottle; body has square cross section. Bottom of neck apparently cut in vertical facets; shoulder narrow and rounded; wall vertical; four pyramidal feet, one at each angle between sides. Each side has cross-shaped linear motif, which splays at bottom to fill space between each pair of feet.

Incomplete. Entire rim, almost entire neck, and parts of two feet are missing. Pitted, with remains of opaque pale brown weathering.

Comment: The bottle was found during excavations directed by Prof. George T. Scanlon. It had no archeological context.

A bottle with similar cross-shaped motifs, also made of dark green glass and with apparently similar weathering, is in the al-Sabah Collection, Dār al-Āthār al-Islāmiyyah, Kuwait National Museum (LNS 289 G: Carboni 2001, p. 127, no. 2.28q).

Bibliography: Scanlon and Pinder-Wilson 2001, p. 97, no. 42r.

233. Small Bottle, "Molar Flask"

9th to 11th century. 56.1.101.
H. (surviving) 5.3 cm, W. (body) 1.7 cm.
Transparent blue, appearing bluish green in reflected light. Blown (probably mold-blown); ground; facet- and linear-cut.

Bottle. Bottom of neck probably has hexagonal cross section; body tall, with flat shoulder, vertical sides, square cross section, and small conical cavity; at bottom of wall, four pointed feet, one at each corner. Decoration is very similar on all four sides, with horizontal line above midpoint. Area above this line has one vertical cut at center and triangular facet at each corner, which it shares with adjoining sides. Area below line has small diamond-shaped cut at each corner, again shared with adjoining sides, and deep triangular cut at bottom, which partly defines feet.

Incomplete. Rim, almost all of neck, and most of one foot are missing. Dull and pitted, with remains of light gray weathering, especially in cuts.

Comment: The object was acquired from a Tehran-based dealer, who reported that it was found in Gurgān Province, northern Iran.

The conical form of the interior suggests that it was not created during the process of inflation. The most likely explanation of the shape is that it was made by grinding the object with a rotating tool, perhaps akin to a bow drill (cf. Contadini 1999, p. 324, on shaping the interiors of rock crystal vessels).

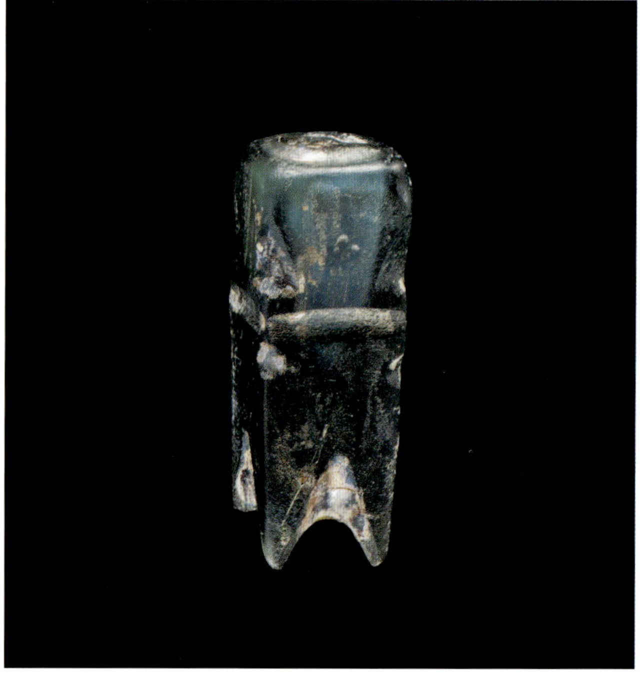

233

234. Small Bottle, "Molar Flask"

9th to 10th century. Found during excavations at Fusṭāṭ (Old Cairo), Egypt (80.10.37). Gift of the American Research Center in Egypt. 81.1.41.
H. (surviving) 5 cm, W. (each side of wall) 1.7 cm.
Transparent deep green. Blown (body blown in dip mold); linear-cut.

Bottle. Lower neck cylindrical; shoulder narrow; wall vertical, with rhomboidal cross section; at bottom of wall, four feet, one at each corner. Decorated on body above and below four horizontal grooves, one on each side. Upper wall has, on each side, one broad V-shaped cut composed of two inclined planes on each side, and at each angle, one short horizontal notch. Lower wall has one narrow cut shaped like inverted V on each side and one short horizontal notch at each angle; legs are defined by inverted Vs, which continue downward and merge at bottom of wall.

Incomplete. All of two legs and most of neck and other two legs are missing. Surface is shiny deep green mottled with light greenish gray and brown.

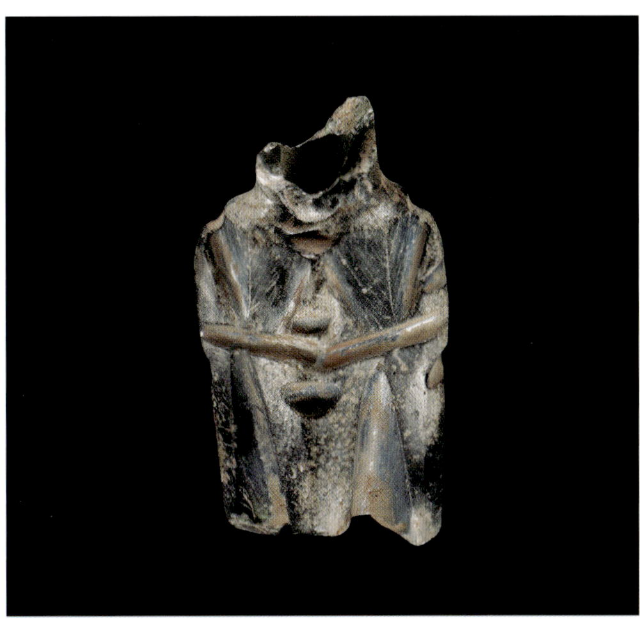

234

Comment: The object was found during excavations directed by Prof. George T. Scanlon. It was recovered from a deposit attributed to the years around 900 (see below).

In earlier publications, Scanlon and Pinder-Wilson described the object as cobalt blue and remarked on the unusual rhomboidal cross section of the body. In strong transmitted light, examination of the broken edge of the neck, which is chipped on both surfaces, reveals that the glass is actually green. The overall appearance of the object suggests that it has been exposed to intense heat, which caused the glass to soften and become distorted: hence the rhomboidal section. In all probability, the original cross section was square.

Bibliography: Scanlon and Pinder-Wilson 2001, p. 97, no. 42o = Pinder-Wilson and Scanlon 1987, p. 68, no. 16.

235. Small Bottle, "Molar Flask"

9th to 11th century. 56.1.130.
H. (surviving) 4.4 cm, W. (body) 1.9 cm.
Almost colorless, with yellowish green tinge.
Blown (probably mold-blown); facet- and linear-cut.

Bottle. Shoulder rounded; body short, with vertical walls and square cross section; at bottom of wall, four feet, one at each corner. Decorated on body above and below single continuous horizontal groove. On each side, upper wall has vertical cut and lower wall has deep triangular cut with apex at top; on each corner, upper part has facet shaped like inverted V and lower part has roughly circular hollow facet.

Incomplete. Rim, neck, and parts of all four feet are missing. Dull, with remains of pale gray weathering.

Comment: See **236** and **237**.

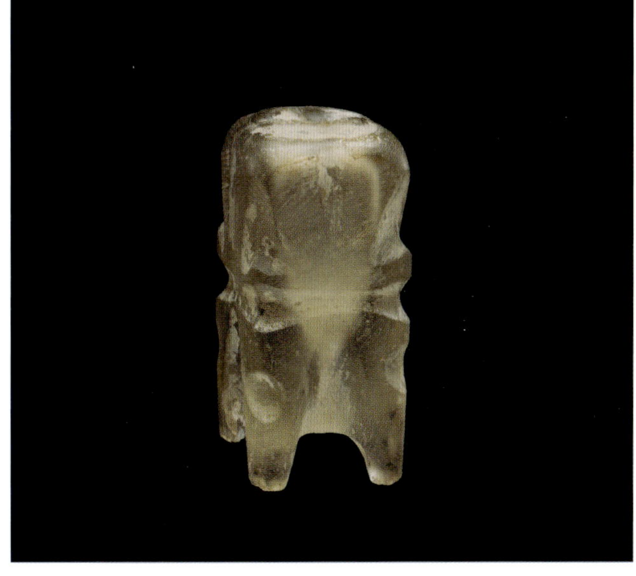

235

236. Small Bottle, "Molar Flask"

9th to 11th century. 56.1.129.
H. (surviving) 4.3 cm, W. (body) 1.9 cm.
Transparent light greenish blue. Blown (probably mold-blown); facet- and linear-cut.

Bottle. Shoulder rounded; body short, with vertical walls and square cross section; at bottom of wall, four feet, one at each corner. Decorated on body above and below single continuous horizontal groove. On each side, upper wall has vertical cut and lower wall has deep triangular cut with apex at top; on each

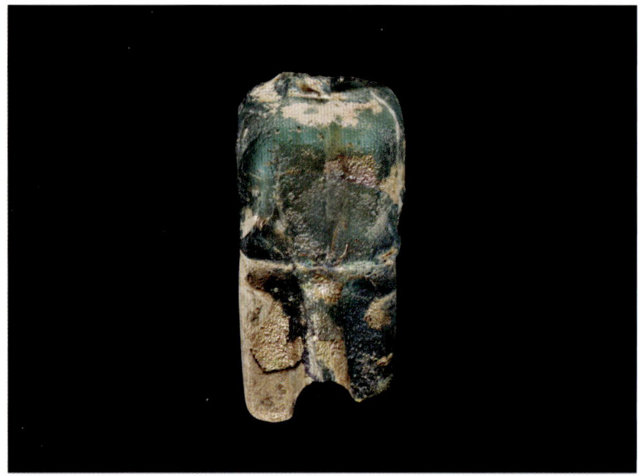

236

corner, upper part has facet shaped like inverted V and lower part has roughly circular hollow facet.

Incomplete. Rim, neck, and two feet are missing; other two feet have major losses. Dull and pitted, with remains of matte pale gray weathering.

Comment: See **235** and **237**.

237. Small Bottle, "Molar Flask"

9th to 11th century. Gift of Abbas Mazda. 55.1.24.
H. (surviving) 3.7 cm, W. (body) 1.8 cm.
Translucent bluish green. Blown (probably mold-blown); facet- and linear-cut.

Bottle. Neck cylindrical at bottom; shoulder slopes; body short, with vertical walls and square cross section; at bottom of wall, four feet, one at each corner. Decorated on body above and below single continuous horizontal groove. On each side, upper wall has vertical cut and lower wall has deep triangular cut with apex at top; on each corner, upper part has facet shaped like inverted V and lower part has hollow circular facet.

Incomplete. Rim, upper neck, and all four feet are missing. Remains of light silvery gray weathering.

Comment: See **235** and **236**.

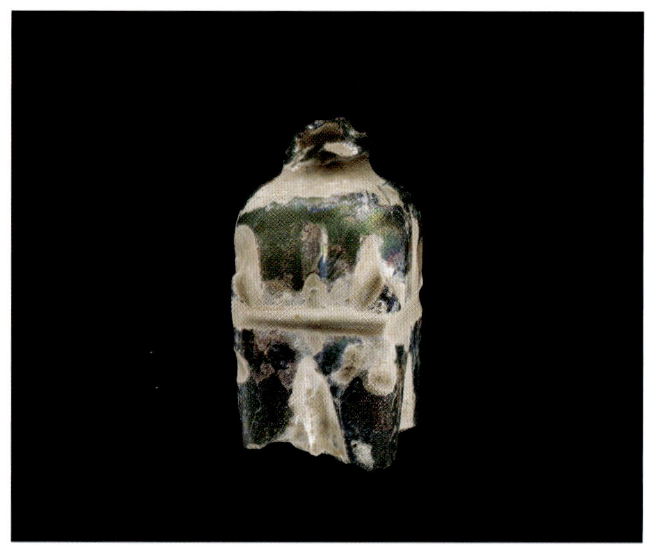

237

12. Pitcher

238. Pitcher

10th to 11th century. Formerly in the Strauss Collection (S2700). Gift of The Ruth Bryan Strauss Memorial Foundation. 79.1.72.
H. (rim) 18.2 cm, (thumb-rest) 20.2 cm, D. (rim) 9.3 cm, (max.) 9.9 cm.
Almost colorless, with yellowish tinge. Blown, applied; linear-cut.

Pitcher: biconical. Rim plain, with bevel on outside; neck in form of truncated cone; base flat, with rounded edge; pontil mark (D. 1.2 cm); handle attached to wall, drawn up and out, then in and reattached to top of neck; circular thumb-rest. Broad, somewhat slipshod linear-cut decoration on neck and wall. On neck: three large U-shaped motifs, joined at the top, with V-shaped motif inside each U and in spaces on either side of central U. On wall: single panel, which begins and ends at sides of handle; it is defined at top by two horizontal lines and at ends by single slanting line, which bends outward at bottom; there is no lower border. Panel contains two ogee arches with double outlines; arches are connected at bottom by short horizontal lines, and they have similar lines extending to edges of panel; each arch contains, at top, two concentric pendent arcs below area of crosshatching and, at bottom, four comma- or hook-shaped motifs and very short, straight cuts. Area between arches contains two concentric arcs with inverted V-shaped motif on each side and trefoil underneath. Areas between arches and sides of panel also have pairs of concentric crescents. Beneath pairs of lines that link and flank arches are groups of comma-shaped motifs and short, straight cuts.

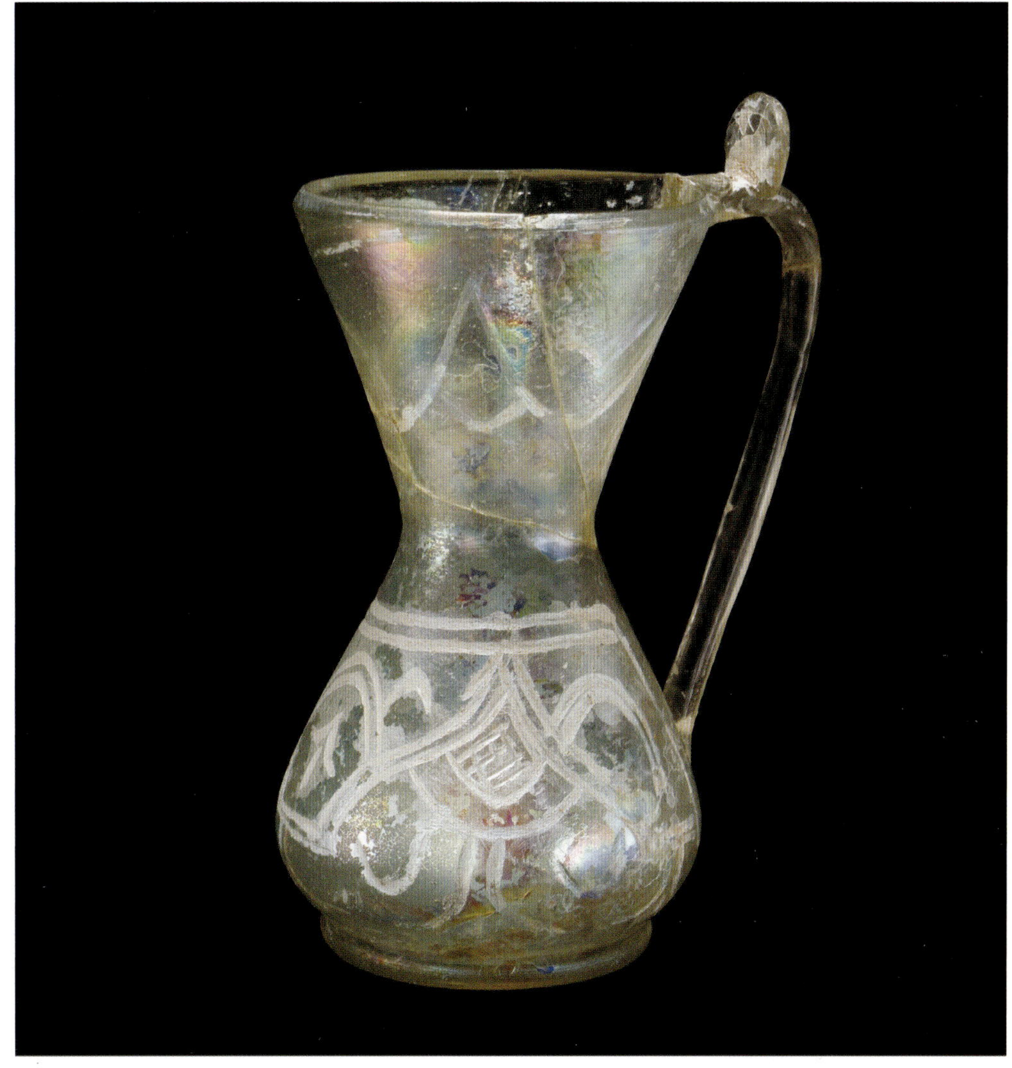

238

Incomplete. Part of rim and neck, small part of lower wall, and most of handle are missing and have been restored. Dull and pitted, with remains of iridescent weathering, especially in cuts.

Comment: The object is not unlike a globular pitcher excavated at Nishapur, northeastern Iran, now in The Metropolitan Museum of Art, New York (39.40.101: Kröger 1995, pp. 174–175, no. 228).

13. Indeterminate

239. Fragment of Bottle(?) with Vegetal Scroll

About 10th century. Formerly in the Smith Collection (555-15). Gift of Carl Berkowitz and Derek Content. 76.1.217.
H. (surviving) 5.1 cm, D. (est.) about 9 cm.
Almost colorless, with yellowish green tinge.
Blown; linear- and slant-cut.

Fragment of bottle(?) with straight, vertical or tapering wall (Th. 0.1 cm). Decoration consists of two horizontal lines, probably forming lower border of panel containing small part of vegetal scroll comprising stem and part of leaf. Stem consists of three parallel curving lines and has three transverse cuts at junction with leaf. Leaf sprouts from stem and expands; it is filled with seven curved longitudinal lines. Between stem and leaf is crescent-shaped shoot. Above and beneath vegetal scroll are several indeterminate cuts. All motifs are linear-cut except for shoot and one cut above it.

Broken on all sides. Somewhat dull, and speckled with transparent pale brown weathering.

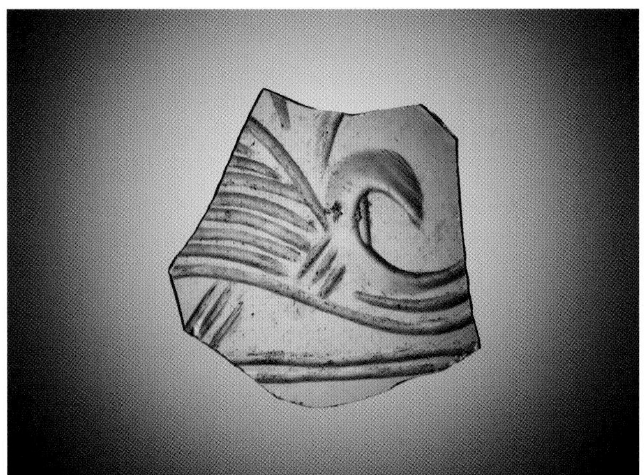

239

COMMENT: The shape and diameter of the fragment indicate that it is part of a bottle with a cylindrical body (cf. **526**) or a tapering body (cf. **272**).

240. Fragment of Beaker(?)

9th to 10th century. Formerly in the Smith Collection. 68.1.59-49.
Max. Dim. 2.8 cm, D. (est.) about 7 cm.
Colorless. Blown; slant- and linear-cut.

Fragment of beaker(?). Wall is straight and vertical or tapering. Decorated with parts of two elements: on right, slant-cut oval motif containing linear-cut herringbone pattern; on left, indeterminate slant- and linear-cut motif.

Broken on all sides. Dull and pitted, with remains of brown weathering, especially in cuts.

COMMENT: The oval motif filled with a herringbone pattern may be compared with the decoration on a bottle in the al-Sabah Collection, Dār al-Āthār al-Islāmiyyah, Kuwait National Museum (LNS 164 G: Carboni 2001, p. 133, no. 2.39).

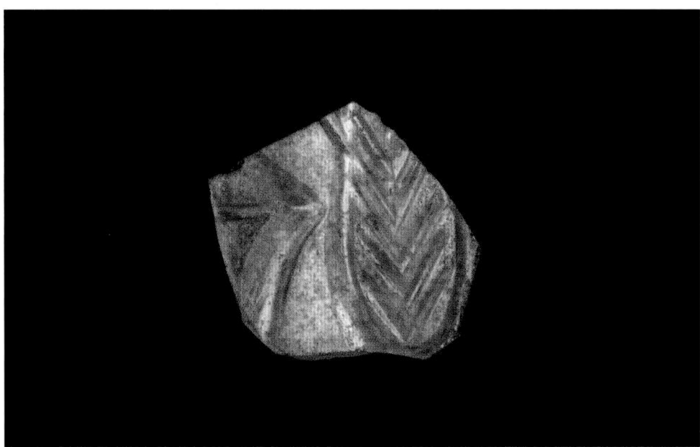

240

241. Fragment

10th to early 11th century. Formerly in the Smith Collection (493-10). Gift of Carl Berkowitz and Derek Content. 76.1.254.
Max. Dim. 6.7 cm.
Almost colorless, with yellowish green tinge.
Blown; linear-cut.

Fragment from wall (Th. 0.15–0.2 cm) of large vessel. It has slightly convex profile and is covered with ornament defined by shallow linear cuts (W. 0.2–0.4 cm) and with areas of crosshatching. At presumed top of fragment, small part of roundel (D. perhaps 6–7 cm) containing unidentified motif surrounded by crosshatching. Below this, horizontal band of guilloche consisting of small roundel (D. 2.6 cm) containing countersunk dot and, on right side, part of larger roundel (D. about 3.8 cm). Below small roundel, tear-shaped motif framed by cuts.

Broken into two pieces and mended; broken on all sides. Partly dull; pale gray weathering, especially in cuts.

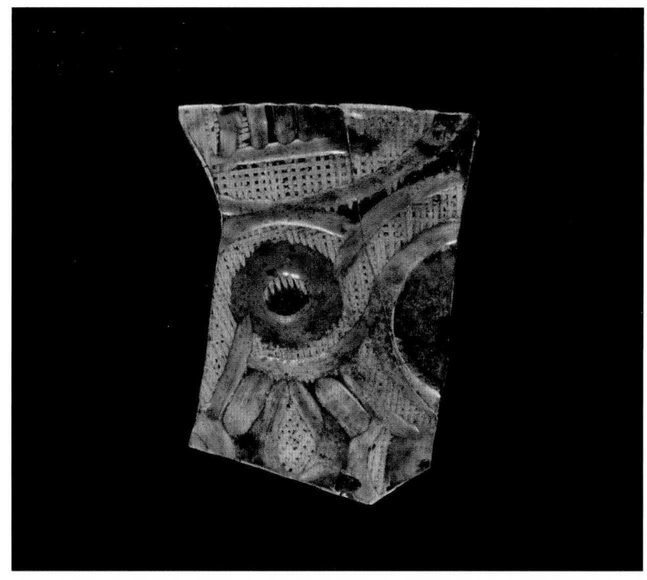

241

COMMENT: If the decoration was symmetrical about a vertical axis running through the centers of the countersunk dot and the tear, the small roundel had a larger roundel on the left side as well as on the right side. Bands of guilloche appear to be uncommon in early Islamic cut glass, although interwoven bands enclose decorated panels on some scratch-engraved objects, including **34** and a bottle in the al-Sabah Collection, Dār al-Āthār al-Islāmiyyah, Kuwait National Museum (LNS 375 G: Carboni 2001, pp. 76–81, no. 17a; *Glass of the Sultans* 2001, p. 166, no. 72).

Bibliography: *Verres antiques* 1954, p. 54, no. 334 (part of group).

242. Fragment

Date uncertain. Formerly in the Smith Collection (1147). 59.1.468.
H. 6.1 cm, D. (rim) 2.3–2.5 cm.
Almost colorless, with green tinge. Blown (perhaps in mold); facet- and linear-cut.

Fragment of rim and upper neck or body of vessel. Rim everted, with rounded lip and somewhat irregular mouth; neck or body has vertical side and square cross section. Each side has panel defined at top and bottom by single horizontal cut, 1.9 cm and 5.4 cm below rim; edges of each panel have two subtriangular or kite-shaped facets, one above the other, with longer sides meeting or almost meeting at midpoint.

Incomplete. Rim is chipped, and lower part of object is missing. Dull and pitted, with traces of pale grayish weathering.

Comment: The fragment is unlike any other object in this catalog, and its date and origin are uncertain. It is also not clear whether the fragment is the neck of a bottle or a tubelike vessel with a square cross section.

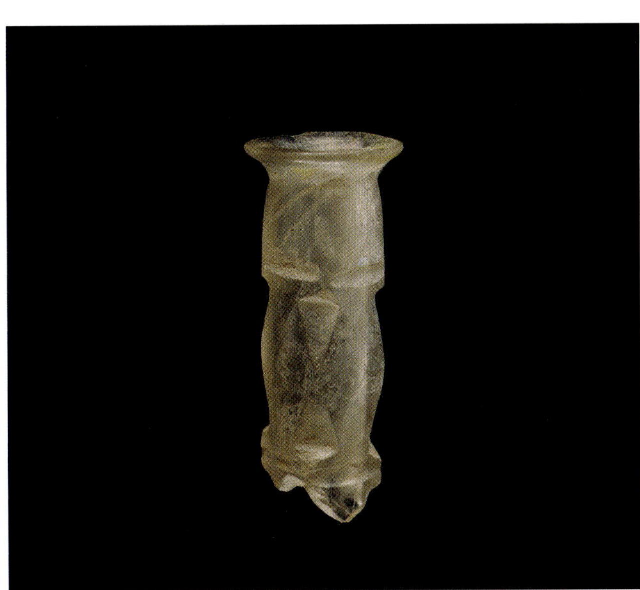

242

243. Fragment

10th to 11th century. Formerly in the Smith Collection (1221-27). Gift of Carl Berkowitz and Derek Content. 76.1.281.
Max. Dim. 4 cm.
Almost colorless, with yellowish tinge. Blown; linear-cut.

Fragment from wall of hollow vessel (Th. 0.1 cm) with unpolished linear-cut ornament consisting of two parallel lines and curvilinear motif, partly filled with transverse hatching.

Broken on all sides. Traces of pale brown weathering, especially in cuts.

Comment: The curvature of the fragment suggests that it is part of a bowl or a bottle.

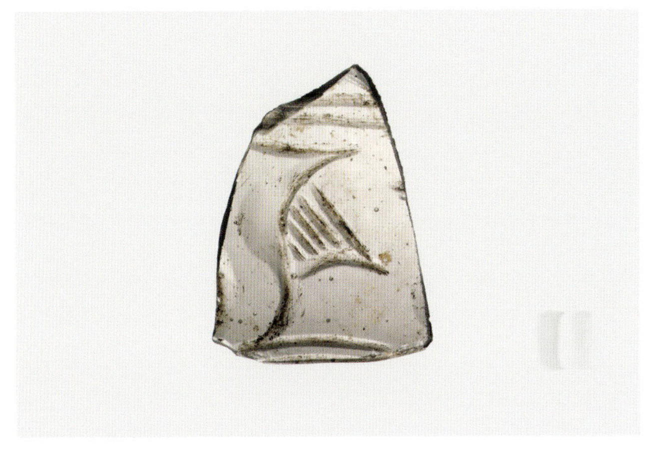

243

244. Fragment

10th to 11th century. Formerly in the Smith Collection. 68.1.59-47.
Max. Dim. 3.5 cm.
Almost colorless, with yellowish tinge. Blown; linear-cut.

Fragment from wall (Th. 0.15–0.25 cm) of vessel with linear-cut decoration consisting of two pairs of

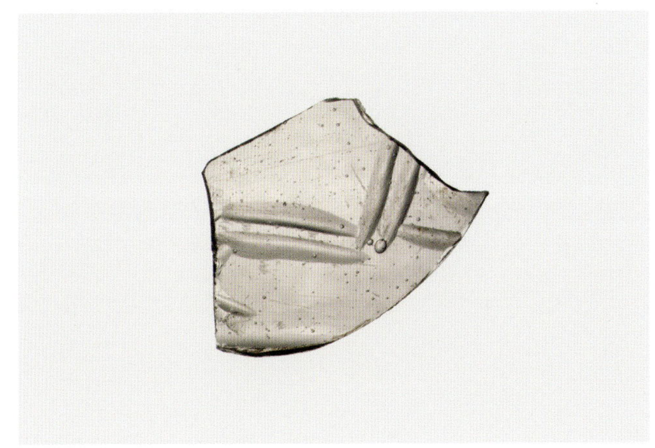

244

parallel lines meeting at right angle, and small parts of several single lines.

Broken on all sides. Slightly pitted.

245. Fragment

9th to 10th century. Formerly in the Smith Collection. Gift of Carl Berkowitz and Derek Content. 76.1.280.
Max. Dim. 3 cm.
Colorless. Blown; linear- and slant-cut.

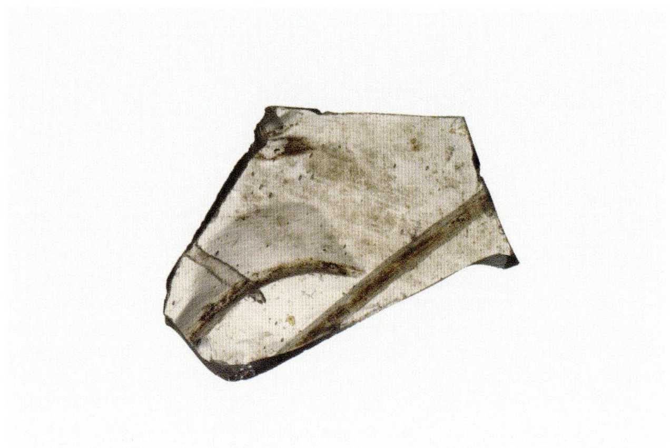

245

Fragment from wall of vessel. Indeterminate decoration includes two linear cuts and slant-cut crescentic motif.

Broken on all sides. Incipient weathering.

246. Fragment

10th to 11th century. Formerly in the Smith Collection. Gift of Carl Berkowitz and Derek Content. 76.1.278.
Max. Dim. 2 cm.
Colorless. Blown; linear- and slant-cut.

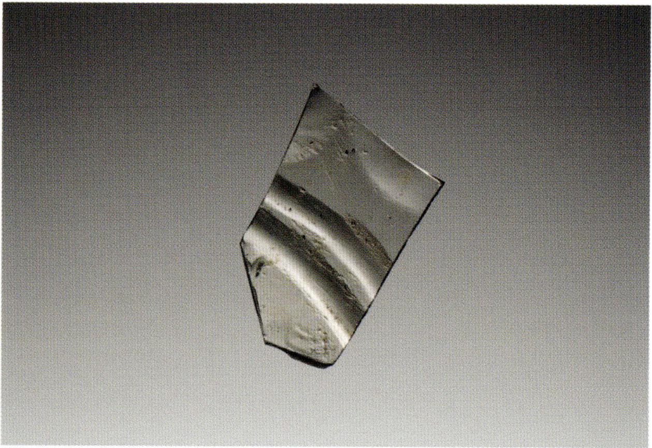

246

Fragment: scrap from wall of vessel (Th. 0.1 cm) with indeterminate linear- and slant-cut ornament.

Broken on all sides. No obvious weathering.

247. Fragment

9th to 11th century. Formerly in the Smith Collection (1221-7). Gift of Carl Berkowitz and Derek Content. 76.1.282.
Max. Dim. 2 cm.
Almost colorless, with yellowish tinge. Blown; linear-cut.

Fragment from wall (Th. 0.1 cm) of small vessel. Decoration of unpolished linear cuts includes geometric motifs and hatching.

Broken on all sides. Somewhat dull.

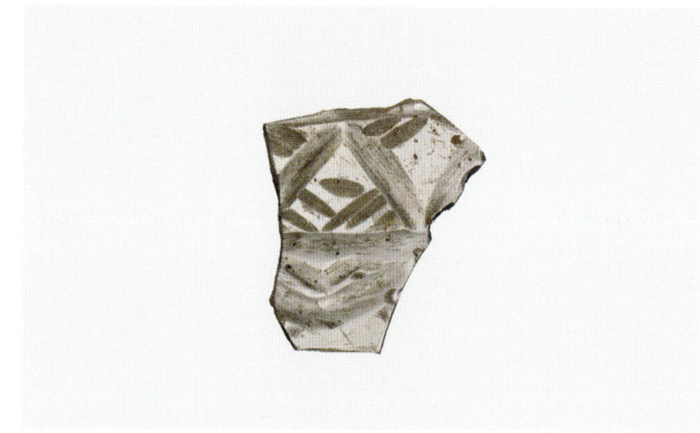

247

248. Fragment

10th to 11th century. Formerly in the Smith Collection. 68.1.59-82.
Max. Dim. 1.9 cm.
Almost colorless, with yellowish tinge. Blown; linear-cut.

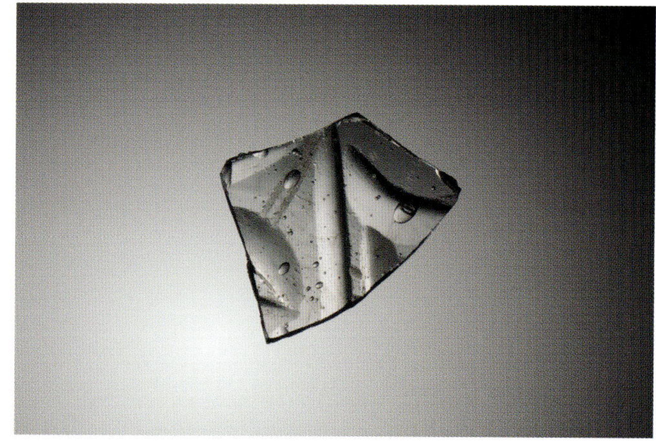

248

Fragment from wall (Th. 0.15 cm) of vessel with linear-cut decoration consisting of lines 0.2–0.3 cm wide.

Broken on all sides. No obvious weathering.

249. Fragment

9th to 11th century. Formerly in the Smith Collection. Gift of Carl Berkowitz and Derek Content. 76.1.277.
Max. Dim. 1.1 cm.
Colorless. Blown; linear-cut.

Fragment from body of vessel (Th. 0.1 cm) with indeterminate linear-cut decoration. Cuts are shallow and up to 0.25 cm wide.

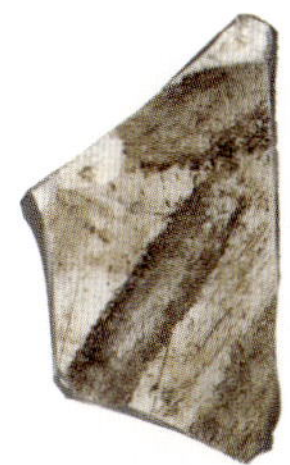

249

Broken on all sides. Outer surface dull; cuts are matte.

Slant-Cut Objects

A large number of early Islamic wheel-cut glasses are decorated in a style that resembles the "beveled" style of stucco, stone, and wood carving that was widely used at Samarra in the ninth century and survived in modified forms until the 14th century (Ettinghausen 1952). A characteristic feature of this style is the beveling of the surface toward the design: that is, the surrounding surface is cut and ground with a cross section shaped like a check (√), so that the ornament is flush with the surface but appears to be raised. In his monograph on the glass from Nishapur, Jens Kröger (1995, p. 161) suggested that, when applied to glass, this distinctive style of cutting should be termed "slant-cut," and I have adopted his suggestion. Often, as on many of the objects in this catalog, slant-cut ornament is combined with linear cutting. Fragments of slant-cut glass, presumably of the ninth century, were excavated at Samarra, and Kröger published 20 examples from Nishapur, which he attributed to the 10th century (*ibid.*, pp. 165–228, nos. 219–228).

The slant-cut objects are described in the following order:

1. Dish or bowl (**250**).
2. Bowls (**251–253**).
3. Beakers (**254–265**).
4. Large and medium bottles (**266–276**).
5. Small bottles (**277–282**).
6. Small bottle, "molar flask" (**283**).
7. Indeterminate (**284–295**).

1. Dish or Bowl

250. Fragment of Dish or Bowl

9th to 10th century. Formerly in the Smith Collection. 68.1.59-27.
Max. Dim. 3.8 cm.
Semitransparent deep green. Blown; linear- and slant-cut.

Fragment from bottom of dish or bowl (Th. 0.1–0.3 cm). Decorated on outside with two parallel curved lines, which may be border of medallion (external D. perhaps as great as 14 cm). Within this border, part of subcircular or oval motif with slant-cut countersunk

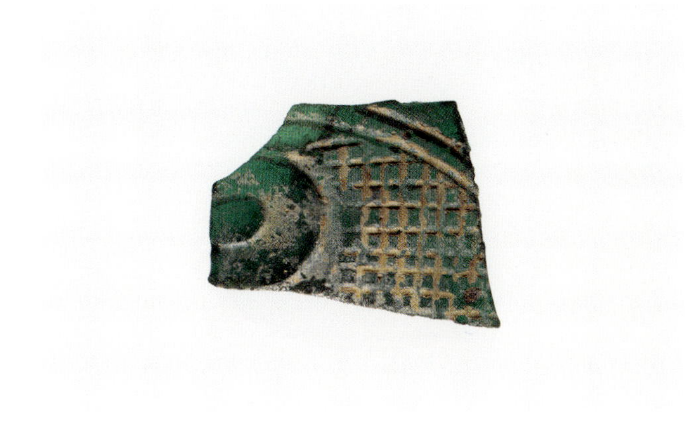

250

3. Beakers

254. Beaker with Animals

10th to 11th century. Formerly in the Strauss Collection (S1426). Bequest of Jerome Strauss. 79.1.45.
H. 13.1 cm, D. (rim) 9.3 cm.
Almost colorless, with yellowish tinge. Blown; linear- and slant-cut.

Beaker: roughly cylindrical. Rim plain, with top ground flat; wall almost straight, but with slightly concave profile, and tapering; base plain; pontil mark consists of irregular scar (L. 1.5 cm). Linear-cut decoration, with few slant-cut embellishments, on wall: single frieze bordered at top by pair of continuous horizontal lines 3.4–3.7 cm below rim, and at bottom by single horizontal line 0.9 cm above base. Frieze is completely filled with two similar animals moving from right to left. Each has head shown en face, and rest of body and limbs in profile. Head is shaped like rectangle, but is narrower at bottom than at top; eyes are indicated by single pointed oval, and muzzle by triangle that consists of bottom of head and two straight lines that converge at oval. Body has double outline; neck is filled with transverse hatching, horizontal band at bottom of neck by zigzag, and rest of body by crosshatching. Left shoulder is long and oval, left leg is very short and extended forward, and foot is hatched. Right foreleg is raised in front of chest; its foot is hatched. Left haunch resembles simple half-palmette, with slant-cut volute at top and hatching lower down; left leg is short, and foot is hatched. Right hind leg is much longer and extends forward; again, foot is hatched. Tail hangs down; it is long, pointed oval filled with hatching. Each animal carries unidentified object on its back: two vertical lines, which are separated by cross, are linked by curved line at top and terminate in outward-pointing slant-cut volutes; volute on viewer's right has curved beaklike projection.

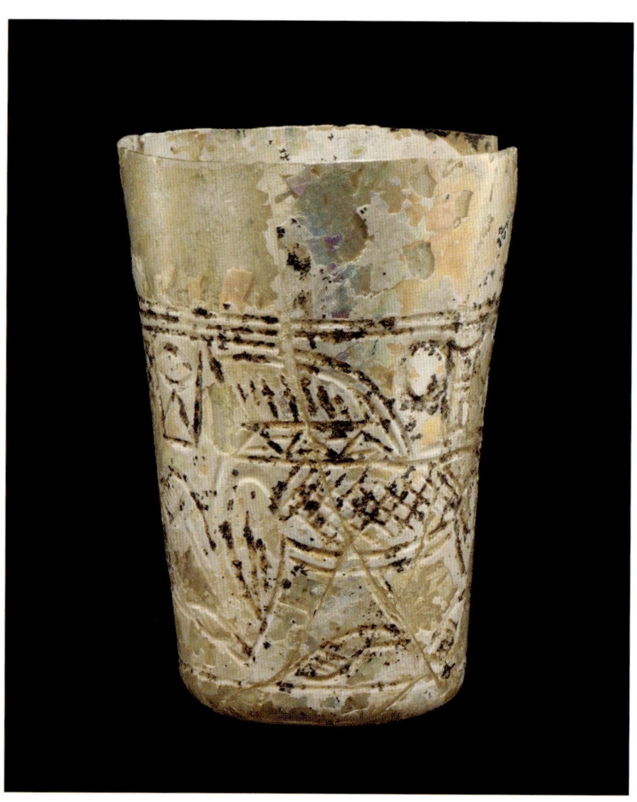

254

Incomplete. Broken, with small losses from rim (about 15 percent), upper wall, and bottom of wall; repaired. Remains of opaque off-white weathering speckled with dark gray.

Comment: The object is said to have come from Nishapur, northeastern Iran.

Three features of the animals set them apart from the great majority of animals on ninth- to 11th-century Islamic cut glass: the heads shown en face, the double outlines, and the prominent crosshatching. The depiction of heads en face, but without the other features mentioned above, occurs on a small number of relief-cut objects, which include **319** (see page 190) and a relief-cut fragment in the Museum für Islamische Kunst, Berlin (I.6569: Kröger 1999a, pp. 227–228, fig. 13 and illus. 29d). Double outlines and prominent crosshatching, however, are not characteristic of relief-cut glasses, but they are occasionally found on slant- and linear-cut objects. Charleston (1942, pp. 212–213) drew attention to a fragmentary linear-cut beaker, said to have come from Rayy or Sāveh, northern Iran, in the National Museum, Stockholm. The fragments are decorated with animals, which have double outlines and crosshatched bodies. Charleston compared this beaker with a bottle in the Victoria and Albert Museum, London, which has a bird with a crosshatched body. A similar bird appears on a fragmentary beaker excavated at Nishapur, now in the Iran Bastan Museum, Tehran (3943: Kröger 1995, p. 165, no. 219), and on a beaker in the Museum für Islamische Kunst, Berlin (I.22/61: *ibid.*, p. 165, fig. 16); the latter object also has a crosshatched animal.

Animals with crosshatched bodies and heads en face are seen on a bottle with linear-cut decoration from Ṣabra al-Mansuriyya, Qairouan, Tunisia (Marçais and Poinssot 1952, pp. 379–380, pl. LVII); and on several objects with linear-cut decoration from the Serçe Limanı shipwreck off the southern coast of Turkey (e.g., Bass 1984, p. 66, fig. 2a, b). Perhaps the closest parallel for **254**, however, is another fragmentary beaker from Serçe Limanı, which is decorated with two animals, not unlike the animals on the object in question, the bodies of which have double outlines and are crosshatched; unfortunately, the heads are not preserved (Bodrum Museum of Underwater Archeology, GW 1167: I am grateful to Prof. George F. Bass for this information). The Serçe Limanı ship sank within a few years of 1025 (Bass and others 2009).

Kröger (1999a, p. 228) and others have drawn attention to the stance of the lions on the Ṣabra al-Mansuriyya and Serçe Limanı glasses and the lions on approximately half of the published Hedwig beakers, including **589**. In addition to extensive hatching, nearly half of the Hedwig beakers have areas of crosshatching (e.g., Allen 1987, pp. 3–13, nos. 1–3, 5–10, and 12). Despite these common features, the overall appearance of the Hedwig beakers is unlike that of any of the objects mentioned above, and their origin remains one of the most tantalizing puzzles for students of medieval glass (see pages 334–337).

BIBLIOGRAPHY: *Glass Drinking Vessels* 1955, p. 31, no. 63.

255. Beaker with Birds

About 10th century. 61.1.23.
H. 9.7 cm, D. 6.4 cm.
Almost colorless, with yellowish tinge. Blown; linear- and slant-cut.

Beaker shaped like truncated cone. Rim plain; wall straight and tapering; base flat; trace of pontil mark. Wall has continuous frieze of irregular linear- and slant-cut decoration, which extends from about 2.5 cm below rim to bottom and consists of one register bordered by two horizontal grooves at top. Register is divided into equal panels by two pairs of vertical grooves. Each panel has, at center, large V-shaped motif with double outlines containing stylized bird standing in profile, facing right, and, on either side of V, standing bird facing side of panel.

Complete. Rim and upper wall broken into many pieces and repaired (see below). Dull and pitted, with silver-colored weathering and iridescence.

COMMENT: For a beaker of the same form, decorated with a single register that extends to the bottom of the wall and is divided into two panels containing large V-shaped motifs, excavated at Nishapur, northeastern Iran, see Kröger 1995, pp. 160–161, no. 218. Although the V-shaped motifs contain plantlike elements, the flanking triangles contain stylized birds similar to the birds on **255**. The close similarity of the two pieces suggests that they may have come from the same workshop, presumably in Iran.

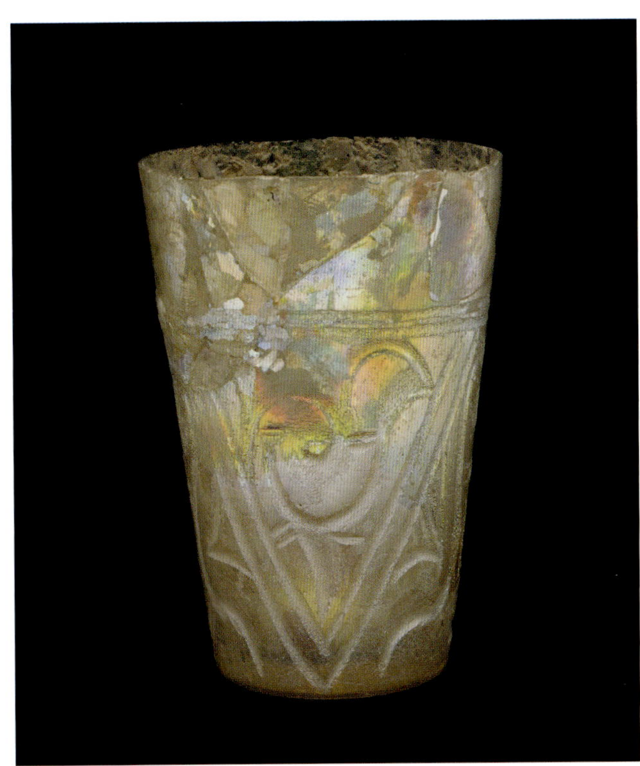

255

It is not certain that all of the fragments in the repaired part of the beaker are original, despite the fact that they fit together convincingly. In any case, it appears that flakes of weathering were deliberately attached to the inner surface of some of the pieces.

256. Beaker with Palmettes

About 10th century. 58.1.26.
H. 10.5 cm, D. (rim) 7 cm, (base) 4.3 cm.
Colorless; small bubbles. Blown; linear- and slant-cut.

Beaker shaped like truncated cone. Rim plain and ground flat; wall straight, tapering slightly, and "stepped" inward 1.2 cm above bottom; base is in form of disk, with shallow countersunk boss (H. 0.1 cm, D. 2.6 cm) at center; no pontil mark. Wall has continuous frieze of irregular linear- and slant-cut decoration, which extends from about 2.7 cm below rim to 1.5 cm above bottom and consists of one register bordered by two horizontal grooves at top and one horizontal groove at bottom. Frieze is slant-cut and consists of two narrow palmettes alternating with

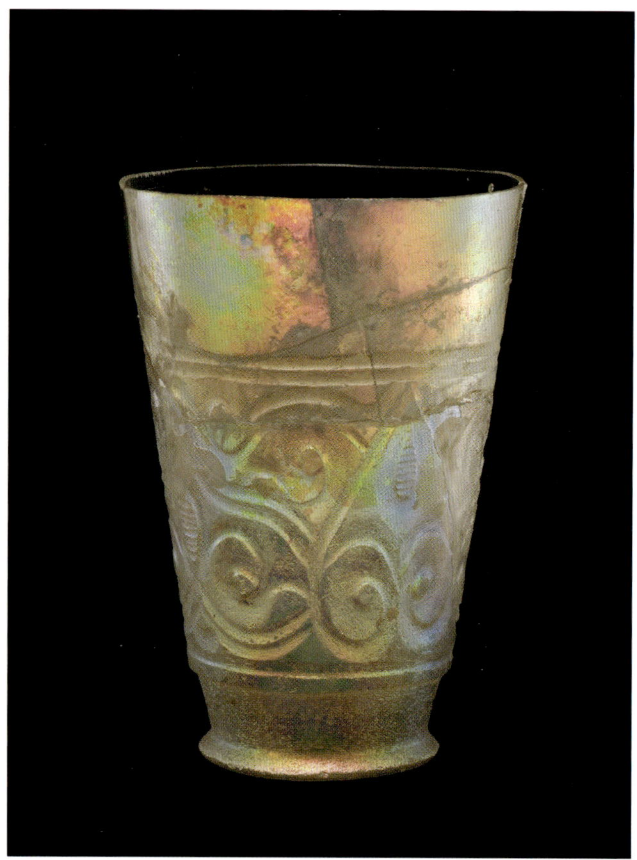

256

two broader palmettes. Each narrow palmette has tip uppermost, two large volutes, and pointed oval motif toward tip. Each broader palmette is similar, but has ogival outline. Spaces between palmettes are filled with scrolling vegetal motifs. Below border at bottom of frieze, wall was cut back to create disklike foot.

Incomplete. Broken, with loss of about 60 percent of rim and small parts of upper wall; restored. Dull and pitted, with remains of light brown weathering and iridescence.

Comment: Beakers with expanded feet, similar to the foot of this object, are not uncommon among glasses with relief-cut decoration, where the removal of a significant amount of glass from the wall allowed the glass cutter to create a relatively broad foot from a straight-sided blank. Such feet are less common on slant-cut objects, where the decorator was required to cut back the bottom of the wall in order to make a relatively narrow expanded foot. For another example of a slant-cut beaker on which the lower wall has been cut back to make an expanded foot, see *Hentrich Collection* 1974, p. 257, no. 402 (in the Museum Kunst Palast, Düsseldorf, P. 1971-104).

For a beaker decorated with palmettes and vegetal motifs, excavated at Nishapur, northeastern Iran, see Kröger 1995, pp. 167–169, no. 223.

257. Fragment of Beaker with Fleur-de-Lis

9th to 11th century. Formerly in the Smith Collection. 68.1.59-2.
H. (surviving) 4.3 cm, D. (base, est.) about 4.5 cm.
Colorless. Blown; linear- and slant-cut.

Fragment of beaker. Lower wall (Th. 0.2–0.4 cm) is straight and tapering; base (Th. 0.35–0.4 cm) flat, with pontil mark. Wall has parts of two motifs, apparently separated by two vertical linear-cut lines: (1) linear- and facet-cut fleur-de-lis, flanked by two transverse lines; and (2) indeterminate motif with curved lines.

Broken on all sides. Dull, with patches of light gray and brownish weathering.

Comment: The fleur-de-lis would have occupied about half the circumference of the beaker, presumably with the second motif filling the other half.

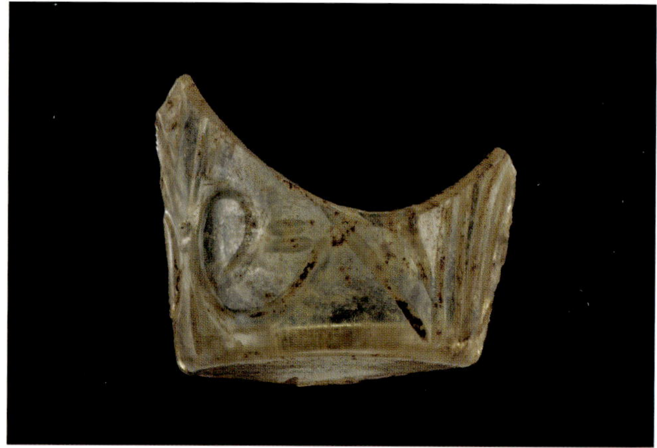

257

258. Fragment of Beaker with Vegetal Motif

10th to 11th century. 51.1.132.
H. (surviving) 7 cm, D. (est.) about 9 cm.
Almost colorless, with greenish yellow tinge; very small bubbles. Blown; linear- and slant-cut.

Fragment of beaker, including small part of rim. Rim plain, with lip ground flat; upper wall (Th. 0.1–0.15 cm) straight and tapering. Exterior has linear- and slant-cut ornament beneath two parallel, and presumably continuous, horizontal grooves, 1.7–2 cm below lip: part of vegetal scroll. Stem curves down from left to right; on outside of curve, (1) tendril, which curves upward and divides into two, and (2) narrow oval shoot at junction of stem and tendril; on inside of curve, part of half-palmette or leaf with curved veins.

Broken on all sides. Traces of incipient very pale gray weathering.

Comment: The fragment was purchased in Cairo, Egypt. The virtual absence of weathering is consistent with the probability that the object was found in Egypt.

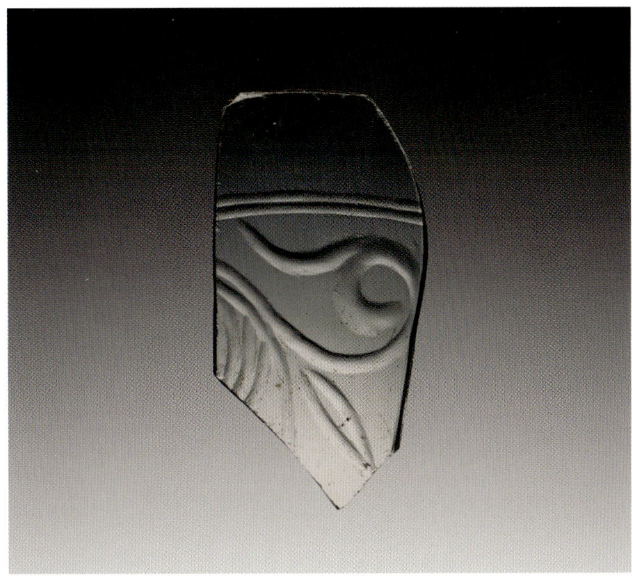

258

259. Fragment of Beaker with Vegetal Ornament

Probably 10th to 11th century. Formerly in the Smith Collection. 68.1.59-26.
H. (surviving) 3.8 cm, D. (est.) about 6 cm.
Colorless or almost colorless. Blown; linear- and slant-cut.

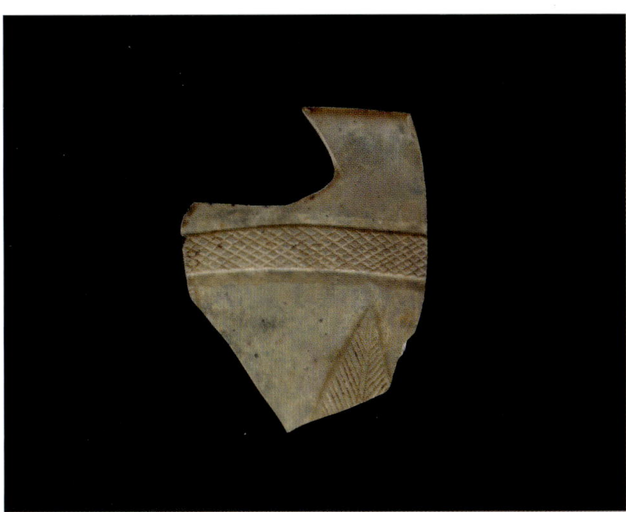

259

Fragment from rim and upper wall of beaker. Rim plain, with rounded lip; wall straight and tapering. Surviving decoration consists of upper border and part of vegetal motif. Border begins 1.3 cm below lip, is 0.9 cm wide, and consists of countersunk band of closely spaced crosshatching. Vegetal motif is vertical leaf or palmette in slant-cut, countersunk relief, with linear-cut central vein and herringbone pattern of hatching.

Very small part of rim survives; all other edges are broken. Patchy brown to silver iridescent weathering, especially on outside.

Comment: The fragment is unusual. Apart from the use of crosshatching, which occurs infrequently on early Islamic cut glass, the small scale and meticulous workmanship make the fragment exceptional and call into question the attribution suggested above.

260. Fragment of Beaker

10th to 11th century. Formerly in the Smith Collection. 68.1.59-20.
H. (surviving) 4.6 cm, D. (est., at top) 6–7 cm.
Almost colorless, with greenish yellow tinge.
Blown; slant- and linear-cut.

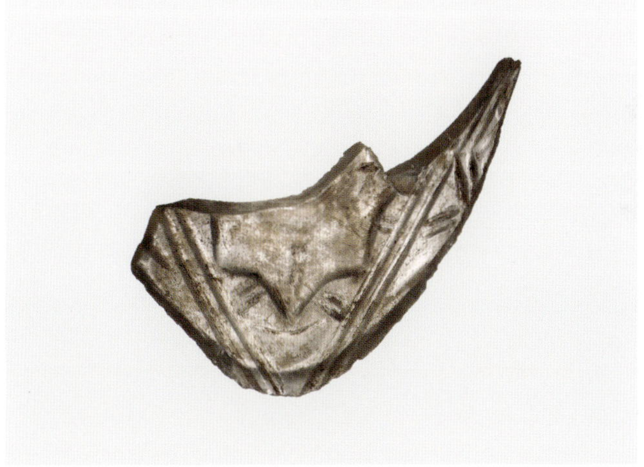

260

Fragment from lower wall of beaker (Th. 0.15–0.4 cm) with straight, tapering side. Decoration apparently consisted of frieze containing overall pattern of horizontal rows of triangular and diamond-shaped panels with double linear-cut outlines. Surviving part of frieze seems to have large diamond-shaped panel flanked, at bottom, by smaller triangular panels with apexes pointing upward, and, above these, possibly by congruent triangular panels with apexes pointing downward. Diamond-shaped panel has indeterminate slant- and linear-cut motif, which is symmetrical about vertical axis. Triangular panels have simple slant- and linear-cut ornament.

Broken on all sides. Dull, with patches of brownish weathering, especially in cuts.

Comment: If the decoration was symmetrical, it consisted of a row of contiguous diamond-shaped panels that extended for the full height of the frieze and were separated above and below the points where they touch by pairs of triangles, the bases of which were formed by the frieze's upper and lower edges.

261. Fragment of Beaker(?)

Probably 10th century. Formerly in the Smith Collection (508). Gift of Mrs. Ray Winfield Smith. 81.1.693.
H. 6.3 cm, D. (max., surviving) 5.5 cm, (base) 4 cm.
Almost colorless, with greenish yellow tinge; small bubbles. Blown; slant-cut.

Fragment of beaker(?), preserving approximately 30 percent of lower wall and entire base. Wall straight, tapering first at steep angle, then at shallower angle near bottom; base slightly splayed, with countersunk boss (D. 2.3 cm) at center of underside; pontil mark probably removed by grinding and polishing. Wall has incised decoration made with broad, slanting cuts: on upper part, two apparently continuous staggered horizontal rows of 15 contiguous tall ovals; each oval has countersunk downward-pointing tear-shaped motif, several of which are hatched with short horizontal cuts; just below lower row, 15 contiguous pendent crescents and, below this, continuous horizontal groove. Beneath groove, wall is cut to form profile of bottom of wall and base.

Dull, with pits and pale grayish weathering, especially in coldworked areas.

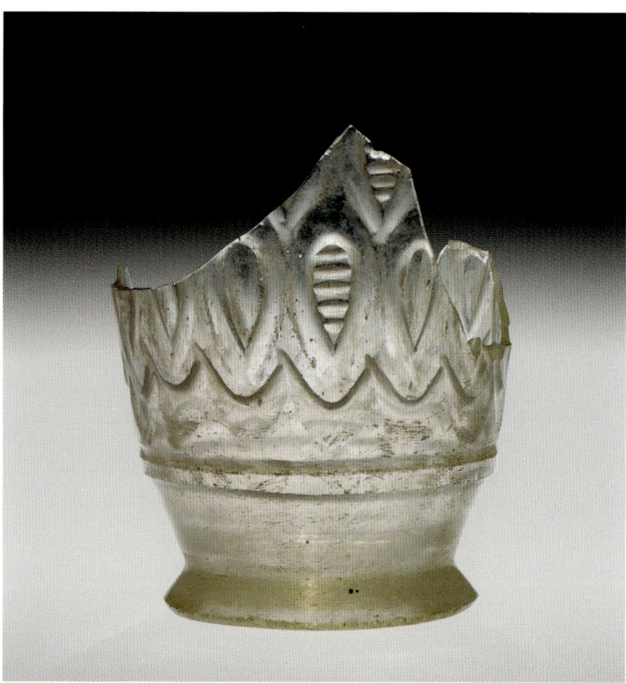

261

Comment: According to the Museum's records, Ray Winfield Smith purchased the fragment from the Tehran- and Paris-based dealer Ayoub Rabenou in 1948.

The size and shape of the fragment suggest that it is the lower part of a beaker, although it may have come from a bottle. A similar pattern of oval motifs is found on a fragment of relief-cut glass from Iran (Lamm 1929–30, p. 153, pl. 57, no. 9).

Bibliography: *Verres antiques* 1954, p. 51, no. 313.

262. Fragment of Beaker(?)

About 10th century. 51.1.131.
H. 5.8 cm, D. (est.) about 10 cm.
Colorless, but broken edges are yellowish green. Blown; slant-cut.

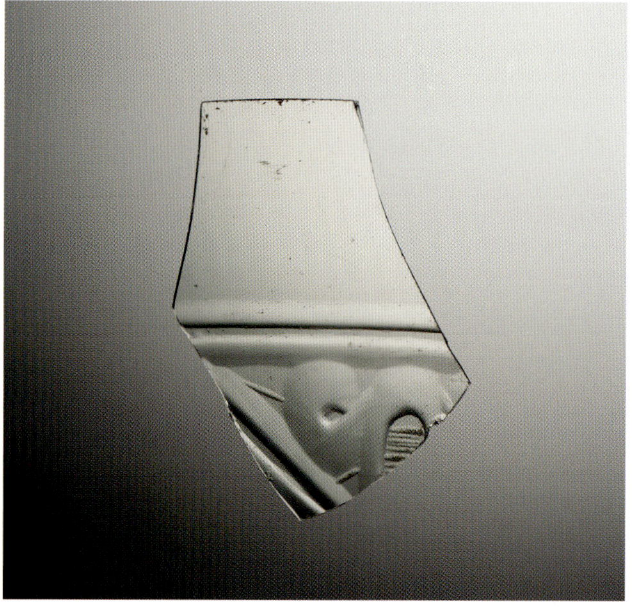

262

Fragment of beaker(?). Rim plain, with top ground flat; wall (Th. 0.1–0.15 cm) straight and tapering slightly. Slant-cut decoration apparently consists of frieze bordered at top by horizontal rib 3.2 cm below rim. Surviving part of frieze contains hatched oval or tear-shaped motif with volute and linear element on one side.

Broken on all sides, except for small part of rim. No obvious weathering.

Comment: The glass is thin, and therefore the cutting is rather shallow. The horizontal rib is defined by two parallel slant cuts, and except for the hatching, all components of the frieze are slant-cut.

263. Fragment of Beaker(?)

10th to 11th century. Formerly in the Smith Collection (1221-18). Gift of Carl Berkowitz and Derek Content. 76.1.300.
Max. Dim. 4.1 cm, D (est.) perhaps about 7 cm.
Almost colorless, with yellowish tinge. Blown; slant- and linear-cut.

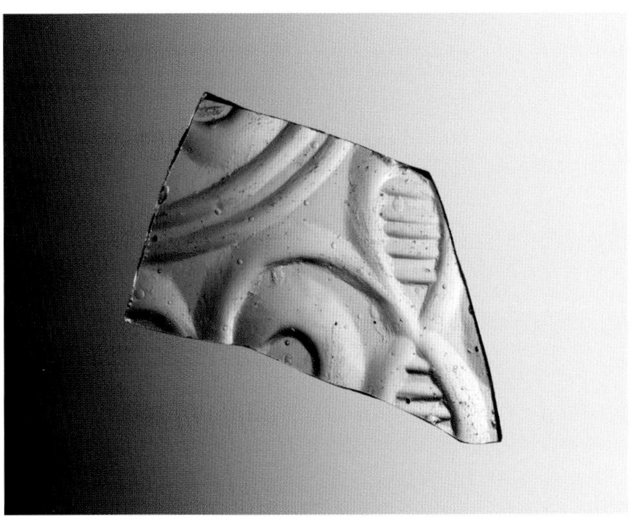

263

Fragment from straight or slightly convex wall (Th. 0.1 cm) of beaker(?) with slant- and linear-cut decoration. Ornament includes part of "fleur-de-lis" or quatrefoil with two contiguous vertical elements, which are elongated, rounded at one end and pointed at other end, and filled with horizontal hatching; and two rounded elements (perhaps with volutes), one on either side. Other ornament consists of curvilinear (circular?) border comprising two linear cuts, with indeterminate motif at center.

Broken on all sides. Lightly pitted.

Comment: The diameter and thickness of the fragment suggest that it is part of a beaker rather than a larger object, such as a bottle. The principal motif may have been similar to the "fleur-de-lis" on **149** and **266**.

264. Fragment of Beaker(?)

10th to 11th century. Formerly in the Smith Collection (1221-21). Gift of Carl Berkowitz and Derek Content. 76.1.255.
H. (surviving) 3.5 cm, D. (est.) about 6–7 cm.
Almost colorless, with yellowish tinge. Blown; slant- and linear-cut.

Fragment from wall (Th. 0.2 cm) of beaker(?) with straight side. Two parallel horizontal linear cuts represent upper or lower border of frieze. Surviving part of frieze has vertical cut, perhaps defining edge of panel, and one crescent-shaped slant-cut motif.

Broken on all sides. Virtually without weathering.

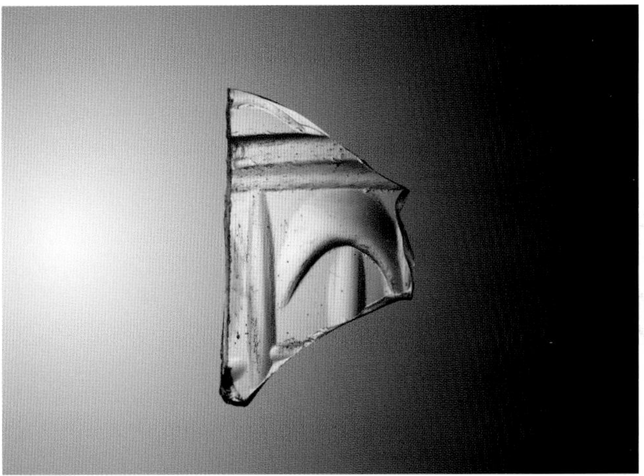

264

265. Fragment of Beaker(?)

About 10th century. Formerly in the Smith Collection. 68.1.59-41.
H. 3.4 cm, D. (rib, est.) 5–6 cm.
Almost colorless, with yellowish tinge. Blown; slant-cut.

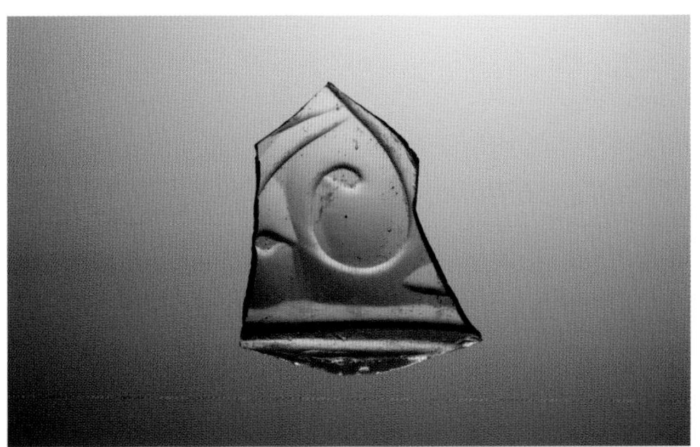

265

267. Globular Bottle with Rosettes

10th century. 64.1.15.
H. 16.9 cm, D. (rim) 2.6 cm, (max.) 10.1 cm.
Colorless or almost colorless. Blown; slant- and linear-cut.

Bottle with almost globular body, but with width greater than height. Rim plain, with internal bevel and top ground flat; neck cylindrical; wall curves smoothly out, down, and in; shallow disklike base, slightly concave on underside; no pontil mark (but see below). Slant- and/or linear-cut decoration on neck, wall, and underside of base. On neck: linear-cut band of chevrons, bordered at top and bottom by pairs of continuous horizontal grooves. Chevrons are arranged in six adjoining columns, each with 11 pairs of diagonal cuts that form inverted Vs. On wall: broad band of slant- and linear-cut ornament with pair of continuous horizontal grooves at top and single groove at bottom. Ornament consists of four identical roundels separated by vegetal ornament. Each roundel is defined by two concentric grooves and contains slant-cut rosette composed of four heart-shaped elements. Space between each pair of roundels is occupied by slant- and linear-cut scrolling stem with leaf resembling half-palmette, but with volute at top and bottom. On underside of base: ring of about 73 short oval cuts at edge and, at center, facet-cut square (W. 1.7 cm) filled with crosshatching, perhaps to eliminate pontil mark.

Incomplete. Broken, with losses from body, including most of one rosette and part of another; restored. Dull and pitted, with pale iridescence.

Comment: The form and decoration of the bottle have several very close parallels. The body of a bottle decorated with roundels containing rosettes was found during excavations at Nishapur, northeastern Iran (The Metropolitan Museum of Art, New York, 40.170.129: Kröger 1995, p. 171, no. 225), and the same deposit—the filling of a well—also contained a neck that is almost identical to the neck of **267** (48.101.263: *ibid.*, pp. 171–172, no. 226; Kröger notes that the body and the neck have different chemical compositions and cannot be from the same vessel). Two similar bottles are in the Hentrich Collection in the Museum Kunst Palast, Düsseldorf (P. 1971-105: *Hentrich Collection* 1974, p. 264, no. 411), and the Heeramaneck Collection at the Los Angeles County Museum of Art (M.73.5.387: *Heeramaneck Collection* 1973, p. 182, no. 369). The bottle in Los Angeles is described as having, in each roundel, "a floral motif resembling an acanthus." Of the two roundels visible in the photograph in the catalog of the collection, one contains a floral or vegetal motif, and the other contains a rosette composed of four heart-shaped elements.

Bibliography: *Persian Glass* 1972, p. 17, no. 29.

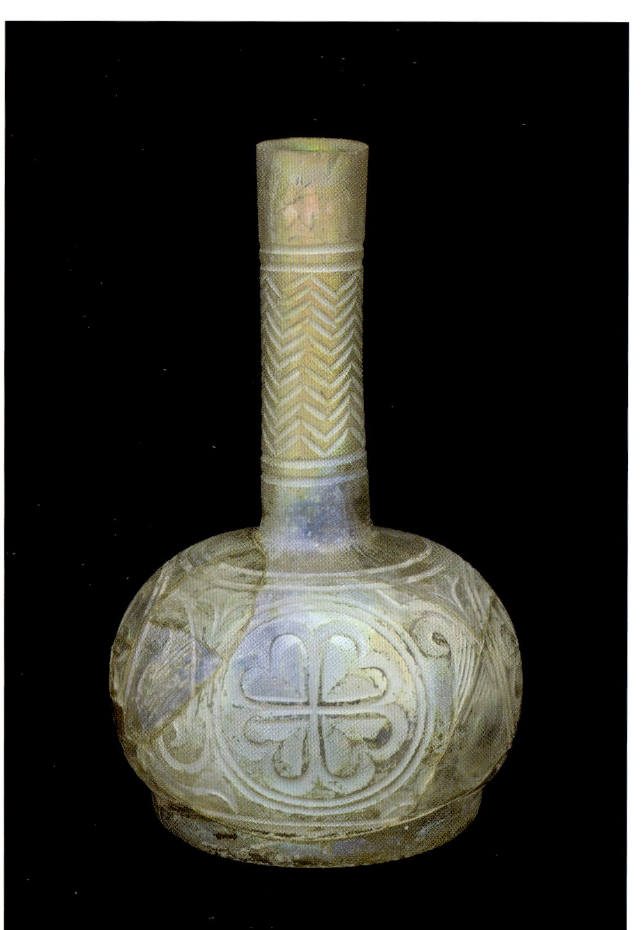

267A

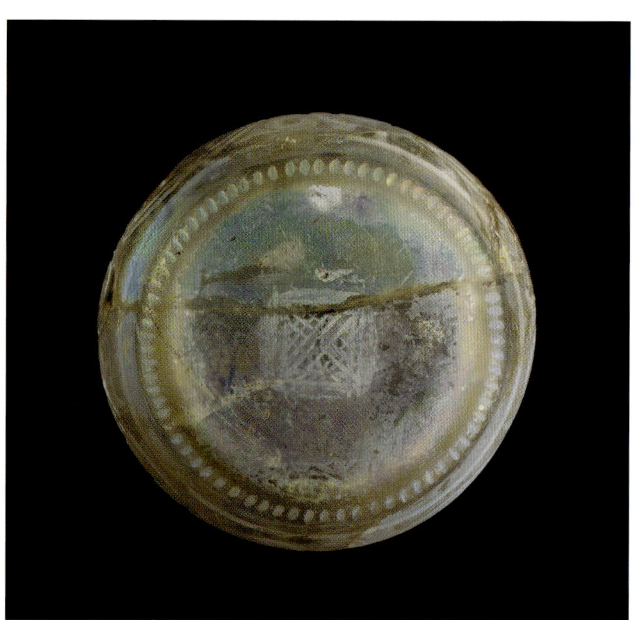

267B

268. Globular Bottle

10th to 11th century. Formerly in the Smith Collection (378). 55.1.133.
H. 20.9 cm, D. (rim) 1.8 cm, (max.) 10.2 cm.
Transparent deep blue. Blown; facet-, linear-, and slant-cut, and probably filed.

Bottle with globular body. Rim plain, with flat top; neck long, narrow, and slightly wider at bottom than at top; wall curves down, out, and in; base has tubular foot-ring made by folding, and is slightly convex at center; apparently no pontil mark. Neck and wall have wheel-cut and probably filed ornament. Neck has four horizontal bands of ornament separated by countersunk ribs (from top to bottom): (1) countersunk molding with convex profile; (2) five vertical facets (H. 4.1 cm) separated by unworked strips; each facet has raised triangle at top and bottom, and raised diamond at midpoint; (3) six contiguous rhomboids (H. 2.2 cm, W. 0.9 cm) forming continuous zigzag; above and below junction of each pair of rhomboids, one short horizontal cut; and (4) six rectangular vertical facets (H. 2.4 cm) and one unworked vertical strip. Body has two continuous horizontal friezes with two parallel border lines at top of upper frieze, single line separating friezes, and single line at bottom of lower frieze. Upper, narrow frieze consists of five arc-shaped cuts with their ends pointing down, alternating with five arc-shaped cuts with their ends pointing up; inside each arc is one more or less horizontal cut, and between two arcs is one cross-shaped motif. Lower, wider frieze has four rather irregular, contiguous motifs with double outlines; two motifs are large horizontal "rectangles" with triangular ends and triangular projections from midpoints of sides; these are separated by one hexagon and one pentagon; each "rectangle" contains row of five countersunk circular bosses, hexagon and pentagon contain four such bosses, and rows of bosses occupy field above and below "rectangles," with one additional boss at junction of "rectangle" and pentagon; short straight or curving cuts are also found inside hexagon, pentagon, and one "rectangle," and in field.

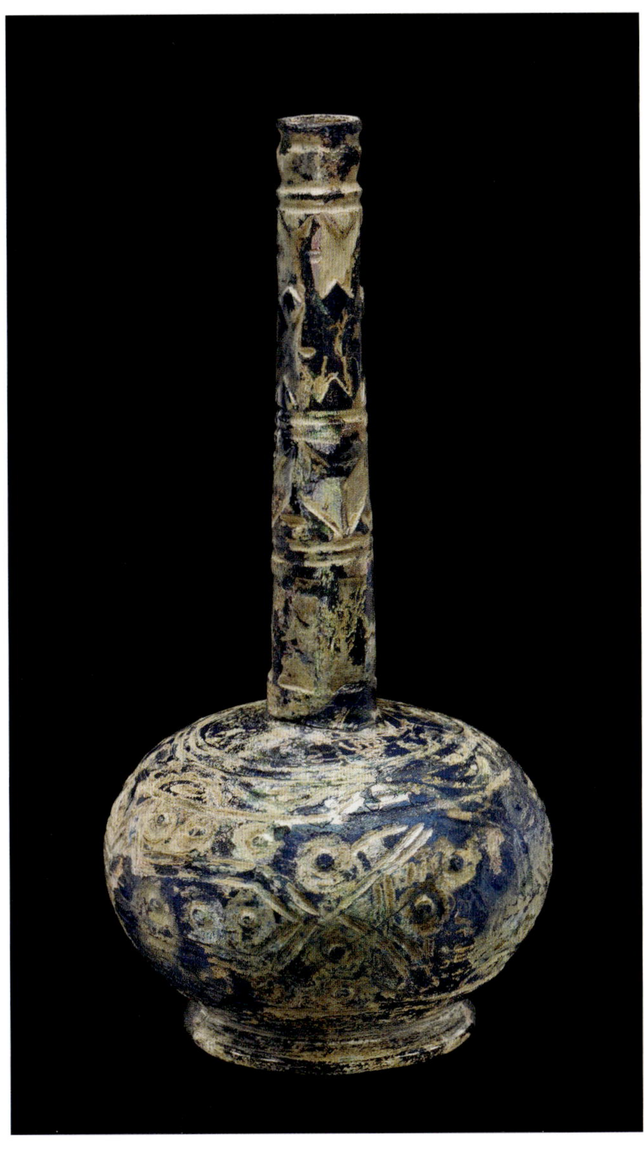

268

Complete. Broken into 10 pieces and repaired. Mostly dull to matte and pitted, with extensive remains of pale gray to silver, slightly iridescent weathering.

Comment: The decoration was carelessly laid out. There is a gap in the otherwise unbroken frieze of facets at the base of the neck, and the pentagonal panel on the wall seems to be the result of misjudging the space needed for a second hexagonal panel.

The object is similar in size, shape, color, and decoration on the neck to another bottle at Corning (**266**), which, Ray Winfield Smith reported, probably came from Iran.

Bibliography: *Glass from the Ancient World* 1957, p. 273, no. 562.

269. Ovoid Bottle

9th to 10th century. Formerly in the Smith Collection (578). 55.1.131.
H. 22.8 cm, D. (max.) 8.7 cm, (base) 4.9 cm.
Almost colorless, with yellowish tinge; many minute bubbles. Blown; facet-, linear-, and slant-cut.

Bottle with ovoid body. Rim plain, with flat top; neck cylindrical; wall curves out, down, and in; base plain, with rounded side; no pontil mark. Decorated

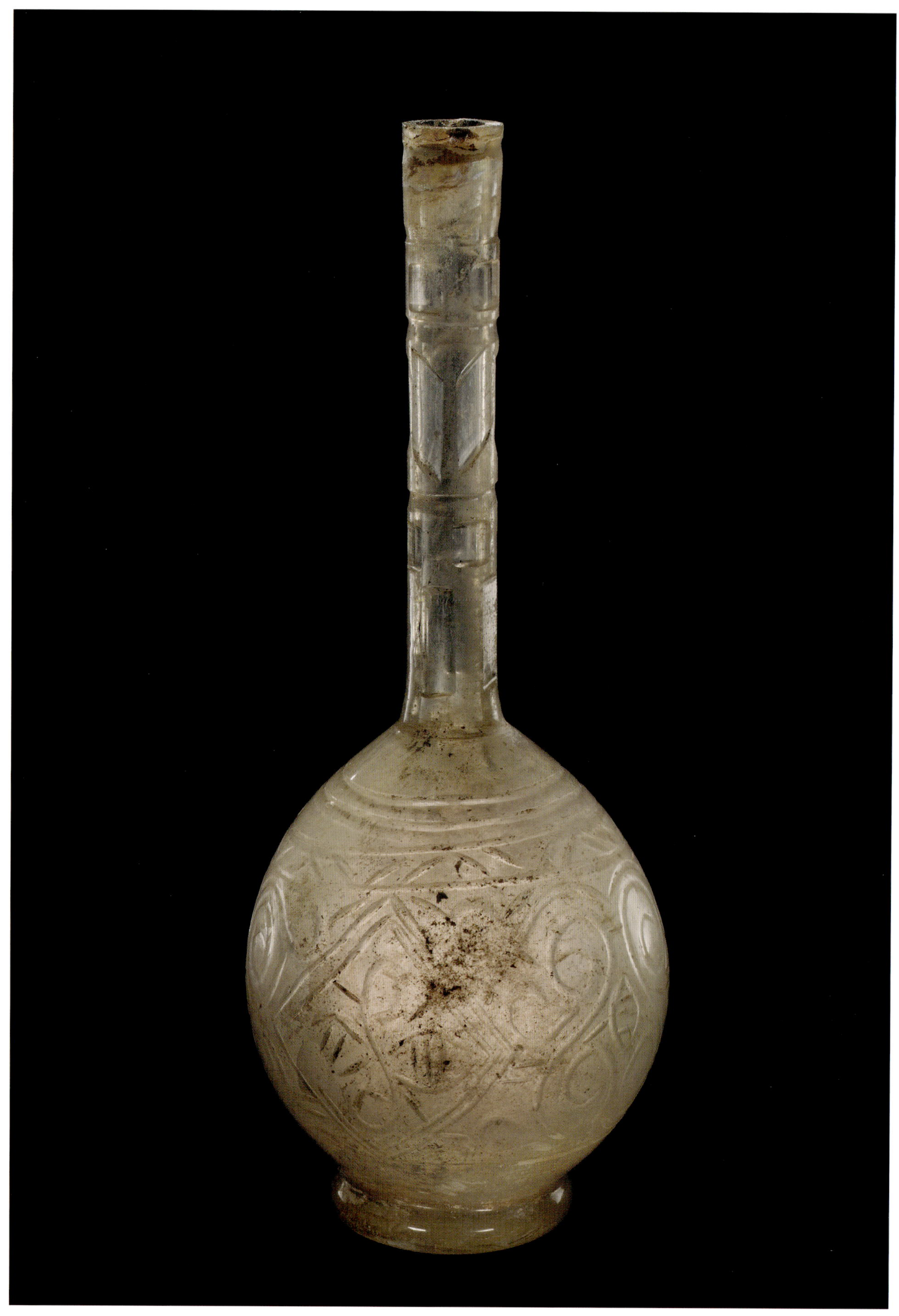

269

on neck and wall. On neck: five continuous horizontal bands (from top to bottom): (1) plain; (2) row of four square facets; (3) six rhomboidal facets forming continuous band of tall, narrow chevrons; (4) row of four square facets; and (5) four tall rectangular facets. Bands 1–3 are separated by continuous grooves, with additional grooves above 1 and below 3. On wall: continuous horizontal frieze of linear- and slant-cut ornament: two rhombuses with double outlines, each containing one elongated S-shaped element between two hatched oval motifs, and with two or three straight cuts in background. Rhombuses are separated on either side by two pairs of S-shaped motifs; in every case, S on left is reversed to create symmetrical design. At centers of three pairs of S-shaped motifs is one tear-shaped motif with horizontal hatching; fourth pair has small area of crosshatching instead; spaces between adjacent pairs also have single tear-shaped motif with horizontal hatching. Frieze is bordered at top by narrow band of rudimentary chevrons and at bottom by single line. Between band of chevrons and top of wall, two continuous horizontal grooves. Tops and bottoms of S-shaped motifs are slant-cut; remainder of decoration is linear-cut.

Intact, except for chips in rim and circular hole (D. 0.6 cm) drilled in base (see below). Somewhat dull, with patches of pitting and silvery gray weathering; slight iridescence.

Comment: According to *Verres antiques* (see below), Ray Winfield Smith acquired the object in Iran. **197** has identical facet-cut decoration on the neck. Similar pairs of S-shaped elements are found, inverted, on a mold-blown bottle in the al-Sabah Collection, Dār al-Āthār al-Islāmiyyah, Kuwait National Museum (LNS 8 G: Carboni 2001, p. 217, no. 55 = *Glass of the Sultans* 2001, p. 91, no. 17). The rhombuses and the band of chevronlike ornament are similar to decoration occupying the same positions on **196**. The hole in the base was presumably drilled by Smith to obtain a sample for spectrographic analysis.

Bibliography: *Verres antiques* 1954, p. 54, no. 331; *Glass from the Ancient World* 1957, p. 273, no. 564; *Persian Glass* 1972, p. 17, no. 31.

270. Ovoid Bottle with Inscription

9th to 10th century. 67.1.3.
H. 18.2 cm, D. (rim) 2.1 cm, (max.) 6.2 cm.
Colorless. Blown; slant-cut.

Bottle with ovoid body. Rim plain, with ground top; neck cylindrical, but narrower at bottom than at top; shoulder slopes; wall curves out, down, and in, and merges with rounded base. Neck, wall, and base are covered with slant-cut ornament arranged in six continuous horizontal bands framed by either one or two continuous horizontal ribs. Upper neck has band of seven vertical oval facets, and lower neck has six contiguous rectangular vertical facets. Shoulder is divided into 10 contiguous vertical facets. Upper wall has narrow band of Kufic: "بركة و سرور لصاحبه" (*baraka wa surur li-sahibihi*; Blessing and happiness to its owner). Below this is broader band containing two small, inverted heart-shaped motifs with vegetal

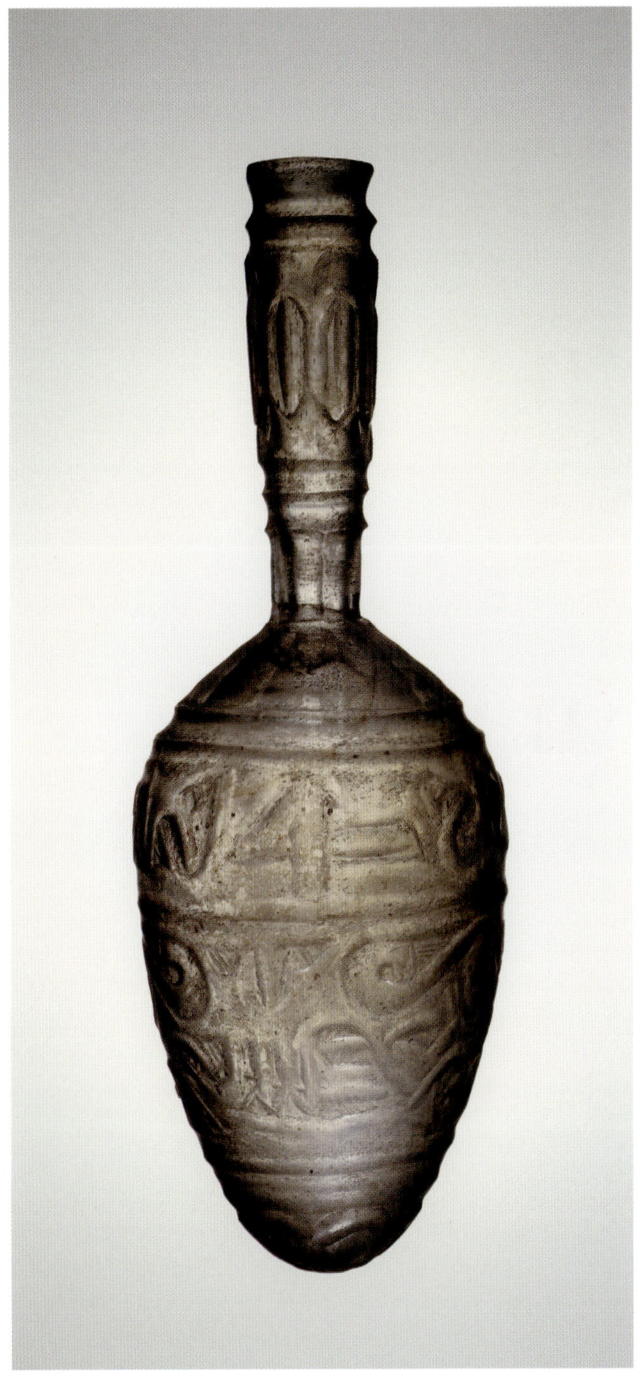

270

scrolls springing symmetrically from their tops and in roughly symmetrical patterns from their bottoms. Base is cut in form of rosette with seven petals.

Complete, except for small chip on rim; broken at base of neck and repaired. Dull and pitted.

Comment: The form is similar to that of a bottle with slant- and linear-cut decoration in the Museum Kunst Palast, Düsseldorf (P. 1973-63: *Hentrich Collection* 1974, p. 275, no. 422), and a bottle in the Iraqi National Museum, Baghdad (IM 30325).

Bibliography: "Recent Important Acquisitions," *JGS*, v. 10, 1968, p. 183, no. 22; *Persian Glass* 1972, p. 16, no. 28; *Glass of the Sultans* 2001, pp. 189–190, no. 94.

271. Cylindrical Bottle with Vegetal Motifs

9th to 10th century. 67.1.2.
H. 15.5 cm, D. (rim) 4.1 cm, (max.) 8.2 cm.
Colorless or almost colorless. Blown; facet-, linear-, and slant-cut.

Bottle with cylindrical body. Rim plain, with rounded lip; neck tapers; shoulder has rounded profile; wall descends vertically and curves in at bottom; base plain; pontil mark irregular (L. 1.6 cm). Decorated on neck, shoulder, and wall. On neck: two continuous bands of facet-cut ornament, each with horizontal groove at top. Upper band has eight adjacent rhomboidal facets creating row of chevrons, with short horizontal cuts in triangular spaces between each pair of rhomboids. Lower band has five adjacent rectangular facets with heights greater than widths. On shoulder: two continuous bands of linear-cut ornament. Upper band consists of pair of closely spaced horizontal grooves, and lower band has two more widely spaced horizontal grooves containing row of small X-shaped motifs. On wall: single register of linear- and slant-cut ornament extending from band of crosses at edge of shoulder to single horizontal groove 0.8–1.0 cm above base. Register contains symmetrical arrangement of two opposed diamond-shaped panels with double borders separated by two shallow ogival arches. Each panel contains vegetal motif shaped like "fleur-de-lis," with slant-cut volutes at sides and linear-cut hatched oval at top. Each arch contains similar but broader motif, while spaces between panels and arches are filled with pairs of volutes separated by two vertical cuts.

Intact. Most of surface is dull, with extensive patches of light to dark gray weathering and glints of iridescence.

Comment: A bottle with the same form and similar decoration is in The Toledo Museum of Art (47.5: *Art in Glass* 1969, p. 38). Other examples of this form with cut decoration include **371**; another bottle at Toledo (47.6: *ibid.*); vessels from Kermānshāh, western Iran, and Baghdad (Lamm 1929–30, p. 156, pl. 58, nos. 12 and 13); and objects in The Chrysler Museum of Art, Norfolk, Virginia (Merrill 1989, p. 22, no. 15 = "Recent Important Acquisitions," *JGS*, v. 9, 1967, p. 137, no. 22); The British Museum, London (OA 1959.2-18.1 and 1959.2-18.2: *Masterpieces of Glass* 1968, p. 107, nos. 139 and 140; the latter is also illustrated in Pinder-Wilson 1991, 1999, and 2004, p. 117, fig. 141, left); and the Los Angeles County Museum of Art (*Cohn Collection* 1980, p. 163, no. 159). For examples of this form with mold-blown decoration, see Pinder-Wilson 1991, 1999, and 2004, p. 123, fig. 151 (in The British Museum: OA 1976.11-2.1); and "Recent Important Acquisitions," *JGS*, v. 39, 1997, p. 157, no. 2 (in The Corning Museum of Glass: 97.1.1).

Bibliography: "Recent Important Acquisitions," *JGS*, v. 10, 1968, p. 184, no. 23; *Persian Glass* 1972, p. 17, fig. 30.

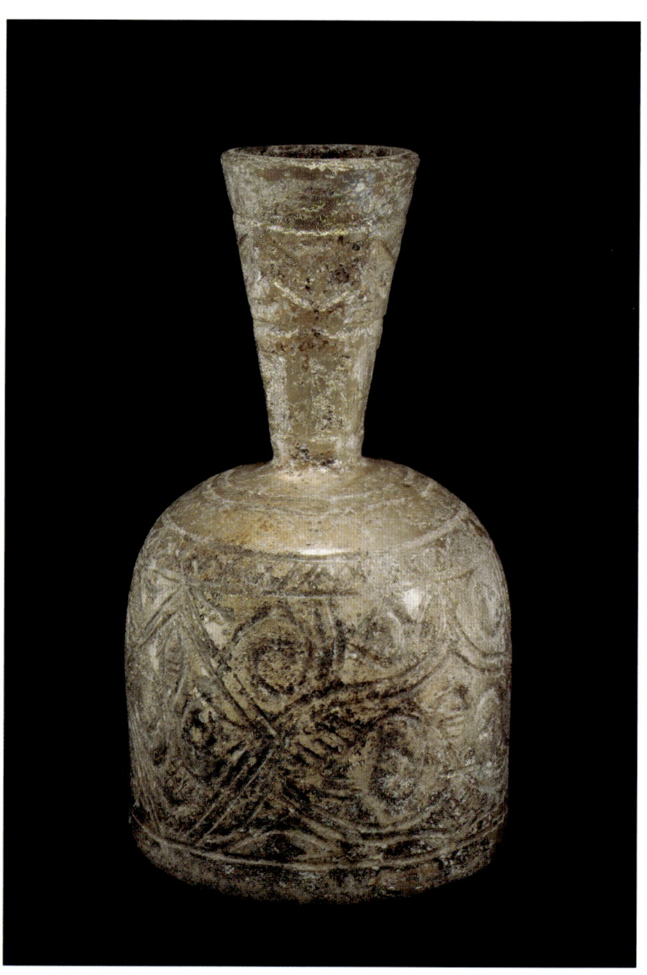

271

272. Cylindrical Bottle with Inscription

10th to 11th century. Formerly in the Smith Collection (667). 55.1.128.
H. 21.7 cm, D. (shoulder) 12.5 cm, (base) 9 cm.
Transparent deep blue; small bubbles and sand impurities. Blown (body probably blown in dip mold); facet-, linear-, and slant-cut, and probably filed.

Bottle with roughly cylindrical body. Rim (probably not original: see below) ground flat; neck cylindrical and wider at bottom than at top; shoulder almost flat, but slightly higher at junction with neck, with rounded edge; wall straight and tapering; base plain; pontil mark roughly circular (D. 1.7–2.1 cm).

Neck, shoulder, and wall have wheel-cut and probably filed ornament. On neck: four narrow friezes separated by single grooves (W. 0.3 cm, Depth 0.1 cm),

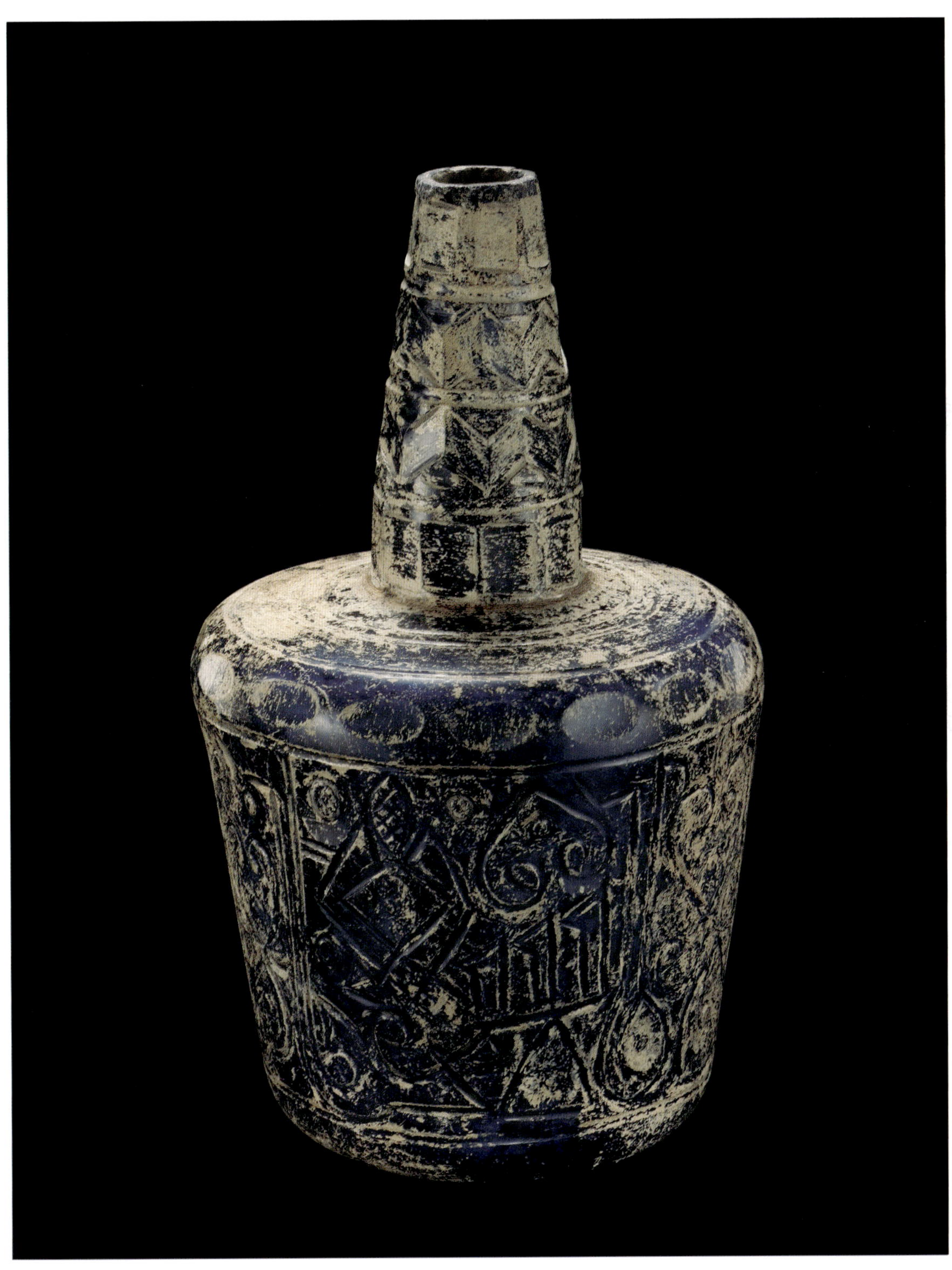

272

from top to bottom: (1) eight vertical rectangular facets (H. 1.6 cm, W. 0.6 cm); (2) 12 contiguous rhomboids (H. 1.1 cm, W. 0.7 cm) forming continuous zigzag, with one short horizontal cut in each triangular area between zigzag and upper and lower borders; (3) as (2), with uppermost angles of zigzag below lowest angles of zigzag in frieze (2); and (4) 11 vertical rectangular facets (H. 1.5 cm, W. 1.0–1.2 cm). On shoulder: three concentric grooves and, at junction with wall, continuous band of 16 horizontal oval facets. On wall: extending from just below band of facets to near base, and bordered at top and bottom by single horizontal grooves, Kufic inscription, "وسلام واقبال و دولة" (*wa salam wa iqbal wa dawla*; and well-being and prosperity and power); field contains palmettes, other vegetal motifs, and countersunk dots.

Incomplete, if original rim was everted (as on **273**, etc.) and is lost. Otherwise, complete, except for concentric hole (D. 0.6 cm) in base, presumably drilled for Ray Winfield Smith to obtain sample for spectrographic analysis. Surface partly covered with smooth, tan-colored scum, with patches of iridescence.

Comment: According to *Glass from the Ancient World* (see below), the object was acquired "from a Persian source" and was said to have come from Nishapur in northeastern Iran.

A colorless bottle with the same form, and with facet-cut decoration on the neck and linear-cut ornament on the wall, was found in the tomb of Princess Chenguo (d. 1018) at Naiman Qi in the Inner Mongolia Autonomous Region, China (An 1991, pp. 130 and 135, and fig. 12; see also *Brilliance of the Silk Road* 1999, p. 144, no. 11, illus. in color on p. 24).

Bibliography: Anon. 1954, illus. on dust jacket; Faider-Feytmans 1954, p. 16; *Verres antiques* 1954, p. 53, no. 323; *Glass from the Ancient World* 1957, pp. 269–271, no. 552.

273. Cylindrical Bottle

10th to 11th century. Formerly in the Smith Collection (381). 55.1.127.
H. 22.7 cm, D. (rim) 7.5 cm, (max., at shoulder) 13.5 cm.
Transparent deep green, appearing opaque deep blue in reflected light. Blown (body probably blown in dip mold); facet-, linear-, and slant-cut, and probably filed.

Bottle with roughly cylindrical body. Rim everted, with beveled edge and grinding on upper surface; neck cylindrical and wider at bottom than at top; shoulder almost flat, but slightly higher at junction with neck, and with rounded edge; wall bulges at top, then descends almost vertically; base plain; pontil mark annular (D. 1.9–2.1 cm). Neck, shoulder, and wall have wheel-cut and probably filed ornament. On neck: three narrow friezes, separated by single horizontal grooves (W. 0.6 cm, Depth 0.1 cm), from top to bottom: (1) eight vertical rectangular facets (H. 2.1 cm, W. about 0.8 cm) separated by narrow unworked strips; (2) 10 contiguous rhombuses (H. 2.1 cm, W. 1.2 cm) forming continuous zigzag; above junction of each pair of rhombuses, one inverted V-shaped cut; at midpoint of junctions, one small triangular or kite-shaped cut; and below junctions, one V-shaped cut; and (3) 11 vertical rectangular facets (H. 1.4 cm, W. 1.2 cm) separated by narrow unworked strips. On shoulder: three concentric grooves near edge and, at junction with wall, continuous band containing five groups of relatively large contiguous horizontal oval facets alternating with five groups of three to five small vertical oval facets. On wall: broad frieze, with single border lines above and below, containing five contiguous lozenges with double borders, with short horizontal cut at junction of each pair of lozenges; each lozenge is divided into four smaller lozenges with double inner borders; at center of each large lozenge, one crosshatched oval motif, and within each smaller lozenge, one slant-cut scroll and one pair of short horizontal cuts; each triangular space above junctions of large lozenges contains oval motif flanked by scrolls; each triangular space below these junctions contains scroll flanked by group of two short, straight cuts and one longer arc-shaped cut.

Almost complete. Broken into numerous pieces and repaired, with small losses restored. Much of surface is covered with opaque weathering, which varies in color from ocher to bluish gray. Circular hole (D. 0.6 cm) in base was made by Ray Winfield Smith to obtain sample for spectrographic analysis.

Comment: At the time of its exhibition at the Musée de Mariemont (Morlanwelz, Belgium) in 1954, the bottle was described as the "seul exemplaire intact [of this type] connu à ce jour." By 1957, when a photograph of the object appeared in *Glass from the Ancient World*, it had been broken and repaired. Bottles with this form and a similar combination of linear- and slant-cut ornament have been found at Nishapur, northeastern Iran, and are generally believed to be Iranian (Kröger 1995, pp. 172–173, no. 227). For another bottle of the same form, with similar ornament on the neck and shoulder, see **67**; for a bottle of the same form, with a pattern of lozenges on the wall, see *Ancient Glass and Glazed Wares*, n.d., back cover; and for

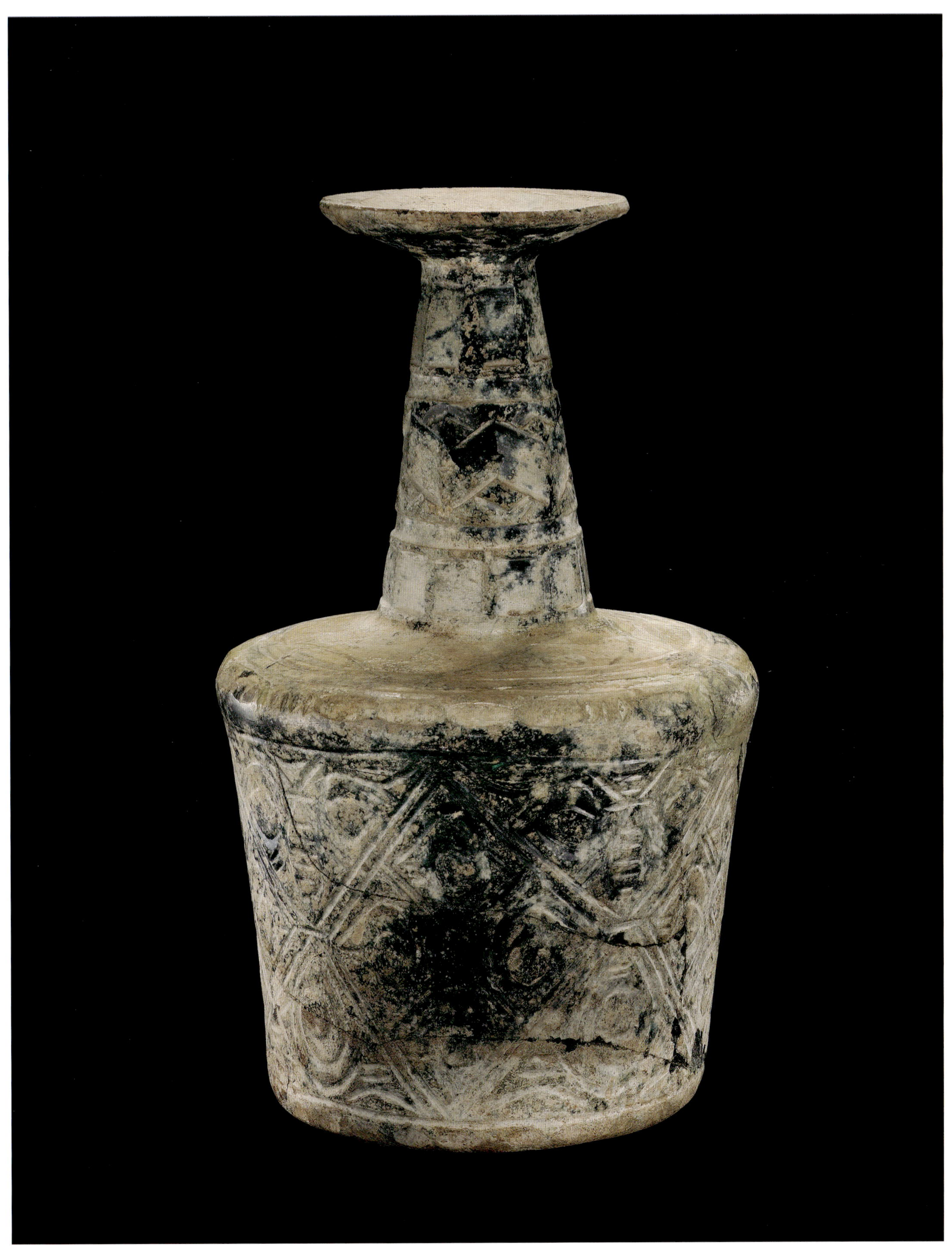

273

5. Small Bottles

277. Small Bottle with Half-Palmettes

9th to 10th century. Formerly in the Smith Collection. 59.1.486.
H. 5.1 cm, D. (rim) 1.1 cm, W. (body, max.) 4.5 cm.
Almost colorless, with green tinge; bubbly. Blown; slant-cut.

Bottle: lentoid. Rim plain, with flat top (but see below); neck short and cylindrical; body is shaped like biconvex lens and has rounded bottom. Decorated on both faces and on sides. Each face has raised oval medallion containing slant-cut half-palmette with volute at top and straight element near right edge, and is embellished with short transverse cuts. Each side is cut in two steps at top, below which are 13 or 15 short horizontal cuts arranged in vertical column that is slightly wider at top than at bottom. Junction of sides is cut in two ribs with square cross sections and, at center, one rib with triangular cross section.

Probably intact (but see below), except for one large and several very small chips in rim. On one face, faint spots of brownish weathering. On inside of neck, "COP" painted in black.

Comment: The bottle cannot stand unsupported. The shortness of the neck suggests that the top of the vessel may have been damaged and a new rim created by grinding the broken edge.

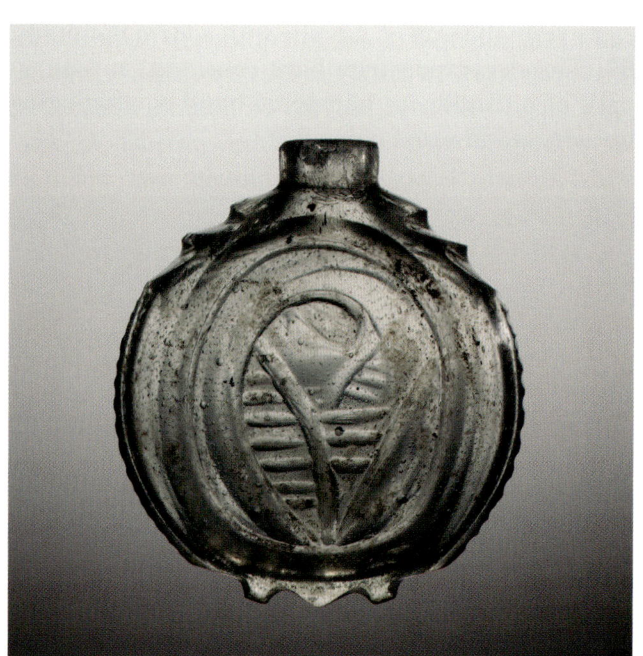

277

278. Small Bottle with Vegetal Ornament

9th to 10th century. Formerly in the collection of Maurice Nahman, Cairo, Egypt. 53.1.51.
H. 6 cm, D. (max.) 3.5 cm.
Almost colorless, with yellow tinge; few minute bubbles and impurities. Blown; linear- and slant-cut.

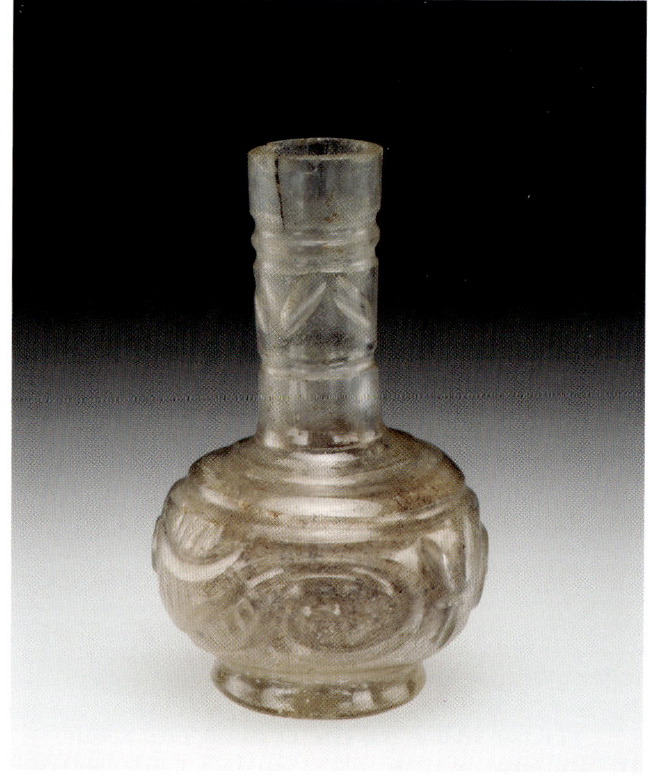

278

Bottle: rim plain, with flat upper surface; neck cylindrical; body roughly globular; base discoid, with splayed side; base plain, with ground and polished underside. Decorated on neck and wall. On neck: band of three linear-cut chevrons, which form one more or less continuous zigzag, bordered by pair of horizontal grooves at top and single groove at bottom. On wall: two similar slant-cut vegetal elements, each consisting of curving stem terminating in volutes at both ends, separated by two linear-cut Y-shaped motifs and bordered by pair of horizontal grooves at top and single groove at bottom.

Intact, except for chips at rim and on underside of base. Traces of weathering, especially on inside.

Comment: The object was acquired in Cairo and probably was found there.

279. Small Bottle

9th to 10th century. Formerly in the Smith Collection (960). Gift of Mrs. Ray Winfield Smith. 81.1.24.
H. 7.4 cm, W. 3.7 cm.
Translucent deep blue, with greenish tinge; many small bubbles. Mold-blown; facet-, linear-, and slant-cut.

Bottle with square body. Rim plain, with rounded top; neck cylindrical and narrower at bottom than at top; shoulder slopes and has rounded edge; wall vertical; base plain; circular pontil mark (D. about 1.1 cm). Decorated on neck, shoulder, and wall. On neck: five vertical rectangular facets (H. 1.7 cm, W. 0.5 cm), separated by narrower strips, of which four are plain and one has two short horizontal cuts; below facets, one continuous horizontal groove. On shoulder: four short diagonal cuts, one above each angle of wall. On each side of wall: schematic slant-cut half-palmettes in upper corners, and schematic centrally placed palmette in lower part.

Almost complete. Broken and repaired, with very small losses from junction of neck and shoulder. Patches of light brown weathering. "RWS / 960" written in black ink on blue paper label attached to base.

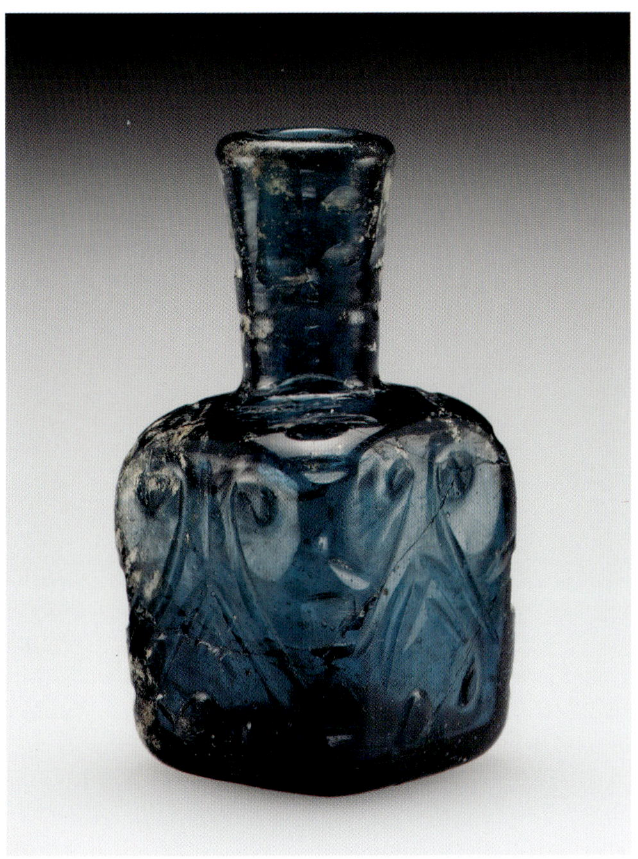

279

Comment: The bottle is rather carelessly decorated. See also **256** (a beaker with related slant-cut palmettes).

Bibliography: *Verres antiques* 1954, p. 47, no. 285; *Glass from the Ancient World* 1957, p. 273, no. 563.

280. Small Bottle

9th to 11th century. Formerly in the collection of Maurice Nahman, Cairo, Egypt. 53.1.43.
H. 6.6 cm, W. (rim) 1.5 cm, (body) 1.6 cm.
Transparent very pale yellowish green. Blown (probably mold-blown); perhaps ground; facet-, linear-, and slant-cut.

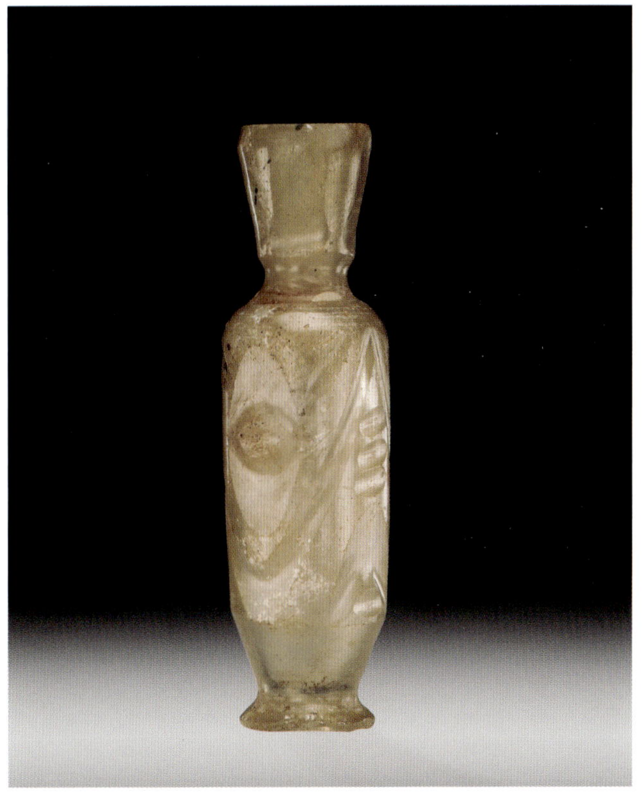

280

Bottle with cylindrical body. Rim plain, with top ground flat; neck wider at top than at bottom; shoulder rounded; upper two-thirds of wall vertical, and lower one-third tapering; foot is shaped like very shallow truncated cone; no pontil mark. Decorated on neck and wall. On neck: four equidistant vertical rectangular facets above continuous horizontal groove. On wall: two pairs of almost identical motifs, which alternate. Motif 1 consists of slant-cut V containing tall oval facet with raised eye-like motif at center and one slanting linear cut on either side; upper ends of Vs touch at top of wall. Motif 2 fills spaces between V-shaped motifs and consists of three short horizontal cuts above slant-cut element shaped like isosceles triangle with hollow base and one short horizontal cut.

Complete, except for chips in edge of foot. Partly covered with dull grayish weathering.

Comment: The object was acquired in Cairo and probably was found there.

281. Small Bottle

10th to 12th century. Formerly in the Smith Collection (1220-[ ]). Gift of Carl Berkowitz and Derek Content. 76.1.191.
H. (surviving) 5.8 cm, W. (max.) 3.2 cm.
Transparent pale greenish yellow. Blown (probably mold-blown); perhaps ground; facet-, linear-, and slant-cut.

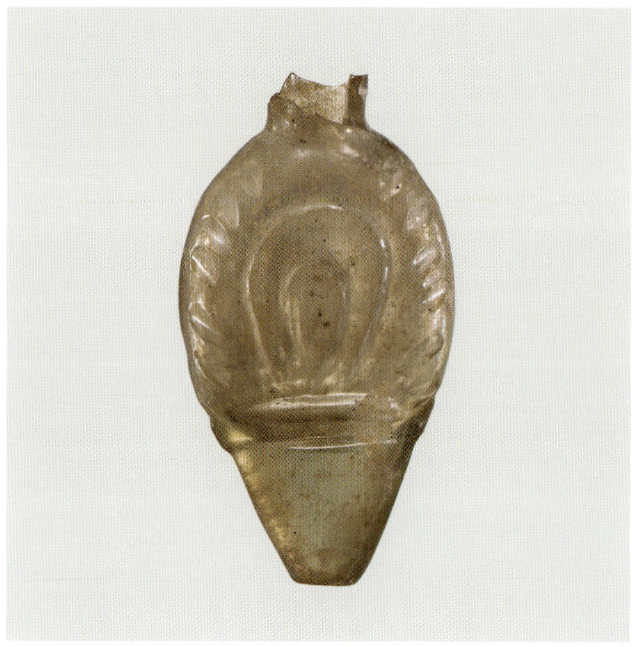

281

Bottle. Lower neck has roughly circular cross section; body has cross section resembling flattened oval, with two broad, flat sides and two narrow, rounded sides; flat sides taper slightly, while rounded sides curve out, down, and in; body has solid, truncated triangular foot with rectangular cross section. On each broad side: horseshoe-shaped panel containing slant-cut almond-shaped motif; at sides of panel, vertical row of six short transverse cuts. On each narrow side: vertical row of four or five small oval facets. On each short side of foot: single vertical facet.

Incomplete. Rim and much of neck are missing. Slightly pitted, with spots of pale yellowish weathering.

282. Small Bottle

9th to 11th century. Formerly in the Smith Collection (1220-6). Gift of Carl Berkowitz and Derek Content. 76.1.193.
H. 5.2 cm, W. (shoulder) 2.1 cm.
Colorless or almost colorless. Blown (probably mold-blown); perhaps ground; linear- and slant-cut.

Bottle with cylindrical body. Lower neck is narrow; shoulder slopes and has rounded edge; wall is straight and slightly tapered, then tapers more sharply at bottom; foot is shaped like very shallow truncated cone; no pontil mark. Decoration on wall: three almost identical motifs, each consisting of slant-cut V-shaped element containing large raised triangle with, at center, slant-cut vertical line, pointed at bottom and filled with horizontal cuts; between each pair of V-shaped motifs, vertical row of short horizontal cuts above slant-cut A-shaped element.

Incomplete. Rim, most of neck, and much of foot are missing. Extensive opaque pale gray weathering.

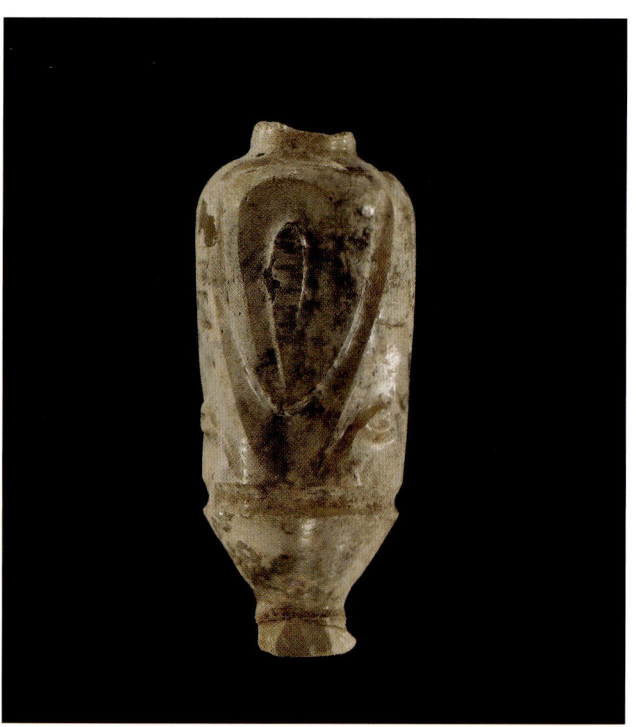

282

6. Small Bottle, "Molar Flask"

283. Small Bottle, "Molar Flask"

9th to 11th century. Formerly in the collection of Maurice Nahman, Cairo, Egypt. 53.1.55.
H. 6.3 cm, W. (rim) 1.1 cm, (body) 1.7 cm.
Colorless or almost colorless. Blown (probably mold-blown); facet- and slant-cut.

Bottle. Rim plain, with flat top; neck roughly cylindrical, but wider at top than at bottom; body tall, with sloping shoulder, vertical walls, and square cross section; at bottom of wall, four very small feet, one below each side. Decorated on neck and body. On neck: five rather irregular contiguous vertical facets above one continuous horizontal groove. On wall: each side is decorated with raised panel, which runs from top to bottom and contains two tall, narrow slant-cut facets, one above the other, each of which has raised eye-shaped motif at center.

Intact. Partly covered with light yellowish gray weathering, with brown specks and patches.

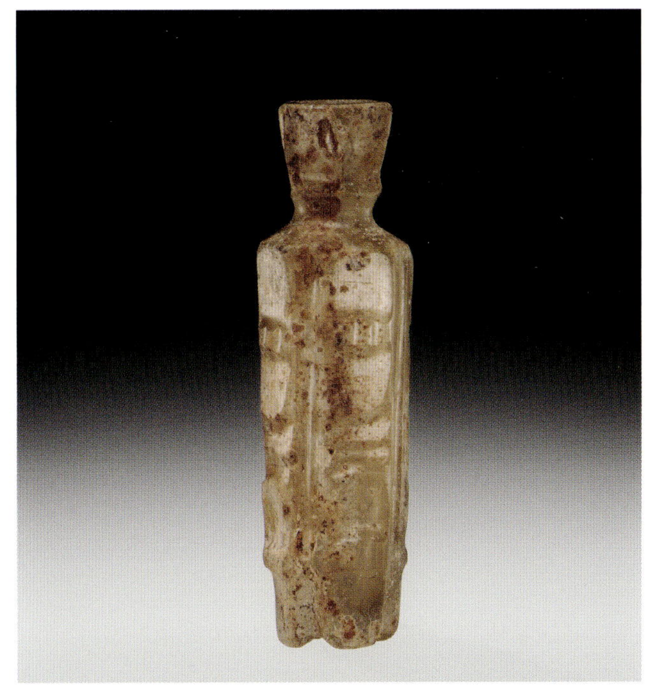

283

7. Indeterminate

284. Fragment with Bird

Probably 9th to 10th century, possibly later.
51.1.128.
H. (surviving) 0.6 cm, D. 4 cm.
Almost colorless, with yellowish tinge; few minute bubbles. Blown; linear- and slant-cut.

Fragment of base or cover (described as base). Lower wall descends vertically; base plain, with, on underside, raised medallion (D. 3.3 cm) filled with linear- and slant-cut ornament: bird shown frontally, with (when seen from inside) head turned to viewer's right. Head has pointed beak; body is short and divides at bottom to form legs; wings are partly extended on either side of body, and each terminates in half-palmette. Neck, body, legs, and wings of bird are enlivened with short linear cuts, usually in pairs, and background has similar treatment.

Broken on all sides. Slightly dull, with transparent light brown weathering in incisions.

COMMENT: The fragment was acquired, together with **204**, **258**, **262**, **276**, **292**, **315**, **356**, **421**, **424**, **460**, **465**, and **488**, in Cairo, Egypt. It is either part of a small vessel decorated on the underside, or a cover decorated on the top. The ornament is tentatively identified as a heraldic bird, presumably an eagle. The quality of the glass and the workmanship are consistent with identifying the fragment as an example of ninth- to 10th-century (more probably, 10th-century) cut glass, although the manner in which the eagle is represented would also be at home at a later date (cf. an early 11th-century Egyptian earthenware dish with luster ornament, signed by Muslim, in The Metropolitan Museum of Art, New York (63.178.1).

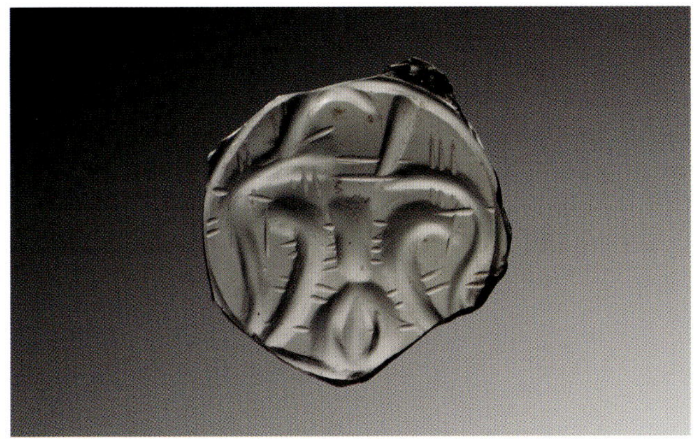

284

285. Fragment with Bird(?)

10th to 11th century. Formerly in the Smith Collection (937). Gift of Carl Berkowitz and Derek Content. 76.1.256.
Max. Dim. 4.5 cm.
Almost colorless, with greenish yellow tinge.
Blown; slant- and linear-cut.

Fragment from wall of vessel (Th. 0.15 cm) with slant- and linear-cut decoration. Identity of ornament is uncertain, but it includes half-palmette with hatched interior and volute at lower extremity. Second element may be head of bird with slant-cut countersunk dot for eye and beak indicated by single linear cut. If identification of head is correct, half-palmette may be wing and other linear-cut elements may be outline of plump body and one upper leg.

Broken on all sides. Dull, with some brownish weathering, especially in cuts.

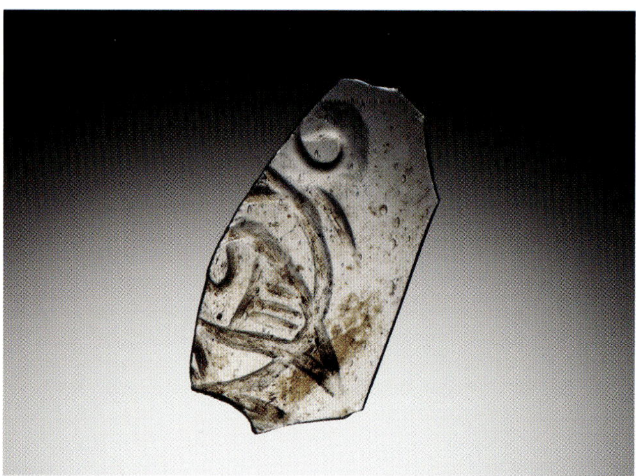

285

Comment: The curvature of the fragment suggests that it was part of the body of a bottle or the wall of a bowl. The interpretation of the ornament as a bird is not without difficulty: the "head" is not completely convincing, and the position of the "wing," folded across the "breast," is unusual.

Bibliography: *Verres antiques* 1954, p. 49, no. 298 (part of group).

286. Fragment with Palmette

9th to 10th century. Formerly in the Smith Collection. 68.1.59-45.
Max. Dim. 4.5 cm, D. (est.) perhaps about 9 cm.
Colorless; small bubbles. Blown; slant-cut.

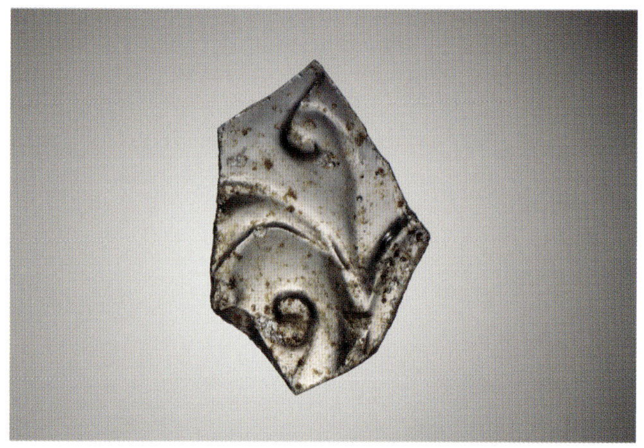

286

Fragment from wall (TTh. 0.25 cm) of vessel with straight, perhaps vertical side. Decoration (Th. 0.1 cm) consists of part of vertical stem with, at top, small palmette, and below this, pair of large curvilinear leaves that terminate in volutes.

Broken on all sides. Somewhat pitted, with specks of light brown weathering, especially in pits.

Comment: The stem surmounted by a palmette is reminiscent of the treelike motif on the underside of the relief-cut Falcon and Ibex Bowl (**296**).

287. Fragment with Palmette

9th to 10th century. Formerly in the Smith Collection. 68.1.59-54.
Max. Dim. 2.9 cm.
Almost colorless, with yellowish tinge; small bubbles. Blown; slant- and linear-cut.

Fragment from wall (Th. 0.2 cm) of vessel with slant- and linear-cut decoration. Ornament consists of two parallel linear cuts, probably transverse and defining side of triangular panel; one cut at opposite edge of panel may define other side, in which case apex

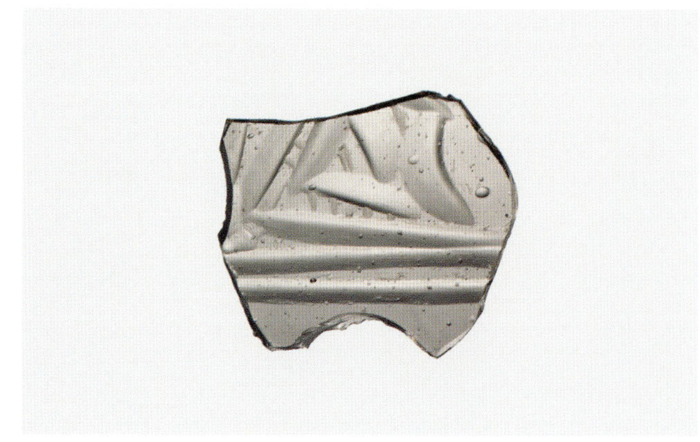

287

was just above top of fragment. Panel contains schematic palmette with notched sides and hatched interior, which would have fitted perfectly into top of triangle.

Broken on all sides. No obvious weathering.

288. Fragment with Vegetal Ornament

9th to 10th century. Formerly in the Smith Collection (938). Gift of Carl Berkowitz and Derek Content. 76.1.284.
H. (surviving) 3.3 cm, D. (est.) about 8–9 cm.
Almost colorless, with yellowish tinge. Blown; slant- and linear-cut.

Fragment from wall (Th. 0.1 cm) of vessel with slightly convex profile. Decoration consists of small part of frieze containing symmetrical arrangement of two stems, side by side, which diverge slightly toward the ends and terminate in outward-pointing slant-cut volutes; each stem also has at least one other outward-pointing volute. Single horizontal linear cut defines top(?) of frieze.

Broken on all sides. Traces of brownish weathering in cuts.

Bibliography: *Verres antiques* 1954, p. 49, no. 298 (part of group).

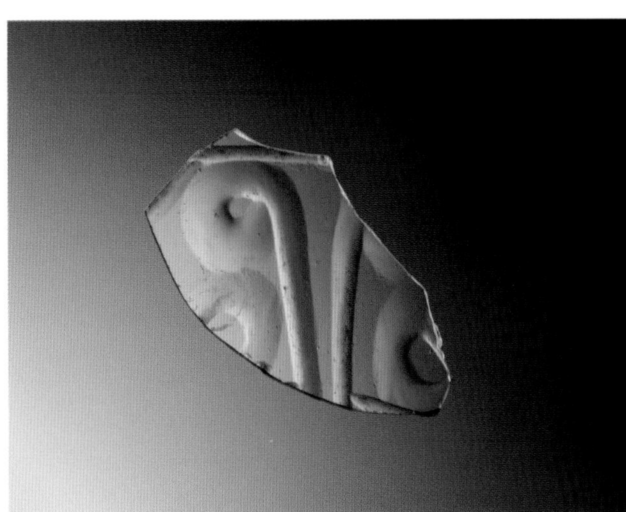

288

289. Two Fragments

10th century. Formerly in the Smith Collection (939 and 940). Gift of Carl Berkowitz and Derek Content. 76.1.303a, b.
Max. Dim. (a and b) 3.4 cm.
Almost colorless, with yellowish tinge; very few minute bubbles. Blown; slant- and linear-cut.

Two fragments from wall of vessel with convex profile. First fragment (a) has curvilinear decoration that includes countersunk circular motif (D. 0.5 cm) and comma-shaped element filled with transverse hatching. Second fragment (b) is similar, but has two countersunk circular motifs and small part of hatched element.

Both fragments are broken on all sides. No obvious weathering.

Comment: The fragments are from the same vessel. Both the glass and the coldworking are of excellent quality.

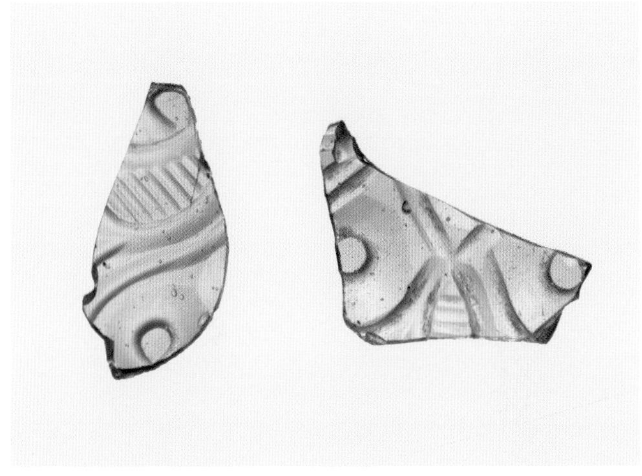

289

290. Fragment

About 10th century. Formerly in the Smith Collection. 68.1.59-22.
Max. Dim. 5.6 cm.
Colorless. Blown; slant-cut.

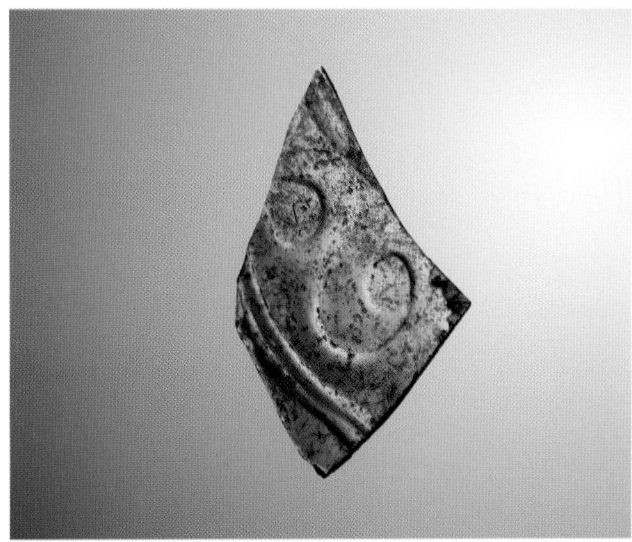

290

Fragment of vessel. Wall apparently straight. Slant-cut ornament consists of curvilinear stems and S-shaped motif terminating in roughly oval "buds."

Broken on all sides. Small areas of gray to pale brown weathering.

Comment: The curvature of the fragment suggests that it came from the wall of a cylindrical object, perhaps a pitcher or a bottle. For the decorative style, see **266**.

291. Fragment

Perhaps 9th to 10th century. Formerly in the Smith Collection (1016). Gift of Carl Berkowitz and Derek Content. 76.1.285.
Max. Dim. 4.8 cm, D. (est.) about 5 cm.
Colorless; few minute bubbles. Blown; slant- and linear-cut.

Fragment of beaker or small bottle. Wall (Th. 0.1–0.15 cm) straight and vertical or almost vertical. Decorated with part of frieze with border at bottom. Frieze has overall pattern consisting of two overlapping rows of ornament (from top): (1) contiguous slant-cut facets, which are either diamond-shaped or triangular with rounded apex, surviving example of which contains countersunk triangular motif with rounded base, partly filled with linear-cut hatching and with one small X-shaped element; and (2) contiguous slant-cut facets (H. 2.1 cm), which are triangular with rounded base, two surviving examples of which contain countersunk triangular motif with rounded base, filled with linear-cut crosshatching. Border is at least 1 cm wide and is filled with vertical hatching.

Broken on all sides. Surfaces appear to be pristine.

Comment: This is an unusual fragment. It was carefully made from glass of very high quality, and carefully cut. The quality of the glass and the presence of slant cutting confirm that the fragment is Islamic in origin and ninth- to 10th-century in date, but the decoration is exceptional. The register of narrow vertical ribs appears to be without parallel among published objects. The kite-shaped motifs recall the so-called shields on Hedwig glasses (see page 333).

The border is assumed to be at the bottom of the frieze because this is where the wall is thickest. I am aware of only one other early Islamic glass object with a band of linear-cut vertical hatching: a bottle found during excavations at Nishapur, northeastern Iran, which has bands of horizontal, transverse, herringbone, and vertical hatching. It is attributed to the 10th

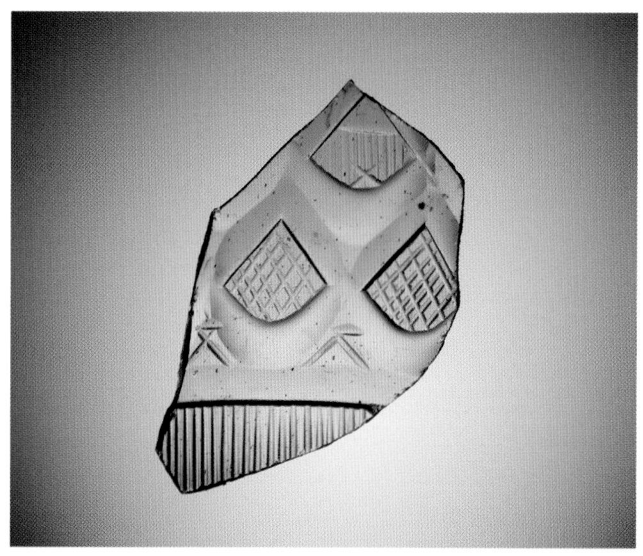

291

century (Kröger 1995, pp. 172–173, no. 227). The date and place of manufacture of **291** are unknown, although the condition of the fragment and the fact that it formerly belonged to Ray Winfield Smith suggest that it may have been acquired in Egypt.

Bibliography: *Verres antiques* 1954, p. 49, no. 298 (part of group).

292. Fragment

About 10th century. 51.1.126.
H. 4.4 cm, D. (grooves, est.) about 13 cm.
Almost colorless, with yellowish tinge; many minute bubbles. Blown; slant-cut.

Fragment from wall of cylindrical vessel. Slant-cut ornament consists of hatched oval motif enclosed by two crescent-shaped elements, one above and one below it; ends of crescents curve outward and terminate

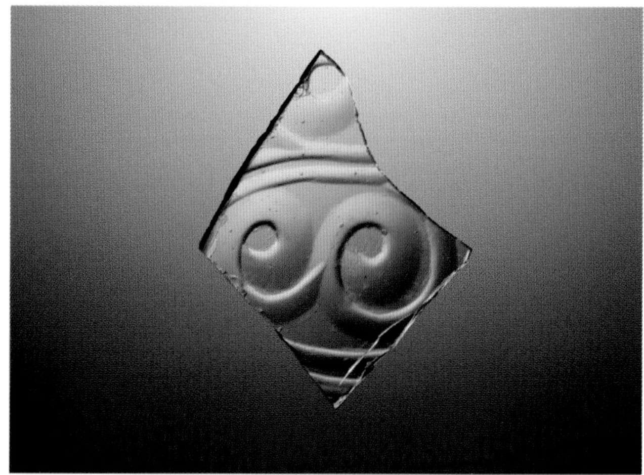

292

in roughly circular "buds." Above (or below) decoration, pair of horizontal grooves: evidently border at top (or bottom) of slant-cut frieze.

Broken on all sides. Patches of cloudy gray to brownish weathering.

Comment: The curvature of the fragment suggests that it came from the wall of a cylindrical object, perhaps a pitcher or a bottle. For the decorative style, see **266**.

293. Fragment

Date uncertain. Formerly in the Smith Collection. 68.1.59-44.
Max. Dim. 4 cm.
Colorless; minute bubbles. Blown; slant-cut.

Fragment from wall of vessel, bearing part of one curving, slant-cut line.

Broken on all sides. Patches of transparent pale brown weathering, especially in cut.

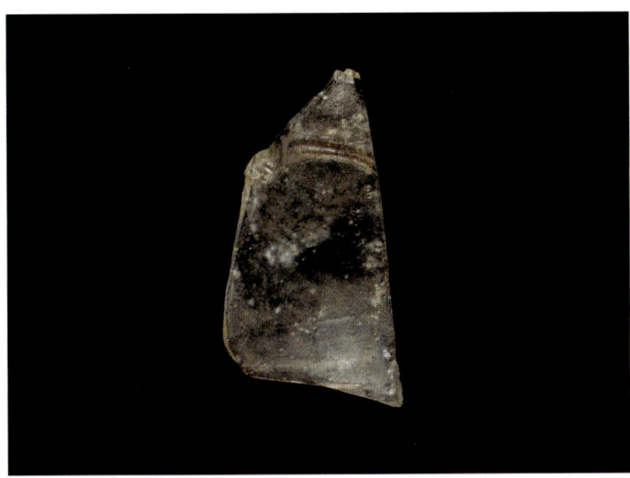

293

294. Fragment

10th to 11th century. Formerly in the Smith Collection (1221-22). Gift of Carl Berkowitz and Derek Content. 76.1.283.
H. (surviving) 3.1 cm, D. (est.) about 9 cm.
Almost colorless, with yellowish tinge. Blown; slant- and linear-cut.

Fragment from wall (Th. 0.15–0.2 cm) of vessel with straight side. Decoration consists of upper part of vertical oval motif with raised border (W. 0.6 cm) containing countersunk oval filled with transverse hatching. Adjoining border on one side is edge of second, possibly similar element.

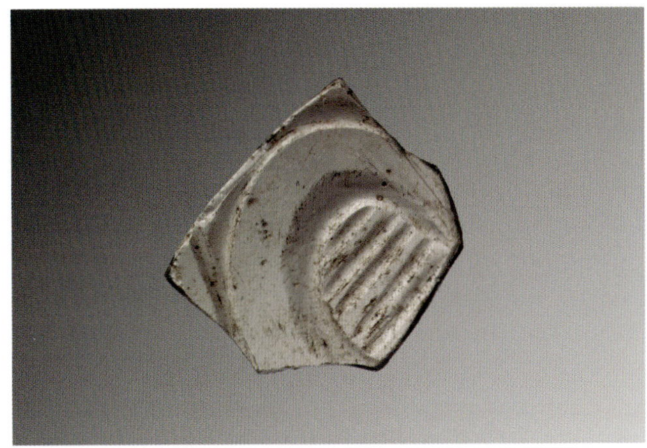

294

Broken on all sides. Transparent grayish brown weathering.

295. Fragment

Probably 10th century. Formerly in the Smith Collection. 68.1.59-39.
H. 2.7 cm, D. (base, est.) about 5 cm.
Almost colorless, with yellowish tinge; bubbles. Blown; slant-cut.

Fragment of vessel, preserving small part of lower wall and even smaller part of base. Lower wall descends almost vertically, then curves down and in; base plain. Wall has incised decoration with broad, slanting cuts: pendent crescents, perhaps part of continuous horizontal row of contiguous crescents; below it, perhaps in space between bottoms of two crescents, small upright triangle; below that, horizontal, presumably continuous, groove.

Broken on all sides. Surface is as new.

Comment: Despite its size, the fragment is identified with confidence as part of a small vessel with typical incised decoration of about the 10th century.

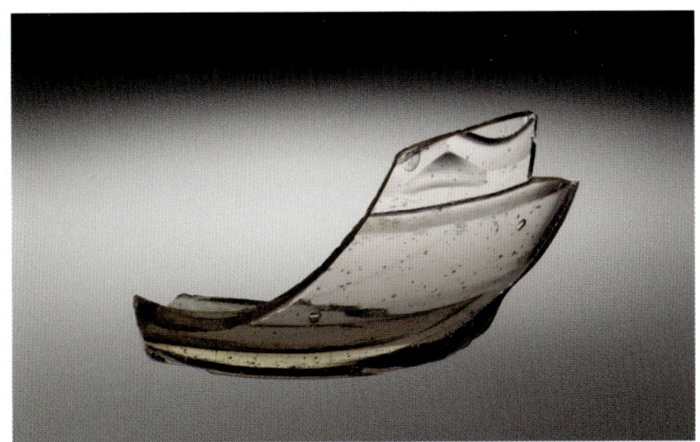

295

Relief-Cut Objects

This large and disparate group, usually known as "relief-cut" glass, is united by a single feature: both the background and most of the interior of the principal motifs have been excavated by cutting and grinding, leaving the outlines and a few internal features in relief. The group may be subdivided in a number of ways, most obviously on the basis of color. The great majority of the objects are monochrome (usually colorless, in imitation of rock crystal), while a small minority consist of cameo glasses, usually with a colorless base glass and a colored overlay (see pages 296–328, **522–585**).

Decoration with raised outlines had a wide distribution in the central Islamic lands in the ninth and 10th centuries. Thus, the excavations at Samarra, Iraq, produced both colorless and cameo glass fragments. The former include part of a bowl decorated with a frieze of hares (Lamm 1928, p. 77, no. 243), which was found in the ruins of the Jawsaq al-Khāqānī, a palace built by Caliph al-Mu^{c}taṣim between 836 and 842, and supposedly abandoned when the caliphs returned to Baghdad in 892. Thirteen hundred kilometers to the northeast of Samarra, colorless relief-cut glass came to light during excavations at Nishapur, northeastern Iran (Kröger 1995, pp. 139–143, nos. 192 and 193). Numerous glasses with raised outlines that appeared on the antiquities market in Tehran are attributed to Nishapur, and although many of the attributions may be apocryphal, there is no reason to suppose that they were not found somewhere in Iran. Twelve hundred fifty kilometers to the southwest of Samarra, excavations at Fusṭāṭ have yielded colorless glasses with raised outlines, including a ewer with a relief-cut inscription and a bowl decorated with a frieze of medallions containing birds (Scanlon and Pinder-Wilson 2001, pp. 99–106, no. A3b and f = Pinder-Wilson and Scanlon 1973, pp. 25–26, nos. 19 and 20). Despite the very wide pattern of distribution of these objects—from Egypt to Khorāsān Province, Iran—they display strong similarities, such as the embellishment of the raised outlines with numerous parallel notches and the use of drilled circular depressions to add texture to the bodies of birds and animals.

The stylistic similarities of objects found over a very wide area are reflected, at least in part, by similarities between the chemical compositions of colorless glasses found at Nishapur and certain colorless glasses excavated at Fusṭāṭ (Brill 1995). In the words of Robert H. Brill: "The analyses match so well that one is tempted to speculate that these particular Fusṭāṭ glasses were made in the same place as the Nishapur colorless glasses; and if that is so, it invites some tantalizing questions. Were they all made at (or near) Nishapur? Were they all made at (or near) Fusṭāṭ? Or were they made somewhere else and exported to both those places?" (*ibid.*, p. 214).

The examples of relief-cut glass in this catalog include a beaker decorated with scrolls, palmettes, and calyx motifs; bowls decorated with a fantastic animal, horses, hares, and lions; a perfume bottle decorated with birds; and a bottle decorated with ibexes.

The relief-cut objects at Corning are described in the following order:

1. Bowls (**296–316**).
2. Box (**317**).
3. Cup (**318**).
4. Beakers (**319–345**).
5. Goblets (**346–353**).
6. Large and medium bottles (**354–382**).
7. Small bottles (**383–387**).
8. Canteen (**388**).
9. Ewers and related objects (**389–396**).
10. Indeterminate (**397–488**).

1. Bowls

296. Bowl with Animals and Birds (Falcon and Ibex Bowl)

9th to 10th century. 53.1.109.
H. 9.2 cm, D. 14.1 cm.
Colorless; minute bubbles. Blown; relief-cut.

Bowl. Rim plain and slightly everted, with rounded lip; upper and middle parts of wall are straight and somewhat tapered; lower wall curves down and in, and merges with convex base; no pontil mark (but see below). Decorated in relief on wall and base. On wall: continuous frieze bordered at top and bottom by pairs of horizontal ribs. Upper ribs are 1.9 cm and 3.1 cm below lip; lower ribs are 7.9 cm and 8.6 cm below lip. Frieze contains four animals alternating with four birds, all shown in profile, facing left. Each animal has pointed snout, eye represented by countersunk dot,

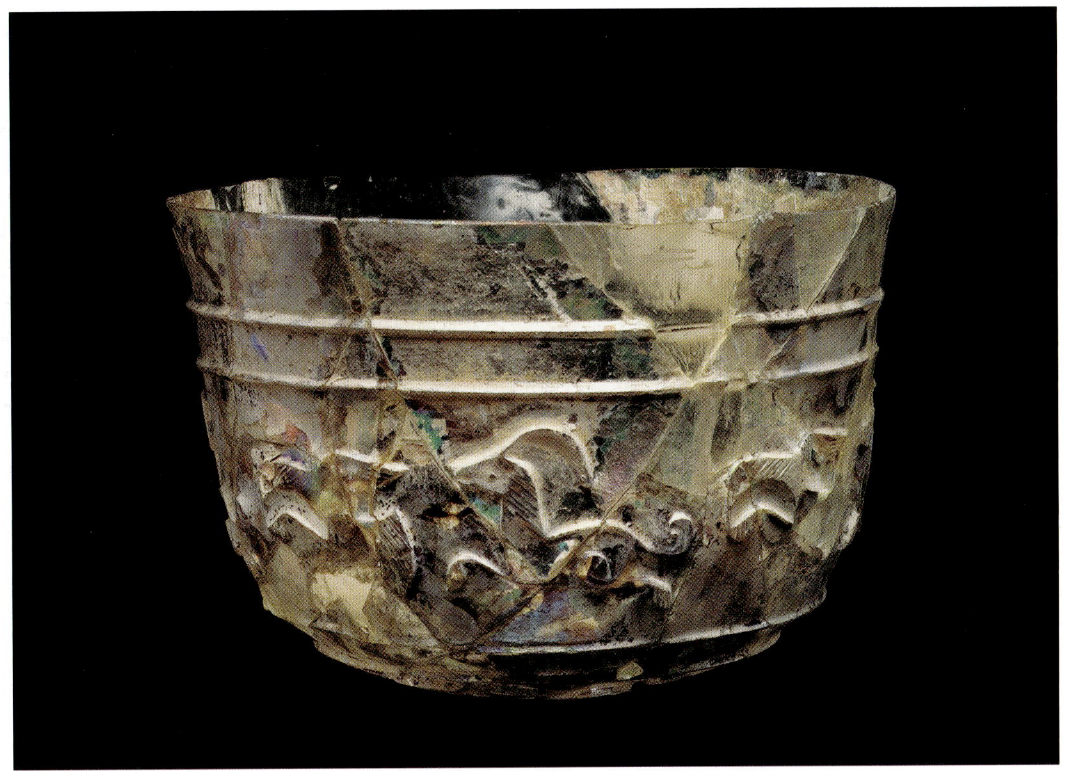

296A

long and curved horn, body with raised outline, foreleg thrust forward, hind leg extended backward, and short, curly tail. Each bird has curved beak, eye represented by countersunk dot, body with raised outline, wing shaped like half-palmette, large tail, and leg pointing forward. Underside of base has two similar birds, standing and facing treelike motif with central circular element, from top of which springs vertical stem terminating in palmette, and from bottom of which descends similar stem, which divides into two scrolls. Necks and feet of animals, as well as necks, wings, feet, and tails of birds, are hatched; some outlines are notched.

Incomplete. Broken into many pieces, with loss of about 35 percent of rim and 15 percent of wall; restored. Pitted, with small patches of brown to black weathering and larger areas of slightly iridescent silver-colored weathering.

COMMENT: The object is said to have been found in Gurgān Province, northern Iran, about February 1953 (letters dated October 6, 1953, and February 22, 1955, from Khalil Rabenou and Abbas Mazda respectively, on file at The Corning Museum of Glass).

The long, curved horns identify the animals as a species of goat or antelope, and the curved beaks identify the birds as raptors: hence the name Falcon and Ibex Bowl, which is sometimes attached to this object. The animals may be compared with the "ibexes" on

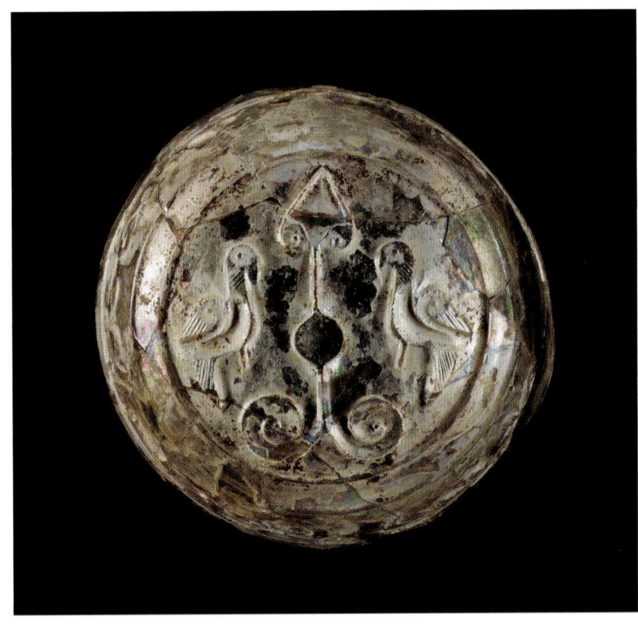

296B

354, while the birds, with their legs extended forward, are similar to some of the birds on a relief-cut bottle in the David Collection, Copenhagen (10/1963: *Glass of the Sultans* 2001, pp. 191–192, no. 96). The latter also has a "tree of life" that divides at the bottom and has a palmette near the top. Other, more distant tree-of-life motifs appear on **490** and on two mold-blown bottles found during excavations at Nishapur, northeastern Iran (Kröger 1995, p. 94, no. 133).

The quality of the design and the cutting led Buechner and others (in *Guide to the Collections* 1958: see below) to describe the bowl as "an achievement of considerable artistic importance." The cutting may be compared with that of **354** and, more closely, with that of the bottle in the David Collection.

Bibliography: Saldern 1955; *Guide to the Collections* 1958, pp. 30–31, no. 26; Oliver, P. 1961, pp. 12–13 and figs. 5 and 6; *Guide to the Collections* 1965, pp. 30–31, no. 32; *Persian Glass* 1972, p. 15, no. 23; *Guide to the Collections* 1974, pp. 30–31, no. 32; Yoshimizu 1983, p. 100; Ettinghausen and Grabar 1987, p. 235, fig. 248; Dolez 1988, p. 40; Yoshimizu 1992, pp. 99 and 291, no. 202; Kröger 1995, p. 140 and fig. 9.

297. Fragment of Bowl with Animal(?) and Bird

9th to 10th century. Formerly in the Smith Collection. Gift of Carl Berkowitz and Derek Content. 76.1.262.
H. (surviving) 7.5 cm, D. (rim, est.) about 12 cm.
Transparent pale greenish blue. Blown; relief-cut.

Fragment from rim and wall of deep bowl (TTh. 0.2 cm) decorated in relief (Th. 0.1 cm). Rim plain, with rounded lip; wall is straight and descends vertically or with slight taper for 7 cm below lip, then it curves down and in. Decoration is restricted to straight part of wall and consists of three horizontal ribs (with centers 0.9 cm, 1.7 cm, and 2.5 cm below lip) and frieze.

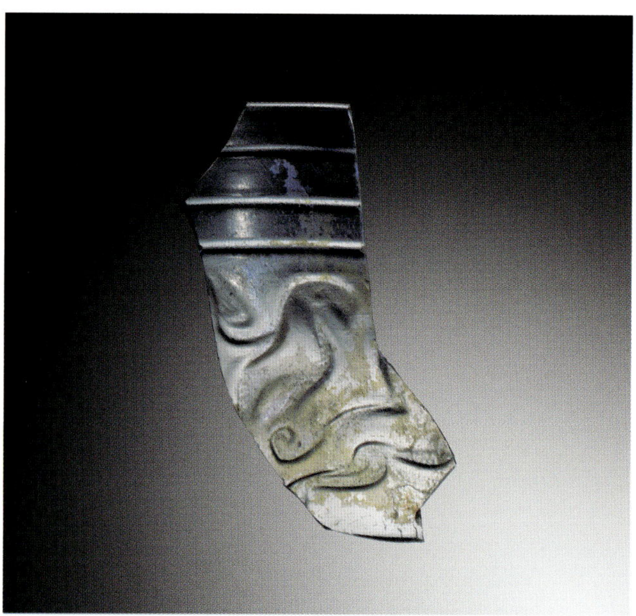
297

Surviving part of frieze consists of three motifs: (1, above, on left) schematic bird, standing in right profile, with small head, large and curved beak, plump body, and perhaps wing extending toward left and terminating in half-palmette; (2, below, on right) uncertain, but possibly long and extremely stylized hind leg of animal moving from left to right; and (3) between bird and animal(?), linear motif terminating in volute at lower left end. Outlines of all motifs are notched.

Broken on all sides, except for very short segment of rim. Decoration is indistinct, perhaps because of cleaning. Patches of violet iridescence.

Comment: The fragment appears to be part of a bowl similar in shape and size to the relief-cut bowl with horses, in the Museum für Islamische Kunst, Berlin (I.20/65: *Glass of the Sultans* 2001, p. 176, no. 82).

298. Fragment of Bowl with Animal

9th to 10th century. Formerly in the Smith Collection (1351). 59.1.438.
Max. Dim. 10.4 cm, D. (rim, est.) 19.6 cm, H. 4.7 cm.
Almost colorless, with yellowish tinge; few small bubbles. Blown; relief-cut.

Fragment of bowl. Rim plain, with rounded lip; wall tapers and is almost straight; base apparently plain. Wall has relief-cut frieze with upper and lower borders each consisting of one continuous horizontal rib. Surviving part of frieze has head, most of body, and hindquarters of relief-cut hare in profile, facing left. Animal has eye represented by countersunk dot, large and pointed ear, body shown in outline, hind leg

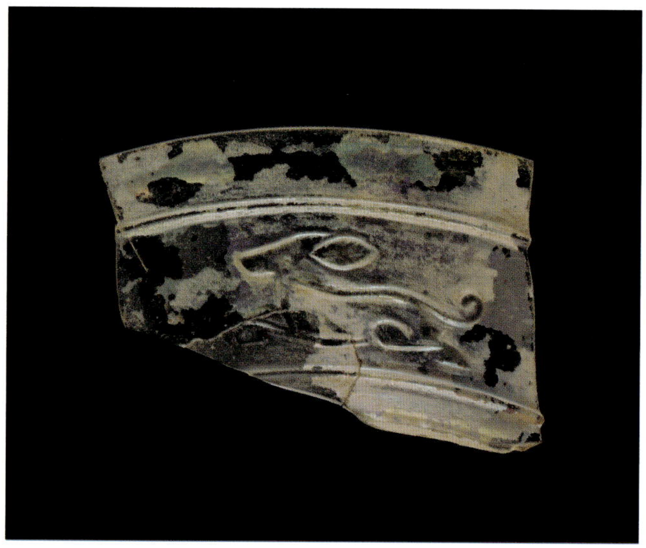
298

extended backward, and curly tail. Ear has incised median line and hatching like veins of leaf; outlines of body and tail are notched.

Fifteen percent of rim survives; all other edges are broken. Mostly covered with iridescent yellowish silver weathering.

Comment: The fragment was part of a shallow bowl with a flat base, similar to **251** and a bowl in the al-Sabah Collection, Dār al-Āthār al-Islāmiyyah, Kuwait National Museum (LNS 113 KG: Carboni 2001, p. 85, no. 19 = *Glass of the Sultans* 2001, pp. 174–175, no. 81). The hare may be compared with the animals on the relief-cut turquoise blue bowl in the Treasury of San Marco, Venice (140: *Glass of the Sultans* 2001, pp. 176–178, no. 83). If the complete frieze depicted a row of more or less identical hares, with no other motifs, it would have contained up to six animals.

Bibliography: *Glass from the Ancient World* 1957, p. 281, no. 588.

299. Fragment of Bowl with Animal

9th to 10th century. Formerly in the Smith Collection (476). 59.1.439.
Max. Dim. 6.7 cm, D. (foot-ring, est.) 6 cm.
Almost colorless, with yellowish tinge; few very small bubbles. Blown; relief-cut.

Fragment of bowl. Lower wall (Th. 0.15 cm) descends in shallow curve; base flat (Th. 0.4 cm with decoration, 0.2 cm without decoration), with foot-ring (H. 0.4 cm), which has narrow, notched rim. Underside of base decorated in relief with animal, shown in profile, facing left, which fills area defined by foot-ring. Animal's head has countersunk eye, mouth indicated by single short cut, and horn (of which only tip survives); neck is curved, narrow, and hatched with parallel transverse incisions; countersunk body has notched outlines and haphazard arrangement of six drilled dots; foreleg, indicated by single notched line, points forward and terminates in oval hoof with two parallel incisions; hind leg, which has roughly comma-shaped haunch and is indicated by single notched line, points forward and downward, and also terminates in oval hoof with parallel incisions; long tail, also indicated by single notched line, curls forward and up, and ends in bulbous tassel. Entire background of animal shows signs of coldworking.

Broken on all sides. Nearly 40 percent of foot-ring and 50 percent of area inside it survive; top of head, most of horn, rump, and part of tail are missing. Small patches of incipient weathering.

Comment: The treatment of the animal, which P. Oliver (see below) described as "mediocre," is reminiscent of, among others, the horses on a relief-cut bowl in the Museum für Islamische Kunst, Berlin (I.20/65: *Glass of the Sultans* 2001, p. 176, no. 82); the ibexes on a bottle in The Corning Museum of Glass (**354**: *ibid.*, p. 181, no. 86); and the ibexes on the Falcon and Ibex Bowl, also at Corning (**296**: Oliver, P. 1961, p. 13, fig. 5; Kröger 1995, p. 141, fig. 9). All of these are also attributed to the ninth or 10th century.

Bibliography: *Glass from the Ancient World* 1957, p. 281, no. 590 (part of group); Oliver, P. 1961, pp. 16–17, fig. 13.

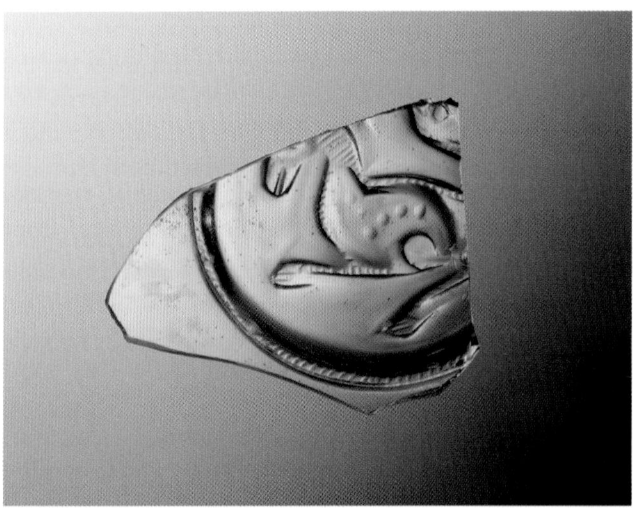

299

300. Fragment of Bowl with Animal

10th century. Formerly in the Smith Collection (475). 59.1.444.
H. (surviving) about 6.5 cm, D. (max., est.) perhaps about 25 cm.
Colorless. Blown; relief-cut.

Fragment from wall of bowl (TTh. 0.4 cm) with convex profile, decorated in relief (Th. up to 0.2 cm). At top of fragment, short section of horizontal rib, presumably upper border of frieze. Surviving part of frieze consists of roundel, perhaps with outer and inner borders (see "Comment"; est. D. of latter is about 7 cm). Roundel contains animal, which stands, facing left. It has triangular head with pointed snout, large oval eye, short ears, and curved horns, which are shown as if from above. Extending downward from its mouth is long, beardlike element. Front legs are incomplete, but hind legs terminate in hooves. Tail is long and thin. Border of frieze is plain, but all other outlines, including borders of roundel, are notched;

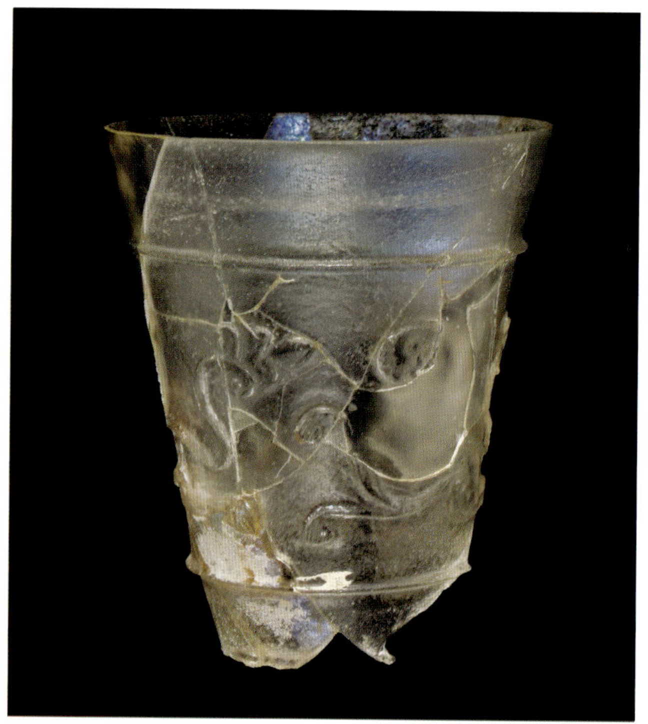

323

two lions on **397** and, more distantly, on several Hedwig beakers. She also likened the tails ending in palmettes to lions' tails on certain Coptic textiles of the sixth century (e.g., *Pagan and Christian Egypt* 1941, p. 60, no. 177).

Bibliography: *Glass from the Ancient World* 1957, p. 265, no. 538; Oliver, P. 1961, pp. 20–21 and fig. 21.

324. Beaker with Animals

9th to 10th century. 58.1.5.
H. 8.7 cm, D. about 9 cm.
Colorless; small bubbles. Blown; relief-cut.

Beaker shaped like truncated cone. Rim plain, with lip ground smooth; wall almost straight, tapering; base plain, with narrow, splayed foot-ring; no pontil mark. Wall decorated in relief with horizontal frieze defined at top and bottom by continuous ribs 1.8 cm and 7.3 cm below rim. Frieze contains three animals shown in profile, running from right to left. Each animal is different. Clockwise, animal 1 has its head down, as if looking at its chest; neck is large and bent; body is relatively small; one foreleg is extended forward; hind leg is bent; tail is raised and forks, terminating in one spiral and one pointed oval motif. Animal 2 is similar, but with head up and forked tail terminating in two half-palmettes. Animal 3 has pointed snout and raised wing. All three animals have hatching on head, feet, and tail, and notched outline.

Incomplete. Broken into many pieces, with loss of about 50 percent of rim and 25 percent of upper wall. Dull and pitted, with remains of silver weathering and some iridescence.

Comment: The object is said to have been found at Nishapur, northeastern Iran.

The winged creature resembles a *senmurv*, a fantastic animal usually represented with a dog's head, a bird's wings, a lion's claws, a peacock's tail, and a fish's scales. These animals originally symbolized the *khvarnah* (glory and good fortune) of the Kayānids, the legendary ancestors of the Sasanians. Their presence on the royal robes depicted in the rock reliefs at Taq-i Bustan, Iran, indicates that they were associated with the *khvarnah* of Sasanian kings as well (Marshak 1998, pp. 84–85). *Senmurvs* appear on a number of post-Sasanian objects, including a seventh- or eighth-century silver-gilt dish in The British Museum, London (BM 124095: *Splendeur des Sassanides* 1993, p. 220, no. 71); an eighth- or ninth-century caftan from Mochtchevaja Balka in the northern Caucasus (*ibid.*, p. 275, nos. 127 and 128); and a ninth- to 10th-century relief-cut glass bowl in the al-Sabah Collection, Dār al-Āthār al-Islāmiyyah, Kuwait National Museum (LNS 113 KG: *Glass of the Sultans* 2001, pp. 174–175, no. 81).

Bibliography: Oliver, P. 1961, p. 18; Ettinghausen and Grabar 1987, p. 234, fig. 246.

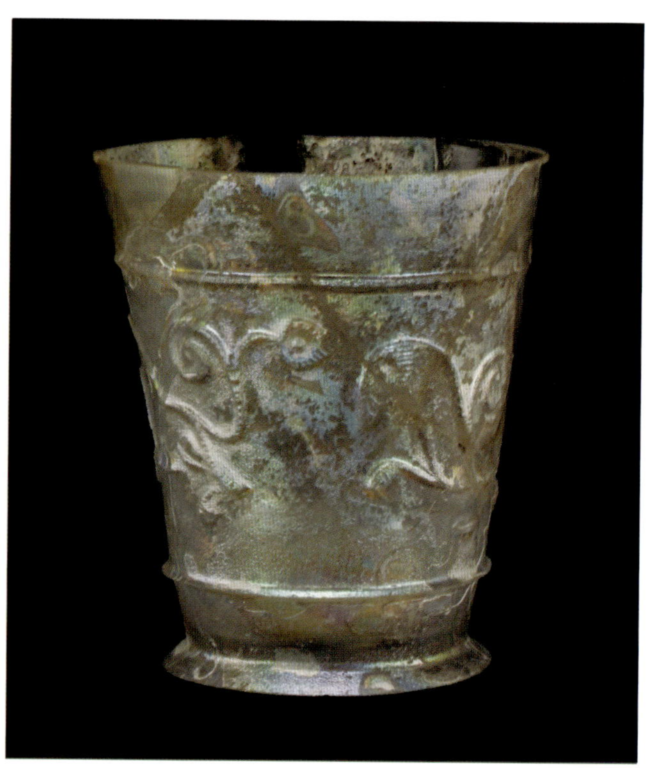

324

325. Fragment of Beaker with Animals

9th to 10th century. Formerly in the Smith Collection (915). 59.1.447.
H. (surviving) 6.5 cm, D. (rim, est.) about 7.5 cm.
Almost colorless, with yellowish brown tinge; many very small bubbles. Blown; relief-cut.

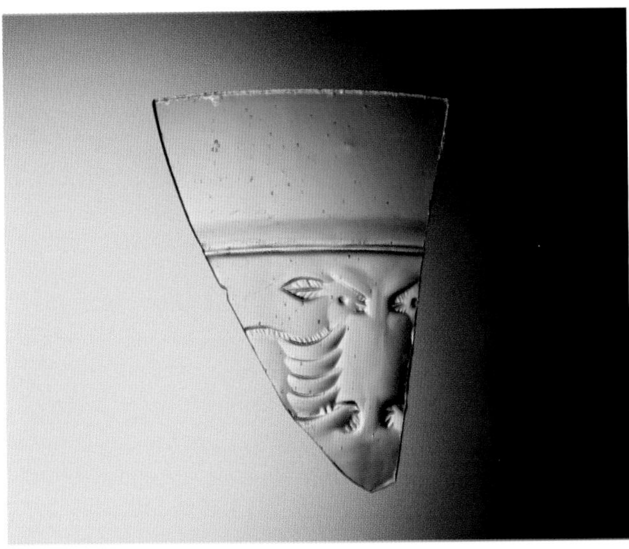

325

Triangular fragment of truncated conical beaker. Rim cracked off and ground. Wall (TTh. 0.15 cm) straight and tapering. Decorated in relief (Th. 0.05 cm): 2.4 cm below rim, horizontal rib, presumably upper border of frieze. Surviving part of frieze has parts of two animals shown in profile, facing each other, with little space between their muzzles and front feet. Animal on left has head with countersunk eye, flat muzzle with short cut separating upper and lower jaws (which have groups of very short parallel cuts), and large oval ear divided by longitudinal cut and with short parallel cuts on either side, together making herringbone pattern; back of neck and back are defined by notched outlines; fleece on chest is indicated by four overlapping crescent-shaped cuts; belly and front leg have notched outlines, with lower leg and hoof bent back underneath upper part of leg. Animal on right, of which only part of head and leg survive, appears to be mirror image of animal on left.

About 25 percent of rim survives; other edges broken. Glass appears to be pristine.

Comment: The object was cut with great delicacy. The shapes of the lower wall and base are unknown; they could have resembled, for example, the relief-cut beaker with a shallow conical foot in The Metropolitan Museum of Art, New York (1974.45: *Glass of the Sultans* 2001, pp. 172–173, no. 79), or the relief-cut beaker with a rounded base in the L. A. Mayer Memorial Institute for Islamic Art, Jerusalem (G73-71: *ibid.*, p. 174, no. 80). The treatment of the fleece recalls the beard of the animal on **300**.

Bibliography: *Verres antiques* 1954, p. 49, no. 298 (part of group); *Glass from the Ancient World* 1957, p. 281, no. 590 (part of group).

326. Fragment of Beaker with Lion

9th to 10th century. Formerly in the Smith Collection (1057). 55.1.147.
H. (surviving) 2.7 cm, D. (max., est.) about 8.5 cm, (rib, est.) about 7 cm.
Transparent pale yellowish green. Blown; relief-cut.

Fragment from lower wall (TTh. 0.2 cm) and base (TTh. 0.4 cm) of beaker decorated in relief. On lower wall: traces of two indeterminate motifs above continuous horizontal rib that presumably defined bottom of frieze. On underside of base: lion walking in left profile. Lion has roughly circular head, with countersunk dot to represent eye, and two vestigial ears; short neck; body with plump breast and straight back and belly; two short front legs, left thrust forward and down, and right raised, both with large paws; one (left) hind leg with misplaced haunch and large paw clutching vegetal scroll; and long tail extending up and forward, and terminating in curl. Front and back of head, outlines of body, and tail are notched; paws are hatched. Interior of body is plain. Outlines of lion are approximately in horizontal plane, so that fragment stands without support.

Small parts of lower wall and almost entire base survive. Broken on all sides. Dull and extensively pitted, with trace of iridescent weathering. Circular hole

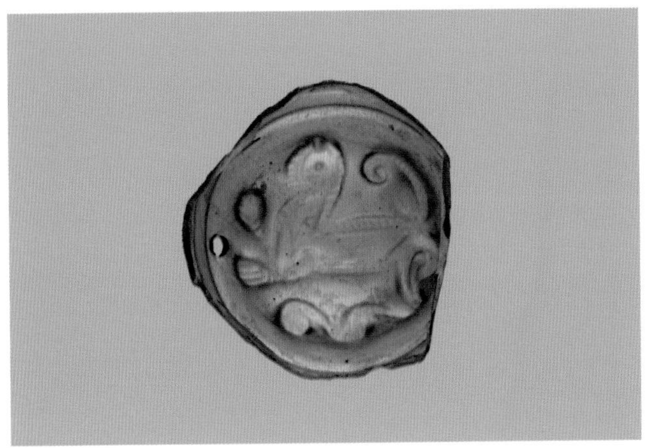

326

(D. 0.4 cm) drilled at junction of wall and base, presumably by Ray Winfield Smith to extract sample for chemical analysis.

Comment: The animal is shown in the posture described in European heraldry as *passant.* It was likened by P. Oliver (1961, p. 20) to the lions on a relief-cut bowl in the Treasury of San Marco, Venice (117: *Glass of the Sultans* 2001, pp. 178–179, no. 84). Like the animal on **326**, each of the San Marco lions has a round head and a single eye; unlike **326**, however, each has a body liberally embellished with printies. Lions on most other early Islamic and related glass vessels, such as **397** and **586**, have the body and limbs shown in profile, but with the head facing the viewer, and both eyes plainly visible.

Bibliography: *Glass from the Ancient World* 1957, p. 283, no. 602; Oliver, P. 1961, pp. 19–20.

327. Fragment of Beaker with Fantastic Animal

9th to 10th century. Formerly in the Smith Collection. 68.1.59-3.
H. (surviving) 4.4 cm, D. (rim, est.) about 6 cm.
Almost colorless, with yellowish tinge. Blown; relief-cut.

Fragment from rim and upper wall of beaker (TTh. 0.2 cm) decorated in relief (Th. 0.1 cm). Rim plain, with narrow rounded lip and shallow bevel on inside; wall straight and tapering. Decoration consists of horizontal rib, 1.7 cm below lip, which forms border of frieze. Surviving part of frieze contains back of neck, most of left wing, and very small part of back of fantastic animal seen in left profile. Neck has notched outline and contains two printies; wing is upright, with backward curl at tip and feathers indicated by hatching arranged in herringbone pattern; back has raised outline.

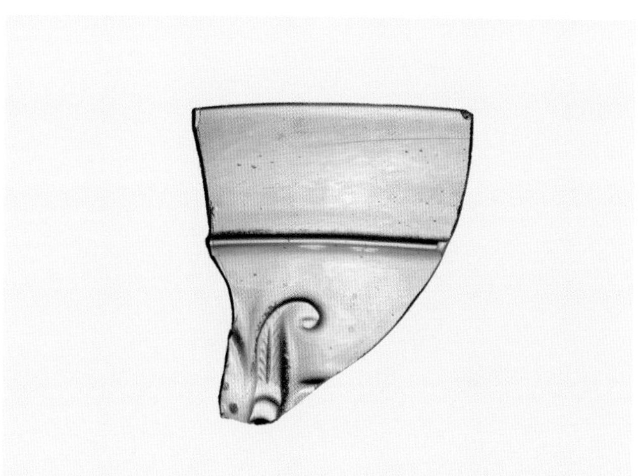

327

Broken on all sides, except for section of rim, which is about 20 percent of original circumference. Glass appears to be as new.

Comment: The quality of the glass and the delicacy of the cutting are exceptional. The identity of the creature cannot be determined; it may have been a *senmurv* (cf. **324**), a griffin (cf. **364**), or some other fantastic animal.

328. Fragment of Beaker(?) with Fantastic Animal

9th to 10th century. Formerly in the Strauss Collection (F78). Bequest of Jerome Strauss. 79.1.309.
Max. Dim. 3.5 cm, D. (est.) about 7 cm.
Almost colorless, with yellowish tinge; minute bubbles. Blown; relief-cut.

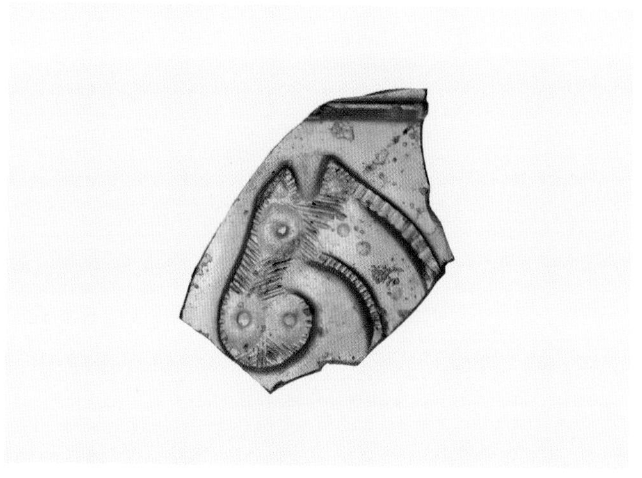

328

Fragment of beaker(?). Wall (Th. 0.2 cm with decoration, 0.1 cm without decoration) straight and perhaps tapering. Decorated in relief with horizontal rib, below which is small part of frieze with fantastic animal seen in profile, facing left. Animal has head with countersunk eye, narrow muzzle terminating in bulbous snout with two countersunk nostrils or eyes, and triangular ears separated by V-shaped cut notch; head is completely covered with hatching, which makes herringbone patterns on muzzle and snout, and each ear has one drilled dot; neck is long and curved, with notched outlines and countersunk interior decorated with row of four drilled dots.

Broken on all sides. Slightly pitted, with traces of transparent pale brown weathering.

COMMENT: The shape, size (the estimated diameter is approximate, but probably not more than one centimeter wrong), and thinness of the fragment suggest that it was part of a beaker. I assume that the rib is the upper border of the frieze, but this is not certain, since we have no idea what the creature looked like. Although fantastic animals are found on other relief-cut glasses (and, indeed, in other media), I have not come across a creature that resembles the beast on **328**.

Cf. the (different) fantastic creature on a fragment from Nishapur in The Metropolitan Museum of Art, New York (40.170.181: Kröger 1995, pp. 140–143, no. 193, with references to other depictions of mythical beasts).

329. Fragment of Beaker(?) with Fantastic Animal (?)

9th to 10th century. Formerly in the Smith Collection. Gift of Carl Berkowitz and Derek Content. 76.1.263.
Max. Dim. 4.4 cm.
Almost colorless, with yellowish tinge. Blown; relief-cut.

Fragment from beaker(?) with straight wall (TTh. 0.25 cm) decorated in relief (Th. 0.1 cm). Decoration is enigmatic, but it may consist of fantastic animal shown in left profile. Its head has large eye indicated by countersunk dot, two small ears, and short, curved horn; neck and breast are represented by single curved line; similar but short line indicates back; and wing is in form of half-palmette. Above head and wing, curvilinear motif, part of which has triangular end. Lines are notched, details in head are incised, and triangular motif has incised lines and one printy.

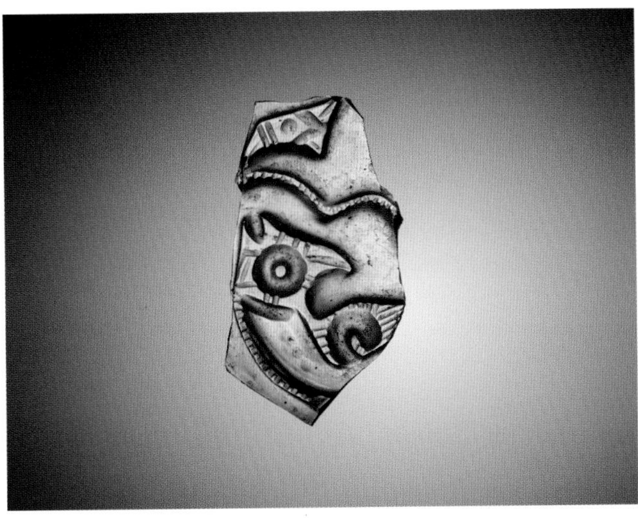

329

Broken on all sides. Some pitting and pale brownish weathering.

330. Fragment of Beaker with Bird

9th to 10th century. Probably from the Smith Collection. Gift of Mansour Mokhtarzadeh. 90.1.2.
Max. Dim. 6 cm, Th. (wall) 0.1 cm, (decoration) 0.1 cm.
Almost colorless, with yellowish green tinge. Blown; relief-cut.

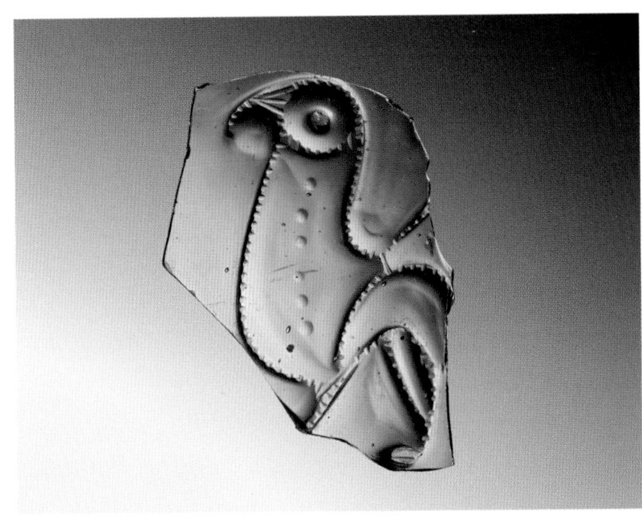

330

Fragment from wall of beaker with straight side that tapers toward bottom. Relief-cut decoration: part of bird strutting to left. Head held high on long neck; rounded breast; one leg in front of the other. All outlines are in relief, with numerous notches. Beak turned down at tip, with upper and lower halves indicated by shallow cuts; head consists of circle with eye in relief at center; row of six small depressions extends along neck, midway between outlines.

Broken on all sides. No trace of weathering.

COMMENT: The fragment is noteworthy on account of the high quality of the glass and of the relief cutting. The bibliographic citations are circumstantial; the donor acquired the fragment as part of a lot, which in 1990 still included a very unusual mold-blown fragment: *Glass from the Ancient World* 1957, p. 239, no. 474, which is mentioned as being part of the lot cited below.

BIBLIOGRAPHY: Probably *Glass from the Ancient World* 1957, p. 281, no. 590 (part of group); also probably *Islamic Antiquities and Works of Art* 1975, lot 593 (part of group).

331. Fragment of Beaker(?) with Birds

9th to 10th century. Formerly in the Smith Collection (919). 59.1.451.
H. (surviving) 5.4 cm, D. (est.) about 6 cm.
Colorless, with few small bubbles. Blown; relief-cut.

Fragment from wall (TTh. 0.25 cm) of beaker(?), decorated in relief (Th. 0.1 cm). At top, plain horizontal rib, presumably upper border of frieze. Surviving part of frieze has parts of two birds facing each other across upward-pointing arrowlike motif and, below it, flat circular boss with notched edge. Both birds stand; each has small, rounded head with countersunk eye and triangular beak with incised line between upper and lower parts. Bird on right has two short incisions indicating nostrils; neck is short, with notched outline at back, parallel incisions indicating feather, and two parallel incisions at junction with body; breast has notched outline.

Broken on all sides. Slightly pitted, with faint trace of weathering, but otherwise in almost pristine condition.

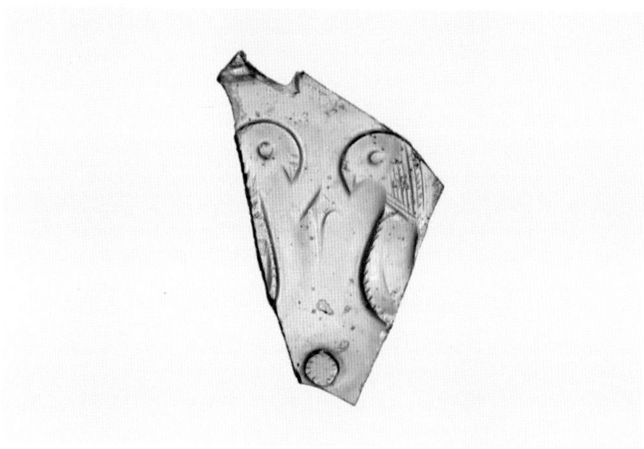

331

Comment: The straight, possibly tapering profile of the fragment indicates that it came from a beaker or possibly a small bottle. The shapes of the birds and the careful cutting in low relief may be compared with the birds on a bottle in the David Collection, Copenhagen (10/1963: *Glass of the Sultans* 2001, pp. 191–192, no. 96) and on the underside of the Falcon and Ibex Bowl (**296**). They share, for example, similar treatments of the head and neck, and the lightly notched outlines.

Bibliography: *Verres antiques* 1954, p. 49, no. 298 (part of group); *Glass from the Ancient World* 1957, p. 281, no. 590 (part of group).

332. Fragment of Beaker(?) with Bird

9th to 10th century. Formerly in the Smith Collection (555-31). Gift of Carl Berkowitz and Derek Content. 76.1.219.
H. (surviving) 3.5 cm, D. (rib, est.) 7 cm.
Colorless. Blown; relief-cut.

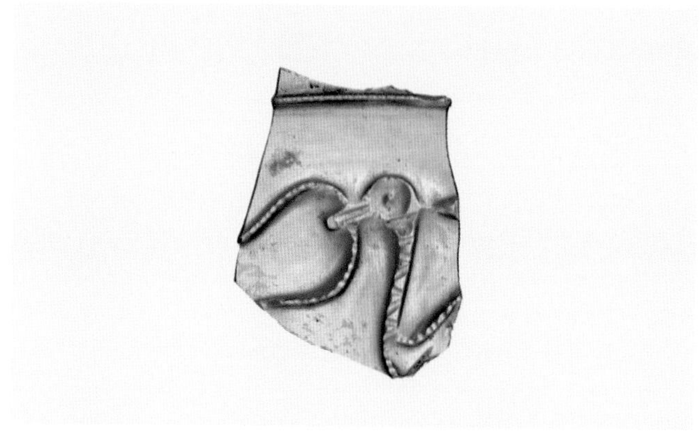

332

Fragment of beaker(?). Wall straight (Th. 0.1 cm) and either vertical or slightly tapered. Decorated in relief (Th. 0.1–0.15 cm): horizontal rib, which presumably formed upper border of frieze; below this, part of bird shown in profile, facing left. Bird has long beak, small head with eye represented by countersunk dot, crest, long neck, and body shown in outline; in its beak, large, perhaps U-shaped object, also shown in outline. Rib and outlines of head, body, and U-shaped object are notched; neck has zigzag pattern of cuts.

Broken on all sides. Virtually unweathered.

Comment: The size and shape of the fragment suggest that it was part of a beaker. The identity of the bird is uncertain. The large beak and long neck suggest that it may be a waterfowl, perhaps a duck. It is tempting to see the U-shaped element in the bird's beak as part of a collar. If this is so, the motif of a bird holding a collar would recall similar scenes in the art of Sasanian Iran and adjoining regions (cf. the bird in the central medallion of a sixth- to seventh-century silver-gilt dish in The State Hermitage Museum, St. Petersburg (S-18: *Splendeur des Sassanides* 1993, p. 217, no. 69).

333. Fragment of Beaker(?) with Bird

9th to 10th century. Formerly in the Strauss Collection (F54). Bequest of Jerome Strauss. 79.1.303.
H. (surviving) 0.7 cm, D. (base) 6.5 cm.
Colorless. Blown; relief-cut.

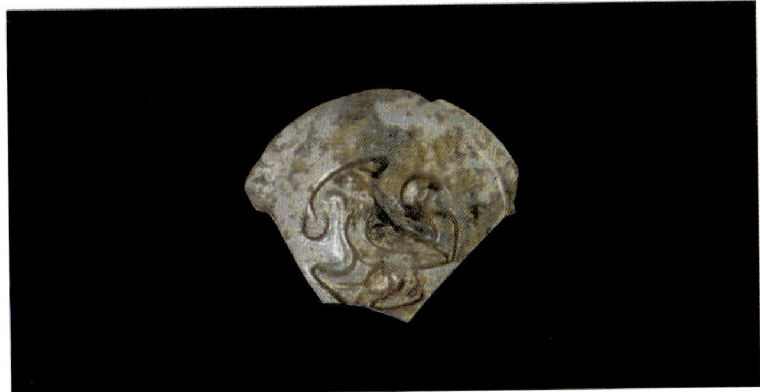

333

Fragment from bottom of beaker (?), consisting of about 60 percent of base. Bottom of wall descends vertically; base shaped like shallow disk with sloping side. Relief-cut decoration (Th. 0.2 cm) on underside of base (when seen from below): stylized bird seen in profile, facing left; it has small head with oval eye and triangular crest, and it holds curly leaf in its beak; body has rounded breast and is pointed at rear; wing is folded; legs are short, and feet are disproportionately large.

Patches of pale grayish weathering, which is slightly iridescent.

Comment: The surface of the decoration, which was made by cutting away parts of the underside of the base, is flush with the edge of the foot. The bird is reminiscent of the roosters that adorn some of the stamped appliqués on such seventh- to eighth-century vessels as the well-known bowl in the collection of the Abegg-Stiftung at Riggisberg, near Bern, Switzerland (4.3.63: Kröger 1998, pp. 305–316; cf. Whitehouse 2005, pp. 34–36, nos. 27–33), although the latter frequently have more flamboyant tail feathers.

334. Beaker with Palmettes and Half-Palmettes

9th to 10th century. Formerly in the Smith Collection (A316). 65.1.9.
H. 12.3 cm, D. about 9 cm.
Colorless. Blown; relief-cut.

Beaker shaped like truncated cone. Rim plain, with rim ground flat; wall (Th. 0.1 cm) straight and tapering; base rounded. Relief-cut decoration (Th. 0.1–0.2 cm) on wall and base. Wall has continuous frieze bordered by one horizontal rib 3.1 cm below rim, and one horizontal rib at junction with base. It contains three large and three smaller motifs; large motifs are identical and equidistant, each consisting of palmette on stem with double outline; lower stem divides into two tendrils, which curve down, out, up, and in, and terminate in half-palmettes; below stem and between tendrils, one kite-shaped boss. Smaller motifs occupy spaces between palmettes; they are (from right to left) inscription, symmetrical arrangement of tendrils and half-palmettes, and inscription(?). Base is decorated with four palmettes pointing toward center. Outlines of large motifs and parts of smaller motifs are notched.

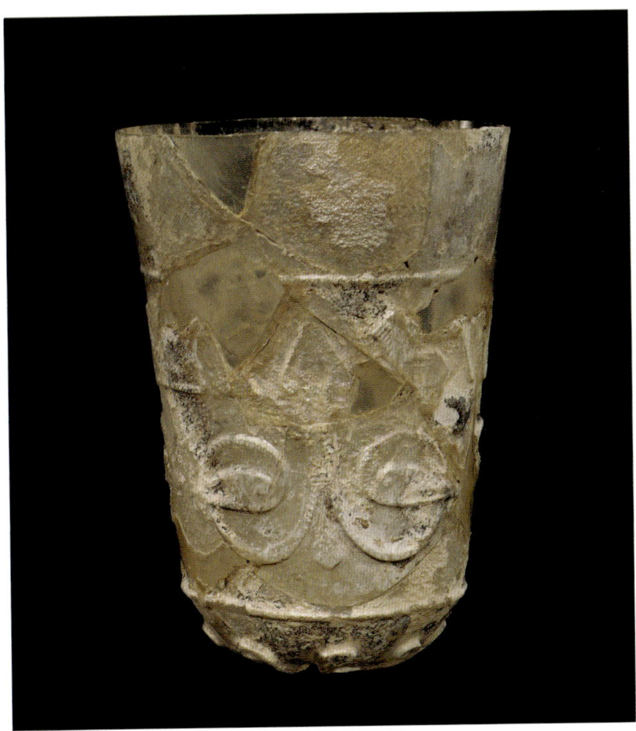

334A

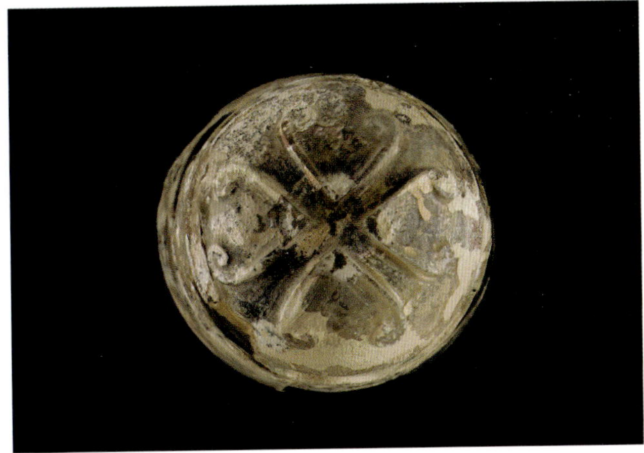

334B

Incomplete. Broken into many pieces, with two large and several smaller losses from rim and wall. Patches of dark brown weathering and, where this is missing, silvery iridescence.

Comment: The four palmettes on the base are similar to the group of palmettes on the rounded base

338. Fragment of Beaker with Vegetal Scroll

9th to 10th century. Formerly in the Smith Collection (555-5). Gift of Carl Berkowitz and Derek Content. 76.1.206.
H. 2.9 cm, D. (base) about 5 cm.
Colorless, with yellowish green tinge. Blown; relief-cut.

Fragment from lower wall and base of beaker (Th. 0.1 cm). Wall is decorated with continuous scroll (Th. 0.1 cm) of rather geometric leaves (H. 1.2 cm) above horizontal rib.

Broken on all sides. Dull, but without obvious weathering.

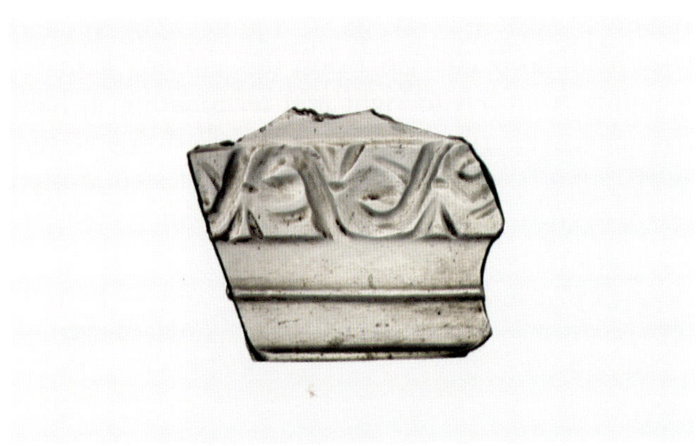

338

339. Fragment of Beaker(?) with Vegetal Motif

9th to 10th century. Formerly in the Smith Collection. 68.1.59-25.
H. (surviving) 4.5 cm, D. (est.) about 6 cm.
Almost colorless, with yellowish green tinge; few minute bubbles. Blown; relief-cut.

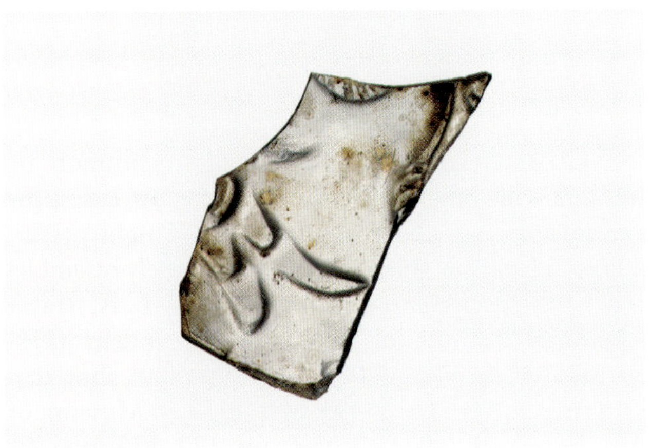

339

Fragment of beaker(?). Wall (Th. 0.1–0.3 cm) straight, possibly tapering. Decorated in relief (Th. 0.1 cm) with narrow leaves on curved stem and unidentified motif. Leaves are embellished with short lateral cuts.

Broken on all sides. Patches of pale brownish weathering or stain.

340. Fragment of Beaker(?) with Vegetal Motif

9th to 10th century. Formerly in the Smith Collection (0921-12). Gift of Carl Berkowitz and Derek Content. 76.1.286.
Max. Dim. 3.8 cm, D. (max., est.) about 6 cm.
Colorless. Blown; relief-cut.

Fragment from wall of beaker(?). Wall (TTh. 0.2 cm) straight and probably tapering. Decorated in relief (Th. 0.1 cm) with small part of frieze that has upper border consisting of horizontal rib. Surviving part of frieze contains vegetal motif represented by two notched lines. One line comprises stem extending upward and curving to left; second line springs from first and spirals outward and down, and terminates in small budlike element.

Broken on all sides. Slightly pitted, with traces of weathering.

COMMENT: The profile and apparent diameter of the fragment suggest that it came from a beaker.

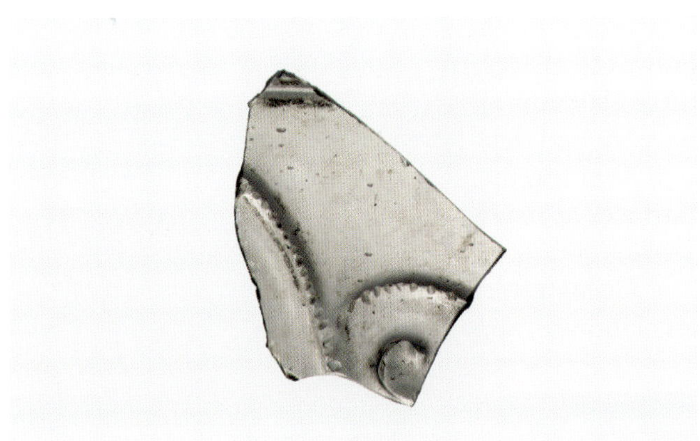

340

341. Fragment of Beaker with Inscription

9th to 10th century. Formerly in the Strauss Collection (F75). Bequest of Jerome Strauss. 79.1.314.
H. (surviving) 6 cm, D. (rim, est.) about 6 cm.
Colorless; few minute bubbles. Blown; relief-cut.

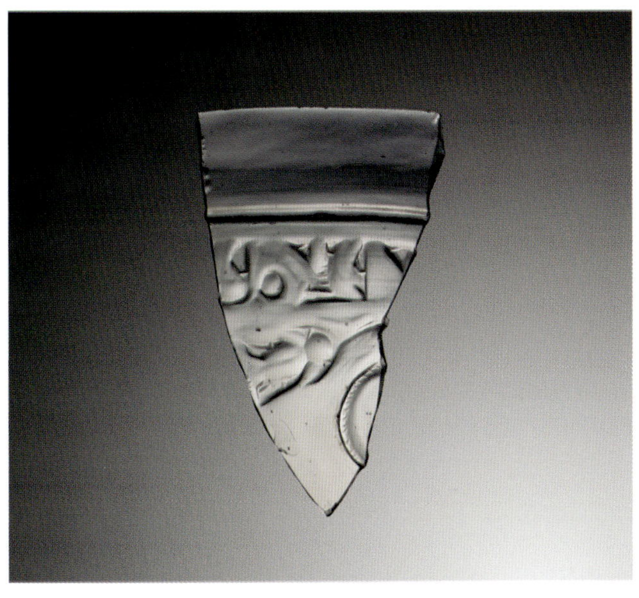

341

Fragment of beaker. Rim plain, with slight bevel on inside; wall (TTh. 0.2 cm) straight and tapering. Decorated in relief (Th. 0.1 cm) with part of frieze bordered at top by horizontal rib. Below rib, Kufic inscription “ للا ” (*lilla* . . .), and below this, unidentified ornament, which includes curved line and stem ending in two foliate elements. Curved line is notched; inscription and foliate terminals are embellished with short cuts.

About 20 percent of rim and small part of upper wall survive. No visible weathering.

342. Fragments of Beaker(?) with Inscription

9th to 10th century. Formerly in the Smith Collection (1288). Gift of Carl Berkowitz and Derek Content. 76.1.264a–c.
Max. Dim. (largest) 2.9 cm, D. (max., est.) about 6 cm.
Colorless. Blown; relief-cut.

Three fragments of beaker(?). Wall (TTh. 0.15 cm) is straight and either vertical or tapering. Each fragment is decorated in relief with part of horizontal inscription (H. 1.9 cm) in elegant Kufic script: “ لا ” (. . . *halw[?]*), “الم” (. . . *al-m*), and “هلو” (*la* . . .). Letters are notched.

All three fragments are broken on all sides. Somewhat dull, with patches of transparent light gray weathering.

Comment: The size, shape, and thinness of the fragments are consistent with the possibility that they came from the wall of a beaker.

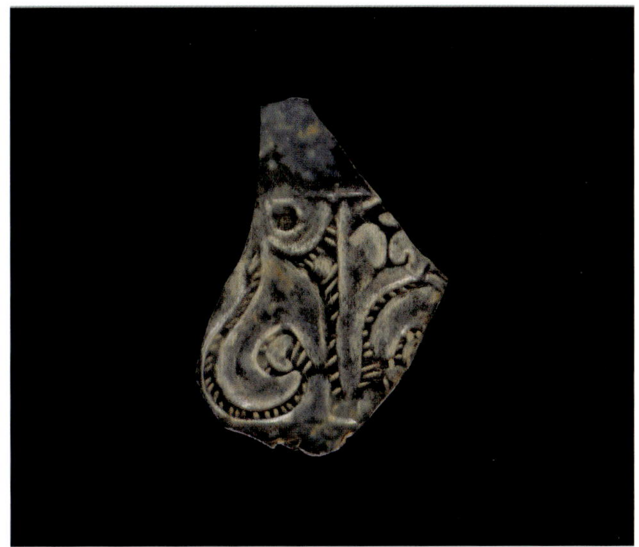

342A

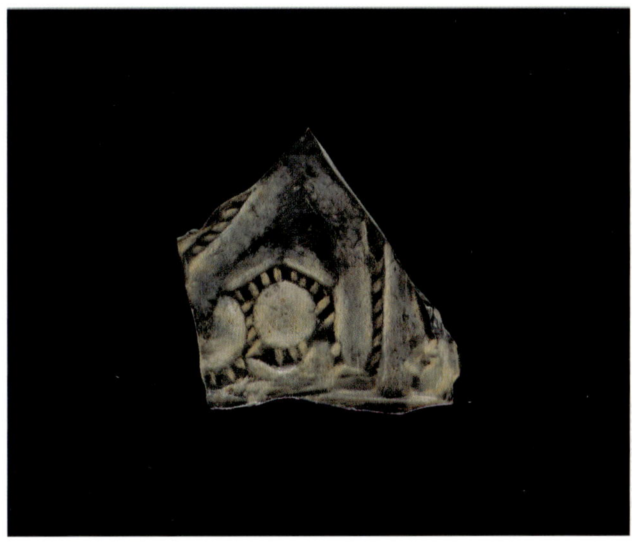

342B

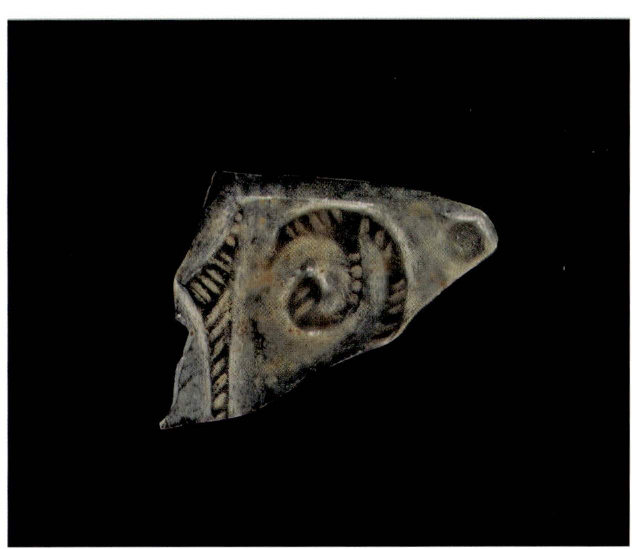

342C

343. Fragment of Beaker(?) with Inscription(?)

Probably 10th century. Formerly in the Smith Collection (926). Gift of Carl Berkowitz and Derek Content. 76.1.221.
Max. Dim. 3.5 cm, D. (est.) about 6 cm.
Almost colorless, with bluish tinge. Blown; relief-cut.

Fragment of beaker(?). Wall (Th. 0.1–0.15 cm) is straight and perhaps tapering. Decorated in relief (H. 0.2 cm) with part of Kufic inscription (?), in which one horizontal element and one vertical element have triangular ends, and one curved element ends in scrolling leaves. Linear elements and leaves are notched; triangles are hatched. One cm below inscription, trace of horizontal rib.

Broken on all sides. Almost pristine, with traces of weathering.

Bibliography: *Verres antiques* 1954, p. 49, no. 298 (part of group); *Glass from the Ancient World* 1957, p. 281, no. 590 (part of group).

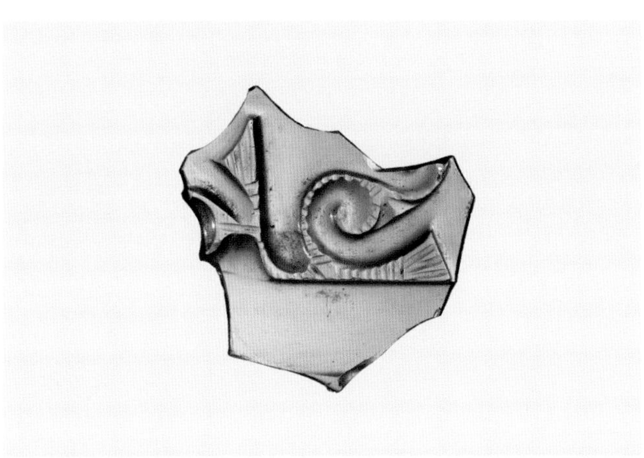

343

344. Fragment of Beaker(?)

9th to 10th century. Formerly in the Smith Collection (1221-16). Gift of Carl Berkowitz and Derek Content. 76.1.293.
Max. Dim. 6.3 cm, D. (rib, est.) about 9–10 cm.
Almost colorless, with yellowish tinge. Blown; relief-cut.

Fragment from straight, perhaps tapering wall (TTh. 0.25 cm) of beaker(?) decorated in relief (Th. 0.1 cm). Decoration consists of horizontal rib, perhaps forming border of frieze, which contained narrow U-shaped motif and traces of other elements, all with notched outlines.

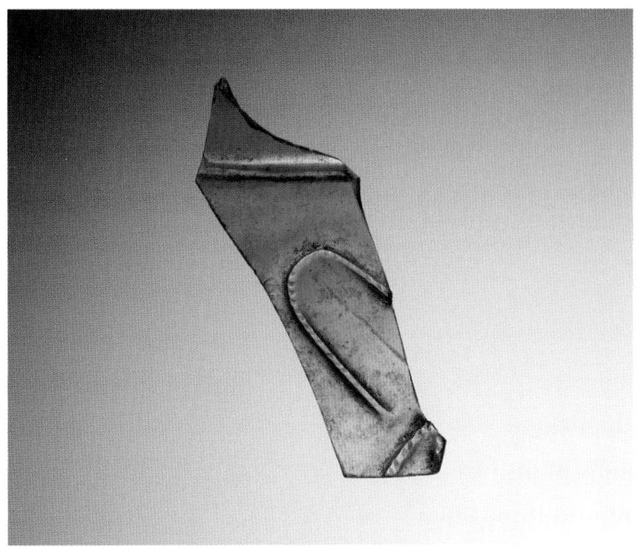

344

Broken on all sides. Dull and lightly pitted, with traces of grayish brown weathering.

Comment: The fragment may have been part of a beaker similar in shape and size to a relief-cut beaker in The Metropolitan Museum of Art, New York (1974.45: *Glass of the Sultans* 2001, pp. 172–173, no. 79). It is not clear whether the rib was the upper or lower border of the frieze.

345. Fragment of Beaker(?)

9th to 10th century. Formerly in the Smith Collection. 68.1.59-64.
H. (surviving) 3.1 cm, D. (est.) about 5 cm.
Colorless. Blown; relief-cut.

Fragment from wall of beaker (?) with slightly concave profile; orientation unknown. Total thickness is less than 0.2 cm; thickness of decoration is less than

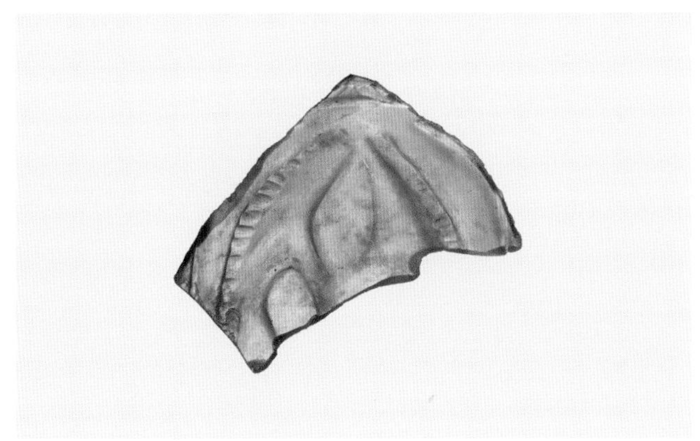

345

0.1 cm. At presumed top, trace of horizontal rib. Below rib, upper part of oval motif with vertical axis greater than horizontal axis, with horizontally hatched, raised outlines. Inside this motif, pointed oval at top, and oval or almost oval motif at left side.

Broken on all sides. Incipient weathering.

Comment: If the decoration was symmetrical, it probably consisted of a tall oval or rhombic motif containing, at the top, an oval leaf or petal, flanked by ovals, all of which possibly formed part of a fleur-de-lis (cf. **266**).

5. Goblets

346. Goblet with Horses

10th to early 11th century. Formerly in the Strauss Collection (S2139). Bequest of Jerome Strauss. 79.1.94.
H. 13.3 cm, D. (rim) 7.8 cm, (foot) 5.3 cm.
Colorless. Blown; relief-cut.

Goblet: conical bowl with rounded bottom. Rim plain, with top ground flat; wall tapers toward narrow horizontal flange, then curves in toward stem; short, slender stem and conical foot with prominent pontil mark belong to another vessel. Body has relief-cut ornament, which leaves wall only 1 mm thick, between raised horizontal border near rim and narrow flange near bottom: frieze of three horses in row, walking to left. Each horse is saddled and bridled. All outlines are in relief and have traces of notches; bodies have rows of dotlike depressions. Above rump of each animal, one word in Kufic script.

Broken into numerous pieces and repaired; losses restored in plastic; bottom of body is entirely restored. Dull and pitted, with traces of yellowish weathering.

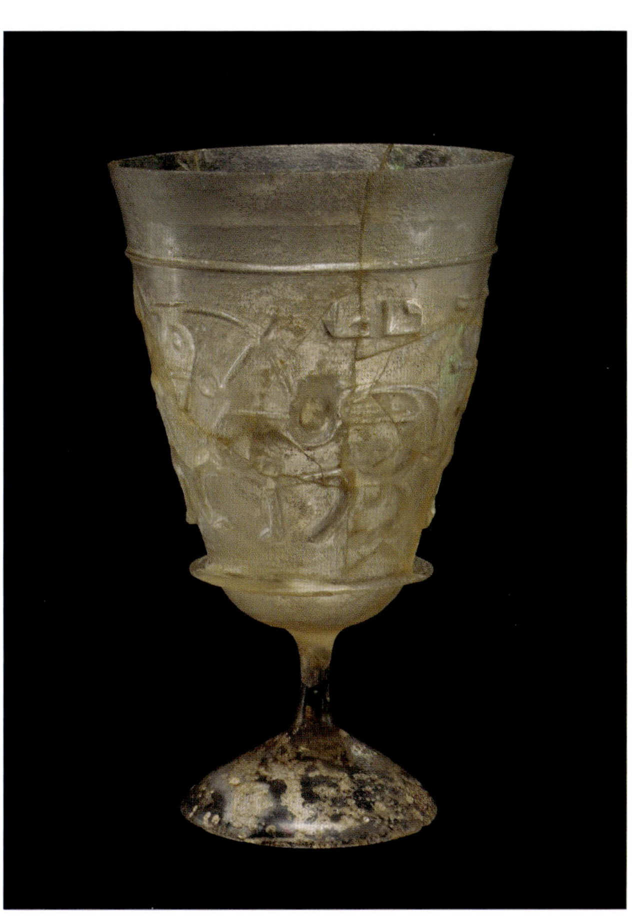

346

Comment: The object belongs to a group of relief-cut goblets with a raised horizontal border near the rim and a flange near the bottom of the wall, which enclose a continuous band of zoomorphic ornament accompanied by Kufic inscriptions.

Cf. *Glass from the Ancient World* 1957, no. 544 (a fragmentary example, which, when complete, was probably decorated with three birds walking to the left, each accompanied by a short Kufic inscription); and two goblets in the al-Sabah Collection, Dār al-Āthār al-Islāmiyyah, Kuwait National Museum: LNS 78 KG (Carboni 2001, p. 87, no. 20b = *3000 Jahre Glaskunst* 1981, p. 139, no. 618: decorated with three humped bulls shown in left profile, but with their heads turned to look behind them, each accompanied by parts of a Kufic inscription) and LNS 84 G (Carboni 2001, p. 88, no. 21: decorated with three birds standing in left profile, each separated from the others by a vertical Kufic inscription). The goblet with three bulls, which was formerly in the Kofler-Truniger Collection, is said to have been found at Nishapur, northeastern Iran (but see page 176).

347. Goblet with Animals

9th to 10th century. Formerly in the Strauss Collection (S2770). Bequest of Jerome Strauss. 79.1.76.
H. (surviving) 5 cm.
Colorless. Blown; relief-cut.

Goblet with bowl shaped like truncated cone. Lower wall straight and tapering to broad horizontal flange, below which it curves down and in, and joins

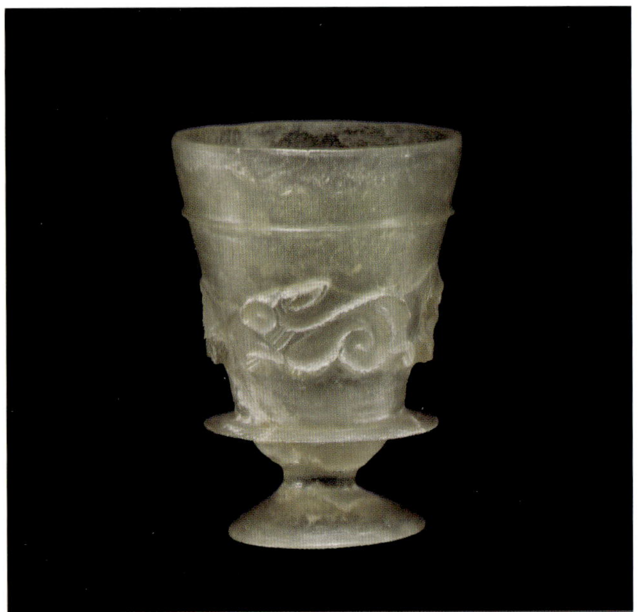

347

very short, solid stem; foot hollow and probably conical; no pontil mark. Wall above flange is decorated in relief with frieze of three very similar animals shown in profile, running from right to left. Each animal has round head with small mouth, eye in form of countersunk dot, and long, pointed ear; body is decorated with raised spiral motif, one short front leg and one short back leg, both with round foot, and tail. All three animals have hatched feet and notched outlines.

Incomplete. Broken, with loss of entire rim and upper wall, and most of foot. Dull and pitted, with remains of pale grayish weathering.

Comment: Friezes of running animals were a popular form of decoration on relief-cut glasses. The numerous examples include **323** and **324**; Kröger 1984, pp. 223–228, nos. 193–195; and *Glass of the Sultans* 2001, pp. 176–181, nos. 82–84 and 86.

The animals on **347** are reminiscent of the "hares" on the turquoise-colored bowl in the Treasury of San Marco, Venice (140: *Glass of the Sultans* 2001, pp. 176–178, no. 83), although the latter were cut with greater delicacy.

For other examples of this form, cf. **348**, which is decorated with three birds of prey and three Kufic inscriptions; **352**, which has three birds and one Kufic inscription; and **353**, which is also decorated with three birds but has no inscription. For two other close parallels, the first decorated with three humped cattle and three Kufic inscriptions, and the second decorated with three eagles, both in the al-Sabah Collection, Dār al-Āthār al-Islāmiyyah, Kuwait National Museum (LNS 78 KG and LNS 84 G), see Carboni 2001, pp. 87–88, nos. 20b and 21.

348. Goblet with Birds and Inscriptions

Probably 10th century. 65.1.4.
H. (surviving) 12.6 cm, D. 11.8 cm.
Colorless; very few bubbles. Blown; relief-cut.

Goblet with truncated conical bowl. Rim plain; wall straight and tapering, with narrow horizontal flange at bottom; base curves down and in; stem cylindrical. Wall is relief-cut with continuous frieze bordered by horizontal rib at top and flange at bottom. Frieze contains three apparently identical birds of prey shown in left profile, but with head turned to right. Each bird has small head with prominent eye and curved beak, short neck, and body and thick tail with rounded end, both defined by single continuous outline; one vestigial wing, extended above body, ends in half-palmette; other wing consists of single curving line in front of body, which terminates in leg with triangular foot; other leg, also with triangular foot, is just behind it. Some outlines are notched; body and tail, and some details, have drilled circular depressions. Above and behind each bird, short inscription in Kufic style and single hook-shaped motif. Inscriptions are: (1) "رعى", (2) "...ية", and (3) "برك"(*baraka …iyya ra*^{c}*i…*; [Perpetual?] blessing . . . [?] protection).

Incomplete. Broken into many pieces, with loss of half of rim, one-fifth of wall, small parts of flange,

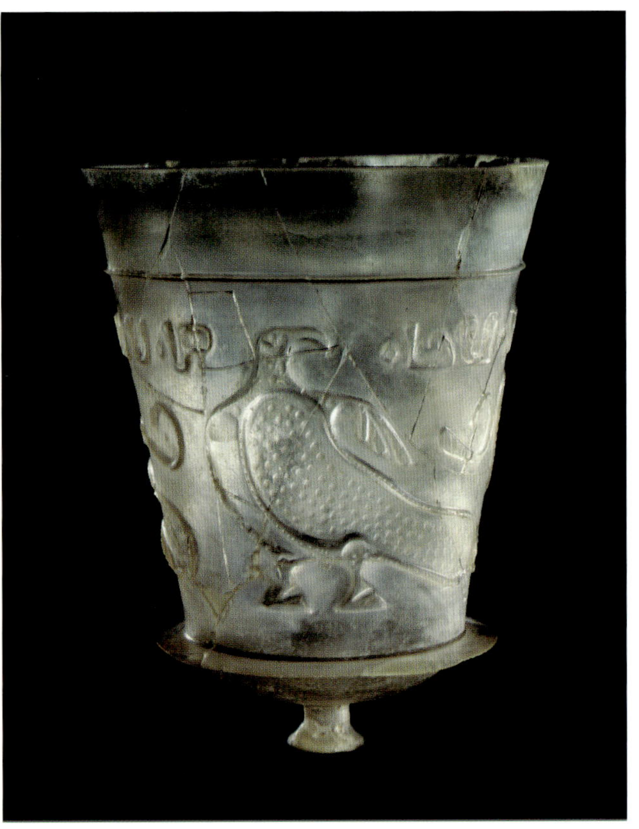

348

most of stem, and entire foot; bowl and flange restored. Dull and pitted, with traces of weathering.

COMMENT: Cf. **352**, which is decorated with three birds and a Kufic inscription, and **353**, which has three birds but no inscription. For two other close parallels, one decorated with three humped cattle and three Kufic inscriptions, and the other with three eagles, both in the al-Sabah Collection, Dār al-Āthār al-Islāmiyyah, Kuwait National Museum (LNS 78 KG and LNS 84 G), see Carboni 2001, pp. 87–88, nos. 20b and 21.

For an example of the same form, also with relief-cut ornament, but made of rock crystal, see Ghirshman 1954, pl. 46a, and *Arts of Islam* 1976, p. 125, no. 102 (said to have been found at Qazvīn, Iran: The British Museum, London, OA 1954 10-131).

BIBLIOGRAPHY: *Guide to the Collections* 1965, p. 28, no. 29; "Recent Important Acquisitions," *JGS*, v. 8, 1966, p. 132, no. 9.

349. Fragment of Goblet with Birds and Inscription

9th to 10th century. Formerly in the Smith Collection (1347). 61.1.14.
H. (surviving) 7 cm, D. (top of fragment, est.) about 5.4 cm, (flange) 4.6 cm.
Colorless or almost colorless. Blown (two gathers); relief-cut.

Fragment of goblet. Wall (TTh. 0.15 cm) of bowl is straight and tapering, with horizontal flange near bottom, below which it tapers with slightly convex

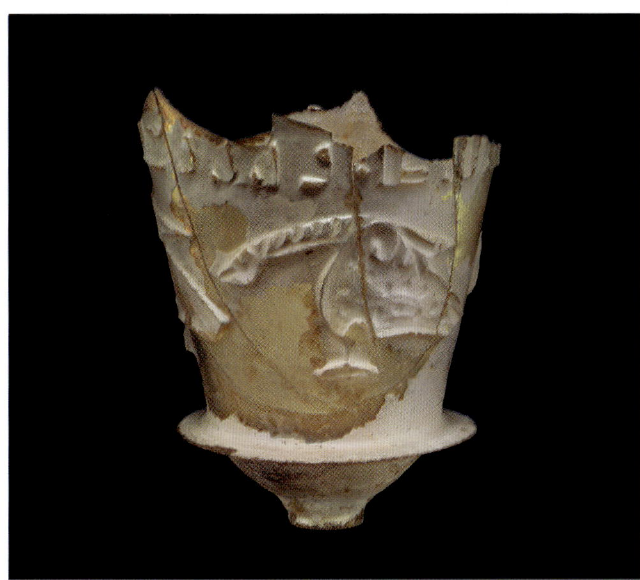

349

profile; solid stem. Wall is decorated in relief (Th. 0.1 cm) with horizontal line of Kufic inscription (H. 0.75 cm) above frieze containing three almost identical birds. Surviving part of inscription reads: "...طا و رد و غبطة ... و و" (. . . *ta wa radd wa ghibta . . . wa wa* . . . ; . . . and accomplishment and happiness . . . and . . .). Each bird is shown in profile and stands facing left, with its head pointing downward. It has small head with pointed beak and eye indicated by countersunk dot, long and thin neck, body with plump breast, small wing represented by half-palmette, tail cut off straight, and short leg with triangular foot; neck is notched, and body is filled with printies.

Incomplete. Entire rim, top of wall, foot, and most of stem are missing. Silver weathering with iridescent sheen; where this is missing, surface is iridescent. Top of stem ground flat to attach modern foot.

COMMENT: The wall is less than 0.1 centimeter thick where glass was removed by the decorator. Despite their distinctive necks, the identity of the birds has not been established.

It appears that goblets of this form seldom carry relief-cut ornament. Other examples include two goblets in the al-Sabah Collection, Dār al-Āthār al-Islāmiyyah, Kuwait National Museum (LNS 78 KG and LNS 84 G: Carboni 2001, pp. 88–90, nos. 20b and 21). **350** and **351** may have been similar, but in both cases the form of the foot is uncertain.

BIBLIOGRAPHY: *Glass from the Ancient World* 1957, p. 265, no. 540.

350. Fragment of Goblet(?) with Birds and Inscription

9th to 10th century. Formerly in the Smith Collection (part of 1058). 2009.1.3a–c.
H. (surviving) 6.2 cm, D. (top of fragment, est.) about 6 cm, (flange) about 4 cm.
Colorless or almost colorless. Blown (two gathers); relief-cut.

Fragment of goblet(?). Wall (TTh. 0.15 cm) of bowl is straight and tapering, with narrow horizontal flange near bottom, below which it tapers with slightly convex profile; solid "stem," which has smooth, concave underside (see below). Wall is decorated in relief (Th. 0.1 cm) with horizontal line of Kufic inscription (H. 0.7 cm): "...ة ملك يمن وعز و س" (. . . *a mulk yumn wa ᶜizz wa s* . . . ; . . . authority prosperity and power and . . .).

Incomplete. Entire rim and top of wall, and large part of lower wall, perhaps also entire foot and most of stem, are missing. Patches of brownish weathering; where this is missing, surface (including underside of stem) is iridescent.

COMMENT: See **349**.

Although the object is described as a goblet, the underside of the "stem" is smooth, and it appears to be weathered. These observations raise the possibility that the vessel was not a goblet similar to **350**, but had a narrow base akin to that of a relief-cut beaker in the L. A. Mayer Memorial Institute for Islamic Art, Jerusalem (G73-71: *Glass of the Sultans* 2001, p. 174, no. 80). **351** may have been similar.

BIBLIOGRAPHY: *Glass from the Ancient World* 1957, p. 267, no. 544; Oliver, P. 1961, p. 23, fig. 26.

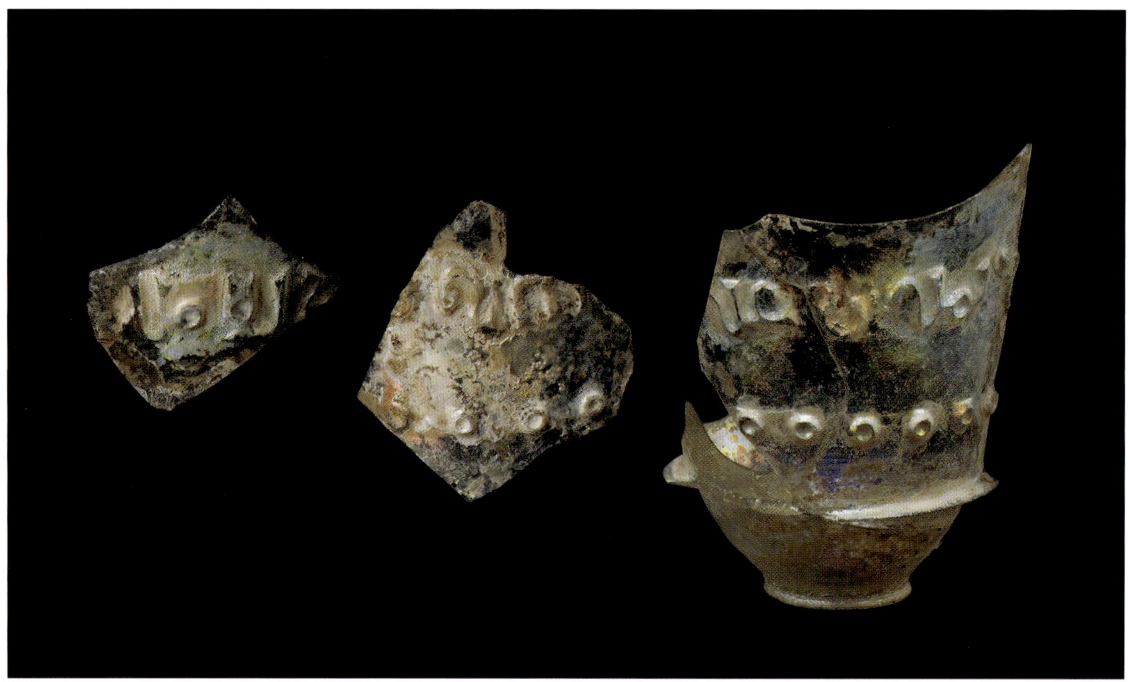

350

351. Fragments of Goblet(?) with Birds and Inscription

9th to 10th century. Formerly in the Smith Collection (part of 1058). 55.1.122.
Max. Dim. (fragment of wall) 5.3 cm, D. (flange) 4.4 cm.
Colorless or almost colorless. Blown (two gathers); relief-cut.

Two fragments of goblet(?): (1) wall (TTh. 0.2 cm) of bowl is straight and tapering; (2) horizontal flange near bottom of wall, below which it tapers with convex profile; short, solid "stem," which splays at bottom and has smooth underside (see below). (1) is decorated in relief (Th. 0.1 cm) with horizontal rib (D. about 7 cm), presumably upper border of frieze, below which is part of bird seen in profile, facing left. It has body with rounded tail, wing represented by half-palmette, and two short legs with triangular feet.

Fragments do not join. (1) appears to be grozed so that top of wall is flush with rib. (2) has circular hole (D. 0.45 cm) below flange, which may have been made by Ray Winfield Smith to obtain sample for chemical analysis. Both fragments are pitted, with remains of silvery iridescent weathering.

COMMENT: When they were acquired by the Museum, the fragments were restored as parts of a goblet similar to **353** (cf. illustrations in *Glass from the Ancient World* 1957 and Oliver, P. 1961). Oliver, however, noting the form of the stem, likened the vessel to a short-stemmed rock crystal goblet from Qazvīn, northern Iran, in The British Museum, London (OA 1954 10-131: *Arts of Islam* 1976, p. 125, no. 102). Both publications allude to a Kufic inscription, but no trace of this survives. Although the Museum's records do not provide confirmation, it seems reasonable to assume that the object was a victim of the Corning flood of 1972 (see page 10).

Although the fragments are described as parts of a goblet, the underside of the "stem" is smooth and it appears to be weathered. These observations raise the possibility that the vessel was similar to neither **353** nor the rock crystal goblet from Qazvīn, which has a broad, conical foot, but had a narrow base akin to that of a relief-cut beaker in the L. A. Mayer Memorial Institute for Islamic Art, Jerusalem (G73-71: *Glass of the Sultans* 2001, p. 174, no. 80). **351** may have been similar.

Bibliography: See **350**.

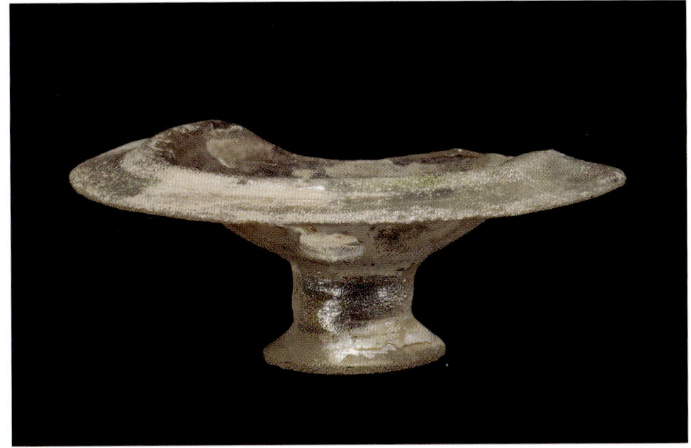

351A

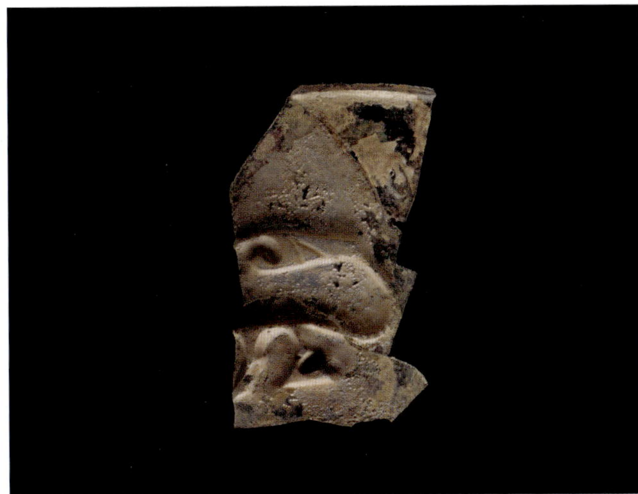

351B

352. Goblet with Birds

Probably 10th century. Formerly in the Strauss Collection (S2308). Bequest of Jerome Strauss. 79.1.50.
H. (surviving) 11.2 cm, D. 9.3 cm.
Colorless; very few bubbles. Blown; relief-cut.

Goblet with truncated conical bowl. Rim plain; wall straight and tapering, with narrow horizontal flange at bottom; bottom curves down and in; stem cylindrical. Wall is relief-cut with continuous frieze bordered by horizontal rib at top and flange at bottom. Frieze contains three apparently identical birds shown in left profile. Each bird has small head with drilled circular eye and curved beak; long, sinuous neck; bulbous body and thick tail with rounded end, both defined by single continuous outline and filled with drilled dots; and one vestigial wing, extended above body. Neck terminates in short leg with triangular foot; other leg, also with triangular foot, is just behind it. Each pair of birds is separated by triangular palmette-like motifs, and above each bird is one tear-shaped motif lying on its side. Between birds and upper border, Kufic inscription: “بركة دا(ئمة) (اقب)ال غبطة شامخة حا” (*baraka da['ima iqb])al ghibta shamikha ha*. . .; Per[petual] blessing, . . . [prosper]ity, high happiness, . . .).

Incomplete. Broken into many pieces, with loss of 35 percent of rim, small areas of wall and flange, most of stem, and entire foot; bowl and flange restored. Dull and pitted, with large areas of ivory-colored weathering.

Comment: Cf. **348**, which is decorated with three birds of prey and three Kufic inscriptions, and **353**, which is also decorated with three birds. For two other close parallels, the first decorated with three humped cattle and three Kufic inscriptions, and the second decorated with three eagles, both in the al-Sabah Collection, Dār al-Āthār al-Islāmiyyah, Kuwait National Museum (LNS 78 KG and LNS 84 G), see Carboni 2001, pp. 87–88, nos. 20b and 21.

For an example of the same form, also with relief-cut ornament, but made of rock crystal, see *Arts of Islam* 1976, p. 125, no. 102 (said to have been found

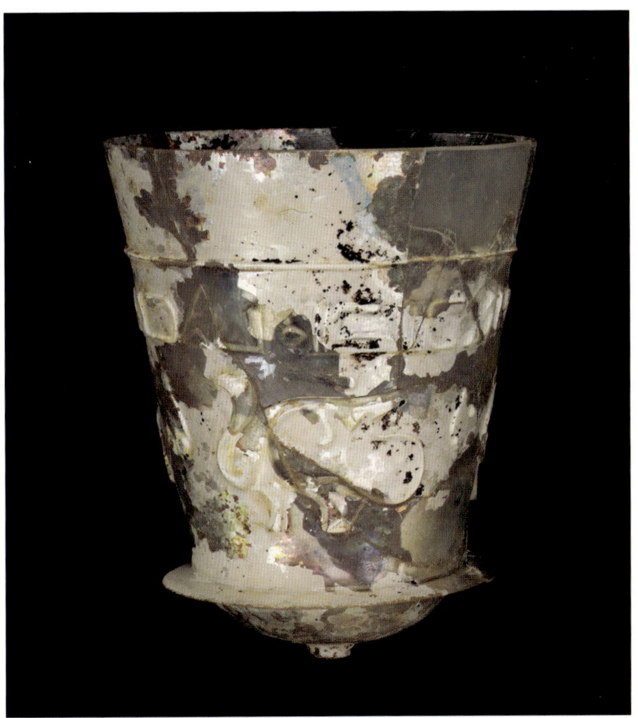

352

at Qazvīn, Iran: The British Museum, London, OA 1954 10-131).

Bibliography: "Recent Important Acquisitions," *JGS*, v. 8, 1966, p. 132, no. 9.

353. Fragment of Goblet with Birds

9th to 10th century. Formerly in the Strauss Collection (S2677). Gift of The Ruth Bryan Strauss Memorial Foundation. 79.1.92.
H. (surviving) 6.1 cm, D. (flange) 3.7 cm.
Colorless. Blown; relief-cut.

Fragment of goblet with truncated conical bowl. Wall straight and tapering until it meets horizontal flange, below which it curves down and in. Relief-cut decoration on wall: continuous frieze bordered at top by horizontal raised rib and at bottom by flange. Frieze contains three birds outlined in relief and shown in profile, walking toward left. Each bird has small circular head with pointed beak, eye represented by dot, and horizontal crest that is as long as body; head and body are separated by raised line; body has plump breast and prominent arched back, and it merges with downward-pointing tail; very small wing is folded across top of back; legs are placed one in front of the other and have feet with two claws. Outlines do not have notches, but bodies are decorated with small circular depressions.

Incomplete. Rim, most of upper wall, small part of flange, and entire stem and foot are missing and have been restored. Dull and pitted, with traces of pale brown weathering.

Comment: The form may be restored with confidence as a goblet with a solid stem and a conical foot by analogy with vessels such as the relief-cut goblet decorated with three bulls, in the al-Sabah Collection, Dār al-Āthār al-Islāmiyyah, Kuwait National Museum (LNS 78 KG: Carboni 2001, pp. 87–88, no. 20b). The same collection also contains the bowl of a relief-cut goblet decorated with three birds (LNS 84 G: *ibid.*, p. 88, no. 21). In both cases, the outlines are notched, and the bodies are filled with circular depressions. The first of them is said to have come from Nishapur.

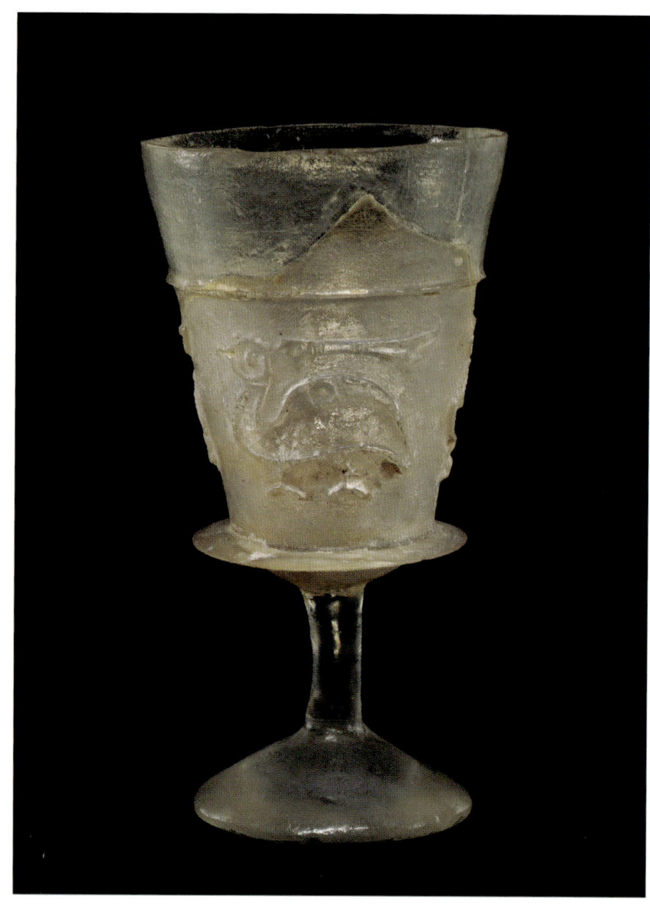

353

6. Large and Medium Bottles

354. Globular Bottle with Ibexes

9th to 10th century. 71.1.7.
H. 16.7 cm, D. (rim) 2.4 cm, (max.) 9 cm.
Colorless. Blown; relief-cut.

Bottle: globular. Rim is very slightly everted and beveled on inside; neck narrow and cylindrical; base has low, splayed foot-ring, within which underside is convex. Relief-cut decoration on neck and wall. On neck: upper part is plain; midsection has five continuous horizontal ribs; lower part is cut in eight contiguous vertical facets; at junction of neck and shoulder, stepped molding. Body is decorated with broad frieze framed by horizontal rib at junction of shoulder and wall, and by rib near bottom of wall. Frieze contains three pairs of ibexes; in each pair, animals face each other across vegetal motif consisting of two S-shaped scrolls terminating below in palmette, with two S-shaped scrolls and heart-shaped motif behind them. Ibexes have long and curving horns, short bodies, and small tails; hip joints of rear legs are marked with scroll; many outlines are notched; heads and feet of ibexes, and some other motifs, are hatched.

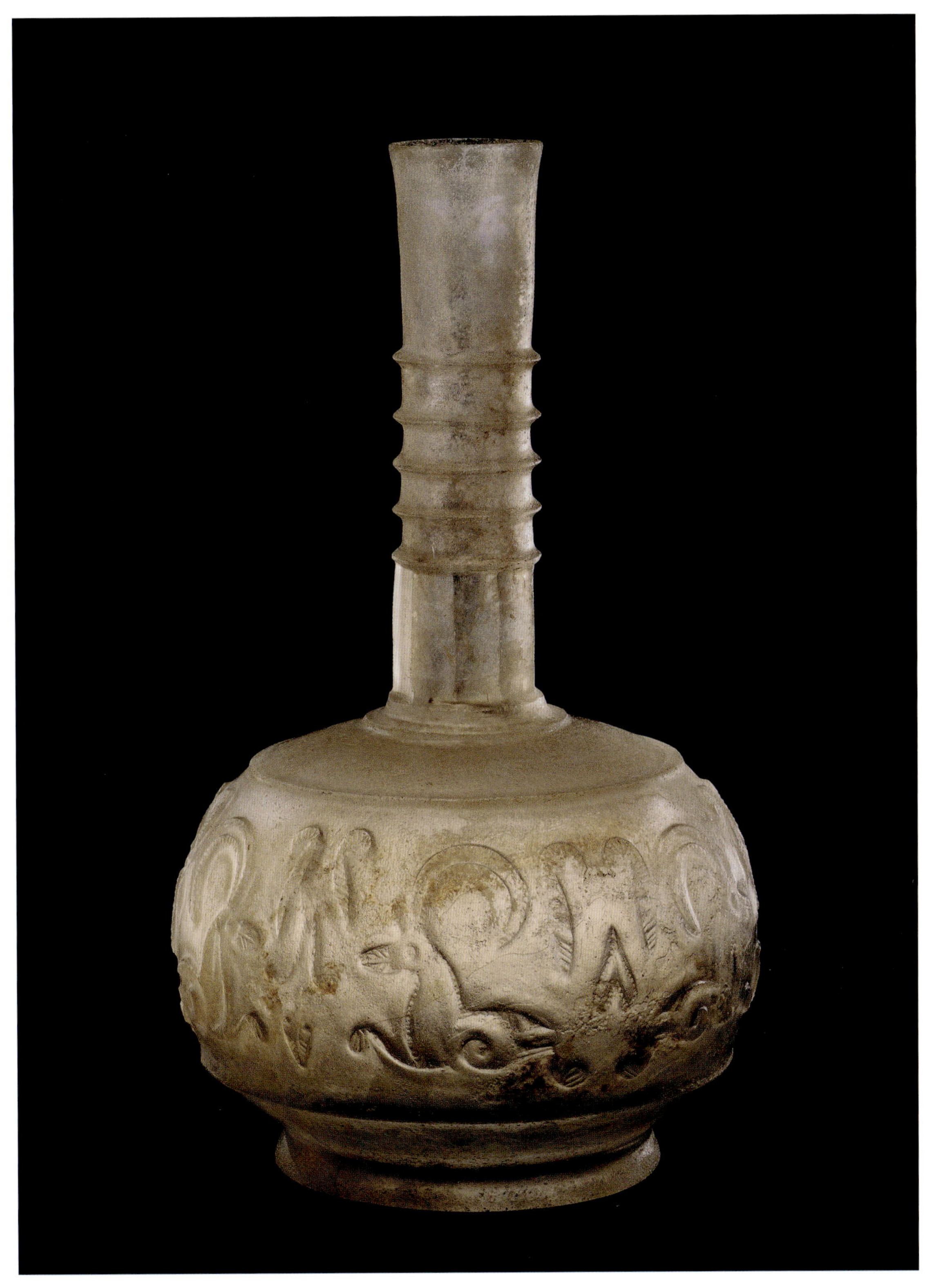

354

Intact. Dull and pitted, with traces of weathering.

Comment: Charleston (see below) remarked on the cutter's meticulous attention to detail and the care with which the inside of the rim and the underside of the base—parts that are not normally visible—were finished.

Bibliography: *Persian Glass* 1972, p. 15, no. 25; "Recent Important Acquisitions," *JGS*, v. 14, 1972, p. 155, no. 20; Charleston 1980, pp. 70–71, no. 27; Dolez 1988, p. 41; Charleston 1990, pp. 70–71, no. 27; *Treasures from Corning* 1992, p. 30, no. 20; Yoshimizu 1992, pp. 100 and 291–292, no. 205; *Glass of the Sultans* 2001, p. 181, no. 86.

355. Fragment of Globular Bottle with Ram

9th to 10th century. Formerly in the Strauss Collection (F53). Bequest of Jerome Strauss. 79.1.316.
Max. Dim. 5.2 cm, H. (surviving) about 4.6 cm, D. (upper rib, est.) about 4 cm, (lower rib, est.) about 6 cm.
Almost colorless, with yellowish tinge. Blown; relief-cut.

Fragment from shoulder and upper wall of globular bottle (TTh. 0.25 cm) decorated in relief (Th. 0.1 cm). Decoration consists of, on shoulder, horizontal rib (D. about 4 cm) and, on wall, frieze defined at top by horizontal rib (D. about 6 cm). Surviving part of frieze contains head of ram in left profile, but with ears and horns shown frontally. Head has mouth represented by short linear cut and eye represented by countersunk dot; ears are short and pointed; horns are large and curve up, out, and down, and almost touch back of head and muzzle. Head and ears have incised details, and neck has transverse hatching; back of head and horns are notched.

Broken on all sides. No obvious weathering.

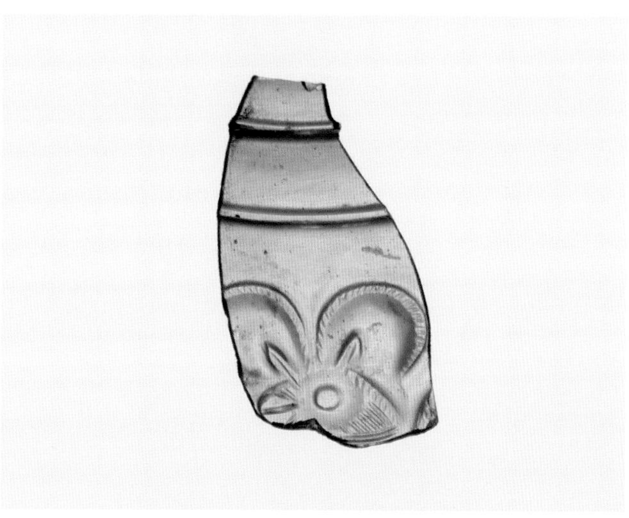

355

Comment: If the bottom of the fragment was at or near the midpoint of the wall, the body of the bottle had a maximum diameter of about eight to nine centimeters, comparable in size, and perhaps also in shape, with **354**. The twisted perspective of the animal, with the head in profile and the ears and horns represented frontally, may be compared with the perspective of the animals on the Corning Ewer (**522**) and of an animal on **298**. This had been a common way to depict rams and similar animals in late Sasanian art (cf. *Splendeur des Sassanides* 1993, p. 147, no. 6; p. 149, no. 8; p. 154, no. 12; p. 188, no. 49; p. 204, no. 60; and p. 206, no. 61; and *Les Perses sassanides* 2006, p. 114, no. 54).

356. Fragment of Globular Bottle with Animal

9th to 10th century. 51.1.120.
Max. Dim. 4.5 cm, D. (rib, est.) about 9 cm.
Colorless. Blown; relief-cut.

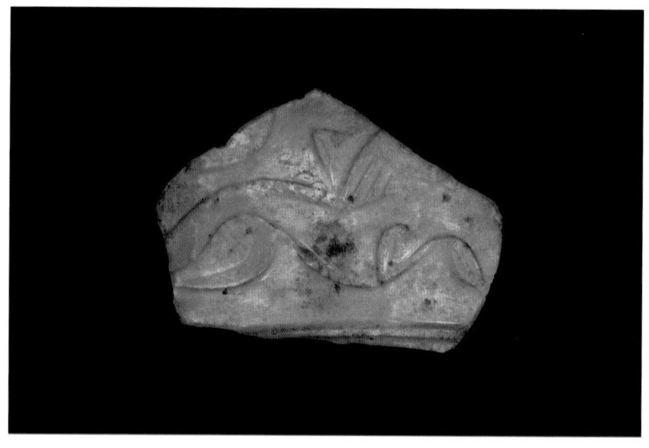

356

Fragment from lower wall of bottle with globular body (TTh. 0.2–0.3 cm) with relief-cut decoration (Th. 0.1 cm). At bottom of fragment, horizontal rib, presumably lower border of frieze. Surviving part of frieze contains animal, shown in profile, moving from left to right. Animal lacks most of head, but has eye represented by countersunk dot, detached triangular "ear," and possibly stem or leaf in mouth; neck is short, and body is slender; right front leg is short and has oval foot; right hind leg has large, tear-shaped haunch; tail is long and curves up and forward above animal's back. Outlines of body are notched; "ear," neck, and front foot are hatched.

Broken on all sides. Matte pale gray, semitransparent weathering with brown spots.

Comment: The fragment is part of a bottle similar in size, shape, and design to the body of **354**. The rib is the lower border of a frieze with animals. The surviving animal, with its hatched triangular neck, notched outlines, and countersunk body without drilled dots, is reminiscent of the animals on the turquoise blue bowl in the Treasury of San Marco, Venice (140: *Glass of the Sultans* 2001, pp. 176–178, no. 83), and the animals on a fragmentary bowl found in the Jawsaq al-Khāqānī, the palace built by Caliph al-Mu^{c}taṣim at Samarra, Iraq, in A.D. 836 (Lamm 1928,

p. 77, nos. 243 and 244). The fragments from Samarra were republished recently by Jens Kröger (2002). The animals on the fragments from Samarra carry, in their mouths, long and curling stems terminating in half-palmettes.

The treatment of the eye and neck, the front foot, and the haunch may be compared with the treatment of the horses on a bowl in the Museum für Islamische Kunst, Berlin (I.20/65: *Glass of the Sultans* 2001, p. 176, no. 82 = Kröger 1984, pp. 223–224, no. 193).

357. Globular Bottle with Birds and Palmettes

9th to 10th century. Formerly in the Smith Collection (610). 55.1.135.
H. (surviving) 15.5 cm, D. (max.) 10.2 cm.
Translucent deep blue. Blown; relief-cut.

Bottle: globular. Neck tall and cylindrical; shoulder slopes, with rounded edge; base plain; no pontil mark. Neck, shoulder, and wall have relief-cut ornament, sometimes with double raised outlines: on lower neck, one continuous horizontal raised band; on shoulder, two shallow steps; on wall, broad continuous frieze of vegetal ornament with birds and other elements; at bottom of wall, two steps. Frieze has, at top, eight contiguous segmental arches, with one tear-shaped motif in each spandrel; descending from springing of each pair of arches is bifurcated vegetal scroll; one stem curves up to left and terminates in palmette, which fills underside of arch, while other descends and terminates in elongated half-palmette; palmettes have alternately three and five leaves, and half-palmettes have three leaves. Lower part of frieze also contains four birdlike creatures; each bird is in two parts, separated by tip of half-palmette; front part (below palmette

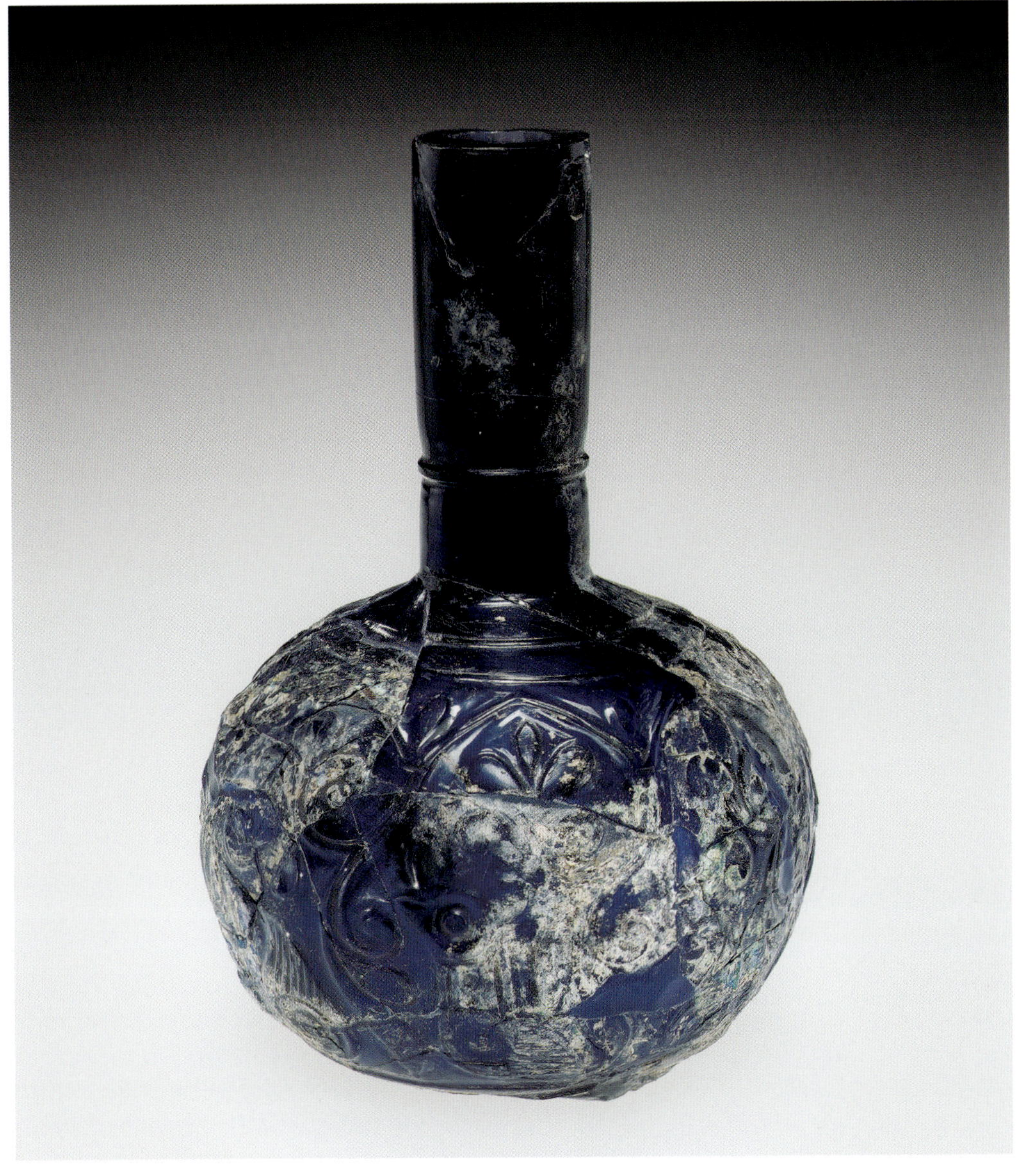

357

with five leaves) has round head with prominent eye, small beak, "ear," and curling crest at back, broad and straight neck decorated with circular depressions, and triangular body decorated with one countersunk dot and horizontal hatching; rear part of bird (below palmette with three leaves) is shaped like "Paisley pine" leaf and is decorated with ring-and-dot motif and curved, transverse hatching; above each rear part is one S-shaped motif.

Incomplete. Broken into many pieces, with loss of rim, top of neck, and small parts of wall and base; restored, except for rim and top of neck. Some parts of surface are matte, with slightly iridescent bluish gray weathering; others are almost pristine.

COMMENT: According to Ray Winfield Smith (in *Glass from the Ancient World* 1957, p. 277, no. 579), he acquired the bottle "from a Persian source," and he believed that it was probably found in Iran.

The contrast between the extensively weathered and virtually unweathered fragments is striking.

BIBLIOGRAPHY: *Antikes Glas* 1951, p. 11, no. 81; *Antikes Glas* 1952–3, p. 20, no. 103; *Verres antiques* 1954, p. 52, no. 318; *Glass from the Ancient World* 1957, p. 277, no. 579.

358. Fragment of Globular Bottle with Bird

9th to 10th century. Formerly in the Smith Collection (555-14). Gift of Carl Berkowitz and Derek Content. 76.1.296.
Max. Dim. 4.6 cm.
Probably almost colorless, with yellowish tinge. Blown; relief-cut.

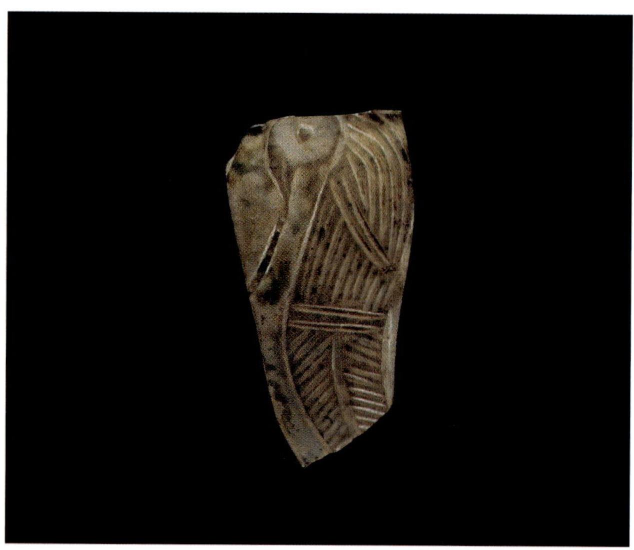

358

Fragment from body of globular bottle (TTh. 0.2 cm) decorated with part of bird in relief (Th. 0.1 cm). Bird has round head with short, pointed beak and eye represented by countersunk dot; no perceptible neck; and narrow body that terminates in pointed wing or tail. Body is filled with hatching, and wing or tail is filled with herringbone pattern. Bird holds lightly notched stem in beak.

Broken on all sides. Translucent yellowish brown weathering. On interior, cross-shaped motif in ink or pencil.

COMMENT: The curvature of the fragment suggests that it is from the body of a more or less globular bottle. The bird appears to be standing with its body almost vertical and its head pointing downward. The overall hatching on the body is unusual.

359. Fragment of Globular Bottle with Palmette and Half-Palmettes

9th to 10th century. Formerly in the Smith Collection. 68.1.59-11.
H. (surviving) about 3.5 cm, D. (rib, est.) about 6 cm.
Colorless. Blown; relief-cut.

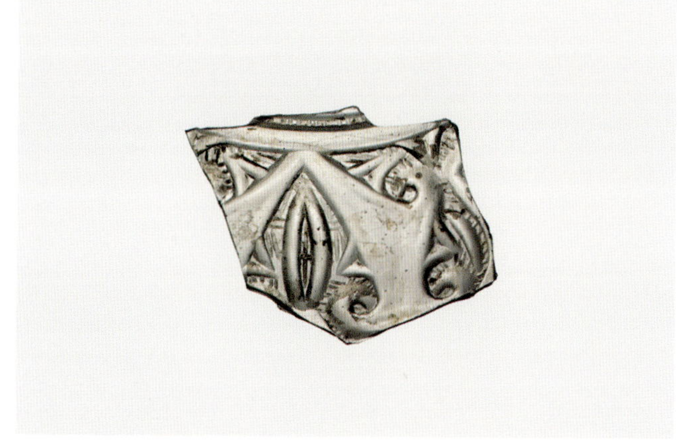

359

Fragment of globular bottle. Minute part of shoulder survives; upper wall curves out and down. Decorated with horizontal rib at junction of shoulder and wall. Below this, fragment has one palmette and parts of three half-palmettes. Palmette springs from two stems, one on each side, and has volutes, triangular insets in sides, and long, narrow countersunk oval motif on interior. On right side of palmette, two smaller outward-pointing half-palmettes emerge from tip of half-palmette, which is also smaller and appears to be on curving stem, possibly attached to right-hand stem of full palmette. On left side of palmette, part of half-palmette, which is mirror image of motif on opposite side. Rib, stems, and volutes are notched; some details are hatched.

Broken on all sides. Dull, with somewhat cloudy surface.

COMMENT: The fragment came from the edge of the shoulder and the upper wall of a bottle with a globular body, perhaps similar in shape and size to **354**. The surviving decoration appears to be a symmetrical arrangement of vegetal motifs, with half-palmettes flanking a full palmette.

360. Fragment of Globular Bottle with Half-Palmettes

9th to 10th century. Formerly in the Smith Collection (1263-j). Gift of Carl Berkowitz and Derek Content. 76.1.265.
H. (surviving) 4 cm, D. (max., est.) about 10 cm, (foot-ring, est.) about 6 cm.
Almost colorless; virtually bubble-free. Blown; relief-cut.

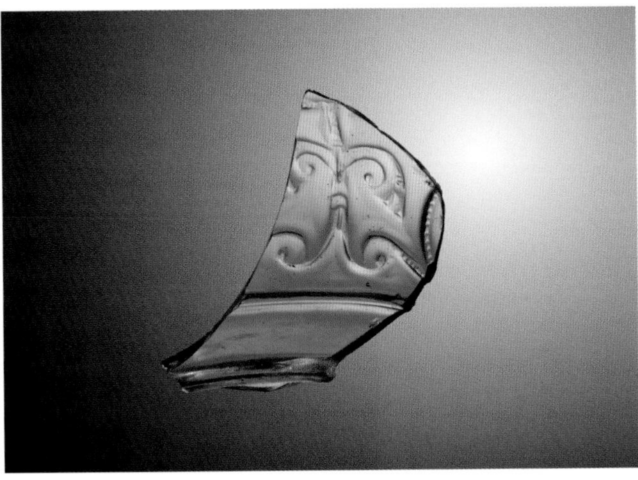

360

Fragment from lower wall (TTh. 0.2–0.35 cm) and base (TTh. 0.7 cm) of bottle with globular body decorated in relief. Wall curves down and in; base plain, with narrow foot-ring. Decoration on wall consists of part of frieze with lower border indicated by horizontal rib. Surviving part of frieze has vertical stem with pair of half-palmettes. Stem divides at bottom and joins scrolls to right and left. Leaves of half-palmettes are separated by cuts, and stem and scroll are notched.

Broken on all sides. Surfaces almost as new.

COMMENT: The fragment is from a bottle with a body that was similar in size and shape to the body of **354**, which also has a foot-ring. The straight, vertical stem decorated with half-palmettes and attached to scrolls at the bottom is distantly reminiscent of the vertical stems on the underside of the Falcon and Ibex Bowl (**296**), the side of the bowl with birds (**490**), and the side of the bottle with pairs of birds in the David Collection, Copenhagen (10/1963: *Glass of the Sultans* 2001, pp. 191–192, no. 96).

BIBLIOGRAPHY: *Verres antiques* 1954, p. 49, no. 298 (part of group).

361. Fragment of Globular Bottle with Half-Palmette

9th to 10th century. Found during excavations at Fusṭāṭ (Old Cairo), Egypt (68.12.65). Gift of the American Research Center in Egypt. 69.1.93.
H. (surviving) 5.1 cm, D. (max., est.) about 9.5 cm, (foot-ring) 6.7 cm.
Colorless or almost colorless. Blown; relief-cut.

Fragment of bottle with globular or roughly globular body. Lower wall (TTh. 0.2 cm) curves out, down, and in; base consists of short, splayed foot-ring and, at center, raised circle (D. 3.6 cm); no trace of pontil mark. Wall is decorated in relief (Th. 0.1 cm) with frieze containing vegetal ornament bordered at bottom by horizontal rib; surviving ornament includes scrolling tendrils, one of which terminates in half-palmette. Tendrils are notched, and half-palmette and one other, indeterminate element are hatched. Circle on underside of base is also notched.

Incomplete; small part of lower wall and almost entire base survive. Speckled charcoal gray to silver weathering.

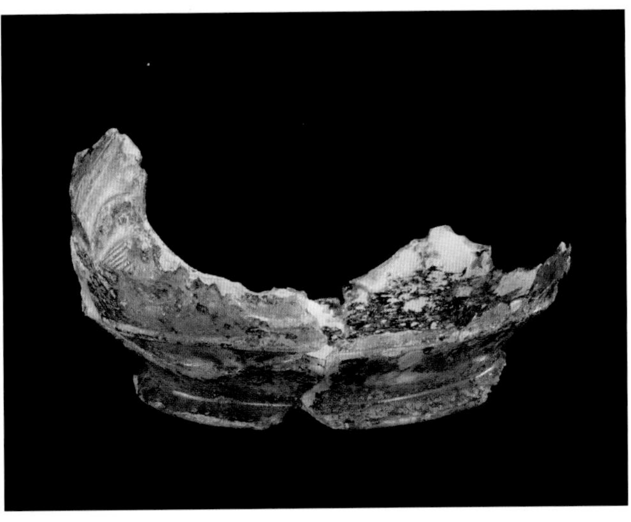

361

Comment: The fragment was found during excavations directed by Prof. George T. Scanlon. The excavator dated the fragments to the ninth to 10th centuries.

Although the drawing published by Scanlon and Pinder-Wilson (2001, p. 101) shows the wall curving down and in, in fact it curves down and out before bending in toward the foot. The object, therefore, was not a beaker, but rather a bottle with a globular body, perhaps similar to the body of **354**.

Bibliography: Scanlon and Pinder-Wilson 2001, p. 104, no. 43e.

362. Fragment of Globular Bottle with Vegetal Motifs

9th to 10th century. Formerly in the Smith Collection. 68.1.59-9.
Max. Dim. 5.4 cm, D. (rib, est.) about 6 cm.
Colorless. Blown; relief-cut.

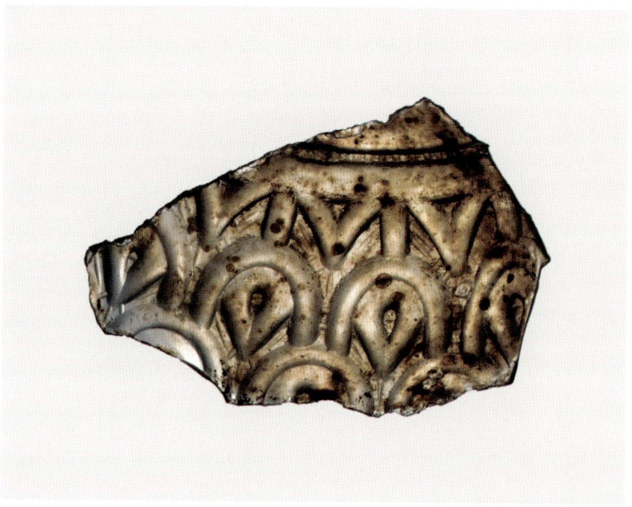

362

Fragment of bottle with globular body. Lower shoulder curves out and down, and merges with wall (TTh. 0.2 cm), which continues to descend in smooth curve. Decorated in relief (Th. 0.05–0.1 cm) with notched horizontal rib that forms upper border of frieze. Surviving part of frieze has overall pattern consisting of three contiguous rows of ornament (from top): (1) pairs of opposed leaflike motifs, which extend up and out from single stem; between each pair of leaves, one small triangular boss; (2) between each pair of stems in (1), scalelike motif, rounded at top, terminating in pair of opposed leaves and stem, similar to those in (1) but smaller, and containing one tear-shaped motif; and (3) apparently similar to (2). Leaves have longitudinal hatching, and stems are notched.

Broken on all sides. Patches of transparent pale grayish weathering.

Comment: The fragment is identified with confidence as part of a bottle similar to **354**. The pairs of opposed leaves establish the orientation of the fragment and show that the horizontal rib is the upper border of the frieze. Kröger (1999c) demonstrated that pairs of opposed leaves in early Islamic decoration are derived from Sasanian winged motifs. The overall pattern of overlapping scales is unusual, although it occurs on **381** and on a fragment of a linear-cut vessel in the al-Sabah Collection, Dār al-Āthār al-Islāmiyyah, Kuwait National Museum (LNS 186 G: Carboni 2001, p. 123, no. 2.25).

363. Ovoid Bottle

9th to 10th century. Formerly in the Smith Collection (1060). 55.1.132.
H. 22.5 cm, D. (rim, est.) about 3.5 cm, (max.) 8.8 cm.
Colorless. Blown; relief-cut.

Bottle with ovoid body. Rim plain, with top flattened by grinding; neck cylindrical; wall (TTh. 0.2 cm) curves smoothly down, out, and in, and merges with rounded base (Th., at center, 0.25 cm); no pontil mark. Relief-cut decoration (Th. 0.1 cm) on neck and wall. On neck: continuous band of five raised oval(?) motifs, each containing one countersunk circular element (D. 0.4 cm) above one continuous horizontal rib. On wall, from top to bottom: (1) continuous band (W. 1.7 cm) of 11 closely spaced horizontal ribs; (2) continuous band of eight identical oval motifs (H. 3.8 cm, W. 2.4 cm); each oval has raised outline with indentations at widest point, and it contains two raised ovals, which almost touch and have single raised tear-shaped motifs between their tops and bottoms, inverted at top and upright at bottom; and (3) separated from (2) by horizontal rib and with similar rib below it, continuous band of 15 identical raised elements (H. 3.8 cm, W. 1.6 cm) conjoined at bottom; each element has straight sides, which curve in to pointed top, and one vertical rib at center; below junction of each pair of sides is one countersunk circle (D. 0.5 cm), and below this all raised elements terminate in row of semicircular scallops, each of which frames one countersunk circle.

Incomplete. Most of rim and parts of neck and wall are missing. Losses include most of two and parts of four oval motifs in (2) and all of one and parts of four pointed elements in (3). Dull and pitted, with traces of weathering. Circular hole (D. 0.5 cm) at center of base was probably made by Ray Winfield Smith in order to obtain sample for chemical analysis.

COMMENT: The catalog entry in *Glass from the Ancient World* (see below) records that the object came "from Persia." No parallel appears to have been published for either the oval motifs in (2) or the pointed elements in (3).

BIBLIOGRAPHY: *Glass from the Ancient World* 1957, p. 275, no. 567.

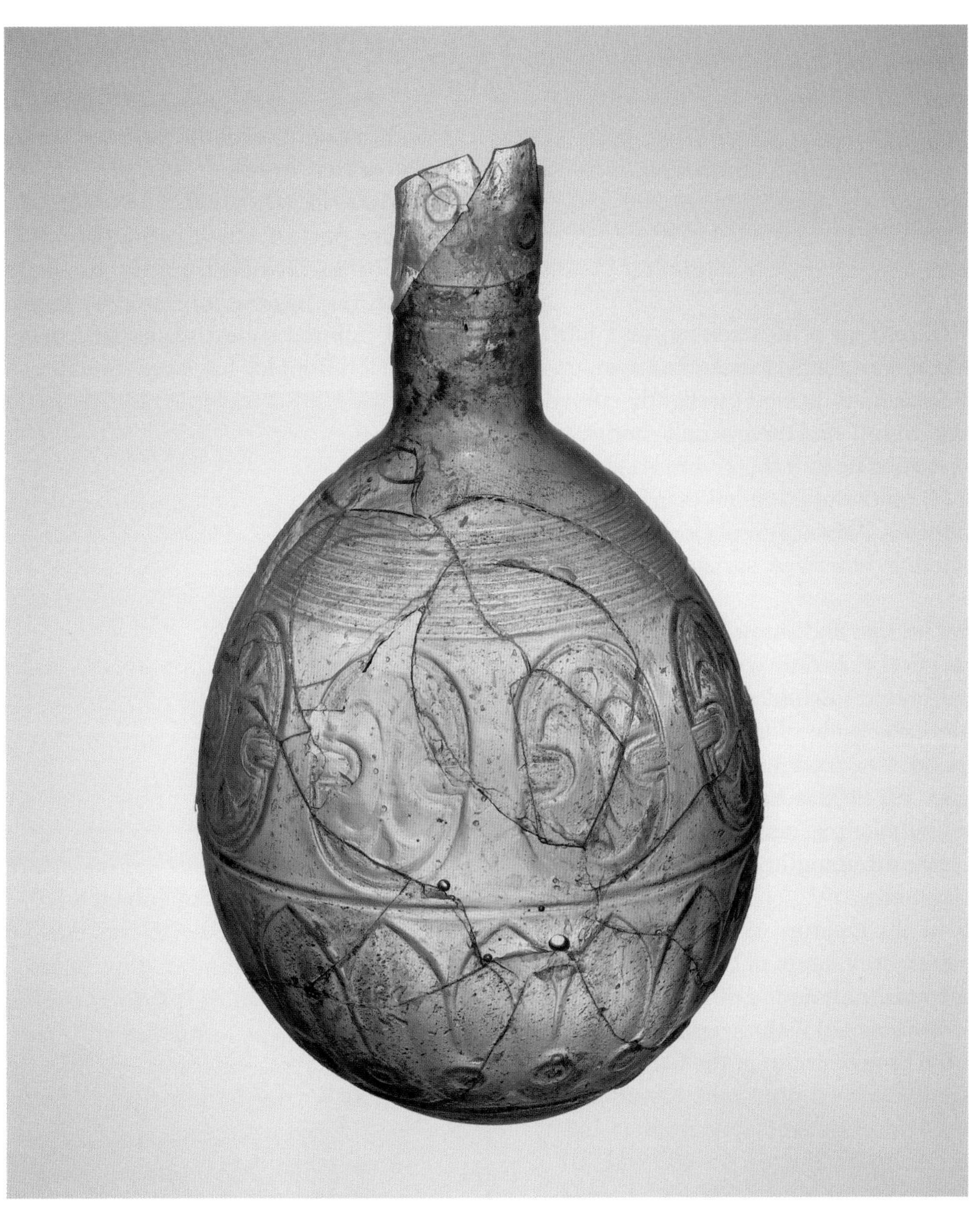

363

364. Fragment of Cylindrical Bottle with Griffin

10th to 11th century. Formerly in the Strauss Collection (F71). Bequest of Jerome Strauss. 79.1.313.
H. (surviving) 5.6 cm, D. (est.) about 15 cm.
Almost colorless, with yellowish tinge; minute bubbles. Blown; slant- and relief-cut.

Fragment from wall of cylindrical bottle (TTh. 0.25 cm) decorated in relief (Th. 0.1 cm) with combination of relief cutting (background is recessed) and slant cutting (most details of decorative motifs are slant-cut). Surviving ornament consists of head, neck, and wing of griffin, apparently shown in left profile but with head turned to look back over body. Griffin has small head with hooked beak, curved tear-shaped eye, and two triangular ears; thick neck with narrow

objects made in Fatimid Egypt. If the decoration was symmetrical, and if the vertical stem of the palmette was divided at the bottom into two scrolling stems bearing palmettes and half-palmettes, the decoration would be comparable with that on a globular rock crystal bottle in the treasury of Saint Stephen's Cathedral in Halberstadt, Germany (49: Shalem 1996, pp. 209–210, no. 52).

368. Cylindrical Bottle with Inscription

9th to 10th century. Formerly in the collections of Maurice Nahman and Ray Winfield Smith (Smith 838). 55.1.119.
H. 9.7 cm, D. (rim) 2 cm, (max.) 6.2 cm.
Almost colorless, with green tinge; few small bubbles. Blown; relief-cut.

Bottle: cylindrical. Rim with flat top and small external bevel; neck has cylindrical, slightly tapering upper part, below which it expands and is roughly hemispherical; shoulder slopes and has rounded edge; wall descends vertically before curving in at bottom; base plain; no pontil mark (but see below). Decorated on neck, shoulder, wall, and base. On neck: upper part is cut in seven flat vertical facets; lower part has seven contiguous hollow oval facets above continuous horizontal groove. On shoulder: shallow "step" at midpoint and continuous narrow band of finely incised crosshatching at edge. On wall: in large letters (H. 2.5 cm), pseudo-Kufic inscription, "برك بر كد كا عد" (*b-r-k b-r-k-d*^{c}*-d*), above continuous horizontal rib; below inscription, near bottom of wall, band of nine contiguous hollow oval facets. On base: shallow disk (D. 3.5 cm).

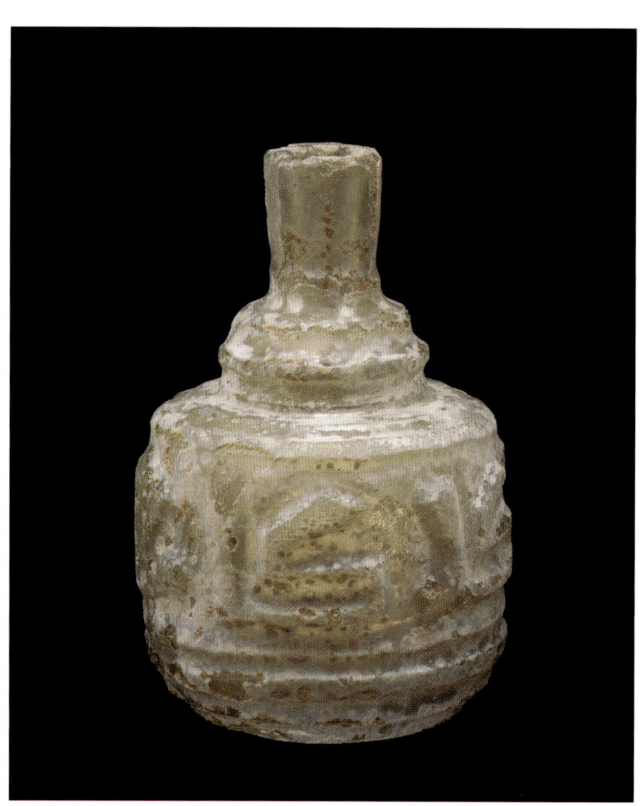

368

Intact, except for numerous small chips. Surface is almost matte, with numerous spots and patches of bluish gray to pale brown weathering. Circular depression (D. 0.2 cm) near center of base may have been made by Ray Winfield Smith to obtain sample for chemical analysis.

Comment: A number of small cylindrical bottles of rock crystal have inscriptions on the wall. They include a bottle in the abbey of Marienberg in Val Venosta, Italy (Shalem 1996, pp. 181–182, no. 9 = Lamm 1929–30, p. 201, pl. 68, no. 11); a bottle in The British Museum, London (FB Is13: Shalem 1996, p. 182, no. 10 = Lamm 1929–30, p. 202, pl. 68, no. 14); a bottle in the church of Saint-Sauveur at Harelbeke, northwestern Belgium (Shalem 1996, pp. 182–183, no. 10a); a bottle in the Landesmuseum at Brunswick, Germany (Lamm 1929–30, p. 207, pl. 73, no. 4); and a bottle formerly in the collection of Harari Bey, Cairo, Egypt (*ibid.*, p. 207, pl. 74, no. 3).

For another vessel with a band of finely incised crosshatching, see **59**.

Bibliography: *Nahman Collection* 1953, no. 73; *Verres antiques* 1954, no. 293; *Glass from the Ancient World* 1957, no. 577.

369. Bell-Shaped Bottle with Hares

9th to 10th century. 73.1.3.
H. 15.3 cm, D. (rim) 3.3 cm, (base) 8.6 cm.
Colorless; some seed. Blown; relief-cut.

Bottle with bell-shaped body. Rim plain, with rounded lip; neck cylindrical, but narrower at bottom than at top; shoulder rounded; wall almost straight, and wider at bottom than at top; base plain; no pontil mark (but see below). Decorated on neck, shoulder, wall, and base. On neck: raised collar (H. 2.9 cm) decorated with 13 tall, narrow tongues, each rounded at top, outlined in relief; below this, continuous horizontal rib and, at junction with shoulder, one continuous "step." On shoulder: two steps, below which is register (H. 2.3 cm) containing 18 tongues, wider than those on neck, each rounded at bottom, outlined in relief. On wall: two registers (H. of each about 3 cm), defined by three horizontal ribs; upper register contains six running hares facing forward in left profile, each with raised outlines, countersunk eye, large ear, and prominent tail; lower register has six similar animals, also running from left to right, but with their heads alternately looking forward and backward; in both registers, some outlines are notched, and heads, ears, and some limbs are hatched. On base: two concentric circles, one at edge and the other (D. 3.6 cm) at center.

Almost complete. Broken, with small losses from rim, shoulder, upper register of animals, and edge of base; restored. Dull and somewhat pitted, with remains of weathering and trace of iridescence.

Comment: The animals are reminiscent of the "hares" on the turquoise blue bowl in the Treasury of San Marco, Venice (140: *Glass of the Sultans* 2001, pp. 176–178, no. 83). A complete bottle with the tongue pattern employed as a panel design is now in the Iran Bastan Museum, Tehran (*7000 Years of Iranian Art* 1964, p. 100, no. 605).

Bibliography: *Guide to the Collections* 1974, p. 28, no. 28; "Recent Important Acquisitions," *JGS*, v. 16, 1974, p. 127, no. 14.

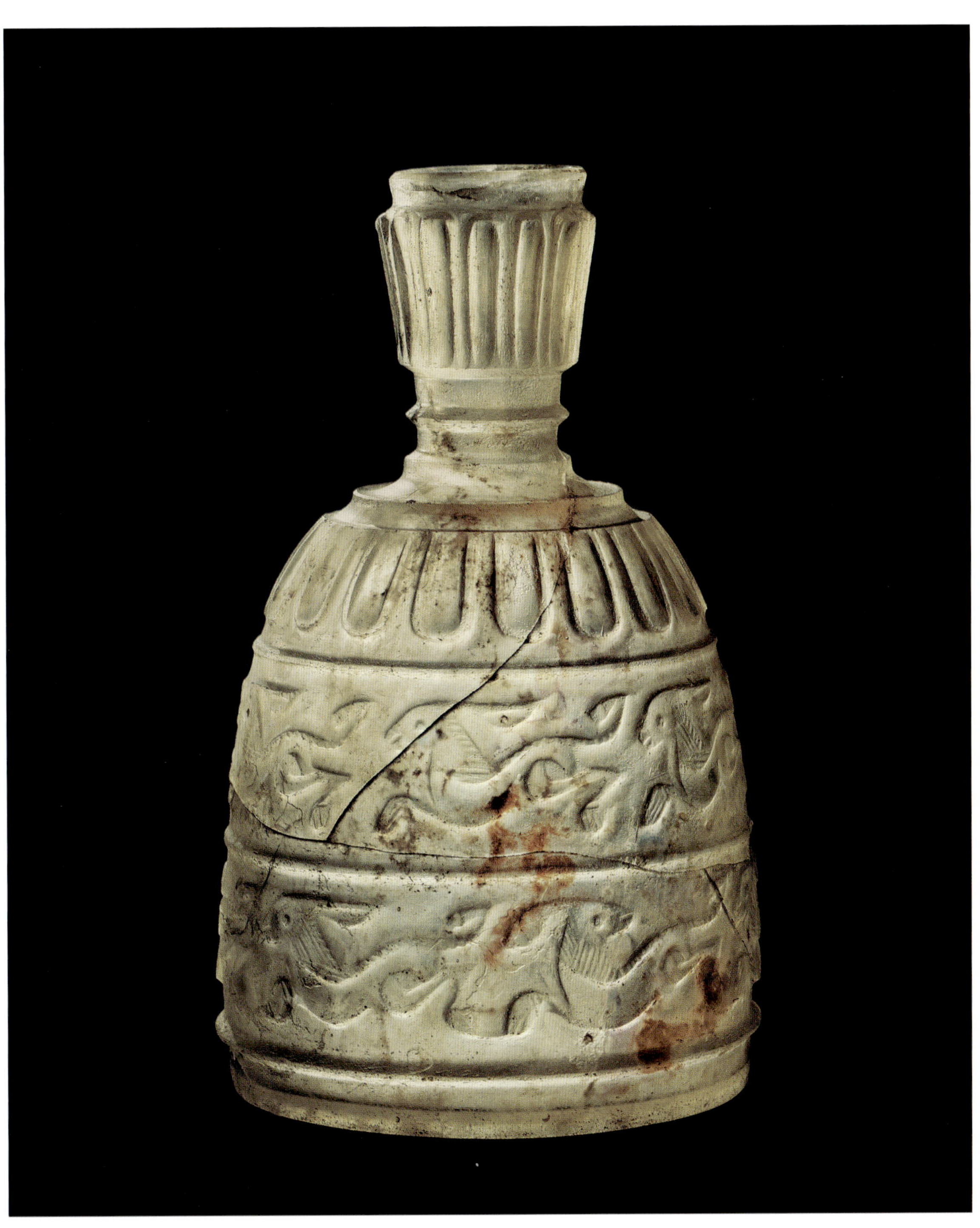

369

370. Bell-Shaped Bottle with Arches

9th to 10th century. 73.1.30.
H. 14.8 cm, D. (rim) 4 cm, (base) 8.3 cm.
Transparent light bluish green; few small bubbles. Blown; relief-cut.

Bottle with body shaped like bell. Rim plain, with pronounced internal bevel; neck cylindrical, but narrower at bottom than at top; shoulder rounded; wall almost straight, splaying slightly toward bottom; base plain; no pontil mark (but see below). Relief-cut ornament on neck, shoulder, wall, and base. On neck: single continuous band of ornament, with one horizontal rib at top and at bottom; ornament consists of five intersecting diamond-shaped facets, each with notched vertical ridge at midpoint. On shoulder: one "step" at junctions with neck and with wall, and between them continuous frieze of seven curved facets. On wall: seven contiguous panels, each containing one large, elongated arch with similar but smaller arch inside it; at top of wall, at junction of each pair of

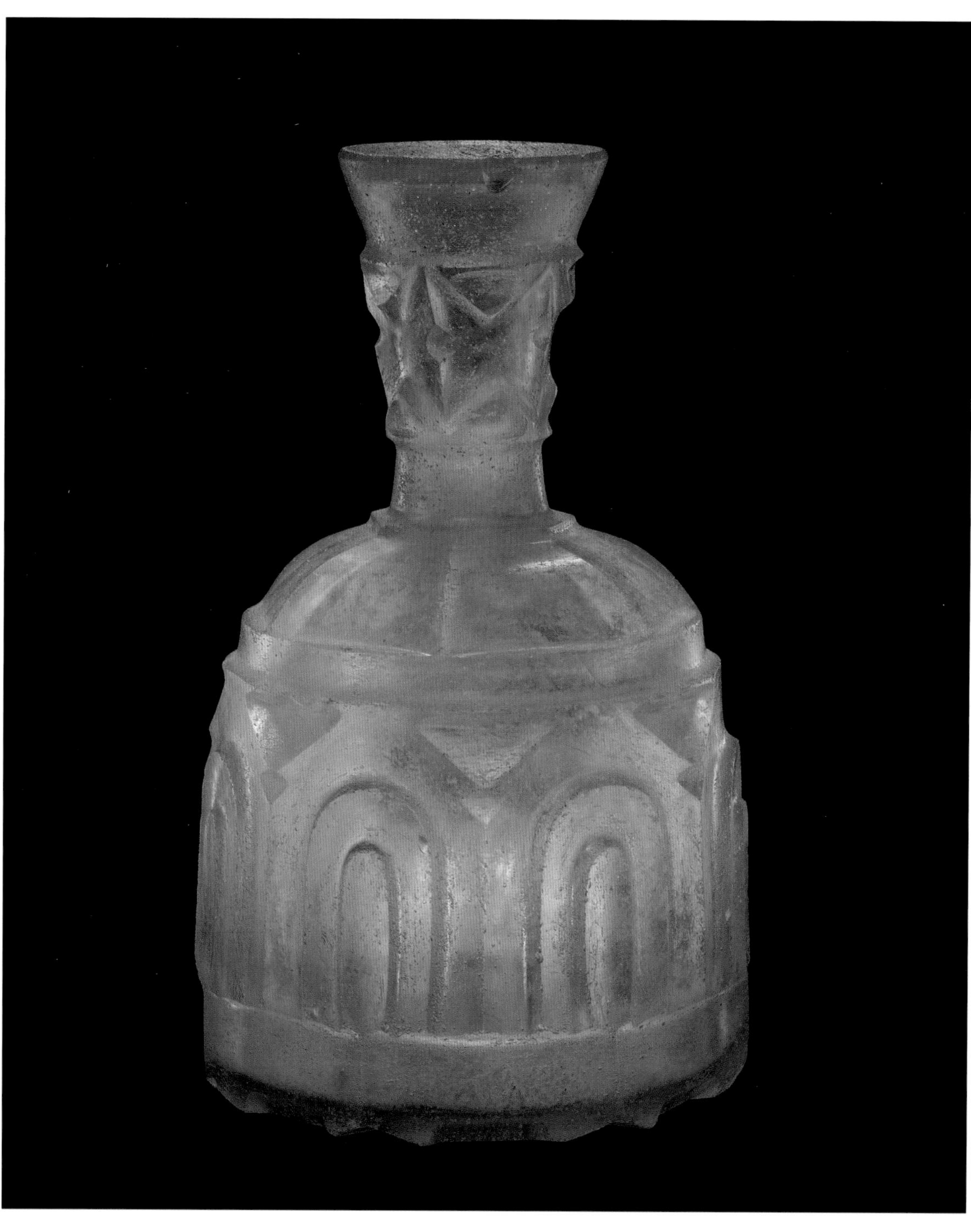

370A

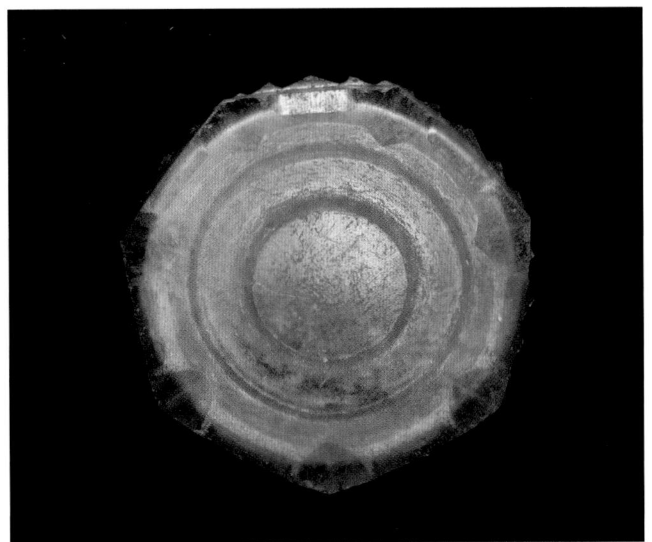

370B

panels, one large triangular facet with small triangular facet beneath it; at bottom of wall, below panels with arches, seven plain contiguous facets with junctions under vertical axes of arches. On base: seven rhomboidal facets, one beneath each junction of pair of plain facets, and two concentric countersunk disks (D. 5.4 cm and 3.4 cm).

Intact, except for chip on rim. Somewhat pitted, with remains of weathering, especially on interior.

COMMENT: The object is said to have come from Bojnūrd in Khorāsān Province, northeastern Iran.

For parallels, see **274**.

BIBLIOGRAPHY: "Recent Important Acquisitions," *JGS*, v. 16, 1974, p. 127, no. 15; Charleston 1980, pp. 68–69, no. 26; *idem* 1990, p. 68, no. 26.

371. Fragment of Bottle with Hare

9th to 10th century. Formerly in the Strauss Collection (F74). Bequest of Jerome Strauss. 79.1.312.
Max. Dim. 6.3 cm, D. (max., est.) about 14 cm.
Almost colorless, with yellowish tinge. Blown; relief-cut.

Fragment from shoulder and upper wall of bottle (TTh. 0.25 cm) decorated in relief (Th. 0.1 cm). Decoration consists of, on shoulder, parts of curving stem and tendril; on upper wall, part of hare running in left profile. It has pointed snout, eye represented by countersunk dot, and long ear extending behind head; neck is filled with transverse hatching; and left leg reaches forward. It carries stem in its mouth. Snout and ear have incised details. Above hare's head is curved stem with curling tendril. Stems on shoulder, above hare, and in hare's mouth are notched.

Broken on all sides. No obvious weathering.

COMMENT: The curvature of the fragment indicates that it is from the rounded shoulder and straight, slightly tapering wall of a bottle similar, among others, to the relief-cut bottle in the David Collection, Copenhagen (10/1963: *Glass of the Sultans* 2001, pp. 191–192, no. 96). The hare may be compared with the running "hares" on the relief-cut, turquoise blue bowl in the Treasury of San Marco, Venice (140: *ibid.*, pp. 176–178, no. 83), although the latter do not carry stems in their mouths.

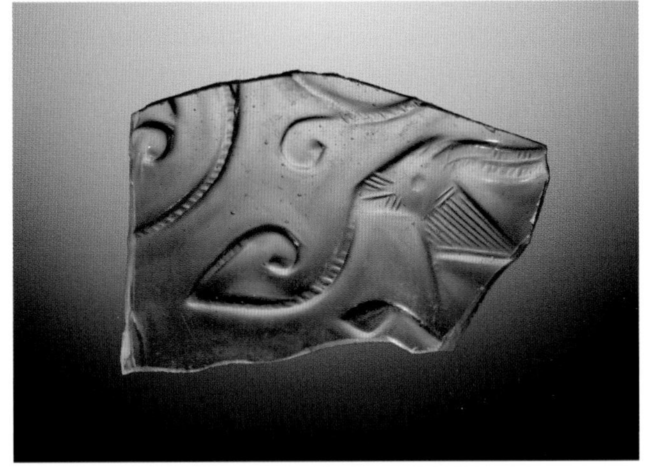

371

372. Fragment of Bottle with Hare

9th to 10th century. Formerly in the Smith Collection (555-28). 59.1.446.
H. (surviving) 6.2 cm, D. (shoulder, est.) about 5 cm.
Almost colorless, with greenish tinge. Blown (perhaps mold-blown); relief-cut.

Fragment from sloping shoulder and vertical wall of bottle (TTh. 0.35 cm) decorated in relief (Th. 0.1 cm). Decoration consists of, at junction of shoulder and wall, prominent rib with incised herringbone motif; on wall, frieze (W. 3.8 cm) with horizontal rib at top and bottom. Surviving part of frieze contains hare running in left profile. It has head with eye represented by countersunk dot and large oval ear extending backward; neck filled with transverse hatching; body with raised outlines, embellished with single row of printies; short, curly tail; and part of rear left foot. Details of snout are indicated by incised lines; ear is hatched from base to tip on either side of incised line; outlines of body and tail are notched.

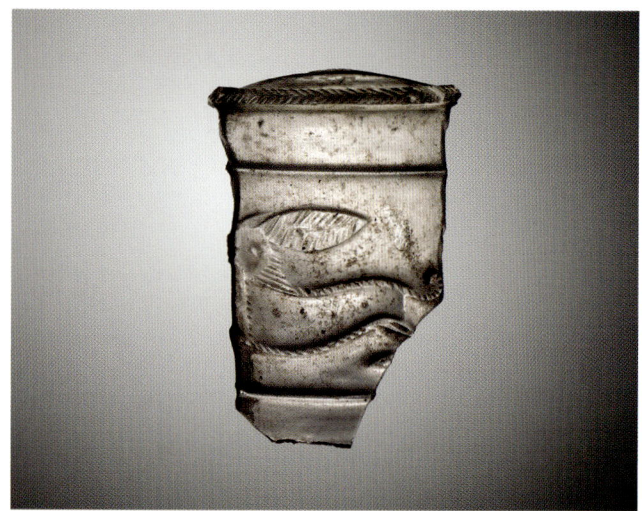

372

Broken on all sides. Exterior is almost matte, with light gray weathered surface; interior is shiny and considerably less weathered.

COMMENT: The glass thickens at the top of the fragment, and this suggests that the bottom of the neck had a diameter of about three centimeters. The form—a medium-size cylindrical bottle with a narrow shoulder and a relatively wide neck—and the relief-cut decoration are most readily matched among rock crystal vessels: for example, a bottle decorated with palmettes and half-palmettes in the Stiftkirchengemeinde at Bad-Gandersheim, Germany (Shalem 1996, p. 177, no. 2), and a bottle with an inscription in the abbey of Marienberg in Val Venosta, Italy (*ibid.*, pp. 181–182, no. 9).

The hare may be compared with a hare (one of two) on a fragmentary bowl in the al-Sabah Collection, Dār al-Āthār al-Islāmiyyah, Kuwait National Museum (LNS 77 G: Carboni 2001, p. 90, no. 22), which has similar ears, a short and hatched neck, and a body with notched outlines and a single row of printies. A somewhat similar hare is found on **390**.

373. Fragment of Bottle with Hare

9th to 10th century. Formerly in the Smith Collection (918). Gift of Carl Berkowitz and Derek Content. 76.1.199.
H. (surviving) 3.4 cm, D. (est., at top of fragment) about 2.5 cm.
Almost colorless, with greenish tinge; no obvious bubbles. Blown; relief-cut.

Fragment from neck of bottle. Straight and wider at bottom than at top. Decorated with hare (Th. 0.15 cm) running toward left. Hare has pointed snout, eye represented by countersunk dot, large hatched ear, body with notched outlines, extended foreleg, and tail that curves out, up, and in, and terminates in hatched scut.

Broken on all sides. Apparently pristine, with no obvious trace of weathering.

COMMENT: The hare was probably one of two such animals occupying a continuous horizontal band on the neck of a bottle. This is suggested by a close parallel: the bottle decorated in relief with a band of hares on the neck and numerous birds on the body, in the David Collection, Copenhagen (10/1963: Leth 1975, p. 15; Folsach 1990, pp. 138 and 143, no. 221; *idem* 2001, pp. 200 and 209, no. 313; *Glass of the Sultans* 2001, pp. 191–192, no. 96). The parallel is sufficiently close to suggest that the two objects may have been decorated in the same workshop.

BIBLIOGRAPHY: *Verres antiques* 1954, p. 49, no. 298 (part of group); *Glass from the Ancient World* 1957, p. 281, no. 590 (part of group).

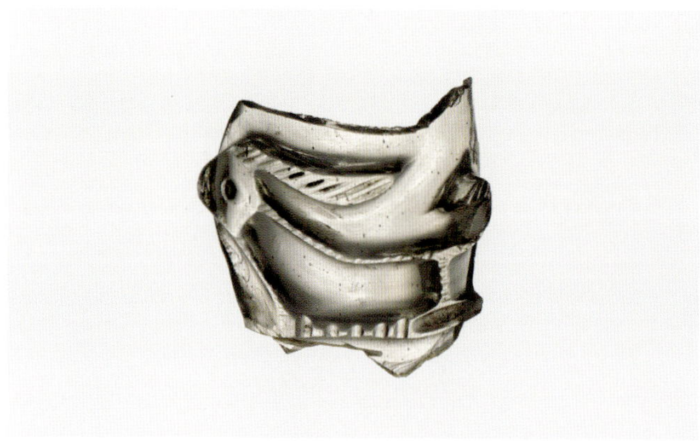

373

374. Fragment of Bottle with Animal

9th to 10th century. Formerly in the Strauss Collection (F73). Bequest of Jerome Strauss. 79.1.315.
H. (surviving) 4.7 cm, D. (bottom of wall, est.) about 10 cm.
Almost colorless, with greenish tinge. Blown (perhaps mold-blown); relief-cut.

Fragment from lower wall and edge of base of bottle (TTh. 0.35 cm) decorated in relief (Th. 0.1 cm). Lower wall straight, with very slight taper; base plain. Decoration on wall consists of frieze defined at bottom by horizontal notched rib. Surviving part of frieze contains two lower front legs and one hind leg of animal apparently in left profile. Front legs have narrow pasterns with single longitudinal grooves, and hatched triangular feet. Hind leg is partly notched; it also has hatched triangular foot. Between hind leg and nearer front leg, notched linear motif and possibly one printy. Underside of base has concentric rib (D., est., about 8 cm), which serves as foot-ring.

Broken on all sides. Patches of transparent brownish weathering.

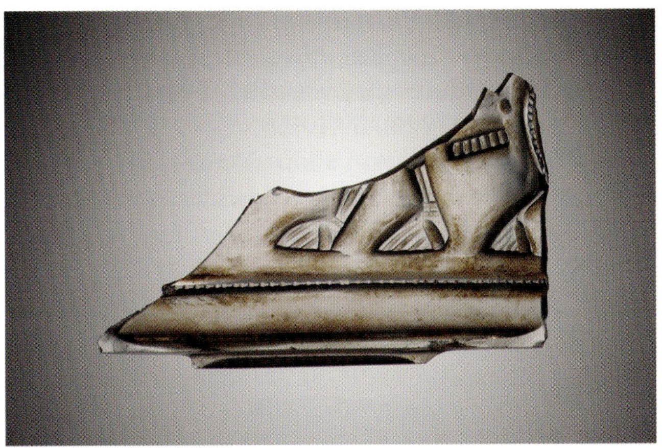

374

375. Fragment of Bottle with Bird or Fantastic Animal (?)

9th to 10th century. Formerly in the Smith Collection. Gift of Carl Berkowitz and Derek Content. 76.1.267.
Max. Dim. 3.8 cm, D. (est.) about 10 cm.
Almost colorless, with yellowish tinge. Blown; relief-cut.

Fragment from vertical or almost vertical wall of bottle (TTh. 0.2 cm) decorated in relief (Th. 0.05 cm). Decoration is difficult to interpret, but it may consist of bird or fantastic animal, shown on its side. If this is correct, surviving parts include back of head, neck with transverse hatching, extended wing with hatching parallel to outer edge, and (if it is animal), outline of back. Beyond wing and head, part of second element, with notched outline.

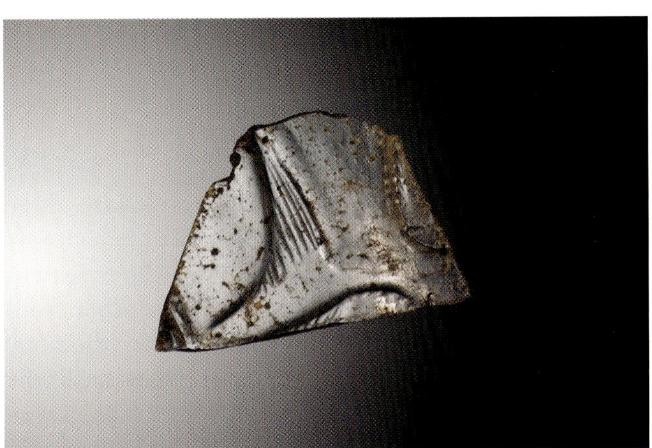

375

Broken on all sides. Dull and pitted, with specks of brown weathering.

Comment: The shape of the fragment indicates beyond doubt that it is part of a vessel with a vertical or almost vertical wall, and the diameter shows that the vessel was a bottle rather than a beaker. Whether the "bird" or "animal" faces up or down, therefore, its orientation is very unusual, to the extent of calling into question its identification. However, the identity of the "wing" seems to be plausible, as are the identities of the "head" and the "neck."

376. Fragment of Bottle with Bird

9th to 10th century. Formerly in the Smith Collection (1263-[?]). Gift of Carl Berkowitz and Derek Content. 76.1.268.
Max. Dim. 5.8 cm.
Almost colorless, with yellowish tinge. Blown; relief-cut.

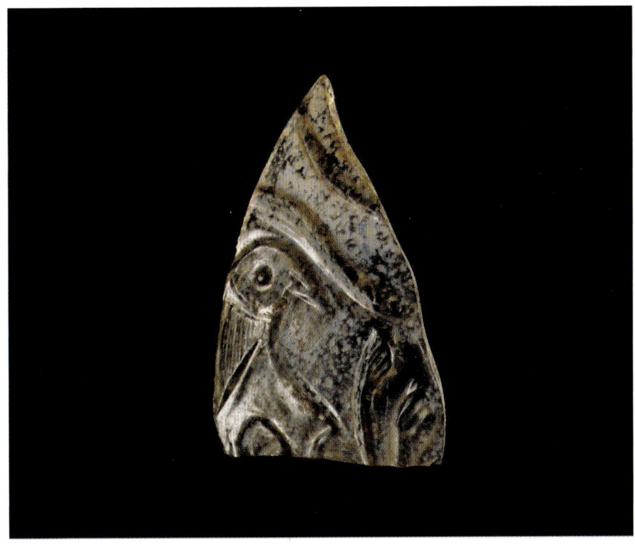

376

Fragment from wall of bottle (TTh. 0.2–0.25 cm) decorated in relief (Th. 0.1 cm). Decoration consists of part of bird in right profile. Bird has head with round top, countersunk dot representing eye, and curved, pointed beak; neck is covered by triangle of vertical hatching; breast is almost upright; wing covert survives at bottom of fragment; both legs are extended out and up, and terminate in hatched triangular feet. On front of bird, two sinuous lines, which are notched.

H. (surviving) 4.4 cm, D. (shoulder) 2 cm. Colorless or almost colorless. Blown (body perhaps blown in dip mold); relief-cut.

Bottle with cylindrical body. Rim evidently everted; neck cylindrical; shoulder slopes; wall descends vertically, then tapers at bottom; base solid and shaped like shallow truncated cone. Relief-cut decoration on neck and wall. On neck: continuous horizontal rib at midpoint. On wall: two horizontal ribs, one at junction with shoulder and other near base; between them, Kufic or pseudo-Kufic inscription.

Incomplete. Broken, with loss of rim, top of neck, and small parts of wall and base. Pale gray enamel-like weathering.

Comment: See **383**.

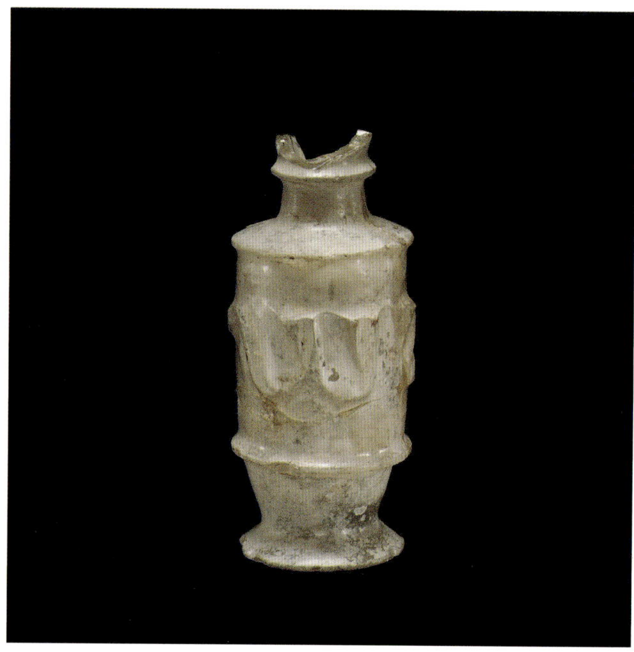

385

386. Small Bottle with Inscription

9th to 10th century. Formerly in the Smith Collection (912). Gift of Carl Berkowitz and Derek Content. 76.1.203.
H. (surviving) 4.3 cm, D. (max.) 2 cm. Almost colorless, with greenish tinge. Blown; relief-cut.

Bottle with cylindrical body. Bottom of neck is narrow; shoulder slopes; wall descends vertically, then tapers; foot is solid and conical; no pontil mark. Decorated on wall: one frieze defined by continuous horizontal ribs at edge of shoulder and on bottom of vertical side. Frieze contains Kufic inscription.

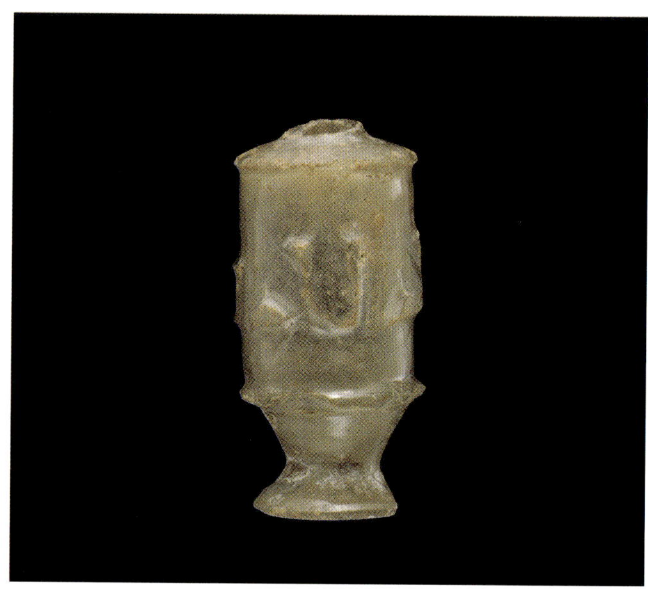

386

Incomplete. Rim, neck, and two-thirds of base are missing. Dull, with patches of enamellike weathering.

Comment: See **383**.

Bibliography: *Verres antiques* 1954, p. 47, no. 283; *Glass from the Ancient World* 1957, p. 283, no. 597.

387. Small Bottle

9th to 10th century. Formerly in the Smith Collection (1220-5). 76.1.192.
H. (surviving) 5.5 cm, W. (max.) 2.8 cm. Perhaps almost colorless. Blown (perhaps in dip mold); linear- and relief-cut.

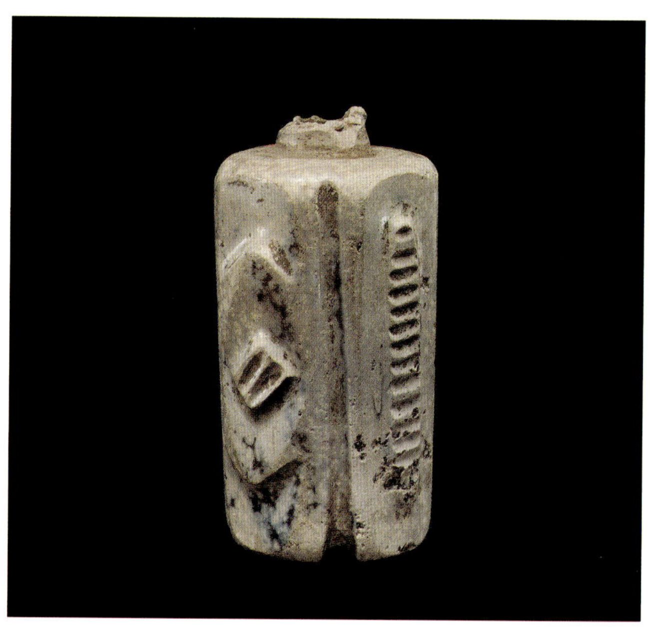

387

Bottle. Bottom of neck cylindrical; shoulder flat, with rounded edge; body has square cross section, and wall descends vertically; base flat; trace of pontil mark (?). Sides of wall are decorated with two opposed pairs of patterns: (1) tall, narrow stripe in low relief, with rounded ends and numerous horizontal notches; and (2) tall hexagonal panel in low relief, with slightly concave surface and hatched diamond-shaped motif at center. Angles between sides have notches from top to bottom, which extend under base, forming cross-shaped element.

Incomplete. Body is complete, but entire rim and most of neck are missing. Almost completely covered with shiny grayish weathering.

Comment: A bottle with similar decoration is in the Benaki Museum, Athens (41/6: Clairmont 1977, p. 89, no. 296).

8. Canteen

388. Canteen with Animals, Birds, Palmettes, and Other Motifs

9th to 10th century. Formerly in the Smith Collection (611). 55.1.125.
Restored: H. 24.4 cm, W. 18.4 cm, Depth 13.1 cm.
Colorless; very small bubbles. Blown; applied, relief-cut.

Canteen: roughly globular, but flattened to form two broad and two narrow sides; one broad side appears to be flat, while the other has convex vertical and horizontal profiles; narrow sides are also convex. Rim everted, with pointed pouring lip; neck cylindrical and wider at bottom than at top; shoulder curves out and down; lower wall tapers and curves in at bottom; base flat; no pontil mark. Two opposed earlike handles project from shoulder; seen from above, they are on vessel's longer axis; each is semicircular, with plain surfaces and circular perforation (D. 0.75 cm) countersunk on both sides.

Rim, neck, and body have vigorous relief-cut ornament up to 0.7 cm deep. On outside of rim: one continuous horizontal rib that follows outline of lip. On neck: one continuous horizontal rib at top and bottom, between which is vegetal scroll terminating in two half-palmettes below pouring lip, with full palmette equidistant from them. On shoulder and upper parts of narrow sides: elaborate cartouche enclosing neck and handles, and terminating at each end in two symmetrical scrolling lines. On upper part of each broad side: cartouche, its upper border parallel to border of cartouche on shoulder, terminating in tendril and half of heart-shaped palmette, and its lower border curving out and down from midpoint; interior of cartouche has two concentric circles with dot at center and, on either side of them, single standing bird shown in profile, facing right, with horizontal body and legs, and head facing down.

Flat side has, below cartouche, heart-shaped palmette on vertical stem at center, and indeterminate motif to left; at bottom of wall, heart-shaped palmette at center, flanked on either side by long-legged animal, shown in profile, leaping toward edge; animal has long tail with hatched tuft, and second "tail" attached to central palmette; space beyond and beneath animal is occupied by vegetal ornament, which includes heart-shaped palmette.

Very little of bulging side survives, but decoration appears to have included bird at left side; bottom may have included leaping animals, as on flat side (one paw and lower leg remain), with vegetal ornament and heart-shaped palmettes.

Underside of base is decorated with two birds shown in profile, facing each other, their beaks touching; beaks are straight, heads small, and necks thick; bodies merge with pointed tails, and wings are folded; legs are straight, with triangular feet. Birds stand on curved stems, which merge with vegetal ornament at bottom of first short side; above their beaks is one straight stem, which also merges with ornament at bottom of second short side.

Many outlines are notched; necks, wings, and legs of birds, as well as paws and tails of animals, are hatched; bodies of birds on underside of base have drilled dots.

Incomplete. Broken into many pieces, with very extensive losses: 35 percent of rim and upper wall, most of lower wall, and small parts of base; circular hole (D. 0.6 cm) drilled in base by Ray Winfield Smith to obtain sample for chemical analysis. Wall at bottom right of flat side appears to be distorted, as if by intense heat. Pitted, with iridescent weathering.

Comment: The object is a tour de force of glass cutting. According to Smith (*Glass from the Ancient World* 1957, p. 267, no. 545), it was "acquired from a Persian source, and [was] probably found there." The condition of the bottom of the flat side suggests that,

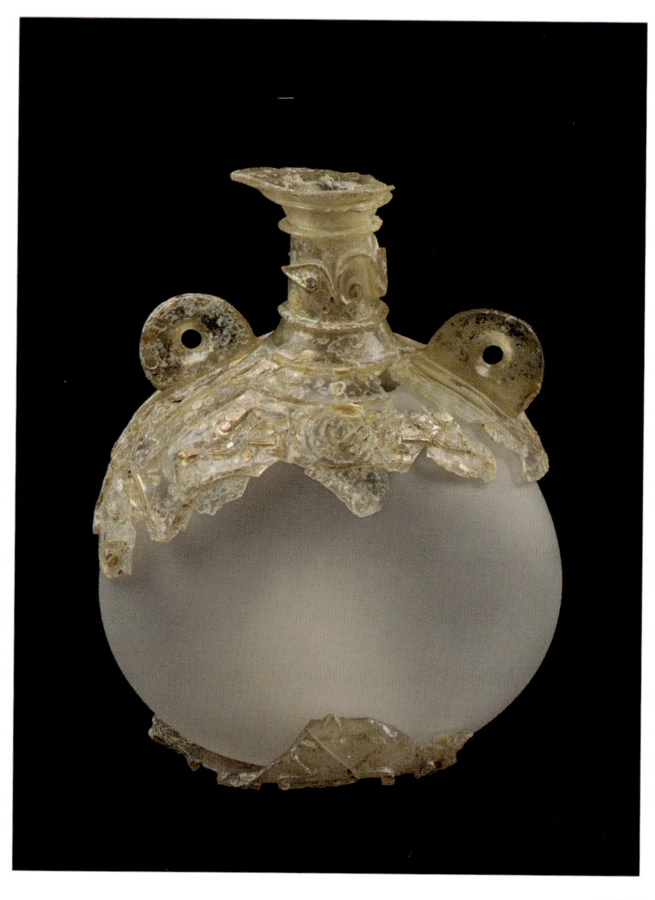

388A

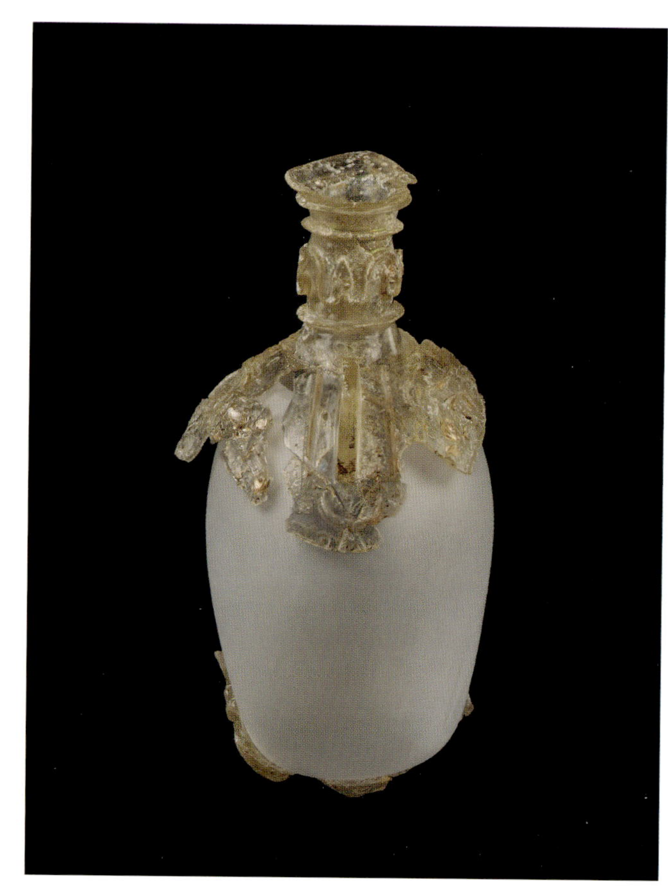

388B

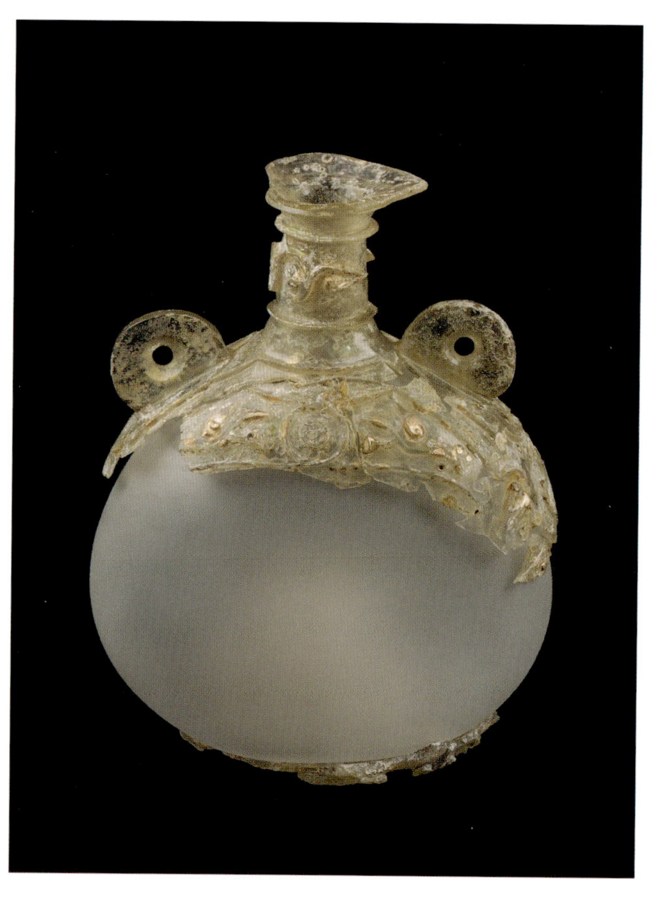

388C

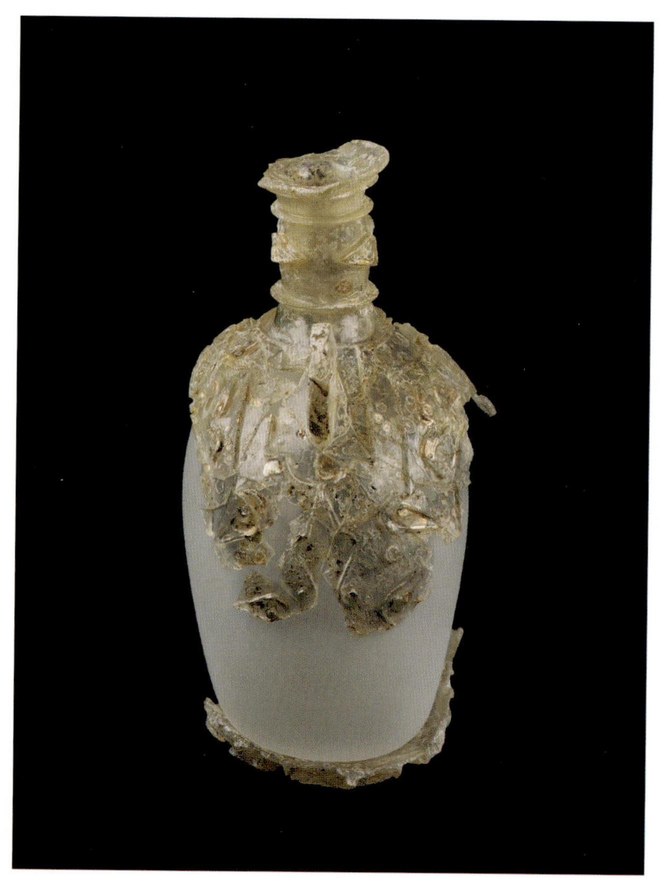

388D

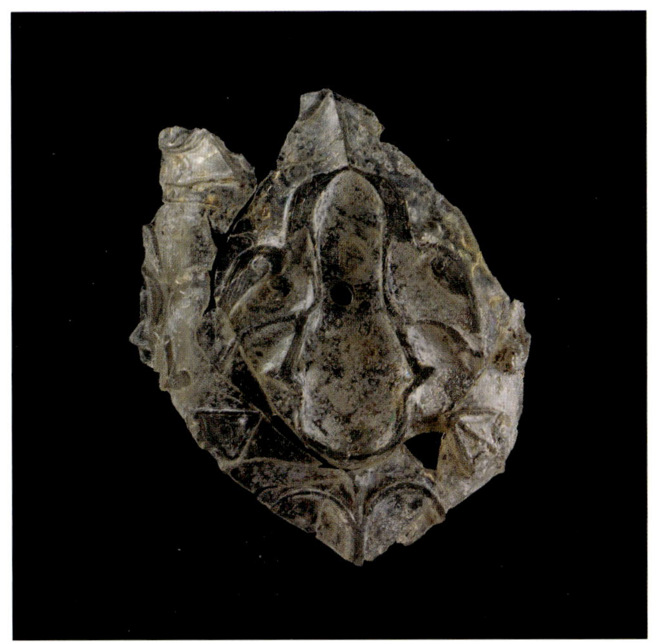

388E

sometime after its completion, it was subjected to intense heat; the other surviving parts, however, do not appear to have been affected.

The size and the form are partly conjectural, given the complete absence of the midsection of the wall. However, as Smith observed, one side of the body is flatter than the other, and consequently the form of the object somewhat resembled that of the celebrated gilded and enameled canteen in The British Museum, London (OA 69.1-23.3: *Glass of the Sultans* 2001, pp. 247–249, no. 123), although in the latter the contrast between the two sides is more pronounced. The form has Parthian and Sasanian antecedents made of pottery (Debevoise 1934, pp. 102–105, nos. 298–306; Langdon and Harden 1934, p. 126, fig. 1, no. 24).

Similarly, the layout of the ornament on the sides is conjectural. The flat side may have had a symmetrical design, with a palmette "tree" at the center, flanked by indeterminate motifs at the top and leaping animals at the bottom, and with an unknown amount of vegetal ornament. The bulging side, too, may have had a symmetrical layout, although the central element was not a palmette "tree." The element seems to have been flanked by an unknown number of birds at the top and by leaping animals at the bottom, again interspersed with vegetal ornament. The ornament on the sides cannot be determined.

P. Oliver (1961, p. 12) placed the flask "at the start of the sequence" of Islamic relief-cut glass and compared it with the Falcon and Ibex Bowl (**296**), which is said to have been found in Gurgān Province, northern Iran. The similarities include the presence on both of heart-shaped palmettes (and perhaps palmette "trees") and the generous use of hatching. Oliver (*ibid.*, p. 28) attributed the two objects to the second half of the ninth century.

BIBLIOGRAPHY: *Verres antiques* 1954, p. 53, no. 325; *Glass from the Ancient World* 1957, pp. 267–269, no. 545; *Guide to the Collections* 1958, p. 28, no. 23; Oliver, P. 1961, p. 12, figs. 1–4; Martin 1977, cover and p. 15, fig. 13.

9. Ewers and Related Objects

389. Ewer with Animals, Birds, Half-Palmettes, and Other Motifs

9th to 10th century. Formerly in the Smith Collection (382). 59.1.480.
H. 17.8 cm, D. (shoulder) 9.2 cm, (base) 8.9 cm.
Colorless; minute bubbles. Blown; relief-cut.

Ewer: cylindrical. Mouth has long, pointed pouring lip and plain rim, which is beveled on inside; neck roughly cylindrical, and wider at bottom than at top; shoulder slopes gently to rounded edge; body has vertical wall; base flat; no trace of pontil mark (but see below); handle with almost square cross section attached to edge of shoulder, drawn up and in, and reattached to outside of rim, with trace of thumb-rest at highest point. Decorated in relief on neck, shoulder, wall, underside of base, and handle. Neck has rectangular panel with continuous raised border, which begins and ends on either side of handle. Panel contains two hare-like animals with raised outlines, seen in profile, with their noses and forefeet touching each other below pouring lip; each animal has head with round and countersunk eye, long and hatched ear, schematic body, and raised tail ending in half-palmette; most outlines are notched, and feet are hatched. Shoulder has horizontal "step" just below neck, raised horizontal rib near midpoint, and, at edge, horizontal band of hollow oval facets alternating with pairs of short transverse cuts. Wall is almost completely filled with rectangular panel, which begins and ends on either side of handle and has horizontal raised border at bottom (it is continuous below handle), but no border at top. Decoration is symmetrical on either side of pouring lip. Central motif consists of short vertical stem;

at top, this divides into two sinuous tendrils, each of which divides and terminates in half-palmettes; at bottom, stem splits into two horizontal lines ending in tendrils that curve down and out, and terminate in half-palmettes. On either side of central motif, single bird stands facing inward; each bird has small head, slender body, folded wing with covert ending in half-palmette, straight tail, and leg and foot extended forward as if grasping support. Behind each bird is one humped bull, shown in profile, facing inward; each animal has head with eye indicated by countersunk dot, ear, and curved horn; body with prominent hump, foreleg extended, and raised tail terminating in half-palmette; some outlines are notched, and hooves, half-palmettes, and other details are hatched. Behind each animal, below handle, are two vertical stems, which extend up and in at top and curve down and in at bottom, and terminate in half-palmettes; stems are notched, and half-palmettes are hatched. Handle has small rectangular protrusion at bottom and remains

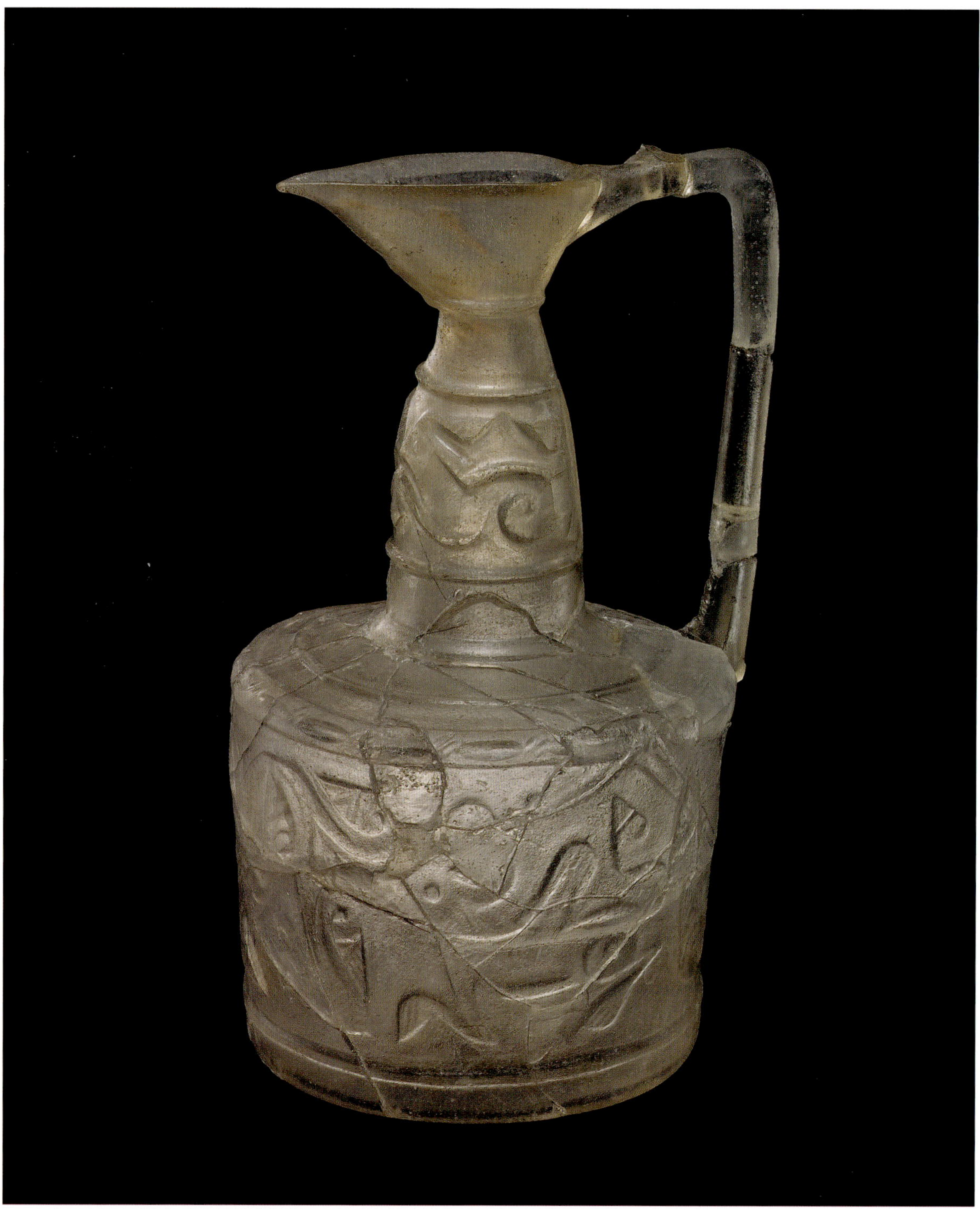

389A

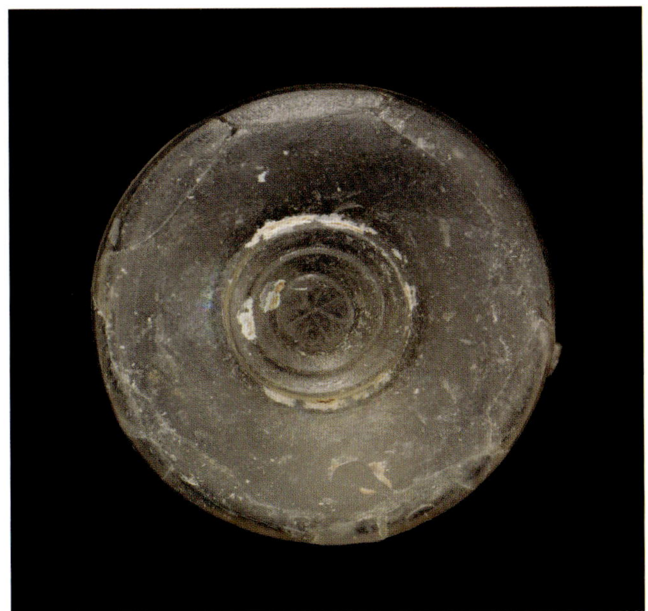

389B

of wheel-cut thumb-rest at top. Decoration on underside of base consists of, at center, countersunk circle (D. 1.2 cm) inscribed with star formed from eight narrow, intersecting cuts and surrounded by two concentric countersunk rings (external D. 2.4 cm and 3.4 cm).

Incomplete. Broken and restored. Losses include nearly 50 percent of shoulder, 25 percent of wall, and about 30 percent of handle, including almost all of thumb-rest. Dull and pitted, with slight iridescence.

Comment: None of the elements in the panel on the wall is complete, and the description is based on the assumption, which observation confirms to be at least partly correct, that the decoration was symmetrical on either side of the pouring lip. The coldworking on the underside of the base has removed all traces of the pontil mark (if such existed).

Several features of the ornament recall a relief-cut bottle in the David Collection, Copenhagen (10/1963: *Glass of the Sultans* 2001, pp. 191–192, no. 96). The decoration on the neck of the bottle includes a frieze of two hares (both running from right to left, however), and the shoulder has a "step" just below the junction with the neck and two horizontal ribs. The decoration on the wall includes a vertical stem that, at the top, has a palmette, above which it divides into two leaflike motifs; at the bottom, the stem splits into two linear elements terminating in tendrils with half-palmettes. On either side of this large and complex motif is a perched or standing bird, similar to the birds on **296**. The hares have numerous parallels on relief-cut glasses of the ninth and 10th centuries, including **298**, **347**, **369**, and **372**.

390. Fragment of Ewer with Animals

9th to 10th century. Formerly in the Smith Collection (part of 1084). 55.1.141.
H. (surviving) 14.4 cm, D. (rim) 4.9 cm.
Colorless; very small bubbles. Blown; applied, facet- and relief-cut.

Fragment of ewer, consisting of all of neck and handle, and small part of upper wall. Rim plain, with lip ground flat; neck shaped like narrow funnel, with slightly concave profile; upper wall curves down and out, and before cutting was barely 0.15 cm thick; handle with rectangular cross section dropped onto wall, drawn up and in, and attached to top of neck, with vertical thumb-rest at highest point. Neck, wall, and handle have relief- and facet-cut ornament. Midsection of neck has broad relief-cut panel, which is interrupted behind handle and framed by raised border; panel contains two confronted animals shown in profile and separated by small oval motif; each animal has eye indicated by countersunk dot, long and curved ear, front leg extended forward and rear leg extended backward, and long tail with tuft; oval motif and ears are hatched with herringbone pattern; necks, feet, and tufts are hatched; outlines of animals are notched.

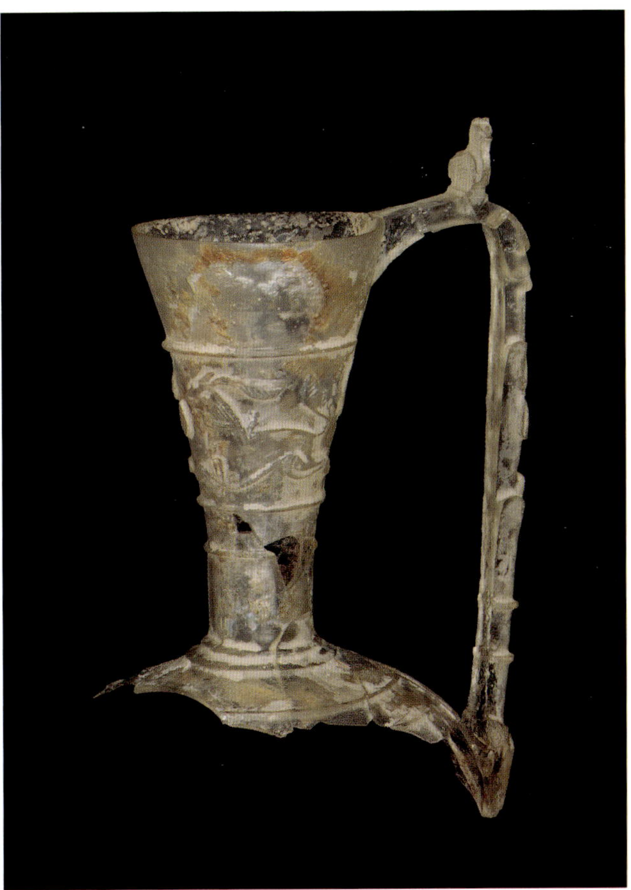

390

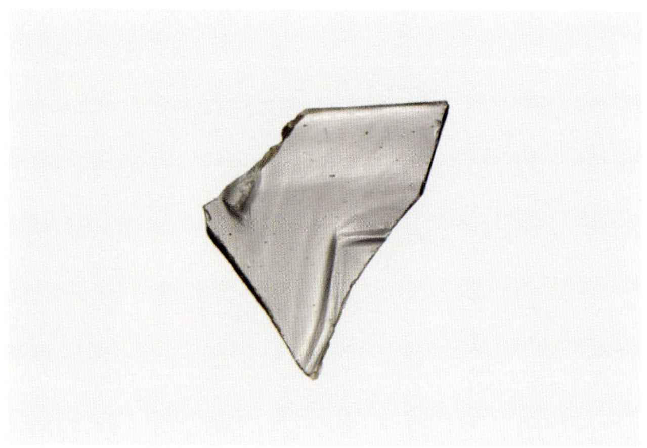

393

Comment: If the projection near the rim is the remains of a handle, as seems likely, the fragment probably came from a pitcher with a tapering neck, perhaps similar in form to a pitcher with slant-cut decoration excavated at Nishapur, northeastern Iran, and now in The Metropolitan Museum of Art, New York (39.40.101: *Glass of the Sultans* 2001, pp. 192–193, no. 97 = Kröger 1995, pp. 174–175, no. 228). On the Corning Ewer (**522**) and its rock crystal counterparts, the ornament occupies a single large panel that begins and ends on either side of the handle, and has a continuous raised border; the area behind the handle is plain. The border on this fragment, however, curves in a manner that suggests it continued behind the handle, and, if symmetrical, it would have risen on the other side and resumed its horizontal course around the neck. This is consistent with the decoration on the pitcher in the Metropolitan Museum, which continues behind the handle.

394. Spout with Animal and Bird

9th to 10th century. Formerly in the Smith Collection (part of 1084). 55.1.141a.
Max. Dim. 10.9 cm, D. 0.65 cm.
Colorless; few very small bubbles. Blown; applied, relief-cut.

Spout: curved, with oval cross section at bottom and circular cross section at top, which may have been ground. Bottom has band of relief-cut decoration at front and sides: at top, countersunk horizontal rib; beneath it, bird shown in profile, facing left, with small beak, eye indicated by countersunk dot, hatched neck, wing in form of half-palmette, and large, hatched tail; just below bird, quadruped, also in profile, facing left, with pointed snout, long ear, hatched neck, front and back legs extended forward, and curving tail; body has notched outlines.

Broken from wall of vessel at bottom; otherwise, apparently complete. Dull and pitted, with traces of dark brown weathering, and iridescence.

Comment: When it was published by Smith and P. Oliver (see below), the spout was attached to a fragmentary ewer (**390**), although Smith was not "entirely certain" that they came from the same object. In fact, the spout appears to have been attached to a vessel with a thicker wall than the ewer, and the cutting is less delicate. It is difficult, too, to imagine how the decoration on the bottom of the spout might be accommodated in the panel on the wall of the ewer.

Bibliography: *Glass from the Ancient World* 1957, pp. 278–279, no. 585; Oliver, P. 1961, p. 15, fig. 11.

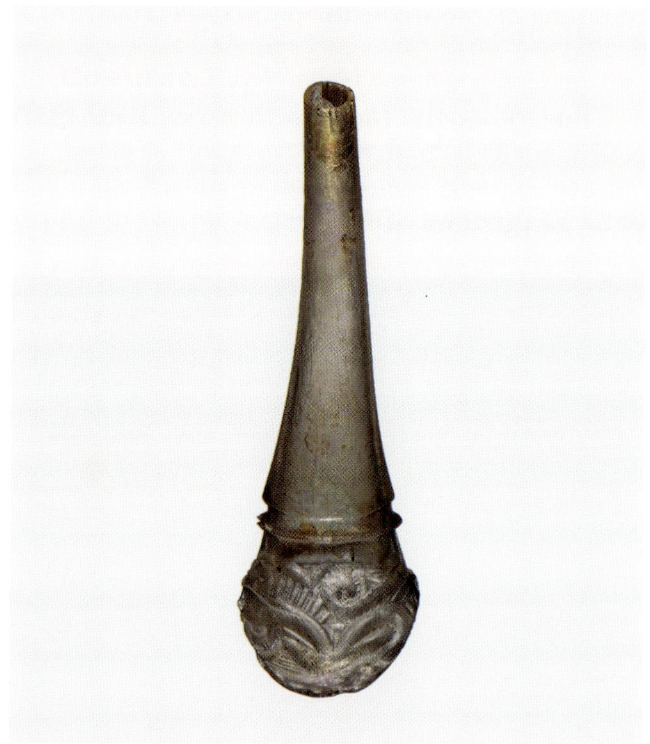

394

395. Handle

9th to 10th century. Formerly in the Smith Collection (1103). 59.1.466.
H. (surviving) 8.5 cm, W. 1.3–1.4 cm,
Th. (without decoration) 0.3–0.4 cm.
Colorless or almost colorless. Applied, relief-cut.

Handle, which curves out and down, then descends vertically. Decorated in three places, once on curved part and twice on vertical part: (1) on curved part, groove (W. 0.4 cm, Depth 0.25 cm) that has

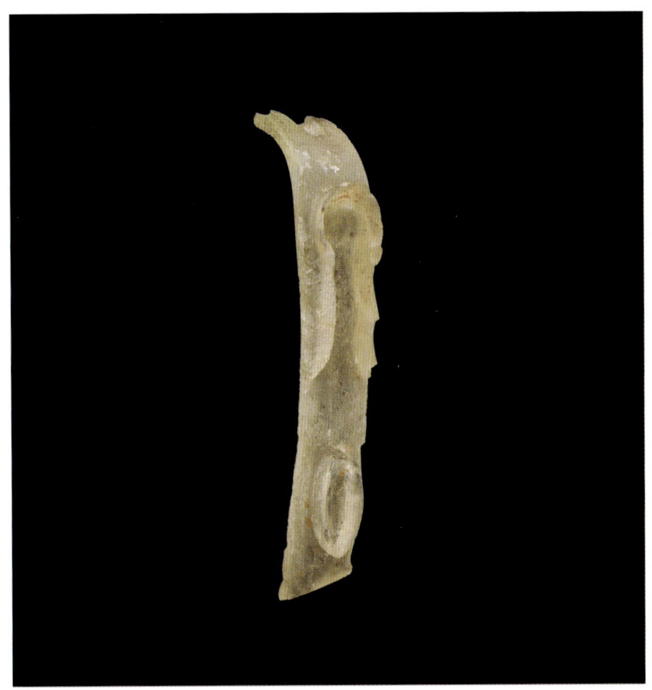

395

rounded end and is on axis of handle; (2) on upper vertical part, in raised outline, motif (L. at least 3.6 cm, Th. up to 0.5 cm) shaped like keyhole, but with bottom open; and (3) below this, also in raised outline (L. 1.75 cm, Th. 0.5 cm), narrow oval motif. Outer sides of keyhole motif have curved elements in low relief. Sides of handle opposite oval motif are indented and have slightly convex edges.

Top, bottom, and parts of decoration are missing. Much of surface is dull and pitted, with patches of pale brown weathering.

COMMENT: The size and shape of the handle suggest that it may have been part of a ewer, perhaps similar to the Corning Ewer (**522**). It is likely that the groove near the top of the handle was associated with an elaborate thumb-rest, such as that which embellished the Corning Ewer.

BIBLIOGRAPHY: *Glass from the Ancient World* 1957, p. 279, no. 582.

396. Fragment of Thumb-Rest with Birds

9th to 10th century. Formerly in the Smith Collection (964). 59.1.467.
H. (surviving) 4.1 cm, W. 3.5 cm.
Colorless. Applied and hotworked; linear-cut, with openwork and minimal slant cutting.

Fragment of vertical thumb-rest from top of handle. Fragment (Th. 0.15–0.25 cm) is flat or almost flat, has two keyhole-shaped vertical perforations (H. 1.7 cm, Max. W. 0.8 cm), and is decorated on one face only. Decoration is symmetrical about vertical axis. It consists of, between perforations, vertical element (W. 0.3 cm) embellished with crescent-shaped notches; outside perforations, two elongated S-shaped elements covered with groups of vertical and horizontal cuts, which terminate at top in outward-facing birds' heads, shown in profile, with hooked beaks and eyes consisting of countersunk dots defined by slant cutting.

Broken at top, bottom, and right side. Surfaces are slightly cloudy, with small spots of light brown weathering.

COMMENT: The object is part of a large and elaborate thumb-rest from the handle of a pouring vessel. At the top, the object continued above the birds' heads, and, at the bottom, it continued below the lowest parts of the S-shaped elements. The original size and shape are unknown.

Glass vessels with large, ornate thumb-rests are not common. The Corning Ewer (**522**) and the cameo glass pitcher (**523**) also have the remains of elaborate thumb-rests, while **396** is a fragmentary thumb-rest with openwork, attached to an elaborate handle that, in addition to openwork, has linear-cut decoration. Another ninth- to 10th-century relief-cut vessel, the Buckley Ewer in the Victoria and Albert Museum, London (C.126-1936: Lamm 1939, v. 3, p. 2597, and v. 6, pl. 1441; Whitehouse 1993a, p. 52, fig. 9), has a large, bifurcated thumb-rest in the form of two birds. Three other relief-cut ewers also have large thumb-rests decorated with openwork (*Khalili Collection* 2005, pp. 203–205, nos. 241–243), but, as Goldstein remarked, "questions have sometimes been raised regarding [their] authenticity" (*ibid.*, p. 241).

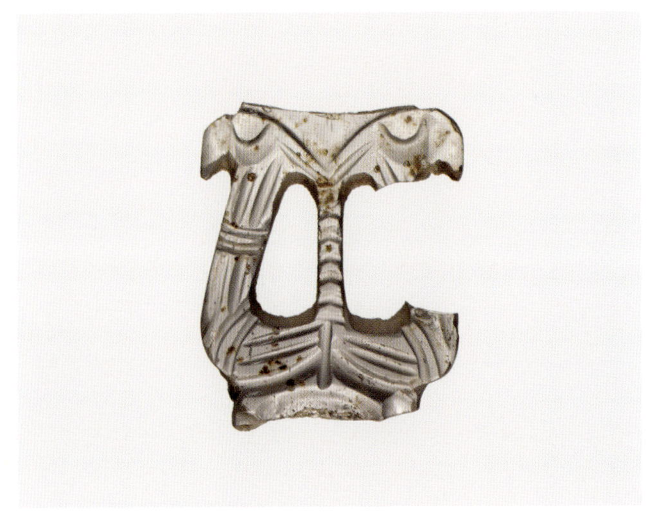

396

10. Indeterminate

397. Fragment with Lions

About 10th century. Formerly in the Smith Collection (914). 55.1.144.
Max. Dim. 5.3 cm, D. (at level of animals' forepaws, est.) about 7 cm.
Colorless; no obvious bubbles. Blown; relief-cut.

Fragment from wall of vessel with globular body. Wall (Th. 0.1 cm) curves out, down, and in. Decoration (Th. 0.1 cm) consists of two identical lions standing on their hind legs and facing each other. Each lion has head shown in twisted perspective, with two eyes represented by countersunk dots, and with two narrow, pointed ears; neck and body are in profile; front leg is raised, and back leg is extended downward; tail curls at tip. Between lions' hind legs is one downward-pointing palmette. Minute parts of other motifs survive above and between lions' heads, behind lion on right, and below palmette. Outlines of lions and palmette are notched, feet are hatched, and heads have incised details.

Broken on all sides. Glass appears to be pristine.

COMMENT: The fragment came from a vessel with a globular body, perhaps a bottle. Both the glass and the cutting are of exceptional quality. Smith (in *Glass from the Ancient World*: see below) rightly described the fragment as "sparkling."

The treatment of the lions' heads, in which both eyes are shown although the rest of the animals is in profile, is found on a number of 10th-century and later Islamic and Islamic-influenced objects, both of glass and of other materials. The glass objects include a relief-cut bowl in the Treasury of San Marco, Venice (117: *Glass of the Sultans* 2001, pp. 178–179, no. 84); a facet- and linear-cut bottle from the site of Ṣabra al-Mansuriyya, Qairouan, Tunisia (Marçais and Poinssot 1952, pp. 379–382 and pls. 55 and 58); a similar bottle and a linear-cut beaker from the shipwreck at Serçe Limanı near the Turkish coast, opposite Rhodes (Bass and others 2009, pp. 64–65, no. BK 87); and several Hedwig beakers, including **586** (see pages 333–334). Examples in other media include fritware bowls of the type associated with Tell Minis, Syria (Folsach 1990, p. 90, no. 88; *idem* 2001, p. 144, nos. 140 and 141); the painted ceiling of the Cappella Palatina in Palermo, Sicily (Grube and Johns 2005, p. 46, pl. 10; p. 50, pl. 14; p. 52, pl. 16; etc.); and, spectacularly, the coronation mantle of King Roger II of Sicily (Gabrieli and Scerrato 1979, [pp. 138–139], fig. 149; Grube and Johns 2005, p. 260, fig. 94.1). The Serçe Limanı ship foundered about 1025; the coronation mantle bears the date 548 in the Muslim calendar, which is equivalent to 1133–1134; the ceiling of the Cappella Palatina was decorated in the 1140s (Grube and Johns 2005, p. 7); and Tell Minis ware is usually attributed to the mid-11th century. The date of the Hedwig beakers is uncertain, but recent discussions support the idea that they were made in the 12th century.

While the (admittedly far from exhaustive) list of parallels for the way in which the lions are represented on **397** focuses on the 11th and 12th centuries, the crisp relief cutting and the use of notched outlines suggest a somewhat earlier date. The latest securely datable example of decoration with relief-cut notched outlines is the rock crystal ewer in the Treasury of San Marco, Venice, which has an inscription naming the Fatimid caliph al-ʿAzīz Biʾllāh (r. 975–996) (80: Erdmann 1971, pp. 112–113, no. 124).

BIBLIOGRAPHY: *Verres antiques* 1954, p. 49, no. 298 (part of group); *Glass from the Ancient World* 1957, pp. 280–281, no. 591; Oliver, P. 1961, pp. 20–22, 26, and 27, fig. 22.

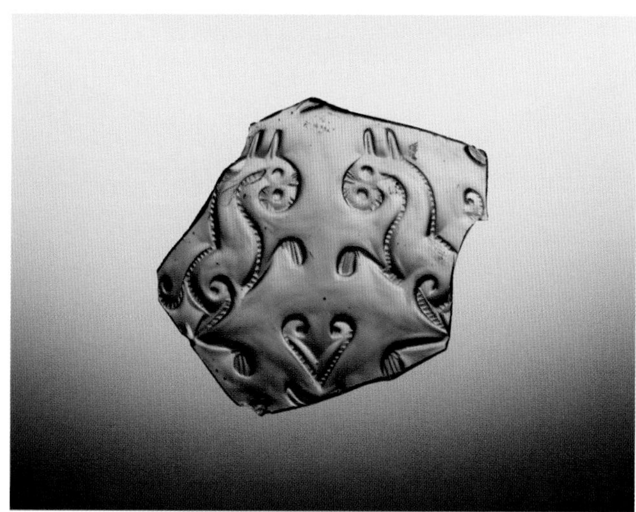

397

398. Fragment with Hares

9th to 10th century. Formerly in the Smith Collection (555-32). 59.1.450.
Max. Dim. 6.2 cm.
Colorless. Blown; relief-cut.

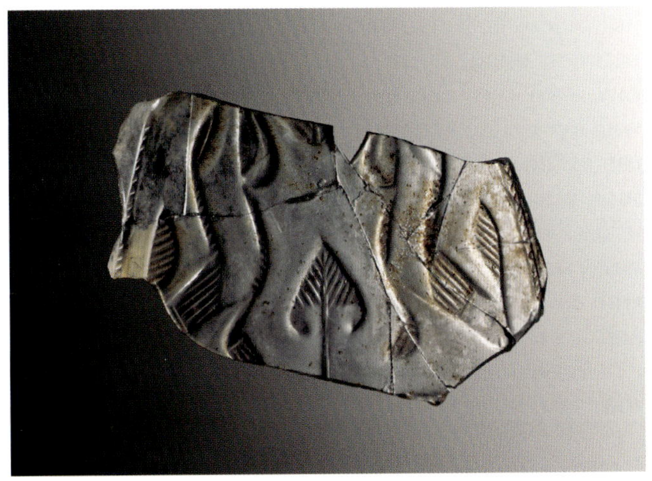

398

Fragment (assembled from seven small fragments) from wall (Th. 0.1–0.15 cm) of vessel of uncertain form (see "Comment"). Decoration includes palmette on straight stem, and following description assumes that stem is vertical and palmette points upward. If this is so, fragment is almost flat both vertically and horizontally, but on both sides, about 3 cm from stem, it begins to curve in horizontal plane. Decoration (Th. 0.1 cm) consists of two hares, one on each side of palmette, running from top to bottom of fragment, with their legs close to palmette and stem, and their heads farther away. On each side of fragment, where wall begins to curve, raised border, which presumably enclosed panel containing symmetrical arrangement of hares and palmette. Ears, neck, and limbs of each hare, as well as palmette, have transverse hatching; outlines of bodies of hares and border are notched.

Broken on all sides. Dull, with transparent pale grayish weathering.

Comment: The fragment appears to be part of the wall of a canteen or "pilgrim flask" with at least one flat face, which was decorated with a panel containing a symmetrical arrangement of hares on either side of a palmette. Hares and other animals are usually shown as though moving on a flat surface, and the vertical stance of the hares on this fragment is very unusual.

Bibliography: *Glass from the Ancient World* 1957, p. 281, no. 590 (part of group).

399. Fragment with Hares

9th to 10th century. Formerly in the Smith Collection (916). Gift of Carl Berkowitz and Derek Content. 76.1.202.
H. (surviving) 3.2 cm, D. (est.) about 9 cm.
Almost colorless, with pale yellowish fracture.
Blown; relief-cut.

Fragment of bottle or bowl. Lower wall curves down and in; it is 0.1 cm thick at top of fragment and 0.3 cm thick at bottom. Decorated with parts of two registers. Upper register has small part of unidentified motif, probably animal, with hatched foot or limb. Lower register has notched upper border and plain lower border; it contains frieze of animals shown in profile, running toward left. One almost complete animal is hare with pointed snout, eye represented by countersunk dot, large ear, body with notched outlines, foreleg thrust forward and embellished with hatching, and rounded haunch. In front of hare, tail and hind limb of another animal.

Broken on all sides. No obvious weathering.

Comment: The fragment may be part of a bottle similar in form to **354**.

Bibliography: *Verres antiques* 1954, p. 49, no. 298 (part of group).

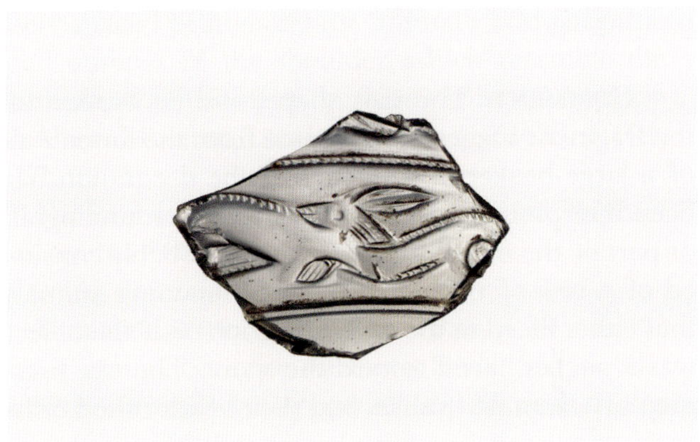

399

400. Fragment with Animals

9th to 10th century. Formerly in the Smith Collection (555-25). Gift of Carl Berkowitz and Derek Content. 76.1.230.
H. (surviving) 5.7 cm, D. (est.) 9 cm.
Colorless. Blown; relief-cut.

Fragment of vessel. Wall (Th. 0.2 cm) apparently almost vertical, but with slightly convex profile. Relief-cut decoration (Th. 0.1 cm) consists of frieze with horizontal border at bottom (top is missing). Frieze contains geometric pattern of contiguous octagons shaped like two squares superimposed at 45 degrees, but with narrow projection at center of top. Parts of two octagons survive: that on right apparently contains chest,

other, from Nishapur in northeastern Iran, see Kröger 1995, pp. 137–138, no. 190.

Bibliography: *Verres antiques* 1954, p. 49, no. 298 (part of group).

408. Fragment with Animal

9th to 10th century. Formerly in the Strauss Collection (F76). Bequest of Jerome Strauss. 79.1.306.
Max. Dim. 4.3 cm.
Almost colorless, with yellowish tinge; few small bubbles. Blown; relief-cut.

Fragment of vessel. Wall (Th. 0.25 cm with decoration, 0.1 cm without decoration) is straight and vertical or almost vertical. Decorated in relief with part of animal seen in right profile. Head has countersunk eye, rounded muzzle with mouth indicated by short cut and with short transverse cuts on upper and lower jaws, and two horns shown in twisted perspective, one short and curling, and the other longer and curved; neck is completely in relief and filled with transverse hatching, with two transverse cuts at different angles marking junction with body; latter has notched outline and is countersunk.

Broken on all sides. Glass appears to be pristine.

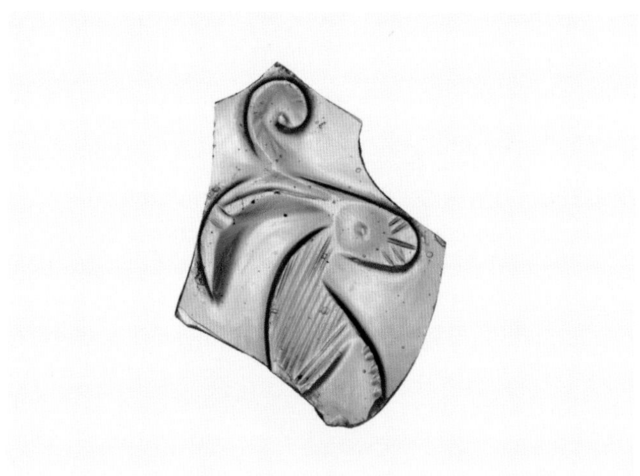

408

409. Fragment with Animal

9th to 10th century. Formerly in the Strauss Collection (F77). Bequest of Jerome Strauss. 79.1.307.
Max. Dim. 4.1 cm, D. (est., at narrowest point) about 6–7 cm.
Almost colorless, with greenish yellow tinge; small bubbles. Blown; relief-cut.

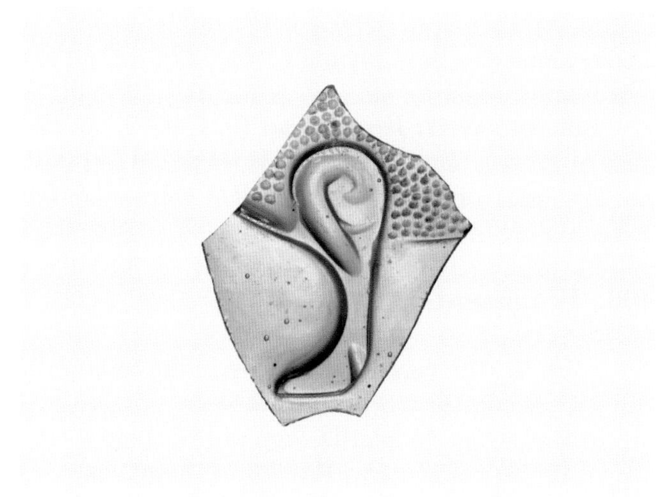

409

Fragment of vessel. Wall (Th. 0.25 cm with decoration, less than 0.1 cm without decoration) descends vertically or almost vertically, with slightly concave profile. Decorated in relief with part of quadruped: chest has narrow notched outline; body is countersunk and filled with closely spaced drilled dots; front leg has tear-shaped shoulder, which is slant-cut to form simple half-palmette; leg is short and straight; foot is triangular, with notch at junction of heel and lower leg.

Broken on all sides. Surface is virtually as new.

Comment: The small diameter and the slightly concave profile of the fragment suggest that it is part of a beaker, perhaps similar to **335**, which is roughly the same size ("Recent Important Acquisitions," *JGS*, v. 9, 1967, p. 137, no. 20). For another animal with a countersunk body filled with a large number of drilled dots, see **403** (*Glass from the Ancient World* 1957, p. 281, no. 589; Oliver, P. 1961, p. 24, fig. 28).

410. Fragment with Animal

9th to 10th century. Formerly in the Smith Collection (923). Gift of Carl Berkowitz and Derek Content. 76.1.215.
H. (surviving) 3.7 cm.
Colorless. Blown; relief-cut.

Fragment from wall of vessel (Th. 0.1 cm). Decorated in relief (Th. 0.1 cm) with curving stems, which are notched, above head of animal seen in profile, facing left. Animal has pointed snout, eye represented by countersunk dot, large ear, and back of head or neck filled with transverse hatching.

Broken on all sides. Traces of incipient weathering.

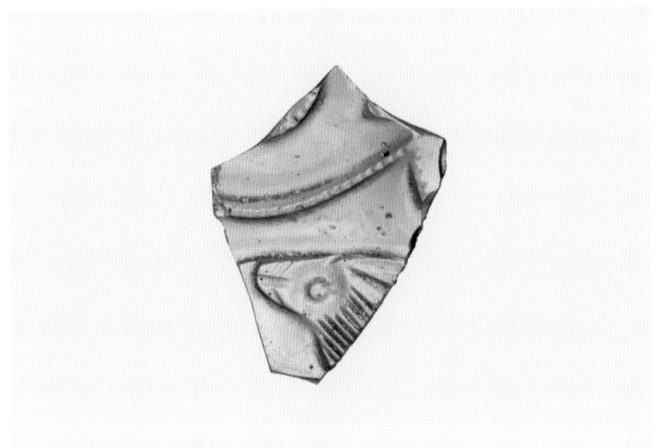

410

Bibliography: *Verres antiques* 1954, p. 49, no. 298 (part of group); *Glass from the Ancient World* 1957, p. 281, no. 590 (part of group).

411. Fragment with Animal

9th to 10th century. Formerly in the Smith Collection (628). Gift of Carl Berkowitz and Derek Content. 76.1.211.
Max. Dim. 3.7 cm.
Colorless. Blown; relief-cut.

Fragment from wall of vessel (Th. 0.1 cm). Decorated in relief (Th. 0.1 cm) with part of animal above horizontal border embellished with more or less contiguous diamond-shaped notches. Fragment shows part of animal's chest and one front leg, which extends forward, with hoof or foot bent down and back. Leg is notched.

Broken on all sides. Pristine, with no obvious weathering.

Bibliography: *Glass from the Ancient World* 1957, p. 281, no. 590 (part of group).

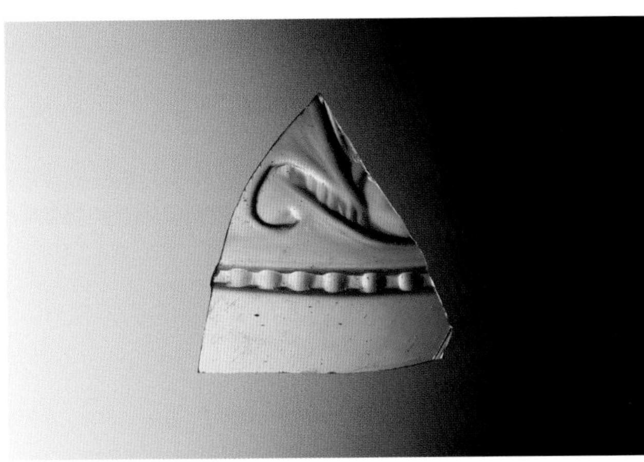

411

412. Fragment with Animal

9th to 10th century. Formerly in the Smith Collection (1098). 55.1.145.
Max. Dim. 3.7 cm.
Colorless or almost colorless. Blown; relief-cut.

Fragment of vessel, with flat, decorated surface and very slightly convex plain surface: perhaps from center of base. Decorated on underside(?) in relief with animal seen in profile, facing left. Head has countersunk eye, triangular muzzle with cut indicating mouth and transverse cuts on upper and lower jaws, and long, curving horn with median incised line and notches above this; neck is represented by triangular area of transverse hatching; body is roughly triangular, with deep chest and narrow rump, defined by notched outlines and countersunk; front leg has tear-shaped shoulder and extends forward; hind leg has countersunk haunch, leg indicated by single line, and oval foot with transverse hatching.

Broken and grozed on all sides. Shiny, with large areas of light grayish violet weathering and some iridescence.

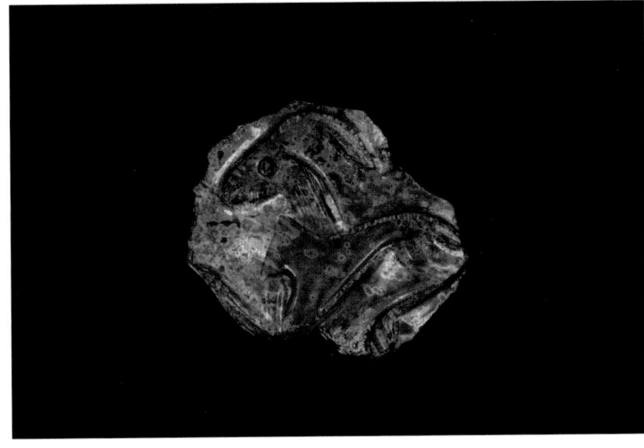

412

Comment: The long, curved horn indicates that the animal is an antelope, possibly an ibex. The treatment of the animal, with its triangular hatched neck, deep chest and narrow rump, and notched outlines, is reminiscent of the long-eared animals on a fragmentary bowl found in the Jawsaq al-Khāqānī, the palace built by Caliph al-Mu^{c}taṣim at Samarra, Iraq, in A.D. 836 (Lamm 1928, p. 77, nos. 243 and 244). The fragments were republished by Kröger (2002), who attributes the object to the first half of the ninth century.

The weathering extends over the grozed edges, showing that the fragment was carefully trimmed, presumably to preserve the animal as an amulet or simply as a curiosity.

BIBLIOGRAPHY: Oliver, P. 1961, pp. 14–15, fig. 10.

413. Fragment with Animal

9th to 10th century. Formerly in the Smith Collection (555-9). Gift of Carl Berkowitz and Derek Content. 76.1.201.
H. (surviving) 3.6 cm, D. (est.) about 6 cm.
Almost colorless, with yellowish green fracture. Blown; relief-cut.

Fragment of beaker or bottle. Wall (Th. 0.1 cm) is straight and tapers. Decorated with animal (Th. 0.1 cm) shown in profile, moving to left. Animal has head down and eye represented by countersunk dot; back of head is covered with transverse hatching; neck and body have notched outlines; leg is extended forward and has hatched foot.

Broken on all sides. Glass is pristine, with no trace of weathering.

COMMENT: The animal resembles the horses on a bowl in the Museum für Islamische Kunst, Berlin, although the latter have shallow circular depressions on their bodies (I.20/65: Kröger 1984, pp. 223–224, no. 193; *Glass of the Sultans* 2001, p. 176, no. 82).

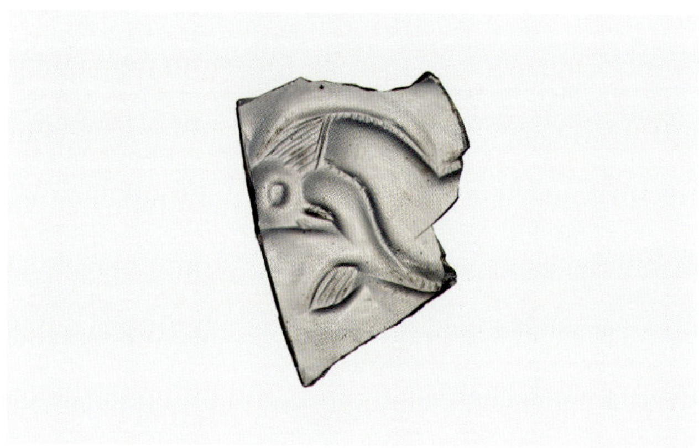

413

414. Fragment with Animal

9th to 10th century. Formerly in the Strauss Collection (F31). Bequest of Jerome Strauss. 79.1.308.
Max. Dim. 3 cm.
Colorless; few very small bubbles. Blown; relief-cut.

Fragment of vessel. Wall (Th. after cutting 0.15 cm) has convex profile and is decorated in very high relief (0.4 cm) with part of animal seen in profile, moving (perhaps running) to left. Animal has head with countersunk eye, long and pointed snout with mouth slightly open, and ear; neck and chest have raised outlines and are countersunk; front leg is extended forward; head has many short incised lines; head and shoulder are embellished with drilled dots; and front leg has median groove and notches.

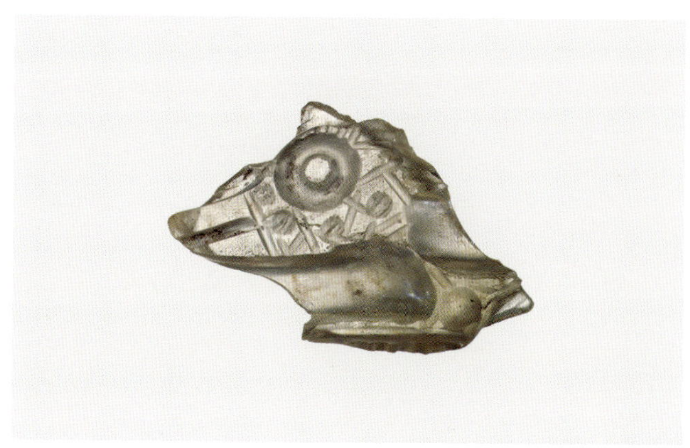

414

Broken on all sides. Dull, with traces of faint iridescence.

COMMENT: The curvature of the fragment suggests that it may have come from the globular body of a bottle or similar form, with a maximum diameter of about eight to nine centimeters. The ornament is in unusually high relief. The long, pointed snout of the animal suggests that it may be a dog, a wolf, or even a bear, despite the fact that such animals do not form part of the usual repertoire of ornament on relief-cut glass.

415. Fragment with Animal

9th to 10th century. Formerly in the Smith Collection. 68.1.59-74.
Max. Dim. 3 cm.
Almost colorless, with yellowish tinge; very few minute bubbles. Blown; relief-cut.

Fragment from wall of vessel (Th. 0.1–0.15 cm) with relief-cut decoration (Th. 0.2 cm) on exterior. Decoration consists of foreleg and hoof of quadruped, moving toward right. Leg is indicated by single notched line, and hoof by triangular area enlivened with short, narrow cuts.

Broken on all sides. Surface is almost as new, except for traces of light brown accretion or weathering.

COMMENT: Although the fragment is very small, the ornament may be identified with confidence as an animal by analogy with the galloping horses on a

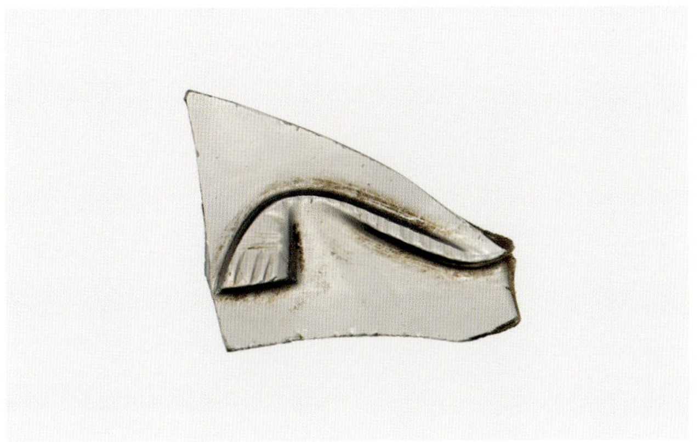

415

relief-cut bowl in the Museum für Islamische Kunst, Berlin (I.20/65: *Glass of the Sultans* 2001, p. 176, no. 82). Each of the horses is shown in profile with one foreleg, which is extended forward and represented by a notched line, and with a hatched triangle representing the hoof. For the legs and hooves of ibexes depicted in the same manner, see **296** and **354**.

416. Fragment with Animal(?) and Half-Palmette

9th to 10th century. Formerly in the Smith Collection. 68.1.59-28.
Max. Dim. 4 cm.
Colorless or almost colorless. Blown; relief-cut.

Fragment of vessel. Wall (TTh. 0.2 cm) is straight, but angle at which it descends is uncertain. Decorated in relief (Th. 0.1 cm) on outside: part of elaborate curvilinear design, which includes half-palmette and area with row of nine very short cuts; outlines are notched, and half-palmette has incised details.

Broken on all sides. Transparent pale gray and light brown weathering.

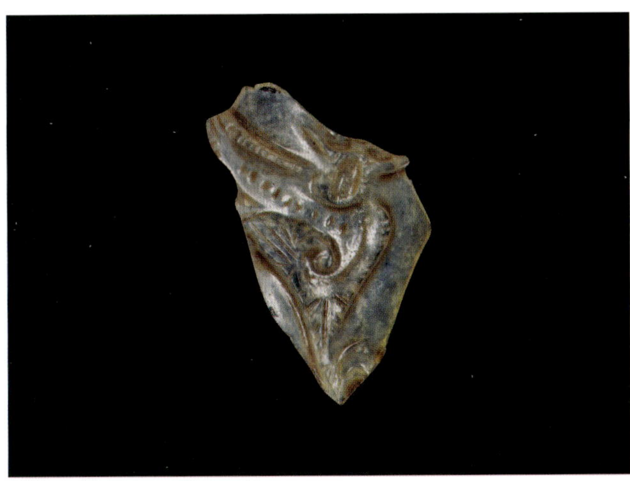

416

Comment: The fragment probably came from the wall of a beaker or a bottle. The half-palmette and the notched outlines place it firmly among Islamic relief-cut glasses of the ninth and 10th centuries. The ornament, however, defies identification. The row of short incisions resembles the rows of drilled dots that were usually employed to decorate the bodies of birds or animals; drilled dots serve this purpose on the Corning Ewer (**522**), where half-palmettes are found on the haunches of the animals and the wing coverts of the birds of prey. It is possible, therefore, that the fragment preserves part of an animal, either real (as on the Corning Ewer) or imagined (as on a fragment from Nishapur, northeastern Iran, now in The Metropolitan Museum of Art, New York: 40.170.181: Kröger 1995, pp. 140–143, no. 193).

417. Fragment with Winged Animal (?)

9th to 10th century. Formerly in the Smith Collection. 68.1.59-10.
Max. Dim. 4.2 cm.
Colorless or almost colorless. Blown; relief-cut.

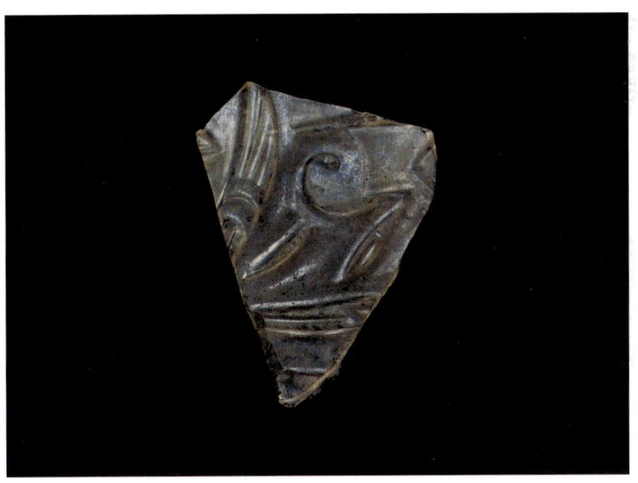

417

Fragment from wall (TTh. 0.2 cm) of vessel with relief-cut ornament (Th. 0.1 cm). Decoration appears to depict winged animal, in left profile, standing on groundline. If this is so, it includes small part of crest on back of head; upright wing, which narrows toward tip and bends slightly forward; back; left hind leg, with haunch represented by volute; part of right hind leg; and belly. Wing is hatched, and belly and groundline are notched.

Broken on all sides. Transparent mottled pale brown weathering.

Comment: If the interpretation of the ornament is correct, the animal may be a *senmurv* with a wing not unlike the wings of the *senmurv* on a Sasanian pressed glass plaque at Corning (64.1.31: Whitehouse 2005, pp. 15–16, no. 1).

418. Fragment with Animal(?)

9th to 10th century. Formerly in the Smith Collection (555-19). Gift of Carl Berkowitz and Derek Content. 76.1.231.
Max. Dim. 4.2 cm, D. (est.) about 8 cm.
Colorless. Blown; relief-cut.

Fragment of vessel, possibly beaker. Wall (Th. 0.1 cm) is probably straight, perhaps tapering. Decoration in relief (Th. 0.1 cm) is meticulous and executed with considerable skill. It apparently includes one front leg and head of animal, with eye represented by countersunk dot. Other fragmentary motifs are curvilinear and may be vegetal. Some outlines are notched, and one motif is hatched.

Broken on all sides. No obvious weathering.

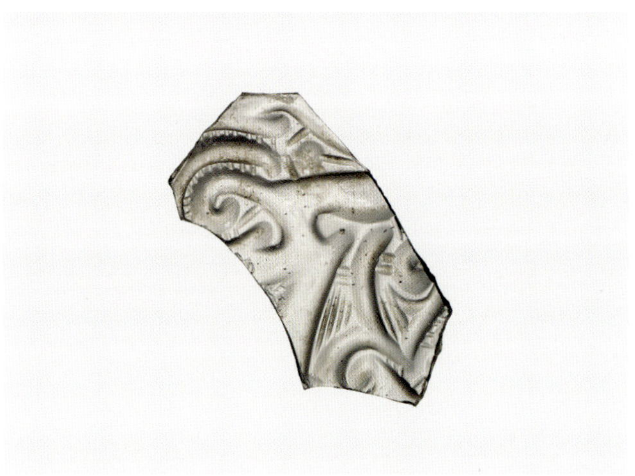

418

419. Fragment with Animal(?)

9th to 10th century. Formerly in the Smith Collection (935). Gift of Carl Berkowitz and Derek Content. 76.1.205.
Max. Dim. 4 cm.
Colorless. Blown; relief-cut.

Fragment from wall of vessel (Th. 0.1 cm). Decorated with part of complex design, which is impossible to elucidate. It includes notched, curving stems(?) and head of animal, facing right, with square snout, eye represented by countersunk dot, and chest with notched outline (?).

Broken on all sides. Pristine, with no obvious weathering.

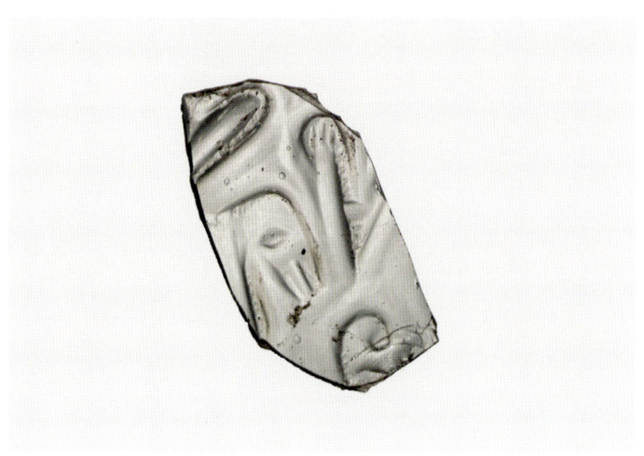

419

Bibliography: *Verres antiques* 1954, p. 49, no. 298 (part of group); *Glass from the Ancient World* 1957, p. 281, no. 590 (part of group).

420. Fragment with Animal(?)

9th to 10th century. Formerly in the Smith Collection. 68.1.59-86.
Max. Dim. 3.2 cm.
Colorless or almost colorless. Blown; relief-cut.

Fragment from wall (TTh. 0.2 cm) of vessel decorated in relief (Th. 0.1 cm) with part of head of animal (?). Surviving ornament appears to have rounded top of head, countersunk dot representing eye, and long, curving horn(s). However, ornament also has part of line projecting up and forward from front of head, for which no explanation is obvious. Raised lines are notched.

Broken on all sides. Dull, with transparent very pale grayish weathering.

Comment: The long, curving horn(s) suggest that the animal—if indeed it is an animal—is an ibex (cf. **350**).

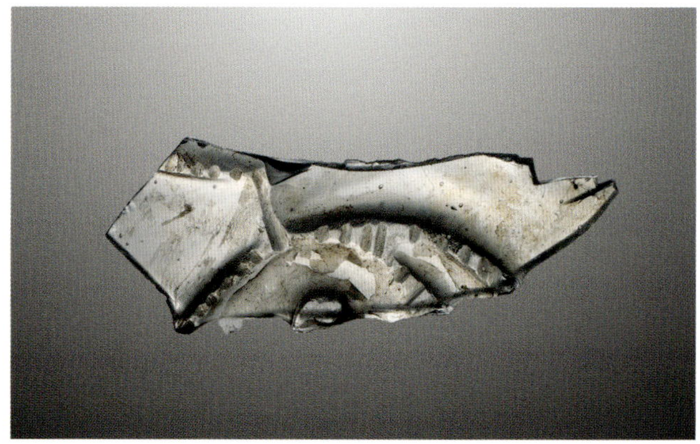

420

421. Fragment with Birds

9th to 10th century. 51.1.123.
Max. Dim. 6 cm, D. (horizontal rib, est.) about 7 cm.
Colorless; very few minute bubbles. Blown; relief-cut.

Fragment of bottle or bowl. Wall (Th. 0.1 cm at top and 0.3 cm at bottom) curves down and in. It is decorated with frieze bordered at bottom by horizontal rib in relief. Above this, parts of three relief-cut birds, apparently identical, shown in profile, facing right. Each bird has small head, with eye indicated by drilled dot and pointed beak with incised line separating upper and lower halves; short neck; plump body with folded wing shaped like teardrop and with single incised line; and fanlike tail.

Broken on all sides. Patches of transparent light gray weathering.

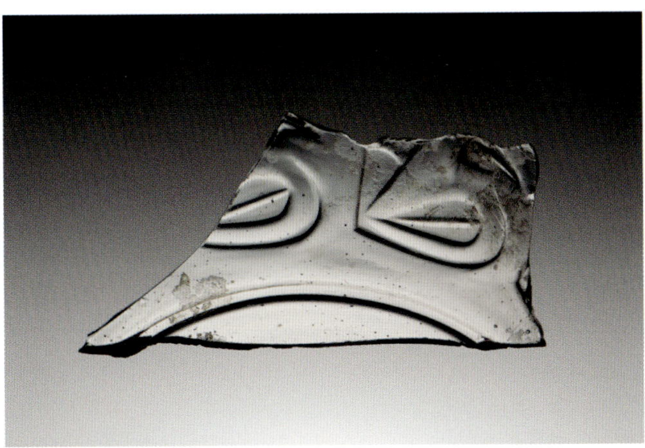

421

Comment: The fragment was acquired, together with **204**, **258**, **262**, **276**, **284**, **292**, **315**, **356**, **424**, **460**, **465**, and **488**, in Cairo, Egypt. It appears to have come from a hemispherical bowl or a bottle with a globular body. If the lower part of the frieze contained a continuous line of identical birds, there were probably seven of them.

422. Fragment with Bird and Inscription

10th to early 11th century. Formerly in the Smith Collection. 68.1.59-37.
H. 5.5 cm, D. (est.) about 5 cm.
Colorless. Blown; relief-cut.

Fragment of vessel. Wall (Th. 0.1 cm) straight and vertical or nearly vertical. Exterior has relief-cut decoration (Th. 0.05–0.1 cm): part of horizontal, and

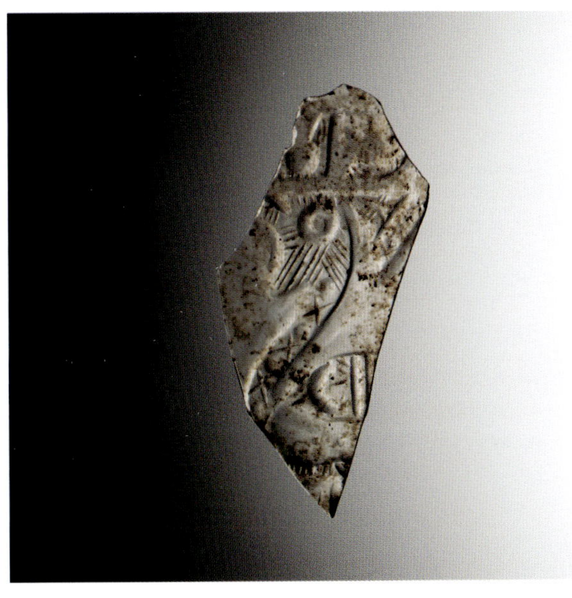

422

presumably continuous, band. At top, Kufic inscription with letters 0.9 cm high. Below this, occupying most of fragment, bird shown in profile, facing left. Head has countersunk boss to indicate eye, beak, wattle, and triangular crest; neck is long and thin; only small parts of body and folded wing survive. Inscription and outline of bird's body are notched; head, beak, wattle, and uppermost part of neck are hatched; rest of neck has row of drilled dots alternating with incised crosses, as does widest part of crest; body has drilled dots, and wing has details indicated by broad cuts and narrow incisions.

Broken on all sides. Dull, with patches of transparent pale brown weathering.

Comment: The fragment is probably from the wall of a beaker or a bottle decorated by an excellent glass cutter. In addition to its generic likeness to numerous examples of Islamic relief-cut glass of the ninth and 10th centuries, it has one specific feature that immediately associates it with some of the latest datable Islamic cut glass: the alternating drilled dots and incised crosses that embellish the neck and the crest of the bird. These have exact parallels on the Corning Ewer (**522**), where they adorn the upper border of the frieze and the necks, wings, and tails of the birds of prey; on the tails, they occupy the same position as on the crest of the bird on this fragment. The ewer is closely similar to a group of rock crystal ewers, two of which bear inscriptions showing that they were made in 975–996 and 1000–1008 or 1011 respectively. It is likely that **422** is of similar date; indeed, given the apparent rarity of rows of dots and crosses, it is not impossible that they came from the same workshop.

423. Fragment with Bird and Inscription

9th to 10th century. Found during excavations at Fusṭāṭ (Old Cairo), Egypt (68.11.1). Gift of the American Research Center in Egypt. 69.1.65c.
H. (surviving) 5.4 cm.
Colorless. Blown; relief-cut.

Fragment from wall of vessel. Wall (TTh. 0.2 cm) curves out, down, and in. Decorated in relief (Th. 0.1 cm) with small part of frieze with two fragmentary elements: (1) three Kufic letters with notched stems and hatched floriated terminals and (2) bird shown in profile, facing left; it has small head with eye indicated by countersunk dot, deep body, and wing raised above back; neck and wing are hatched.

Broken on all sides. Dull, with remains of weathering; slight iridescence.

Comment: The object was found during excavations directed by Prof. George T. Scanlon. It was discovered, together with **380**, **456**, **470**, and other fragments, among the contents of a pit that the excavator dated to the ninth or 10th century.

See **380**, **456**, and **470**. Scanlon and Pinder-Wilson 2001 (pp. 105–106, no. 43j) reported that all four fragments are of "uniform metal and curvature and so possibly come from a single vessel." It seems unlikely that **423** came from the same vessel as **380** because the letters in the inscriptions are of different sizes and thicknesses.

The bird on **423** recalls the birds on a relief-cut bottle in the David Collection, Copenhagen (10/1963: *Glass of the Sultans* 2001, pp. 191–192, no. 96).

Bibliography: Scanlon and Pinder-Wilson 2001, pp. 105–106, no. 43j(c).

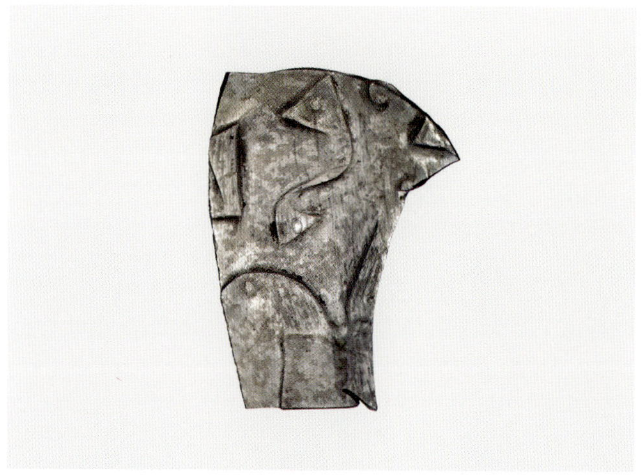

423

424. Fragment with Bird

9th to 10th century. 51.1.121.
H. 6.6 cm, D. (est.) about 6–7 cm.
Colorless or almost colorless; very few bubbles.
Blown; relief-cut.

Fragment of beaker or bottle. Wall (Th. 0.2 cm with decoration, 0.1 cm without decoration) is straight and descends vertically or almost vertically. Decorated in relief with two horizontal ribs, which form upper and lower borders of frieze (W. 4.7 cm). Frieze contains part of standing bird seen in profile, facing left. Its neck is hatched; body is narrow, with breast and belly defined by notched line, and with broader, partly notched line indicating back; wing, extended above body, is indicated by curving notched line that terminates in hatched half-palmette; leg is suggested by cusp in contour of background; foot or perch is indicated by arc-shaped notched line, higher at center than at edges.

Broken on all sides. Pitted and speckled, with small streaks and patches of brown weathering.

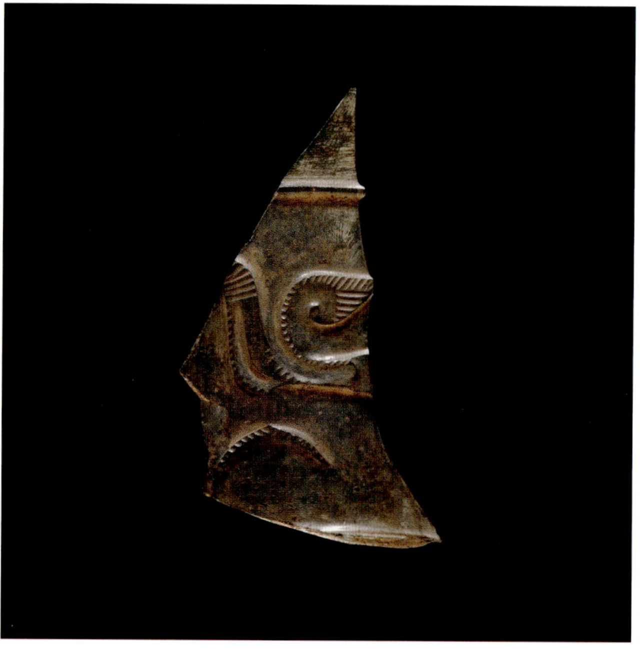

424

Comment: The fragment was acquired, together with **204**, **258**, **262**, **276**, **284**, **292**, **315**, **356**, **421**, **460**, **465**, and **488**, in Cairo, Egypt. The diameter of the fragment is consistent either with a beaker (or goblet) or with a bottle. The treatment of the foot (if that is what it is) recalls the feet on some of the birds on a relief-cut bottle in the David Collection, Copenhagen (10/1963). The illustration in *Glass of the Sultans* 2001 (pp. 191–192, no. 96) does not show the birds in question. However, they appear clearly in Kröger 1999a, p. 222, fig. 6.

425. Fragment with Bird

9th to 10th century. Formerly in the Smith Collection (928). 59.1.448.
H. 5 cm, D. (max., est.) about 6 cm.
Colorless; very few tiny bubbles. Blown; relief-cut.

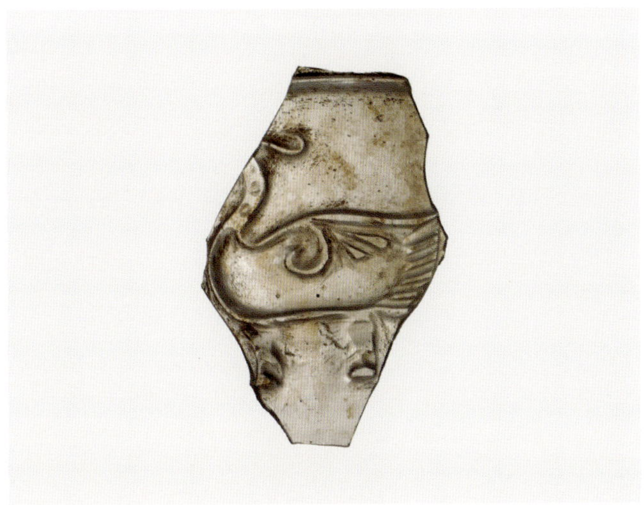

425

Fragment of beaker or goblet with straight, probably tapering wall (Th. 0.2 cm with decoration, less than 0.1 cm without decoration). Decorated in relief with bird seen in profile, facing left. Head is missing, except for oval crest; neck consists of single curved line embellished with two drilled dots; body is elongated, with curved chest and flat, horizontal belly; wing is folded and represented by half-palmette; tail is indicated by stack of five transverse lines; legs are widely separated and short, and they terminate in triangular feet.

Broken on all sides. Dull, with patches of thin grayish weathering.

Comment: With its wing in the form of a half-palmette and its short, widely spaced legs, the bird is reminiscent of the three relief-cut birds on a goblet in the al-Sabah Collection, Dār al-Āthār al-Islāmiyyah, Kuwait National Museum (LNS 84 G: Carboni 2001, p. 88, no. 21), although the latter have notched outlines.

Bibliography: *Verres antiques* 1954, p. 49, no. 298 (part of group); *Glass from the Ancient World* 1957, p. 281, no. 590 (part of group); Oliver, P. 1961, p. 24, fig. 27b.

426. Fragment with Bird

9th to 10th century. Formerly in the Strauss Collection (F32). Bequest of Jerome Strauss. 79.1.310.
Max. Dim. 4.75 cm.
Colorless; few minute bubbles. Blown; relief-cut.

Fragment of vessel, possibly bottle. Wall (Th. 0.25 cm with decoration, 0.1 cm without decoration) descends in convex curve. Decorated in relief with part of bird seen in profile, facing left. Bird's neck is broad and merges with body, both having notched outlines and continuous countersunk interior with row of four drilled dots; leg is short, extends forward, and terminates in two notched lines representing foot with two talons or two feet; wing folded, shown as elaborate half-palmette, with notched stem and hatched leaves. Above wing, curving notched lines, presumably parts of vegetal ornament.

Broken on all sides. Faint incipient weathering, but surface is almost as new.

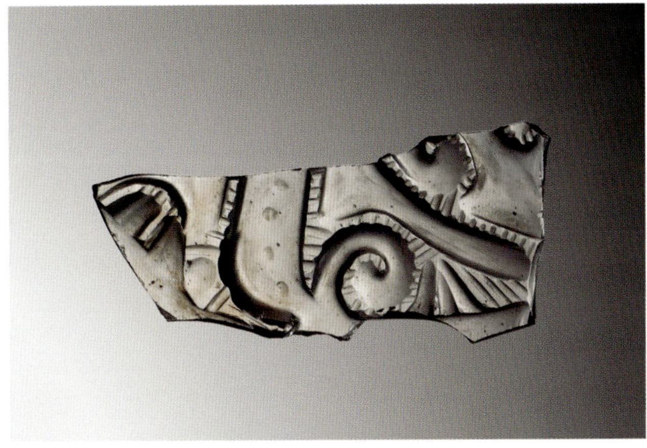

426

Comment: The bird is not immediately obvious. However, the notched lines, the countersunk area between them, and the drilled dots indicate that we are dealing with part of a bird or animal, and the use of a half-palmette to represent a bird's wing is not uncommon: cf. **305**, **425**, and three relief-cut birds on a goblet in the al-Sabah Collection, Dār al-Āthār al-Islāmiyyah, Kuwait National Museum (LNS 84 G: Carboni 2001, p. 88, no. 21).

427. Fragment with Bird

9th to 10th century. Formerly in the Smith Collection. 68.1.59-18.
Max. Dim. 4.5 cm, D. (max., est.) about 6 cm.

Almost colorless, with greenish tinge. Blown; relief-cut.

Fragment from wall of globular(?) vessel (TTh. 0.3 cm), decorated in relief (Th. 0.1 cm) with bird shown in left profile. Bird has small head with pointed beak and eye indicated by countersunk dot; thin, curving neck; plump body with folded wing and short, pointed tail; and two short legs with relatively large feet. Behind bird, small part of another motif. Some outlines are notched, and part of head, upper legs, and other areas are hatched.

Broken on all sides. Dull, with transparent grayish weathering.

COMMENT: The fragment appears to have come from the body of a bottle with a globular body, perhaps not unlike **354**. The bird may have been intended to be a stylized guinea fowl, which has a small head with a pointed beak, a slender neck, a plump body with a short tail, and large feet. Similar birds adorn the upper register of ornament on a relief-cut beaker in the L. A. Mayer Memorial Institute for Islamic Art, Jerusalem (G73-71: Hasson 1979, pp. 15 and 35, no. 23; *Glass of the Sultans* 2001, p. 174, no. 80).

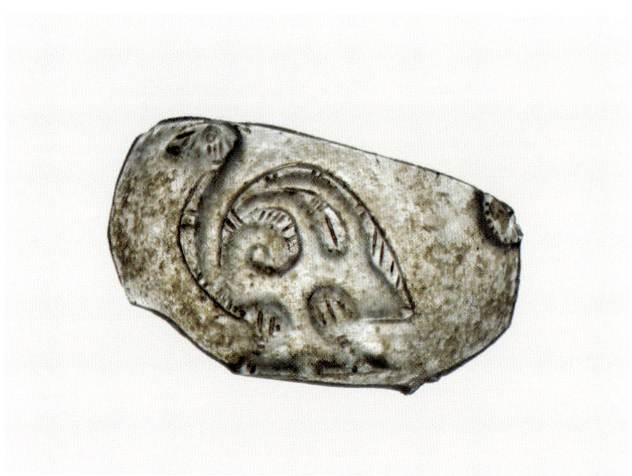

427

428. Fragment with Bird

9th to 10th century. Formerly in the Smith Collection (555-29). 59.1.449.
H. 4.1 cm, D. (est.) about 3.5 cm.
Almost colorless, with yellowish tinge; minute bubbles. Blown; relief-cut.

Fragment of vessel. Neck or wall (Th. 0.3 cm with decoration, less than 0.1 cm without decoration) descends vertically or almost vertically. Decorated with part of frieze containing bird seen in profile, facing right, above horizontal rib. Bird has small head with countersunk eye and pointed beak; neck merges with body, and both have notched outlines; neck has three faint drilled dots; wing is seen folded, represented by curl; one short leg has long, triangular foot.

Broken on all sides. Incipient pale gray weathering.

COMMENT: The small diameter of the fragment suggests that it is part of the neck of a bottle decorated with a frieze that perhaps contained two birds. For a frieze of hares on the neck of a cylindrical bottle, see the bottle with hares and birds in the David Collection, Copenhagen (10/1963: *Glass of the Sultans* 2001, pp. 191–192, no. 96).

BIBLIOGRAPHY: Oliver, P. 1961, p. 24, fig. 27a.

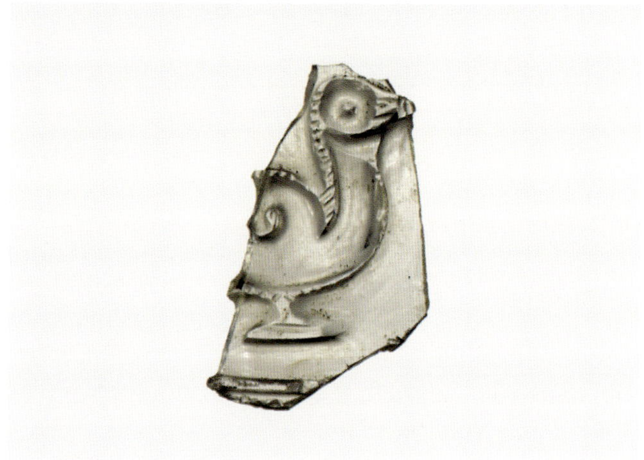

428

429. Fragment with Bird

9th to 10th century. Formerly in the Smith Collection (1089). 59.1.452.
H. (surviving) 3.8 cm, D. (est.) about 6 cm.
Colorless. Blown; relief-cut.

Fragment of small vessel. Wall (TTh. 0.2 cm) straight and perhaps tapering. Decorated in relief (Th. 0.1 cm) with bird shown in profile, facing right. Head is rounded on top, with eye represented by countersunk dot and with short, curved beak; neck has two curved lines, one of which touches eye; breast has single notched outline; wing covert terminates in comma-shaped element.

Broken on all sides. No visible weathering.

COMMENT: The shape of the head and the beak recall the parrot-like birds on **306** and **522** (the Corning Ewer).

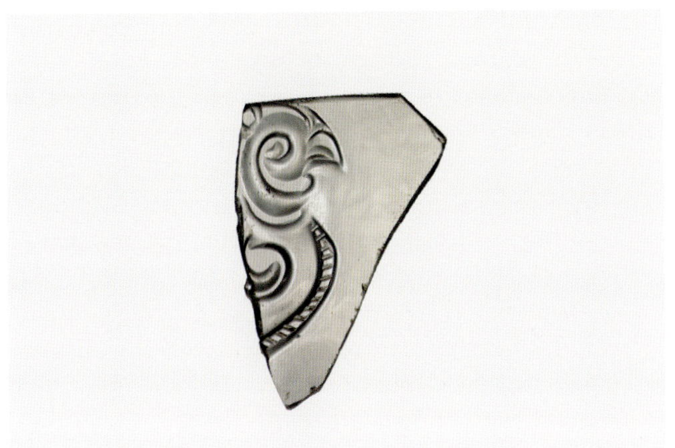

429

430. Fragment with Bird

9th to 10th century. Formerly in the Smith Collection. 68.1.59-65.
H. 3.3 cm, D. (est.) 6–7 cm.
Colorless; virtually bubble-free. Blown; relief-cut.

Fragment of vessel. Wall (Th. 0.1 cm) straight and vertical or almost vertical. Exterior has relief-cut ornament (Th. 0.1 cm): standing bird shown in profile, facing left. Neck is long, curves down to head, and is hatched; breast and underside of body are indicated by notched outline; wing is tear-shaped and folded, with hatched details; tail is upright and wedge-shaped, also with hatched details.

Broken on all sides. Small areas of transparent pale brown weathering.

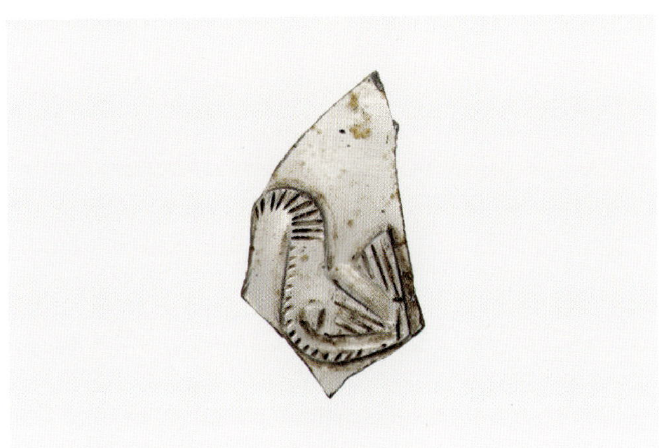

430

Comment: The fragment is part of a small, straight-sided vessel, perhaps a beaker. The relief cutting and the presence of a notched outline show beyond question that the fragment is Islamic and of the ninth or 10th century.

431. Fragment with Bird

9th to 10th century. Formerly in the Smith Collection (932). Gift of Carl Berkowitz and Derek Content. 76.1.232.
Max. Dim. 2.9 cm, D. (est.) perhaps about 7 cm.
Colorless. Blown; slant- and relief-cut.

Fragment from wall (Th. 0.1 cm) of vessel. Decoration (Th. 0.1 cm) includes part of bird, with breast shown by notched outline in relief, legs by slant cuts, and wing by relief-cut hatched motif resembling half-palmette.

Broken on all sides. Virtually unweathered.

Comment: The relative positions of the elements identified above as the breast, wing, and legs support the interpretation of the element as a bird, and the "wing" invites comparison with the wings of birds on a relief-cut bottle in the David Collection, Copenhagen (10/1963: *Glass of the Sultans* 2001, pp. 191–192, no. 96). Nevertheless, the identity of the motif as a bird is less than certain.

Bibliography: *Verres antiques* 1954, p. 49, no. 298 (part of group).

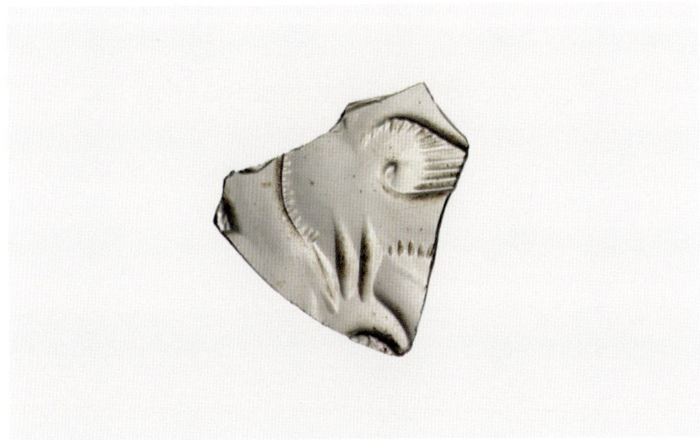

431

432. Fragment with Bird

9th to 10th century. Formerly in the Smith Collection. 68.1.59-83.
Max. Dim. 2 cm.
Colorless. Blown; relief-cut.

Fragment from wall of vessel (Th. 0.1 cm) with convex profile and relief-cut ornament (Th. 0.1 cm) on exterior. Ornament consists of head and neck of bird shown in profile, facing left. Head has small countersunk boss to represent eye and short, hooked

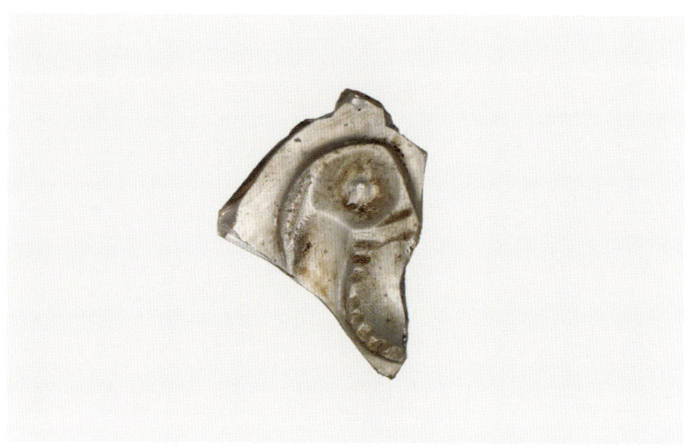

432

beak, below which neck has notched outline. Beak and top of neck are hatched.

Broken on all sides. Dull, with transparent pale grayish weathering.

433. Fragment with Bird(?)

9th to 10th century. Formerly in the Smith Collection (917). 59.1.453.
Max. Dim. 4.7 cm.
Colorless. Blown or cast; relief-cut.

Fragment from floor of plate or plaque (TTh. 0.5 cm) decorated in prominent relief (Th. 0.35 cm). Decoration may show bird, standing in right profile, with small head, long and pointed beak, folded wing, and large fanlike tail. Background between head and tail is filled with small printies.

Broken on all sides. Decorated surface is dull and pitted, with light brownish weathering; plain surface has little weathering.

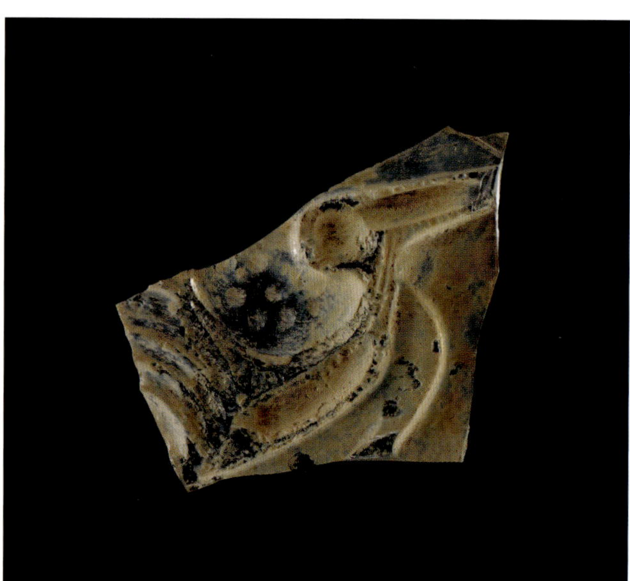

433

Comment: The plain surface is completely flat: hence the identification of the fragment as part of the floor of a plate or plaque. The identity of the ornament is more difficult, and it is described as a bird with no great confidence. Indeed, the "head" lacks the countersunk dot that almost always indicates the eye of a relief-cut bird or animal, and the occurrence of printies in the background is very unusual.

Bibliography: *Verres antiques* 1954, p. 49, no. 298 (part of group); *Glass from the Ancient World* 1957, p. 281, no. 590 (part of group).

434. Fragment with Bird(?)

9th to 10th century. Formerly in the Smith Collection (931). Gift of Carl Berkowitz and Derek Content. 76.1.287.
H. (surviving) 3.8 cm, D. (est.) about 5 cm.
Colorless. Blown; relief-cut.

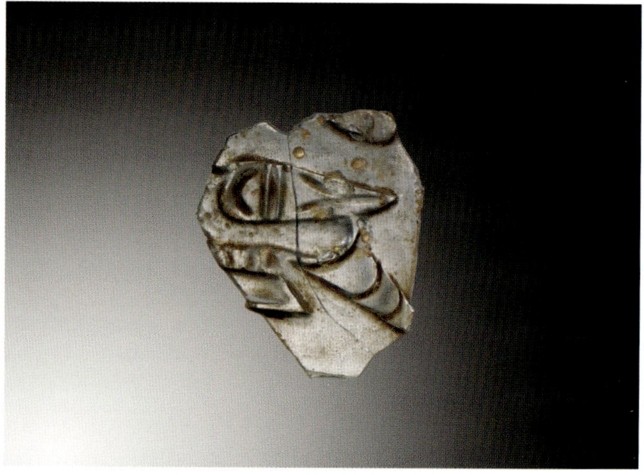

434

Fragment probably from neck or wall of bottle. Side (TTh. 0.3 cm) is straight and either vertical or nearly vertical. Decorated in relief with part of bird or birdlike creature with body shown in outline, which is partly notched; folded wing with semicircular covert and pointed tip; long, tapering tail; and short leg indicated by single line. Details of wing are linear-cut, and tail extends in crescent-shaped stages.

Broken on all sides. Some brownish weathering, especially in cuts.

Comment: The shape of the body and the disproportionately long tail suggest that the subject may not be a bird but some mythical, perhaps composite creature (cf. **326**). The treatment of the tail recalls the tail of the fantastic animal and the border of the medallion on a slant- and relief-cut bowl in the al-Sabah

Collection, Dār al-Āthār al-Islāmiyyah, Kuwait National Museum (LNS 113 KG: Carboni 2001, p. 85, no. 19; *Glass of the Sultans* 2001, pp. 174–175, no. 81).

435. Fragment with Bird(?)

9th to 10th century. Formerly in the Smith Collection. 68.1.59-79.
Max. Dim. 3.3 cm.
Colorless; very few minute bubbles. Blown; relief-cut.

Fragment of vessel. Wall (Th. 0.1 cm) is straight and decorated in relief (Th. 0.1 cm) with neck of bird (?) shown in profile, facing left. Neck has notched outlines and transverse hatching at top; neck is wider at bottom than at top, and begins to expand at front in order to merge with breast. Small raised area behind neck may be edge of wing.

Broken on all sides. Slightly dull, with incipient weathering.

Comment: There is little doubt that the fragment shows the neck of an animal or a bird; horizontal or transverse hatching is a common feature at the top of the necks of animals and birds on ninth- to 10th-century relief-cut vessels (cf. *Glass of the Sultans* 2001, p. 176, no. 82; pp. 179–180, no. 85; and pp. 191–192, no. 96). The element behind the creature's neck is most easily explained as a wing: hence the opinion that it may have been a bird.

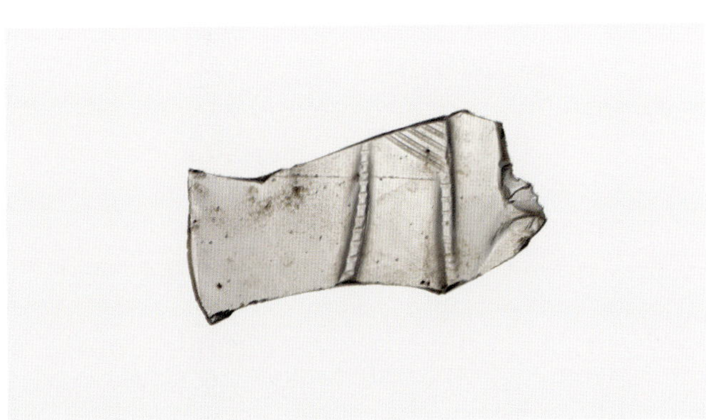

435

436. Fragment with Bird(?)

9th to 10th century. Formerly in the Smith Collection. 68.1.59-85.
Max. Dim. 1.9 cm.
Colorless. Blown; relief-cut.

Fragment from wall (TTh. 0.2 cm) of vessel with relief decoration (Th. 0.1 cm). Very little ornament survives, but it may consist of rounded outline of back of bird's head and eye represented by countersunk dot.

Broken on all sides. Traces of brownish weathering.

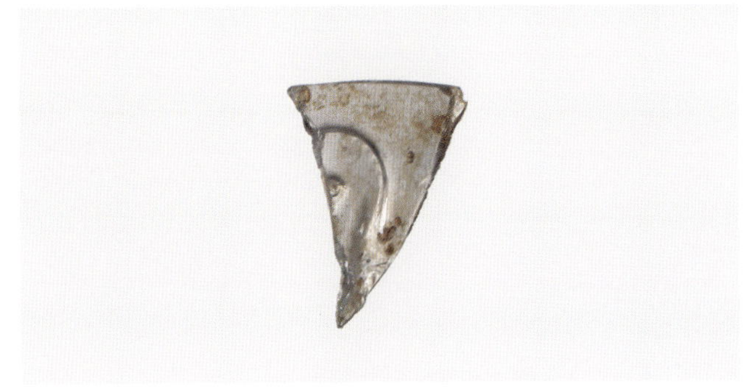

436

437. Fragment with Palmette and Half-Palmette

9th to 10th century. Formerly in the Smith Collection. 59.1.455.
Max. Dim. 4.1 cm, D. (est.) about 8 cm.
Colorless; small bubbles. Blown; relief-cut.

Fragment of beaker or bottle. Wall (Th. up to 0.4 cm with decoration, 0.1–0.25 cm without decoration) straight and perhaps tapering, thickening at bottom. Decorated in relief with palmette-like motif, which points upward and has notched outlines, lower ends terminating in volutes, and small horizontal cut at center; palmette was apparently flanked by two similar motifs with notched lines and, surviving only on right, half-palmette.

Broken on all sides. Somewhat dull, with patches of transparent grayish weathering and few iridescent spots.

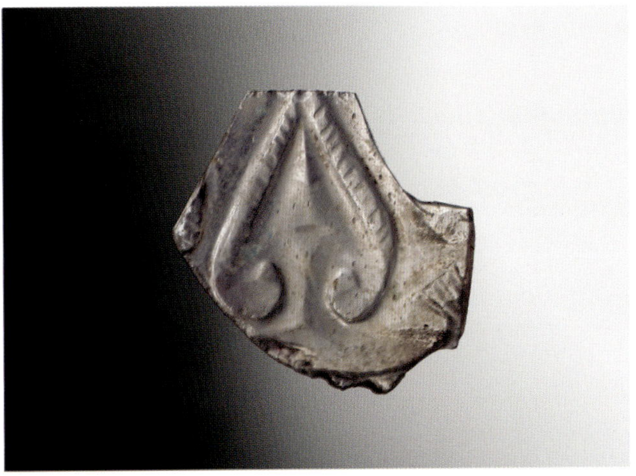

437

Comment: The marked thickening at the bottom of the fragment may be the edge of a horizontal rib or of the foot. The simple palmette-like motif is similar to four downward-pointing palmettes on a small relief-cut bottle, decorated with birds, in The Toledo Museum of Art (1983.79: *Glass of the Sultans* 2001, pp. 179–180, no. 85), and on a bottle in the Benaki Museum, Athens (Clairmont 1977, pp. 97–98, no. 323).

438. Fragment with Palmette

9th to 10th century. Formerly in the Smith Collection (555-18). Gift of Carl Berkowitz and Derek Content. 76.1.204.
H. (surviving) 3.4 cm, D. about 5 cm.
Colorless. Blown; relief-cut.

Fragment of beaker or bottle. Wall (Th. 0.1 cm) is almost straight. Decorated in relief (Th. 0.2 cm) with palmette that grows out of two curved stems and has, springing from its top, another motif. Palmette has pair of volutes and circular depression at center; stems are notched. Fragment also has small part of unidentified curvilinear motif.

Broken on all sides. Pristine, with no obvious weathering.

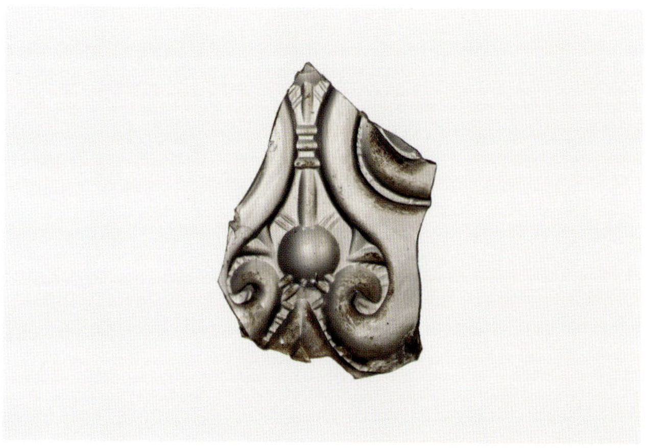

438

439. Fragment with Palmette

9th to 10th century. Formerly in the Smith Collection. 68.1.59-76.
H. 3.2 cm, D. (est.) about 7 cm.
Colorless; few very small bubbles. Blown; relief-cut.

Fragment. Wall straight and vertical or almost vertical. Outside is decorated in relief: tear-shaped element in and above V-shaped element, whose sides curve up and out and terminate in volutes; short

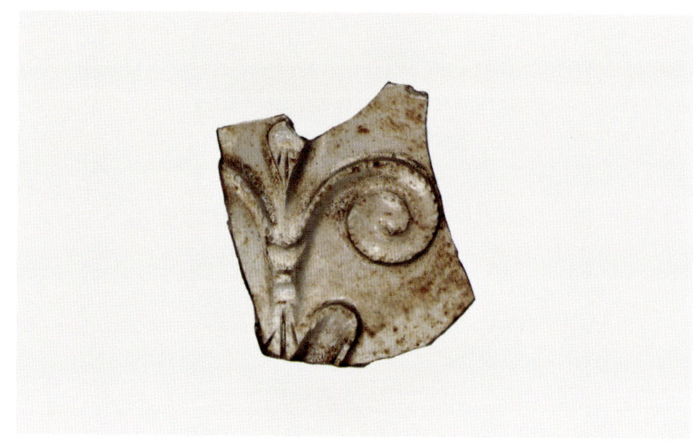

439

stem projects down from V and terminates in simple, downward-pointing palmette; V-shaped element, volutes, and edges of palmette are notched; tear-shaped motif and part of palmette are hatched.

Broken on all sides. Dull, with transparent pale gray and light brown weathering.

Comment: The description assumes that the tear-shaped motif is pointed at the bottom. This, however, is not at all certain, and the ornament could equally well have the palmette at the top and the tear at the bottom (the Corning Ewer [**522**] has two tear-shaped motifs; one is pointed at the top, and the other is pointed at the bottom). Treelike designs that include palmettes and/or volutes are not uncommon on relief-cut vessels; the two motifs are found together, for example, on the base of the Falcon and Ibex Bowl (**296**).

440. Fragment with Palmette

9th to 10th century. Formerly in the Smith Collection. 68.1.59-53.
Max. Dim. 2.9 cm.
Colorless or almost colorless. Blown; linear- and relief-cut.

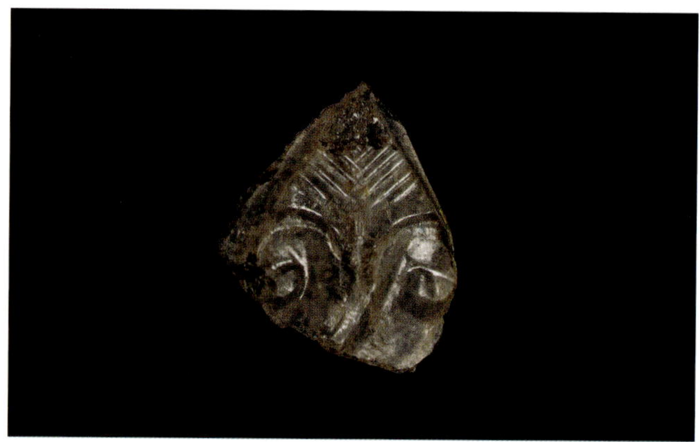

440

Fragment from wall or base of vessel (TTh. 0.3 cm). Decorated in relief (Th. 0.1 cm) with palmette, which is hatched with linear-cut herringbone pattern.

Broken on all sides. Pitted, with yellowish weathering.

441. Fragment with Palmette

9th to 10th century. Formerly in the Smith Collection. 68.1.59-63.
Max. Dim. 2.8 cm, D. (est.) about 7 cm.
Colorless; few very small bubbles. Blown; relief-cut.

Fragment of vessel. Wall (Th. 0.2 cm) apparently straight and possibly vertical. Exterior has decoration in relief (Th. 0.2 cm): part of palmette with notched outlines; lower end terminates in volutes; interior is cut in shallow facets.

Broken on all sides. Patches of transparent light brown weathering.

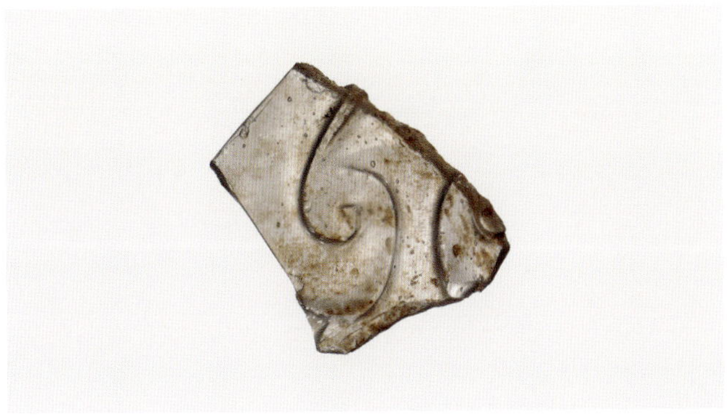

441

Comment: The simple palmette with notched outlines is a frequent component of ninth- to 10th-century relief-cut glass, and so, despite its size, the identity of the fragment is certain. It appears to have come from a vertical part of the vessel, probably a bottle. Given its estimated diameter (about seven centimeters), presumably it came from the body rather than from an exceptionally wide neck.

442. Fragment with Palmette

9th to 10th century. Formerly in the Smith Collection. 68.1.59-68.
Max. Dim. 2.4 cm.
Colorless. Blown; relief-cut.

Fragment from wall (Th. 0.15–0.2 cm) of vessel decorated in relief (Th. 0.1 cm) with palmette, which has four V-shaped veins.

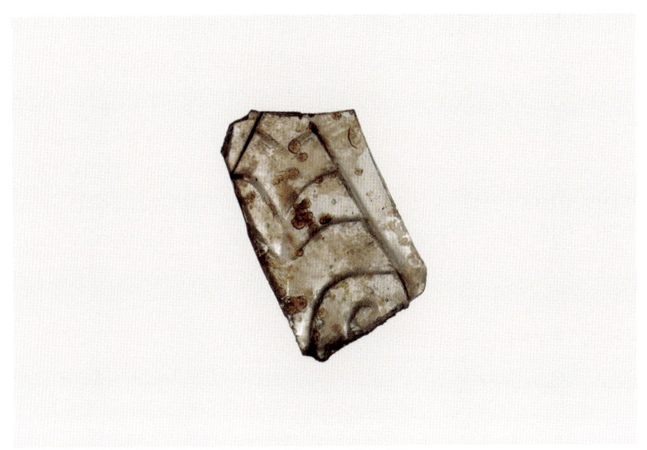

442

Broken on all sides. Patches of light brown to pinkish gray weathering.

443. Fragment with Palmette

9th to 10th century. Formerly in the Smith Collection. 68.1.59-87.
Max. Dim. 2 cm.
Colorless. Blown; relief-cut.

Fragment from wall (Th. 0.2 cm) of vessel with relief-cut decoration (Th. 0.1 cm) on outside: small part of palmette. If so, and if it points upward, surviving ornament consists of lower left side, which has parts of two petals and straight edge terminating in volute.

Broken on all sides. Patches of transparent pale brown weathering.

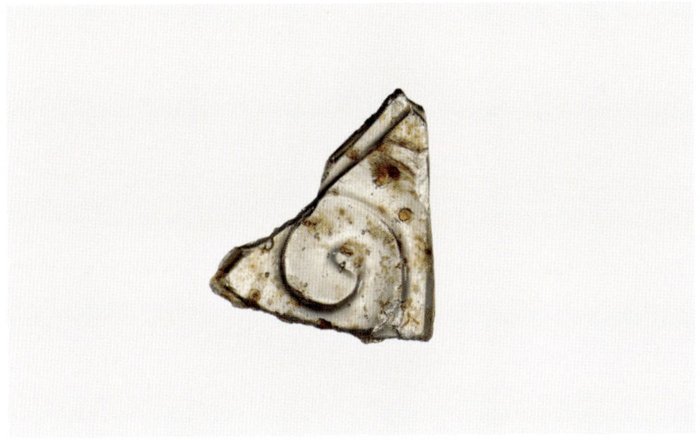

443

Comment: The motif is a triangular palmette, similar in shape to the palmette on the top of the "tree" on the underside of the Falcon and Ibex Bowl (**296**). Despite its size, the fragment is identified with confidence as Islamic relief-cut glass of the ninth or 10th century.

444. Fragment with Half-Palmettes, Vegetal Scroll, and Inscription

10th century. Formerly in the Smith Collection (555-21). Gift of Carl Berkowitz and Derek Content. 76.1.257.
H. (surviving) 5 cm, D. (max., est.) about 7 cm.
Almost colorless, with yellowish tinge. Blown; relief-cut.

Fragment of vessel with straight, vertical or tapering wall (TTh. 0.2 cm) decorated in relief (Th. 0.1 cm). Decoration consists of parts of two horizontal elements, one above the other: (above) elaborate vegetal scroll extending from left to right with, on left, downward-pointing tendril that terminates in sketchy half-palmette and, on right, upward-pointing tendril that terminates in well-formed half-palmette; (below) small part of foliated Kufic inscription, part of which is embellished with half-palmette. Stem, tendrils, and letters are notched; half-palmettes are embellished with pairs of short, incised lines.

Two fragments, which join. Broken on all sides. Patches of pale to light brownish weathering.

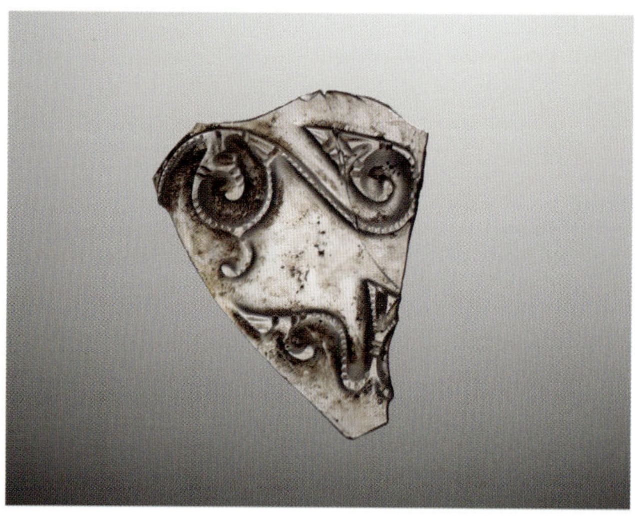

444

Comment: The size and shape of the fragment suggest that it is from the wall of a bottle or, more probably, a beaker. The glass is remarkably thin: scarcely 0.1 centimeter in places where the background has been removed. The foliated character of the inscription suggests that the object was made in the 10th century.

445. Fragment with Half-Palmettes

9th to 10th century. Formerly in the Smith Collection. 68.1.59-14.
Max. Dim. 6 cm.
Colorless; very small bubbles. Blown; relief-cut.

Fragment of vessel. Wall (Th. 0.15 cm) splays, then curves out and down. Outside decorated in relief (Th. 0.2 cm): parts of two half-palmettes, side by side. Each half-palmette had two stems that curved up, out, over, and down, terminating in curling leaf and at least one or, probably, two triangular or kidney-shaped leaves; between stems, narrow tear-shaped motif, which is rounded at top and pointed at bottom.

Broken on all sides. Patches of transparent pale gray weathering.

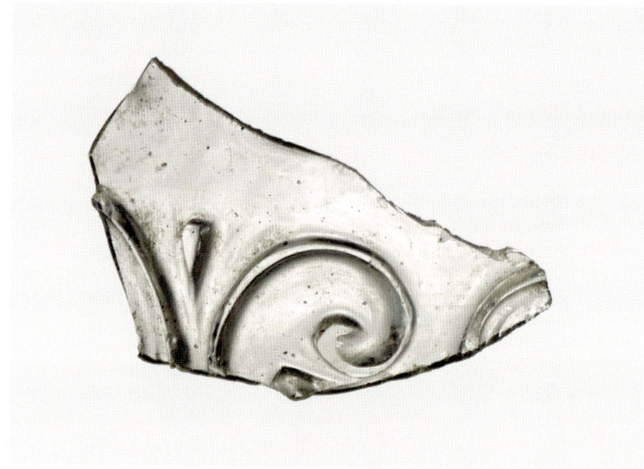

445

Comment: The profile suggests that the fragment is part of a ewer roughly similar to the Corning Ewer (**522**). The identification of the ornament as two half-palmettes is based on the assumptions that (1) the tear marks the center of a symmetrical motif and (2) the second motif was identical to the first (the small surviving part of the second motif is a mirror image of part of the first motif).

446. Fragment with Half-Palmettes

9th to 10th century. Formerly in the Smith Collection. 68.1.59-50.
Max. Dim. 4.2 cm, D. (est.) about 10 cm.
Colorless or almost colorless. Blown; relief-cut.

Fragment of vessel with convex profile. Wall (Th. 0.1 cm) is decorated in relief (Th. 0.1 cm) on outside: upper part of "tree" with pair of half-palmettes at top, above triangular or tear-shaped element inside kite-shaped motif with raised outlines, above stem, which is wider near bottom than at top; on either side of "tree," parts of curvilinear motifs. Outlines of kite are

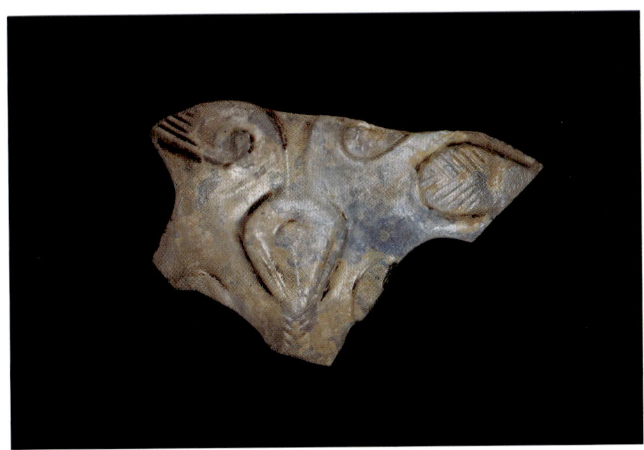

446

lightly notched, and other motifs are hatched, in some cases in herringbone pattern.

Broken on all sides. Remains of light brown, slightly iridescent weathering.

Comment: The fragment is convex in both the vertical and the horizontal planes, and it is likely, therefore, that it came from a globular or hemispherical vessel such as a bottle or a bowl. The treelike motif is reminiscent of the "trees" on **490** and a bottle in the David Collection, Copenhagen (10/1963: *Glass of the Sultans* 2001, pp. 191–192, no. 96). The bottle in the David Collection also provides a parallel for hatching in a herringbone pattern.

447. Fragment with Half-Palmette

9th to 10th century. Formerly in the collection of George McKearin. Gift of Betty Gruene Speir. 73.1.24.
H. 4.7 cm, W. 4.4 cm, D. (max., est.) about 11 cm.
Almost colorless, with bluish green tinge; very small bubbles. Blown; relief-cut.

Fragment of vessel with convex profile. Wall (Th. 0.2 cm) has relief-cut decoration (Th. 0.35 cm) on outside: part of frieze with horizontal line, presumably continuous, forming upper or lower border. If line is upper border, fragment has broad half-palmette, each half with three leaves, which is inverted, above similar, perhaps identical motif, which is upright.

Broken on all sides. Patches of transparent grayish brown weathering.

Comment: The fragment is part of a vessel with a markedly convex wall: a bottle (cf. **354**), a ewer (cf. **522**), or a bowl (cf., very roughly, *Glass of the Sultans* 2001, pp. 178–179, no. 84). It is not clear, however, whether it came from the top or the bottom of the frieze. If the estimated diameter of the vessel is approximately correct, the frieze could have contained continuous bands of half-palmettes, with five in each band.

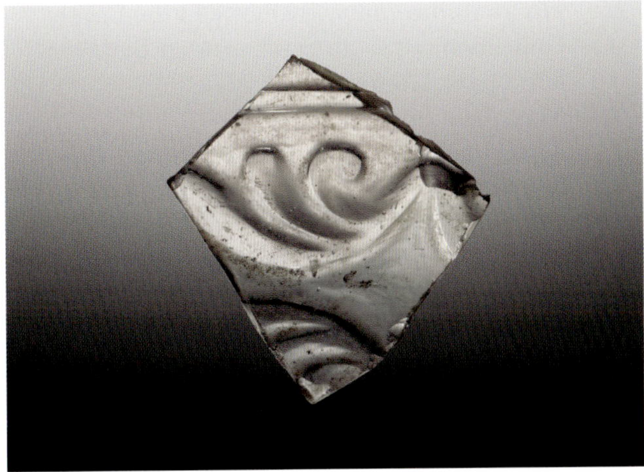

447

448. Fragment with Half-Palmette

9th to 10th century. Formerly in the Smith Collection (555-4). Gift of Carl Berkowitz and Derek Content. 76.1.218.
Max. Dim. 4.6 cm.
Almost colorless, with greenish tinge. Blown; relief-cut.

Fragment from wall of vessel (Th. 0.1–0.2 cm), decorated on outside with parts of four elements: curving line, straight line terminating in half-palmette, straight line from which spring two opposed volutes, and curving line. All lines are notched, and half-palmette is hatched.

Broken on all sides. Dull, with spots of light brown weathering.

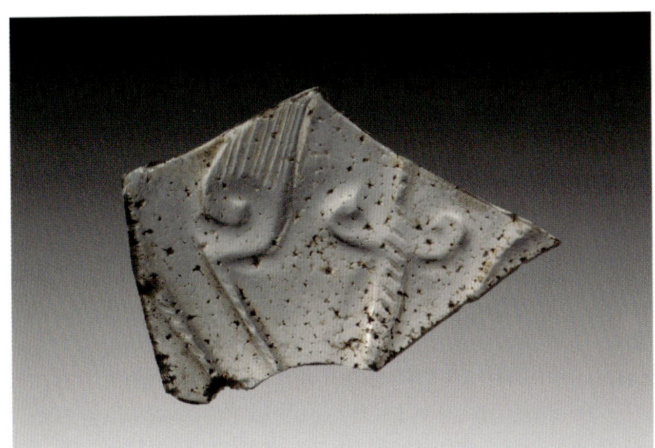

448

465. Fragment with Inscription(?) and Vegetal Scroll

9th to 10th century. 51.1.130.
H. 4.9 cm, D. (max., est.) about 8 cm.
Almost colorless, with yellowish green tinge; minute bubbles. Blown; relief-cut.

Fragment of beaker or bottle. Lower wall (Th. 0.15–0.4 cm with decoration, 0.1–0.4 cm without decoration) straight and probably tapering, and considerably thicker at bottom than at top. Decorated in relief (from top to bottom): (1) small part of inscription(?) consisting of straight plain and notched lines, terminating at right in hatched triangle; (2) scroll, apparently with coiled stems that point alternately up and down, and terminate in hatched leaves or buds; and (3) horizontal rib.

Broken on all sides. Dull, with patches of transparent yellowish weathering and slight iridescence.

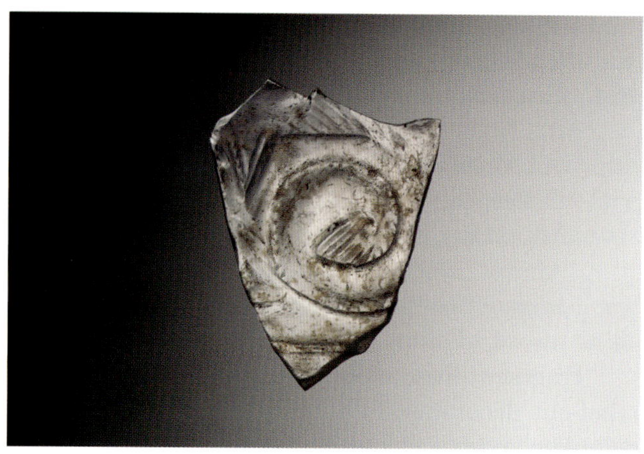

465

COMMENT: The fragment is part of the lower wall of a beaker or bottle, and to judge from the sudden increase in thickness in the vicinity of the rib, the bottom was very close to the base of the vessel. Evidently the object was decorated with a frieze bordered by horizontal ribs and containing vegetal ornament and perhaps also a Kufic inscription.

466. Fragment with Inscription(?)

9th to 10th century. Formerly in the Smith Collection (1263-b). Gift of Carl Berkowitz and Derek Content. 76.1.251.
Max. Dim. 3.9 cm, D. (est., at rib) about 9 cm.
Colorless; minute bubbles. Blown; relief-cut.

Fragment, probably from shoulder of bottle, which is 0.2 cm thick at top and 0.1 cm thick at bottom. Decorated in relief (Th. 0.15 cm) on outside: horizontal, presumably continuous rib; above this, small part of Kufic inscription (?); below, and roughly parallel to rib, part of stemlike motif, which divides at one end and has trace of second motif beneath it. Stem, but not other elements, is notched.

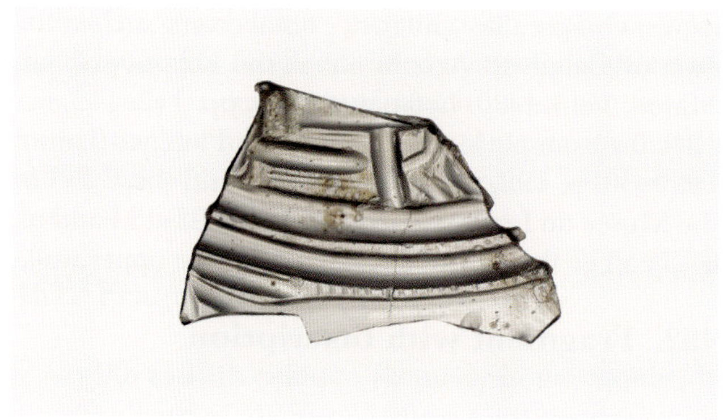

466

Broken on all sides. Small patches of abrasion and pale brownish weathering.

COMMENT: The fragment is from the shoulder of a ewer or, more probably, a bottle with a more or less globular body. If this is so, the rib is the upper border of a broad band of ornament covering most of the wall, and the inscription(?) surrounded the neck.

467. Fragments

9th to 10th century. Formerly in the Smith Collection (1222-8). Gift of Carl Berkowitz and Derek Content. 76.1.292.
Max. Dim. (1) 5 cm, (2) 4.1 cm, D. (base, est.) about 7 cm.
Almost colorless, with yellowish tinge. Blown; slant- and relief-cut.

Two fragments from lower wall (TTh. 0.25–0.4 cm) and edge of base (Th. 0.55 cm) of vessel. Wall tapers, with slightly convex profile and small ridge at junction with base, which is flat. On lower wall, slant- and relief-cut decoration. Fragment 1 has pair of contiguous motifs with raised outlines; each is semicircular at bottom and contains slant-cut tear-shaped element with circular depression at center. Fragment 2 has part of one such motif.

Both fragments broken on all sides (see below). Dull, with patches of pale gray weathering.

COMMENT: The fragments do not join. In both cases, one edge is smooth and has no weathering, presumably the result of sawing to remove samples for analysis.

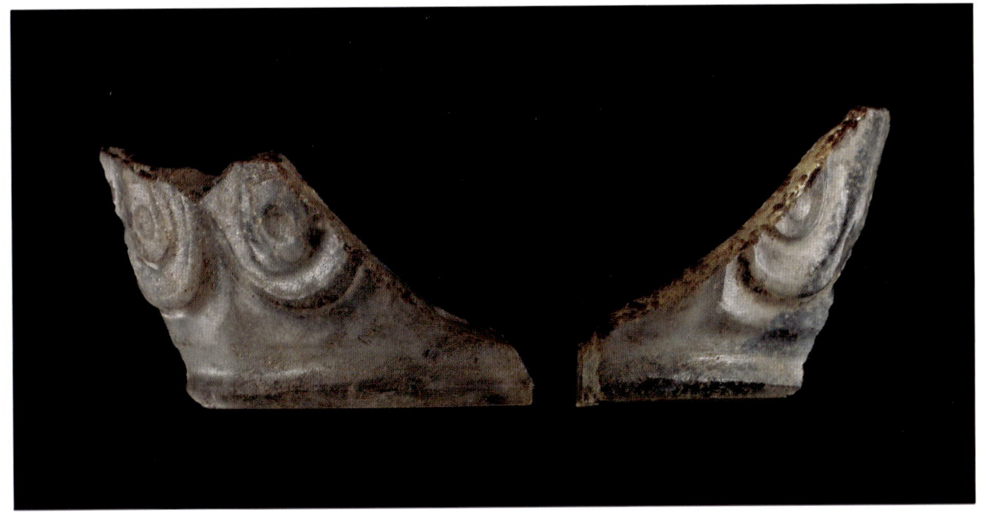

467

468. Fragment

Probably about 11th century. Formerly in the Smith Collection. 59.1.567-15.
Max. Dim. 5 cm, H. (surviving) 1.4 cm, D. (base, est.) about 11 cm.
Colorless; very small bubbles. Blown; linear- and relief-cut.

Fragment. Lower wall straight and tapering, rounded at bottom; base flat. Decorated near bottom of wall and on underside of base. On wall: one horizontal rib; on base: two concentric grooves (D. about 10 cm and 9.5 cm).

Broken on all sides. Dull and lightly pitted. Evidently cleaned, since no weathering survives.

Comment: The profile and the horizontal rib suggest that the fragment came from a bottle with a panel of relief-cut ornament on the wall, perhaps similar in shape to the bottle with relief-cut ornament in the David Collection, Copenhagen (10/1963: *Glass of the Sultans* 2001, pp. 191–192, no. 96).

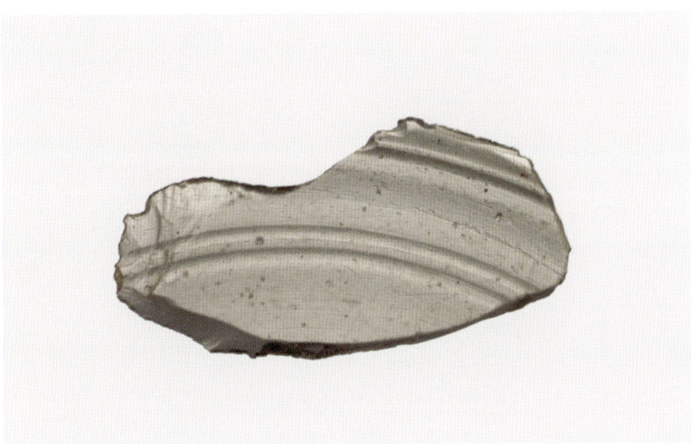

468

469. Fragment

Probably 9th to 10th century (but see below). Formerly in the Smith Collection (1221-3). 59.1.459.
Max. Dim. 4.9 cm, H. (surviving) 1.7 cm, D. (est.) about 9 cm.
Almost colorless, with yellowish green tinge; very small bubbles. Blown; relief-cut.

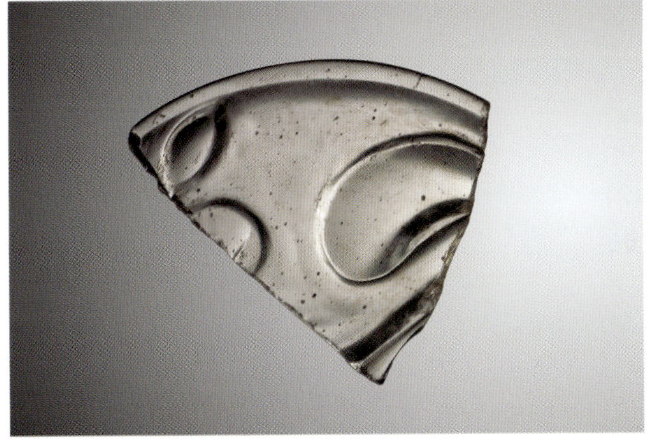

469

Fragment of shallow bowl or cover (description assumes bowl), including approximately one-fifth of rim. Rim plain, with rounded outer edge and narrow bevel on inside; wall (Th. 0.3 cm at top and 0.4 cm at bottom) curves down and in, and is decorated in relief (Th. 0.2 cm) on outside. Decoration consists of single stemlike line and three curvilinear flowerlike motifs, each of which has raised edge and hollow center; largest motif is shaped like kidney, smallest is pointed oval, and third, incomplete motif is indeterminate.

Surface is almost as new, except for traces of transparent pale grayish weathering.

COMMENT: Since it entered the Museum (and possibly before this), the fragment has been taken to be Islamic and of the eighth, ninth, or 10th century. The quality of the glass is consistent with this view, but it is not conclusive. A ninth- to 10th-century date is certainly possible, although the combination of raised edges and hollow interiors and the kidney-shaped motif are difficult to parallel among early Islamic cut glasses. Similar motifs, also with raised edges and hollow interiors, are found on a Roman relief-cut vessel from Cologne (RGM Glas 967: *Glass of the Caesars* 1987, p. 191, no. 101, where it was assigned to the second half of the first century). We should not exclude the possibility, therefore, that **469** is pre-Islamic.

470. Fragment

9th to 10th century. Found during excavations at Fusṭāṭ (Old Cairo), Egypt (68.11.1). Gift of the American Research Center in Egypt. 69.1.65b.
H. (surviving) 4.8 cm, D. (rib, est.) about 5.5 cm.
Colorless. Blown; relief-cut.

Fragment from wall of vessel. Wall (TTh. 0.2 cm) tapers at top, then curves down and in. Decorated in relief (Th. 0.1 cm) with, at top, small part of frieze with two fragmentary elements: (1) perhaps part of lower leg and hatched foot and (2) indeterminate; below them, single horizontal rib and, below rib, part of arcade consisting of narrow vertical line, which is notched, and three segmental arches.

Broken on all sides. Dull, with remains of weathering; slight iridescence.

COMMENT: The object was found during excavations directed by Prof. George T. Scanlon. It was discovered, together with **380**, **423**, **456**, and other fragments, among the contents of a pit that the excavator dated to the ninth or 10th century.

See **380**, **423**, and **456**. Scanlon and Pinder-Wilson 2001 (pp. 105–106, no. 43j) reported that all four fragments are of "uniform metal and curvature and so possibly come from a single vessel." If **380** and **470** are parts of the same vessel, it would have been decorated with a frieze containing an inscription above a row of ornament, which may have contained animals, above a continuous arcade. This is not impossible, but it is difficult to imagine **423** and **456** as parts of the same object.

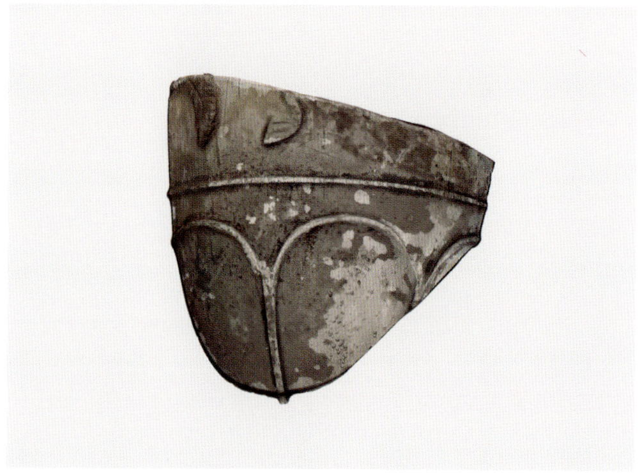

470

BIBLIOGRAPHY: Scanlon and Pinder-Wilson 2001, pp. 105–106, no. 43j(b).

471. Fragment

Probably 9th to 10th century. Formerly in the Smith Collection. 68.1.59-34.
Max. Dim. 4.7 cm.
Almost colorless, with yellowish tinge. Blown; relief-cut.

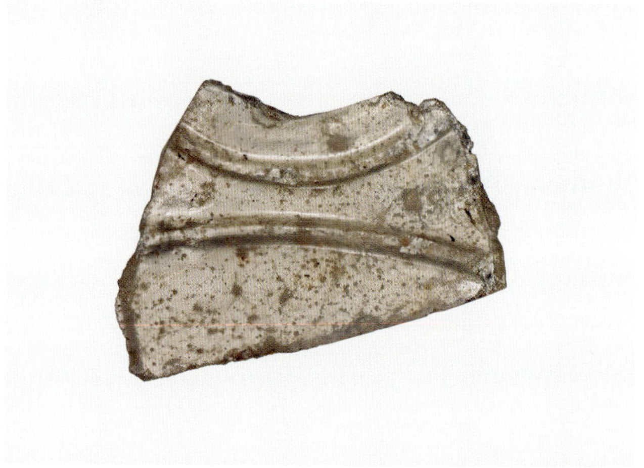

471

Fragment from wall (TTh. 0.5 cm) of vessel decorated in relief (Th. 0.15 cm). Decoration consists of one almost straight line, one curved line, and trace of third, apparently curved line. Curved line is lightly notched.

Broken on all sides. Dull and pitted, with patches of transparent pale brown weathering.

472. Fragment

9th to 10th century. Formerly in the Smith Collection (1221-20). Gift of Carl Berkowitz and Derek Content. 76.1.291.

Max. Dim. 4.5 cm, D. (est.) about 6 cm (but see below).
Almost colorless, with yellowish tinge. Blown; relief-cut.

Fragment from wall of vessel (TTh. 2.5 cm), possibly cylindrical, with linear decoration in relief (Th. 0.1 cm). Motifs include stem, from which springs simple half-palmette with volute at lower extremity; and bent element, which curls and expands slightly at end, resembling limb or tail of animal. Outline of half-palmette and one other line are notched.

Broken on all sides. Some transparent grayish weathering.

Comment: Both the form of the object and the identity of the ornament are uncertain. The curvature suggests that the fragment may be part of a cylindrical vessel (D. about 6 cm) with a slightly convex profile, in which case the half-palmette was horizontal and the limb- or taillike element was vertical. In any case, it is impossible to determine the nature of the decoration that included a half-palmette, a "limb," and one other raised element.

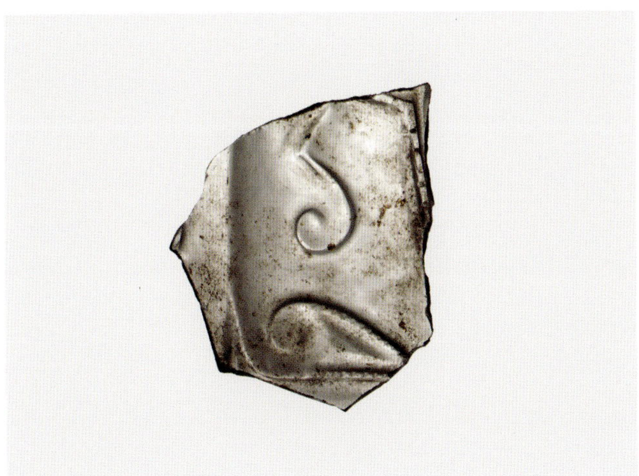

472

473. Fragment

About 10th century. Formerly in the Smith Collection (936). Gift of Carl Berkowitz and Derek Content. 76.1.290.
Max. Dim. 4 cm.
Colorless, with few very small bubbles. Blown; relief-cut.

Fragment from wall (TTh. 0.25 cm) of vessel decorated in relief (Th. 0.1 cm). Decoration consists of small part of complex design of indeterminate character, composed of curving lines (W. 0.25–0.3 cm) with median grooves punctuated by pairs of perpendicular cuts; one line expands into hatched triangular area and branches.

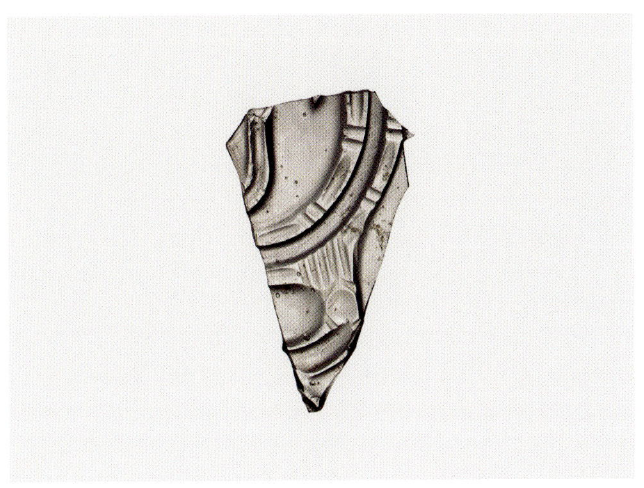

473

Broken on all sides. Virtually without weathering.

Comment: The glass is completely colorless, and were it not for the bubbles, it would closely resemble rock crystal. The decoration of the relief-cut lines with median grooves and perpendicular cuts is very unusual.

Bibliography: *Verres antiques* 1954, p. 49, no. 298 (part of group); *Glass from the Ancient World* 1957, p. 281, no. 590 (part of group).

474. Fragment

9th to 10th century. Formerly in the Smith Collection. 68.1.59-38.
H. 3.9 cm, D. (rib, est.) about 7 cm.
Almost colorless, with yellowish tinge; almost bubble-free. Blown; relief-cut.

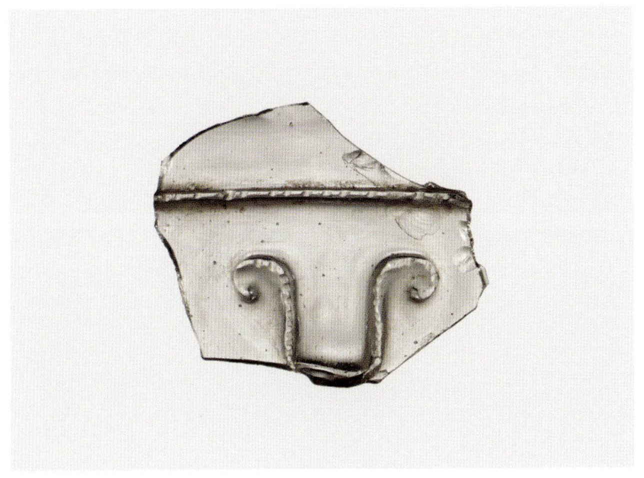

474

Fragment from wall of beaker or bowl. Wall (Th. 0.1–0.15 cm) descends almost vertically, then curves down and in. Relief-cut decoration (Th. 0.2 cm) consists of horizontal rib, below which is one complete U-shaped linear motif, but with ends of uprights curling out, down, and in. Both rib and U-shaped element are notched.

Broken on all sides. Virtually unweathered.

Comment: The fragment may have come from the lower wall of a beaker similar to the relief-cut beaker in the L. A. Mayer Memorial Institute for Islamic Art, Jerusalem (G73-71: *Glass of the Sultans* 2001, p. 174, no. 80), or from the midsection of a roughly hemispherical bowl. The U-shaped motif recalls a relief-cut bowl in The British Museum, London, which has U-shaped elements that turn outward at the top and terminate in half-palmettes (OA 1966.4-18.1: "Recent Important Acquisitions," *JGS*, v. 9, 1967, p. 137, no. 19; *Masterpieces of Glass* 1968, pp. 109–110, no. 146, "found in Persia"; Pinder-Wilson 1991, 1999, and 2004, p. 118, fig. 146).

475. Fragment

9th to 10th century. Formerly in the Smith Collection. 68.1.59-30.
Max. Dim. 3.8 cm, D. (rim, est.) about 11 cm.
Almost colorless, with greenish yellow tinge; very few minute bubbles. Blown; relief-cut.

Fragment of cup or bowl, including small part of rim. Rim plain, with rounded lip; wall straight and almost vertical. Outside has horizontal rib in prominent relief, top of which is 2.1 cm below lip; inside of rim and top of wall have slight bevel, which extends 1.7 cm below lip.

Surfaces are virtually as new.

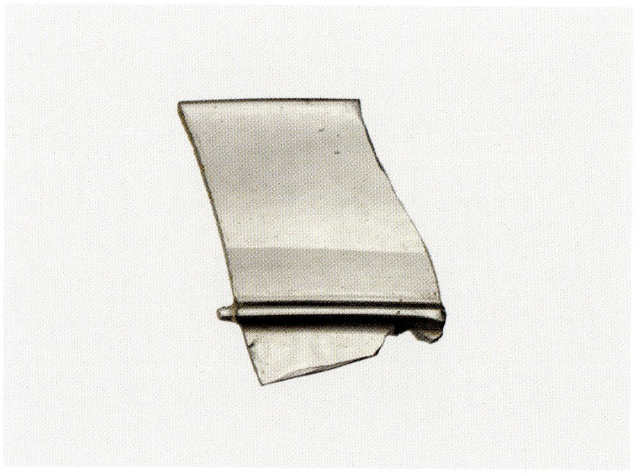

475

Comment: So little of the rim survives that the estimated diameter may be inaccurate (perhaps the vessel was somewhat, but not very much, smaller). The bevel on the inside of the rim is not uncommon on early Islamic cut glass, and a date in the ninth or 10th century is suggested with confidence.

476. Fragment

9th to 10th century. Formerly in the Smith Collection. 68.1.59-80.
Max. Dim. 3.3 cm, D. (est.) about 6 cm.
Almost colorless, with greenish tinge; few minute bubbles. Blown; relief-cut.

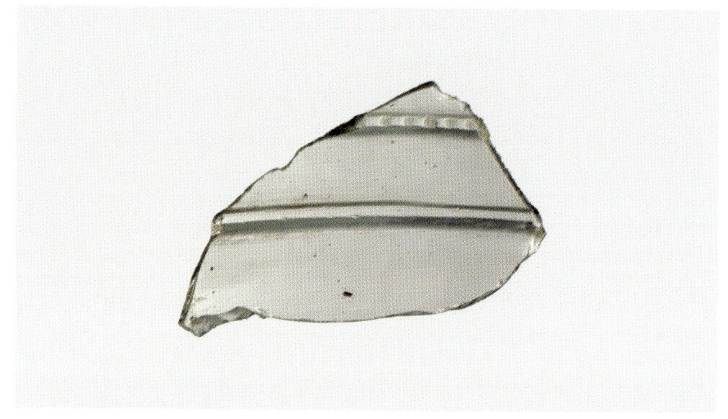

476

Fragment from wall (Th. 0.1 cm) of vessel, which is straight and either vertical or tapering, and decorated in relief: horizontal rib and, parallel to it, straight section of line with shallow notches.

Broken on all sides. Surface is virtually as new.

477. Fragment

9th to 10th century. Formerly in the Smith Collection. 59.1.556.
Max. Dim. 3.3 cm.

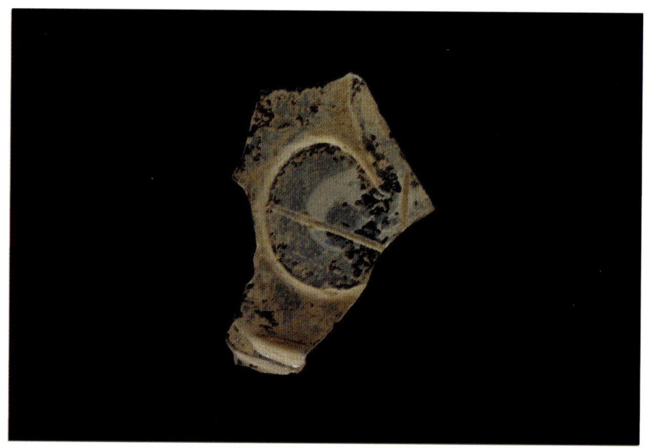

477

Colorless or almost colorless. Blown; slant- and relief-cut.

Fragment from wall of vessel (TTh. 0.25 cm). Decorated with vegetal motif (?), which may be part of trefoil leaf with edges in relief (Th. 0.1–0.15 cm) and interior slant-cut; each lobe has incised axial vein. Adjacent to leaf is narrow rib, which may be part of stem.

Broken on all sides. Dull, with remains of grayish weathering.

478. Fragment

9th to 10th century. Formerly in the Smith Collection (1263-h). Gift of Carl Berkowitz and Derek Content. 76.1.294.
Max. Dim. 3.2 cm.
Colorless; very few minute bubbles. Blown; relief-cut.

Fragment from wall (TTh. 0.2 cm) of vessel decorated in relief (Th. 0.1 cm) with (1) horizontal rib and (2) small part of curvilinear, probably vegetal, motif. (1) presumably was part of continuous border at top or bottom of frieze. Assuming (1) was at bottom, (2) consists of two symmetrical stems, upper parts of which descend, converge, and join before separating and curving down to right and left; stem on left appears to terminate in leaf.

Broken on all sides. Scattered spots of pale brown weathering or stain.

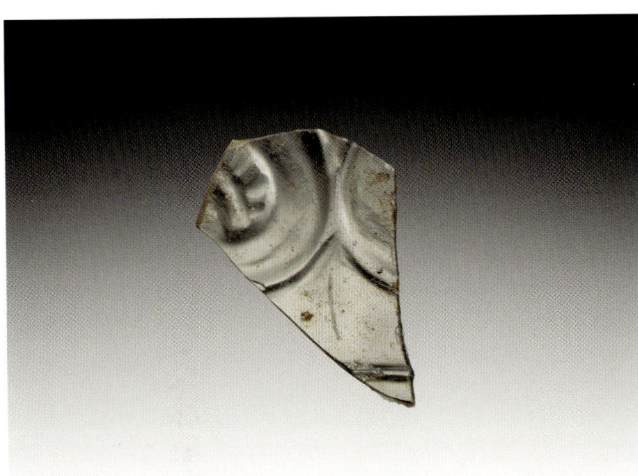

478

Comment: The fragment seems to preserve a small part of a frieze containing (perhaps among other elements) vegetal ornament that includes a symmetrical arrangement of scrolling stems terminating in leaves.

479. Fragment

9th to 10th century. Formerly in the Smith Collection (1263-f). Gift of Carl Berkowitz and Derek Content. 76.1.295.
H. (surviving) 3.1 cm, D. (est.) about 5–6 cm.
Almost colorless, with yellowish tinge. Blown; relief-cut.

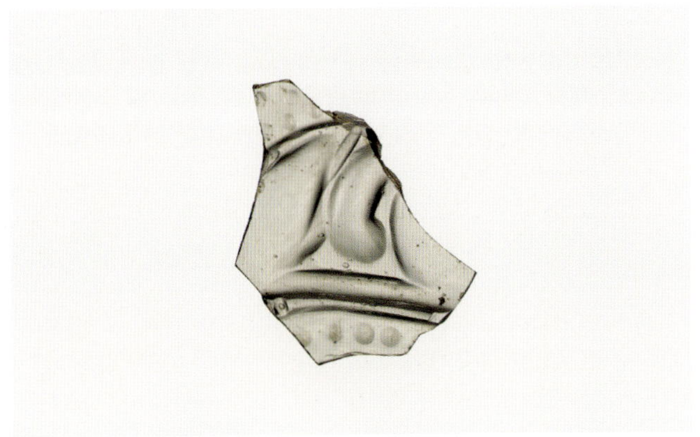

479

Fragment from wall (TTh. 0.1 cm) of vessel with straight side decorated in relief (Th. 0.05 cm) with small parts of two motifs filled with printies.

Broken on all sides. Pitted, with specks of light brownish weathering.

Comment: The shape, profile, and thinness of the fragment suggest that it came from a small object, perhaps a beaker or the neck or wall of a bottle.

480. Fragment

9th to 10th century. Formerly in the Smith Collection. 68.1.59-59.
Max. Dim. 3 cm, D. (est.) about 6 cm.
Colorless. Blown; relief-cut.

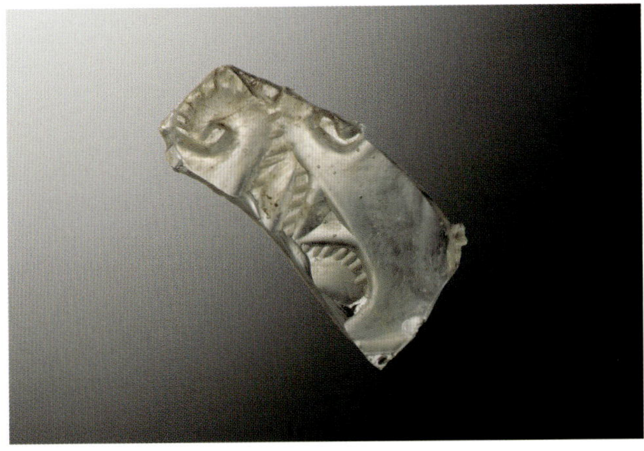

480

Fragment from straight or slightly convex wall (TTh. 0.2 cm) of vessel with relief-cut decoration (Th. 0.1 cm). Surviving part of may include vegetal motif. Some outlines are notched.

Broken on all sides. Dull, with traces of weathering.

481. Fragment

9th to 10th century. Formerly in the Smith Collection. 68.1.59-70.
Max. Dim. 2.9 cm.
Almost colorless, with yellowish green tinge.
Blown; relief-cut.

Fragment. Wall (Th. 0.1 cm) apparently straight. Decorated in relief (Th. 0.1 cm) with horizontal rib (?), above or below which are one incomplete notched L-shaped element and trace of second, curvilinear(?) motif.

Broken on all sides. Somewhat dull, with cloudy weathering.

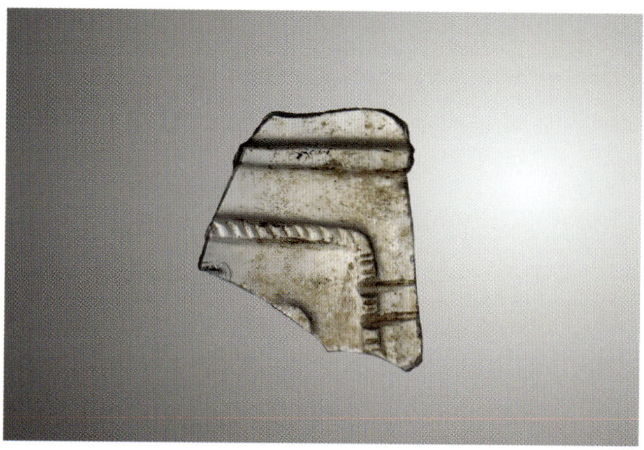

481

482. Fragment

9th to 10th century. Formerly in the Smith Collection. 68.1.59-69.
Max. Dim. 2.6 cm, D. (rib, est.) about 9 cm.
Almost colorless, with yellowish tinge; very small bubbles. Blown; relief-cut.

Fragment from wall (TTh. 0.2 cm) of vessel with straight, probably tapering wall. Decorated in relief (Th. 0.1 cm) with parts of horizontal rib and unidentified curvilinear motif with notched outline.

Broken on all sides. Virtually unweathered.

Comment: The rib may be the upper border of a frieze. The shape and size of the fragment suggest that it may have been part of a goblet (cf. *Glass of the Sultans* 2001, pp. 172–173, no. 79) or possibly a bowl (*ibid.*, p. 176, no. 82).

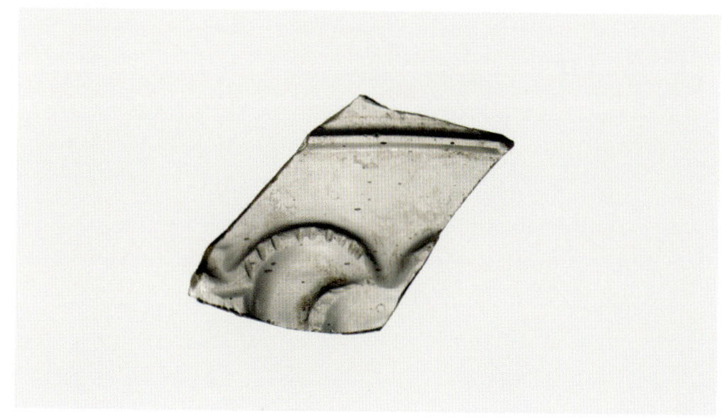

482

483. Fragment

9th to 10th century. Formerly in the Smith Collection. Gift of Carl Berkowitz and Derek Content. 76.1.259.
Max. Dim. 2.6 cm.
Colorless. Blown; relief-cut.

Fragment from wall of small vessel (TTh. 0.15 cm) decorated in relief (Th. 0.05 cm). Decoration consists of small part of horizontal rib and, below it, traces of unidentified motifs.

Broken on all sides. Slightly pitted, but with very little weathering.

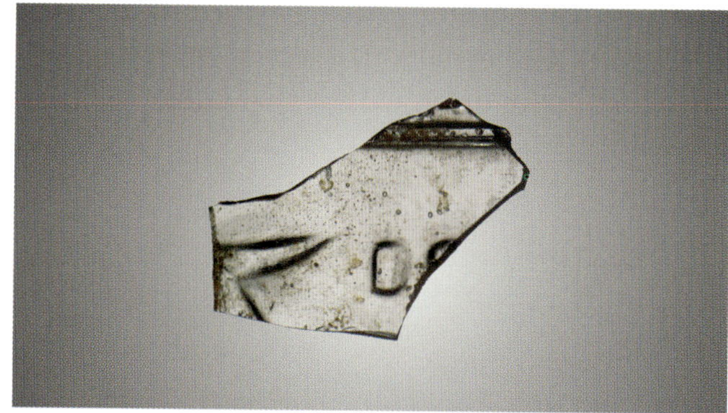

483

484. Fragment

9th to 10th century. Formerly in the Smith Collection. 68.1.59-71.
Max. Dim. 2.6 cm.
Almost colorless. Blown; relief-cut.

Fragment from wall (TTh. 0.2 cm) of vessel decorated in relief (Th. 0.1 cm). Surviving decoration

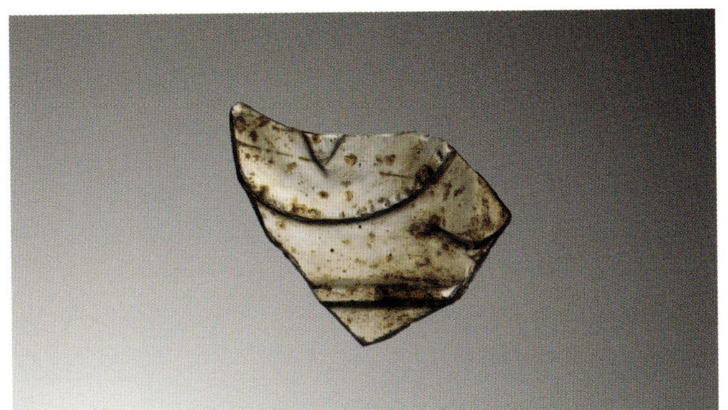

484

consists of one straight element, possibly part of horizontal rib, and one curved element, which is notched.

Broken on all sides. Dull, with spots of light brown weathering.

485. Fragment

9th to 10th century. Formerly in the Smith Collection. 68.1.59-75.
Max. Dim. 2.2 cm.
Colorless. Blown; relief-cut.

Fragment from wall (Th. 0.1–0.25 cm) of vessel with relief-cut decoration (Th. 0.1 cm) on outside: notched line, which curves in two directions (like tall, narrow S) and curls at end.

Broken on all sides. Patches of transparent pale gray and brownish weathering.

Comment: The motif is too fragmentary to identify with certainty. One possibility, however, is that it is the tail of an animal: cf. the S-shaped tails of the humped cattle depicted on a relief-cut beaker in the al-Sabah Collection, Dār al-Āthār al-Islāmiyyah, Kuwait National Museum (LNS 31 KG: Carboni 2001, p. 87, no. 20a). Despite its size, the fragment is identified with confidence as Islamic relief-cut glass of the ninth or 10th century.

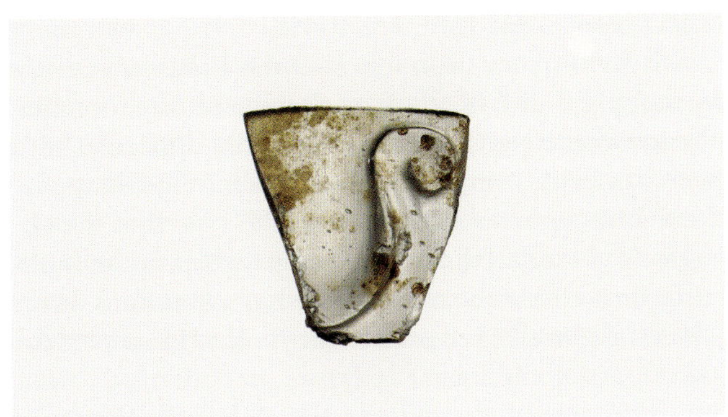

485

486. Fragment

Date uncertain. Formerly in the Smith Collection. 68.1.59-93.
Max. Dim. 2.2 cm.
Colorless. Blown; perhaps relief-cut.

Fragment from wall of vessel (Th. 0.1 cm) with one raised line (W. 0.1 cm, Th. 0.05 cm) that was either relief-cut or applied.

Broken on all sides. Small patches of light brown weathering.

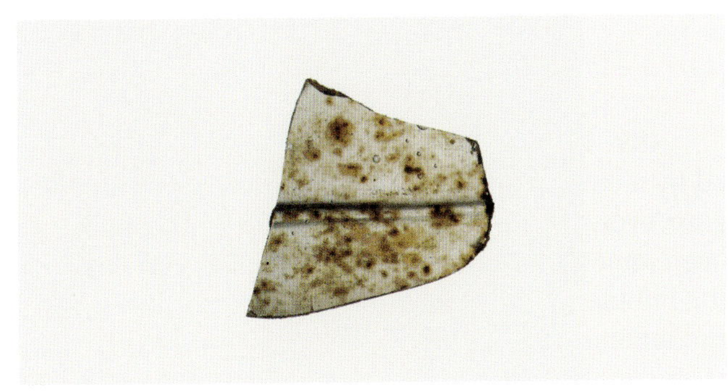

486

487. Fragment

9th to 10th century. Formerly in the Smith Collection (555-22). Gift of Carl Berkowitz and Derek Content. 76.1.289.
Max. Dim. 2 cm.
Colorless. Blown; relief-cut.

Fragment from wall of vessel (TTh. 0.2 cm) with small part of horizontal(?) rib (Th. 0.1 cm).

Broken on all sides. No obvious weathering.

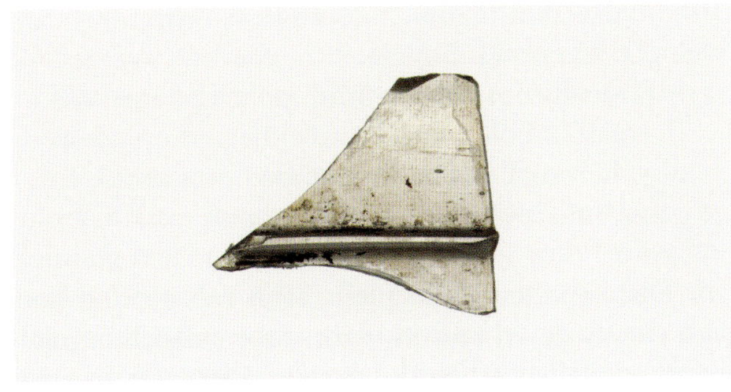

487

488. Fragment

9th to 10th century. 51.1.124.
Max. Dim. 1.9 cm.
Colorless or almost colorless. Blown; relief-cut.

Khorāsān, who ruled from 874 to 1001, claimed to be descendants of Bahrām VI (r. 590); and the Ṣaffārid dynasty of Sistan claimed descent from the founder of the Sasanian dynasty, Ardashīr I.

It is not surprising, therefore, to find that craftsmen in Iran revived Sasanian motifs in the 10th and early 11th centuries (see, for example, Ghuchani 1998).

Bibliography: *Glass from the Ancient World* 1957, p. 231 and p. 263, no. 530; *Guide to the Collections* 1958, p. 28, no. 24; *idem* 1965, p. 28, no. 28; *Glass of the Sultans* 2001, pp. 196–197, no. 101; *Guide to the Collections* 2001, p. 57.

490. Bowl with Birds and "Tree of Life" Motifs

9th to 10th century. Formerly in the Smith Collection (1062). 55.1.136.
H. 7.6 cm, W. 17.8 cm.
Translucent deep green; few spherical bubbles. Probably slumped over mold; slant- and relief-cut.

Bowl: hemispherical, with eight lobes. Rim has flat top and beveled inner surface formed by grinding; wall curves down and in, and has on inside, at junctions of lobes, sharp cusps that extend from rim to center of floor; base is slightly convex, with solid foot-ring; no pontil mark.

Wall is decorated on outside with slant- and relief-cut ornament consisting of two alternating motifs, each repeated four times: (1) standing bird, facing left, with curved beak, small head, elongated body, tiny wing, and pointed tail; its neck is embellished with band of horizontal cuts, and wing and tail have transverse parallel cuts; and (2) "tree of life," with trunk divided at top into two scrolling half-palmettes, and at midpoint into inverted palmette flanked by long, curving leaves.

Incomplete. Slightly less than half survives. Surviving part has been broken into 14 pieces and restored. Dull, with remains of weathering. Hole (D. 0.6 cm), near center of floor, was made by previous owner to obtain sample for spectrographic analysis.

Comment: Ray Winfield Smith reported that the object came from Iran.

Evidently the blank was made by sagging a disk of glass, perhaps with the foot-ring already formed by stamping (it does not appear to have been applied), over a lobed form. The shape of the bubbles supports the view that the object was not inflated, and it is

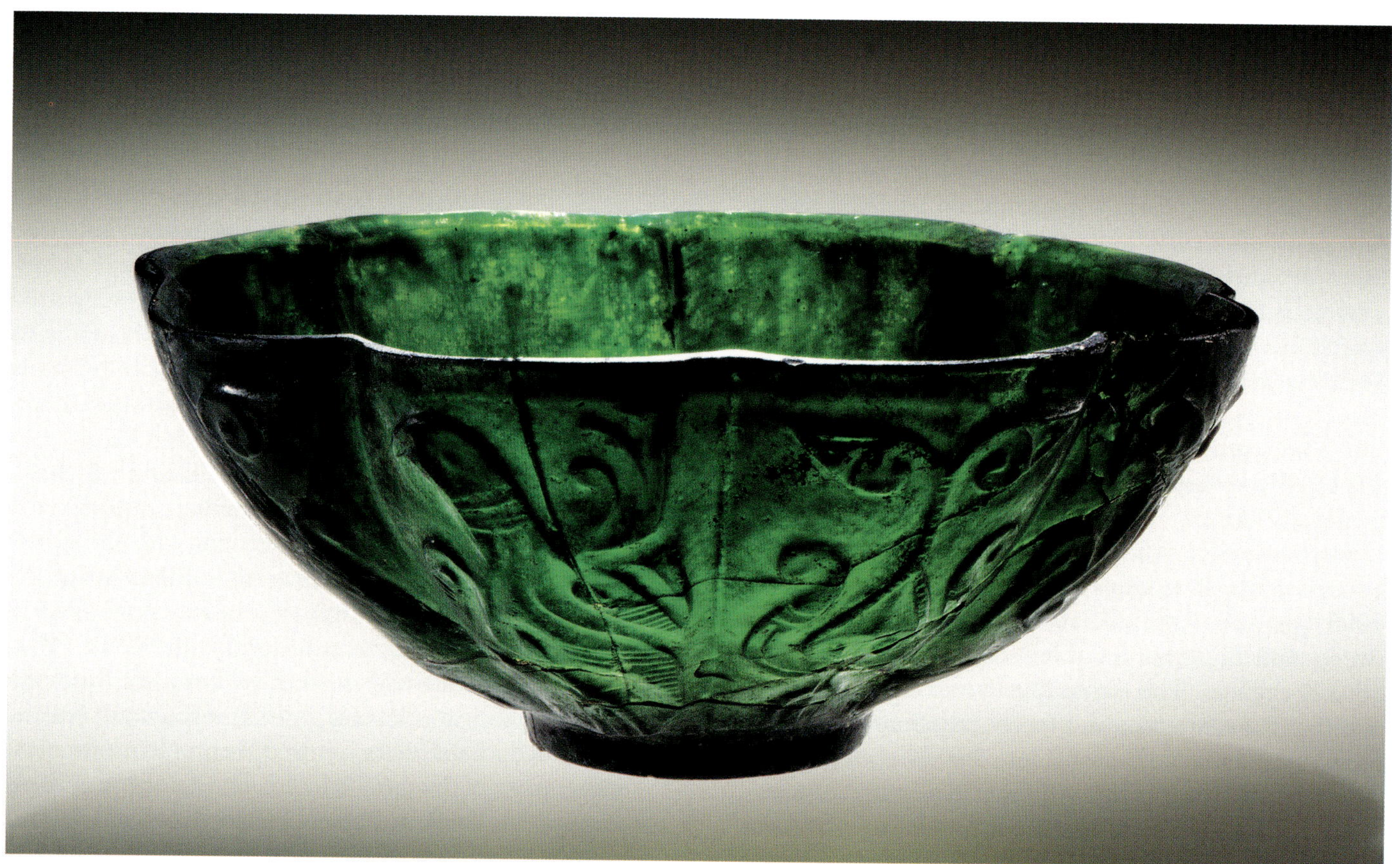

490

difficult to imagine that the cusps on the interior of the vessel could have emerged so crisp if the parison had been blown in a mold.

The decoration displays a combination of slant and relief cutting. P. Oliver (1961, p. 26) likened the birds and the tree-of-life motifs to the birds and vegetal form on the Falcon and Ibex Bowl at Corning (**296**: Kröger 1995, p. 141, fig. 9). Parallels for the form include the famous turquoise blue bowl with slant-cut hares in the Treasury of San Marco, Venice, which has five lobes (140: *Glass of the Sultans* 2001, pp. 176–178, no. 83 = Erdmann 1971, pp. 103–104, no. 117), and a bowl in The Metropolitan Museum of Art, New York (1970.20: Jenkins 1986, p. 24, no. 22). The latter object has the same sharp cusps on the interior as **490**.

The object belongs to a group of medieval Islamic green glass objects with an unusually high lead content. Chemical analysis showed that the glass of **490** contains 73.9 percent lead oxide (Brill 1999, v. 1, p. 101, and v. 2, p. 204, no. 5197). A dish in the Shōsō-in Treasury at the Tōdaiji Temple at Nara, Japan, has a similar color and is reported to contain 55 percent lead oxide (Harada and others 1965, pp. iii–iv and 19, color pl. 5, and black-and-white pls. 42–45). Although the Shōsō-in Treasury was consecrated in 756, it also contains objects transferred to it from a second shrine at the Tōdaiji Temple in 950.

Bibliography: *Glass from the Ancient World* 1957, p. 263, no. 532; *Guide to the Collections* 1958, p. 29, no. 24; Oliver, P. 1961, pp. 25–26, fig. 30; *Guide to the Collections* 1965, p. 29, no. 30; *Persian Glass* 1972, p. 15, no. 24; *Guide to the Collections* 1974, p. 29, no. 30; Martin 1977, pp. viii–ix; Marshall 1990, dust jacket; Yoshimizu 1992, pp. 99 and 291, no. 204; *Glass of the Sultans* 2001, pp. 188–189, no. 93; *Guide to the Collections* 2001, p. 56.

491. Fragment with Horse(?)

Perhaps 8th to 10th century; possibly earlier.
Formerly in the Smith Collection (956).
59.1.463.
Max. Dim. 10.8 cm.
Almost colorless, with greenish tinge. Probably molded; coldworked.

Fragment of large object (TTh. 1.4 cm) decorated in relief (Th. 1 cm). Decoration consists of horse or horselike animal running in right profile. Entire animal is in solid relief, with virtually flat surface. It has triangular, downward-pointing head with two broad cuts across muzzle, eye indicated by printy, and two short, pointed ears; neck is long, with single incised

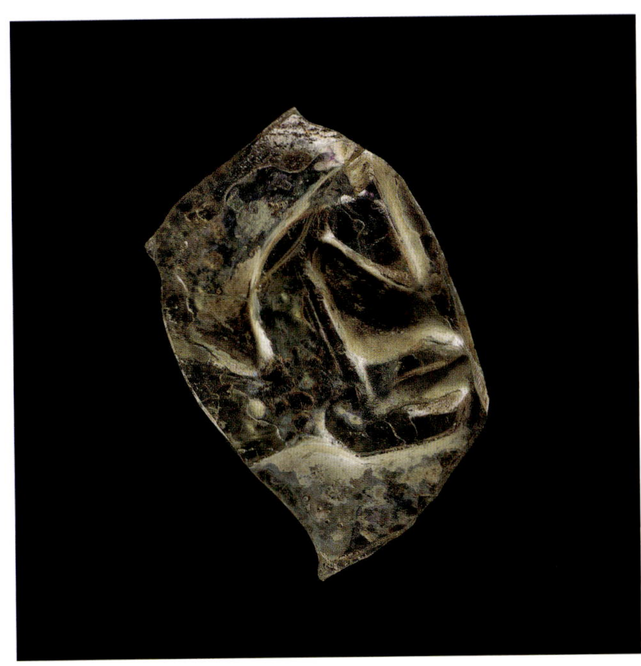

491

lines across top and bottom, and along sides, and with two printies; body has single incised lines along back and belly, and printy behind shoulder; legs are extended forward. Beneath animal, at edge of fragment, trace of second raised element.

Undecorated surface is completely smooth. It has concave profile on axis parallel to animal's neck, but is almost flat along perpendicular axis.

Two fragments, which join. Broken on all sides. Pitted, with patches of iridescent pale brown to silver weathering.

Comment: Uncertainty surrounds almost every aspect of this fragment, despite the fact that it has been published on at least three earlier occasions. The author of the catalog entry in *Verres antiques* (see below) noted: "Son style aberrant ne permettrait pas de le classer parmi la production islamique, s'il n'avait fait parti d'un lot d'objets provenant de l'Iran. La superbe irisation argentée que la recouvre permet de croire qu'il s'agit d'un objet de fouille persan. X^{e}–XIe s." (Its abnormal style would not allow one to classify it as an Islamic product if it had not been part of a group of objects from Iran. The superb silvery iridescence, which covers it, allows one to believe that we are dealing with an object from an excavation in Iran. 10th to 11th century). Thus, the author (presumably Ray Winfield Smith) reported that the fragment came from Iran and, despite its unusual character, concluded that it is Islamic and of the 10th to 11th century.

In *Glass from the Ancient World* (see below), the author, who in this case certainly was Smith, described the fragment as part of a "large, extremely heavy . . .

the year 900. Nevertheless, cameo glasses appear to have been made for more than 100 years. The linear-cut cup (**494**) and several fragments are similar to the cameo glass cup (*Glass of the Sultans* 2001, pp. 193–194, no. 98 = Lamm 1928, pp. 68–69, no. 187) found during excavations in the Jawsaq al-Khāqānī, the palace built by Caliph al-Mu[c]taṣim in 836–842 at Samarra, Iraq. Samarra ceased to be the capital of the [c]Abbāsid caliphs in 892, and it is widely assumed that most of the finds from the city's several palaces were deposited no later than this date, although the site was never completely abandoned. (The mint at Samarra continued to issue coins until 953: see Miles 1954; however, for evidence that most of the site was indeed abandoned after 892, see Northedge 1996.) The excavations at Samarra also yielded cameo glass fragments with relief decoration (*Glass of the Sultans* 2001, p. 182, no. 87 = Lamm 1928, p. 78, no. 249).

At the other end of the chronological spectrum, **522** so closely resembles a group of rock crystal ewers made in the late 10th and early 11th centuries (inscriptions show that one was made between 975 and 996, and another between 1000 and 1011) that we may reasonably suppose it was made at about the same time. Thus relief-cut cameo glasses seem to have been made between the ninth and early 11th centuries.

Provenance

Similarly, we are ill-informed about the place or places where early Islamic cameo glass was made. The possibilities cover an arc that extends from Egypt to Iran, but we should be cautious about concluding that an object was made at a particular place simply because it or objects like it were found there. Archeological excavations at Fusṭāṭ have yielded one fragment of cameo glass (**529**). Three of the fragments described here (**505**, **517**, and **549**) were acquired in Cairo in 1951, and it is likely that a bowl in the Museum of Islamic Art, Cairo (2463: *Cameo Glass* 1982, p. 33, fig. 14 = *Arts of Islam* 1976, p. 140, no. 130), was also acquired in Egypt. Other fragments at Corning were acquired from Ray Winfield Smith, who collected extensively in Egypt, and it is possible that they, too, came from Cairo (their often pristine condition would support this conjecture). We may be confident, therefore, that cameo glass was available in medieval Egypt. Similarly, excavations at Samarra brought to light several fragments of cameo glass, and so we also know that it was available in Iraq. The same claim may be advanced for Iran, since several objects were found or are said to have been found in that country: they include **492**, fragments from Rayy or Sāveh (Lamm 1935, pp. 13–14 and pls. 7D and 39B and C), a vessel in the L. A. Mayer Memorial Institute for Islamic Art in Jerusalem (G24-69: *Glass of the Sultans* 2001, p. 182, no. 88), and a bottle in The British Museum, London (OA 1966.12-11.1: *ibid.*, pp. 194–195, no. 99). A blue fragment with white and blue overlays was excavated at Nishapur, a large medieval site in northeastern Iran, in 1939 (The Metropolitan Museum of Art, New York, 40.170.181: Kröger 1995, pp. 140–143, no. 193, erroneously described as "dark blue"), and both **492** and the vessel in the Mayer Memorial Institute are associated with Nishapur, although this is a popular provenance among dealers in Islamic antiquities, and the reports should be treated with caution.

* * *

The catalog entries are arranged as follows:

1. Blank with an applied overlay (**492**).
2. Probably with an applied overlay, and facet-cut (**493**).
3. With applied overlays and linear-cut, sometimes in combination with slant cutting (**494**–**521**).
4. Cased or with applied overlays, and relief-cut (**522**–**585**).

1. Blank

492. Beaker

9th to 10th century. 81.1.4.
H. 11.7 cm, D. 9.6 cm.
Transparent deep blue over colorless; both with bubbles. Blown, applied.

Beaker. Rim plain, with slight external bevel; wall (Th. 0.3 cm) curves down and in, then is straight and slightly splayed; base plain, with roughly circular pontil mark (W. 1.5 cm). Irregular continuous blue band (W. 2.5–3.1 cm, Th. 0.1 cm) applied to wall between 4.5 cm and 8 cm below rim.

Incomplete. Approximately 65 percent of rim and upper wall, and small part of lower wall, missing and restored in plastic. Dull. Blue glass has several internal cracks; colorless glass is pitted in places and has remains of pale tan-colored weathering.

Comment: The object, which is said to have been found at Nishapur, northeastern Iran, is the only known blank for an Islamic cameo glass beaker.

The blue overlay was applied to the colorless parison and marvered before the vessel was blown to its intended size and shape. It is possible that the internal cracks developed when the beaker was annealed and are the reason why it was never finished. At present, the fragments do not fit together well. This has been taken to be because the object "sprang" as a result of poor annealing (*Cameo Glass* 1982, p. 128, no. 148); however, the beaker was inexpertly restored, and the poor fit may be remediable.

For a relief-cut colorless beaker of the same form, see **335**.

Bibliography: *Cameo Glass* 1982, p. 128, no. 148; "Recent Important Acquisitions," *JGS*, v. 24, 1982, p. 90, no. 11; Whitehouse 2003, pp. 149–150, fig. 2.

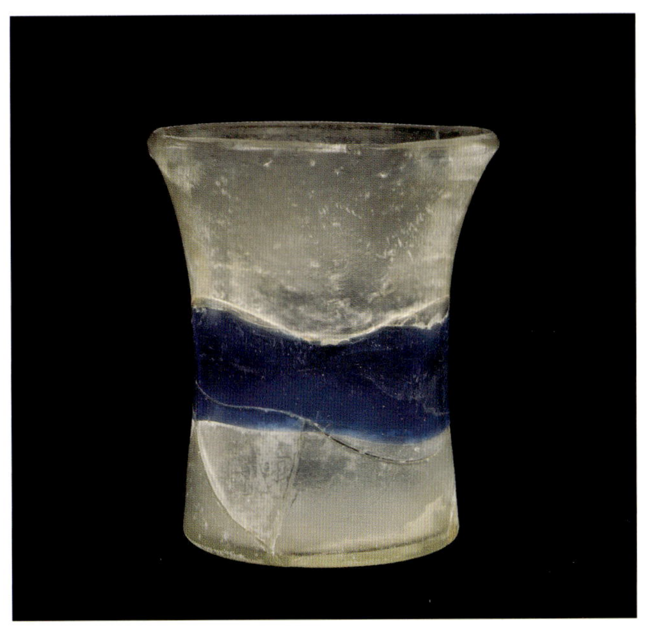

492

2. Facet-Cut Fragment

493. Fragment

9th to 10th century. Formerly in the Smith Collection. 68.1.95.
Max. Dim. 4.2 cm, D. (est.) about 7 cm.
Transparent green over colorless; both with very small bubbles. Blown, applied; facet-cut.

Fragment from wall (TTh. less than 0.2 cm) of vessel, which is straight and apparently vertical or almost vertical. Most, but not all, of exterior has green overlay (Th. 0.05 cm). Entire surface is decorated with four horizontal (presumably continuous) rows of almost contiguous, more or less circular hollow facets (each: D. about 0.9 cm), which are cut through green overlay to colorless base glass or cut directly in colorless glass.

Broken on all sides. Green and colorless glasses are slightly pitted and have patches of brown weathering.

Comment: The fragment came from a straight-sided vessel with an overall pattern of hollow facets.

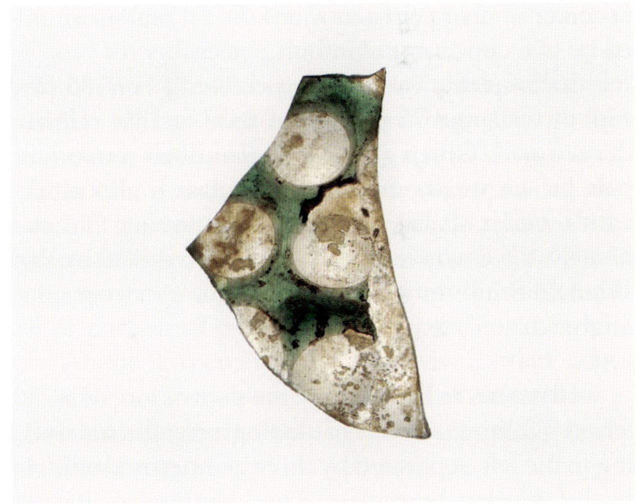

493

The extent of the green overlay or overlays cannot be determined. Only one other example of facet-cut cameo glass is known to me: a colorless beaker with a yellowish brown patch, reputedly from Nishapur (Berlin, Museum für Islamische Kunst, I.54/71: Kröger 1984, pp. 153–154, no. 134).

the animal's head may be missing, suggests that the beaker may have been cut down, presumably after the original rim had sustained damage.

Bibliography: Whitehouse 2003, pp. 150–151, fig. 6, right.

497. Fragment of Beaker with Animal (?)

9th to 10th century. Formerly in the Smith Collection. 68.1.83.
H. (surviving) 4.9 cm, D. (est., at top of fragment) about 10 cm.
Transparent green over colorless; both with small bubbles. Blown, applied; linear-cut.

Fragment of beaker(?). Lower wall straight and tapering; edge of base plain. Decorated at bottom of wall with green pad (H. at least 4.9 cm, W. at least 2.7 cm). Pad is cut in form of stylized animal (?) seen in profile, facing left, with two curved cuts at base of neck, one small limb raised and pointing forward, two limbs standing on ground, and haunch indicated by parabolic cut.

Broken on all sides. Green glass has patches of pale grayish brown weathering; colorless glass is extensively pitted, with traces of weathering.

Comment: No trace of coldworking is apparent on the (admittedly very pitted) colorless glass, and it is probably safe to assume that the overlay was applied as a pad. The tapering wall and the dimensions of the fragment indicate that it is probably part of a beaker similar to such more or less complete cameo glass beakers as *Cohn Collection* 1980, p. 156, no. 149; Goldstein and others 2001, p. 208, no. 181; and *Islamic Art and Manuscripts* 2001, p. 194, lot 329. If the fragment was not part of a beaker, it could have come from a bottle similar to, but smaller than, the bottle in the David Collection, Copenhagen (2/1972: *Glass of the Sultans* 2001, pp. 195–196, no. 100), which has two green pads, two brown pads, and extensive linear cutting.

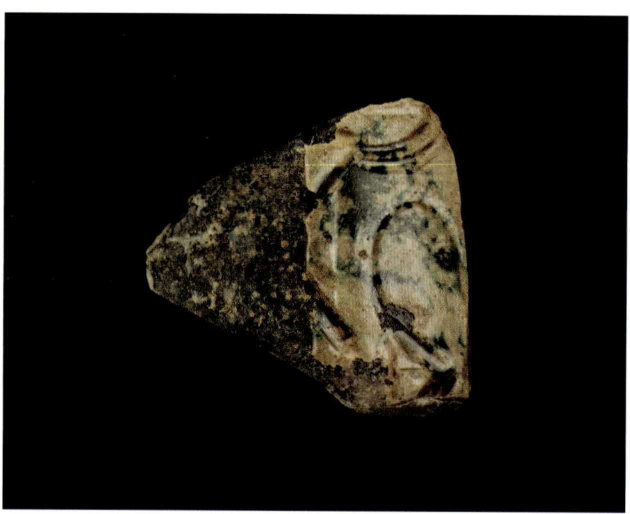

497

498. Fragment of Beaker or Bottle with Animal(?)

9th to 10th century. Formerly in the Smith Collection. 68.1.90.
Max. Dim. 4 cm, H. (surviving) about 2.9 cm, D. (est., at top) about 6 cm.
Transparent green over colorless. Blown, applied; linear-cut.

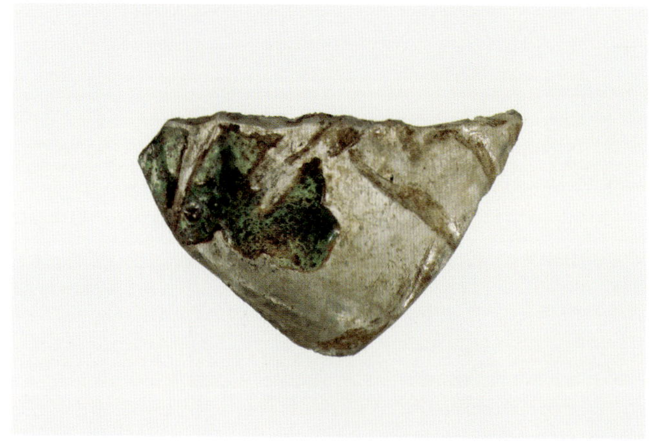

498

Fragment of beaker or bottle. Lower wall straight, tapering, and becoming markedly thicker as it approaches base (Th. 0.2 cm at top and 0.6 cm at bottom). Decorated with applied green pad (H. more than 1.8 cm, W. more than 2.4 cm) and linear cutting, perhaps in form of stylized animal facing right, with foot at bottom right corner. Colorless glass below and to right of pad is also linear-cut.

Broken on all sides. Dull, with patches of light yellowish brown weathering.

Comment: The pronounced thickening toward the lower edge of the fragment indicates that it came from the bottom of the wall, just above the base. The green motif is tentatively identified as an animal facing right on the basis of the roughly triangular element at the bottom right corner, which is similar to the "foot" of an "animal" on a beaker in the Los Angeles County Museum of Art (*Cohn Collection* 1980, p. 156, no. 149—if, indeed, the motif shown in the photograph is intended to represent an animal with a large, bushy tail).

499. Fragment of Bottle with Animal (?)

9th to 10th century. Formerly in the Smith Collection. 68.1.82.
H. (surviving) 5.4 cm, D. (est.) 12 cm.
Transparent green over colorless; both with few minute bubbles. Blown, applied; linear-cut.

Fragment of bottle(?): cylindrical. Wall vertical (TTh. 0.25 cm). Decorated with green pad (Th. 0.05 cm), which was at least 4.5 cm wide and 4.7 cm high, and is linear-cut. Pad is too fragmentary to permit identification of motif with certainty (but see below). At assumed top right, one green dot at center of circular or roughly circular area is cut through to colorless glass; projecting from circular area toward left is large green lunette with straight upper surface and one curved cut and one straight cut on interior; below lunette, large irregular green area with several cuts; at left edge of pad, element with vertical left edge and one or possibly two triangular projections toward right.

Broken on all sides. Green glass has patches of pale yellowish brown enamellike weathering; colorless glass has patches of brown weathering.

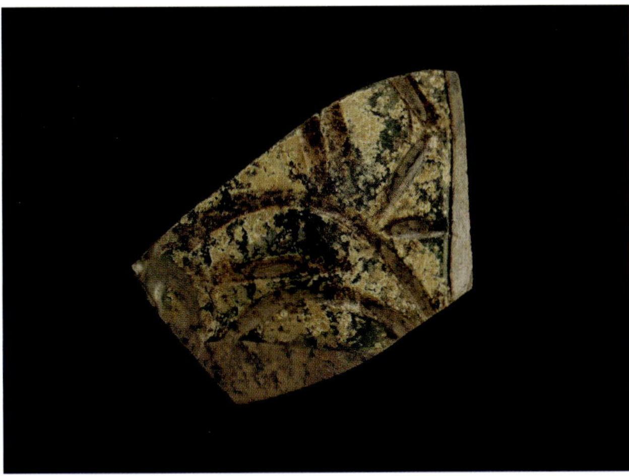

499

Comment: The fragment is thought to be from the wall of a bottle, although it is possible that the vessel was a large cylindrical cup. The ornament is difficult to interpret. If, however, the countersunk dot at the assumed top right corner is an eye (cf. the eyes of the animals on the cameo glass bottle in The British Museum, London (OA 1966.12-11.1: *Glass of the Sultans* 2001, pp. 194–195, no. 99), the ornament could be interpreted as an animal facing right, with a large lunette-shaped ear and a vertical tail with a triangular tip. Such a creature would be far from realistic, but so are the animals on other cameo glasses with applied overlays: e.g., the bottle in the David Collection, Copenhagen (2/1972: *ibid.*, pp. 195–196, no. 100); a fragment in the Museum für Islamische Kunst, Berlin (I.1993.8: Kröger 1999c, pp. 328–329, pl. 43c); and a beaker in the Los Angeles County Museum of Art (*Cohn Collection* 1980, p. 156, no. 149). In this respect, cf. **498**.

500. Fragment of Beaker with Bird

9th to 10th century. 2009.1.5.
H. (surviving) 4.9 cm, D. (est.) about 6 cm.
Transparent deep green over almost colorless with yellowish tinge; latter with small bubbles. Blown, applied; linear-cut.

Fragment from wall of beaker (Th. 0.1–0.2 cm). Wall is straight and probably slightly tapered. Fragment retains part of applied green pad with linear-cut decoration: bird, standing and shown in profile, facing left. Surviving parts are breast and lower body, perhaps with part of tail; wing, folded and shaped like half-palmette, but without volute; and, in front of body, wing tip. Colorless glass has no trace of coldworking, other than in vicinity of green appliqué.

Broken on all sides. Colorless glass is cloudy and has small patches of pale brown weathering; green glass is somewhat dull.

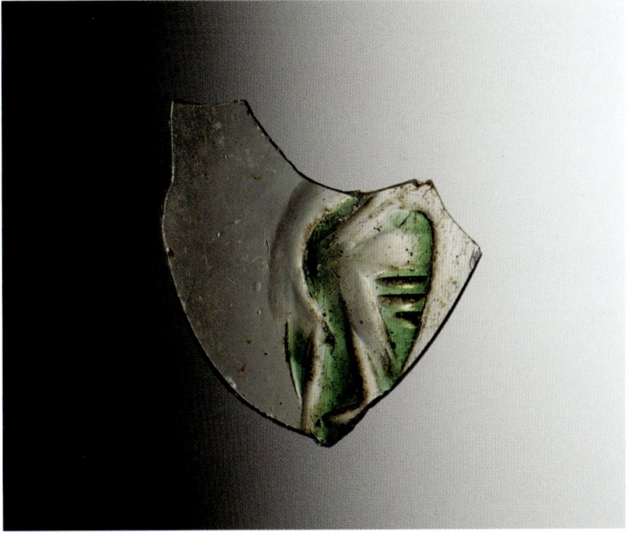

500

501. Fragment of Beaker or Bottle (?) with Bird

9th to 10th century. Formerly in the Smith Collection (555-6). Gift of Carl Berkowitz and Derek Content. 76.1.304.
H. (surviving) 5.8 cm, D. (est.) about 8 cm.

Transparent green over colorless; latter with small bubbles. Blown, applied; linear- and slant-cut.

Fragment of beaker or bottle (?) with straight, vertical or nearly vertical wall (TTh. 0.15–0.25 cm) and part of green overlay (Th. 0.05 cm). Overlay is cut in form of bird standing in profile, facing right, with folded wing, long and narrow tail, and two long legs. Lower body is embellished with single cut; wing has two horizontal cuts and is separated from body by long, curving cut. To left of bird, colorless glass has large curvilinear motif with slant-cut volutes.

Broken on all sides. Green glass is slightly pitted; colorless glass has patches of transparent pale brown weathering.

COMMENT: The size and shape of the fragment suggest that it is part of a beaker or a bottle. The bird resembles the standing bird on **530**, which also has slant-cut ornament in the colorless glass.

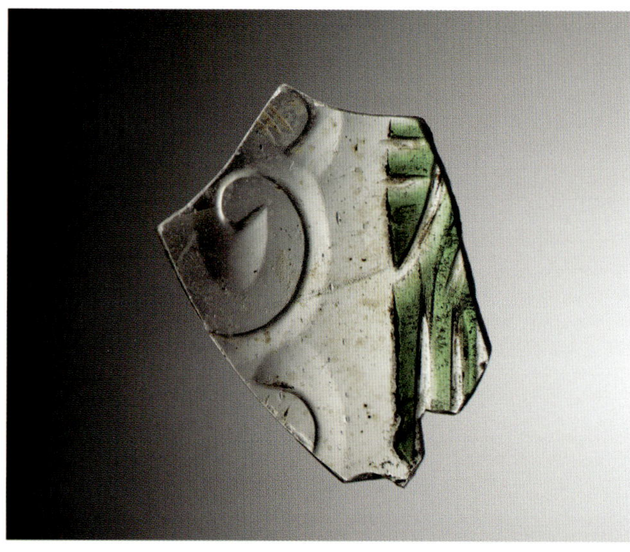

501

502. Fragment of Bottle(?) with Bird

9th to 10th century. Formerly in the Smith Collection (1287-A). 59.1.506.
H. (surviving) 4.1 cm, D. (est.) about 11 cm.
Transparent yellowish brown and transparent green over colorless. Blown, applied; linear-cut.

Fragment of bottle(?): cylindrical. Wall probably vertical (TTh. 0.2 cm). Decorated with brown pad (H. at least 2.9 cm, W. at least 3 cm, Th. 0.1 cm), below which is minute trace of green overlay. Pad and colorless background are linear-cut. Pad is cut in form

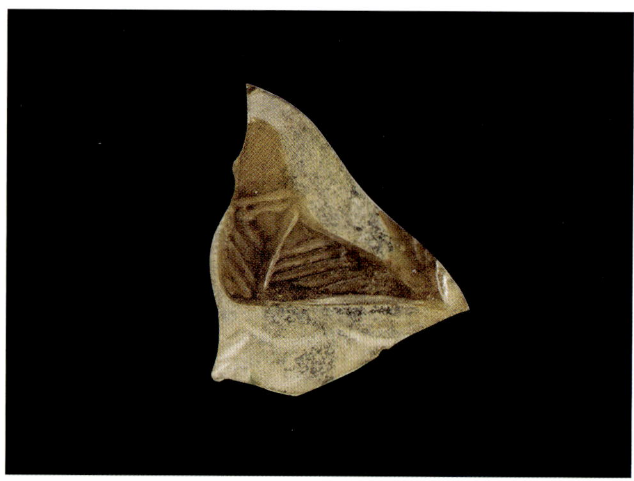

502

of bird seen in left profile; beak and front of head are missing; top of head is rounded; short neck is inclined slightly forward; body is roughly triangular, with long, flat underside and no legs; tail is upright, with plumage spreading forward; junction of neck and body is indicated by two parallel cuts; body is divided into unequal halves by transverse cut, with groups of parallel cuts on either side; tiny fragment of brown survives 0.3 cm above top of head. Below bird, colorless glass has horizontal row of three contiguous arcs, and other cuts; below this, trace of green overlay.

Broken on all sides. Dull and somewhat pitted, with pale brownish gray weathering.

COMMENT: The brown speck above the head of the bird may be the remains of a tendril held in its beak.

503. Fragment of Bottle(?) with Bird

Perhaps 9th to 10th century. Formerly in the Smith Collection. 68.1.94.
Max. Dim. 3.6 cm.
Transparent green over almost colorless with yellowish tinge; former with dark brown scale. Blown, applied; linear-cut.

Fragment from convex wall (TTh. 0.2 cm) of bottle(?), decorated with applied green pad (Th. 0.1 cm): tip of folded wing, with plumage indicated by two cuts parallel to upper edge and two transverse cuts.

Broken on all sides. Green glass is dull in places, with gray to light brown weathering; colorless glass has brownish weathering.

COMMENT: The absence of traces of coldworking on the colorless glass indicates that the overlay was applied locally rather than gathered over most of the parison. The motif is identified with confidence as the wing of a bird (cf. the wing of the bird on **528**). The wing is linear-cut, but the bird on **528** has a linear-cut wing and a relief-cut body, and it is possible that this bird, too, was partly relief-cut.

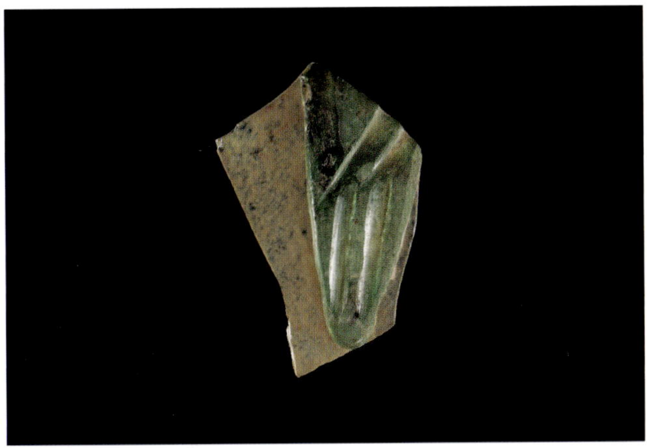

503

504. Fragment of Bottle(?) with Palmette

9th to 10th century. Formerly in the Smith Collection (1221-4). Gift of Carl Berkowitz and Derek Content. 76.1.305.
H. (surviving) 5.1 cm, D. (base, est.) 9 cm.
Transparent green over almost colorless with yellowish green tinge. Blown, applied; linear- and slant-cut.

Fragment of bottle(?): cylindrical. Lower wall (TTh. 0.25 cm) straight, tapering slightly, and curving in at bottom; base plain. Two very small patches of green overlay (Th. 0.05 cm) survive. Colorless glass has linear- and slant-cut decoration: large palmette framed by apparently symmetrical arrangement of curving lines; palmette and lines are separated by groups of two or three short transverse and horizontal cuts. On underside of base, one corner of large square motif with borders consisting of pairs of parallel cuts.

Broken on all sides. Green glass is pitted and has matte light green weathering; colorless glass is slightly pitted and has patches of transparent pale gray weathering.

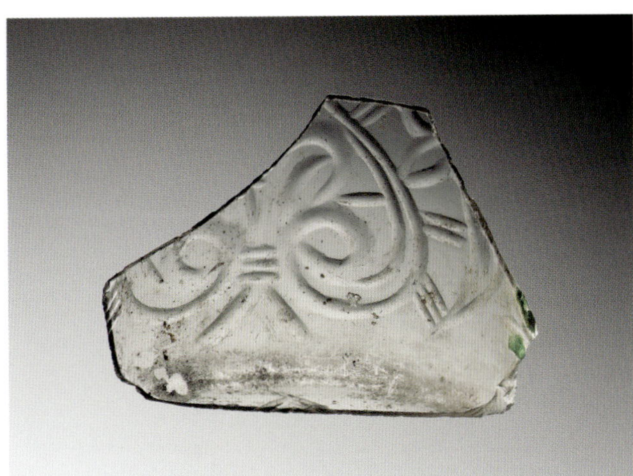

504

Comment: The fragment was probably part of a bottle similar in size and shape to the cameo glass bottle with applied green and brown pads in the David Collection, Copenhagen (2/1972: *Glass of the Sultans* 2001, pp. 195–196, no. 100).

505. Fragment of Cup with Half-Palmette

9th to 10th century. 51.1.168I.
H. (surviving) 5.5 cm, D. (est.) 10 cm.
Transparent green over almost colorless with yellowish tinge. Blown, applied; linear-cut.

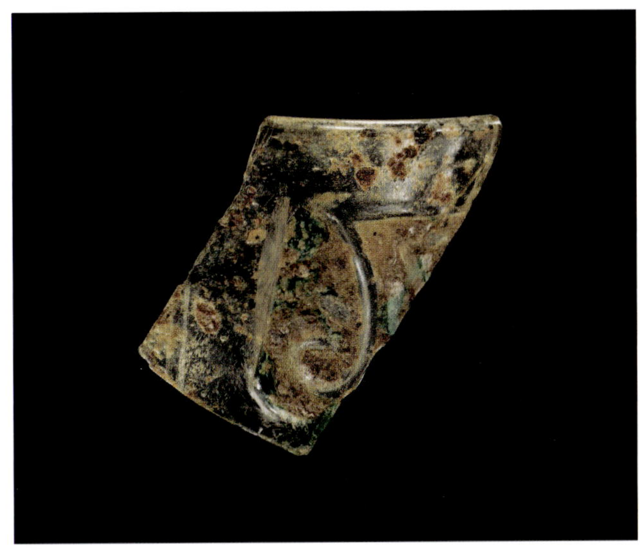

505

Fragment of cylindrical cup, consisting of approximately 10 percent of rim and upper wall. Rim plain, with rounded lip; wall (TTh. 0.3–0.4 cm) descends vertically. Decorated in relief (Th. 0.1 cm) with part of green motif: vertical half-palmette on short stem, which curves to right and connects with second green element with concave left side and horizontal top that is at almost same level as tip of half-palmette. Green glass is embellished with, and bordered by, linear cuts; colorless glass has single vertical cut 1.2 cm from half-palmette. This cut apart, colorless glass has no trace of coldworking.

Green glass has patches of pale brown enamellike weathering; colorless glass is pitted, deeply in places, with brown weathering in pits.

Comment: The fragment, which was acquired in Cairo, Egypt, was part of a cylindrical cup similar to the cameo glass cup found during excavations in the Jawsaq al-Khāqānī, the palace built by Caliph al-Muᶜtaṣim in 836–842 at Samarra, Iraq. Samarra ceased to be the capital of the ᶜAbbāsid caliphs in 892, and it is widely assumed that most of the finds from the city's several palaces were deposited no later than this date (*Glass of the Sultans* 2001, pp. 193–194, no. 98 = Lamm 1928, pp. 68–69, no. 187). If the green motif was symmetrical, with half-palmettes flanking a central element, it may have been a "tree of life" similar to the two stylized trees on a green over colorless cylindrical cameo glass cup in The Chrysler Museum of Art, Norfolk, Virginia (68.6: Merrill 1989, p. 22, no. 14 = *Cameo Glass* 1982, p. 105, no. 20).

506. Fragment of Cup with Half-Palmette

9th to 10th century. Formerly in the Smith Collection. 68.1.105.
H. (surviving) 3.7 cm, D. (est.) 10 cm.
Transparent blue over almost colorless with green tinge; both with very small bubbles.
Blown, cased; slant-cut.

Fragment of cup: apparently cylindrical. Rim plain, with ground and polished lip; wall (TTh. 0.3 cm) descends vertically. Blue relief decoration (Th. 0.1 cm) begins 1.1 cm below rim: part of slant-cut scrolling half-palmette and tip of adjacent motif.

Approximately 10 percent of rim survives; all other edges broken. Little weathering.

Comment: The area between the rim and the blue overlay has traces of coldworking, and this suggests that the object was cased. The color of the overlay and the slanting cuts may be compared with a fragment from Samarra, Iraq, which is generally believed to date from the period when the caliphs were in residence, between 836 and 892 (*Glass of the Sultans* 2001, p. 182, no. 87 = Lamm 1928, p. 78, no. 24).

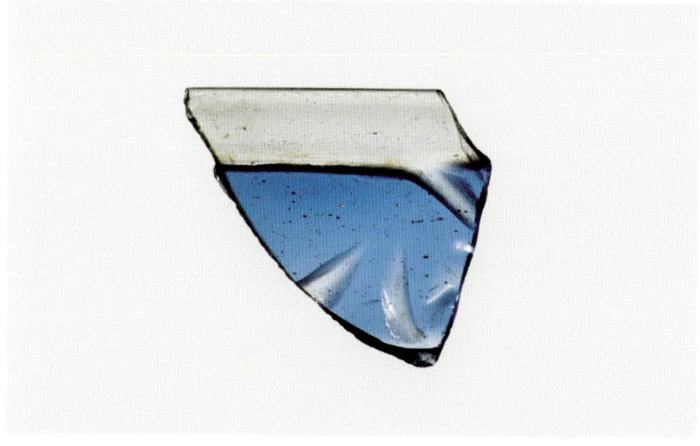

506

507. Fragment of Beaker or Bottle with Half-Palmette

9th to 10th century. Formerly in the Smith Collection. Not accessioned.
H. (surviving) 4.9 cm, D. (wall, est.) about 5 cm.
Transparent green over almost colorless with yellowish tinge; latter has very small bubbles.
Blown, applied; linear-cut. (Not illustrated.)

Fragment of beaker or bottle. Wall (TTh. 0.2 cm) vertical or almost vertical. Decoration consists of green pad (H. more than 3.5 cm, W. 1.9 cm, Th. 0.1 cm) with linear-cut decoration that includes one half-palmette.

Broken on all sides. Colorless glass has patches of transparent light brown weathering; green glass is slightly pitted.

Comment: The colorless glass shows signs of coldworking only in the immediate vicinity of the green overlay. This observation shows conclusively that (1) the green glass was applied as a pad and (2) the original width of the pad was about 2.7 centimeters..

508. Fragment with Half-Palmette(?)

Perhaps 9th to 10th century. Formerly in the Smith Collection. 68.1.93.
Max. Dim. 3.2 cm, H. (surviving) about 2.6 cm, D. (est.) about 7 cm.
Transparent green over colorless; both with very small bubbles. Blown, applied; linear-cut.

Fragment of vessel with straight, probably vertical wall (TTh. 0.2–0.25 cm). Decorated in relief with green linear-cut pad (Th. 0.1 cm). Orientation of fragment and identity of motif uncertain; perhaps it is part of half-palmette (see below). Traces of coldworking on colorless glass extend up to 0.5 cm beyond edge of green pad.

Broken on all sides. Green glass is dull and pitted, with pale silvery gray weathering; colorless glass has pristine unworked surfaces, but traces of weathering in cuts.

Comment: The limited extent of the coldworking on the colorless glass indicates that the overlay was applied rather than gathered. The surviving decoration

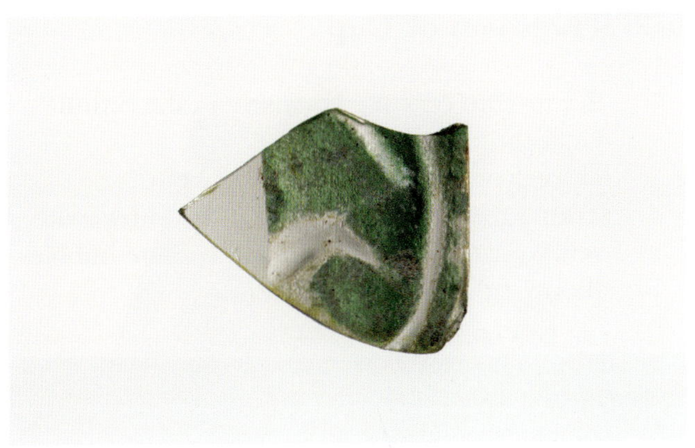

508

is reminiscent of ornament on the cylindrical cameo glass cup found during excavations in the Jawsaq al-Khāqānī, the palace built by Caliph al-Mu[c]taṣim in 836–842 at Samarra, Iraq (see **506**). The surviving decoration on **508** may be a (reversed) variation on the half-palmette that appears in the top right corner of plate V.187 in Lamm 1928 and the illustration on page 193 in *Glass of the Sultans* 2001. Alternatively, it may be the tail of an animal.

509. Fragment of Cup with Lozenge

9th to 10th century. Formerly in the Smith Collection. 68.1.80.
H. (surviving) 6.8 cm, D. (est., base) about 9 cm.
Transparent green over colorless. Blown, applied; linear-cut.

Fragment from lower wall (TTh. 0.3–0.4 cm) and base of cylindrical cup. Decoration consists of applied green pad (W. 4.6 cm, Th. 0.1 cm) extending from above top of fragment to within 0.3 cm of base. Pad has linear-cut decoration: at presumed center, lozenge (H. 1.9 cm) inside larger lozenge (H. 5 cm). If ornament was symmetrical, single oval motifs extended from midpoints of sides of larger lozenge to edge of pad (and, in one case, beyond edge), and two parallel horizontal lines extended to edge of pad from each angle at side of lozenge.

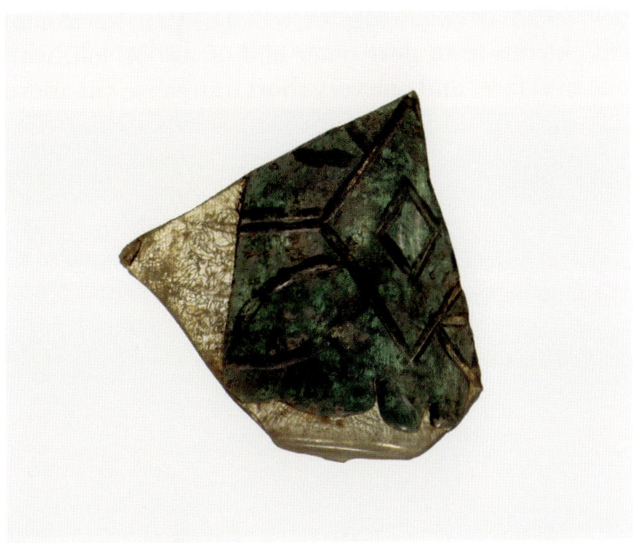

509

Broken on all sides. Patches of grayish weathering and network of fine white lines on inner surface.

COMMENT: For the decoration, cf. **513**.

BIBLIOGRAPHY: Brill and Fenn 1992, p. 256, no. 6341.

510. Fragment of Cup

9th to 10th century. Formerly in the Smith Collection. 59.1.593.
H. (surviving) 6.8 cm, D. (rim, est.) 8 cm.
Transparent green over almost colorless with green tinge. Blown, applied; linear-cut.

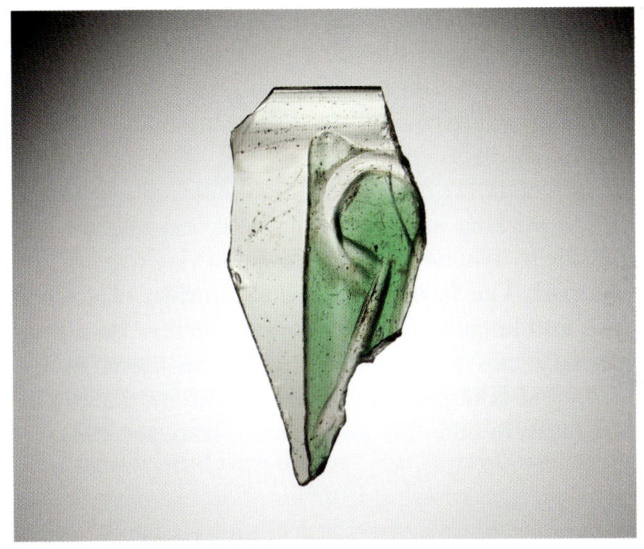

510

Fragment of cylindrical cup. Rim plain, with narrow, rounded top; wall (TTh. 0.4 cm) vertical. Decoration consists of applied green pad (Th. 0.1 cm) with indeterminate linear-cut details.

Broken on all sides, except for small part of rim. Colorless glass is unweathered; green glass is slightly dull.

COMMENT: Cf. **494**.

Chemical analysis revealed that, unlike the almost colorless base glass, the green overlay contains 54.9 percent lead oxide (Brill 1999, v. 1, p. 93, and v. 2, p. 189, nos. 5382 and 5383).

Transparent green over colorless; both with very small bubbles. Blown, applied; linear-cut.

Fragment of cup, beaker, or bottle. Lower wall (TTh. 0.15–0.3 cm) is straight and either vertical or tapering. Decorated with green pad, which, like colorless glass, is linear-cut; identity of motif on pad, which includes thick tear-shaped element, is unknown.

Broken on all sides. Green glass is extensively pitted and has pale green to brown weathering; colorless glass is almost unweathered.

Comment: The variable thickness of the wall indicates that the fragment came from near the bottom of a vessel, the base of which probably had a diameter of between five and six centimeters.

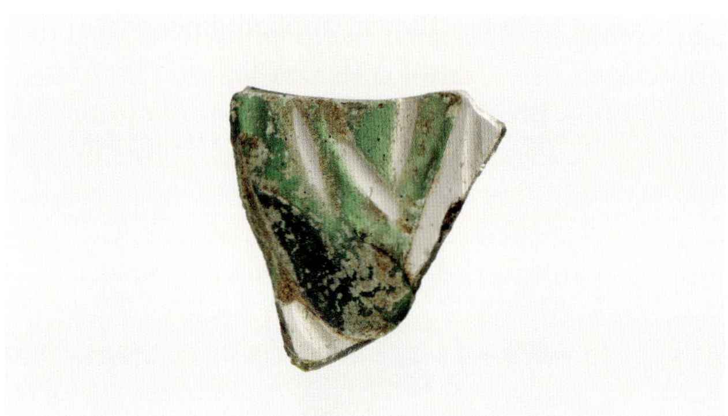

516

517. Fragment of Beaker or Bottle

9th to 10th century. 51.1.168III.
H. (surviving) 4.3 cm, D. (est.) perhaps about 6 cm.
Transparent green over colorless; both with small bubbles. Blown, cased or more probably applied; linear-cut.

Fragment from wall of beaker or bottle (TTh. 0.15 cm) that was either vertical or almost vertical. Decorated with tall, narrow green overlay (Th. 0.05 cm) with slightly convex sides and rounded (presumably upper) end. Overlay has several cuts: notch near top of right side; groove near and parallel to right side, which expands and curves to left at top; shallow horizontal line in rounded top of overlay; and four shallow horizontal lines near left side. Just above overlay, shallow, presumably continuous horizontal line cut in colorless glass.

Broken on all sides. Green glass is dull, with some grayish weathering; colorless glass has patches of transparent pale grayish weathering; both have small patches of opaque white weathering or encrustation.

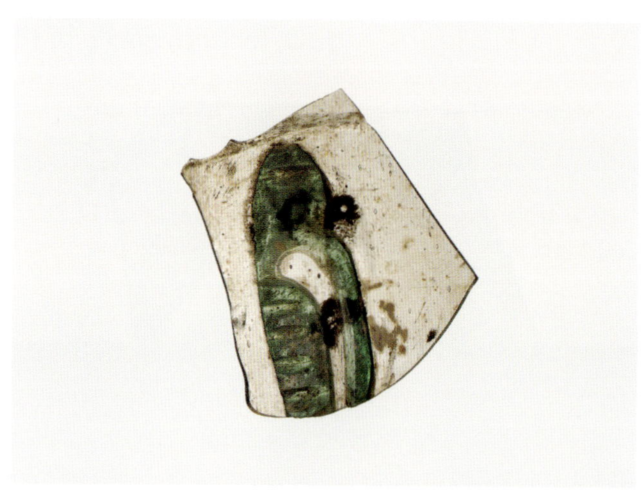

517

Comment: The fragment, which was acquired in Cairo, Egypt, was part of a beaker or a bottle. Apart from the horizontal cut noted above, the colorless glass has no obvious signs of coldworking, and this indicates that the overlay was applied rather than cased. If the rounded end is at the top of the overlay, the decoration may be a schematic bird standing in profile, facing right, with its wing folded (cf. the more elaborate standing birds on a colorless relief-cut bottle in the David Collection, Copenhagen, 10/1963: *Glass of the Sultans* 2001, pp. 191–192, no. 96). For a similar but smaller motif, see **528**.

518. Fragment of Beaker or Bottle

9th to 10th century. Formerly in the Smith Collection. 68.1.100.
H. (surviving) 2.3 cm, D. (est., at top of fragment) about 6 cm, (base) about 5 cm.
Transparent green over almost colorless with yellowish tinge; green glass has few small bubbles; colorless glass has rather more bubbles. Blown, applied; linear-cut.

Fragment of beaker or bottle. Lower wall (TTh. 0.3–0.8 cm) straight, tapering, and rounded at bottom; base (Th. 0.5 cm) plain, with trace of pontil mark. Decorated near bottom of wall with green pad (H. at least 1.3 cm, W. at least 3.1 cm, Th. 0.1 cm). Pad is linear-cut in indeterminate form. One curved line extends down wall to right of and below pad, and end of one other cut survives below left side of pad.

Broken on all sides. Green glass is dull and somewhat pitted, with traces of weathering; colorless glass is almost as new.

Comment: The bottom of the wall and the base are unusually thick.

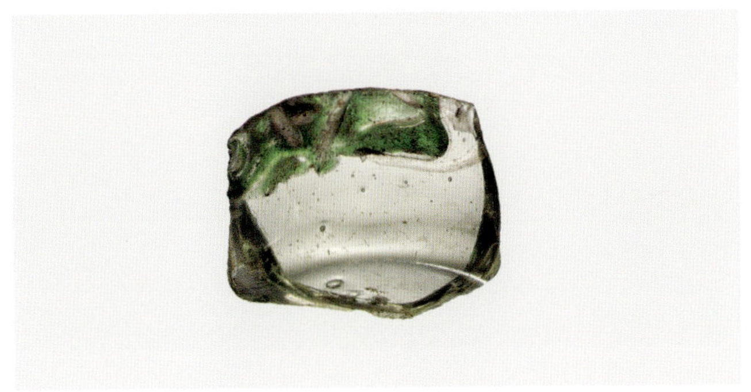

518

The upper edge of the fragment is parallel to the base and retains traces of grozing and polishing. Evidently the object was broken and the base was cut down to form a shallow dish. The date at which this occurred is unknown.

519. Fragment of Bottle(?)

9th to 10th century. Formerly in the Smith Collection. 68.1.87.
Max. Dim. 5.2 cm, H. (surviving) about 3.1 cm, D. (max., est.) about 12 cm.
Transparent light yellow over colorless; both with few very small bubbles. Blown, applied; linear-cut.

Fragment of bottle(?). Wall (TTh. 0.25–0.35 cm) appears to descend vertically and to curve in slightly at bottom. Decorated with yellow pad (Th. 0.1 cm), probably with vertical left edge, rounded corner, and roughly horizontal lower edge, and with three transverse linear cuts and one crescent-shaped cut. Colorless glass to left of overlay has no trace of coldworking.

Broken on all sides, with crack in colorless glass. Yellow glass is pitted and has pale yellowish brown weathering in pits; colorless glass has incipient weathering.

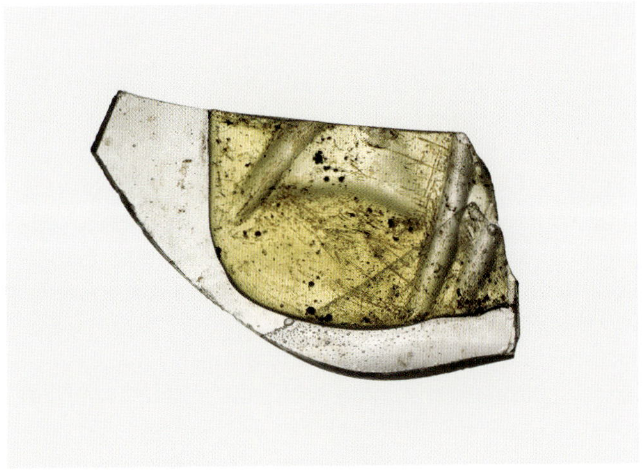

519

Comment: The shape, diameter, and thickness of the fragment are consistent with the suggestion that it was part of the lower wall of a bottle that may have had a shape similar to that of the bottle with green and brown linear-cut pads in the David Collection, Copenhagen (2/1972: *Glass of the Sultans* 2001, pp. 195–196, no. 100). The apparent absence of coldworking on the colorless glass to the left of the pad indicates that the overlay was applied rather than gathered. The color of the overlay is unusual among the fragments of early Islamic cameo glass at Corning, the nearest approximations being the bosses on a fragment of uncertain origin (**585**) and the overlay on **531**.

520. Fragment

9th to 10th century. Formerly in the Smith Collection. 68.1.106.
Max. Dim. 4.5 cm.
Transparent green over colorless; both with bubbles. Blown, probably applied; linear-cut.

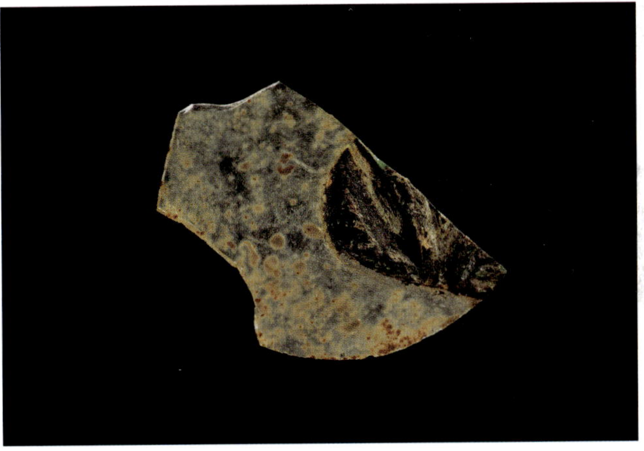

520

Fragment from wall (TTh. 0.25 cm) of vessel with green overlay (Th. 0.05 cm). Overlay covers entire exterior surface and has parts of three linear cuts, which penetrate to base glass.

Broken on all sides. Green glass is almost completely weathered to matte brown with gray spots; colorless glass has patches of thin light brown weathering.

Comment: The character of the cutting suggests that the fragment is from a vessel with applied rather than cased overlays. The ornament has not been identified.

521. Fragment

9th to 10th century. Formerly in the Smith Collection. 68.1.99.
Max. Dim. 3.9 cm, D. (est.) about 9 cm.
Transparent green over almost colorless with greenish yellow tinge. Blown, applied; linear-cut.

Fragment of vessel with straight, vertical or almost vertical wall (TTh. 0.2 cm). Decorated in relief with green pad (Th. almost 0.1 cm) embellished with cuts. No trace of coldworking exists on colorless glass.

Broken on all sides. Green glass is almost matte, with brown and gray weathering; colorless glass has patches of slightly iridescent pale gray weathering.

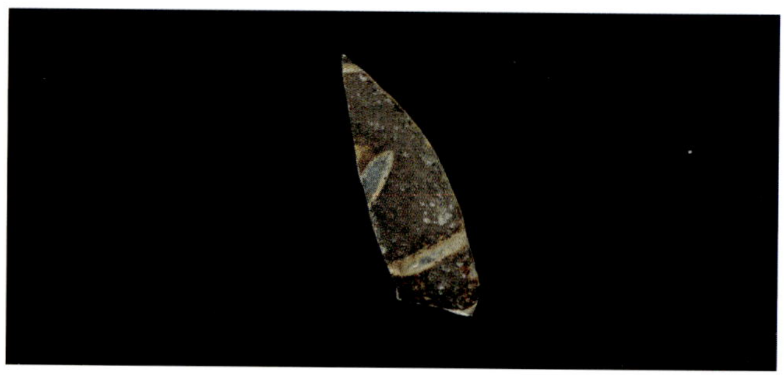

521

Comment: The size and shape of the fragment suggest that it may have been part of a cylindrical cup or a beaker. The absence of coldworking on the colorless glass indicates that the overlay was applied rather than gathered. The decoration is indeterminate.

4. Relief-Cut Objects

522. The Corning Ewer

About 1000. Formerly in the collection of Edmund de Unger. Acquired with funds from the Clara S. Peck Endowment. 85.1.1.
H. 16 cm, D. (max.) 9.3 cm.
Translucent pale green over colorless. Blown, cased; relief-cut, drilled; handle applied.

Ewer with pear-shaped body. Rim plain, outsplayed, with oval mouth and pointed pouring lip; neck narrow; foot hollow, splayed; ribbon handle attached to lower part of body and rim. Decorated in relief: one band on lip; two bands on neck, one curving up toward pouring lip; panel with birds and animals on body, defined at top by border with superficial incised crosses alternating with deeper printies, and at bottom by plain line that turns up at extremities and follows line of handle until it meets upper border; inside panel, pair of opposed, regardant horned quadrupeds with crossed forelegs, each with bird of prey perched on rump and pecking at back of neck; behind these, at each edge of panel, parrot-like bird on branch, its back to bird of prey and head turned back over shoulder, with scrolling palmette spray in beak; hind leg joints of animals and wing coverts of raptors terminate in half-palmettes; bodies of animals and raptors enlivened with printies; behind handle, green overlay cut in tall, tapering form; lower end of handle cut in relief with heart-shaped palmette above two volutes; at highest point of handle, remains of elaborate bifurcated thumb-rest.

Broken into approximately 50 pieces; restored; restorations include most of rim, lower part of handle, parts of parrot to left of pouring lip, and most of base; upper part of handle may be replacement from ewer of similar size and shape; traces of grayish weathering.

Comment: Mr. de Unger acquired the object in Tehran, Iran.

There are marked differences in the degree to which the colorless glass has been removed. Around the central part of the body, where the colorless glass was thinnest, hardly any of it is missing. Near the top and bottom, on the other hand, a considerable amount of colorless glass has been removed: at least two millimeters at the top of the neck and almost as much at the bottom of the panel.

The motif of a bird of prey attacking an animal has a long history in Egypt and Western Asia. It is found, for example, on a Sasanian seal of about the fifth century, in The British Museum, London (1772.3-15.302 = WAA Seals 119521: *Vases & Volcanoes* 1996, p. 199, no. 78).

The Corning Ewer has few close parallels in glass. The most notable example is the colorless Buckley Ewer in the Victoria and Albert Museum, London (Buckley 1935). A number of similar, elaborately relief-cut ewers and other vessels have appeared on the market in recent years (see, for example, *Earthly Beauty, Heavenly Art* 1999, pp. 204–206, nos. 171–174; Shindo 2002, p. 32, no. 49; and *Khalili Collection* 2005, pp. 203–205, nos. 241–243), but the chemical composition of the glass from which some of them were formed

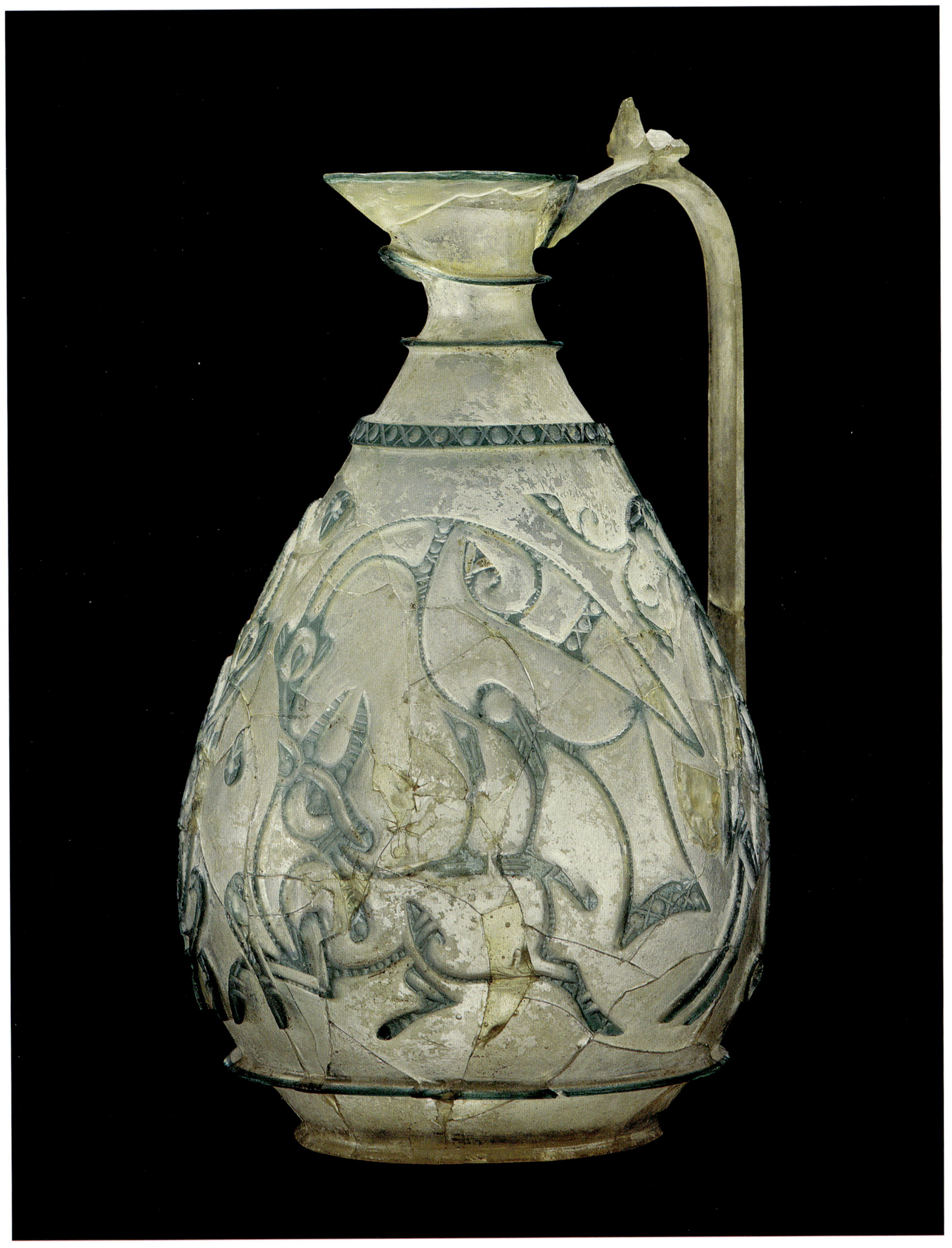

522A

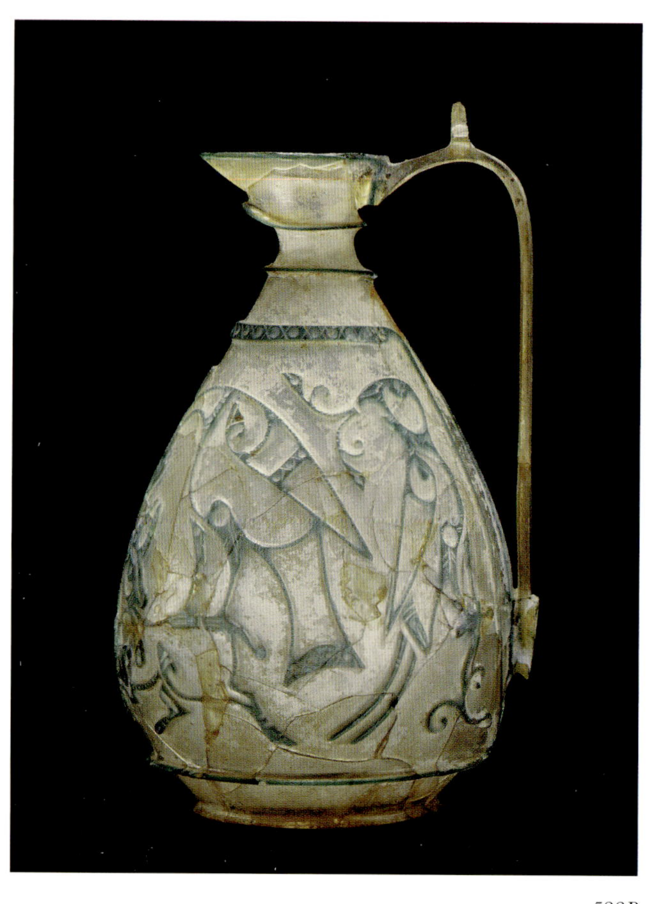

522B

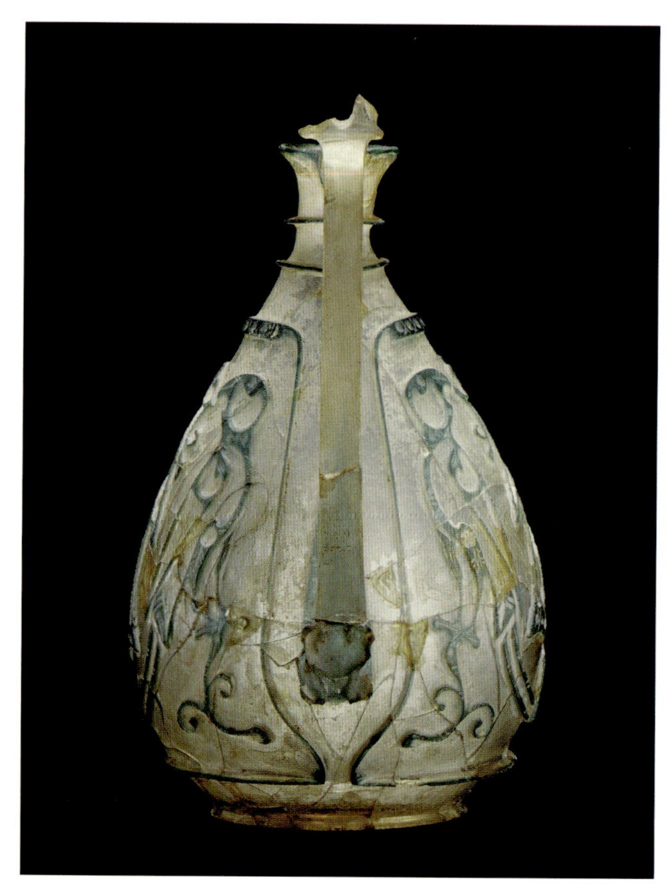

522C

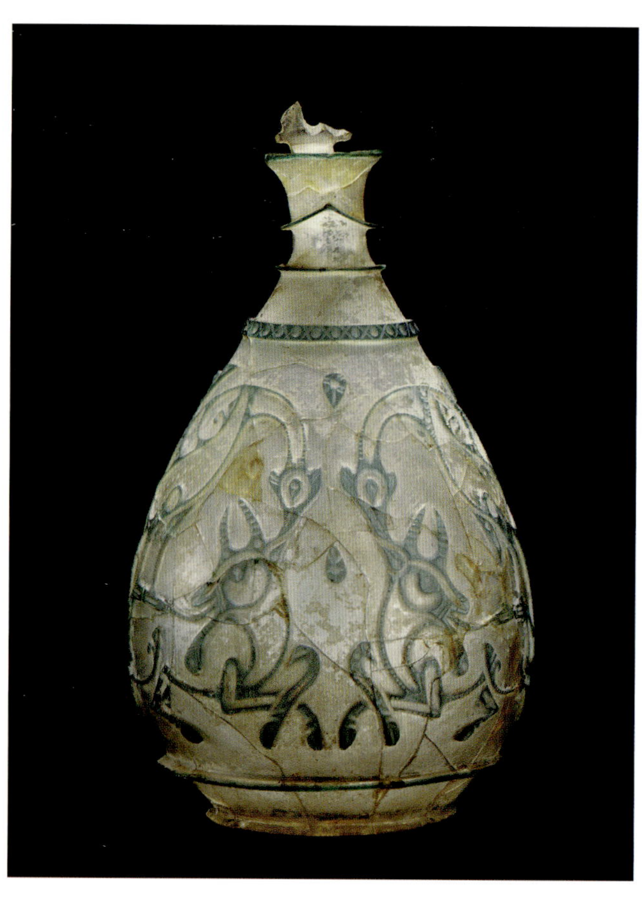

522D

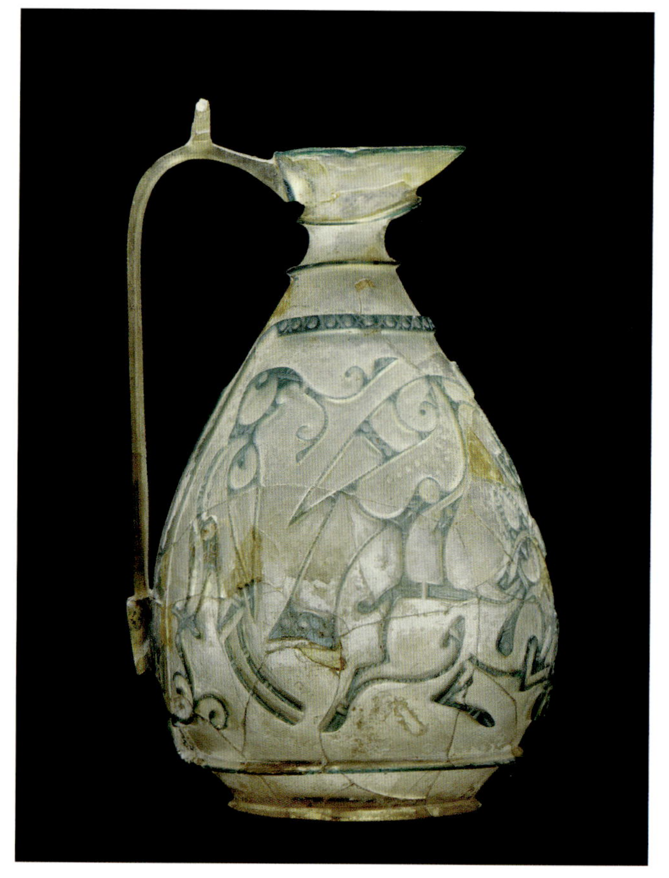

522E

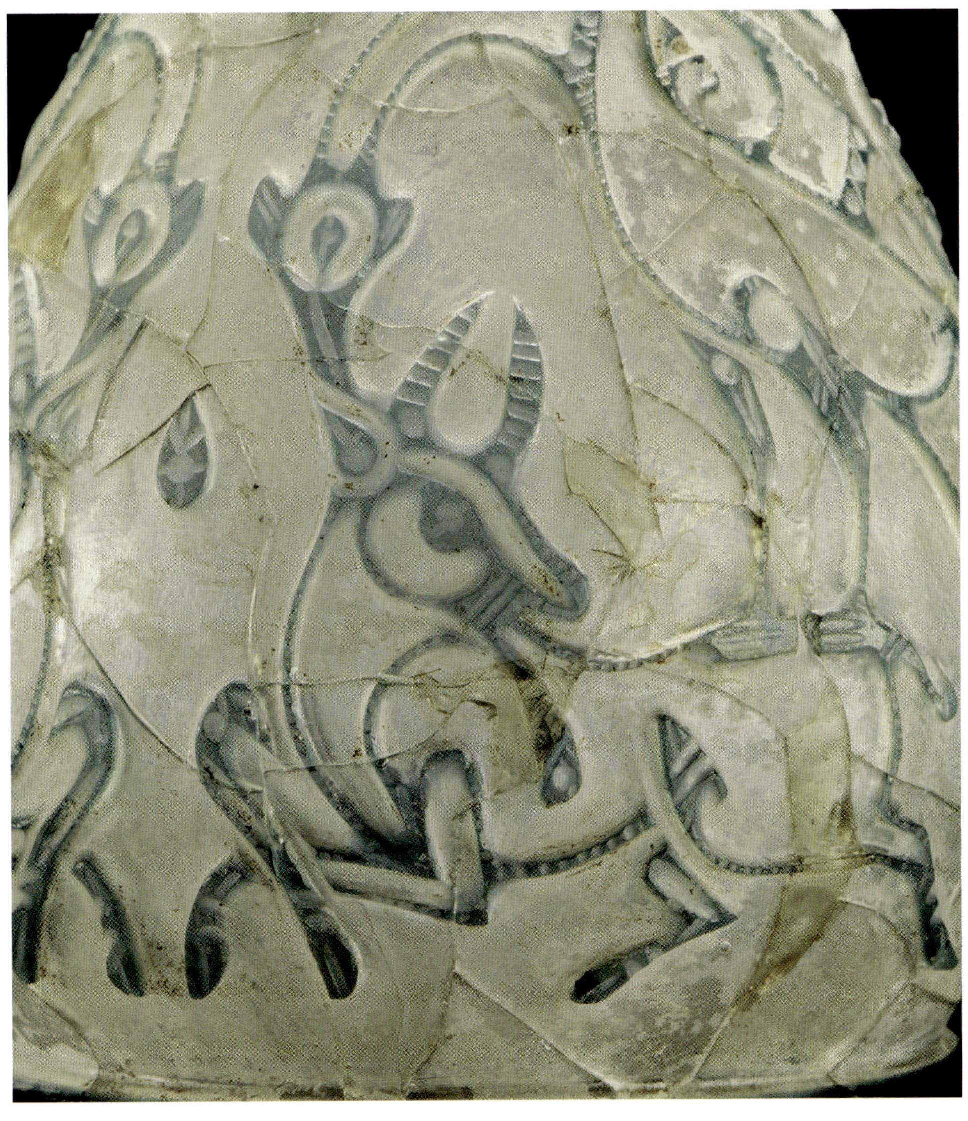

522F

raises questions about where and when they were made. However, the Corning Ewer does have parallels in another, related medium: rock crystal. These are the six ewers that form such a conspicuous element in the group of rock crystal objects usually attributed to workshops in Fatimid Cairo (Rice 1956; Scerrato 1979). A seventh rock crystal ewer, in the David Collection, Copenhagen, has an unusual form and no decoration on the body (27/1999: Folsach 2001, pp. 227–228 and 237, no. 368). Perhaps the best known of the group is a ewer in the Treasury of San Marco, Venice (80). Like the Corning Ewer, it has an everted rim and a narrow neck with two relief bands; a pear-shaped body, the bottom of which is emphasized by a third, sharply defined relief band; a foot-ring; and a concave base (Scerrato 1979, p. 527, fig. 592; *Eredità dell'Islam* 1993, p. 153, no. 61). The elaborate strap handle is surmounted by an ibex. The body is decorated with a single panel containing two seated lions, separated by arabesques. Above them, a Kufic inscription invokes "the blessing of God on the Imam al-ᶜAzīz Biᵓllāh." Al-ᶜAzīz Biᵓllāh was the fifth Fatimid caliph, who reigned in Cairo from 975 to 996. Since the Iranian traveler Naṣir-i Khusraw identified Cairo as a center for the working of rock crystal in the mid-11th century, it seems reasonable to suppose that the ewer was made there.

The five other rock crystal ewers are closely similar, each having a pear-shaped body with a single panel of ornament divided below the lip by luxuriant arabesques. The first of these, also in the Treasury of San Marco, has (instead of lions) a pair of rams (Scerrato 1979, p. 527, fig. 591; *Eredità dell'Islam* 1993, pp. 151–153, no. 60). The second, formerly among the treasures of the Medici and now in the Palazzo Pitti, Florence, has a pair of birds and an inscription indicating that it was made either between 1000 and 1008 or in 1010–1011 (*Eredità dell'Islam* 1993, p. 155, no. 62). The third ewer, in the treasury of the cathedral at Fermo, on the Adriatic coast of Italy, also has a pair of birds and an inscription (Scerrato 1979, p. 479, fig. 521; *Eredità dell'Islam* 1993, pp. 148–149, no. 58). The fourth, now in the Musée du Louvre, Paris, again depicts a pair of birds, which have a family likeness to the parrots on the Corning Ewer. It is, however, the last example, in the Victoria and Albert Museum, that bears the closest resemblance to the Corning Ewer. Surrounded by arabesques are two versions of the same familiar scene. On each side, a short-horned animal runs toward the center of the panel. A bird of prey, its wings outspread as though it has only just alighted, perches on the rump of the animal and pecks at its neck. The animal turns to look at its attacker. (For a small fragment that may have come from another rock crystal ewer, see **590**.)

The striking similarity between the Corning Ewer and the ewer in London solves one problem but raises another. The problem that it raises (or, better, restates) concerns connections. The Corning Ewer is said to have been found, and perhaps was made, in Iran; the rock crystal ewers apparently were made in Egypt. What, if any, mechanism connected Iran and Egypt and perhaps led to the production of such closely similar objects in two widely separated regions? Was it the result of the mobility of craftsmen, who moved (perhaps either sent or summoned) between Egypt and Iran? Are we looking at objects commissioned in one of these places and executed in the other? Or are the ewers, glass and rock crystal alike, manifestations of an "international" style created by all of these factors? The questions remain open, but as far as glass objects are concerned, one day chemical analyses may provide us with some of the answers.

The problem that it solves concerns chronology. Thanks to the inscriptions on the first ewer at San Marco and the ewer in the Palazzo Pitti, we know that the rock crystal ewers were made in the late 10th and early 11th centuries. If one suggested that all six were produced between about 975 and 1025, one would probably be correct. Presumably, the Corning Ewer belongs to the same period. It was made, therefore, within a generation of the year 1000. Wherever its decorator worked, it is not unreasonable to claim that he was a glass cutter whose skill rivaled that of the lapidaries who decorated the rock crystal ewers, and that the ewer stands comparison with the work of the greatest glass cutters of any period, before or since.

BIBLIOGRAPHY: *Arts of Islam* 1976, p. 141, no. 132; *Cameo Glass* 1982, pp. 30–31; Whitehouse 1985a, p. 67; *idem* 1985b; *JGS*, v. 28, 1986, cover and frontispiece; Charleston 1989, p. 301, fig. 11; Whitehouse 1990a; Yoshimizu 1992, pp. 101 and 292, no. 206; Ellis 1993, p. 63; Whitehouse 1993a; *idem* 1993b, p. 13, no. 20; *Glass of the Sultans* 2001, pp. 184–186, no. 90; *Guide to the Collections* 2001, p. 55; Whitehouse 2001a, p. 56; *idem* 2003, pp. 149–150, fig. 1.

523. Pitcher with Animals and Birds

Late 10th to early 11th century. Formerly in the Smith Collection (1494). 59.1.489.
H. (rim) 17.1 cm, D. (rim) 8.7 cm, (max.) 10.7 cm.
Translucent deep green over colorless. Blown (body probably blown in dip mold), cased; relief-cut, drilled; handle applied.

Pitcher with cylindrical body. Rim plain, with top ground flat and bevel on interior; neck shaped like funnel, with straight, tapering side; shoulder slopes, with rounded edge; wall descends vertically and turns in at bottom; base plain, with low kick; no pontil mark. Handle dropped onto edge of shoulder, drawn up and out, then bent in and attached to top of neck, with folded and pinched thumb-rest, which projects above rim.

Most of neck and entire body cased with green glass, which has been cut away to create three registers of ornament in relief: (1) on neck, (2) on shoulder, and (3) on wall. Register on neck is contained within panel that begins and ends behind handle; sides of panel have curved recesses at top, but are straight at bottom; space between them is bisected by vertical line extending from bottom of upper handle attachment to top of lower attachment, or close to it. Panel contains two animals running toward each other. Each animal has short horns, open mouth, body shown in outline, forelegs projecting forward, hind legs projecting backward, and long tail. Register on shoulder is framed at top by pair of continuous horizontal ribs, and at bottom by horizontal row of alternating oval and circular motifs shown in outline. Panel contains two snakes with heads almost touching and tails near lower handle attachment. Each has kite-shaped head with eyes close together, open mouth, and sinuous body shown in outline. Register on wall is continuous; it is framed at top by ovals and circles (see above), and at bottom by identical row of ovals and circles at junction of wall and base. Panel contains two animals running toward each other. Each animal has body and tail shown in outline and cloven hooves; above the back is stem, which divides and terminates in two half-palmettes separated by detached oval leaf with pointed ends. Behind and above each animal is bird shown in profile. Each bird faces in same direction as animal and has body and one wing shown in outline.

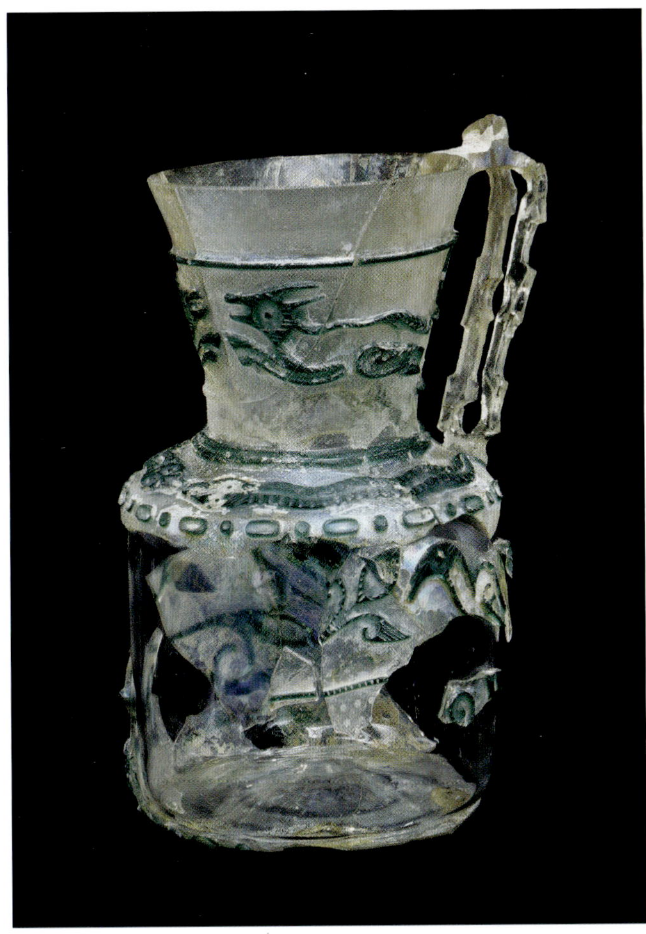

523A

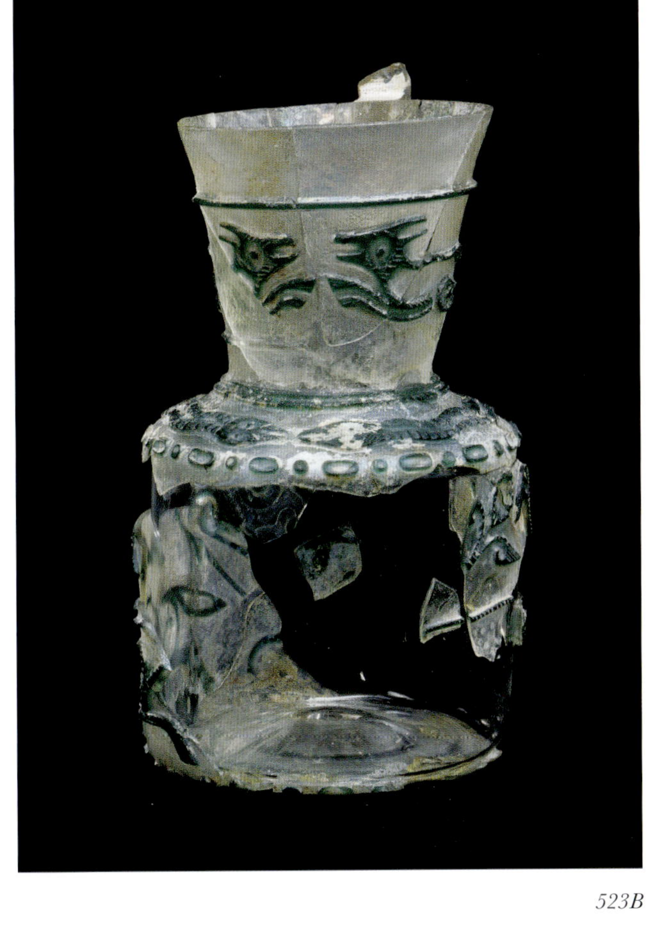

523B

Behind animals and birds are curvilinear stems and tendrils. Underside of base has two concentric circles (D. 4.3 cm and 6.9 cm). Most edges of raised decoration are vertical or nearly vertical, with very few slanting cuts. Most linear elements are notched; solid green elements, such as heads of animals on neck, head of one snake on shoulder, and heads of birds and half-palmettes on wall, are hatched. Bodies of birds and quadrupeds, but not snakes, are decorated with small circular depressions made by drilling.

Handle has openwork pattern consisting of three connected circular holes with raised borders; on edges of handle, opposite each hole, are shallow projections with slightly concave profiles; thumb-rest was cut in indeterminate design.

Incomplete. Approximately 35 percent of rim and neck, small part of shoulder, half of body, and small part of base are lost (but see below). Green glass is dull and somewhat pitted, and it has remains of greenish gray weathering; colorless glass has remains of silver to light gray weathering and some iridescence.

Comment: A large triangular fragment from the rim and neck, decorated with the head, shoulder, and forelimbs of one of the animals, is in the collection of

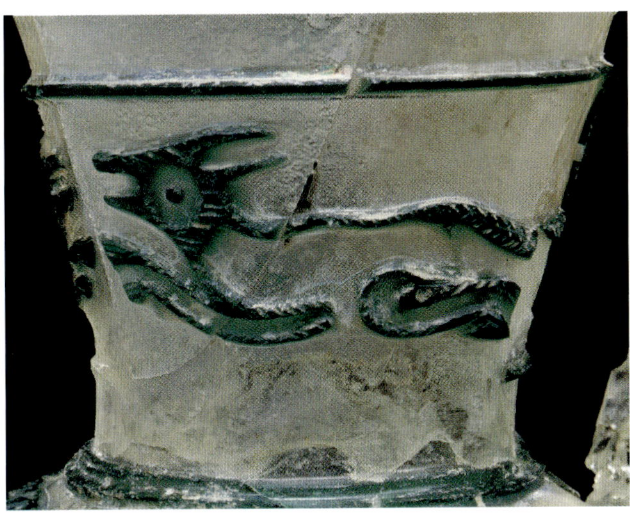

523C

the Museum für Islamische Kunst, Berlin (I.1993.7: Kröger 1999c, p. 329 and pl. 43d). In 2002, that museum kindly lent the fragment to the Corning Museum so that it could be reunited with the other surviving fragments.

A sample of the colorless glass was collected for chemical analysis, but so far the result has not been published (Brill 1999, v. 1, p. 93, no. 5388).

perhaps with part of animal moving to right, represented by outline of haunch, tail terminating in triangular tip, and small part of leg; above haunch, trace of second motif; outline of leg is notched, and tip of tail is hatched.

Broken on all sides. Transparent very pale gray weathering on interior.

Comment: The fragment came from a vessel with a markedly convex profile; perhaps it was a bottle, a ewer, or a hemispherical bowl. The tentative identification of the main motif as part of an animal derives from its general similarity to the hindquarters of animals on relief-cut objects, such as the bowl decorated with horses, in the Museum fur Islamische Kunst, Berlin (I.20/65: Kröger 1984, pp. 223–224, no. 193; *Glass of the Sultans* 2001, p. 176, no. 82), and the celebrated turquoise blue bowl in the Treasury of San Marco, Venice (140: *ibid.*, pp. 176–177, no. 83).

528. Fragment of Cup or Beaker with Bird

9th to 10th century. Formerly in the Smith Collection (1262-D). 59.1.493.
Max. Dim. 5.4 cm, D. (est.) about 7 cm.
Transparent green over colorless; both with very few small bubbles. Blown, applied; relief- and linear-cut.

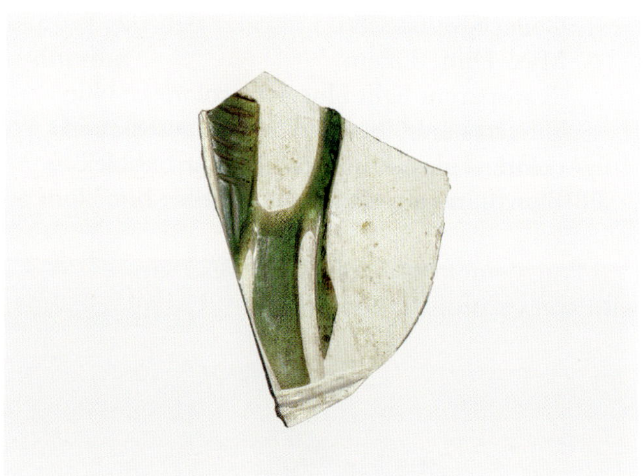

528

Fragment from wall of cup or beaker (TTh. 0.25 cm), which is straight and either vertical or tapering. Relief decoration (Th. 0.1 cm): part of standing bird in profile, facing right; lower body shown in outline; leg indicated by single line of uneven thickness; wing, folded against back, appears as solid green triangle, with plumage indicated by straight cuts through to colorless glass; tail, too, is solid green; just below tail, colorless horizontal rib, presumably continuous, in countersunk relief. Colorless glass has traces of coldworking only in vicinity of bird.

Broken on all sides. Green glass is dull, with faint brown to grayish weathering; colorless glass has incipient weathering.

Comment: The absence of coldworking in the area farthest from the bird indicates that the green glass was applied to a small part of the wall rather than gathered. If the wall is vertical, the fragment probably came from a cylindrical object similar to the cameo glass vessel decorated with ibexes, in the L. A. Mayer Memorial Institute for Islamic Art, Jerusalem (G24-69: *Glass of the Sultans* 2001, p. 182, no. 88). Alternatively, if the wall tapers, it may have come from a beaker similar to the colorless relief-cut glass beaker in The Metropolitan Museum of Art, New York (1974-45: *ibid.*, pp. 172–173, no. 79), or the rock crystal relief-cut beaker in The British Museum, London (OA 1954 10-131: *Arts of Islam* 1976, p. 125, no. 102).

529. Fragments of Beaker with Bird

9th to 10th century. Found during excavations at Fusṭāṭ (Old Cairo), Egypt (73.9.16). Gift of the American Research Center in Egypt. 79.1.16.
H. (surviving) 5.7 cm, D. (rim) 5 cm, (base) 4.3 cm.
Green over colorless. Blown, cased; relief-cut.

Two groups of fragments representing approximately half of rim, one-third of lower wall, and entire base of one beaker. Rim plain, with upper surface ground flat; lower wall straight and tapering; base plain, but slightly outsplayed; no pontil mark. Lower wall has green decoration in relief: bird shown in left profile, with narrow neck, plump body, small folded wing with hollow circle at inner end and four short parallel cuts, and single leg and foot; to right and left of bird, unidentified motifs; below it, cut in colorless glass, horizontal rib, presumably continuous.

Surfaces have thick layer of opaque deep brown weathering; where this is missing, glass has off-white to silver weathering.

Comment: The fragments were found during excavations directed by Prof. George T. Scanlon in 1973 (Scanlon 1981: see below). Scanlon and Pinder-Wilson (2001: see below) attributed them to the years around 900.

It is not certain that the fragmentary rim and the base were parts of the same object. For beakers with

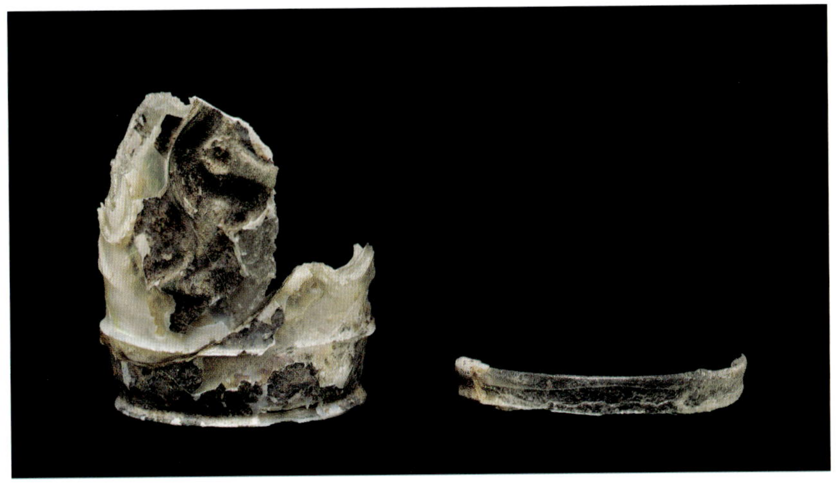

529

a similar shape, see Kröger 1984, pp. 225–226, no. 194 (a colorless beaker with a frieze of relief-cut animals, in the Museum für Islamische Kunst, Berlin, I.70/62); and *idem* 1995, pp. 137–138 (also colorless, with relief-cut ornament, found at Nishapur, northeastern Iran). In previous publications (see below), this object was described as colorless, presumably because the weathering almost conceals the color of the bird. There is no doubt, however, that it has a bright green overlay.

Bibliography: Scanlon 1981, pp. 428–429, fig. 9; Pinder-Wilson and Scanlon 1987, p. 68, no. 17 (which does not mention the fragmentary rim or the green overlay); Scanlon and Pinder-Wilson 2001, pp. 103–104, no. 43d (which again does not mention the rim or the overlay).

530. Fragment of Beaker(?) with Bird

9th to 10th century. Formerly in the Strauss Collection (F82). Bequest of Jerome Strauss. 79.1.293.
H. (surviving) 6.6 cm, D. (est., at highest point) about 5 cm.
Transparent bright green over colorless; both with very small bubbles, and green glass has specks of scale. Blown, applied or cased; relief-cut.

Fragment of beaker(?). Wall (TTh. 0.25 cm) straight, perhaps tapering. Decorated in relief in both green (Th. 0.1 cm) and colorless base glass: near center of fragment, standing green bird, shown mainly in outline, facing left, with thin neck, folded wing with dot on covert and feathers indicated by hatching, triangular or wedge-shaped tail, and one or two legs; to left of bird, one detached vertical line; on either side of bird, colorless curvilinear elements with some notched outlines; below these motifs, part of continuous horizontal rib, which is also colorless.

Broken on all sides. Apart from specks of incipient weathering on green, glass is in pristine condition.

Comment: The estimated diameter of the fragment (about five centimeters) suggests that it came from the wall of a beaker rather than from the neck of a bottle. The surviving part of the rib (L. 1.8 cm) is too short to permit a reliable estimate of the angle at which the wall descends, but it appears to taper. The fragment, therefore, is probably from a beaker with a frieze of decoration bordered above and below by horizontal ribs (cf. a beaker in The Metropolitan Museum of Art, New York, 1974.45: *Glass of the Sultans* 2001, pp. 172–173, no. 79). It is impossible to determine whether the greater part of the object was cased with green glass, or whether one or more overlays were applied locally. However, given the relatively small extent of the green decoration, it seems reasonable to

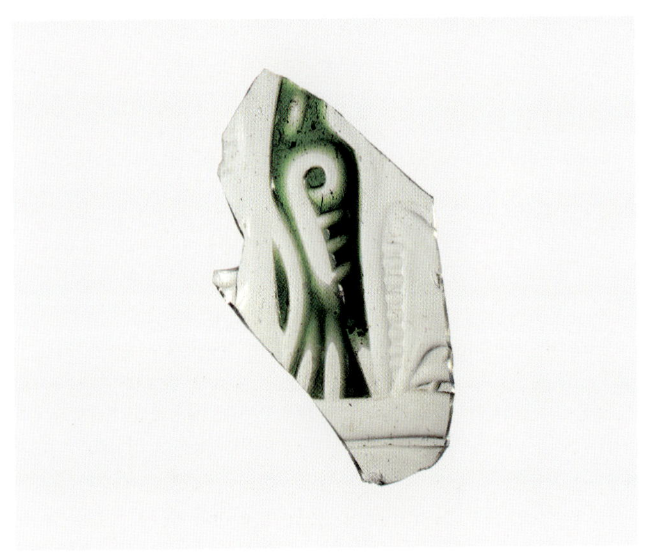

530

assume that the color was applied locally, thereby avoiding the task of removing large areas of unwanted overlay.

531. Fragment of Beaker(?) with Bird

9th to 10th century. Formerly in the Strauss Collection (F79). Bequest of Jerome Strauss. 95.1.19.
Max. Dim. 4.1 cm, H. (surviving) about 2.5 cm, D. (est.) about 6 cm.
Transparent light greenish yellow over colorless. Blown, probably applied; relief-cut, drilled.

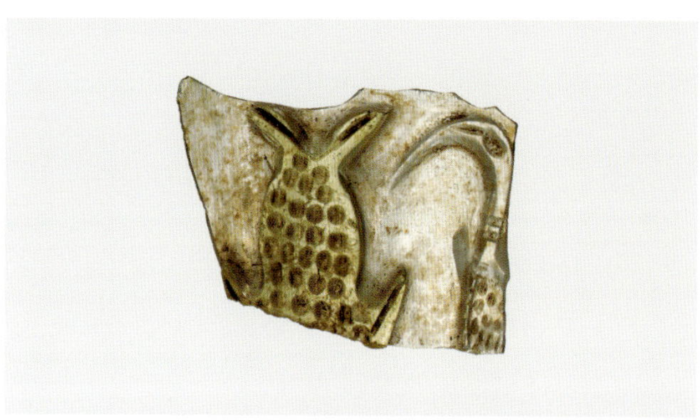

531

Fragment of beaker(?). Wall (TTh. less than 0.2 cm) straight and vertical or nearly vertical, with patch of yellow overlay (Th. 0.1 cm). Decoration relief-cut in both yellow and colorless glasses. Yellow glass has upper part of unidentified object, shown in silhouette. Object is symmetrical about vertical axis; it is bulbous, terminates in two earlike projections at top, and has two similar projections at bottom of surviving portion. Each "ear" has one short cut, and bulbous part is covered with small circular depressions. To right of yellow object, cut in colorless glass, bird is seen standing in profile, facing left. It has long and curved beak, small head with large eye, narrow neck, and part of body. Lower neck has two horizontal cuts, outline of body is at least partly notched, and body is filled with drilled circular depressions.

Broken on all sides. Yellow and colorless glasses have patches of transparent gray to pale brown weathering.

COMMENT: The size and shape of the fragment suggest that it was part of a beaker. If the bird was intended to represent a real species, it may be an egret or a heron. Although the yellow motif is symmetrical and one might expect it to be part of a symmetrical design, the area to the left, which corresponds to the beak and head of the bird on the right, is empty. The color of the overlay is close to that of the overlay on **502**.

532. Fragment of Bottle with Bird

9th to 10th century. Formerly in the Smith Collection. Gift of Carl Berkowitz and Derek Content. 76.1.306.
Max. Dim. 4.9 cm, H. (surviving) about 3.4 cm, D. (max., est.) about 10 cm.
Transparent green over colorless. Blown, applied; relief-cut.

Fragment of bottle, probably globular. Wall (TTh. 0.2 cm) is decorated in relief (Th. 0.1 cm) with green silhouette of bird, which faces left and has plump body and tail terminating in schematic half-palmette; body is embellished with shallow cuts.

Broken on all sides. Green glass is matte, with pale brown weathering; colorless glass is extensively pitted, with silvery gray weathering.

COMMENT: The bird is roughly comparable with the birds on a cylindrical bottle in the David Collection, Copenhagen (2/1972: *Glass of the Sultans* 2001, pp. 195–196, no. 100). The form of the object, however, resembles that of a globular bottle in The British Museum, London, that is decorated with animals (OA 1966.12-11.1: *ibid.*, pp. 194–195, no. 99).

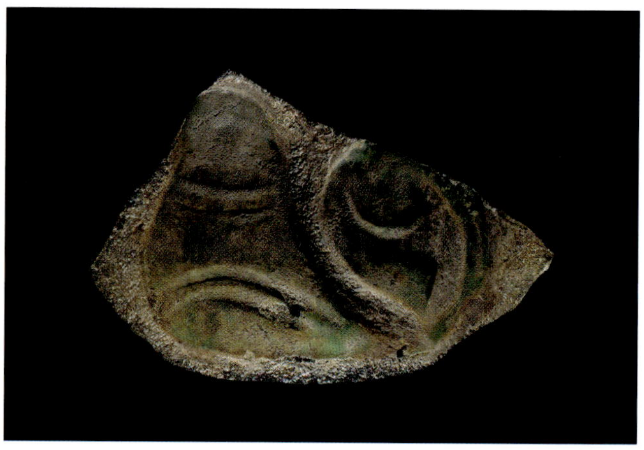

532

533. Fragment of Bottle or Pitcher with Bird

9th to 10th century. Formerly in the Smith Collection (1088). 59.1.503.
Max. Dim. 4.5 cm, D. (max., est.) about 9 cm.
Transparent green over colorless; both with few minute bubbles. Blown, cased; relief-cut.

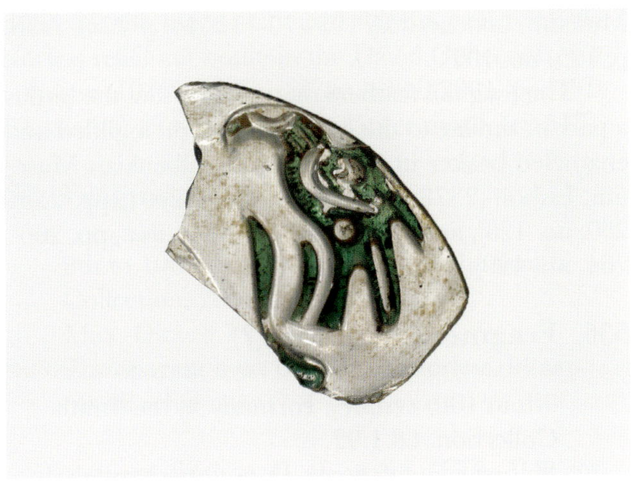

533

Fragment of bottle or pitcher with globular body. Lower wall (TTh. 0.2–0.25 cm) curves out, down, and in. Green relief-cut decoration (Th. 0.1 cm): standing bird, facing left, with curved beak, small head with prominent eye, small and oval body shown in outline and partly notched, folded wing, two legs indicated by single curving lines, and narrow tail that is also shown in outline; below and to left of feet, branching stem; below tail, trace of third, unidentified element.

Broken on all sides. Green glass has patches of light yellow enamellike weathering; colorless glass has faint grayish weathering.

Comment: Traces of coldworking cover the exterior surface of the fragment, indicating that the blank was completely, or almost completely, cased. The curvature of the fragment shows that it came from the wall of a more or less globular vessel: presumably a bottle, the body of which would have been approximately the same size and shape as that of a cameo glass bottle in The British Museum, London (OA 1966.12-11.1: *Glass of the Sultans* 2001, pp. 194–195, no. 99), or a pitcher. It is possible that the raised element at the bottom of the fragment, of which only a trace remains, was a horizontal rib (cf. the rib that borders the frieze of ibexes on **354**).

Bibliography: *Glass from the Ancient World* 1957, p. 285, no. 610 (part of group).

534. Fragment with Bird

9th to 10th century. Formerly in the Smith Collection (961). 59.1.491.
Max. Dim. 6.5 cm.
Transparent green over colorless; both with very few bubbles. Blown, cased or applied; relief-cut.

Fragment from wall of vessel (TTh. 0.4 cm), which appears to splay, then curve down and in. Decorated with green overlay (Th. 0.2 cm): standing bird, facing left; head is narrow, terminating in pointed beak, with eye(s) indicated by two intersecting oval cuts; body is shown in outline, with four shallow circular depressions in colorless interior; wings are of unequal size and consist of curving lines that terminate in half-palmettes with straight, shallow cuts indicating plumage; one leg is indicated by short, straight line; tail with rounded end is outlined in relief and has row of five oval cuts in colorless interior. Traces of coldworking are visible around bird, but may or may not exist at bottom of fragment.

Broken on all sides. Green glass is almost matte, with gray to brown weathering; colorless glass has patches of pale green to brown weathering.

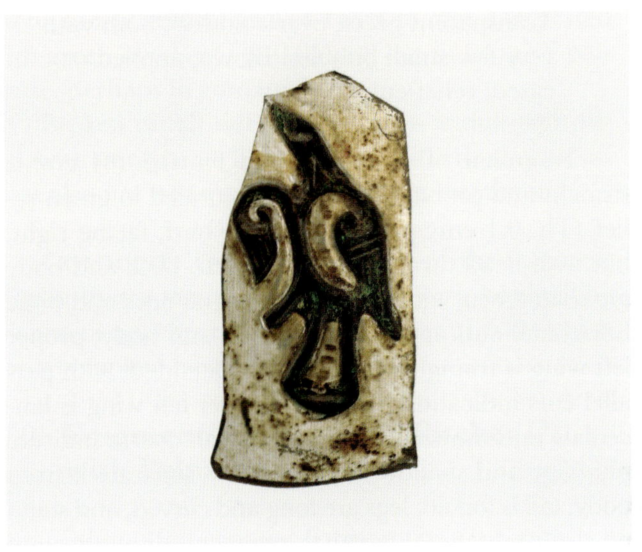

534

Comment: The fragment appears to have come from the lower wall of a vessel with a pear-shaped body. Although the relief cutting is not of the same quality, the conceit of decorating the bird's wings with half-palmettes is reminiscent of the birds of prey on the Corning Ewer (**522**).

Bibliography: *Verres antiques* 1954, p. 49, no. 297 (part of group); *Glass from the Ancient World* 1957, p. 285, no. 610 (part of group).

535. Fragment with Bird

9th to 10th century. Formerly in the Strauss Collection (F83). Bequest of Jerome Strauss. 79.1.288.
H. (surviving) about 5.7 cm, D. (est.) about 7 cm.

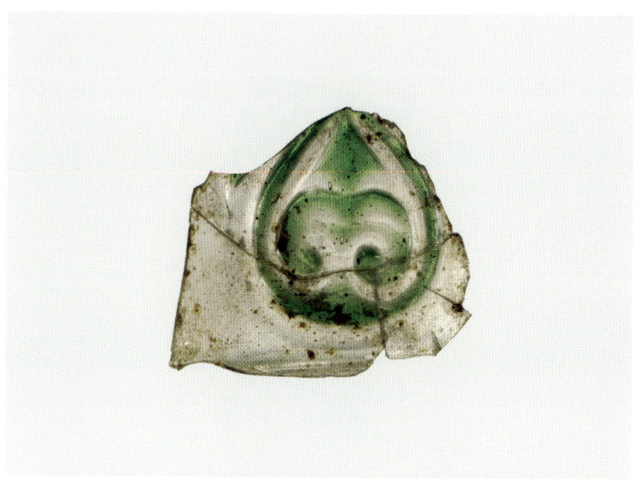

539

Comment: The fragments came from a vessel with a cylindrical body and either a shallow, sloping shoulder or a base that was slightly convex, at least near the edge. In either case, the vessel is most likely to have been a bottle (perhaps similar to *Glass of the Sultans* 2001, pp. 195–196, no. 100, which has green and brown appliqués and linear-cut ornament) or a pitcher (perhaps similar to **523**). For another palmette, perhaps contained in a cordate frame, see **538**.

Bibliography: *Glass from the Ancient World* 1957, p. 285, no. 610 (part of group).

540. Fragment of Pitcher(?) with Palmette

9th to 10th century. Formerly in the Smith Collection. 68.1.91.
H. (surviving) 3.3 cm, D. (base, est.) about 11 cm.
Transparent green over colorless; both with very few minute bubbles. Blown, cased; relief-cut.

Fragment of pitcher(?). Lower wall descends vertically, then curves in at bottom; base flat. Wall and junction of wall and base have green decoration in relief (Th. 0.2 cm). On wall: two descending lines converge in V and terminate in downward-pointing palmette, which is flanked by two lines that slant down and in, and terminate at the same level as the tip of the palmette; at junction of wall and base, horizontal band, presumably continuous, of overlapping elongated Z-shaped motifs, which together resemble two-ply cable. Ornament on wall, but not at junction of wall and base, is embellished with short, straight cuts and notches.

Broken on all sides. Interior has intermittent very thin pale gray weathering.

Comment: The fragment is tentatively identified as part of a pitcher by analogy with **523**, which has continuous horizontal bands of geometric ornament at the edge of the shoulder and the junction of the wall and the base. The palmette resembles the palmettes on the underside of a colorless relief-cut bowl in the Museum für Islamische Kunst, Berlin (I.20/65: *Glass of the Sultans* 2001, p. 176, no. 82 = Kröger 1984, pp. 223–224, no. 193), and on a number of rock crystal objects, such as the ewer decorated with recumbent rams, in the Treasury of San Marco, Venice (86: Erdmann 1971, pp. 113–114, no. 125). Two similar rock crystal ewers, one also in the Treasury of San Marco and the other in the Palazzo Pitti, Florence, bear inscriptions datable to 975–996 and 1000–1008 or 1011 (80: *ibid.*, pp. 112–113, no. 124; Rice 1956).

The color of the overlay and the condition of the fragment are very similar to those of **534**.

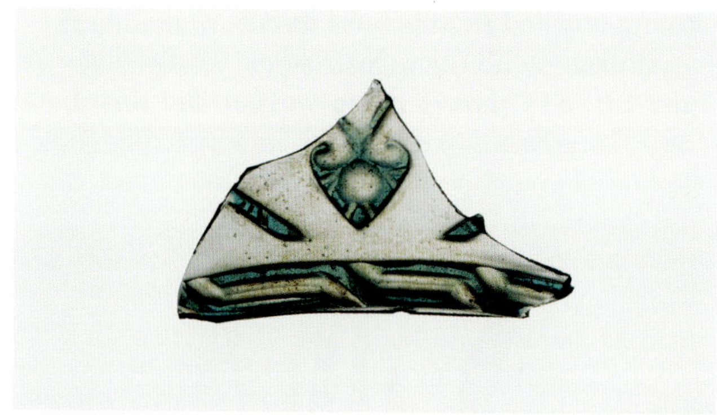

540

541. Fragment of Bowl with Half-Palmettes

9th to 10th century. Formerly in the Smith Collection (1353). 59.1.490.
Max. Dim. 10.5 cm, H. (surviving) 5.6 cm, D. (est.) 26 cm.
Transparent blue over colorless; both with very few minute bubbles. Blown, cased; relief-cut.

Fragment of bowl. Rim plain, with rounded lip; wall (TTh. 0.4 cm) tapers, with slightly convex profile. Outside has blue decoration in relief (Th. 0.2 cm) on colorless background. This consists of parts of two vegetal motifs: (1) pair of half-palmettes, which terminate in small, outward-facing volutes; and (2) on viewer's right, pair of larger half-palmettes, which also terminate in outward-facing volutes.

Small areas of colorless glass are almost pristine; elsewhere, both glasses are extensively pitted, with remains of brown to silver iridescent weathering.

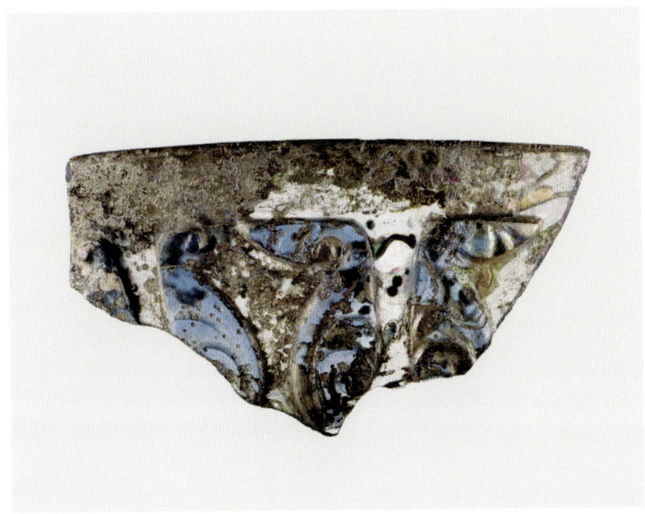

541

Comment: Unless the surviving part of the rim is distorted, the diameter of the vessel was about 26 centimeters. It may have had a tapering wall and a broad, flat base, similar to **251** and a bowl in the al-Sabah Collection, Dār al-Āthār al-Islāmiyyah, Kuwait National Museum (LNS 113 KG: *Glass of the Sultans* 2001, pp. 174–175, no. 81), both of which are colorless vessels with relief-cut ornament. In any case, **541** appears to have come from one of the largest known Islamic cameo glass vessels. If the diameter of the vessel was about 26 centimeters and the decoration consisted of a continuous frieze of alternating pairs of larger and smaller half-palmettes, the wall was decorated with seven (or possibly eight) motifs of each type. On the colorless vessels mentioned above, the principal decoration is on the underside of the base: a bird on **251** and a *senmurv* on the bowl in Kuwait.

542. Fragment of Bottle(?) with Half-Palmette

10th century. Formerly in the Smith Collection.
68.1.98.
Max. Dim. 4.6 cm, H. (surviving) about 4.4 cm, D. (est.) about 10 cm.
Transparent green over colorless. Blown, cased; relief-cut.

Fragment from wall (TTh. 0.3 cm) of bottle(?), which is almost straight and vertical or nearly vertical. Decorated in relief in green (Th. 0.15 cm) on colorless background: part of frieze with horizontal border, presumably continuous; above (or below) this, parts of two tendrils, one of which terminates in half-palmette and other in triangular leaf, and one tear-shaped element. Border and tendrils are notched; half-palmette, leaf, and tear are lightly hatched.

Broken on all sides. Green glass has patches of reddish brown weathering; colorless glass has slightly iridescent pinkish gray weathering.

Comment: It is not clear whether the fragment is from the top or the bottom of the frieze. Nevertheless, the size and shape suggest that it came from a bottle. The tear-shaped motif recalls two similar elements on the Corning Ewer (**522**), the decoration of which also has notched outlines and hatched details. The Corning Ewer is believed to date from about 1000.

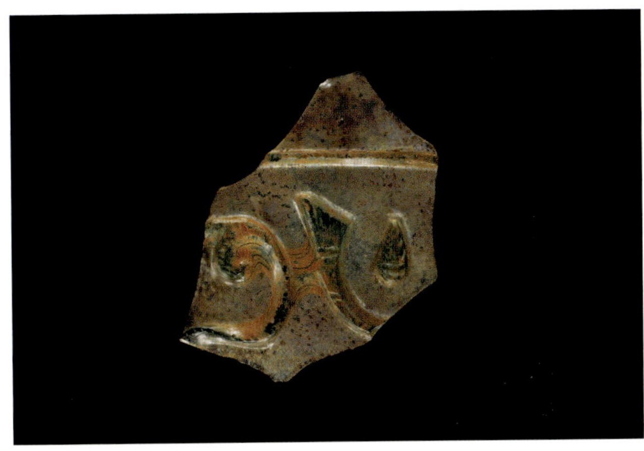

542

543. Fragment of Ewer or Bottle with Half-Palmette

10th century. Formerly in the Smith Collection.
68.1.111.
Max. Dim. 2.5 cm.
Transparent bluish green over colorless; both with very few minute bubbles. Blown, cased; relief-cut.

Fragment of ewer or bottle. Wall or shoulder (TTh. 0.2 cm) descends in smooth convex curve, with green decoration in relief (Th. 0.1 cm) on colorless background: single, presumably continuous horizontal line, above (or below) which is stem terminating in half-palmette with four leaves; stem and outer leaves are notched.

Broken on all sides. No apparent weathering.

Comment: The profile of the fragment indicates that it came from a ewer or a bottle. If it came from a ewer, it is probably from the lower wall (cf. the profile of the Corning Ewer [**522**] and the rock crystal ewers of the same form). If this is the case, the horizontal line is the lower border of the frieze on the wall and the half-palmette faces upward. If the fragment came from a bottle, it may have come from the shoulder of an object resembling the cameo glass bottle in the David Collection, Copenhagen (3/1971: *Glass of the Sultans* 2001, p. 183, no. 89). If so, the horizontal line decorates the shoulder and the half-palmette faces down; on the bottle in the David Collection, there is a line on the shoulder, and the two pairs of birds in the frieze have crests that terminate in downward-pointing half-palmettes. Alternatively, the fragment may have come from the shoulder or the lower wall of a globular bottle such as the rock crystal bottle in Saint Stephen's Cathedral in Halberstadt, Germany (Shalem 1996, pp. 209–210, no. 52 = Lamm 1929–30, p. 197, pl. 67.12).

The half-palmette may be compared with the half-palmettes that decorate the haunches of the animals and the wing coverts of the birds of prey on **522**. The quality of the workmanship is excellent.

The color of the overlay and the condition of the fragment are very similar to those of **540**.

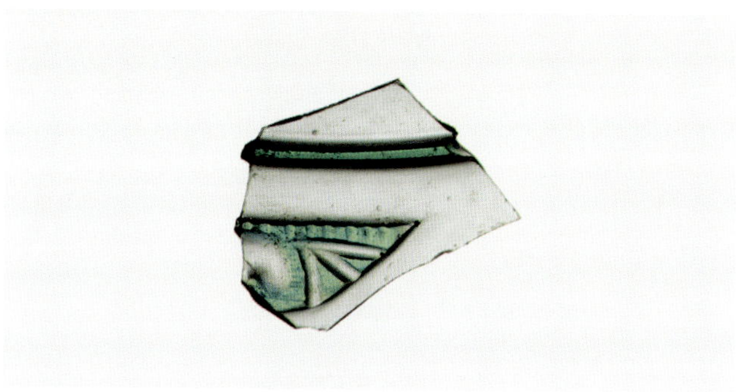

543

544. Fragment of Ewer(?) with Half-Palmettes

9th to 10th century. Formerly in the Smith Collection (1287-B). 59.1.501.
H. (surviving) 4.3 cm, D. (est., at bottom of fragment) 6–7 cm.
Transparent green over colorless; both with few very small bubbles. Blown, cased; relief-cut.

Fragment from wall of ewer(?), which is straight and appears to have a wider diameter at bottom than at top. Decorated in relief (from top to bottom): at highest point, colorless horizontal rib; 0.5 cm below rib, green element that consists of elongated, reversed S-shaped stem, wider at bottom than at top, and terminates in rather open half-palmettes. Entire surface shows signs of coldworking on exterior.

Broken on all sides. Colorless glass has small patches of incipient weathering.

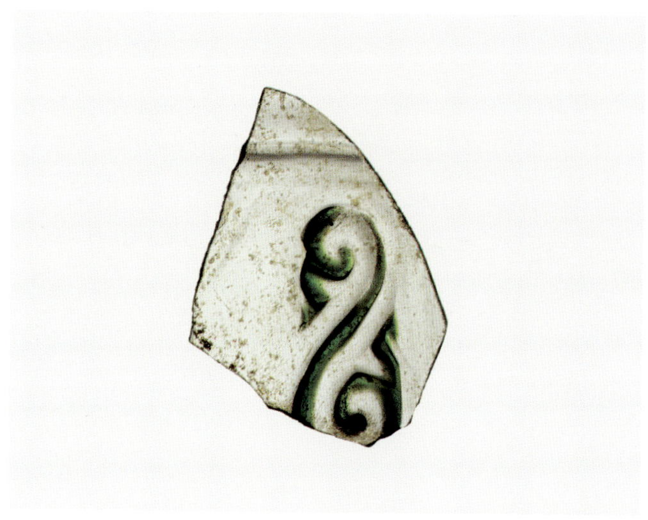

544

Comment: The presence of coldworking over the entire exterior indicates that the overlay was cased rather than applied.

The surviving section of the rib is so short that it is very difficult to estimate the angle at which the wall descends. However, it does appear that the fragment had a greater diameter at the bottom than at the top. If this observation is correct, the fragment may have come from the upper wall of a ewer similar to, but slightly narrower than, the Corning Ewer (**522**). The principal ornament on the Corning Ewer and its rock crystal counterparts is a continuous panel with a pictorial composition on either side, separated by the handle and by small or larger motifs beneath the pouring lip. If the fragment did come from a ewer, the green panel may have been below the lip, separating the two compositions. If the object was not a ewer, presumably it was a pitcher or a bottle.

Bibliography: Whitehouse 2003, pp. 150–151, fig. 5.

545. Fragment with Half-Palmette

9th to 10th century. 59.1.594.
Max. Dim. 3.4 cm.
Transparent light blue over colorless. Blown, probably cased; relief-cut.

Fragment from wall of vessel (TTh. 0.2–0.25 cm). Decoration consists of blue overlay (Th. 0.1 cm) with half-palmette, tear-shaped motif, and other elements. Tear has circular depression at center and short vertical and horizontal cuts. Half-palmette is notched and hatched, and other elements are notched.

Broken on all sides. Small patches of transparent pale brown weathering.

Comment: The fragment came from an object of exceptional quality. The two glasses are virtually bubble-free, and the cutting is exceptional. The tear-shaped motif is very similar to two such motifs on the Corning Ewer (**522**), one pointed at the top and the other pointed at the bottom. The tears on the ewer are placed, one above the other, below the pouring lip; one has the point at the top, and the other has it at the bottom. The decoration on either side of the tears is symmetrical. These observations may indicate the orientation of **545**, which may have had a symmetrical arrangement of half-palmettes and other vegetal motifs. The fragment may have come from the same object as **537**.

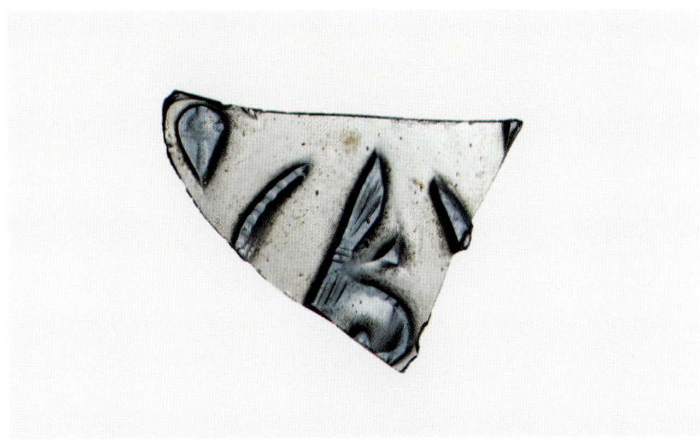

545

546. Fragment with Half-Palmette

9th to 10th century. Formerly in the Smith Collection. 68.1.109.
Max. Dim. 2.9 cm, H. (surviving) about 2.6 cm, D. (at half-palmette, est.) about 9 cm.
Transparent blue over colorless; both with very small bubbles. Blown, probably cased; relief-cut.

Fragment of vessel with convex wall (TTh. 0.3 cm). Decoration relief-cut in blue overlay (Th. 0.1 cm):

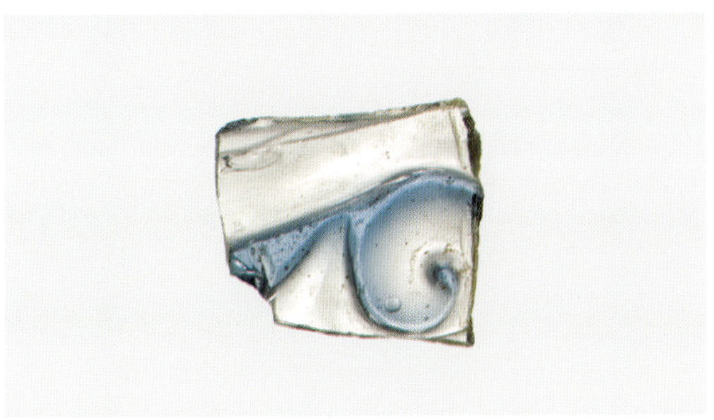

546

at assumed top of fragment, trace of unidentified element; 0.9 cm below this, part of horizontal or nearly horizontal half-palmette on curved stem. Colorless glass is covered with traces of coldworking.

Broken on all sides. Blue and colorless glasses are virtually unweathered.

Comment: Although the fragment is small, the presence of coldworking on the entire surface suggests that the vessel was probably cased. If the half-palmette is from the top or bottom of a decorative frieze, the unidentified element may be part of a continuous horizontal rib. If the fragment is from the top of the frieze, the vessel may have been a bottle, possibly similar to the cameo glass bottle in the David Collection, Copenhagen (3/1971: *Glass of the Sultans* 2001, p. 183, no. 89), on which the frieze contains two pairs of birds with crests terminating in horizontal half-palmettes, just below the border. On the other hand, the fragment may have come from the lower wall of a globular bottle such as the colorless relief-cut bottle with a frieze of ibexes (**354**).

547. Fragment with Half-Palmette(?)

9th to 10th century. Formerly in the Smith Collection. 68.1.59-62.
Max. Dim. 3.6 cm.
Transparent green over colorless. Blown, applied; relief-cut.

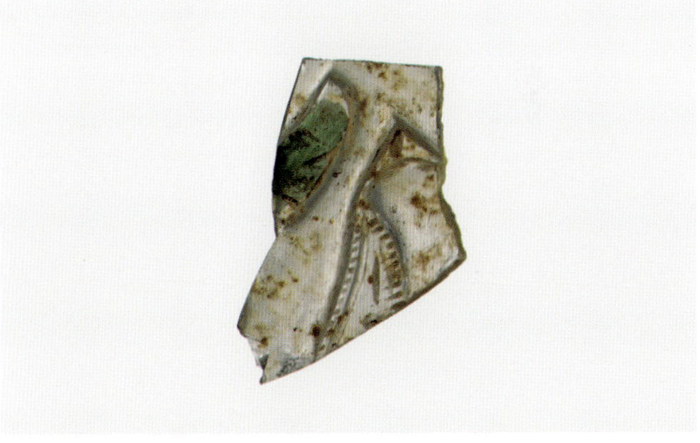

547

Fragment. Wall (Th. 0.1–0.15 cm) is straight and has both green and relief-cut colorless decoration. Green glass has part of narrow, curved motif, possibly half-palmette; colorless glass has part of curvilinear motif with notched outlines and one drilled depression.

Broken on all sides. Green glass has light gray weathering; colorless glass has transparent pale gray weathering.

Comment: The combination of a colored overlay and relief-cut colorless ornament is unusual, but see **531**, **552**, and **585**.

548. Fragment of Cup or Bottle with Animal(?) and Vegetal Scroll

9th to 10th century. Formerly in the Smith Collection. 59.1.595.
H. 5.7 cm, D. (est.) 10 cm.
Transparent light blue over almost colorless; latter has few small bubbles. Blown, cased; relief-cut.

Fragment of cylindrical cup or bottle, including approximately 12 percent of rim. Rim, which may not be original (see below), plain and ground flat; wall descends vertically or almost vertically. Decorated in relief in blue (Th. 0.1 cm) on colorless background (Th. 0.1–0.15 cm): just below rim, one horizontal rib forming upper border of frieze. At top of frieze, narrow vegetal scroll; below this, parts of indeterminate element, possibly animal shown in profile, facing right, with small head, single raised dot representing eye, and horns; curving line at bottom of fragment may be part of body.

Aside from rim, all edges broken. Transparent pale gray weathering, especially on colorless glass.

Comment: The fragment presents two problems: (1) the nature of the rim and (2) the identity of the principal element in the decoration. The rim and the border of the frieze are improbably close together, and one wonders whether the upper part of the vessel was removed after sustaining damage. If this conjecture is correct, the fragment may have come from a bottle rather than a cup. (The same observations apply to the cameo glass "cup" in the L. A. Mayer Memorial Institute for Islamic Art, Jerusalem [G24-69: *Glass of the Sultans* 2001, p. 182, no. 88], the rim of which is not even horizontal.) The decoration is highly stylized (like the decoration on the cup in Jerusalem). The main reason for suspecting that the principal element is an animal is the headlike element with an "eye" and two "horns."

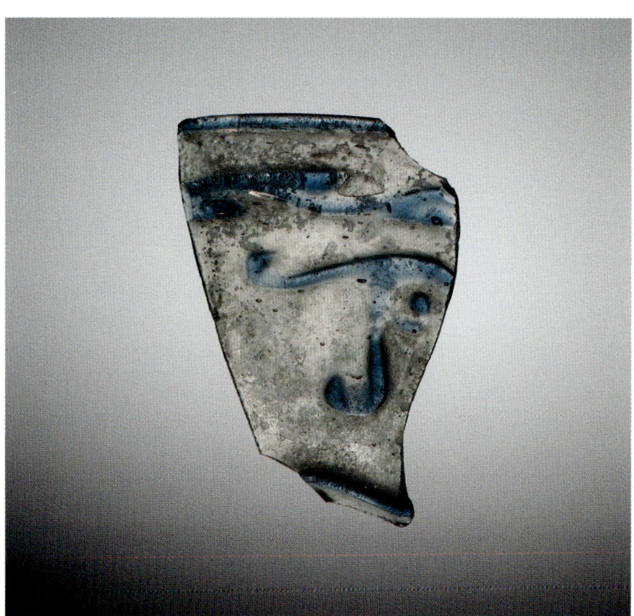

548

549. Fragment of Cup, Beaker, or Bottle with Vegetal Motif

9th to 10th century. 51.1.168II.
H. (surviving) 5 cm, D. (est.) about 8 cm.
Transparent green over colorless. Blown, cased or applied; relief-cut.

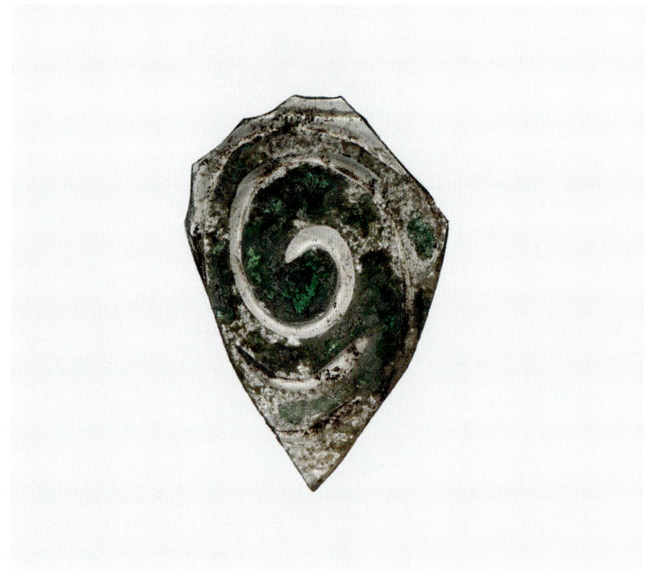

549

Fragment of cup, beaker, or bottle. Wall (TTh. 0.2 cm) straight and vertical or almost vertical, with, below lightly incised horizontal line, relief decoration in green (Th. 0.1 cm): scrolling tendrils, one of which terminates in volute.

Broken on all sides. Green glass is partly missing, is very extensively pitted, and in places has been reduced to opaque light green weathering; colorless glass has patches of light brown weathering.

Comment: The fragment was acquired in Cairo, Egypt.

Its diameter and its vertical or nearly vertical wall suggest that it was part of a cylindrical cup, a beaker, or a bottle.

550. Fragment of Bottle or Pitcher with Leaves

9th to 10th century. Formerly in the Smith Collection. 68.1.85.
H. (surviving) 4 cm, D. (est.) 5.5 cm.
Transparent light blue over almost colorless with yellowish tinge; blue glass has very few bubbles, and colorless glass has somewhat more bubbles. Blown, cased; relief-cut.

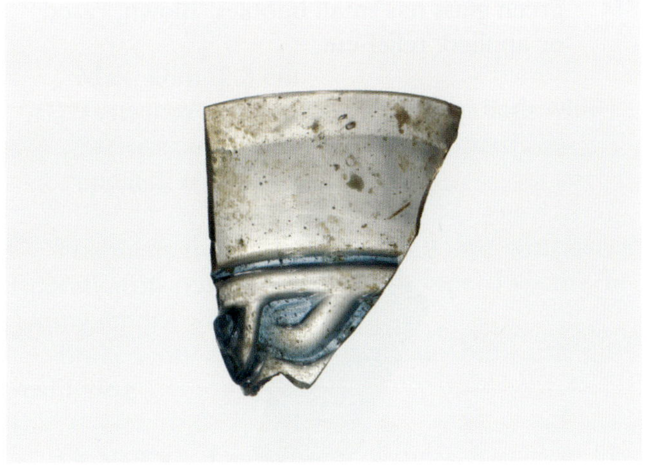

550

Fragment of bottle or pitcher with upper neck shaped like funnel. Rim plain, with flat top and beveled inner surface, both finished by grinding and polishing; neck (TTh. 0.3–0.35 cm) tapers. Decoration in relief (Th. 0.1 cm) begins 2.4 cm below lip: horizontal line, presumably continuous, below which is band, again presumably continuous, of scrolling oval leaves with pointed tips.

Just over 25 percent of rim survives. Blue and colorless glasses have patches of transparent very pale gray weathering.

Comment: Traces of coldworking on the upper neck suggest that most, if not all, of the blank was cased. The object may have been a bottle similar to, but somewhat larger than, the bottle in the David Collection, Copenhagen (3/1971: *Glass of the Sultans* 2001, p. 183, no. 89), which has a rim 3.7 centimeters across and a funnel-shaped upper neck with a continuous relief-cut horizontal line.

551. Fragment with Vegetal Motifs

9th to 10th century. Formerly in the Smith Collection. 59.1.500.
Max. Dim. 4.9 cm, D. (max., est.) about 10 cm.

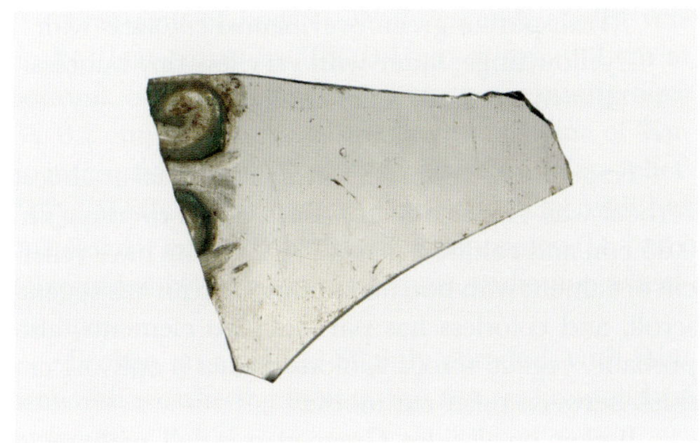

551

Transparent green over almost colorless with yellowish green tinge. Blown, applied; relief-cut.

Fragment from wall of vessel (TTh. 0.25 cm) of uncertain form. Decorated in relief (Th. 0.1 cm) with small parts of three green elements: volute, which appears to terminate in half-palmette, and second, opposed volute; third element is represented by minute patch of green. Exterior surface has traces of coldworking, but only near green overlay.

Broken on all sides. Green glass is almost matte, with light grayish green weathering; colorless glass is dull, with pale gray weathering in coldworked areas.

Comment: The absence of coldworking on the colorless surface, except near the green overlay, indicates that the green glass was applied rather than gathered.

552. Fragment with Leaf Scroll

9th to 10th century. Formerly in the Smith Collection. 68.1.59-55.
Max. Dim. 4.5 cm, H. (surviving) perhaps 4.1 cm, D. (est.) about 6 cm.

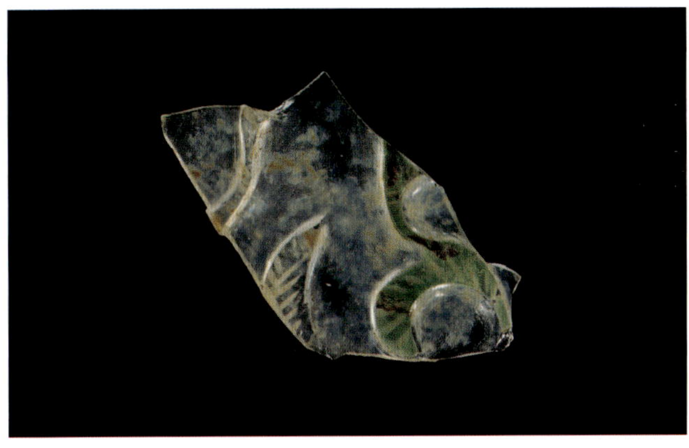

552

Broken on all sides. Both colorless and green glasses are slightly weathered.

Comment: The fragment may have come from a small beaker or the neck or wall of a bottle. Although the surface of the colorless glass displays clear signs of coldworking between the letters of the inscription and up to 0.5 centimeter above it, no such signs (apart from the groove) are apparent at the top of the fragment or below the inscription. It is likely, therefore, that the green glass was applied in a horizontal band that did not extend to the top of the fragment. The narrow lines, which appear to be on the outer surface of the colorless glass, have no obvious explanation.

563. Fragment with Inscription

9th to 10th century. Formerly in the Smith Collection. 59.1.498.
Max. Dim. 2.8 cm, D. (est., at inscription) about 11 cm.
Transparent green over colorless; both with very few minute bubbles. Blown, applied or cased; relief-cut.

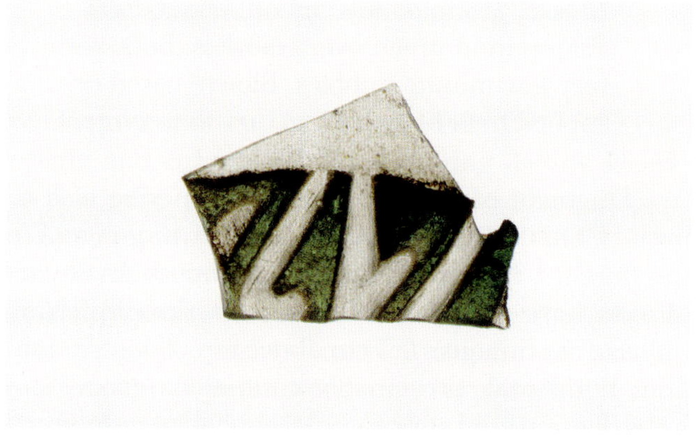

563

Fragment of vessel. Wall (TTh. 0.2 cm) has convex profile and is decorated in relief (Th. less than 0.1 cm): small part of one horizontal line of Kufic inscription.

Broken on all sides. Green glass has grayish green weathering; colorless glass is virtually unweathered.

Comment: The form of the vessel cannot be determined; it may have been a bottle, a ewer, or even a beaker with a bulbous lower section such as the colorless relief-cut vessel in the L. A. Mayer Memorial Institute for Islamic Art, Jerusalem (G73-71: *Glass of the Sultans* 2001, p. 174, no. 80). Although the surface of the colorless glass displays clear signs of coldworking between the letters of the inscription, no such marks are apparent above the inscription. It is likely, therefore, that the green glass was applied in a horizontal band that did not extend to the top of the fragment.

564. Fragment with Inscription

9th to 10th century. Formerly in the Smith Collection (1287-C). 59.1.502.
Max. Dim. 2.6 cm, H. (surviving) 2.5 cm, D. (est., at top of inscription) about 8 cm.
Transparent green over colorless; both with very few minute bubbles. Blown, applied; relief-cut.

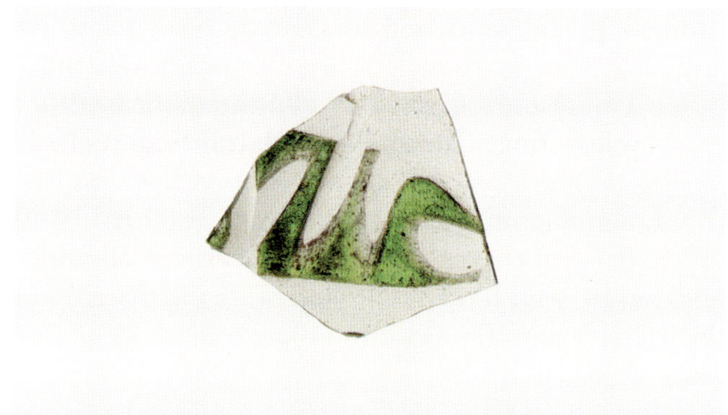

564

Fragment of vessel with straight or very slightly tapering wall or neck (TTh. 0.2 cm) decorated in relief in green (Th. less than 0.1 cm) on colorless background: part of one horizontal line of Kufic inscription: "عز" (*ʿizz*; power, strength); 0.4 cm above top of inscription, shallow horizontal (and presumably continuous) groove cut in background; similar groove just below inscription.

Broken on all sides. Green glass is dull and pitted, with some brownish weathering; colorless glass is virtually unweathered.

Comment: The fragment may have come from the wall of a beaker or the neck or wall of a bottle. The bottom of the inscription slants down from right to left. Perhaps the green glass was applied as a horizontal band, with an uneven lower edge.

565. Fragment with Inscription

9th to 10th century. Formerly in the Smith Collection. 68.1.119.
Max. Dim. 2.4 cm, H. (surviving) 2.3 cm.
Transparent green over colorless; both with very few minute bubbles. Blown, applied; relief-cut.

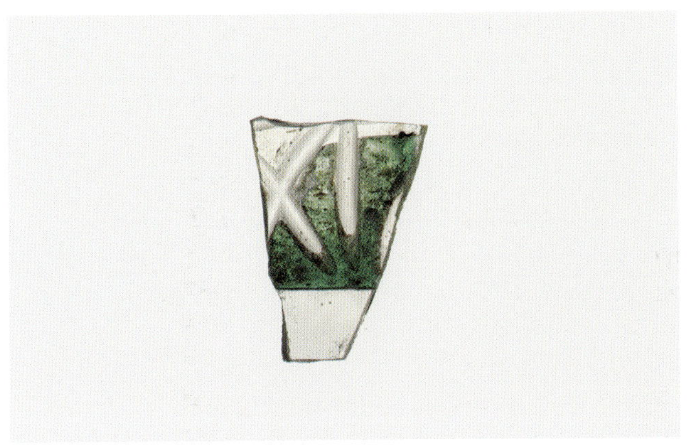

565

Fragment of vessel with straight, vertical or slightly tapering wall (TTh. 0.2–0.25 cm) decorated in relief in green (Th. less than 0.1 cm) on colorless background: part of one horizontal line of Kufic inscription: "بر(كة)" (*bara[ka]*; blessing). Colorless glass below inscription does not appear to have been coldworked.

Broken on all sides. Green glass is dull and pitted, with spots of greenish white weathering; colorless glass is virtually unweathered.

Comment: The absence of coldworking below the inscription indicates that the overlay was applied as a strip or pad.

566. Fragment with Inscription(?)

9th to 10th century. Formerly in the Smith Collection. 68.1.116.
Max. Dim. 2.2 cm.
Transparent green over colorless. Blown, cased or applied; relief-cut.

Fragment. Wall (TTh. 0.2 cm) has convex profile and is decorated with green overlay (Th. 0.1 cm), which has been cut away, leaving small part of elaborate vegetal scroll or possibly inscription in relief.

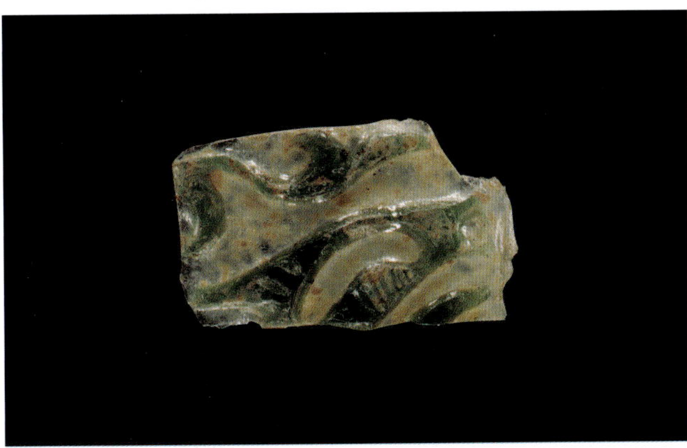

566

Broken on all sides. Green glass has patches of light green weathering; colorless glass has iridescent light gray weathering with brownish spots.

Comment: The shape of the fragment suggests that it may be from a bottle with a globular body or from a bowl.

567. Fragment of Bowl(?)

9th to 10th century. Formerly in the Smith Collection. 68.1.115.
Max. Dim. 2.8 cm, H. (surviving) about 2.5 cm, D. (est.) about 8 cm.
Transparent light blue over colorless. Blown, cased or applied; relief-cut.

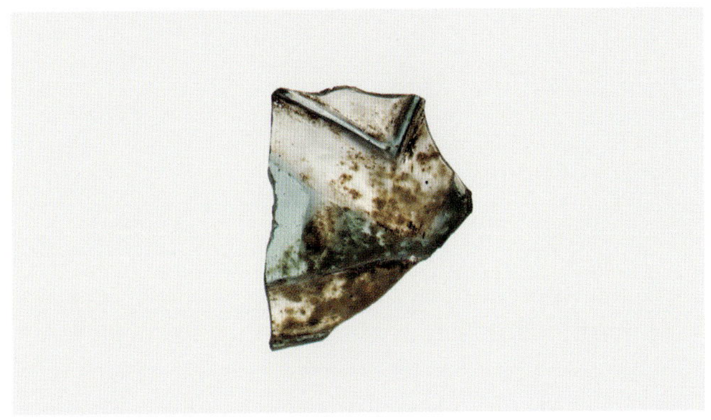

567

Fragment of bowl(?). Wall (TTh. 0.2 cm) has convex profile and is decorated with indeterminate relief-cut blue motifs (Th. 0.1 cm): V-shaped element framed at bottom by larger motif, with, below this, one (presumably continuous) horizontal line.

Broken on all sides. Blue glass has patches of pale bluish brown weathering; colorless glass has patches of transparent gray and brown weathering.

Comment: The convex profile of the fragment suggests that it may have been part of a bowl.

568. Fragment of Ewer(?)

9th to 10th century. Formerly in the Smith Collection (1262-B). 59.1.504.
H. (surviving) 6.5 cm, D. (est., at bottom of fragment) about 5 cm.
Transparent green over colorless; both with few very small bubbles. Blown, cased; relief-cut.

Fragment from wall of ewer(?), which is straight and appears to have wider diameter at bottom than

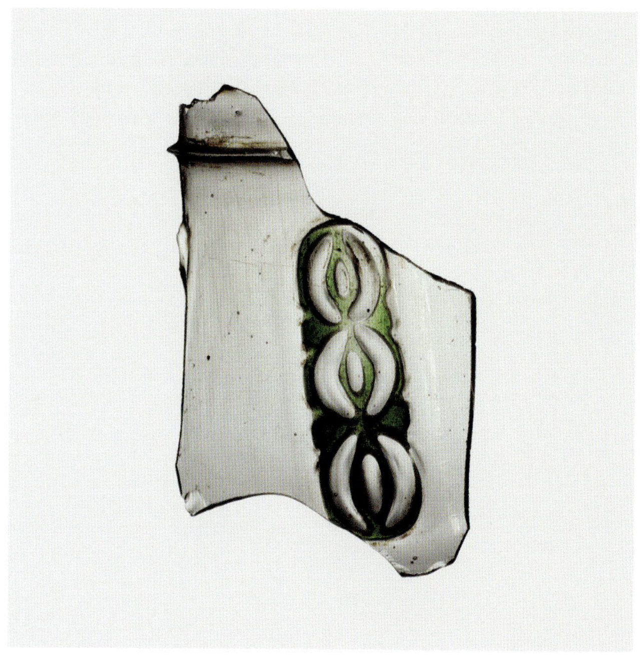

568

at top. Decorated in relief (from top to bottom): at highest point, trace of horizontal rib (?), and 0.7 cm below this, distinct horizontal rib, both cut in colorless glass; 0.8 cm below rib, almost vertical panel (H. 4 cm, W. 1.3 cm) consisting of three contiguous oval motifs shown in outline, each containing oval motif with pointed ends, also shown in outline, with solid semicircular projections at junctions of each pair of large ovals, all in green glass; to left of top of green panel, trace of indeterminate motif. Entire exterior surface shows signs of coldworking.

Broken on all sides. Except for traces of clay above and below rib (probably "flood mud": see page 10), glass is almost as new.

Comment: The traces of coldworking all over the exterior indicate that the overlay was cased rather than applied.

Such a short section of the rib remains that it is very difficult to estimate the angle at which the wall descends. However, the fragment does seem to have a greater diameter at the bottom than at the top. If this observation is correct, the fragment may have come from the upper wall of a ewer similar to, but slightly narrower than, **522**. The principal ornament on **522** and its rock crystal counterparts consists of a continuous panel with a pictorial composition on either side, separated by the handle and by small or larger motifs beneath the pouring lip. If the fragment did come from a ewer, the green panel may have separated two compositions, of which only a trace survives to the left. If the object was not a ewer, presumably it was a pitcher or a bottle.

Bibliography: Whitehouse 2003, pp. 150–151, fig. 5.

569. Fragment

9th to 10th century. Formerly in the Smith Collection. 68.1.107.
Max. Dim. 3.6 cm, H. (surviving) 3 cm, D. (est.) about 7 cm.
Transparent green over colorless. Blown, cased or applied; relief-cut.

Fragment. Wall (TTh. 0.2 cm) is straight and has green overlay (Th. 0.1 cm), which was cut away, leaving small part of indeterminate motif in relief. At least part of motif has notched outlines.

Broken on all sides. Green glass is pitted, with gray to pale brown weathering; colorless glass has transparent light gray weathering.

Comment: The ornament, which appears to have been elaborate, defies interpretation. The straight side and diameter of the fragment suggest that it was part of a cylindrical cup or a beaker.

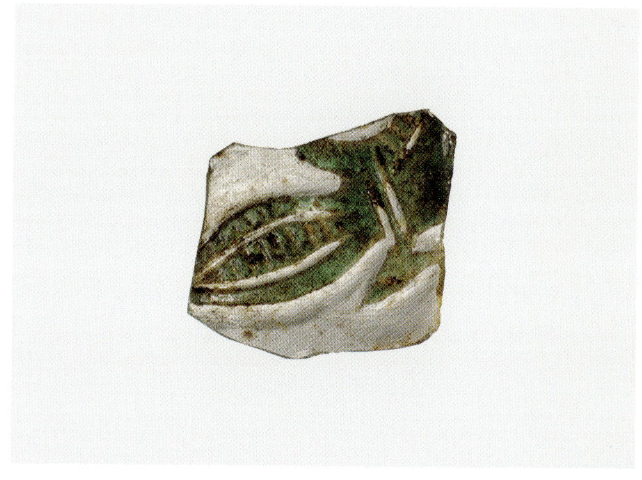

569

570. Fragment

9th to 10th century. Formerly in the Smith Collection. 68.1.112.
Max. Dim. 3 cm.
Transparent light blue over colorless; both with very few minute bubbles. Blown, cased or applied; relief-cut.

Fragment of vessel, apparently with fairly straight wall (TTh. 0.3 cm), with blue relief-cut ornament (Th. 0.1 cm): part of complex curvilinear design with notched borders.

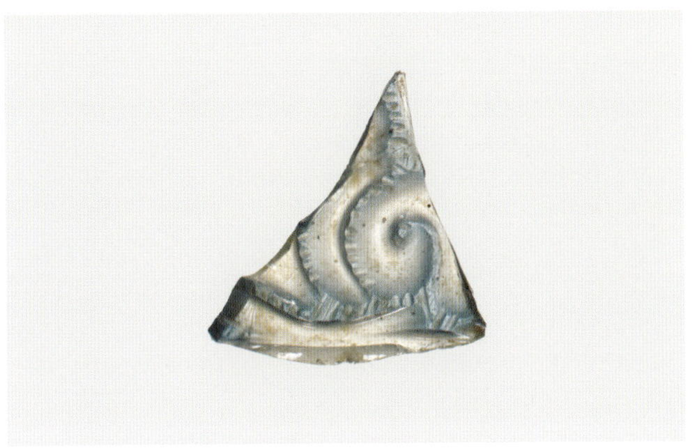

570

Broken on all sides. Both glasses have patches of transparent pale grayish weathering.

Comment: The small size of the fragment prevents identification of either the form of the vessel or the decoration. The ornament seems more likely, however, to consist of a stylized (possibly fantastic) animal than a vegetal motif.

571. Fragment

9th to 10th century. Formerly in the Smith Collection. 68.1.117.
Max. Dim. 2.6 cm.
Transparent brown over colorless; both virtually bubble-free. Blown, applied; relief-cut.

Fragment from wall of vessel (TTh. 0.3 cm). Decorated in relief with indeterminate brown motif (Th. less than 0.05 cm) embellished with broad cut, and with one broad cut in colorless glass.

Broken on all sides. Brown glass is dull, with traces of weathering; colorless glass has patches of transparent light brown weathering.

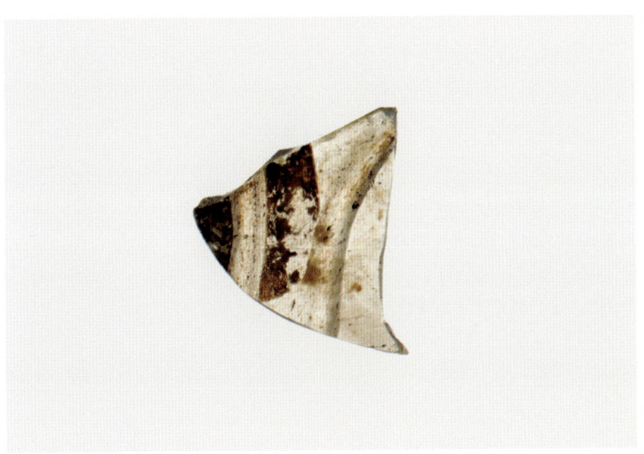

571

Comment: The fragment appears to have been part of a vessel with a straight wall and a diameter of approximately 10 centimeters; perhaps it was a bottle.

572. Fragment

9th to 10th century. Formerly in the Smith Collection. 68.1.120.
Max. Dim. 2.6 cm.
Transparent green over colorless. Blown, probably applied; relief-cut.

Fragment of wall (TTh. 0.2 cm). Decorated in relief (Th. 0.05 cm) with indeterminate green motif embellished with shallow cuts.

Broken on all sides. Green glass is matte, with patches of pale grayish green weathering; colorless glass is virtually as new.

Comment: The fragment was probably part of a vessel (possibly a cylindrical cup) decorated with patches of colored glass with wheel-cut details.

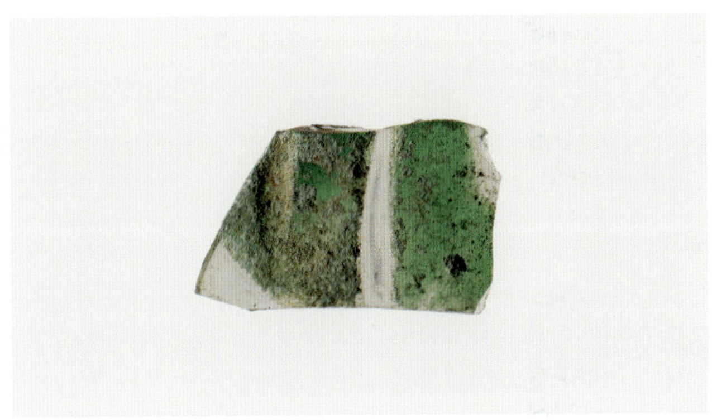

572

573. Fragment

9th to 10th century. Formerly in the Smith Collection. 68.1.122.
Max. Dim. 2.5 cm.
Transparent blue over colorless. Blown, cased or applied; relief-cut.

Fragment: flat. Colorless glass (Th. 0.15 cm) has relief-cut overlay (Th. 0.1 cm) with part of apparently symmetrical motif: rectangular central portion (L. more than 1 cm, W. 0.45 cm) bifurcates at one end, with trace of element in relief between forks, and appears to expand or bifurcate at other end; central elements, five symmetrically placed cuts and forks, are notched.

Broken on all sides. Both glasses have transparent pale gray weathering.

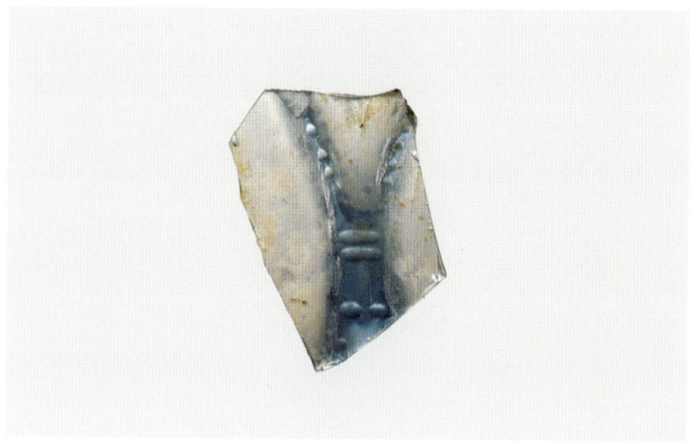

573

Comment: The fragment is completely flat, and it is impossible to suggest the form of the object from which it came, unless it was a plate or an inlay. If the ornament was symmetrical, it may have somewhat resembled the relief-cut tree-of-life motifs on the monochrome green bowl with an eight-lobed rim (**490**). On the latter, each tree has a trunk divided at the top into two scrolling half-palmettes, and at the midpoint into an inverted palmette.

574. Fragment

9th to 10th century. Formerly in the Smith Collection. 68.1.59-78.
Max. Dim. 2.5 cm, H. (surviving) perhaps 2.3 cm.
Transparent yellowish brown over colorless; both with few tiny bubbles. Blown, cased or applied; relief-cut.

Fragment of vessel with convex profile. Wall (TTh. 0.35 cm) is decorated with brown overlay (Th. 0.05 cm) relief-cut in form of scrolling motif with notched and drilled outlines. Colorless glass (original Th. 0.3 cm) has been removed to depth of 0.15–0.2 cm, so that parts of wall are only 0.1 cm thick.

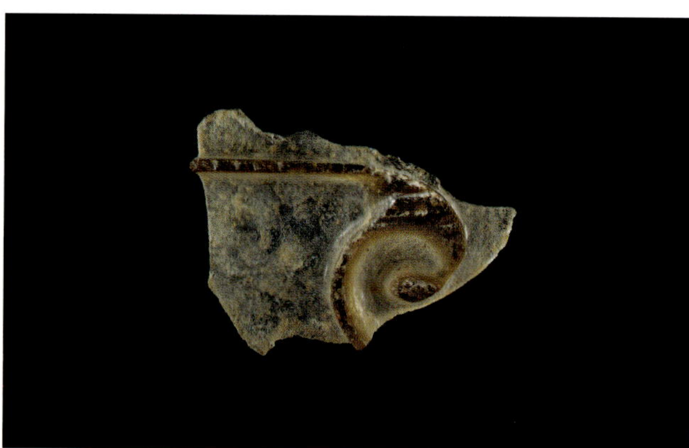

574

Broken on all sides. Brown glass is dull to matte, with pale brown weathering; colorless glass has patches of transparent pale brown weathering.

Comment: For the ornament, perhaps cf. *Glass of the Sultans* 2001, pp. 172–173, no. 79, a relief-cut beaker in The Metropolitan Museum of Art, New York (1974.45), on which opposed pairs of scrolls are united by V-shaped motifs. The removal of up to two-thirds of the colorless glass has created unusually high relief.

575. Fragment

9th to 10th century. Formerly in the Smith Collection. 68.1.118.
Max. Dim. 2.5 cm.
Transparent green over colorless; latter with very small bubbles. Blown, applied; relief-cut.

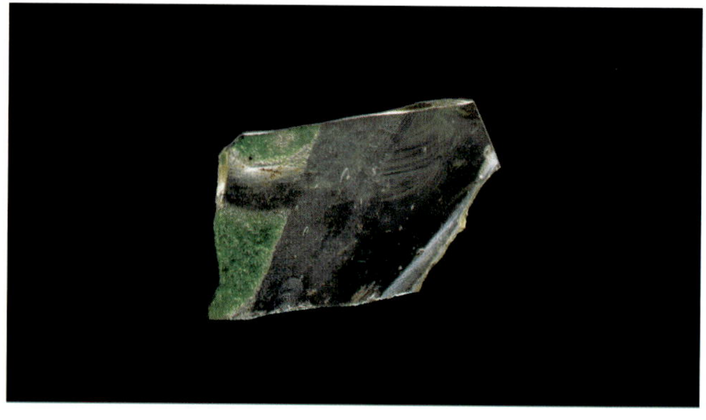

575

Fragment from wall of vessel (TTh. 0.25 cm). Decorated in relief with indeterminate green motif (Th. 0.1 cm) embellished with broad cut, and with one cut in colorless glass.

Broken on all sides. Green glass is dull, with patch of matte pale green weathering; colorless glass is almost as new.

Comment: The fragment may have been part of a vessel with a straight side and a small diameter, possibly a beaker. Apart from one cut, the colorless glass has traces of coldworking only in the immediate vicinity of the green overlay, and this indicates that the overlay was applied as a patch.

576. Four Fragments

9th to 10th century. Formerly in the Smith Collection. 68.1.125a–d.
Max. Dim. (a) 2.4 cm, (b) 1.2 cm, (c) 1.2 cm, (d) 1.4 cm.

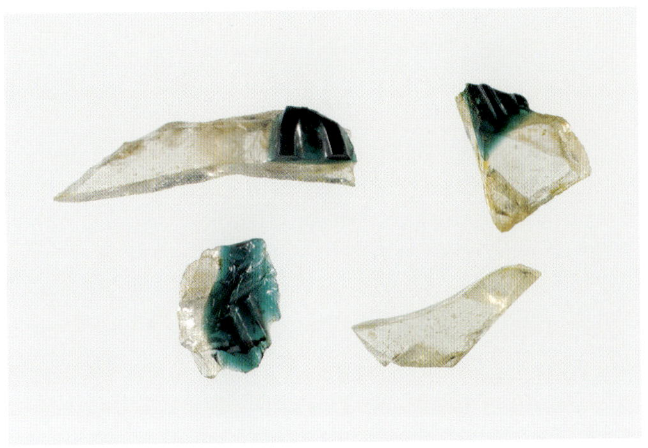

576

Transparent emerald green over colorless. Blown, cased or applied; relief-cut.

Four fragments, apparently from wall (TTh. 0.5 cm) of same vessel, three of which (a, b, and c) have green overlay (Th. 0.15 cm) that was cut.

(a–d) Broken on all sides. Slightly dull, with little weathering.

COMMENT: The fragments, which appear to have come from the same object, are too small to permit identification of the form or the ornament.

577. Fragment

9th to 10th century. Formerly in the Smith Collection. 68.1.114.
Max. Dim. 2.2 cm.
Transparent green over colorless; latter with many small bubbles. Blown, applied; relief-cut.

Fragment from wall of vessel (TTh. 0.2 cm). Decorated in relief with indeterminate green motif (Th. 0.1 cm) embellished with cuts.

Broken on all sides. Green glass is dull, with patches of matte pale green weathering; colorless glass has transparent very pale brown weathering and slight iridescence.

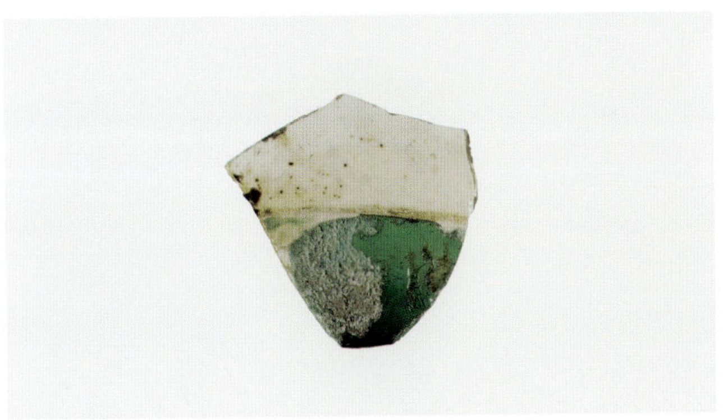

577

COMMENT: The colorless glass has traces of cold-working only in the immediate vicinity of the green overlay, and this indicates that the overlay was applied as a patch.

578. Fragment

9th to 10th century. Formerly in the Smith Collection. 68.1.121.
Max. Dim. 2.2 cm.
Transparent green over colorless. Blown, cased or applied; relief-cut.

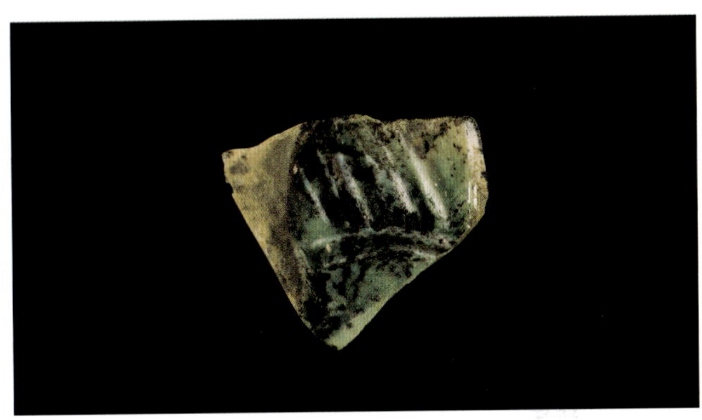

578

Fragment from wall of vessel (TTh. 0.2 cm). Decorated in relief with indeterminate green motif (Th. 0.1 cm) embellished with four parallel cuts and one curved cut that is roughly perpendicular to them.

Broken on all sides. Green glass has patches of glossy light green weathering; colorless glass has patches of transparent light brown weathering.

579. Fragment

9th to 10th century. Formerly in the Smith Collection. 68.1.127.

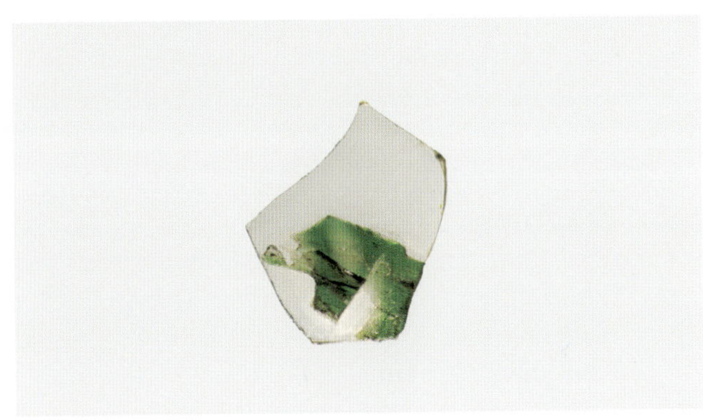

579

Max. Dim. 2 cm.
Transparent green over colorless; both virtually bubble-free. Blown, cased or applied; relief-cut.

Fragment from wall of vessel (TTh. 0.15 cm). Decorated in relief with indeterminate green motif (Th. 0.05 cm) embellished with broad cuts.

Broken on all sides. Green glass is dull, with incipient weathering; colorless glass is pristine, except in cuts.

580. Fragment

9th to 10th century. Formerly in the Smith Collection. 68.1.128.
Max. Dim. 1.7 cm.
Green over colorless; latter with few very small bubbles. Blown, applied; relief-cut.

Fragment from wall of vessel (TTh. 0.15 cm). Decorated in relief with indeterminate green motif (Th. 0.05 cm) embellished with cuts.

Broken on all sides. Green glass is dull, with greenish brown weathering; colorless glass is lightly pitted and has patches of transparent light brown weathering.

Comment: The condition of the fragment is similar to that of **584**, but the fragments do not join.

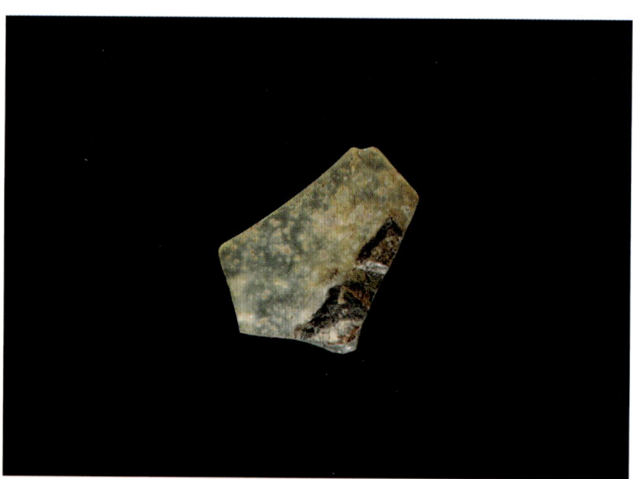

580

581. Fragment

9th to 10th century. Formerly in the Smith Collection. 68.1.126.
Max. Dim. 1.5 cm.
Transparent green over colorless. Blown, cased or applied; relief-cut.

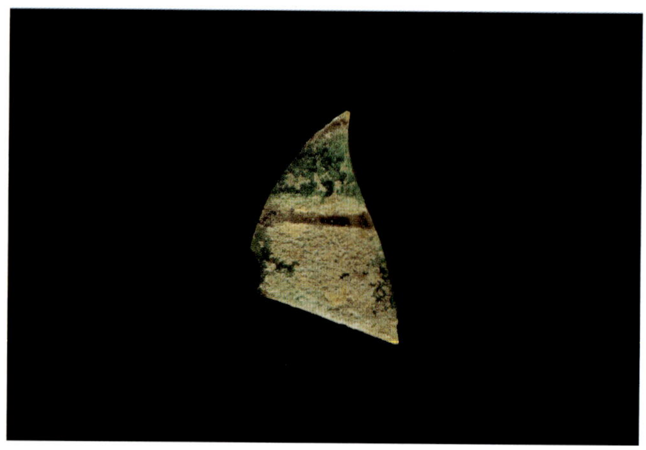

581

Fragment from wall (TTh. 0.25 cm) with small area of indeterminate green decoration in relief (Th. 0.1 cm).

Broken on all sides. Green glass is dull, with pale grayish green weathering; colorless glass has no obvious weathering.

Comment: The thinness of the wall suggests that the fragment came from a small vessel. The form, however, cannot be identified.

582. Fragment

9th to 10th century. Formerly in the Smith Collection. 68.1.129.
Max. Dim. 1.5 cm.
Green over colorless. Blown, cased or applied; relief-cut.

Fragment of wall (TTh. 0.15 cm). Decorated in relief (Th. 0.05 cm) with small part of indeterminate green motif.

Broken on all sides. Colorless glass has small area of incipient weathering.

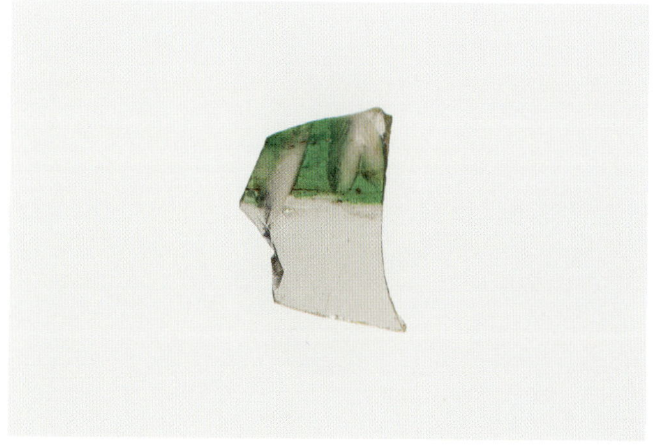

582

583. Fragment

9th to 10th century. Formerly in the Smith Collection. 68.1.130.
Max. Dim. 1.3 cm.
Transparent green over colorless. Blown, cased; relief-cut.

Fragment from wall of vessel (TTh. 0.15 cm). Overlay (Th. 0.5 cm) consists of small S-shaped part of unidentified motif.

Broken on all sides. Colorless and green glasses are dull; green glass has some brown weathering.

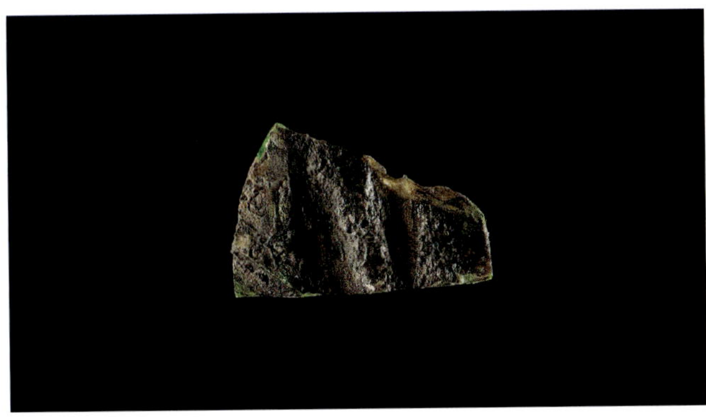

583

584. Fragment

9th to 10th century. Formerly in the Smith Collection. 68.1.59-97.
Max. Dim. 0.9 cm.
Green over colorless. Blown, cased or applied; relief-cut.

Fragment of wall (TTh. 0.15 cm). Decorated in relief (Th. 0.05 cm) with indeterminate green motif embellished with shallow cuts.

Broken on all sides. Green glass is matte, with greenish brown weathering; colorless glass has traces of weathering.

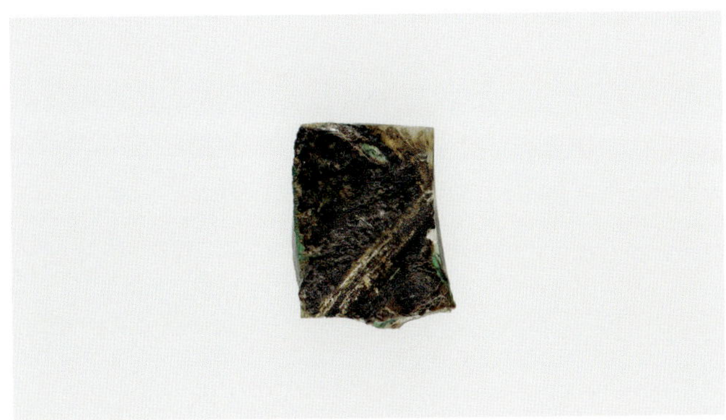

584

COMMENT: The condition of the fragment is similar to that of **580**, but the fragments do not join.

585. Fragment

Perhaps 9th to 10th century. Formerly in the Smith Collection (1076). 59.1.509.
Max. Dim. 6.5 cm, H. (surviving) about 4.8 cm, D. (rib, est.) about 12 cm.
Transparent brownish yellow over almost colorless with yellowish green tinge. Blown, applied or cased; relief-cut.

Fragment, perhaps from bottle (but see below). Shoulder is rounded, and upper wall appears to be roughly straight. Entire exterior surface has clear traces of coldworking. Decoration is relief-cut and consists of: on upper shoulder, parts of three colorless, adjoining swags embellished with notches, which appear to be part of one continuous band of nine or 10 swags surrounding rim or neck; on lower shoulder, two yellow horizontal oval bosses separated by one circular yellow boss, which appear to be part of continuous band of alternating oval and circular bosses (overlay on oval bosses is thick and brownish yellow; overlay on circular boss is thin and yellow); at junction of shoulder and wall, colorless horizontal rib, which presumably was continuous; on upper wall, part of what appears to be colorless animal's head, with circular eye in countersunk tear-shaped element.

Broken on all sides. Yellow glass on circular boss is pitted; yellow glass on oval bosses and colorless glass are almost as new.

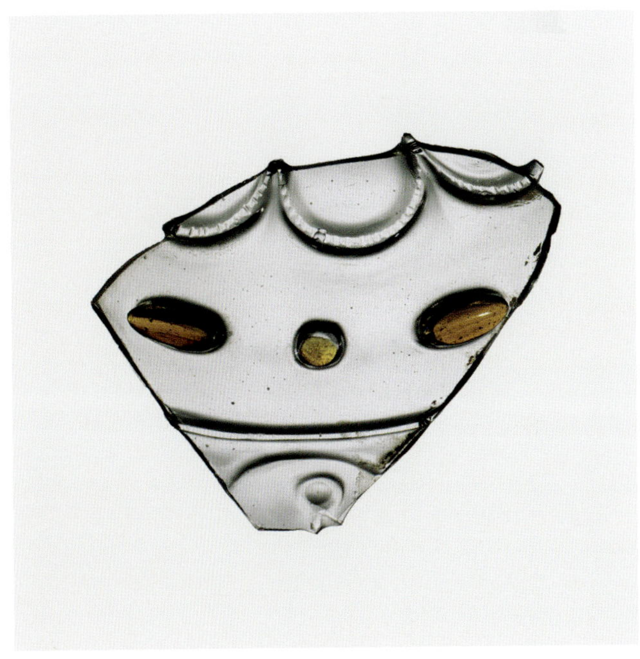

585

COMMENT: The description is based on the assumption that the fragment is part of the wall of a bottle with a globular or perhaps pear-shaped body. It is not impossible, however, that the object was a bowl, with swags surrounding the foot, although in that case the "animal's head" would be difficult to explain.

Regardless of the orientation of the object, the bosses clearly resemble cabochons, and it is reasonable to assume that the different thicknesses of the overlays were intentional, so that, when the object was complete, brown ovals alternated with yellow circles.

The object appears to be without parallel. Ray Winfield Smith regarded it as Islamic and of the ninth or 10th century; in the absence of comparable objects from other cultures or periods, this attribution is plausible. The swags, for example, are notched in a manner that is characteristic of many early Islamic relief-cut glasses, and the motif below the horizontal rib appears to be part of the head of an animal, such as appears on a bowl in the Treasury of San Marco, Venice (117: *Glass of the Sultans* 2001, pp. 178–179, no. 84). The swags themselves, however, have only one parallel in Islamic relief-cut glass or rock crystal: on **365**, which without doubt was made in the ninth or 10th century. Similarly, although the bosses are distantly comparable with the circular bosses on the Hedwig beaker at Veste Coburg, Germany (Lierke 2005, p. 97 = Shalem 1996, pp. 235–236, no. 91 = Allen 1987, pp. 9–11, no. 10), they have no known counterpart on relief-cut glasses of undisputed Islamic origin.

This leads us to admit the possibility that the fragment is not Islamic. The most likely alternative is that it is Byzantine, although our almost total ignorance of medieval Byzantine glass makes it very difficult to pursue this possibility.

BIBLIOGRAPHY: *Glass from the Ancient World* 1957, p. 285, no. 610 (part of group); Whitehouse 2008.

Discussion

Relief-Cut Glass with Zoomorphic Decoration

In terms of quantity, the early Islamic relief-cut glass at Corning offers the student an almost irresistible challenge. Although it has long been recognized as one of the characteristic products of ninth- to 11th-century Islamic glass, few attempts have been made to analyze its ornament and to divide it into regional or chronological variants.

This is not surprising. The total number of complete objects and fragments that have been published is relatively small, and we have very little evidence for where or when particular objects were made, or even where they were found. The most striking exceptions to this "rule" are the fragments found at Samarra in Iraq, Nishapur in Iran, and Fusṭāṭ in Egypt. But even known find-places sometimes prompt more questions than answers. I have already quoted (on page 176) Dr. Robert H. Brill, who, in discussing chemical analyses of fragments from Nishapur and Fusṭāṭ, threw up his hands and wryly asked, "Were [the fragments] all made at (or near) Nishapur? Were they all made at (or near) Fusṭāṭ? Or were they made somewhere else and exported to both those places?" (Brill 1995, p. 214). These questions are complicated by the fact that raw glass was an item of trade and objects may have been formed and decorated at considerable distances from the furnaces where the glass was made (see, for example, Carboni, Lacerenza, and Whitehouse 2003 for the export of raw glass from Tyre, Lebanon, in and after the 11th century).

The entries in this catalog include descriptions of 14 complete or somewhat complete relief-cut objects and 244 fragments: 193 colorless objects (**296–488**), one monochrome green object (**490**), and 64 examples of cameo glass (**522–585**). The following pages contain a preliminary survey of the 115 objects with zoomorphic or apparently zoomorphic ornament: animals, animals and birds, birds, and, in one case, horses and riders. The purpose of the survey is to determine (1) the repertoire of zoomorphic ornament, (2) whether distinct styles of relief cutting exist, and (3), if so, whether they are associated with particular types of vessels. This exercise should be approached with one important caveat. Unlike the objects recovered from an archeological excavation, which presumably comprise everything that was found, almost all of the objects in this catalog were acquired in the marketplace, and we have no means of knowing the extent to which they were selected by vendors and purchasers. In other words, we cannot know whether they do or do not accurately represent the full repertoire of relief-cut glass with zoomorphic decoration. The size of the sample, however, suggests that it may provide a more complete representation than other, smaller samples.

The Repertoire of Zoomorphic Decoration

The defining characteristic of Islamic relief-cut glass is that both the background and the interior of the ornament are cut away to leave the outline in relief. Some of these outlines are plain, and others are notched (the outlines on an object are recorded as "notched" when some, but not necessarily all, of them have notches). In the zoomorphic decoration, almost all of the animals and birds are shown in profile. Some of their bodies are plain, and others are decorated with small circular depressions ("printies") made by drilling. Parts of the bodies may be embellished with simple hatching (e.g., animals' paws and the necks of birds), hatching arranged in a herringbone pattern (e.g., animals' ears), or half-palmettes (e.g., the haunches of animals and the wings of birds). The purpose of the next few paragraphs is to see whether these features occur in consistent combinations that may indicate different tastes or traditions.

The most common component of the zoomorphic decoration consists of animals, which appear on 56 objects, followed by birds (on 48 objects), animals and birds (eight), and humans and animals (one). The animals that can be identified with some confidence are lions (on **323** and **397**), horses (on **319** and **346**), ibexes (on **296** and **354**), other caprids (on **300**, **320**,

355, **408**, **522**, and **523**), hares (on **369**, **371**–**373**, **398**, and **399**), snakes (on **523**), and fantastic creatures (on no fewer than nine objects: **301**, **302**, **321**, **327**–**329**, **364**, **375**, and **417**). Very few of the birds are identifiable, although those on **296** have been described as falcons, two other raptors appear on **522**, the bird on **427** may be a guinea fowl, and the birds on **306**, **429**, and **522** resemble parrots. It may be significant that, if we exclude objects on which animals and birds appear together, animals (52) outnumber birds (38) on the monochrome objects, but they are outnumbered (10 to four) on the cameo glass.

Styles of Relief Cutting

Many of the relief-cut fragments are small, and consequently they display only one or two of the characteristics noted above (this is why some of the numbers in the following paragraphs and tables are inconsistent). Nevertheless, the main components of the relief-cut style are apparent. All of the birds are shown in profile, as are the animals on all but eight objects. These are the exceptions: the bodies of the caprids appear in profile on **300**, **323**, **355**, and **522**, but their horns are represented as if seen from above or from the front; both eyes are shown on the snakelike creature on **301**, the snakes on **523**, and the lions on **397**; and the riders on **319** are turned to face the viewer.

Outlines or parts of the raised outlines of birds and animals appear on 108 objects. Those on which at least some of the outlines are notched outnumber objects with exclusively plain outlines by 92 to 16. On the other hand, objects with no evidence of drilled depressions embellishing the body outnumber objects with printies by 56 to 27. A total of 82 objects preserve sufficient ornament to determine the association of plain or notched outlines and plain or drilled depressions. The associations are as follows:

Notched outline and plain body	45
Notched outline and drilled body	23
Plain outline and plain body	11
Plain outline and drilled body	3
Total	82

If the sample is indicative, the notched outlines of relief-cut animals and birds are approximately five times as common as plain outlines, and plain bodies are approximately twice as common as bodies with drilled dots. The combination of plain outlines and plain bodies is unusual, and the combination of plain outlines and bodies with drilled dots is rather rare.

In addition to drilled dots, the bodies and limbs of animals and birds may be embellished by simple hatching, hatching in a herringbone pattern, or half-palmettes. Simple hatching, usually applied to the necks of animals and birds, and to animals' paws, is the most common of these embellishments; it is found on 60 objects. Herringbone hatching is considerably less common; it is present on the muzzles, ears, or wings of animals and birds on just 17 objects. The most elaborate ancillary motif, the half-palmette, adorns the haunches or wings of animals and birds on 19 objects. Half-palmettes are associated with plain or notched outlines and plain or drilled depressions on 17 of the 19 objects; their occurrence is as follows:

Notched outline and plain body (45)	8
Notched outline and drilled body (23)	7
Plain outline and plain body (11)	1
Plain outline and drilled body (3)	1
Total (82)	17

These observations suggest that the most elaborate relief-cut objects, such as **296** and **522**, have notched outlines, hatching, and half-palmettes. On **296**, the animals and birds have plain bodies, while the bodies of the animals and birds on **522** are drilled.

Ornament and Form

The quality of the best relief cutting of glass stands comparison with some of the best relief-cut rock crystal (see the "Comment" on the Corning Ewer [**522**] on pages 296–300). Indeed, the form, the scale, and the layout and quality of the ornament of the Corning Ewer may be compared with the half-dozen relief-cut rock crystal ewers that are known to exist, and in particular with the example in the Victoria and Albert Museum, London, which also has a single panel containing two short-horned animals running toward each other and being attacked by two birds of prey. One of two similar rock crystal ewers in the Treasury of San Marco, Venice, has an inscription that names the fifth Fatimid caliph, al-ᶜAzīz Biᵓllāh (r. 975–996), and establishes the object as the ruler's property.

Cutting of a much less refined quality is found on the most unusual form with relief-cut ornament: a goblet with a flange at or near the bottom of the bowl. The collection contains eight objects certainly or probably of this type (**346**–**353**). All have zoomorphic decoration (two with animals and six with birds), and six of them are inscribed. Two very similar goblets, both with zoomorphic decoration and Kufic inscriptions, are in the al-Sabah Collection, Dār al-Āthār al-Islāmiyyah, Kuwait National Museum (Carboni 2001, pp. 87–88, nos. 20b and 21). The first goblet in the al-Sabah Collection is said to be from Nishapur, northeastern Iran, and it is possible that the entire group was made in Iran. Vessels of the same form, but with applied decoration, are in a number of collections (e.g., *Cohn Collection* 1980, p. 181, no. 185; Oliver, A. 1980, p. 143, nos. 247 and 248, in the Carnegie Museum of Natural History, Pittsburgh; and *Khalili Collection* 2005, p. 248, no. 287).

One further example of a coherent group of decorated fragments is provided by eight relief-cut cameo glasses (**528**–**530** and **533**–**537**), all of which have small, rather schematic birds. These are similar to birds on three linear- or slant-cut fragments of cameo glass (**500**, **501**, and **503**). The almost perfunctory cutting of these objects is in stark contrast to the exquisite artistry of the Corning Ewer, and it underlines the fact that the quality of early Islamic relief-cut glass runs the gamut from excellent to poor.

Summary

As noted above, the early Islamic relief-cut glass at Corning comprises some 14 complete or more or less complete objects and 244 fragments: 193 are colorless, one is bright green, and 64 are cameo glass. The objects include bowls, a box, a cup, beakers, goblets, bottles, a canteen, ewers and related objects, and numerous indeterminate fragments. Almost half of these objects have zoomorphic decoration. Animals appear on 56 of them, birds on 48, animals and birds on eight, and humans and animals on one.

This discussion has focused on five characteristics of the zoomorphic decoration: the treatment of outlines and bodies, and the presence or absence of simple hatching, herringbone hatching, and half-palmettes. It led to two conclusions: (1) that the more elaborate decoration included notched outlines, drilled bodies, and half-palmettes; and (2) that the more common decoration is characterized by notched outlines and plain bodies, with or without hatching and half-palmettes. Examples of the more elaborate ornament include **320**, **323**, and **522**, while **369** and **389** represent the more common decoration.

The attempt to discover relationships between relief-cut ornament and form, if such existed, was hampered by the fact that so much of the sample consists of small fragments. Nevertheless, it seems possible, for example, that colorless goblets with a flange at or near the bottom of the bowl have zoomorphic decoration, usually birds and usually accompanied by inscriptions.

The chronology remains obscure. The finds from Samarra, attributed to the ninth century, include both monochrome relief-cut glass with notched outlines and half-palmettes, and cameo glass (e.g., *Glass of the Sultans* 2001, p. 178, no. 78a and b, and p. 182, no. 87); 10 monochrome relief-cut fragments (four with zoomorphic decoration), found at Nishapur, are assigned to the ninth century or to the ninth to 10th centuries (Kröger 1995, pp. 137–146, nos. 190–197); and relief-cut glass from excavations at Fusṭāṭ is variously dated between the ninth and 10th centuries (Scanlon and Pinder-Wilson 2001, pp. 99–106, no. 43a–j). It is not always clear, however, whether these chronologies were established on the basis of independently datable archeological contexts or received opinion. The Corning Ewer (**522**) is attributed to the years around 1000 because of its similarity to datable rock crystal objects (see pages 299–300), and the almost complete absence of relief-cut fragments from fully two-thirds of a ton of broken glass vessels in the Serçe Limanı shipwreck in the 1020s (Bass and others 2009) may suggest that relief cutting went out of fashion in the early 11th century. If this is so, we can do no better at present than to attribute early Islamic relief-cut glass to the broad period between about 850 and 1000.

with the Hedwig beaker in the cathedral at Cracow, Poland (Allen 1987, pp. 3–4, no. 2; Shalem 1996, p. 231, no. 83; Lierke 2005, pp. 98–100), while another associates it with a beaker formerly in the Schlesisches Museum für Kunstgewerbe und Altertüme at Wrocław, Poland, which disappeared in 1944 (Allen 1987, pp. 6–7, no. 6; Shalem 1996, pp. 231–232, no. 84; Lierke 2005, p. 96).

History of the Object. **586** is one of two similar beakers from Saint Stephen's Cathedral at Halberstadt. Discovered in the sacristy about 1820, it was acquired by the local commissioner of police, and, at an unknown date, it passed into the hands of a Bad Harzburg bookbinder named Stolle, who is said to have used it as a paste pot. Subsequent owners are listed above.

The cathedral treasury contains a second Hedwig beaker, which is believed to have belonged to Bishop Konrad von Krosigk, who participated in the Fourth Crusade. It has 14th-century mounts and is said to contain relics of the apostles James and Thomas (Allen 1987, pp. 7–8, no. 7; Shalem 1996, p. 234, no. 89; Lierke 2005, p. 98).

Date. Thirteen Hedwig beakers are, or once were, in church treasuries in Europe (Lierke 2005, pp. 16–17 and 95–103). Fragments of up to 11 others have been found in archeological excavations, all in Europe (*ibid.*, pp. 18–19 and 103–106; Wedepohl and others 2007). Two of the beakers that have survived aboveground, in the treasury of the monastery of Saint Nicolas d'Oignies, preserved in the convent of the Soeurs de Notre Dame at Namur, Belgium, are said to have arrived as gifts of Jacques de Vitry, bishop of Acre from 1216 to 1226; they have mounts made in and after 1228 by Brother Hugo, a younger sibling of Giles de Walcourt, the founder of the monastery (Allen 1987, pp. 11–12, nos. 11 and 12; *Phönix aus Sand und Asche* 1988, pp. 97–99, nos. 41 and 42; note, however, that Kröger 2006, p. 28, quotes Ingeborg Krueger as commenting that the list of the bishop's gifts does not specify any glass). One of the excavated fragments, from Novogrudok, Belarus, is reported to have come from a 12th-century context (Gurevich 1963; Shelkovnikov 1966, pp. 109–112; Gurevich 1981, p. 79); another, from Hilpoltstein, Germany, was found in a context attributed to the period 1170–1180 (Platz 2000); and a third, from Pistoia, Italy, is from a deposit datable to the decades around 1300 (Vannini 1987, v. 2, p. 633). Thus the known find-places of Hedwig beakers are in Europe, and the earliest datable examples belong to the 12th or early 13th century.

Place of Manufacture. From the moment the Hedwig beakers attracted scholarly attention, the place of their manufacture has been the subject of considerable debate. The history of this debate has been summarized by Kröger (2006, pp. 29–34). Instead of repeating Kröger's narrative, the following paragraphs contain a list of suggested places of manufacture, together with brief comments. The list is long:

1. The Islamic world
2. Novogrudok
3. Byzantium
4. Central Europe
5. Southern Italy
6. The Latin East
7. Sicily

1. *The Islamic world.* Czihak (1890), Schmidt (1912), Lamm (1929–30, p. 171), and others compared the ornament on Hedwig glasses with that of rock crystal objects made in Egypt during the reign of the Fatimids (969–1171) and concluded that the beakers were made in the Islamic world: in Egypt, Syria (cf. Gray 1987 and Hillenbrand 1999, p. 84), or Iran. However, no fragment of a Hedwig glass has been reported from Egypt or Western Asia, despite the recovery of many hundreds, if not thousands, of relief-cut glass fragments from Fusṭāṭ, Nishapur, and other places. In any case, Hedwig glasses, which have thick walls and are boldly cut, are unlike the great majority of Islamic glass and rock crystal objects, which have thin walls and fine lines.

2. *Novogrudok.* The discovery of a fragmentary Hedwig glass and, "nearby," a small piece of unworked glass of the same color led Shelkovnikov (1966, pp. 109–112) to reject the view that the glasses are Islamic and to attribute them to a local workshop. Nevertheless, we may discount the possibility that the Hedwig glasses were made at Novogrudok on the grounds that the find-place is some 400 miles/640 kilometers from the next specimen (in the cathedral at Cracow) and it is difficult to imagine the circumstances in which objects made in Belarus reached sites in Germany and Italy.

3. *Byzantium.* The notion that Hedwig beakers are Byzantine derives from three hypotheses. The first of these is that the beakers were among luxury items produced at Constantinople and from time to time sent as gifts to rulers in the West (Philippe 1970, pp. 125–141, esp. p. 134). The second, not dissimilar hypothesis maintains that they were brought to western Europe as part of the dowry of Theophanu, daughter of the Byzantine emperor John I Tzimisces, when she married the Holy Roman Emperor Otto II in 972

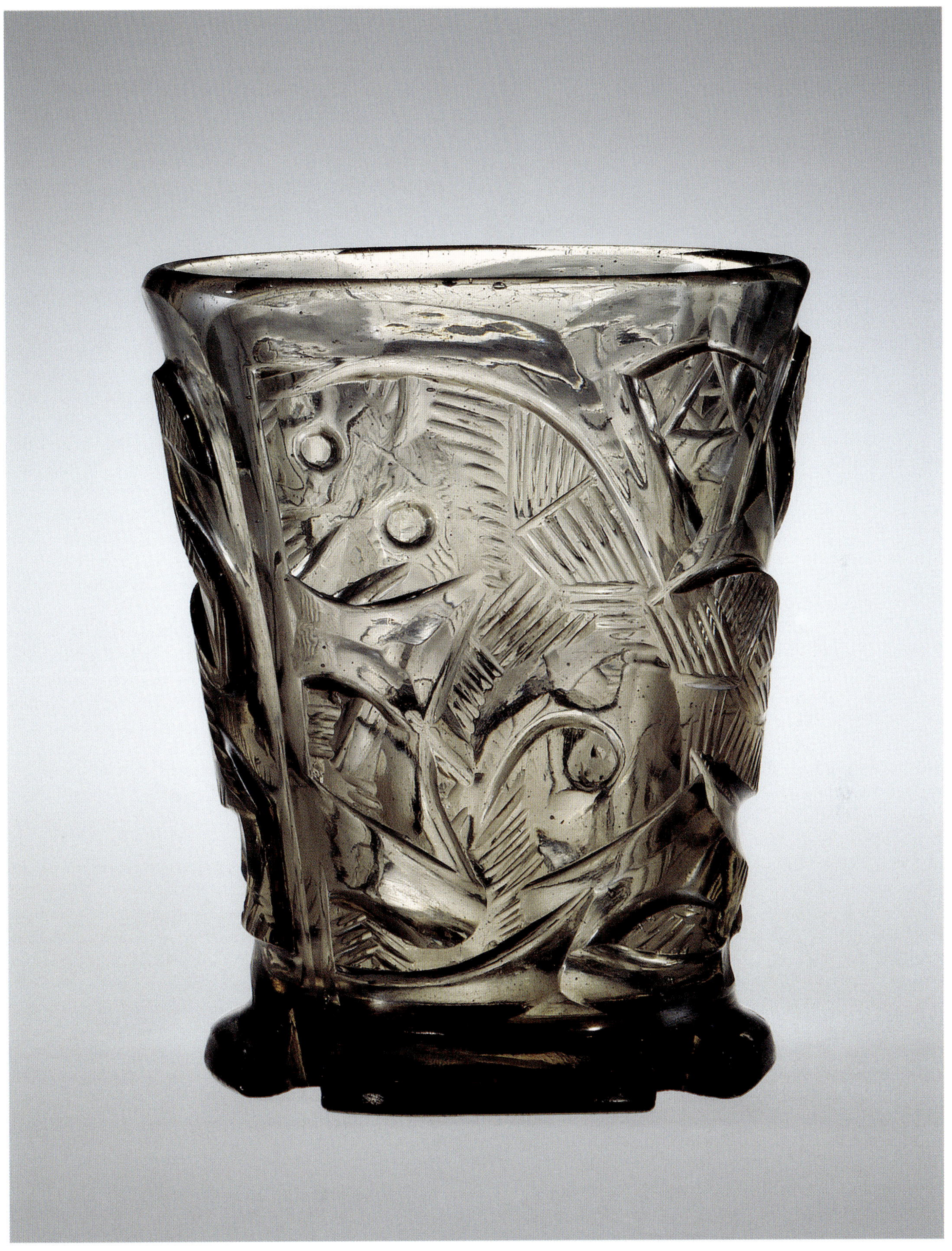

586

(Wentzel 1972, 1973). Finally, Philippe and others noted that booty from the sack of Constantinople in 1204, preserved in the Treasury of San Marco in Venice, includes a number of relief-cut glasses. However, only one of these objects (a bowl decorated with lions: 117: *Glass of the Sultans* 2001, pp. 178–179, no. 84) even remotely resembles a Hedwig glass, and, in any case, scholars are still undecided about the date and origin of many of the San Marco glasses. The evidence in favor of the view that Hedwig beakers are Byzantine, therefore, is purely circumstantial.

4. *Central Europe.* More recently, some scholars have maintained that the Hedwig beakers were made in central Europe and are medieval (cf. Lierke 1999, pp. 140–145) or, in most cases, modern (Ščapova 1978). We may safely reject the explanation that they are modern. Seven of the glasses have 13th- to 15th-century metal mounts, and archeological excavations have yielded additional examples from medieval contexts (see above).

Similarly, despite the exclusively European distribution of the Hedwig glasses, the explanation that they were made in central or eastern Europe in the Middle Ages is untenable. Chemical analyses of six examples have shown that they are made of soda-lime glass, and this alone would render them very unusual if they had been made in Europe in the later medieval period, when glassmakers habitually produced potash glasses (Wedepohl 2005, pp. 22–29). Moreover, no other cut glass vessels are known to have been made in central or eastern Europe between the fifth and 16th centuries.

5. *Southern Italy.* The late Basil Gray believed that the technique used to finish the Hedwig beakers was derived from Islamic glass cutters. At the same time, he was puzzled by the wholly un-Islamic distribution of the surviving examples. Consequently, Gray sought an origin in one of the melting pots of Mediterranean cultures: southern Italy. Hedwig glasses, he maintained (in a colloquium at Basel in 1988, noted by Whitehouse 2002, p. 256), were made in the reign of the Hohenstaufen king Frederick II (1194–1250), either in Sicily or on the mainland of southern Italy. Later, Pinder-Wilson (1991, p. 128) likened the lions, eagles, and griffins on some Hedwig beakers to the same creatures "seen on the exteriors and interiors of the churches of south Italy." Pinder-Wilson's comparison is attractive, but we have no evidence for the cutting of glass or hard stone vessels in southern Italy in the 12th century.

6. *The Latin East.* Saldern (1995a, pp. 239–242) suggested that the beakers were made in the Latin East at the time of the Crusades and were taken to Europe by crusaders, pilgrims, or merchants. He noted that tradition associates the two Hedwig beakers at Namur with Jacques de Vitry, bishop of Acre between 1216 and 1226 (but see above), and that a fragment excavated on the site of the royal palace in Budapest *may* (my italics) have been brought home by King Andrew II, who collected relics in the Holy Land in 1217. In this context, it is noteworthy that Wedepohl (2005) and Wedepohl and others (2007), on the basis of chemical analyses of six Hedwig beakers and their similarity to analyses of certain Islamic low-magnesium soda-ash glasses, concluded that the objects were made in the Levant. We know, however, that raw glass was exported from the Levant between the 11th and 13th centuries (Carboni, Lacerenza, and Whitehouse 2003, pp. 141–149), and so the conclusion that the raw glass was made in the Levant is not necessarily at odds with the view that the beakers were produced elsewhere.

7. *Sicily.* Despite the similarities that unite the Hedwig glasses, their ornament falls into two groups: (A) beakers decorated with, *inter alia*, one or two lions, plus an eagle and/or a griffin, or a tree-of-life motif; and (B) beakers decorated with palmettes, crescents, or geometric motifs, but neither animals nor birds. All four of the main motifs in Group A have Christological significance. Hedwig glasses, therefore, are not only un-Islamic in form and execution, but at least some of them are also non-Islamic in purpose. Indeed, so appropriate are the form and (in Group A) the decoration for incorporation in monstrances and chalices that it is logical to infer that this was their primary function; indeed, in Groups A and B, seven Hedwig glasses are known to have served these purposes by the 15th century, and the feet of six others are notched for attachment to metal mounts. Thus, we may reasonably suspect that the owners of Hedwig beakers were Christian.

Wedepohl's analyses and the iconography of the glasses in Group A are compatible with the idea that Hedwig beakers were made in the Latin East. On the other hand, we are not aware of a tradition in that region of cutting glass or rock crystal in a similar style.

Recently, however, a number of rock crystal objects have been associated with the *nobiles officinae* at the court of the Norman kings at Palermo, Sicily (Shalem 1996, p. 365; Distelberger 2004, pp. 109–113). Distelberger later attributed additional rock crystal vessels to the Palermo workshop and noted that the facets on some of them are similar to the facets on the Hedwig beakers. Indeed, the Hedwig beakers, he concluded, are Sicilian (Distelberger 2005). If this is so, they were made with raw glass imported from the Levant (William of Tyre, writing before 1185, noted that "the glass [of Tyre] is exported to distant provinces, and it provides material suitable for vessels that are remarkable and of outstanding clarity": Carboni, Lacerenza, and Whitehouse 2003, p. 146).

While there are parallels in Apulia for images on Hedwig beakers, equally close or closer parallels are found in the decoration of buildings constructed by the Norman kings of Sicily (Tronzo 1997). The ceiling mosaic of the Stanza Normanna in the Norman palace at Palermo, for example, includes lions, griffins, and an eagle that resemble the creatures on some of the Hedwig beakers. The mosaic, and perhaps the beakers, were made during the reign of William II (1166–1189).

Thus it is attractive to attribute the Hedwig beakers to Sicily, perhaps during the reign of William II. If this is correct, can we explain the presence of most of these Sicilian objects in central Europe? The answer is, yes. In 1177, William II arranged the marriage of his aunt, Constance, to Henry VI, son of the Holy Roman Emperor Frederick Barbarossa, whose family, the Hohenstaufen, were extraordinarily powerful in central Europe. Henry became king of Sicily in 1194. The "migration" of Palermitan luxury goods to central Europe in the late 12th century, therefore, is explicable in terms of Constance's dowry when she married Henry, or of the subsequent movement of treasures between the many branches of the Hohenstaufen family.

The earliest archeological find of a Hedwig beaker, from Hilpoltstein, discovered in a context attributed to the period 1170–1180 (see above), is consistent with this hypothesis.

Bibliography: Czihak 1890, no. 10; *idem* 1891, pp. 196–197, no. 10; Dillon 1907, p. 117, no. 6; Schmidt 1912, p. 55; Lamm 1929–30, p. 173, pl. 63, no. 5; *Important Works of Art* 1967, pp. 12–13, lot 24; Anon. 1968; "Recent Important Acquisitions," *JGS*, v. 10, 1968, p. 184, no. 24; Yoshimizu 1983, p. 102; Whitehouse 1985a, p. 70; Allen 1987, p. 6, no. 5; *Phönix aus Sand und Asche* 1988, pp. 95–96, no. 40; Rebourg 1988, p. 18; Marshall 1990, p. 42; Welander-Berggren 1990, p. 47; Yoshimizu 1992, pp. 127 and 298, no. 254; Saldern 1995a, pp. 239–242; Shalem 1996, p. 233, no. 86; *Glass of the Sultans* 2001, pp. 160–161, fig. 96; *Guide to the Collections* 2001, p. 58; Whitehouse 2002, pp. 257–258, no. 5; Lierke 2005, pp. 97–98.

Appendix 2

An Unusual Polychrome Fragment

587. Fragment of Beaker(?) with Inscription

Perhaps 9th to 10th century. Formerly in the Smith Collection (1286). 59.1.507. H. (surviving) 3.7 cm, D. (est.) 11 cm. Transparent light purple, transparent greenish blue, and colorless. Method of forming uncertain (see below); finished by cutting, grinding, and polishing.

Fragment of beaker(?). Rim plain, with flat top, which is ground and polished; wall vertical. Wall has five presumably continuous horizontal bands (from top to bottom): colorless (W. 1.2 cm), purple (W. 0.8 cm), colorless (W. 0.7 cm), blue (W. 0.6 cm), and colorless (W. at least 0.4 cm). In purple band, outer surface protrudes 0.1 cm beyond colorless surfaces, and its inner surface is flush with the inner colorless surfaces; outside has Kufic or pseudo-Kufic inscription with incised outlines: "د ا بد ا" (*d . . . a . . . db[?] . . . a*). Blue band has both surfaces flush with surfaces of colorless glass, and is plain. Interior has narrow horizontal groove just above top of purple band.

Pristine, except for patches of faint grayish weathering on colorless glass.

Comment: As Ray Winfield Smith noted (in *Glass from the Ancient World* 1957: see below), the fragment is extraordinary. All five colored bands occupy the entire thickness of the wall, and the straightness of their edges and uniform widths are remarkable. Five different glasses, therefore, were assembled within the space of three centimeters. Today, glassworkers might use one of several methods to achieve this effect. For example, they could employ the *incalmo* technique to attach gathers of a different color to the original gather, perhaps by assembling them on two blowpipes to reduce the difficulty of assembling five separate gathers. An alternative method of construction would be to blow five cylinders of different colors but the same diameter, cut them into horizontal sections, stack the sections in the desired order, and heat them until they fuse. The striped cylinder would be picked up on a blowpipe and reheated, the other end would be closed, and the parison would be inflated to the desired shape and size. A third method would be to use the traditional Venetian technique of constructing *vetro a fili* by placing strips of colorless and colored glass side by side, fusing them, and picking them up on a blowpipe (Gudenrath 1991, 1999, and 2004, pp. 238–239). Of these three methods, only *incalmo* is known to have been practiced by medieval Islamic glassworkers (e.g., Clairmont 1977, p. 71, no. 231; *Cohn Collection* 1980, p. 177, no. 180; and Folsach 2001, p. 206, no. 305 = *idem* 1990, p. 144, no. 223), and so this may be the technique—carried out with remarkable precision—that was used to create **587**.

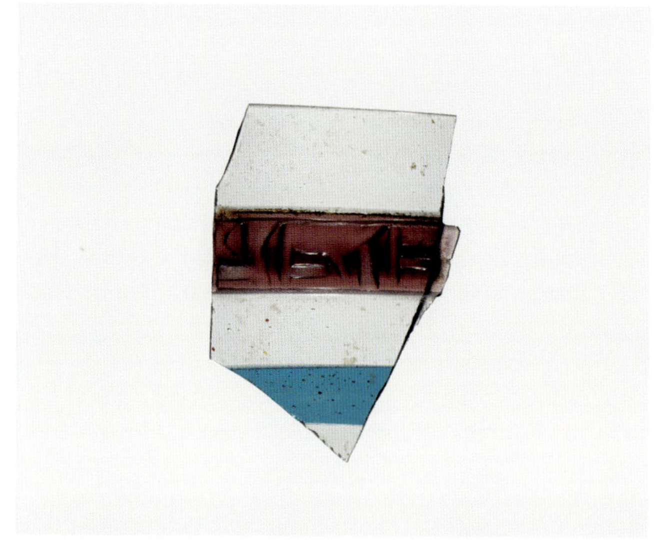

587

The coldworking, while not of the same order of virtuosity, is notable for the precision of the cutting. The result was a drinking vessel of great refinement, which simultaneously reminded the user of rock crystal, amethyst, and turquoise. No parallel is known.

Bibliography: *Glass from the Ancient World* 1957, p. 285, no. 608.

Appendix 3

Fragments of Rock Crystal Objects

588. Fragment of Bowl or Cup with Animal(?)

9th to 10th century. Formerly in the Smith Collection. 68.1.59-81.
H. (surviving) 2.1 cm, D. (rim, est.) 6 cm.
Colorless. Relief-cut.

Fragment of bowl or cup. Rim plain, with flat top; wall curves slightly down and in. Decorated in relief on outside, probably with animal shown in profile, facing left. If so, surviving parts are outlines of back of neck and of body, left haunch, and tail in form of half-palmette, which is above body and extends forward. Outlines are notched, haunch is contoured, and tail is hatched.

About 10 percent of rim survives. Surface is as new.

Comment: The profile of the fragment suggests that it may have come from a bowl rather than a cup. The suggestion that the ornament is probably an animal is made with some confidence, after reviewing images of animals on relief-cut glass of the same period (e.g., on a bowl in the Museum für Islamische Kunst, Berlin (I.20/65: *Glass of the Sultans* 2001, p. 176, no. 82).

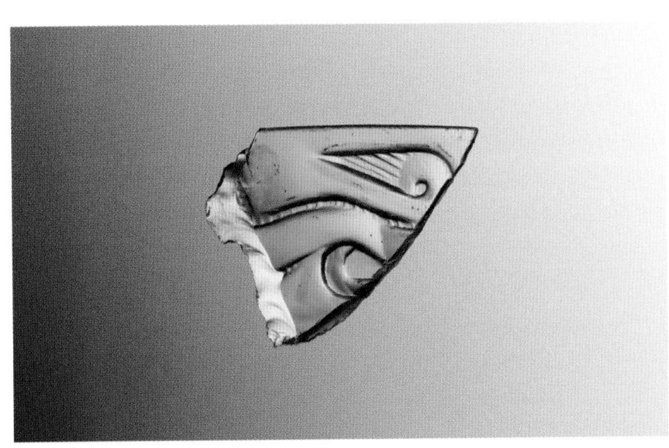

588

589. Fragment of Bowl with Palmette

9th to 10th century. Formerly in the Smith Collection (1267). 59.7.3.
H. (surviving) 2.6 cm, D. (rim, est.) about 10 cm.
Colorless. Relief-cut.

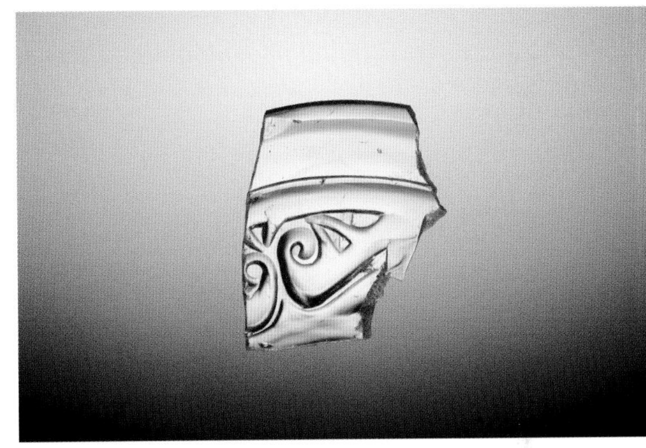

589

Fragment of shallow bowl. Rim has rounded lip and flat, ground, and polished top; wall curves down and in, with hint of foot-ring (D. about 3 cm) at bottom. Exterior decorated in relief with horizontal rib above frieze of vegetal motifs. Surviving ornament consists of short stem that divides at top and terminates in flat palmette with its halves separated by small triangular boss. Stem also divides at bottom, and on each side it curves down, out, and (on surviving side) gently up.

Broken on all sides, except for short section of rim. Surface as new.

Comment: The palmette resembles the palmettes in the upper part of the frieze on a relief-cut glass beaker in The Metropolitan Museum of Art, New York (1974.45: *Glass of the Sultans* 2001, pp. 172–173, no. 79), and on the rim of a rock crystal dish in the

Treasury of San Marco, Venice (102: Erdmann 1971, pp. 115–116, no. 126).

BIBLIOGRAPHY: *Glass from the Ancient World* 1957, p. 285, no. 611a (part of group).

590. Fragment of Ewer(?) with Palmettes and Half-Palmettes

Late 10th to early 11th century. Formerly in the Strauss Collection (F72). 79.7.18.
Max. Dim. 5.6 cm, D. (rib, est.) about 6–7 cm.
Colorless. Relief-cut.

Fragment from wall of ewer(?) (described here as if from lower wall), which curves down and in to horizontal rib, then straightens and tapers. Decorated in relief with part of frieze, with rib forming lower border. Ornament consists of continuous, presumably symmetrical pattern of scrolling stems, which terminate in palmettes, half-palmettes, and leaves. Near top of fragment, small oval motif with partly countersunk center, traces of two stems rising from top, and pair of stems descending from bottom, curving to right and left, then curling inward and terminating in half-palmettes. Below these, and directly beneath oval motif, smaller, downward-pointing tear-shaped motif. To left of tear-shaped motif and below it, extending almost to rib, downward-pointing palmette, from which rise two stems that curve up and out, then divide with (surviving only to right of palmette) one branch curving down and terminating in curling, partly countersunk leaf; other branches (surviving on both sides) curve in and up, and meet, thereby enclosing countersunk diamond-shaped area. All stems are notched, and left stem in upper pair has point of attachment with right stem in lower pair.

Broken on all sides. Surfaces are as new.

COMMENT: The fragment came from the wall of a hollow vessel, probably—but not certainly—a ewer similar to the seven celebrated rock crystal ewers in the Treasury of San Marco in Venice (two examples), in the Palazzo Pitti in Florence, in the cathedral at Fermo (Italy), in the Musée du Louvre in Paris, in the Victoria and Albert Museum in London, and on the London market in 2008. (An eighth, somewhat asymmetrical rock crystal ewer with an elaborately cut handle but no decoration on the body is in the David Collection, Copenhagen (27/1999: Folsach 2001, pp. 227 and 237, no. 368).) The scale and the quality of the cutting of **590** are comparable with these objects, and the profile, which curves on one side of the rib and

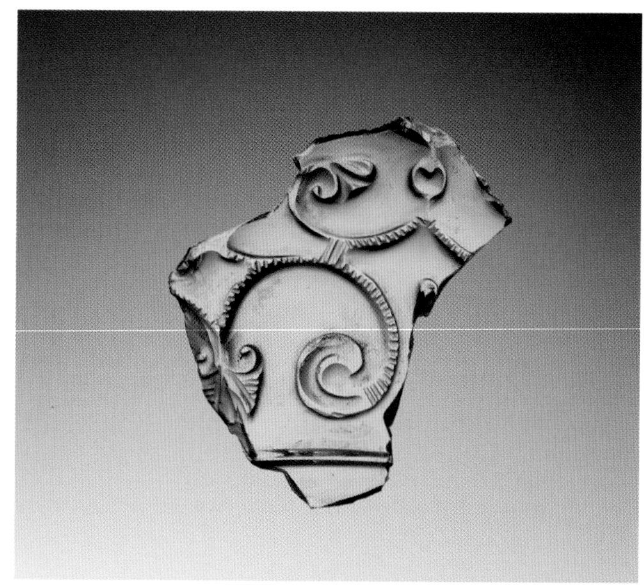

590

straightens to a shallow taper on the other, further suggests that the fragment may be part of the lower wall of a ewer. Moreover, the arrangement of two small elements, one above the other, with an apparently symmetrical pattern of vegetal ornament on either side, is consistent with supposing that the fragment is from the front of a ewer, below the pouring lip and opposite the handle. Indeed, all seven ewers (and their counterparts in glass: e.g., the Corning Ewer [**522**]) have a continuous panel of ornament running around most of the circumference, from one side of the handle to the other, occupied on each side of the vessel by birds and/or animals. In every case, the creatures are separated by a more or less extensive pattern of vegetal scrolls, which are symmetrical about the vertical axis below the lip. On **522**, the scrolls are lacking, but the axis is accentuated by two tear-shaped motifs. It is possible, therefore, that the fragment is part of a ewer that, when complete, was comparable with the ewers mentioned above. One of the ewers in Venice (80) bears an inscription naming Caliph al-ᶜAzīz Biʾllāh (r. 975–996), and the ewer in the Palazzo Pitti has an inscription indicating that it was made between 1000 and 1008 or 1010. The date of the ewers and of **590**, therefore, is likely to fall within the period between about 975 and 1025.

591. Fragment of Jar with Half-Palmettes

9th to 10th century. Formerly in the Smith Collection. 68.1.59-7.
H. 3.4 cm, D. (est.) 4 cm.
Colorless; apparently with patch of very small brown needle-like inclusions.
Relief-cut.

Fragment of jar: cylindrical. Rim plain, beveled on inside; wall vertical; base plain, with narrow splayed foot-ring and at least one concentric circular rib on underside. Wall decorated in relief with frieze of scrolling half-palmettes bordered at top and bottom by horizontal ribs.

Approximately 25 percent of object survives, with complete profile of wall.

COMMENT: The complete jar probably had eight half-palmettes. The size and shape of the object suggest that it was intended to contain a medicinal or cosmetic ointment that was used in small quantities.

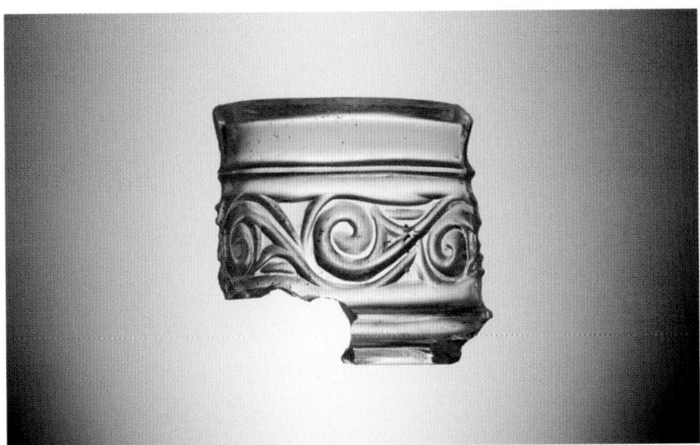

591

592. Fragment with Vegetal Scroll

About 10th century. Formerly in the Smith Collection (1267). Gift of Carl Berkowitz and Derek Content. 76.7.7.
H. (surviving) 3.8 cm, Th. 0.4–0.8 cm.
Colorless. Relief-cut.

Fragment consisting of wall and small section of rim of vessel. Rim has flat top and may have had narrow flange; upper wall has slightly convex profile (but see "Comment"). Wall is decorated on outside with small section of horizontal vegetal scroll (H. 1.3 cm) containing half-palmette with horizontal hatching.

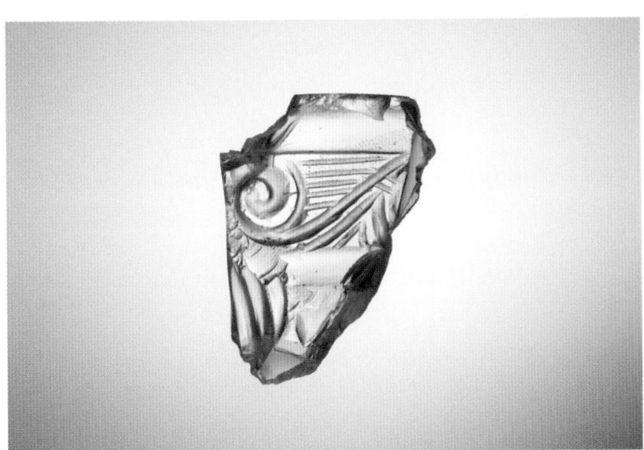

592

Broken on all sides except rim. Extensively chipped below scroll.

COMMENT: The fragment is described as part of a bowl or similar hollow vessel. It is possible, however, that it came from the broad, more or less horizontal rim of a plate similar to a rock crystal object in the Treasury of San Marco, Venice (102: Erdmann 1971, pp. 115–116, no. 126).

593. Miniature Bowl

Date uncertain. Formerly in the Smith Collection. Gift of Carl Berkowitz and Derek Content. 76.7.3.
H. 1.1 cm, L. 3.5 cm, W. 2.3 cm.
Colorless. Ground, cut, and polished.

Bowl: oval. Rim plain, with rounded lip; wall curves down and in; disklike oval base. Decorated in relief just below rim: continuous horizontal row of 21 pyramid-shaped bosses.

Intact, except for small chip in rim.

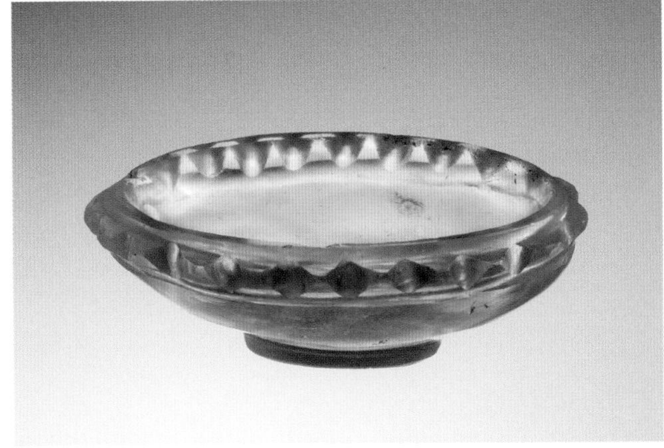

593

COMMENT: For another miniature rock crystal vessel decorated with a row of pyramid-shaped bosses, see **594**. The two objects were acquired at the same time, presumably from the same source, and it is not unlikely that they were part of a set of miniature vessels.

594. Miniature Bowl

Date uncertain. Formerly in the Smith Collection. Gift of Carl Berkowitz and Derek Content. 76.7.4.

H. 1 cm, D. 2.7 cm.
Colorless. Ground, cut, and polished.

Bowl. Rim plain, with rounded lip; wall curves down and in; disklike base. Decorated on wall: just below rim, continuous horizontal row of 30 pyramid-shaped bosses; on lower wall, eight rather irregular pairs of short transverse cuts.

Intact, except for chips and bruise on base.

Comment: See **593**.

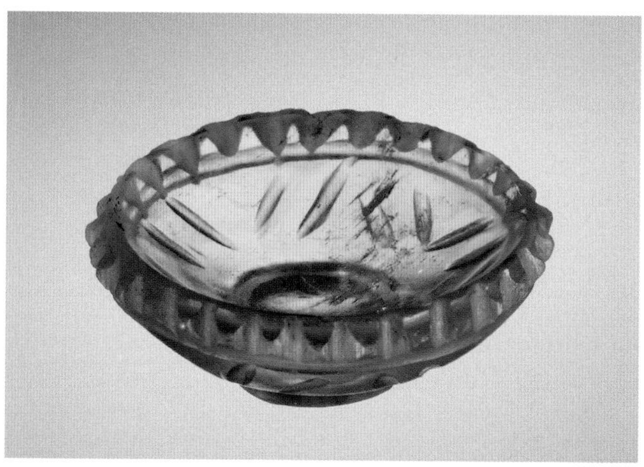

594

595. Fragment

Date unknown. Gift of Dr. George Scanlon.
81.7.83.
Max. Dim. 3.6 cm.
Colorless. Chipped.

Fragment, very roughly trapezoidal.
Broken on all surfaces.

Comment: Presumably the fragment is waste from a lapidary's workshop. The only possible use for it would have been to manufacture a bead or some other small object.

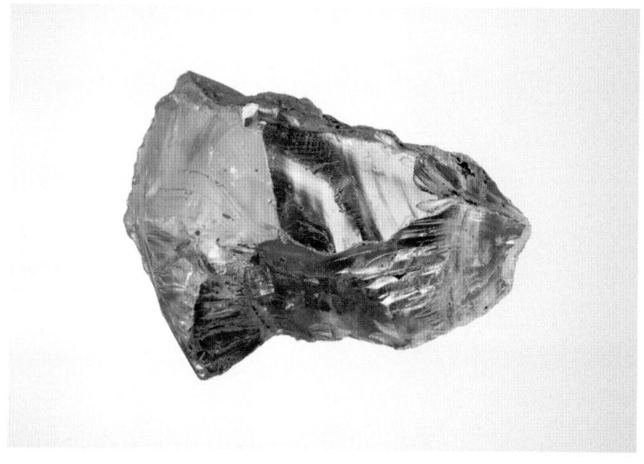

595

Bibliography

Most works are cited by author(s) and date (e.g., Brill 1999). When the same author(s) published more than one work in a single year, the works are distinguished by lowercase letters immediately after the date (e.g., Saldern 1995a, 1995b). When two or more authors have the same surname, they are identified by the initial letters of their given names (e.g., Oliver, A. 1980; Oliver, P. 1961). Exhibition catalogs are cited by name and date (e.g., *Arts of Islam* 1976). Catalogs (including sale catalogs) of well-known private collections are cited by owner's name and date (e.g., *Constable-Maxwell Collection* 1979). Entries beginning with a cardinal or ordinal number, expressed either as a numeral or spelled out, will be found after the alphabetical entries, arranged numerically.

The following abbreviations are used in both the bibliography and the text:

A. Names of Publications

AnnAIHV	*Annales de l'Association Internationale pour l'Histoire du Verre*
JARCE	*Journal of the American Research Center in Egypt*
JGS	*Journal of Glass Studies*

B. Other

cols.	columns
ed.	editor
edn.	edition
esp.	especially
ff.	folios
fig., figs.	figure, figures
illus.	illustrated, illustration
ms.	manuscript
n.	note
n.d.	date not stated
no., nos.	number, numbers
n.p.	not paginated
n.s.	new series
p., pp.	page, pages
pl., pls.	plate, plates
pt.	part
rev.	revised
s.l.	*sine loco* (place not stated)
v., vv.	volume, volumes

Anon. 1930
Anon., *The Islamic Collection/Bulletin of the Bachstitz Gallery*, Berlin: S.B.K., 1930.

Anon. 1954
Anon., *Art-Price Annual*, v. 9, 1953/1954, London: Art and Technology Press, 1954.

Anon. 1968
Anon., "Hedwig Glass Acquired by The Corning Museum of Glass," *Oriental Art*, n.s., v. 14, Summer 1968, pp. 134–135.

Anon. 1982
Anon., "Ray Winfield Smith, 1897–1982," *JGS*, v. 24, 1982, p. 122.

ʿAbd al-Khaliq 1976
H. ʿAbd al-Khaliq, *Al-Zujaj al-islami fi matahif wa-makhazin al-athar fi al-ʿIraq* (The Islamic glass in the Iraqi museums and stores), Baghdad: Wizarat al-I'lam, 1976 (in Arabic).

Afghanistan 2002
Anon., *Afghanistan: Une histoire millénaire*, Paris: Editions de la Réunion des Musées Nationaux, 2002.

Allen 1987
F. N. Allen, *The Hedwig Glasses: A Survey*, Hyattsville, Maryland: the author, 1987.

An 1991
An J., "Dated Islamic Glass in China," *Bulletin of the Asia Institute*, n.s., v. 5, 1991, pp. 123–137.

Ancient Glass and Glazed Wares n.d.
Ancient Glass and Glazed Wares, Second Catalogue, London: Gawain McKinley Ltd., n.d. [1974].

Antikes Glas 1951
Antikes Glas aus der Sammlung Ray Winfield Smith: Sonderausstellung im Museum Dahlem, Arnimallee 23, Berlin, September bis November 1951, Berlin: the museum, 1951.

Antikes Glas 1952–3
Antikes Glas aus der Sammlung Ray Winfield Smith: Ausstellung im Kurpfälzischen Museum Heidelberg, November 1952 bis Herbst 1953, Heidelberg: the museum, 1952.

Antiquities and Islamic Works of Art 1975
Greek, Roman, Egyptian, Western Asiatic, Islamic Antiquities & Works of Art, sale catalog, New York: Sotheby Parke Bernet, May 2, 1975.

Art in Glass 1969
Art in Glass: A Guide to the Glass Collections, Toledo, Ohio: The Toledo Museum of Art, 1969.

Art of the Islamic and Indian Worlds 2008
Art of the Islamic and Indian Worlds, sale catalog, London: Christie's, April 8, 2008.

Arts d'Orient 2004
Arts d'Orient, sale catalog, Paris: Boisregard & Associés, March 19, 2004.

Arts of Islam 1976
The Arts of Islam: Hayward Gallery, 8 April–4 July 1976, [London]: The Arts Council of Great Britain, 1976.

Arts of the Islamic World 2005
Arts of the Islamic World, sale catalog, London: Sotheby's, April 27, 2005.

Arts of the Islamic World 2008
Arts of the Islamic World, sale catalog, London: Sotheby's, April 9, 2008.

Galerie Bachstitz, 's-Gravenhage, v. 2, *Antike, byzantinische, islamische Arbeiten der Kleinkunst und des Kunstgewerbes, antike Skulpturen*, sale catalog, Berlin: Albert Frisch, [1921].

Ghirshman 1954
R. Ghirshman, *Iran: From the Earliest Times to the Islamic Conquest*, Harmondsworth, U.K., and Baltimore, Maryland: Penguin Books, 1954.

Ghuchani 1998
A. Ghuchani, "Sasanian Motifs and Early Islamic Metalwork," in *The Art and Archaeology of Ancient Persia: New Light on the Parthian and Sasanian Empires*, ed. V. S. Curtis, R. Hillenbrand, and J. M. Rogers, London and New York: I. B. Tauris in association with the British Institute of Persian Studies, 1998, pp. 188–191.

Gilded Dragons 1999
C. Michaelson, *Gilded Dragons: Buried Treasures from China's Golden Ages*, London: British Museum Press, 1999.

Glass Drinking Vessels 1955
[J. Strauss], *Glass Drinking Vessels from the Collections of Jerome Strauss and The Ruth Bryan Strauss Memorial Foundation*, Corning: The Corning Museum of Glass, 1955.

Glass from the Ancient World 1957
[R. W. Smith], *Glass from the Ancient World: The Ray Winfield Smith Collection*, Corning: The Corning Museum of Glass, 1957.

Glass from the Ancient World 1991
E. L. Higashi, ed., *Glass from the Ancient World: So Diverse a Unity*, Dearborn, Michigan: University of Michigan–Dearborn, 1991.

Glass of the Caesars 1987
D. B. Harden and others, *Glass of the Caesars*, Milan: Olivetti, 1987.

Glass of the Sultans 2001
S. Carboni and D. Whitehouse, with contributions by R. H. Brill and W. Gudenrath, *Glass of the Sultans*, New York: The Metropolitan Museum of Art in association with The Corning Museum of Glass, Benaki Museum, and Yale University Press, 2001.

Goldstein and others 2001
S. M. Goldstein and others, *Ancient Glass = Kodaī garasu*, [Shiga, Japan]: Miho Museum, 2001.

Gray 1987
B. Gray, "Thoughts on the Origin of 'Hedwig' Glasses," in B. Gray, *Studies in Chinese and Islamic Art*, v. 2, *Chinese Ceramics and Islamic Art*, London: The Pindar Press, 1987. First published in *Colloque Internationale sur l'Histoire du Caire*, 1969, pp. 191–194.

Grube and Johns 2005
E. J. Grube and J. Johns, *The Painted Ceilings of the Cappella Palatina*, Islamic Art Supplement 1, Genoa: The Bruschettini Foundation for Islamic and Asian Art, and New York: The East–West Foundation, 2005.

Gudenrath 1991
W. Gudenrath, "Techniques of Glassmaking and Decoration," in *Five Thousand Years of Glass*, ed. H. Tait, London: British Museum Press, 1991, pp. 213–241.

Gudenrath 1999
W. Gudenrath, "Techniques of Glassmaking and Decoration," in *Five Thousand Years of Glass*, reprinted, with revisions, ed. H. Tait, London: British Museum Press, 1999, pp. 213–241.

Gudenrath 2001
W. Gudenrath, "A Survey of Islamic Glassworking and Glass-Decorating Techniques," in S. Carboni and D. Whitehouse, with contributions by R. H. Brill and W. Gudenrath, *Glass of the Sultans*, New York: The Metropolitan Museum of Art in association with The Corning Museum of Glass, Benaki Museum, and Yale University Press, 2001, pp. 46–67.

Gudenrath 2004
W. Gudenrath, "Techniques of Glassmaking and Decoration," in *Five Thousand Years of Glass*, rev. edn., ed. H. Tait, Philadelphia: University of Pennsylvania Press, 2004, pp. 213–241.

Gudenrath and Whitehouse 1990
W. Gudenrath and D. Whitehouse, "The Manufacture of the [Portland] Vase and Its Ancient Repair," *JGS*, v. 32, 1990, pp. 108–121.

Guide to the Collections 1955
T. S. Buechner and others, *Glass from The Corning Museum of Glass: A Guide to the Collections*, Corning: Corning Glass Center, 1955.

Guide to the Collections 1958
T. S. Buechner and others, *Glass from The Corning Museum of Glass: A Guide to the Collections*, Corning: Corning Glass Center, 1958.

Guide to the Collections 1965
P. N. Perrot and others, *Glass from The Corning Museum of Glass: A Guide to the Collections*, Corning: Corning Glass Center, 1965.

Guide to the Collections 1974
R. H. Brill and others, *Glass from The Corning Museum of Glass: A Guide to the Collections*, Corning: the museum, 1974.

Guide to the Collections 2001
The Corning Museum of Glass: A Guide to the Collections, Corning: the museum, 2001.

Gurevich 1963
F. D. Gurevich, "Stekliannyi rezno bokal iz Novogrudka" (Engraved glass goblet from Novogrudok), *Sovetskaia Arkheologia*, 1963, no. 2, pp. 243–246 (in Russian).

Gurevich 1981
F. D. Gurevich, *Drevnii Novogrudok: Posad–okol'nyi gorod* (Ancient Novogrudok: The artisanal quarter), Leningrad: "Nauka" Leningradskoe Otdelenie, 1981 (in Russian).

Hadad 2000
S. Hadad, "Incised Glass Vessels from the Umayyad and Abbasid–Fatimid Periods at Bet Shean, Israel," *Bulletin of the American Schools of Oriental Research*, no. 317, February 2000, pp. 63–73.

Harada and others 1965
Y. Harada and others, *Shōsōin no garasu = Glass Objects in the Shôsôin*, Tokyo: Nihon Keizai Shimbun Sha, 1965.

Hardy-Guilbert 1984
C. Hardy-Guilbert, "Les Niveaux islamiques du secteur Apadana–Ville Royale," *Cahiers de la Délégation Archéologique Française en Iran*, v. 14, 1984, pp. 121–210.

Hasson 1979
R. Hasson, *Early Islamic Glass*, Jerusalem: L. A. Mayer Memorial Institute for Islamic Art, 1979.

Heeramaneck Collection 1973
P. Pal, *Islamic Art: The Nasli M. Heeramaneck Collection, Gift*

of Joan Palevsky, Los Angeles: Los Angeles County Museum of Art, 1973.

Hentrich Collection 1974
A. von Saldern, *Glas. Band 3. Glassammlung Hentrich: Antike und Islam*, Kataloge des Kunstmuseums Düsseldorf, v. 1, pt. 3, Düsseldorf: the museum, 1974.

Hillenbrand 1999
R. Hillenbrand, *Islamic Art and Architecture*, London: Thames and Hudson, 1999.

Honey 1946
W. B. Honey, *Glass: A Handbook for the Study of Glass Vessels of All Periods and Countries & a Guide to the Museum Collection*, London: Victoria and Albert Museum, 1946.

Horton 1996
M. Horton, with contributions by H. W. Brown and N. Mudida, *Shanga: The Archaeology of a Muslim Trading Community on the Coast of East Africa*, Memoirs of the British Institute in Eastern Africa, no. 14, London: the institute, 1996.

Important Works of Art 1967
Important Mediaeval and Renaissance Works of Art . . ., sale catalog, London: Sotheby & Co., May 18 and 19, 1967.

Insoll 1998
T. Insoll, "Islamic Glass from Gao, Mali," *JGS*, v. 40, 1998, pp. 77–88.

Islam and the Medieval West 1975
S. Ferber, ed., *Islam and the Medieval West*, Binghamton: State University of New York at Binghamton, Center for Medieval and Early Renaissance Studies, 1975.

Islamic Antiquities and Works of Art 1975
Greek, Etruscan, Roman, Byzantine, Egyptian, Western Asiatic, Islamic Antiquities and Works of Art, . . . Ancient and Islamic Glass from the Collection of Ray Winfield Smith, sale catalog, New York: Sotheby's, November 20 and 21, 1975.

Islamic Art 1970
T. Bowie, *Islamic Art across the World*, Bloomington: Indiana University Art Museum, 1970.

Islamic Art 1994
Islamic Art and Indian Miniatures and Rugs and Carpets, sale catalog, London: Christie's, April 26 and 28, 1994.

Islamic Art and Manuscripts 2000
Islamic Art and Manuscripts, sale catalog, London: Christie's, October 10, 2000.

Islamic Art and Manuscripts 2001
Islamic Art and Manuscripts, sale catalog, London: Christie's, October 16, 2001.

Islamic Works of Art 1984
Islamic Works of Art . . ., sale catalog, London: Sotheby's, October 17, 1984.

Islamic Works of Art 1991
Indian, Himalayan and South-East Asian Art; Islamic Works of Art, sale catalog, London: Sotheby's, April 25, 1991.

Jenkins 1986
M. Jenkins, "Islamic Glass: A Brief History," *The Metropolitan Museum of Art Bulletin*, v. 44, no. 2, Fall 1986, pp. 3–56.

Kervran 1984
M. Kervran, "Les Niveaux islamiques du secteur oriental du tépé de l'Apadana. III: Les Objets en verre, en pierre et en métal," *Cahiers de la Délégation Archéologique Française en Iran*, v. 14, 1984, pp. 211–235.

Khalili Collection 2005
S. M. Goldstein, with contributions by J. M. Rogers, M. Gibson, and J. Kröger, *The Nasser D. Khalili Collection of Islamic Art*, v. 15, *Glass: From Sasanian Antecedents to European Imitations*, London: The Nour Foundation in association with Azimuth Editions, 2005.

Koch 1995
A. Koch, "Der Goldschatzfund des Famensi: Prunk und Pietät im chinesischen Buddhismus der Tang-Zeit," *Jahrbuch des Römisch-Germanischen Zentralmuseums Mainz*, v. 42, no. 2, 1995, pp. 403–542.

Kolbas 1983
J. G. Kolbas, "A Color Chronology of Islamic Glass," *JGS*, v. 25, 1983, pp. 95–100.

Kröger 1984
J. Kröger, *Glas* (Staatliche Museen Preussischer Kulturbesitz, Museum für Islamische Kunst, Berlin), v. 1 of *Islamische Kunst: Loseblattkatalog unpublizierter Werke aus Deutschen Museen*, ed. K. Brisch, Mainz am Rhein: Verlag Philipp von Zabern, 1984.

Kröger 1995
J. Kröger, *Nishapur: Glass of the Early Islamic Period*, New York: The Metropolitan Museum of Art, 1995.

Kröger 1998
J. Kröger, "Gläser aus spätantiker und islamischer Zeit in der Abegg-Stiftung," *Riggisberger Berichte*, v. 6, *Entlang der Seidenstrasse: Frühmittelalterliche Kunst zwischen Persien und China in der Abegg-Stiftung*, 1998, pp. 299–380.

Kröger 1999a
J. Kröger, "Fusṭāṭ and Nishapur: Questions about Fatimid Cut Glass," in *L'Egypte fatimide: Son art et son histoire*, ed. M. Barrucand, Paris: Presses de l'Université de Paris-Sorbonne, 1999, pp. 219–232.

Kröger 1999b
J. Kröger, "Vom Flügelpaar zur Flügelpalmette: Sasanidische Motive in der islamischen Kunst," in *Bamberger Studien: Rezeption in der islamischen Kunst*, Beiruter Texte und Studien, v. 61, ed. B. Finster, C. Fragner, and H. Hafenrichter, Würzburg: Ergon-Verlag, 1999, pp. 193–204.

Kröger 1999c
J. Kröger, "Zu einem 1991 erworbenen smaragdgrünem Glasfragment aus frühislamischer Zeit im Museum für Islamische Kunst in Berlin," *Damaszener Mitteilungen*, v. 11, 1999, pp. 317–330.

Kröger 2002
J. Kröger, "The Samarra Bowl with the Half-Palmette Animals Reconsidered," in *Cairo to Kabul: Afghan and Islamic Studies Presented to Ralph Pinder-Wilson*, ed. W. Ball and L. Harrow, London: Melisende, 2002, pp. 151–156.

Kröger 2005
J. Kröger, "Scratched Glass," in S. M. Goldstein, with contributions by J. M. Rogers, M. Gibson, and J. Kröger, *The Nasser D. Khalili Collection of Islamic Art*, v. 15, *Glass: From Sasanian Antecedents to European Imitations*, London: The Nour Foundation in association with Azimuth Editions, 2005, pp. 140–155.

Kröger 2006
J. Kröger, "The Hedwig Beakers: Medieval European Glass Vessels Made in Sicily around 1200," in *The Phenomenon of "Foreign" in Oriental Art*, ed. A. Hagedorn, Wiesbaden: Reichert, 2006, pp. 27–46.

Kubiak and Scanlon 1973
W. Kubiak and G. T. Scanlon, "Fusṭāṭ Expedition: Preliminary Report 1966," *JARCE*, v. 10, 1973, pp. 11–25.

Kucharczyk 2009
R. Kucharczyk, "Islamic Scratch-Engraved Glass from Alexandria (Kom el-Dikka)," *JGS*, v. 51, 2009, pp. 40–52.

Küçükerman 1999
Ö. Küçükerman, *A 500 Years' Heritage in Istanbul: The Turkish Glass Industry and Şişecam*, Istanbul: Türkiye Şişe ve Cam Fabrikaları A.Ş., 1999 (English edition of book published in Turkish in 1998).

Lamb 1965
A. Lamb, "A Note on Glass Fragments from Pengkalan Bujang, Malaya," *JGS*, v. 7, 1965, pp. 35–40.

Lamm 1928
C. J. Lamm, *Das Glas von Samarra*, v. 4 of *Die Ausgrabungen von Samarra*, Forschungen zur Islamischen Kunst, ed. F. Sarre, pt. 2, Berlin: Verlag von Dietrich Reimer/Ernst Vohsen, 1928.

Lamm 1929–30
C. J. Lamm, *Mittelalterliche Gläser und Steinschnittarbeiten aus dem Nahen Osten*, 2 vv., Forschungen zur Islamischen Kunst, ed. F. Sarre, pt. 5, Berlin: Verlag Dietrich Reimer/Ernst Vohsen, 1929–1930.

Lamm 1931
C. J. Lamm, "Les Verres trouvés [à] Suse," *Syria*, v. 12, 1931, pp. 358–367.

Lamm 1935
C. J. Lamm, *Glass from Iran in the National Museum, Stockholm*, Stockholm: C. E. Fritzes K. Hovbokh., and London: Kegan Paul, Trench, Trubner & Co. Ltd., 1935.

Lamm 1939
C. J. Lamm, "Glass and Hard Stone Vessels," in *A Survey of Persian Art: From Prehistoric Times to the Present*, ed. A. U. Pope assisted by P. Ackerman, London and New York: Oxford University Press, 1939, v. 3, pp. 2592–2606, and v. 6, pls. 1439–1459.

Lane 1938
A. Lane, "Medieval Finds at Al Mina in North Syria," *Archaeologia*, v. 87, 1938, pp. 19–78.

Lang 1982
G. Lang, "Fragrance: A Sensual Marriage of Crystal and Essence," *United: The Magazine of the Friendly Skies*, April 1982, pp. 12–15.

Langdon and Harden 1934
S. Langdon and D. B. Harden, "Pottery and Glass from Kish: Excavations at Kish and Barghuthiat," *Iraq*, v. 1, 1934, pp. 124–136.

Leth 1970
A. Leth, *Davids Samling: Islamisk Kunst*, Copenhagen: the collection, 1970 (in Danish, with English captions).

Leth 1975
A. Leth, *Davids Samling: Islamisk Kunst*, Copenhagen: the collection, 1975 (in Danish, with English captions).

Lierke 1999
R. Lierke, *Antike Glastöpferei: Ein vergessenes Kapitel der Glasgeschichte*, Zaberns Bildbände zur Archäologie, Mainz am Rhein: Verlag Philipp von Zabern, 1999.

Lierke 2005
R. Lierke, *Die Hedwigsbecher: Das normannisch-sizilische Erbe der staufischen Kaiser*, Ruhpalding, Germany: Rutzen, 2005.

Marçais and Poinssot 1952
G. Marçais and L. Poinssot, *Objets kairouanais, IXe au XIIIe siècle: Reliures, verreries, cuivres et bronzes, bijoux*, Direction des Antiquités et Arts, Notes & Documents, v. 11, pt. 2, Tunis: Tournier, and Paris: Klincksieck, 1952.

Marshak 1998
B. I. Marshak, "The Decoration of Some Late Sasanian Silver Vessels and Its Subject-Matter," in *The Art and Archaeology of Ancient Persia: New Light on the Parthian and Sasanian Empires*, ed. V. S. Curtis, R. Hillenbrand, and J. M. Rogers, London and New York: I. B. Tauris in association with the British Institute of Persian Studies, 1998, pp. 84–92.

Marshall 1990
J. Marshall, *Glass Source Book*, London: Collins & Brown, 1990.

Martin 1977
J. H. Martin, ed., *The Corning Flood: Museum under Water*, Corning: The Corning Museum of Glass, 1977.

Masterpieces of Glass 1968
D. B. Harden and others, *Masterpieces of Glass*, London: Trustees of The British Museum, 1968.

Matcham and Dreiser 1997
J. Matcham and P. Dreiser, *The Techniques of Glass Engraving*, London: B. T. Batsford Ltd., 1982, reissued in 1997.

Merrill 1989
N. O. Merrill, *A Concise History of Glass Represented in The Chrysler Museum Glass Collection*, Norfolk, Virginia: the museum, 1989.

Miles 1954
G. C. Miles, "The Sāmarrā Mint," *Ars Orientalis: The Arts of Islam and the East*, v. 1, [Washington, D.C.]: Freer Gallery of Art, Smithsonian Institution, and [Ann Arbor]: Fine Arts Department, University of Michigan, 1954, pp. 187–191.

Morrison 1984
H. M. Morrison, "The Glass," in [H.] N. Chittick, *Manda: Excavations at an Island Port on the Kenya Coast*, Memoir 9, Nairobi: The British Institute in Eastern Africa, 1984, pp. 159–179.

Nahman Collection 1953
Succession de Mr Maurice Nahman du Caire, Egypte: Antiquités égyptiennes, grecques et romaines, sale catalog, Paris: Ader, February 26 and 27, 1953.

Newby 1991
M. S. Newby, "The Glass from Farfa Abbey: An Interim Report," *JGS*, v. 33, 1991, pp. 32–41.

Northedge 1996
A. Northedge, "Friedrich Sarre's *Die Keramik von Samarra* in Perspective," in *Continuity and Change in Northern Mesopotamia from the Hellenistic to the Early Islamic Period*, ed. K. Bartl and S. R. Hauser, Berliner Beiträge zum Vorderen Orient, v. 17, Berlin: Dietrich Reimer Verlag, 1996, pp. 229–258.

Oliver, A. 1980
A. Oliver Jr., *Ancient Glass in the Carnegie Museum of Natural History, Pittsburgh*, Pittsburgh: Carnegie Institute, 1980.

Oliver, P. 1961
P. Oliver, "Islamic Relief Cut Glass: A Suggested Chronology," *JGS*, v. 3, 1961, pp. 9–29.

Pagan and Christian Egypt 1941
Pagan and Christian Egypt: Egyptian Art from the First to the

Tenth Century A.D., Brooklyn, New York: Brooklyn Museum, 1941.

Perrot 1968
P. N. Perrot, "The Corning Museum of Glass Loan Exhibit: 'Glass Drinking Vessels through the Ages,'" *East Side House Winter Antiques Show*, New York: East Side House Settlement, 1968, pp. 32–47.

Perrot 1978
P. N. Perrot, "Jerome Strauss, 1893–1978," *JGS*, v. 20, 1978, pp. 159–160.

Les Perses sassanides 2006
Les Perses sassanides: Fastes d'un empire oublié, 224–642, Paris: Musée Cernuschi and Musée des Arts de l'Asie de la Ville de Paris, and Suilly-la-Tour: Findakly, 2006.

Persian Glass 1972
P. N. Perrot, *A Tribute to Persia: Persian Glass*, Corning: The Corning Museum of Glass, 1972.

Philippe 1970
J. Philippe, *Le Monde byzantin dans l'histoire de la verrerie (V^e–XVIe siècle)*, Bologna: Casa Editrice Prof. Riccardo Pàtron, 1970.

Phönix aus Sand und Asche 1988
E. Baumgartner and I. Krueger, *Phönix aus Sand und Asche: Glas des Mittelalters*, Munich: Klinkhardt & Biermann, 1988.

Pinder-Wilson 1963
R. Pinder-Wilson, "Cut-Glass Vessels from Persia and Mesopotamia," *British Museum Quarterly*, v. 27, no. 2, 1963, pp. 33–39.

Pinder-Wilson 1991
R. Pinder-Wilson, "The Islamic Lands and China," in *Five Thousand Years of Glass*, ed. H. Tait, London: British Museum Press, 1991, pp. 112–143.

Pinder-Wilson 1996
R. H. Pinder-Wilson, "Glass from the Islamic World," in G. Fehérvári and others, *Art of the Eastern World*, London: Hadji Baba Ancient Art, 1996, pp. 90–115.

Pinder-Wilson 1999
R. Pinder-Wilson, "The Islamic Lands and China," in *Five Thousand Years of Glass*, reprinted, with revisions, ed. H. Tait, London: British Museum Press, 1999, pp. 112–143.

Pinder-Wilson 2004
R. Pinder-Wilson, "The Islamic Lands and China," in *Five Thousand Years of Glass*, rev. edn., ed. H. Tait, Philadelphia: University of Pennsylvania Press, 2004, pp. 112–143.

Pinder-Wilson and Scanlon 1973
R. H. Pinder-Wilson and G. T. Scanlon, "Glass Finds from Fustat: 1964–71," *JGS*, v. 15, 1973, pp. 12–30.

Pinder-Wilson and Scanlon 1987
R. H. Pinder-Wilson and G. T. Scanlon, "Glass Finds from Fustat: 1972–1980," *JGS*, v. 29, 1987, pp. 60–71.

Platz 2000
K. T. Platz, "Hilpoltstein vom Frühmittelalter bis zur frühen Neuzeit," *Arbeiten zur Archäologie Süddeutschlands*, v. 12, 2000, pp. 71–73.

Rebourg 1988
A. Rebourg, "La Resurrection des verres médiévaux," *Archéologia* (Dijon), no. 239, October 1988, pp. 18–23.

Rice 1956
D. S. Rice, "A Datable Islamic Rock Crystal," *Oriental Art*, n.s., v. 2, no. 3, Autumn 1956, pp. 85–93.

Riis and Poulsen 1957
P. J. Riis and V. Poulsen, *Hama: Fouilles et recherches de la Fondation Carlsberg, 1931–1938*, v. 4, pt. 2, *Les Verreries et poteries médiévales*, Nationalmuseets Skrifter, Større Beretninger III, Copenhagen: Nationalmuseet, 1957.

Royal Hunter 1978
P. O. Harper, *The Royal Hunter: Art of the Sasanian Empire*, New York: The Asia Society in association with John Weatherhill Inc., 1978.

Saldern 1955
A. von Saldern, "An Islamic Carved Glass Cup in The Corning Museum of Glass," *Artibus Asiae*, v. 18, 1955, pp. 257–270, pls. 1 and 2.

Saldern 1963
A. von Saldern, "Achaemenid and Sassanian Cut Glass," *Ars Orientalis: The Arts of Islam and the East*, v. 5, [Washington, D.C.]: Freer Gallery of Art, Smithsonian Institution, and [Ann Arbor]: Department of the History of Art, University of Michigan, 1963, pp. 7–16.

Saldern 1968
A. von Saldern, *Ancient Glass in the Museum of Fine Arts, Boston*, Greenwich, Connecticut: New York Graphic Society, 1968.

Saldern 1995a
A. von Saldern, "Early Islamic Glass in the Near East: Problems of Chronology and Provenances," *AnnAIHV*, v. 13, Pays Bas, 1995 (Lochem, 1996), pp. 225–246.

Saldern 1995b
A. von Saldern, *Glas: Antike bis Jugendstil. Die Sammlung im Museum für Kunst und Gewerbe Hamburg*, Stuttgart: Arnoldsche, 1995.

Sangiorgi 1914
G. Sangiorgi, *Collezione di vetri antichi dalle origini al V sec. d.C.*, Milan and Rome: Casa Editrice d'Arte Bestetti e Tumminelli, 1914.

Scanlon 1972–3
G. T. Scanlon, "Recent Glass from Fusṭāṭ," *Bulletin de la Société Archéologique d'Alexandrie*, no. 43, 1972–1973, pp. 81–89.

Scanlon 1974
G. T. Scanlon, "Fusṭāṭ Expedition: Preliminary Report 1968, Part I," *JARCE*, v. 11, 1974, pp. 81–91.

Scanlon 1981
G. T. Scanlon, "Fusṭāṭ Expedition: Preliminary Report, Back to Fustat-A 1973," *Annales Islamologiques*, v. 17, 1981, pp. 407–436.

Scanlon 1984
G. T. Scanlon, "Fusṭāṭ Expedition: Preliminary Report 1978," *JARCE*, v. 21, 1984, pp. 1–38.

Scanlon and Pinder-Wilson 2001
G. T. Scanlon and R. Pinder-Wilson, *Fustat Glass of the Early Islamic Period: Finds Excavated by The American Research Center in Egypt, 1964–1980*, London: Altajir World of Islam Trust, 2001.

Sčapova 1978
J. Sčapova, "A propos des coupes dites de Sainte Hedwige," *AnnAIHV*, v. 7, Berlin-Leipzig, 1977 (Liège, 1978), pp. 255–269.

Scerrato 1979
U. Scerrato, "I cristalli di rocca," in F. Gabrieli and U. Scerrato, *Gli Arabi in Italia: Cultura, contatti e tradizioni*, Milan: Libri Scheiwiller for Credito Italiano, 1979, pp. 497–520.

Schmidt 1912
R. Schmidt, "Die Hedwigsgläser und die verwandten fatimidischen Glas- und Kristallschnittarbeiten," *Jahrbuch des Schlesischen Museums für Kunstgewerbe und Altertümer*, n.s., v. 6, 1912, pp. 53–78.

Shalem 1996
A. Shalem, *Islam Christianized: Islamic Portable Objects in the Medieval Church Treasuries of the Latin West*, Ars Faciendi: Beiträge und Studien zur Kunstgeschichte, v. 7, Frankfurt am Main: Peter Lang, 1996.

Shelkovnikov 1966
B. A. Shelkovnikov, "Russian Glass from the 11th to the 17th Century," *JGS*, v. 8, 1966, pp. 95–115.

Shindo 2002
Y. Shindo, *Islamic Glass: Finds from Fusṭāṭ, and Collections of Idemitsu and the Middle Eastern Culture Center in Japan*, Tokyo: the center, 2002.

Smith 1952
R. W. Smith, "Gläser der Antike," *Atlantis*, v. 24, no. 12, December 1952, pp. 496–497.

Smith 1957
R. W. Smith, "New Finds of Ancient Glass in North Africa," *Ars Orientalis: The Arts of Islam and the East*, v. 2, [Washington, D.C.]: Freer Gallery of Art, Smithsonian Institution, and [Ann Arbor]: Fine Arts Department, University of Michigan, 1957, pp. 91–117.

Smith 1964
R. W. Smith, "History Revealed in Ancient Glass," *National Geographic*, v. 126, no. 3, September 1964, pp. 346–369.

Splendeur des Sassanides 1993
Splendeur des Sassanides: L'Empire perse entre Rome et la Chine (224–642), Brussels: Musées Royaux d'Art et d'Histoire and Crédit Communal, 1993.

Strube 2003
C. Strube, "Androna/al Andarin: Vorbericht über die Grabungskampagnen in den Jahren 1997–2001," *Archäologischer Anzeiger*, no. 1, 2003, pp. 25–115.

Taniichi 1987
T. Taniichi, *Catalogue of Near Eastern Glass in the Okayama Orient Museum*, v. 4, *Catalogue of Ancient Glass*, Okayama: the museum, 1987.

Treasures from Corning 1992
S. K. Frantz and others, *Treasures from The Corning Museum of Glass*, s.l.: Nihon Keizai Shimbun, 1992.

Treasures in Glass 1966
Treasures in Glass, Kutztown, Pennsylvania: Kutztown Publishing Co., 1966.

Trésors fatimides 1998
M. Barrucand, *Trésors fatimides du Caire*, Ghent: Snoeck-Ducaju & Zoon, and Paris: Institut du Monde Arabe, 1998.

Tronzo 1997
W. Tronzo, *The Cultures of His Kingdom: Roger II and the Cappella Palatina in Palermo*, Princeton, New Jersey: Princeton University Press, 1997.

Al ᶜUsh 1971
M. A. Al ᶜUsh, "Incised Islamic Glass," *Archaeology*, v. 24, no. 3, June 1971, pp. 200–203.

Vannini 1987
G. Vannini, ed., *L'Antico Palazzo dei Vescovi a Pistoia*, v. 2, Florence: Leo S. Olschki Editore, 1987.

Vases & Volcanoes 1996
I. Jenkins and K. Sloan, *Vases & Volcanoes: Sir William Hamilton and His Collection*, London: British Museum Press, 1996.

Verres antiques 1954
Verres antiques de la collection Ray Winfield Smith, [Morlanwelz, Belgium]: Musée de Mariemont, and Gembloux, Belgium: J. Duculot, 1954.

Watson 2004
O. Watson, *Ceramics from Islamic Lands*, New York: Thames & Hudson in association with the al-Sabah Collection, Dar al-Athar al-Islamiyyah, Kuwait National Museum, 2004.

Wedepohl 2005
K. H. Wedepohl, *Die Gruppe der Hedwigsbecher*, Nachrichten der Akademie der Wissenschaften zu Göttingen II. Mathematisch-Physikalische Klasse, Göttingen: Vandenhoeck & Reprecht, 2005, no. 1.

Wedepohl and others 2007
K. H. Wedepohl and others, "A Hedwig Beaker Fragment from Brno (Czech Republic)," *JGS*, v. 49, 2007, pp. 266–268.

Welander-Berggren 1990
E. Welander-Berggren, "Från Mesopotamien till medeltid," *Antik et Auktion*, no. 1, January 1990, pp. 42–47.

Wentzel 1972
H. Wentzel, "Das byzantinische Erbe der Ottonischen Kaiser: Hypothesen über den Brautschatz der Theophano [pt. 2]," *Aachener Kunstblätter*, v. 43, 1972, pp. 11–96.

Wentzel 1973
H. Wentzel, "Byzantinische Kleinkunstwerke aus dem Umkreis der Kaiserin Theophano," *Aachener Kunstblätter*, v. 44, 1973, pp. 43–86.

Whitehouse 1985a
D. Whitehouse, "The Corning Museum of Glass," *Arts and the Islamic World*, v. 3, no. 3, Autumn 1985, pp. 67–70.

Whitehouse 1985b
D. Whitehouse, "Transparent Mystery: Where Was This Ancient Islamic Masterpiece [the Corning Ewer] Made?" *Connoisseur*, December 1985, pp. 130–131.

Whitehouse 1990a
D. B. Whitehouse, "Islamic Cameo Glass Ewer," in R. J. Charleston, with contributions by D. B. Whitehouse and S. K. Frantz, *Masterpieces of Glass: A World History from The Corning Museum of Glass*, expanded edn., New York: Harry N. Abrams Inc., 1990, pp. 72–73.

Whitehouse 1990b
D. Whitehouse, "Late Roman Cameo Glass," *AnnAIHV*, v. 11, Basel, 1988 (Amsterdam, 1990), pp. 193–198.

Whitehouse 1991
D. Whitehouse, "Islamic Glass," in *Sotheby's Concise Encyclopedia of Glass*, ed. D. Battie and S. Cottle, Boston, Toronto, and London: Little, Brown and Company, 1991, pp. 38–45.

Whitehouse 1993a
D. Whitehouse, "The Corning Ewer: A Masterpiece of Islamic Cameo Glass," *JGS*, v. 35, 1993, pp. 48–56.

Whitehouse 1993b
D. Whitehouse, *The Corning Museum of Glass and the Finger Lakes Region, Corning, New York*, Little Compton, Rhode Island: Fort Church Publishers Inc., 1993.

Whitehouse 1997
D. Whitehouse, *Roman Glass in The Corning Museum of Glass, Volume One*, Corning: the museum, 1997.

Whitehouse 2001a
D. Whitehouse, "On Exhibit: Glass of the Sultans, Islamic Artistry," *Veranda*, v. 15, no. 4, July–August 2001, p. 52+.

Whitehouse 2001b
D. Whitehouse, *Roman Glass in The Corning Museum of Glass, Volume Two*, Corning: the museum, 2001.

Whitehouse 2002
D. Whitehouse, "A Note on Hedwig Glasses," in *Cairo to Kabul: Afghan and Islamic Studies Presented to Ralph Pinder-Wilson*, ed. W. Ball and L. Harrow, London: Melisende, 2002, pp. 255–259.

Whitehouse 2003
D. Whitehouse, "Early Islamic Cameo Glass in The Corning Museum of Glass," *AnnAIHV*, v. 15, New York and Corning, 2001 (Nottingham, 2003), pp. 149–152.

Whitehouse 2005
D. Whitehouse, *Sasanian and Post-Sasanian Glass in The Corning Museum of Glass*, Corning: the museum, 2005.

Whitehouse 2008
D. Whitehouse, "An Unusual Fragment of Cameo Glass," *JGS*, v. 50, 2008, pp. 309–311.

Wilkinson 1973
C. K. Wilkinson, *Nishapur: Pottery of the Early Islamic Period*, Greenwich, Connecticut: New York Graphic Society on behalf of The Metropolitan Museum of Art, 1973.

Yoshimizu 1983
T. Yoshimizu, *Garasu nyūmon* (Introduction to glass), Tokyo: Heibon Kabushiki Kaisha, 1983 (in Japanese).

Yoshimizu 1992
T. Yoshimizu, ed., *The Survey of Glass in the World*, v. 1, *Antique and Medieval Glass*, text by A. von Saldern and D. B. Harden, Tokyo: Kyuryudo Art Publishing, 1992 (in Japanese).

2000 Jahre persisches Glas 1963
K. Erdmann, *2000 Jahre persisches Glas*, Brunswick: Waisenhaus, Henri Leonhardt, 1963.

3000 Jahre Glas 1975
A. Ohm, *3000 Jahre Glas aus Privatsammlung Frankfurt am Main, Sonderausstellung Ruhrlandmuseum Essen*, Zwiesel: Stadt Zwiesel, 1975.

3000 Jahre Glaskunst 1981
M. Kunz, ed., *3000 Jahre Glaskunst: Von der Antike bis zum Jugendstil*, Lucerne: Kunstmuseum, 1981.

7000 Years of Iranian Art 1964
E. Porada and R. Ettinghausen, *7000 Years of Iranian Art*, [Washington, D.C.: Smithsonian Institution, 1964].

Concordances

1. Accession Numbers

Accession No.	Cat. No.
50.1.36	**59**
51.1.54	**274**
51.1.110	**9**
51.1.111	**25**
51.1.112	**37**
51.1.113	**19**
51.1.114	**41**
51.1.115	**38**
51.1.116	**29**
51.1.117A	**21**
51.1.117B	**17**
51.1.118A	**33**
51.1.118B	**30**
51.1.119	**11**
51.1.120	**356**
51.1.121	**424**
51.1.122	**276**
51.1.123	**421**
51.1.124	**488**
51.1.125	**205**
51.1.126	**292**
51.1.127	**315**
51.1.128	**284**
51.1.129	**460**
51.1.130	**465**
51.1.131	**262**
51.1.132	**258**
51.1.136	**217**
51.1.142	**15**
51.1.143	**3**
51.1.144	**23**
51.1.168I	**505**
51.1.168II	**549**
51.1.168III	**517**
52.1.1	**143**
53.1.8	**67**
53.1.31	**71**
53.1.32	**70**
53.1.39	**209**
53.1.40	**208**
53.1.42	**210**
53.1.43	**280**
53.1.44	**213**
53.1.45	**385**
53.1.46	**100**
53.1.47	**384**
53.1.51	**278**
53.1.54	**228**
53.1.55	**283**
53.1.56	**230**
53.1.57	**110**
53.1.58	**227**
53.1.59	**225**
53.1.60	**139**
53.1.61	**229**
53.1.62	**221**
53.1.69	**219**
53.1.70	**224**
53.1.71	**223**
53.1.90	**72**
53.1.99	**87**
53.1.109	**296**
54.1.106	**197**
54.1.107	**61**
55.1.24	**237**
55.1.32	**222**
55.1.41	**78**
55.1.42	**80**
55.1.48	**202**
55.1.110	**1**
55.1.111	**2**
55.1.112	**6**
55.1.113	**220**
55.1.114	**207**
55.1.115	**104**
55.1.116	**114**
55.1.117	**133**
55.1.118	**58**
55.1.119	**368**
55.1.120	**494**
55.1.121	**323**
55.1.122	**351**
55.1.123	**165**
55.1.124	**201**
55.1.125	**388**
55.1.126	**200**
55.1.127	**273**
55.1.128	**272**
55.1.129	**55**
55.1.130	**198**
55.1.131	**269**
55.1.132	**363**
55.1.133	**268**
55.1.134	**266**
55.1.135	**357**
55.1.136	**490**
55.1.137	**145**
55.1.139	**489**
55.1.140	**142**
55.1.141	**390**
55.1.141a	**394**
55.1.142	**392**
55.1.144	**397**
55.1.145	**412**
55.1.146	**403**
55.1.147	**326**
55.1.149	**120**
56.1.101	**233**
56.1.107	**48**
56.1.119	**195**
56.1.120	**215**
56.1.129	**236**
56.1.130	**235**
56.1.131	**193**
57.1.6b	**77**
58.1.5	**324**
58.1.20	**4**
58.1.26	**256**
58.1.39	**66**
59.1.1	**314**
59.1.432	**131**
59.1.433	**132**
59.1.434	**391**
59.1.436	**310**
59.1.437	**304**
59.1.438	**298**
59.1.439	**299**
59.1.440	**407**
59.1.441	**406**
59.1.442	**366**
59.1.443	**365**
59.1.444	**300**
59.1.445	**405**
59.1.446	**372**
59.1.447	**325**
59.1.448	**425**
59.1.449	**428**
59.1.450	**398**
59.1.451	**331**
59.1.452	**429**
59.1.453	**433**
59.1.454	**379**
59.1.455	**437**
59.1.456	**378**
59.1.457	**450**
59.1.458	**117**
59.1.459	**469**
59.1.460	**301**
59.1.461	**173**
59.1.462	**152**
59.1.463	**491**
59.1.464	**179**
59.1.465	**153**
59.1.466	**395**
59.1.467	**396**
59.1.468	**242**
59.1.469	**401**
59.1.470	**204**
59.1.471	**49**
59.1.472	**62**
59.1.473	**63**
59.1.474	**154**
59.1.475	**319**
59.1.476	**322**
59.1.477	**166**
59.1.478	**56**
59.1.479	**57**
59.1.480	**389**
59.1.481	**116**
59.1.482	**73**
59.1.483	**90**
59.1.484	**89**
59.1.485	**136**
59.1.486	**277**
59.1.487	**119**
59.1.489	**523**
59.1.490	**541**
59.1.491	**534**
59.1.492	**495**
59.1.493	**528**
59.1.494	**539**
59.1.495	**560**
59.1.496	**556**
59.1.497	**561**
59.1.498	**563**
59.1.499	**559**
59.1.500	**551**
59.1.501	**544**
59.1.502	**564**
59.1.503	**533**
59.1.504	**568**
59.1.505	**557**
59.1.506	**502**
59.1.507	**587**
59.1.508	**118**
59.1.509	**585**
59.1.556	**477**
59.1.567-15	**468**
59.1.582	**196**
59.1.593	**510**
59.1.594	**545**
59.1.595	**548**
59.1.596	**553**
59.1.597	**513**
59.7.3	**589**
60.1.2	**103**
61.1.14	**349**
61.1.23	**255**
62.1.3	**46**
63.1.12	**252**
63.1.19	**134**
64.1.1	**251**
64.1.15	**267**
64.1.24	**175**

76.1.252	**381**
76.1.253	**171**
76.1.254	**241**
76.1.255	**264**
76.1.256	**285**
76.1.257	**444**
76.1.258	**312**
76.1.259	**483**
76.1.260	**336**
76.1.261	**302**
76.1.262	**297**
76.1.263	**329**
76.1.264a–c	**342**
76.1.265	**360**
76.1.266	**461**
76.1.267	**375**
76.1.268	**376**
76.1.269a, b	**172**
76.1.270	**150**
76.1.271	**185**
76.1.272	**183**
76.1.273	**187**
76.1.274	**188**
76.1.275	**191**
76.1.276	**206**
76.1.277	**249**
76.1.278	**246**
76.1.279	**216**
76.1.280	**245**
76.1.281	**243**
76.1.282	**247**
76.1.283	**294**
76.1.284	**288**
76.1.285	**291**
76.1.286	**340**
76.1.287	**434**
76.1.288	**458**
76.1.289	**487**
76.1.290	**473**
76.1.291	**472**
76.1.292	**467**
76.1.293	**344**
76.1.294	**478**
76.1.295	**479**
76.1.296	**358**
76.1.297	**449**
76.1.298	**65**
76.1.299	**181**
76.1.300	**263**
76.1.301	**105**
76.1.302	**189**
76.1.303a, b	**289**
76.1.304	**501**
76.1.305	**504**
76.1.306	**532**
76.7.3	**593**
76.7.4	**594**
76.7.7	**592**
77.1.12	**138**
79.1.15	**313**
79.1.16	**529**

79.1.17	**85**
79.1.22	**12**
79.1.45	**254**
79.1.50	**352**
79.1.51	**318**
79.1.52	**52**
79.1.72	**238**
79.1.76	**347**
79.1.90	**47**
79.1.92	**353**
79.1.93	**158**
79.1.94	**346**
79.1.172	**157**
79.1.190	**122**
79.1.206	**69**
79.1.211	**320**
79.1.216	**148**
79.1.222	**177**
79.1.224	**160**
79.1.229	**125**
79.1.263	**127**
79.1.265	**321**
79.1.268	**126**
79.1.273	**60**
79.1.288	**535**
79.1.293	**530**
79.1.302	**305**
79.1.303	**333**
79.1.304	**167**
79.1.305	**24**
79.1.306	**408**
79.1.307	**409**
79.1.308	**414**
79.1.309	**328**
79.1.310	**426**
79.1.311	**311**
79.1.312	**371**
79.1.313	**364**
79.1.314	**341**
79.1.315	**374**
79.1.316	**355**
79.7.18	**590**
81.1.4	**492**
81.1.24	**279**
81.1.26	**176**
81.1.30	**94**
81.1.31	**98**
81.1.34	**99**
81.1.41	**234**
81.1.46	**96**
81.1.48	**64**
81.1.692	**81**
81.1.693	**261**
81.1.694	**54**
81.1.695	**86**
81.1.696	**137**
81.1.697	**182**
81.1.698	**82**
81.1.699	**68**
81.1.700	**115**
81.1.702	**76**

81.7.83	**595**
85.1.1	**522**
90.1.2	**330**
95.1.19	**531**
95.1.94	**113**
98.1.23	**14**
2006.1.1	**526**
2009.1.1	**180**
2009.1.2	**537**
2009.1.3a–c	**350**
2009.1.4	**51**
2009.1.5	**500**
Not accessioned	**507**
2009.1.18	**211**
2009.1.20	**146**

2. Smith Collection

0921-12	**340**
0981-8	**189**
15C49	**335**
124	**107**
235	**95**
287	**220**
358	**137**
367	**56**
378	**268**
381	**273**
382	**389**
384	**73**
475	**300**
476	**299**
477	**308**
480	**301**
489	**218**
493-5	**93**
493-10	**241**
495	**55**
498	**58**
504	**142**
505	**145**
508	**261**
510d	**50**
512	**79**
519	**201**
545	**322**
555-4	**448**
555-5	**338**
555-6	**501**
555-7	**120**
555-9	**413**
555-11	**454**
555-14	**358**
555-15	**239**
555-18	**438**
555-19	**418**
555-20	**163**
555-21	**444**
555-22	**487**
555-25	**400**
555-28	**372**

555-29	**428**
555-31	**332**
555-32	**398**
578	**269**
579	**198**
610	**357**
611	**388**
627-A	**187**
627-B	**188**
628	**411**
629	**302**
658	**2**
667	**272**
709	**392**
744	**149**
810	**207**
838	**368**
839	**90**
848	**365**
856	**1**
867	**133**
897	**57**
900	**6**
912	**386**
913	**104**
914	**397**
915	**325**
916	**399**
917	**433**
918	**373**
919	**331**
920	**405**
922	**407**
923	**410**
926	**343**
927	**402**
928	**425**
929	**378**
931	**434**
932	**431**
934	**379**
935	**419**
936	**473**
937	**285**
938	**288**
939	**289**
940	**289**
944	**114**
954	**266**
955	**165**
956	**491**
957	**304**
960	**279**
961	**534**
963	**306**
964	**396**
965	**403**
966	**275**
967	**450**
1009	**383**
1012	**381**

1016	**291**
1026	**173**
1046	**119**
1055	**310**
1056	**494**
1057	**326**
1058 (part of)	**350**
1058 (part of)	**351**
1059	**323**
1060	**363**
1062	**490**
1076	**585**
1077	**118**
1084 (part of)	**390**
1084 (part of)	**394**
1088	**533**
1089	**429**
1090	**495**
1098	**412**
1099	**539**
1101	**172**
1102	**116**
1103	**395**
1104	**22**
1105	**40**
1106	**31**
1109	**105**
1110	**231**
1111	**26**
1112	**35**
1113	**8**
1115	**42**
1116	**32**
1118	**43**
1119	**36**
1120	**154**
1123	**62**
1131	**81**
1132	**203**
1135	**204**
1136	**83**
1137	**54**
1139	**115**
1141	**172**
1142	**86**
1143	**76**
1144	**82**
1145	**102**
1146	**51**
1147	**242**
1148	**68**
1149	**141**
1150	**153**
1152	**109**
1153	**117**
1156	**179**
1158	**152**
1160	**162**
1190	**401**
1218-1	**13**
1218-2	**16**
1218-3	**5**
1218-4	**39**
1218-6	**44**
1218-7	**20**
1218-8	**28**
1218-9	**27**
1218-[ ]	**4**
1220-5	**387**
1220-6	**282**
1220-7	**101**
1220-8	**108**
1220-[ ]	**281**
1221-2	**150**
1221-3	**469**
1221-4	**504**
1221-5	**136**
1221-7	**247**
1221-13	**63**
1221-15	**206**
1221-16	**344**
1221-18	**263**
1221-19	**168**
1221-20	**472**
1221-21	**264**
1221-22	**294**
1221-23	**49**
1221-24	**183**
1221-26	**161**
1221-27	**243**
1221-29	**181**
1221-30	**449**
1221-35	**65**
1222-7	**182**
1222-8	**467**
1236	**489**
1237	**200**
1262-A	**557**
1262-B	**568**
1262-C	**556**
1262-D	**528**
1263-b	**466**
1263-c	**461**
1263-e	**458**
1263-f	**479**
1263-g	**171**
1263-h	**478**
1263-j	**360**
1263-[?]	**376**
1263-[?]	**406**
1267	**589, 592**
1286	**587**
1287-A	**502**
1287-B	**544**
1287-C	**564**
1287-D	**561**
1288	**342**
1343	**131**
1346	**130**
1347	**349**
1348	**391**
1351	**298**
1352	**166**
1353	**541**
1385	**45**
1386	**129**
1399	**319**
1419	**89**
1494	**523**
1514	**91**
1515	**132**
A316	**334**
No number	**3**
No number	**14**
No number	**18**
No number	**84**
No number	**151**
No number	**155**
No number	**164**
No number	**169**
No number	**170**
No number	**174**
No number	**184**
No number	**185**
No number	**186**
No number	**190**
No number	**191**
No number	**216**
No number	**240**
No number	**244**
No number	**245**
No number	**246**
No number	**248**
No number	**249**
No number	**250**
No number	**253**
No number	**257**
No number	**259**
No number	**260**
No number	**265**
No number	**277**
No number	**286**
No number	**287**
No number	**290**
No number	**293**
No number	**295**
No number	**297**
No number	**309**
No number	**312**
No number	**314**
No number	**327**
No number	**329**
No number	**330**
No number	**336**
No number	**337**
No number	**339**
No number	**345**
No number	**359**
No number	**362**
No number	**366**
No number	**375**
No number	**377**
No number	**382**
No number	**393**
No number	**404**
No number	**415**
No number	**416**
No number	**417**
No number	**420**
No number	**422**
No number	**427**
No number	**430**
No number	**432**
No number	**435**
No number	**436**
No number	**437**
No number	**439**
No number	**440**
No number	**441**
No number	**442**
No number	**443**
No number	**445**
No number	**446**
No number	**451**
No number	**452**
No number	**453**
No number	**455**
No number	**457**
No number	**459**
No number	**462**
No number	**463**
No number	**464**
No number	**468**
No number	**471**
No number	**474**
No number	**475**
No number	**476**
No number	**477**
No number	**480**
No number	**481**
No number	**482**
No number	**483**
No number	**484**
No number	**485**
No number	**486**
No number	**493**
No number	**496**
No number	**497**
No number	**498**
No number	**499**
No number	**503**
No number	**506**
No number	**507**
No number	**508**
No number	**509**
No number	**510**
No number	**511**
No number	**512**
No number	**513**
No number	**514**
No number	**515**
No number	**516**
No number	**518**
No number	**519**

No number	**520**
No number	**521**
No number	**524**
No number	**525**
No number	**527**
No number	**532**
No number	**536**
No number	**537**
No number	**538**
No number	**540**
No number	**542**
No number	**543**
No number	**546**
No number	**547**
No number	**548**
No number	**550**
No number	**551**
No number	**552**
No number	**554**
No number	**555**
No number	**558**
No number	**559**
No number	**560**
No number	**562**
No number	**563**
No number	**565**
No number	**566**
No number	**567**
No number	**569**
No number	**570**
No number	**571**
No number	**572**
No number	**573**
No number	**574**
No number	**575**
No number	**576**
No number	**577**
No number	**578**
No number	**579**
No number	**580**
No number	**581**
No number	**582**
No number	**583**
No number	**584**
No number	**588**
No number	**591**
No number	**593**
No number	**594**

3. Strauss Collection

F12	**24**
F31	**414**
F32	**426**
F33	**311**
F34	**167**
F53	**355**
F54	**333**
F70	**305**
F71	**364**
F72	**590**
F73	**374**
F74	**371**
F75	**341**
F76	**408**
F77	**409**
F78	**328**
F79	**531**
F82	**530**
F83	**535**
S262	**60**
S1136	**122**
S1426	**254**
S1508	**69**
S1589	**194**
S1680	**121**
S1725	**320**
S1834	**178**
S1868	**147**
S2046	**138**
S2091	**148**
S2139	**346**
S2157	**157**
S2160	**158**
S2227	**177**
S2229	**160**
S2308	**352**
S2317	**318**
S2318	**52**
S2319	**125**
S2522	**113**
S2677	**353**
S2682	**47**
S2700	**238**
S2708	**127**
S2713	**321**
S2735	**126**
S2770	**347**

4. American Research Center in Egypt

65.4.25	**112**
66.5.117	**192**
68.4.84	**74**
68.10.41	**106**
68.11.1	**380, 423, 456, 470**
68.11.2	**144**
68.11.8	**159**
68.11.25	**226**
68.11.40	**92**
68.11.41	**111**
68.11.49	**232**
68.11.77	**75**
68.11.88	**7**
68.12.26	**97**
68.12.27	**88**
68.12.49	**212**
68.12.61	**123**
68.12.65	**361**
68.12.67	**53**
73.9.16	**529**
73.9.17	**313**
78.9.25	**85**
78.10.24	**12**
80.9.28	**96**
80.9.32	**99**
80.10.18	**98**
80.10.36	**176**
80.10.37	**234**
80.10.44	**94**
80.10.53	**64**

5. Chemical Analyses

The following is a concordance of all objects described in this catalog that also appear in Robert H. Brill's *Chemical Analyses of Early Glasses* (Brill 1999). In the first part of the concordance, the numbers on the left are those assigned to objects in the present catalog, while the numbers on the right are those assigned to the samples removed from the objects for chemical analysis. These samples are described in volume one of Dr. Brill's book, and the analyses appear in volume two. In the second part of the concordance, the numbers on the left are the Museum's accession numbers, while those on the right are the numbers assigned to the samples by Dr. Brill.

Brill (1995, pp. 218 and 220; and 1999, v. 1, p. 85, and v. 2, p. 163) published an analysis of a fragment with wheel-cut decoration that was found on the surface at Nishapur and is now stored in the Scientific Research Department at the Corning Museum. The fragment (3081) has not been accessioned into the Museum's collection and does not appear in this catalog. A second wheel-cut fragment from Nishapur (3082) was sampled, but the analysis has not been published.

A. Catalog and Analysis Numbers

Catalog	Analysis
1	6349
2	6350
3	6344
4	6343
6	6348
9	6353
10	6341
11	6357
16	6368
18	6351
19	6360
21	6356
23	6342
25	6352
27	6367
29	6354
30	6358
33	6358
34	6340
37	6359
38	6355
44	6369
67	3099
121	3087
490	5197
510	5382, 5383
523	5388
553	5386, 5387

B. Accession and Analysis Numbers

Accession	Analysis
51.1.110	6353
51.1.111	6352
51.1.112	6359
51.1.113	6360
51.1.115	6355
51.1.116	6354
51.1.117A	6356
51.1.118A	6358
51.1.118B	6358
51.1.119	6357
51.1.143	6344
51.1.144	6342
53.1.8	3099
55.1.110	6349
55.1.111	6350
55.1.112	6348
55.1.136	5197
58.1.20	6343
59.1.489	5388
59.1.593	5382, 5383
59.1.596	5386, 5387
66.1.266	3087
68.1.1	6340
68.1.59-1	6351
68.1.60	6341
76.1.236	6368
76.1.240	6367
76.1.248	6369

Index

The index contains the names of persons (other than authors cited in the Bibliography), places, and things. Collections in museums and other institutions are listed by city; private collections are listed by name. Names of regions and countries are listed only when more precise information is not available. Names of shapes and techniques are listed only when they are discussed. Numerals in boldface indicate catalog numbers.

Drawings

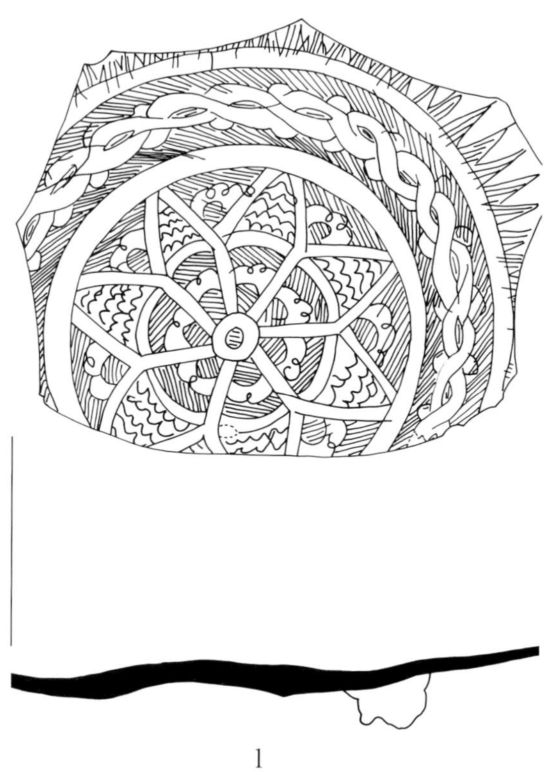

1

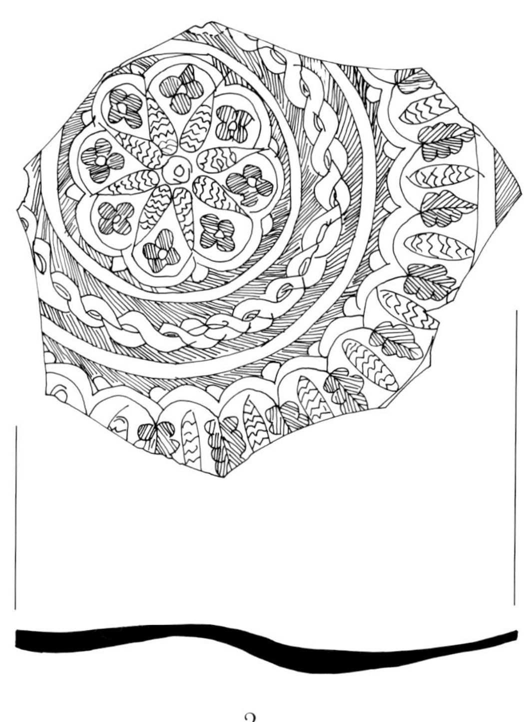

2

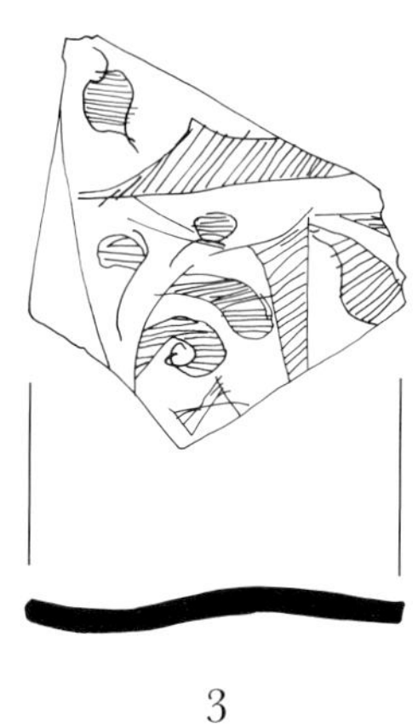

3

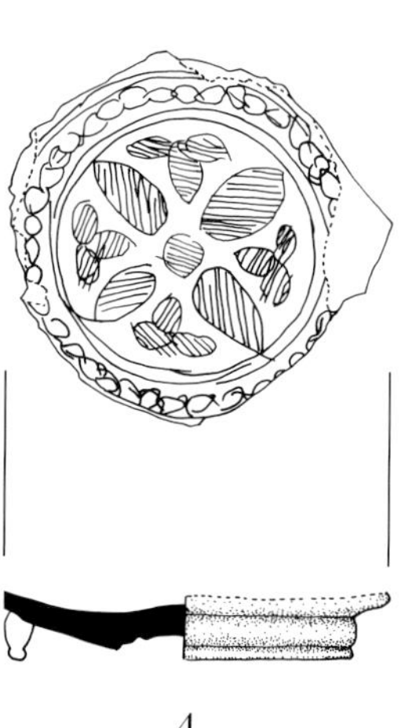

4

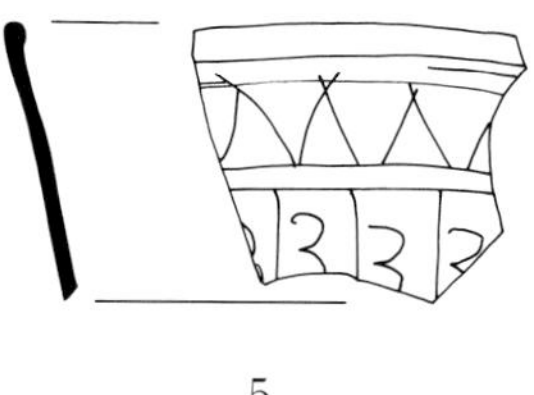

5

Objects with scratch-engraved ornament (1:2).

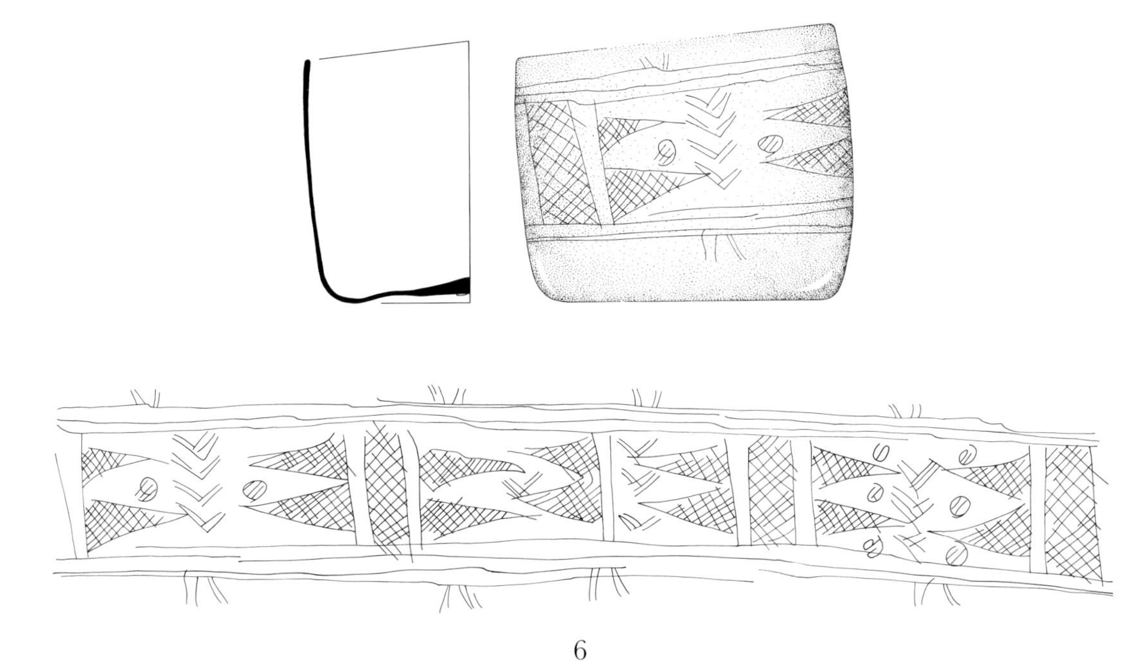

6

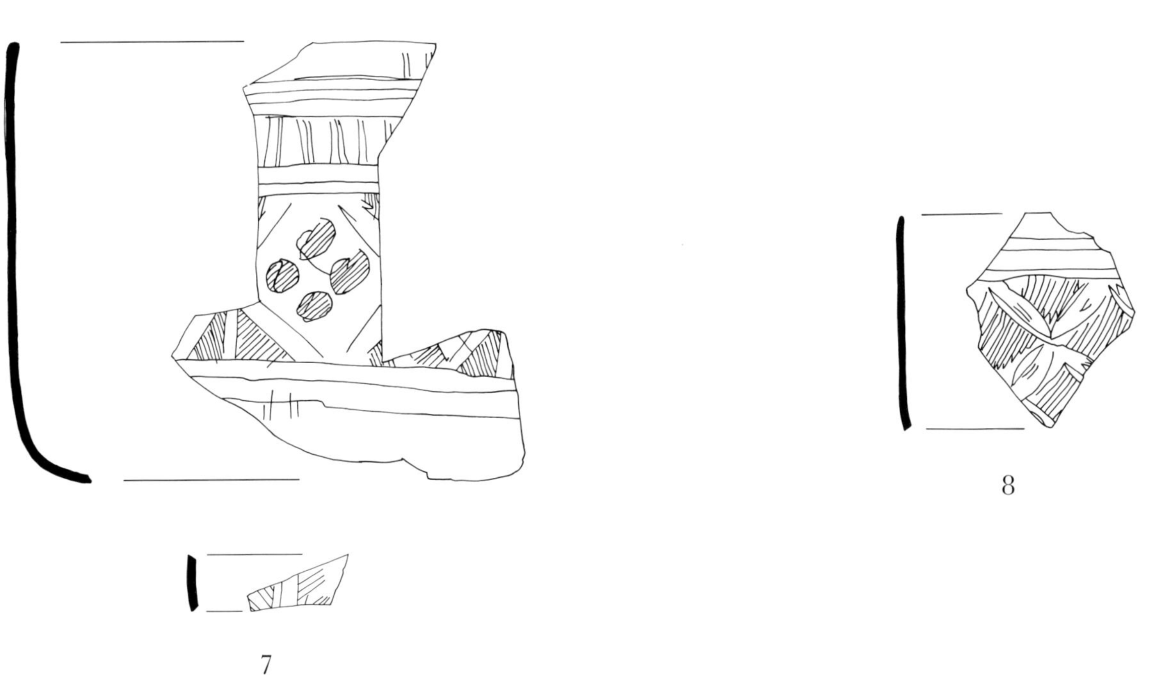

7

8

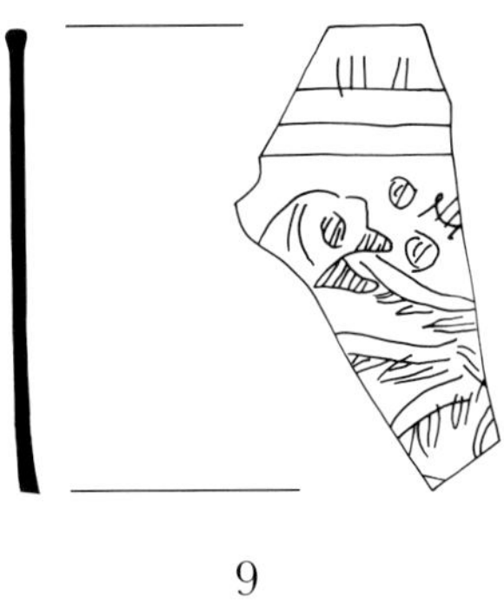

9

*Objects with scratch-engraved ornament (1:2 except **6**, which is 1:3).*

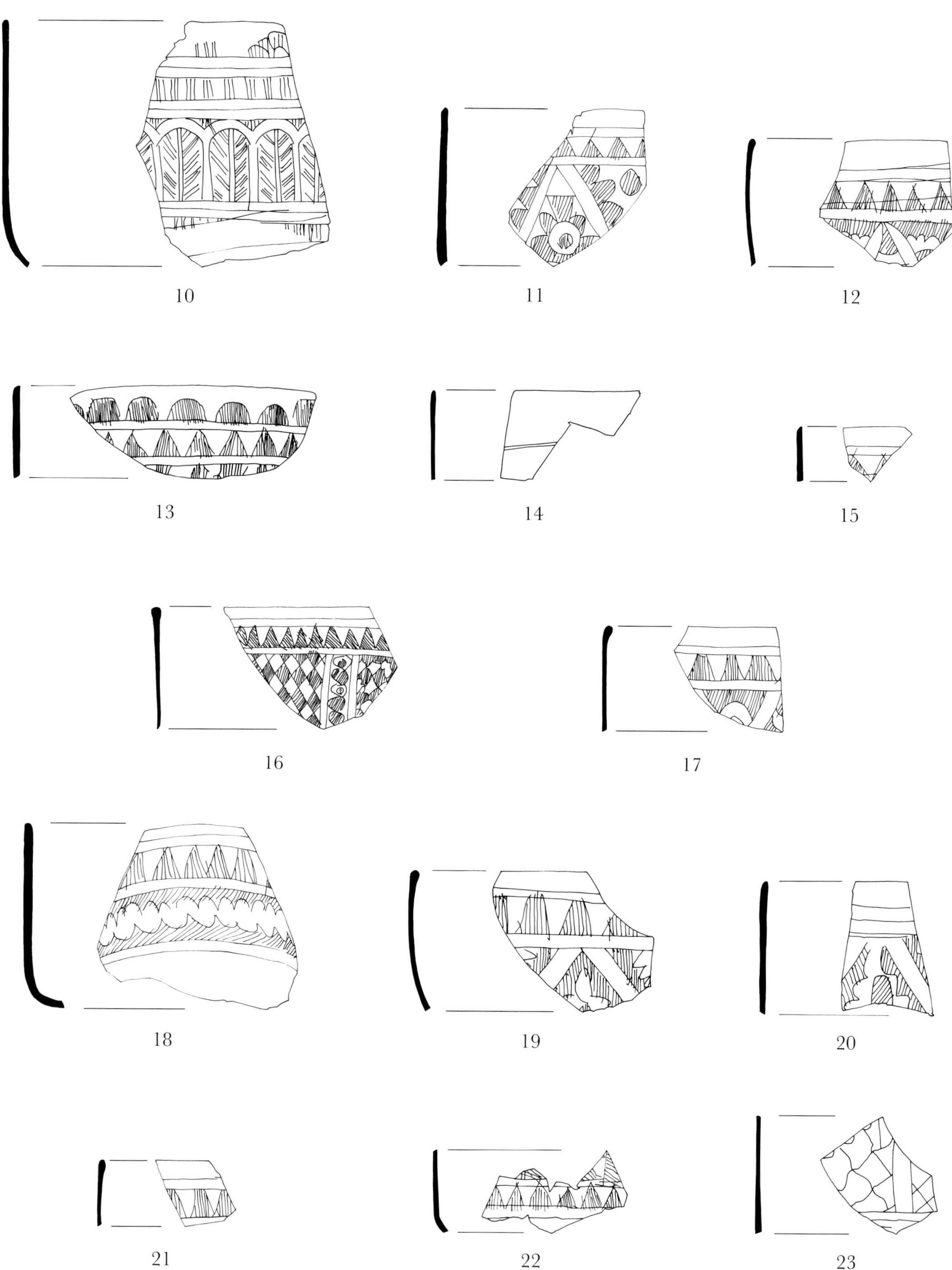

Objects with scratch-engraved ornament (1:2).

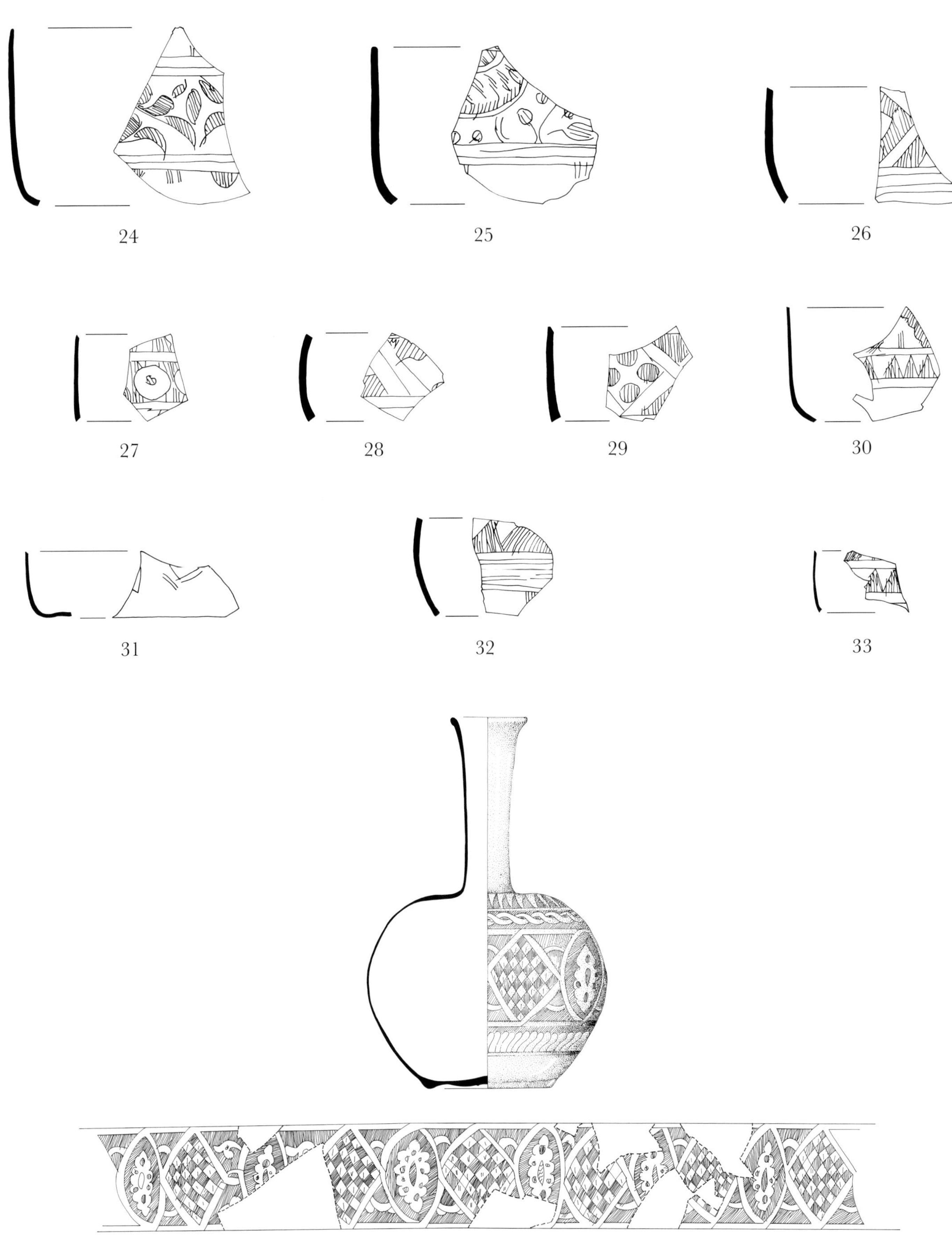

Objects with scratch-engraved ornament (1:2 except ***34****, which is 1:3).*

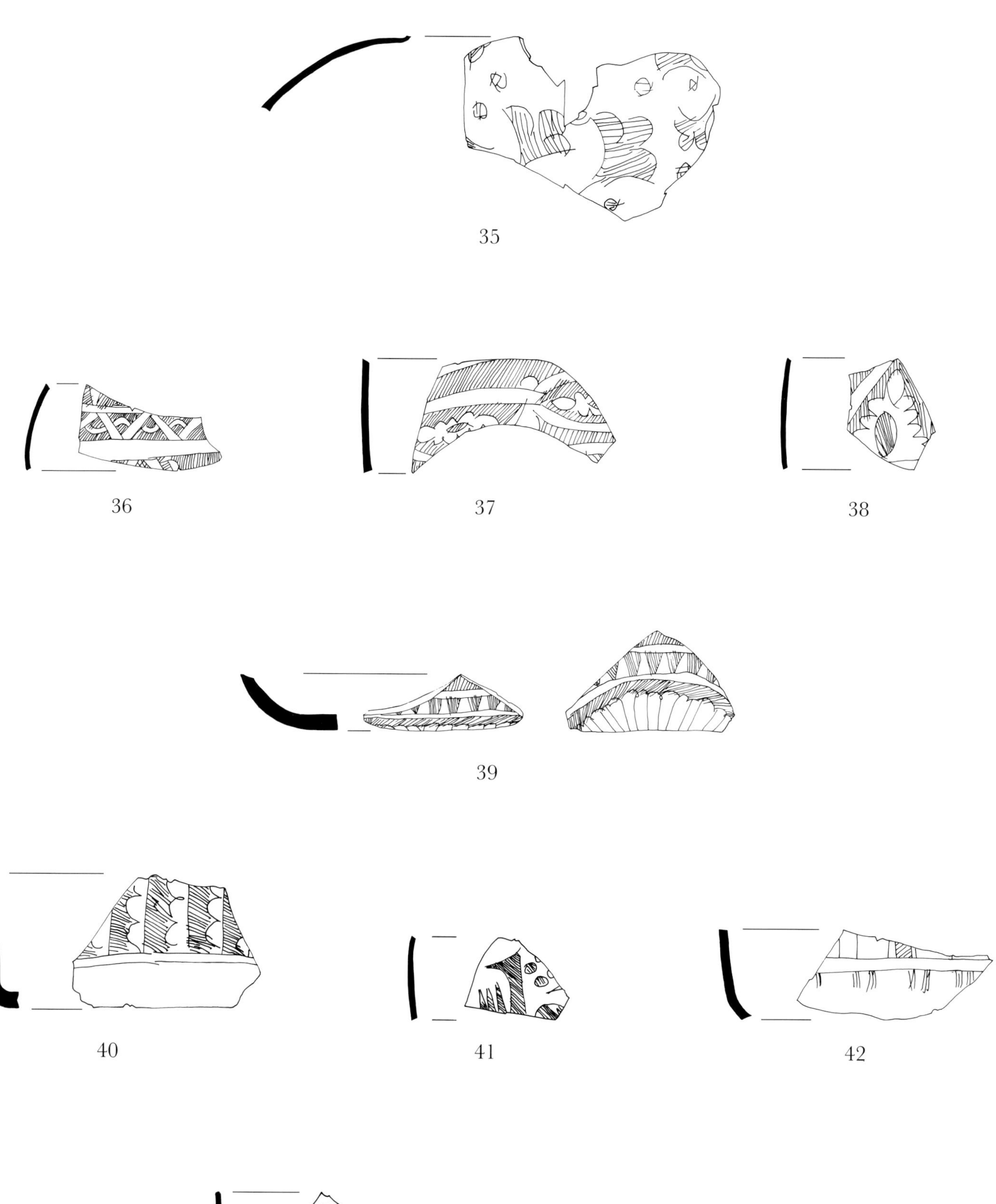

*Objects with scratch-engraved ornament (1:2 except **44**, which is 1:1).*

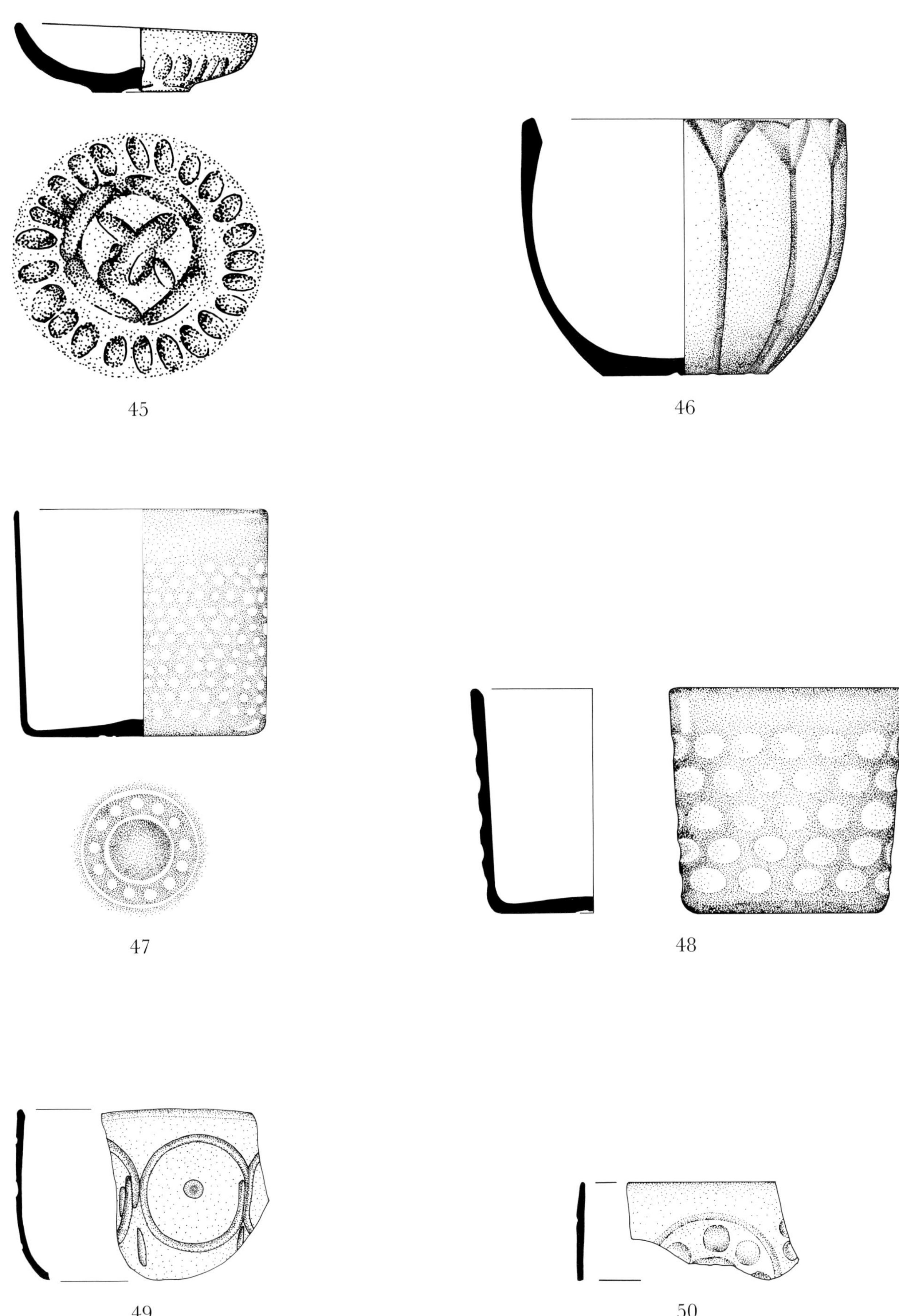

*Facet-cut objects (1:2 except **45**, which is 1:1).*

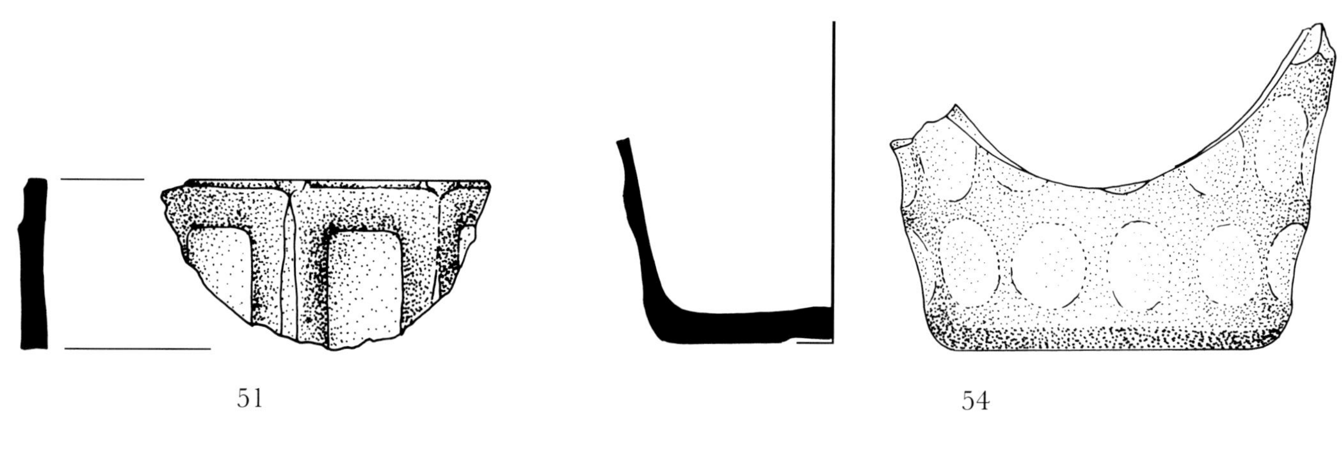

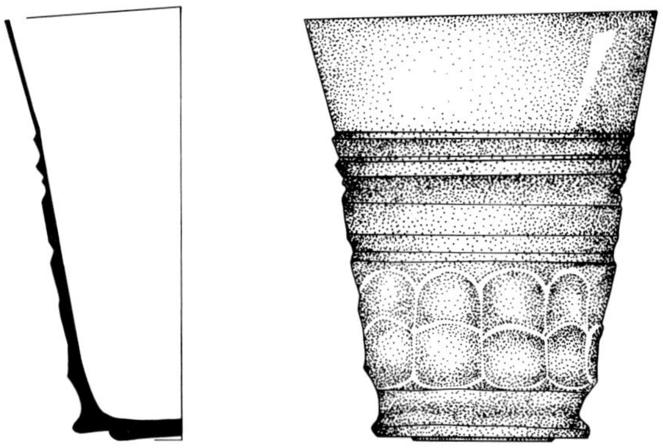

52

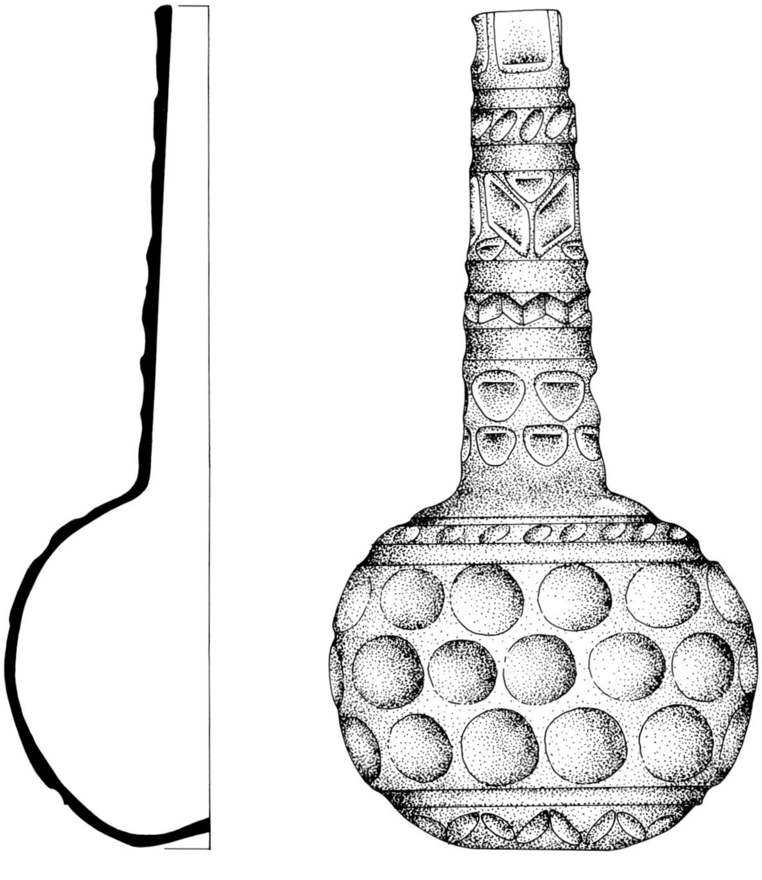

55

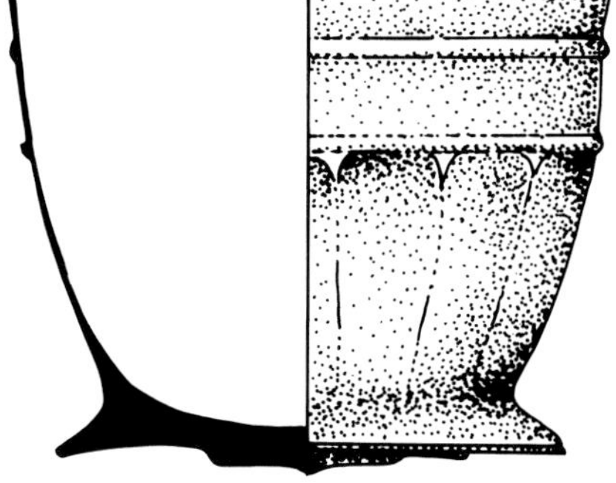

53

*Facet-cut objects (1:2 except **51**, **53**, and **54**, which are 1:1).*

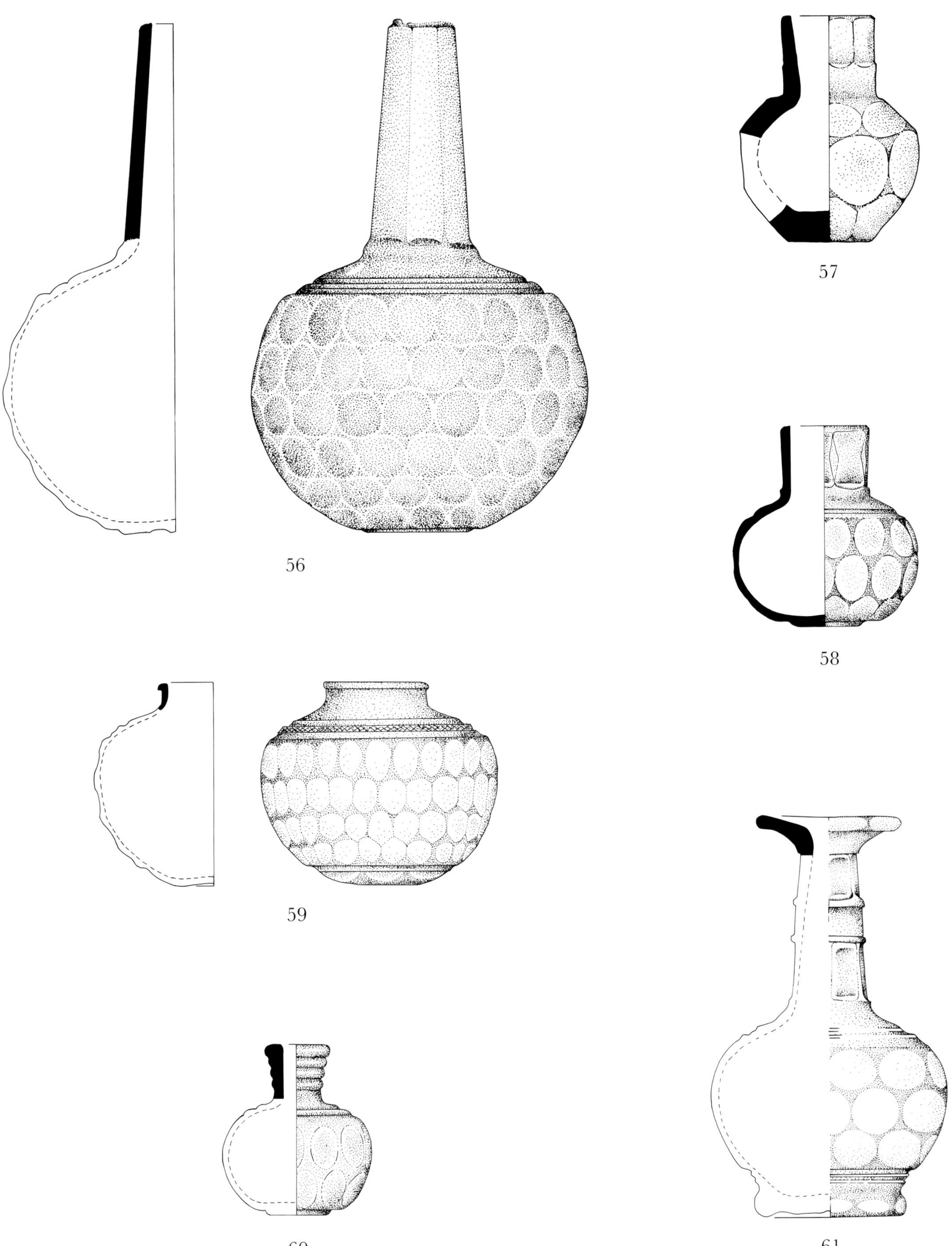

Facet-cut objects (1:2).

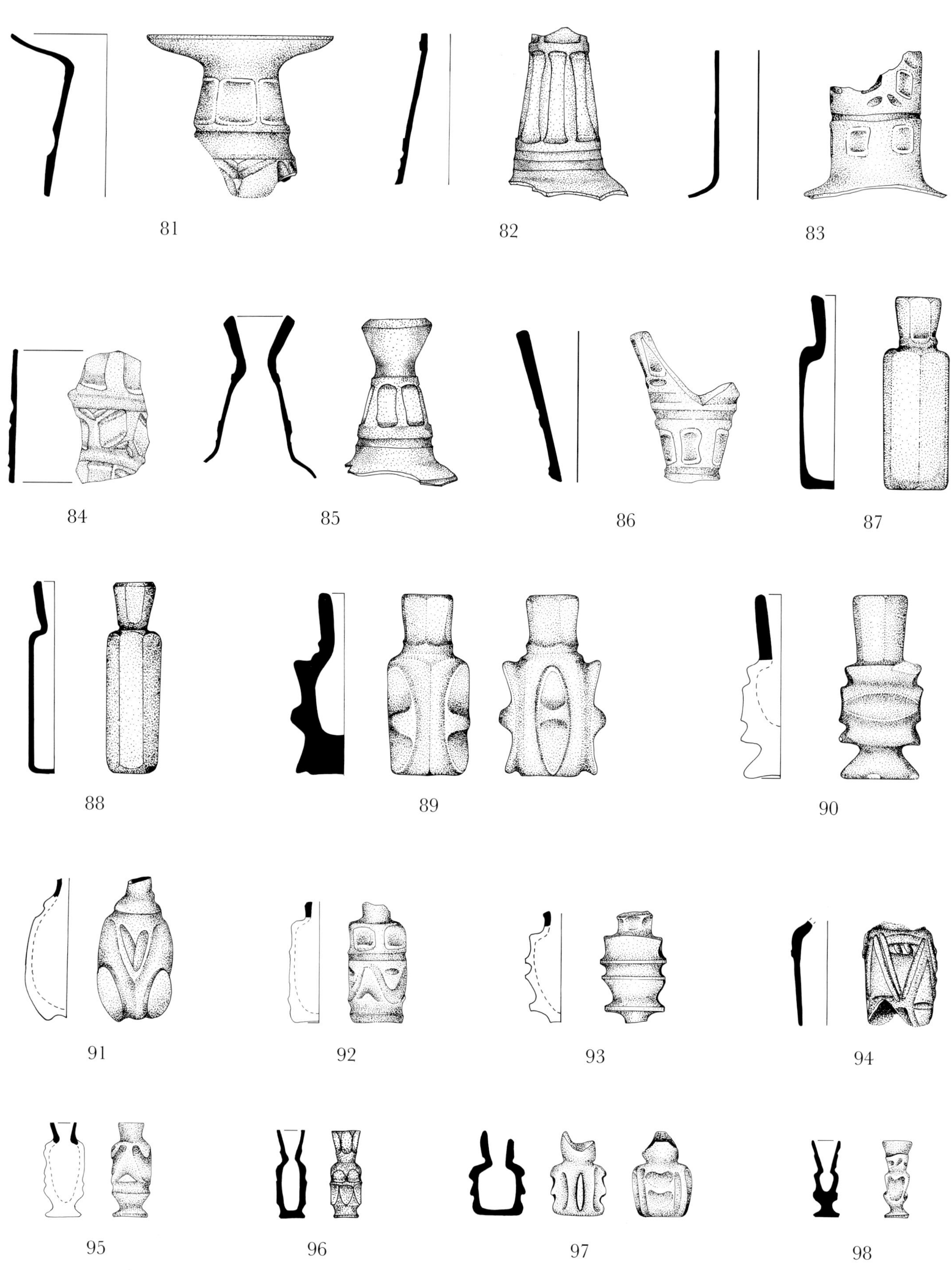

Facet-cut objects (1:2).

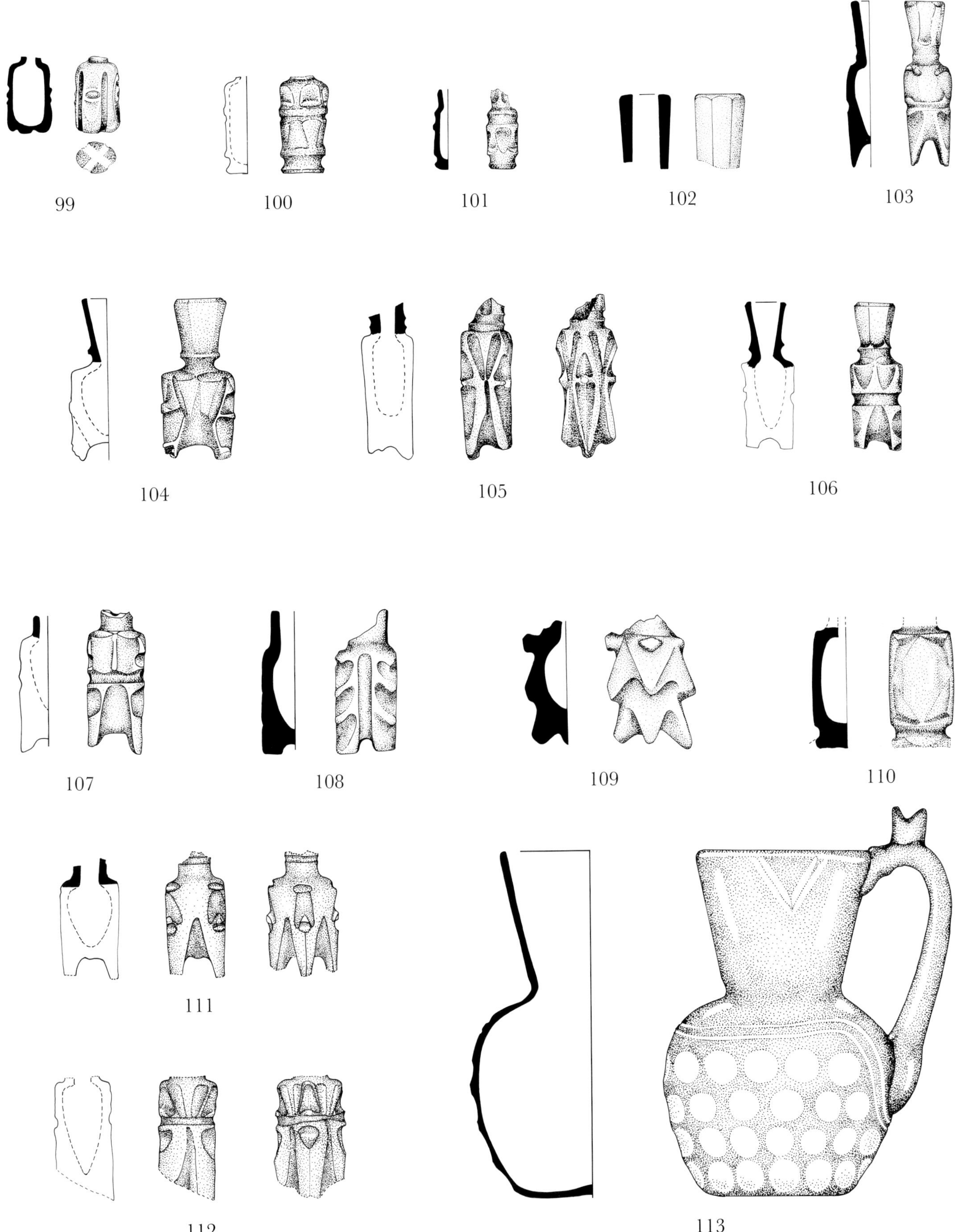

Facet-cut objects (1:2).

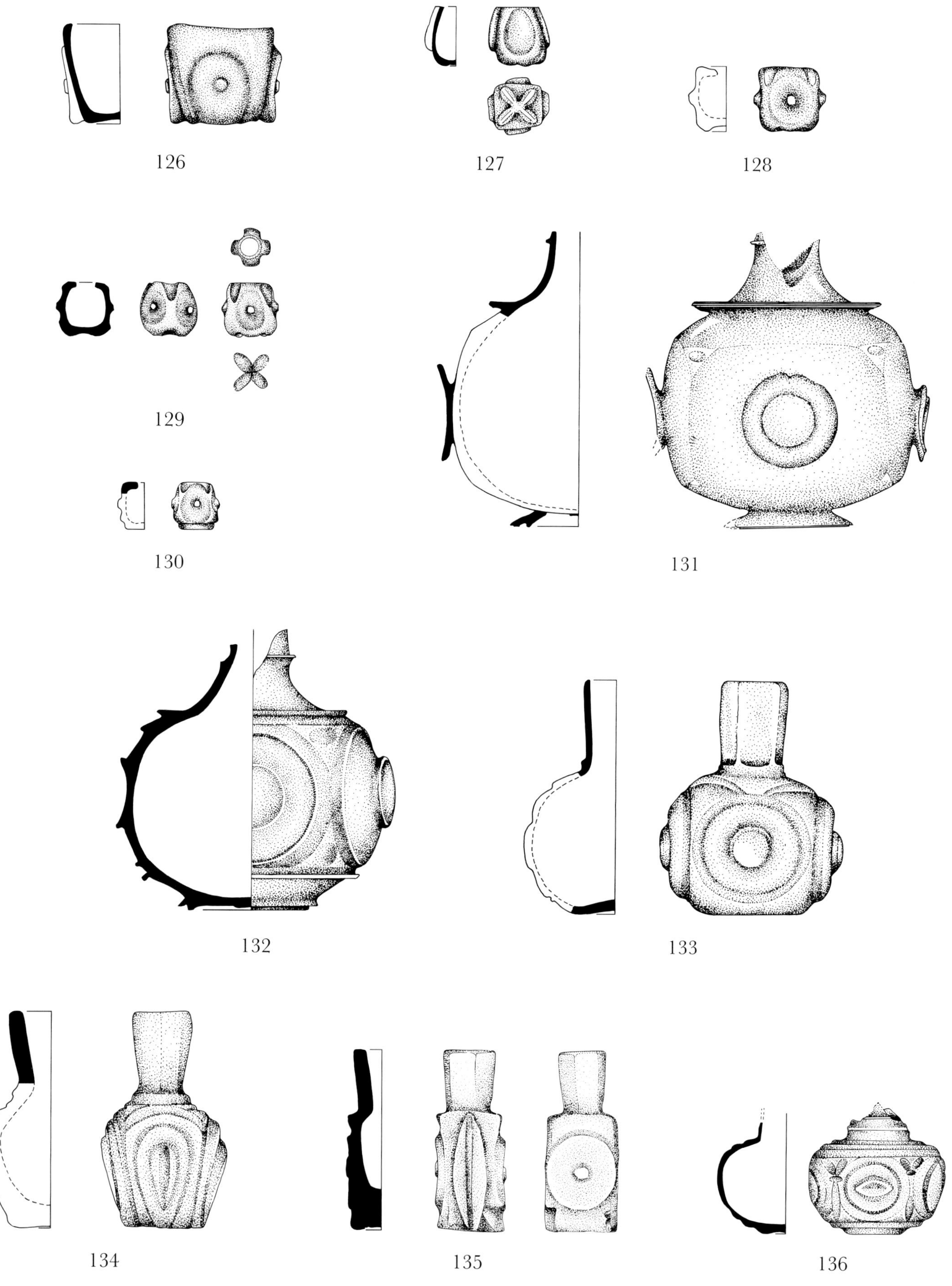

Objects decorated with disks and related motifs (1:2).

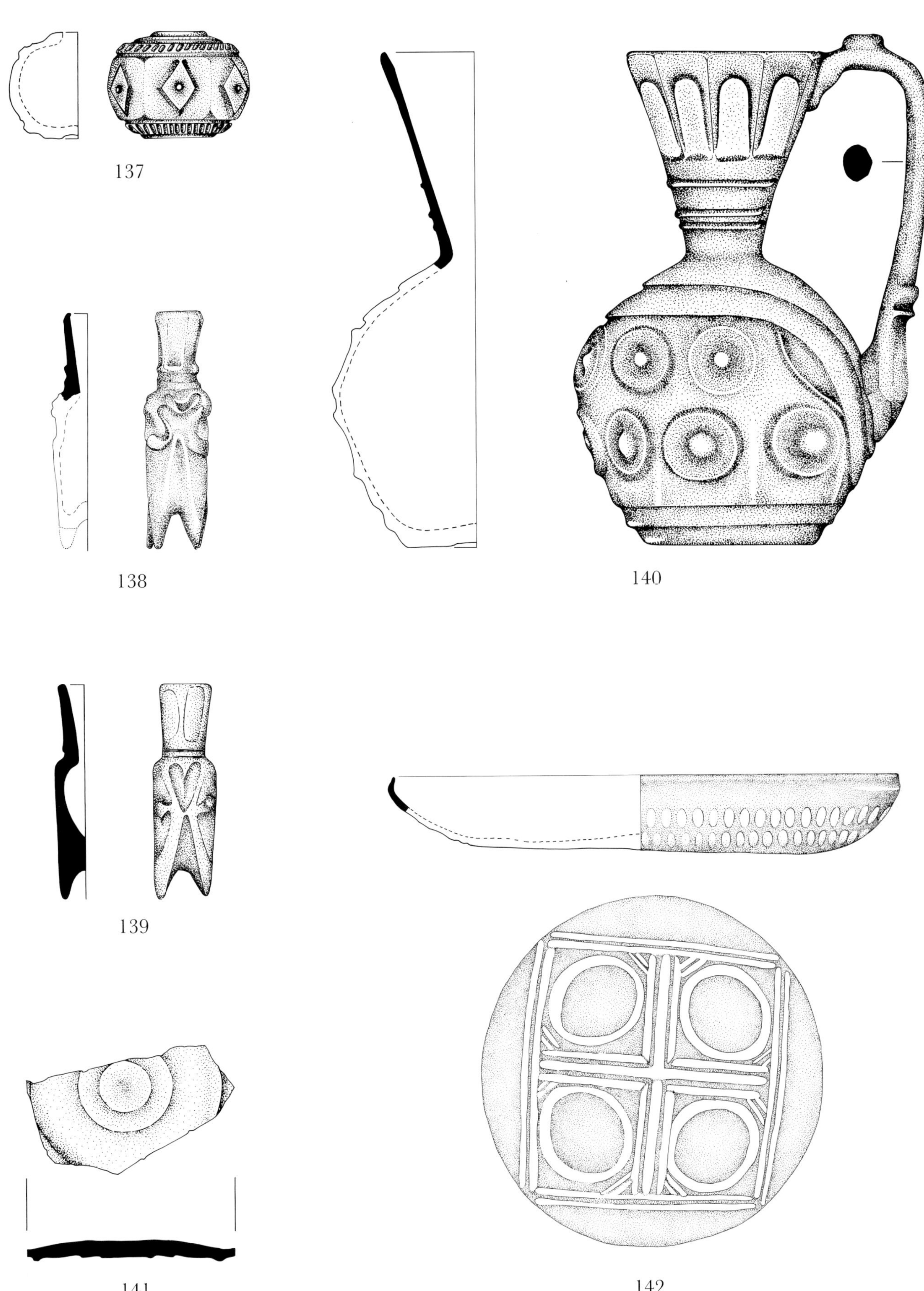

Objects decorated with disks and related motifs (1:2) and linear-cut object (1:3).

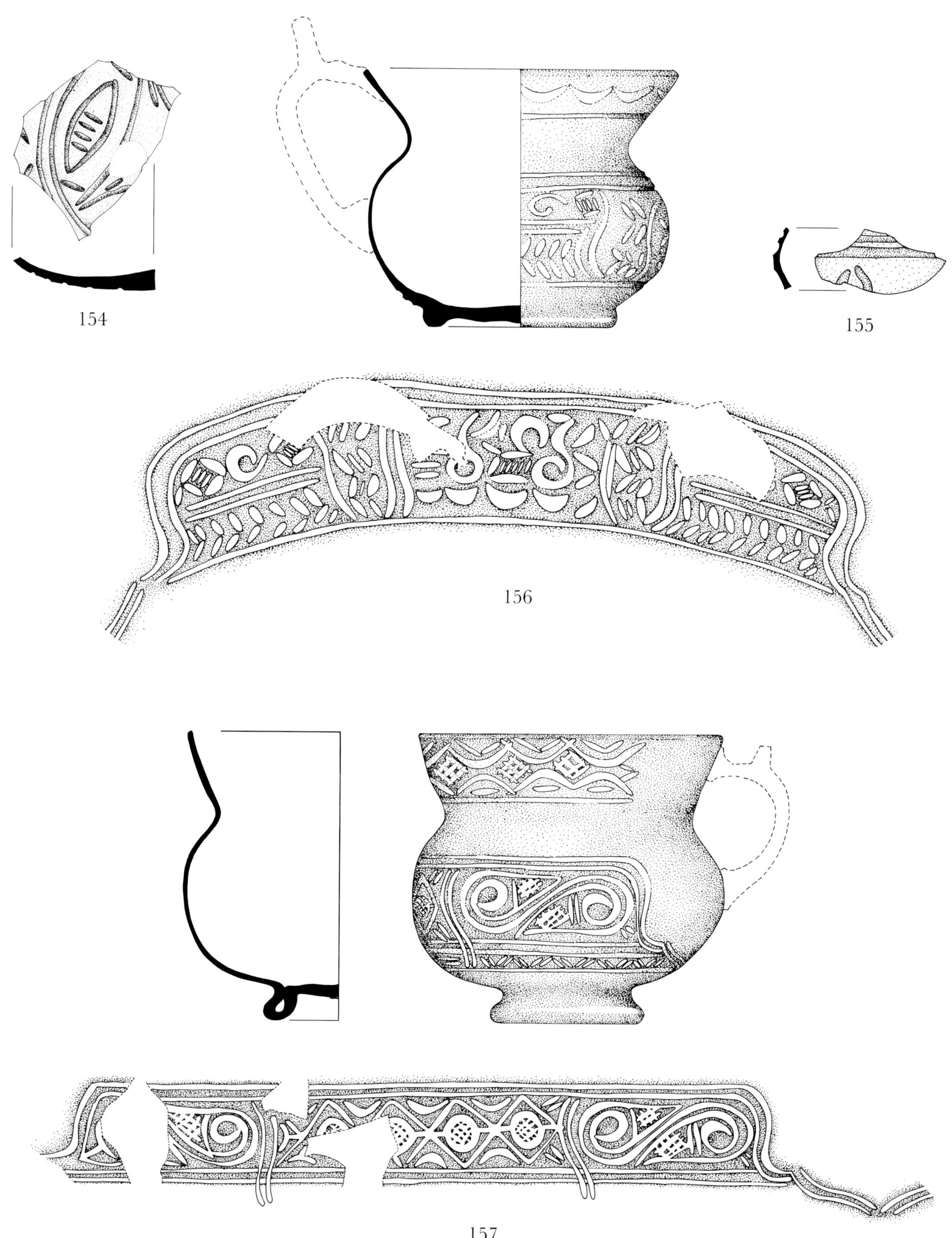

Linear-cut objects (1:2).

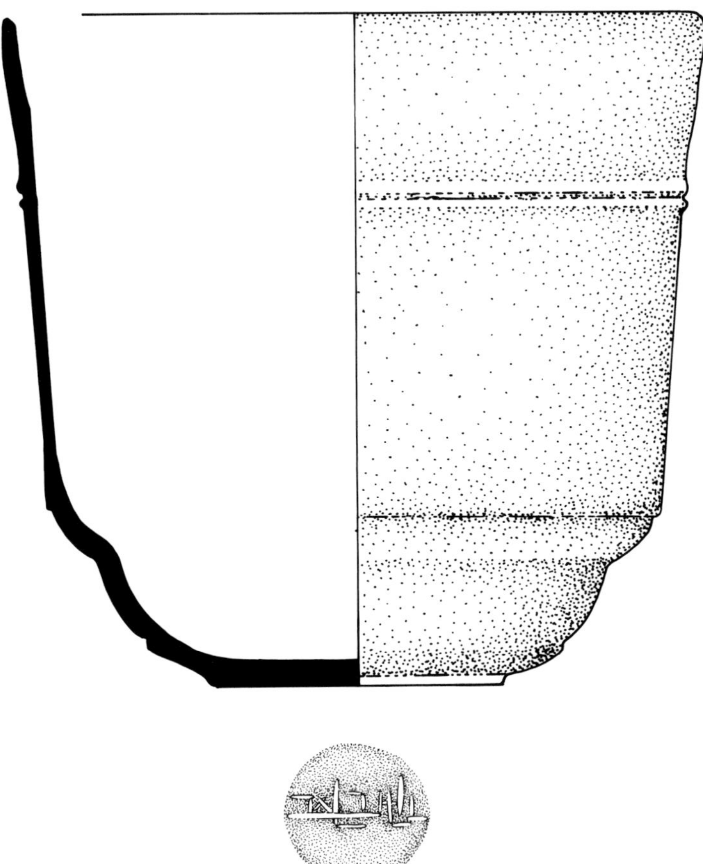

158

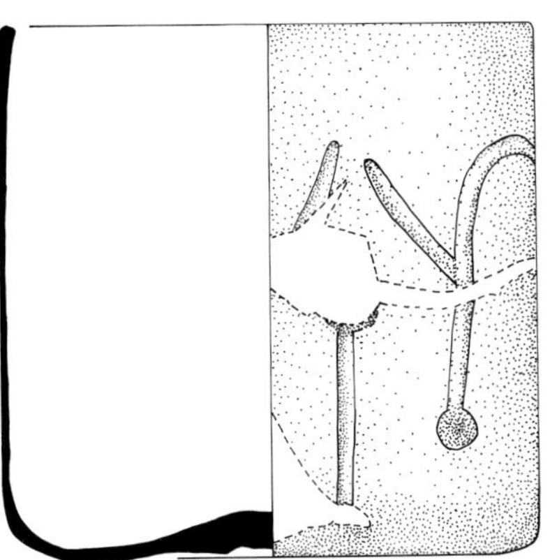

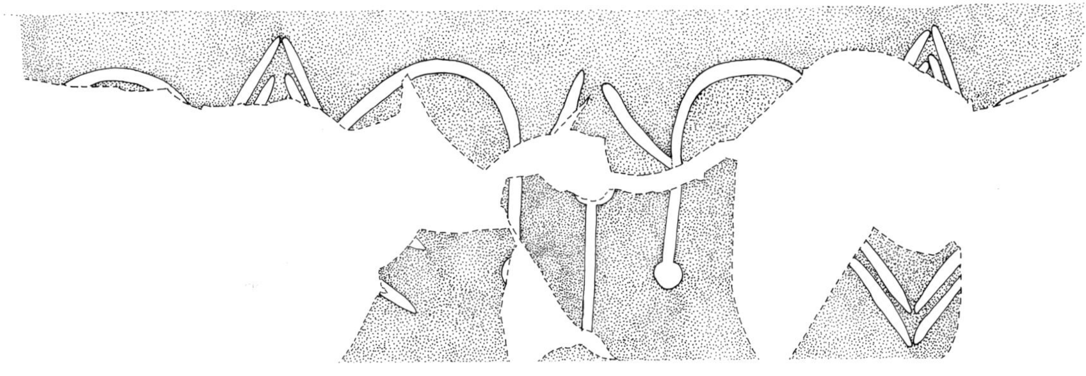

159

Linear-cut objects (1:2).

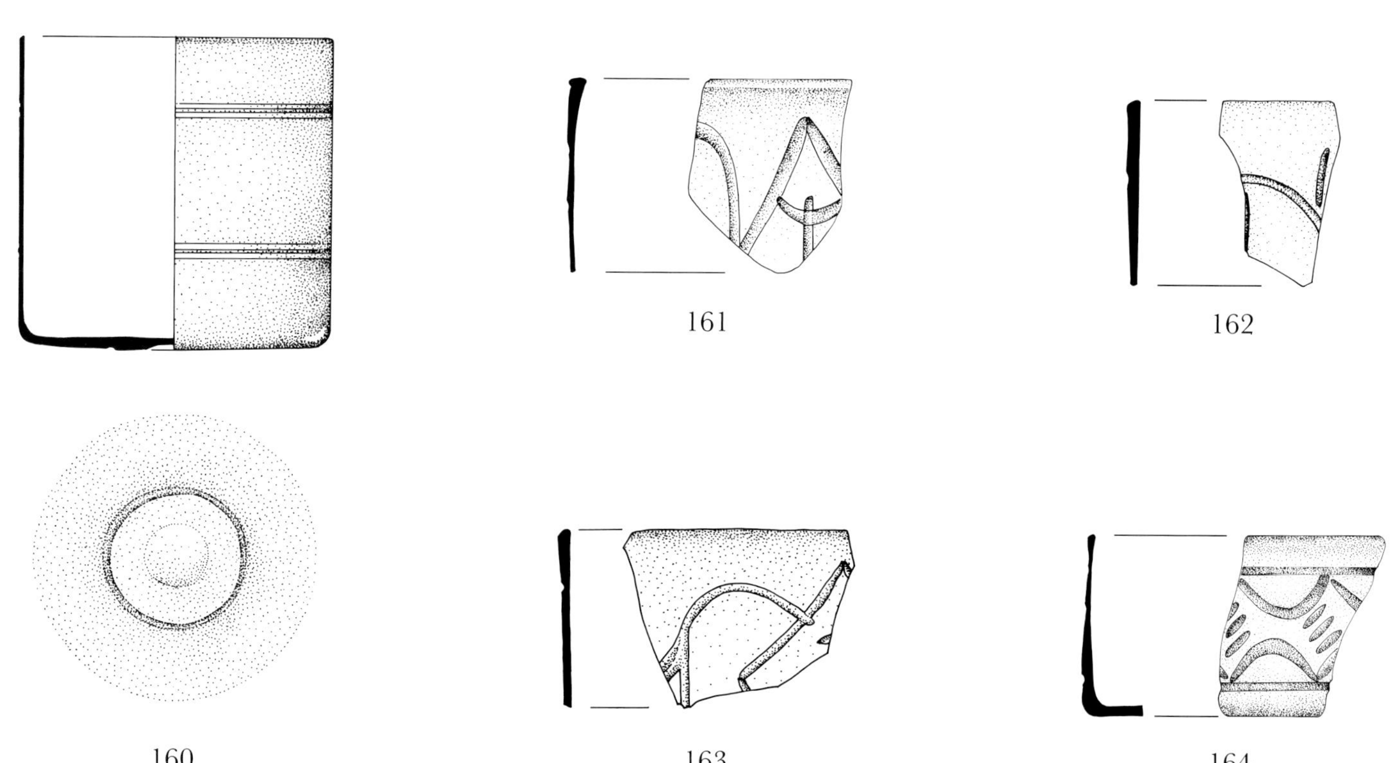

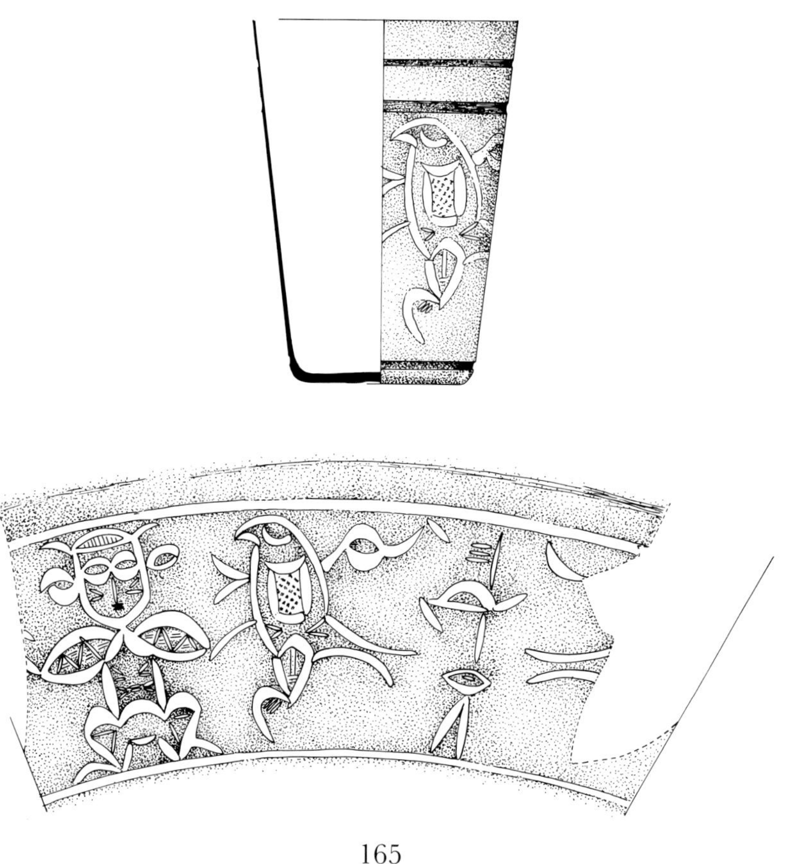

Linear-cut objects (1:2).

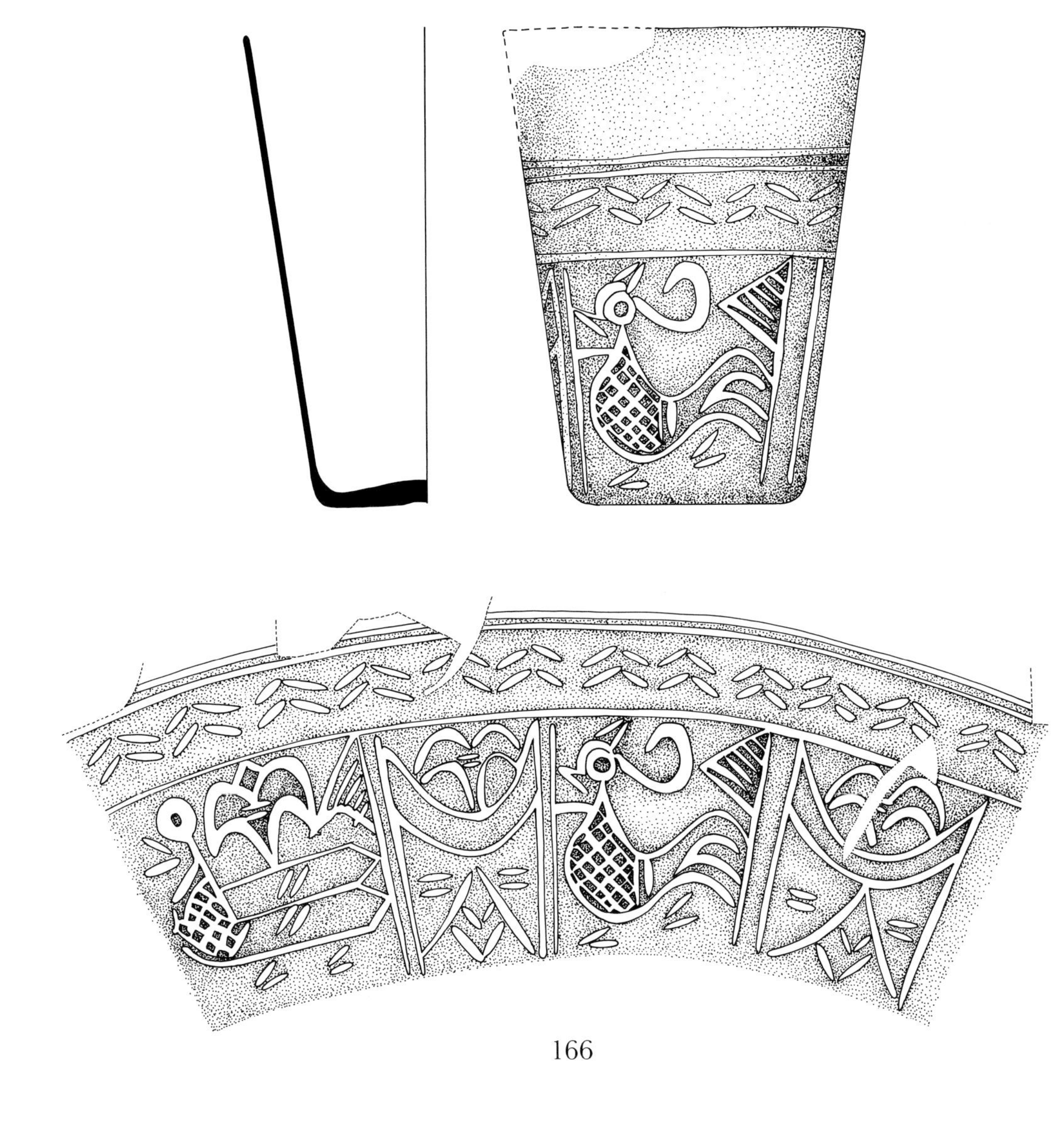

166

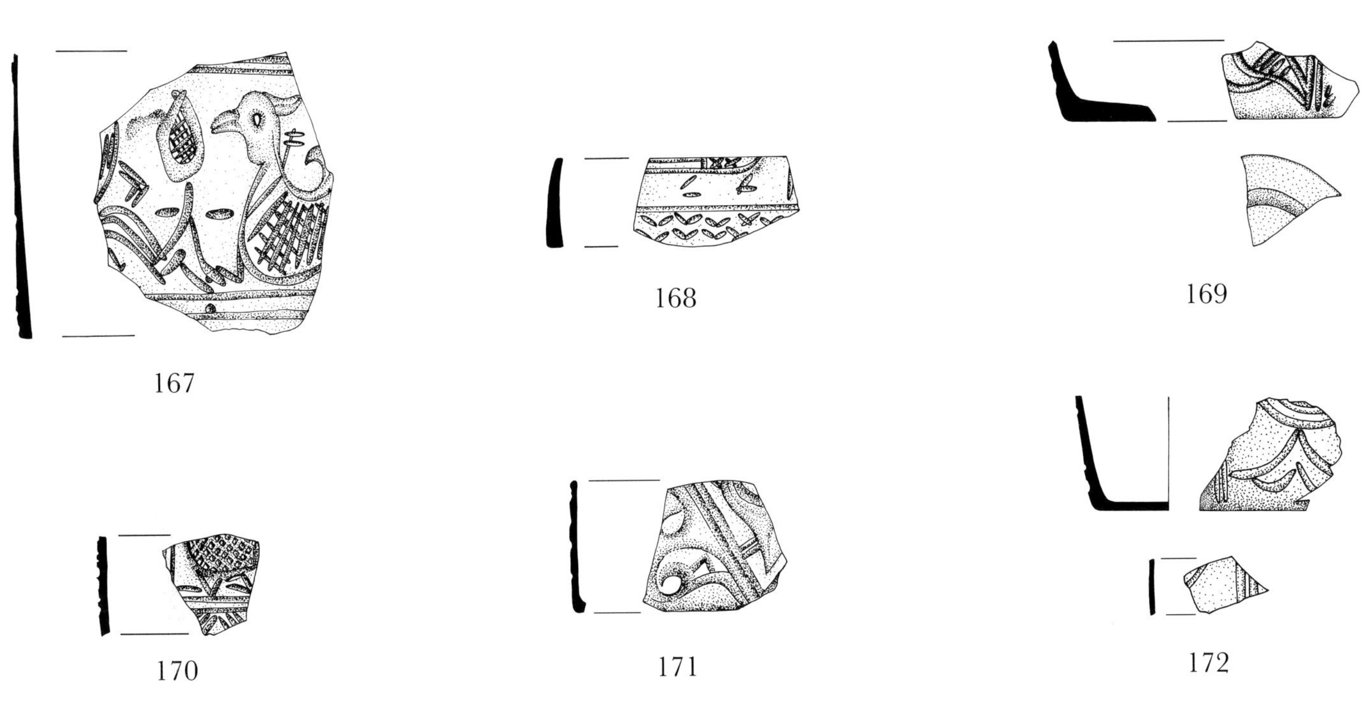

167 168 169 170 171 172

Linear-cut objects (1:2).

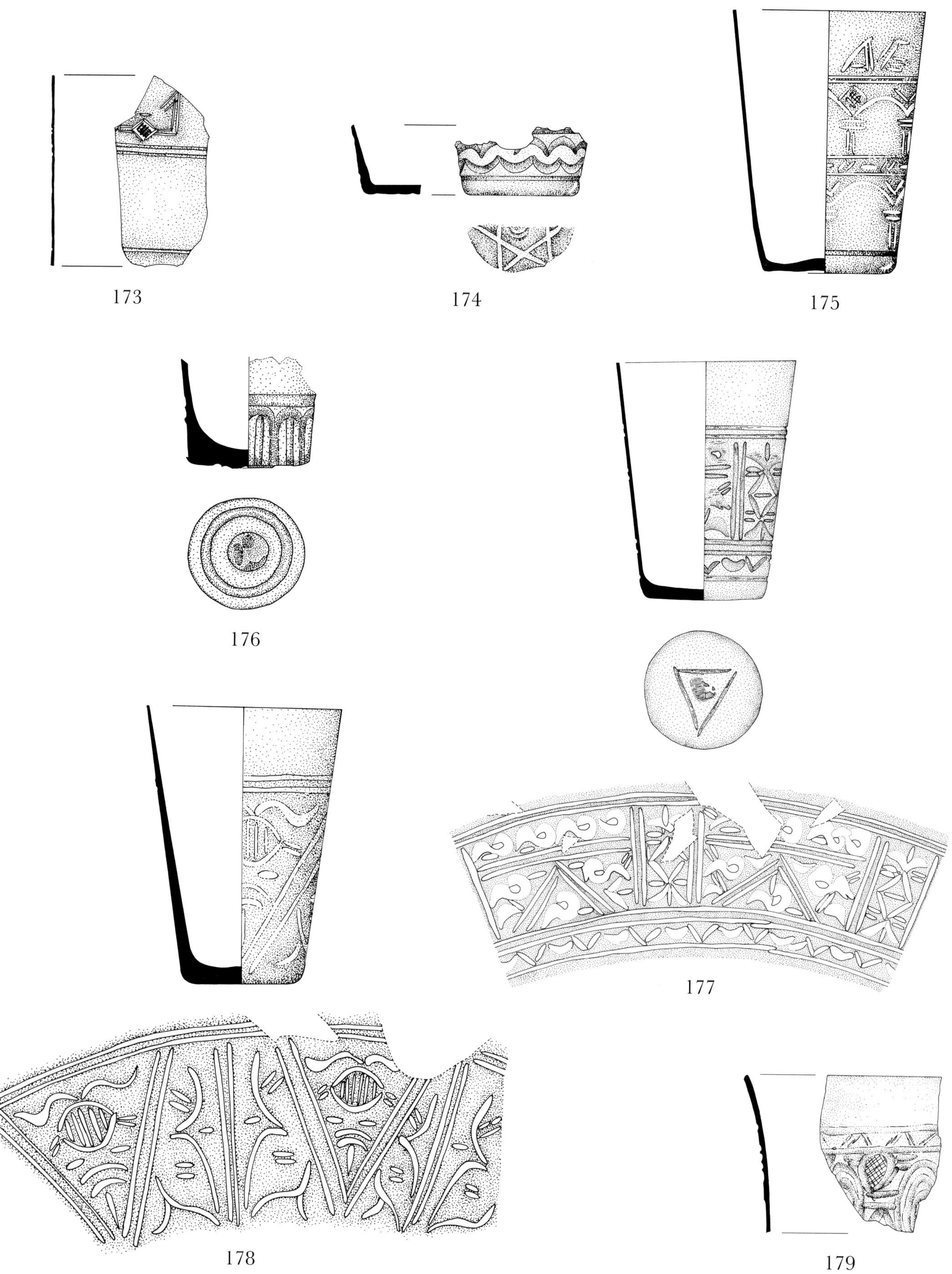

Linear-cut objects (1:2 except ***177*** *and* ***179****, which are 1:3).*

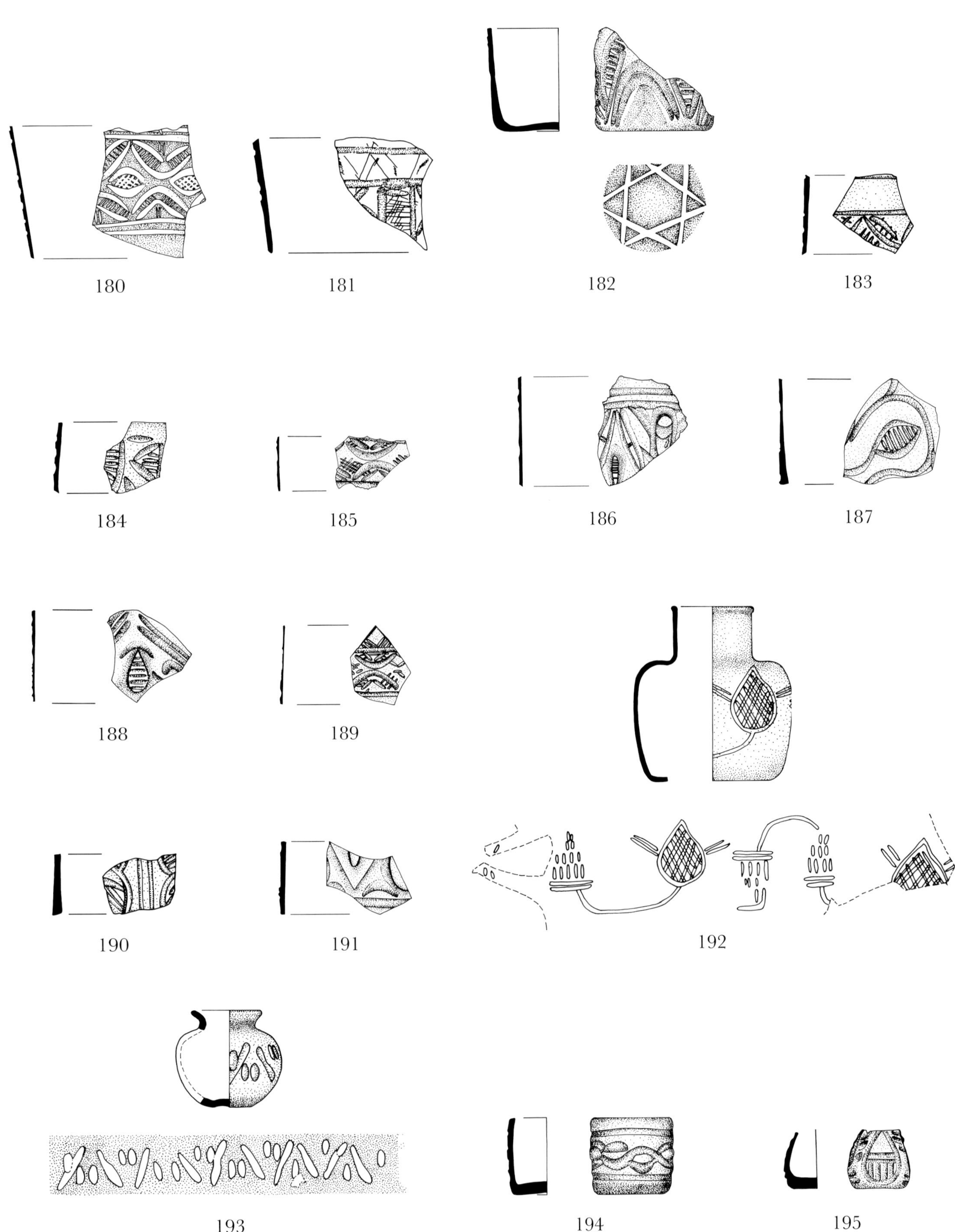

Linear-cut objects (1:2).

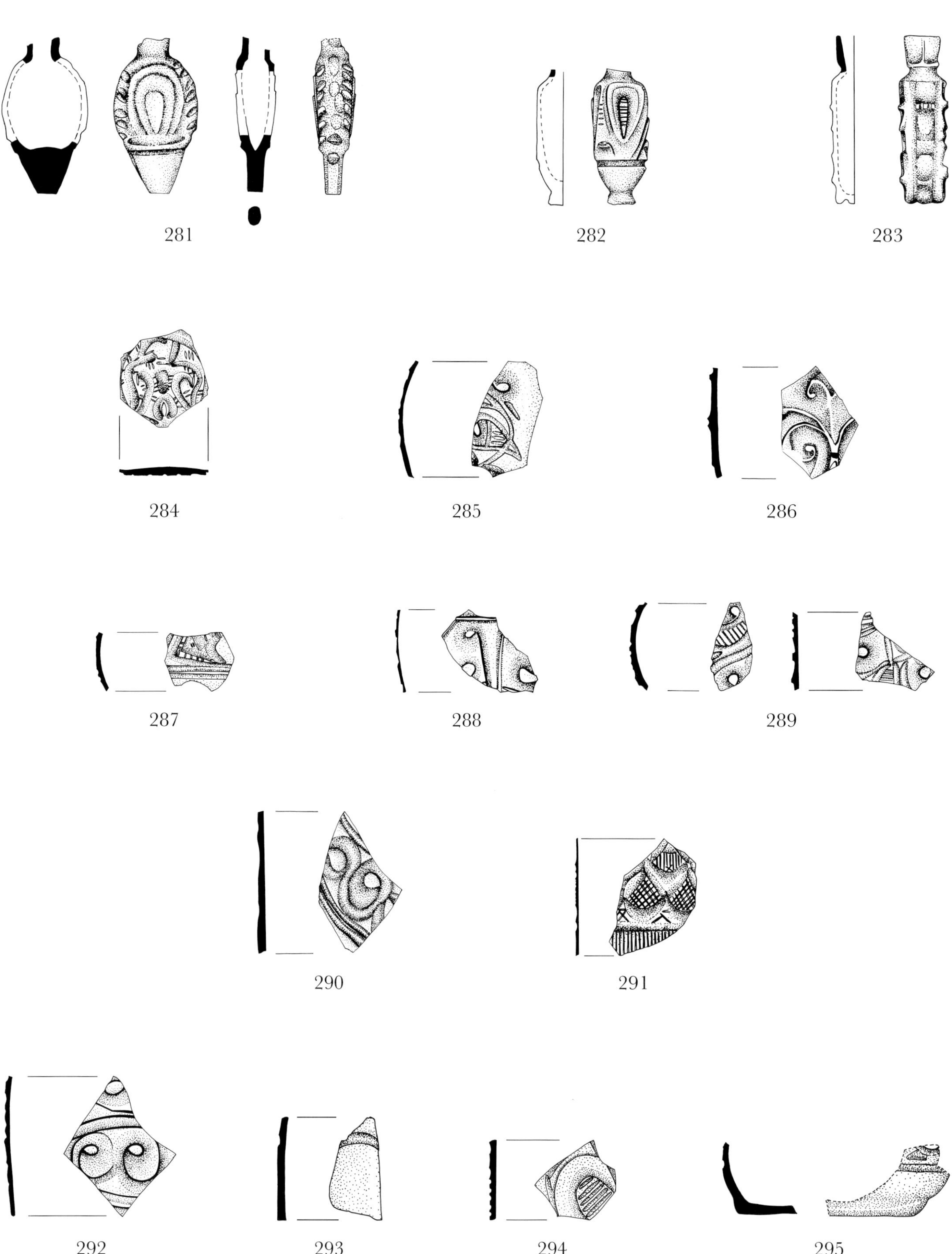

Slant-cut objects (1:2).

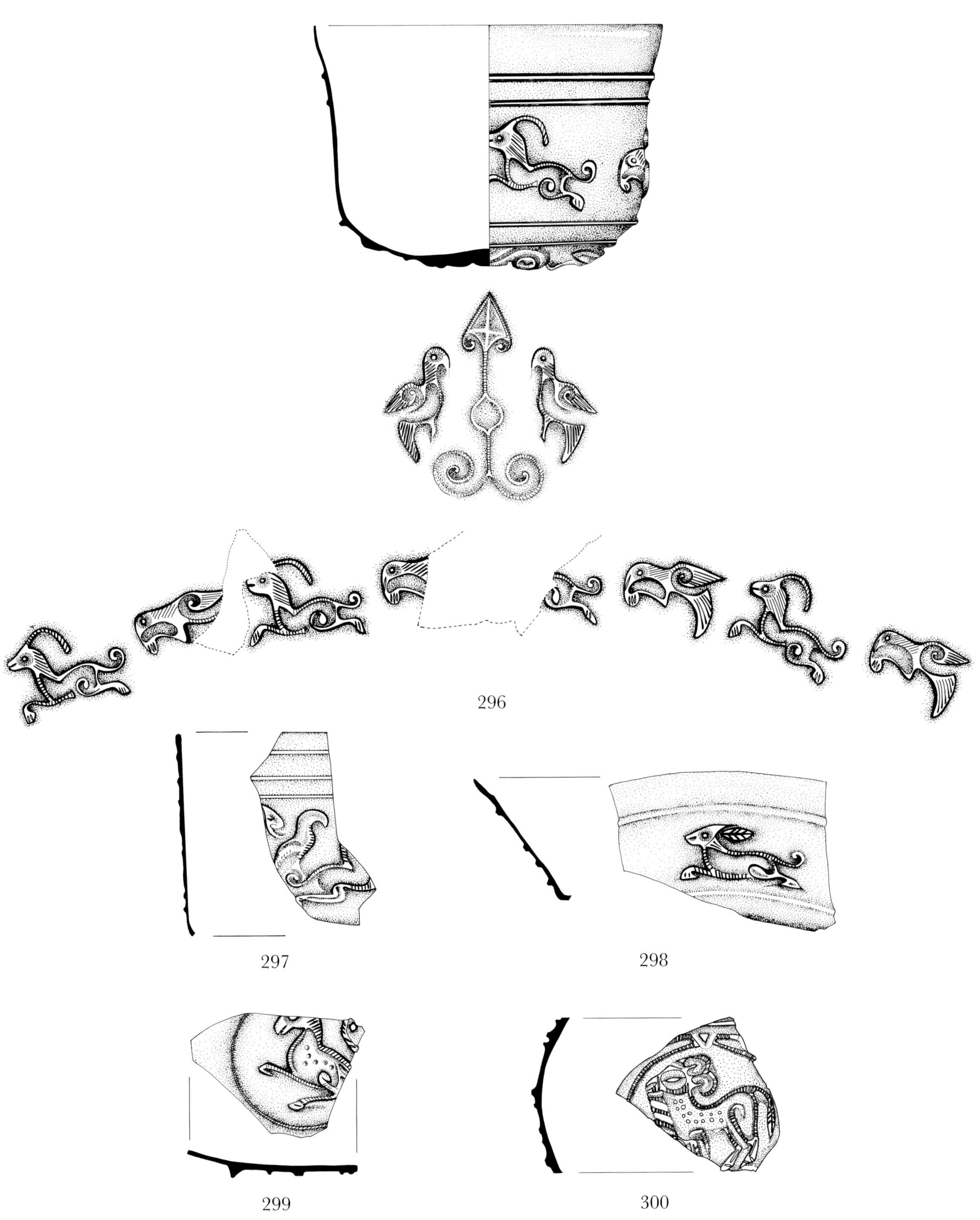

Relief-cut objects (1:2).

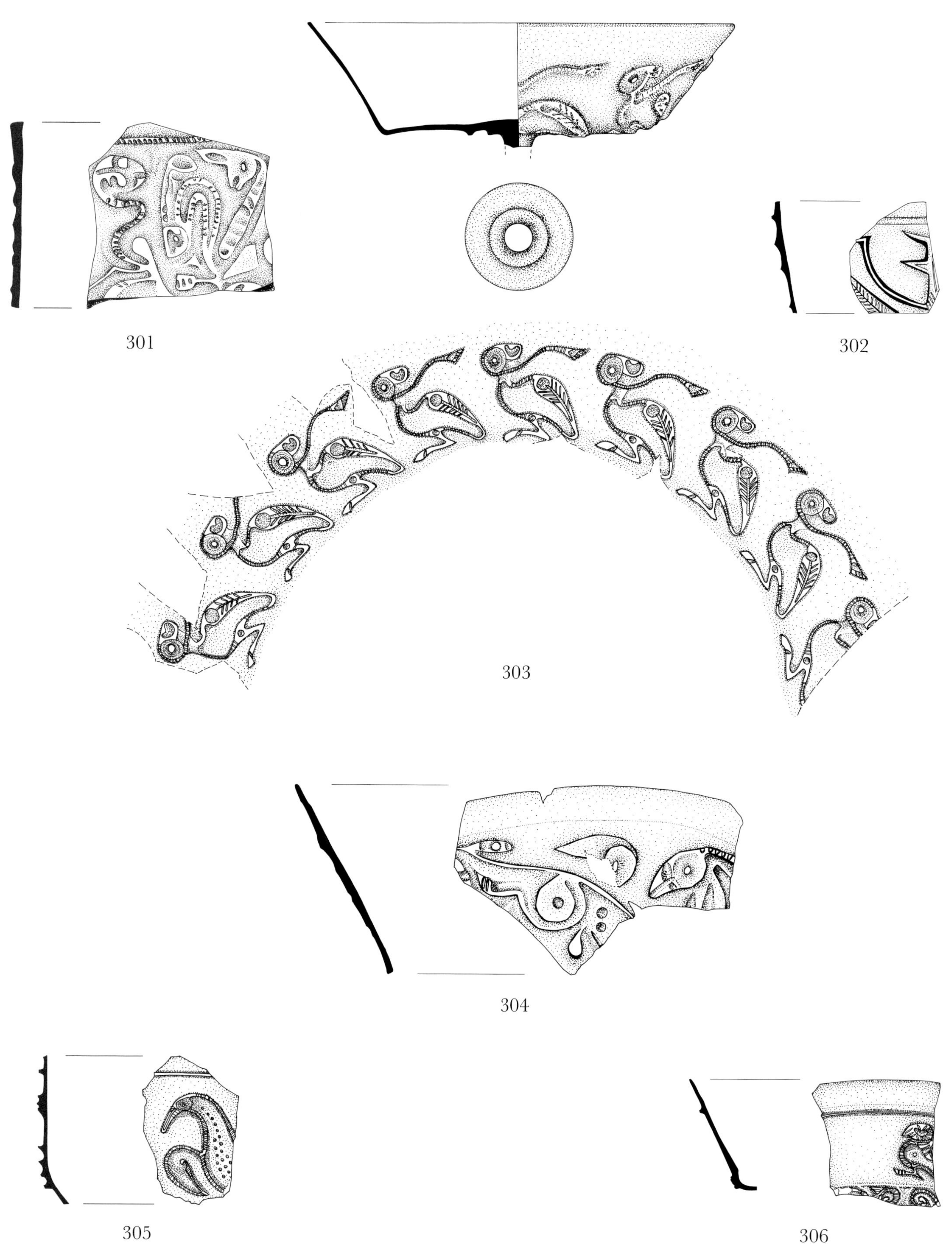

Relief-cut objects (1:2).

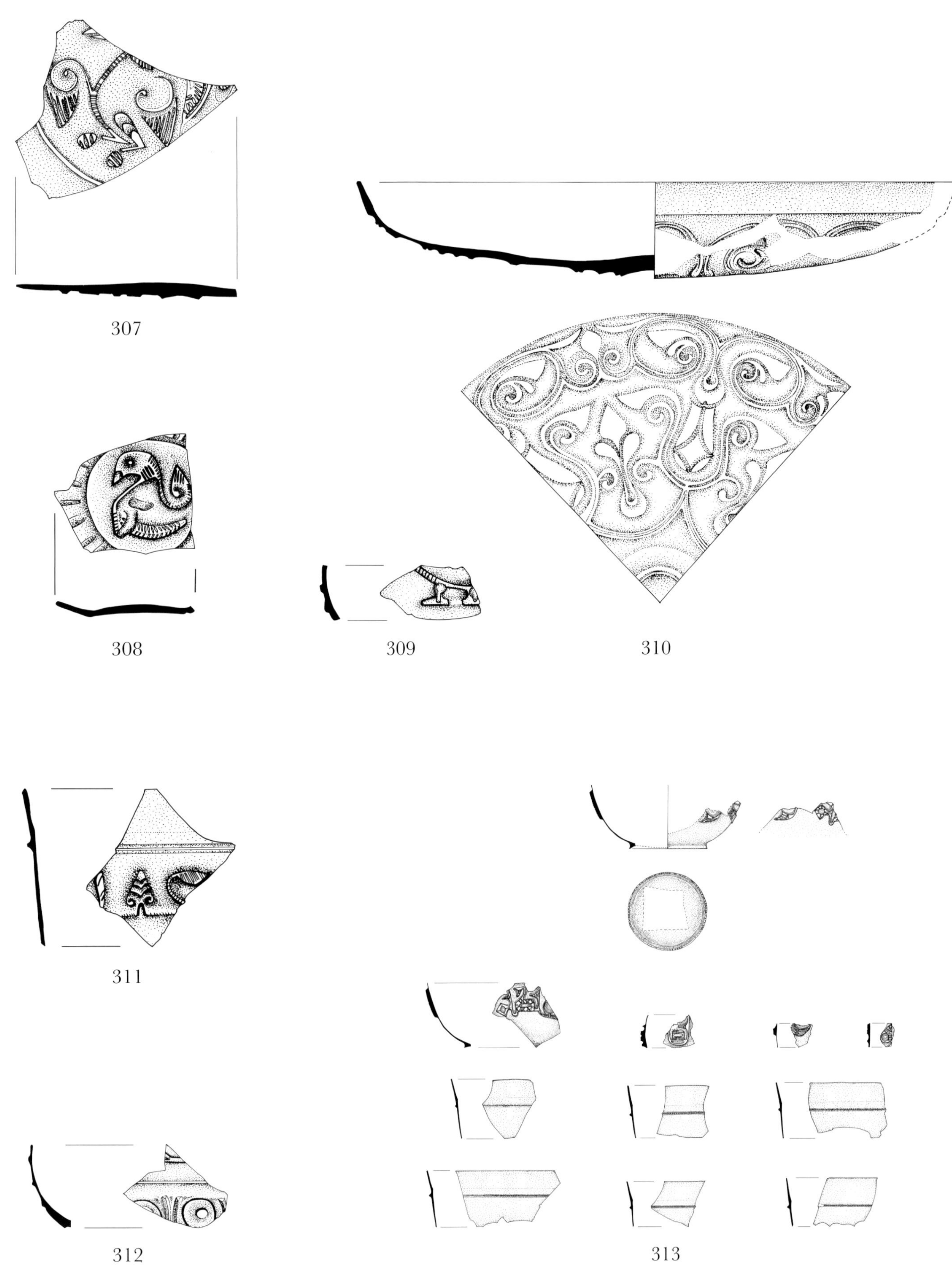

Relief-cut objects (1:2).

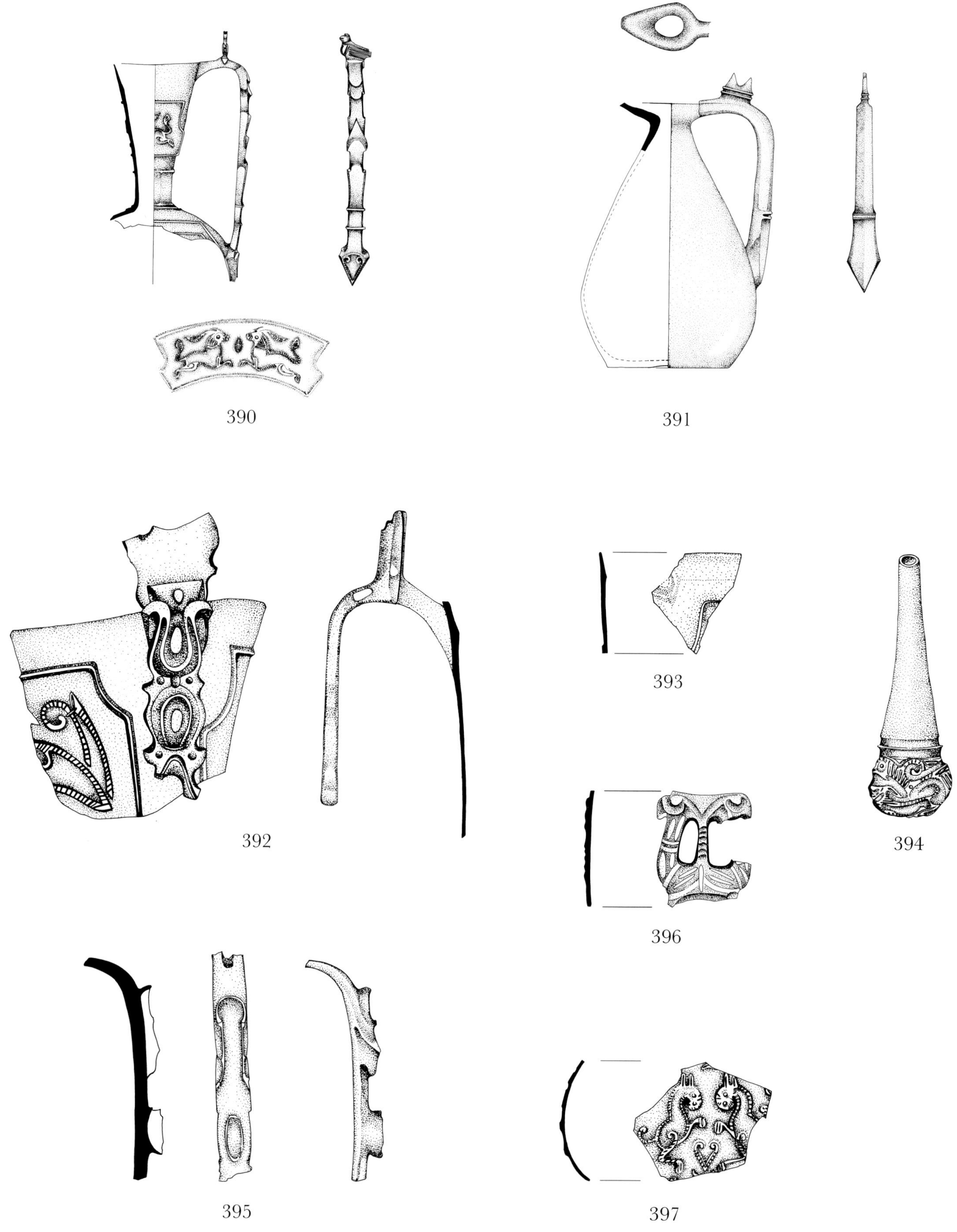

*Relief-cut objects (1:2 except **390** and **391**, which are 1:3).*

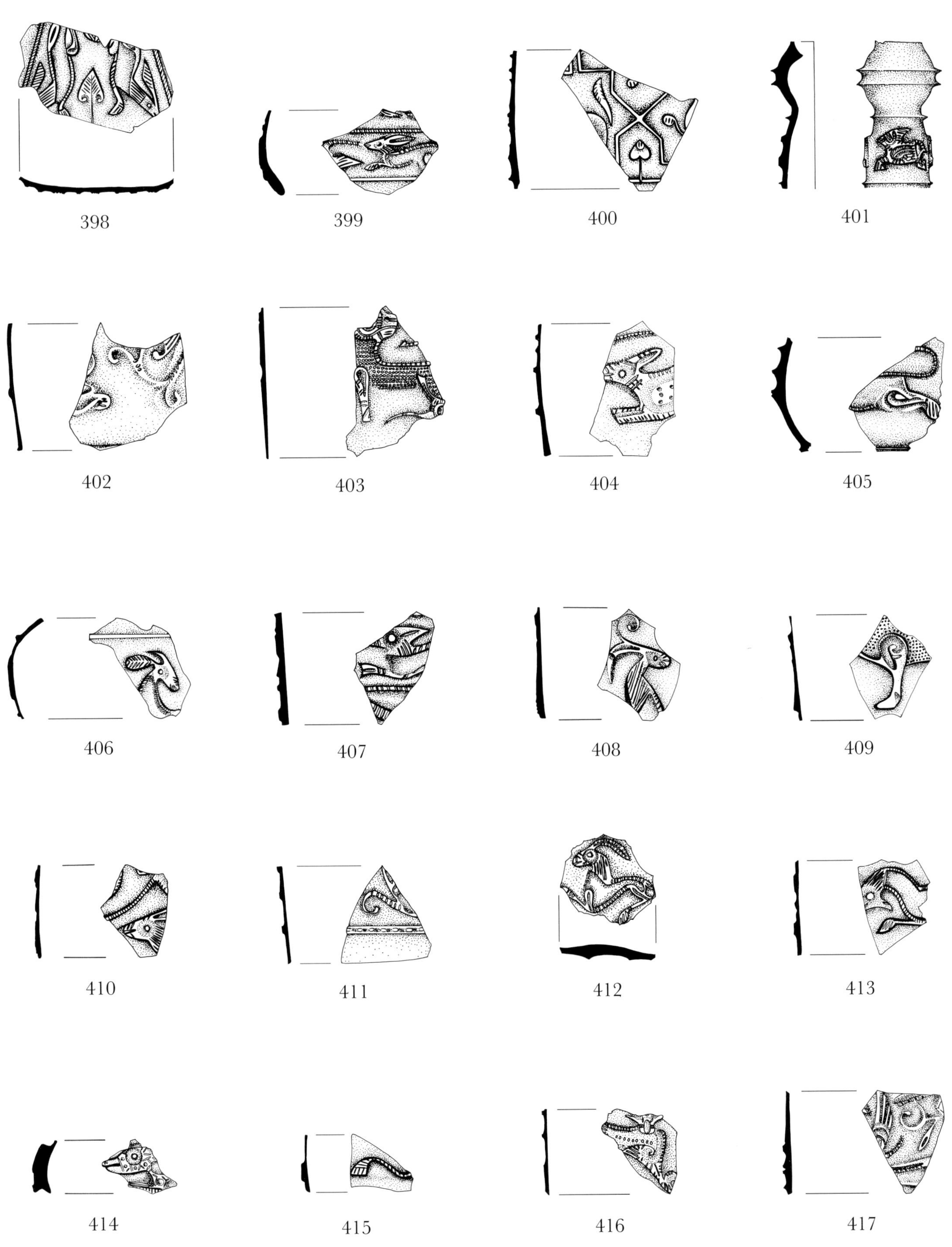

Relief-cut objects (1:2).

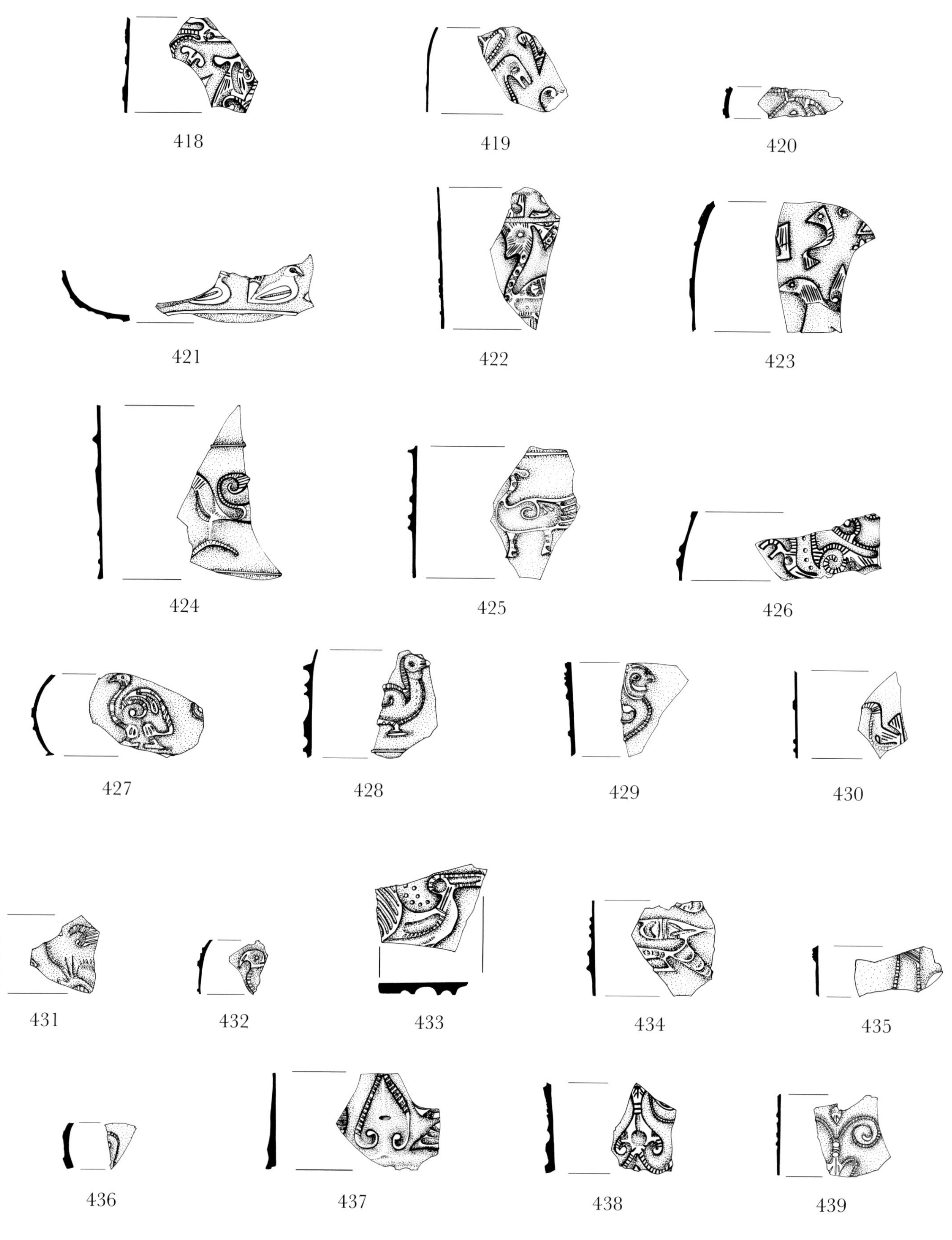

Relief-cut objects (1:2).

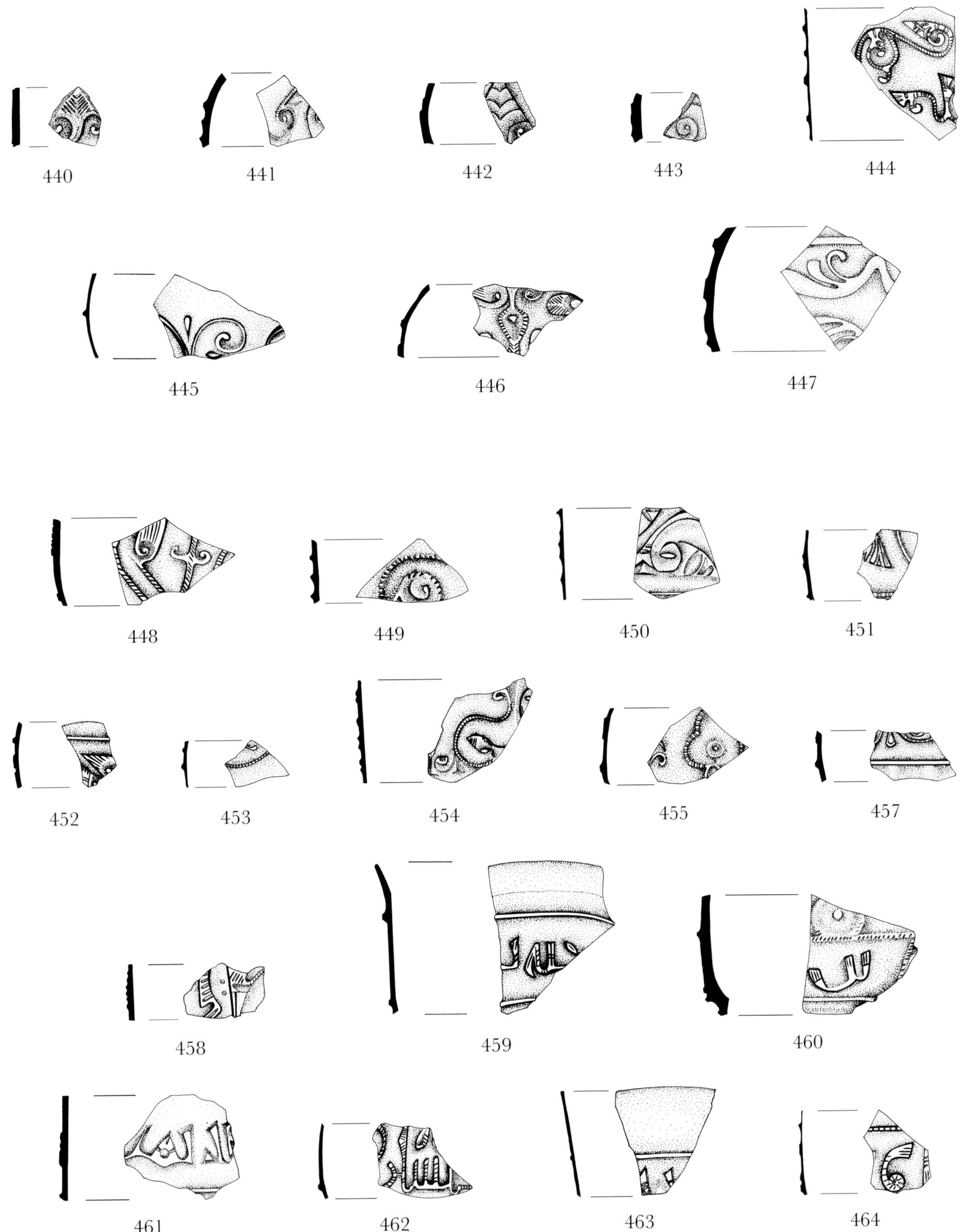

Relief-cut objects (1:2). ***456*** *is not illustrated.*

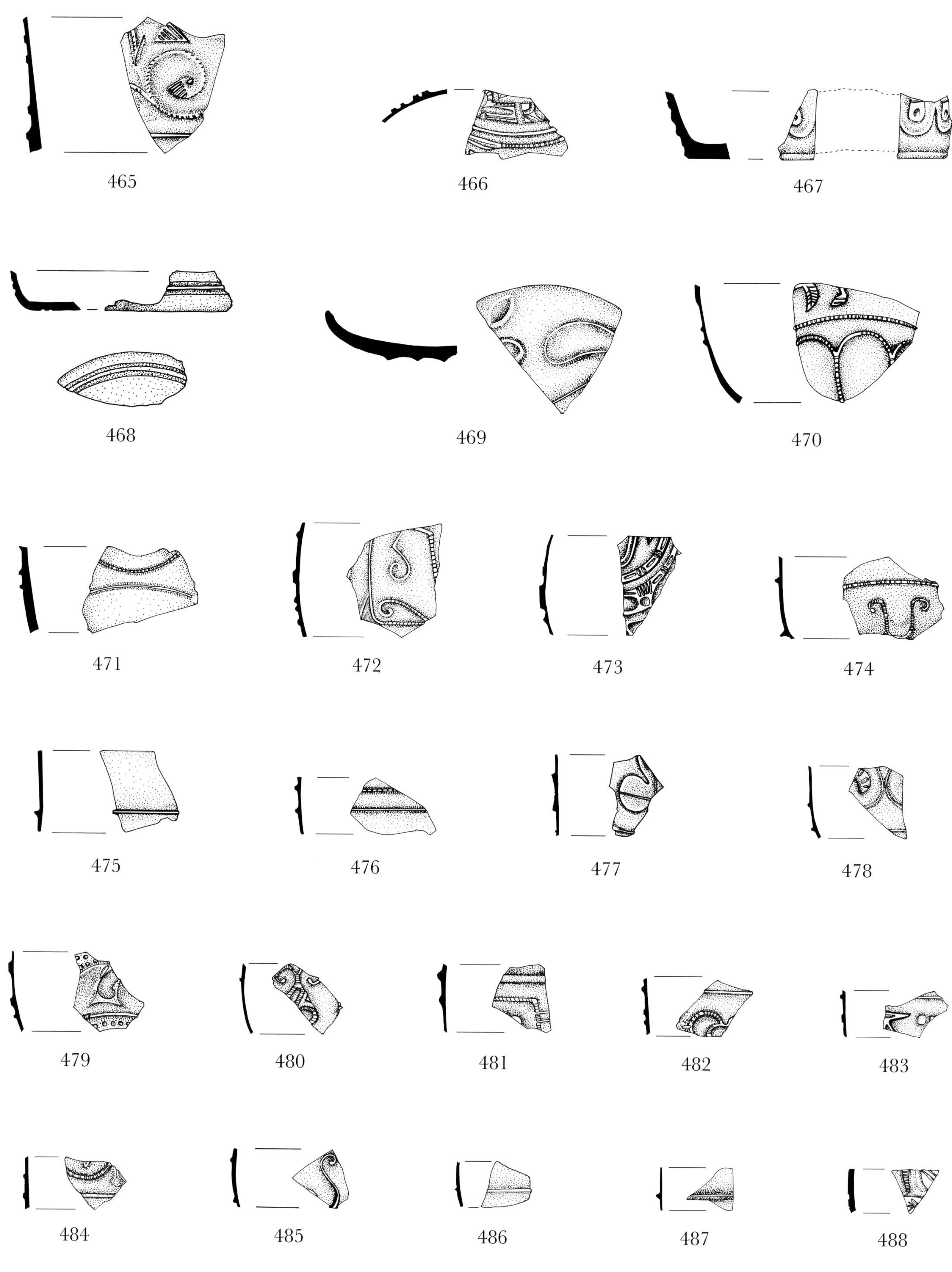

Relief-cut objects (1:2).

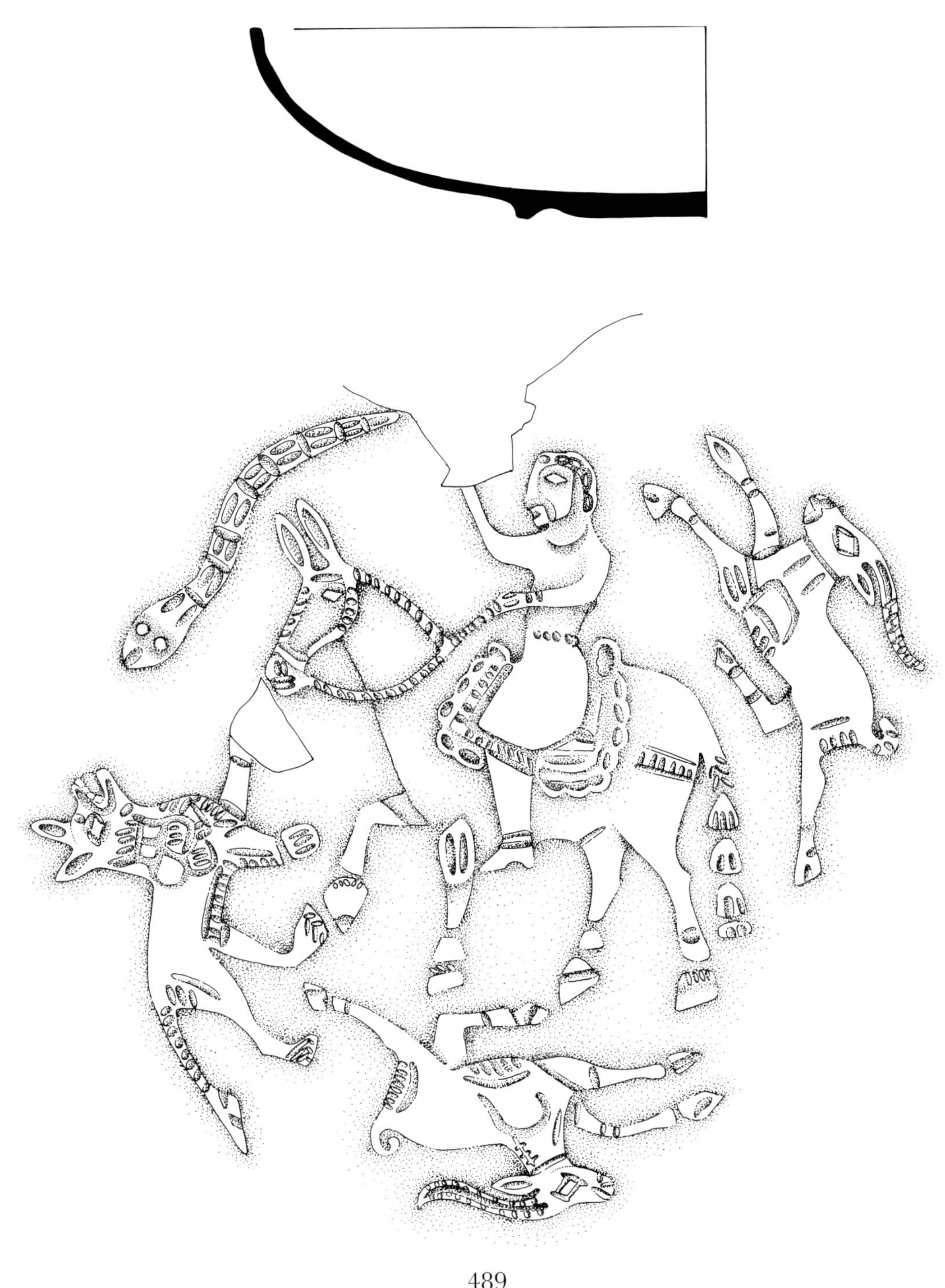

489

Object decorated by molding and cutting (1:2).

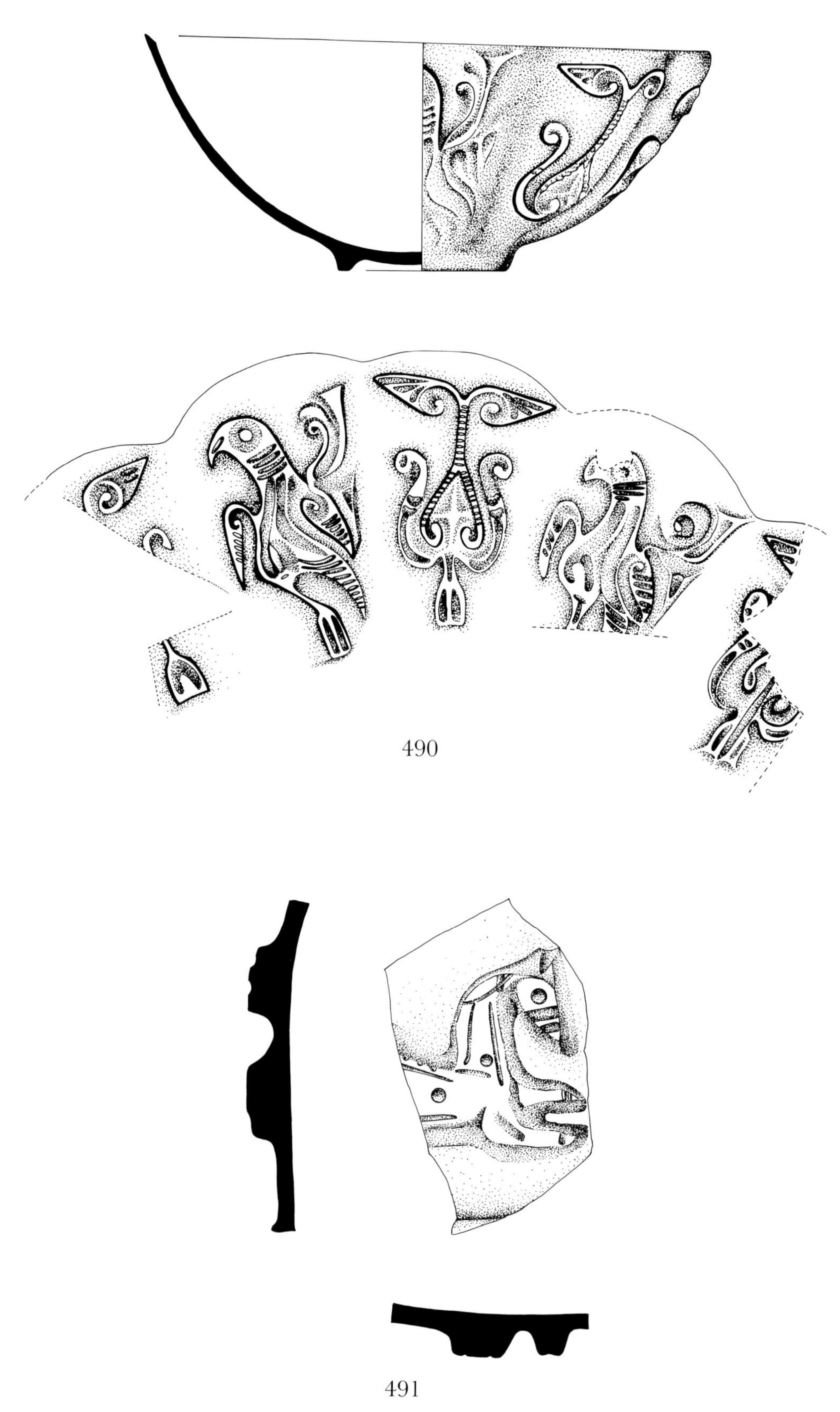

Objects decorated by molding and cutting (1:2).

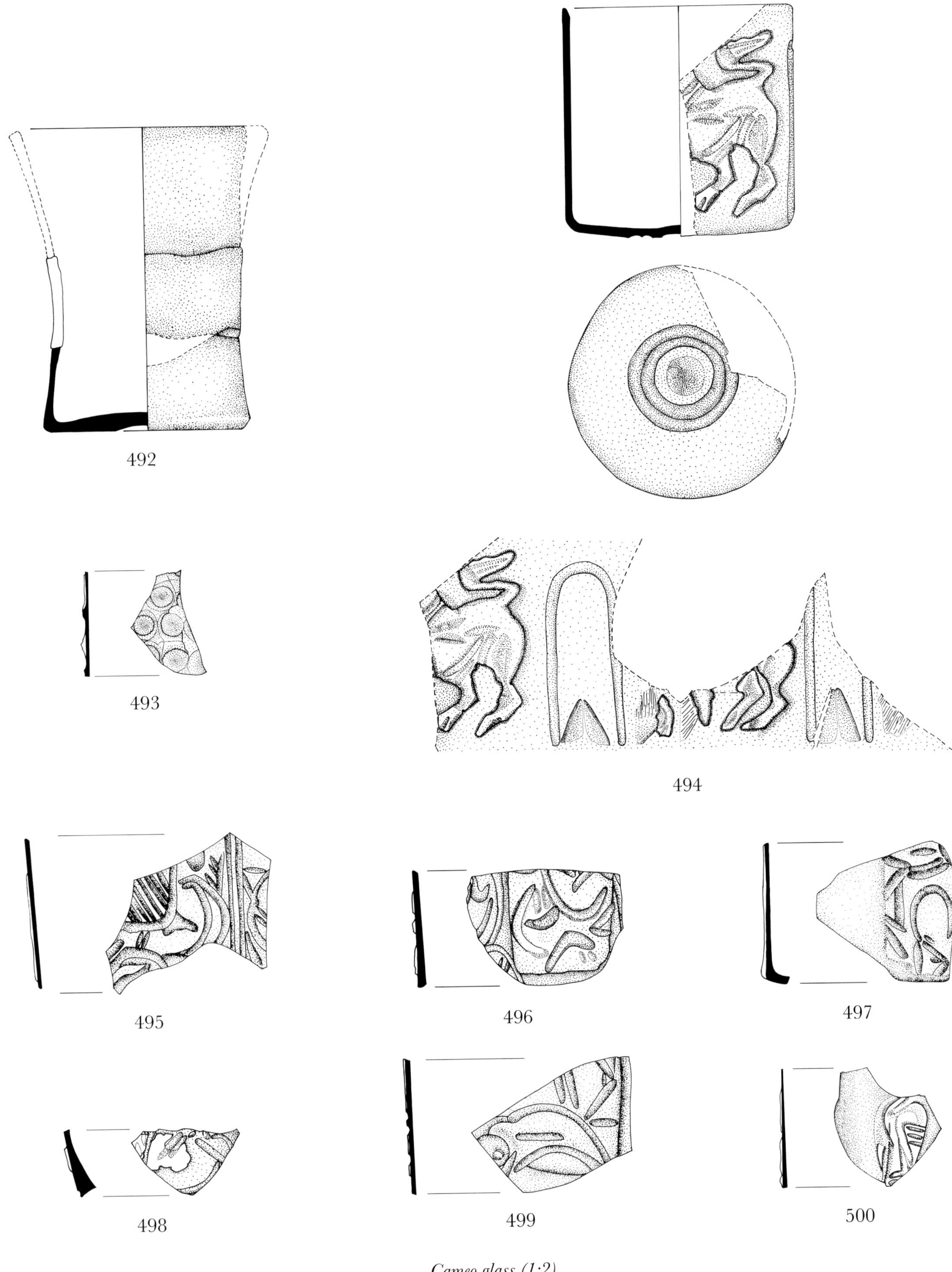

Cameo glass (1:2).

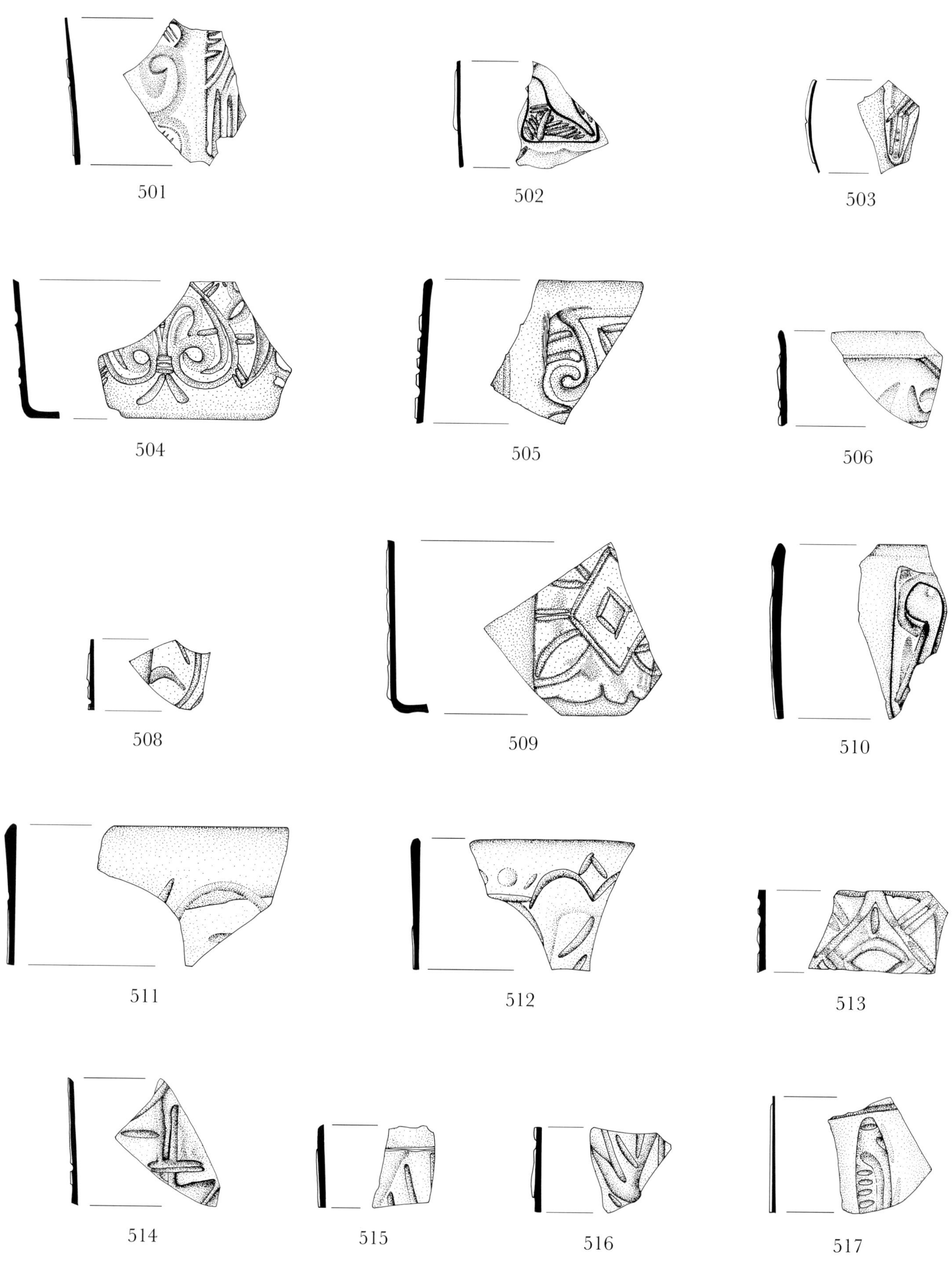

Cameo glass (1:2). ***507*** *is not illustrated.*

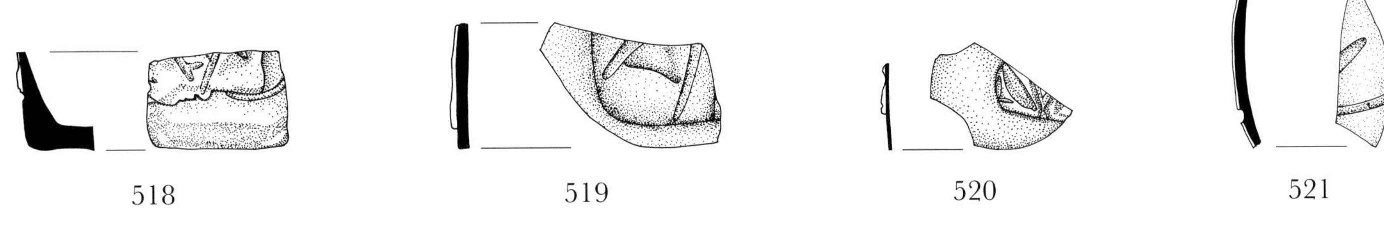

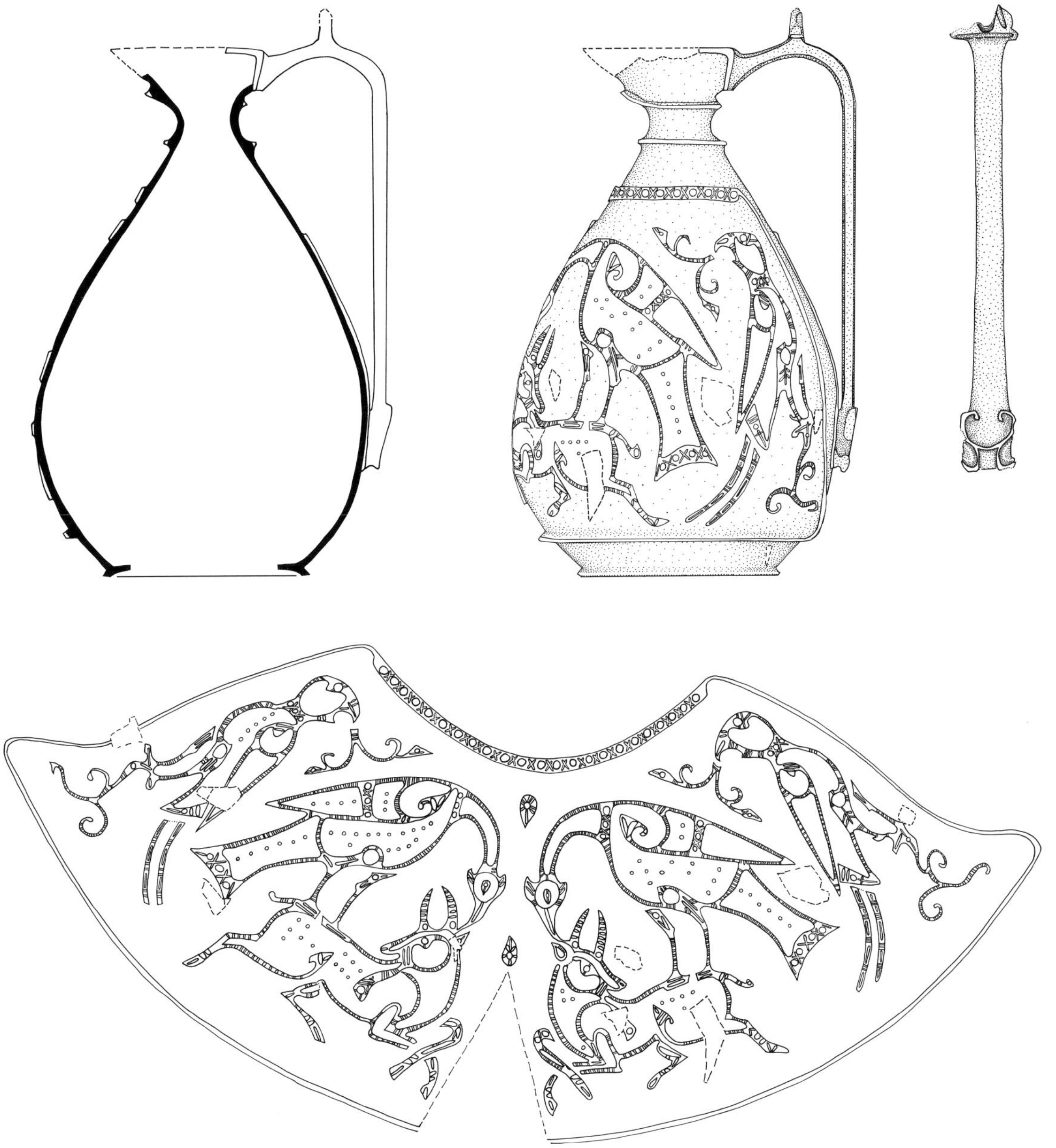

522

Cameo glass (1:2).

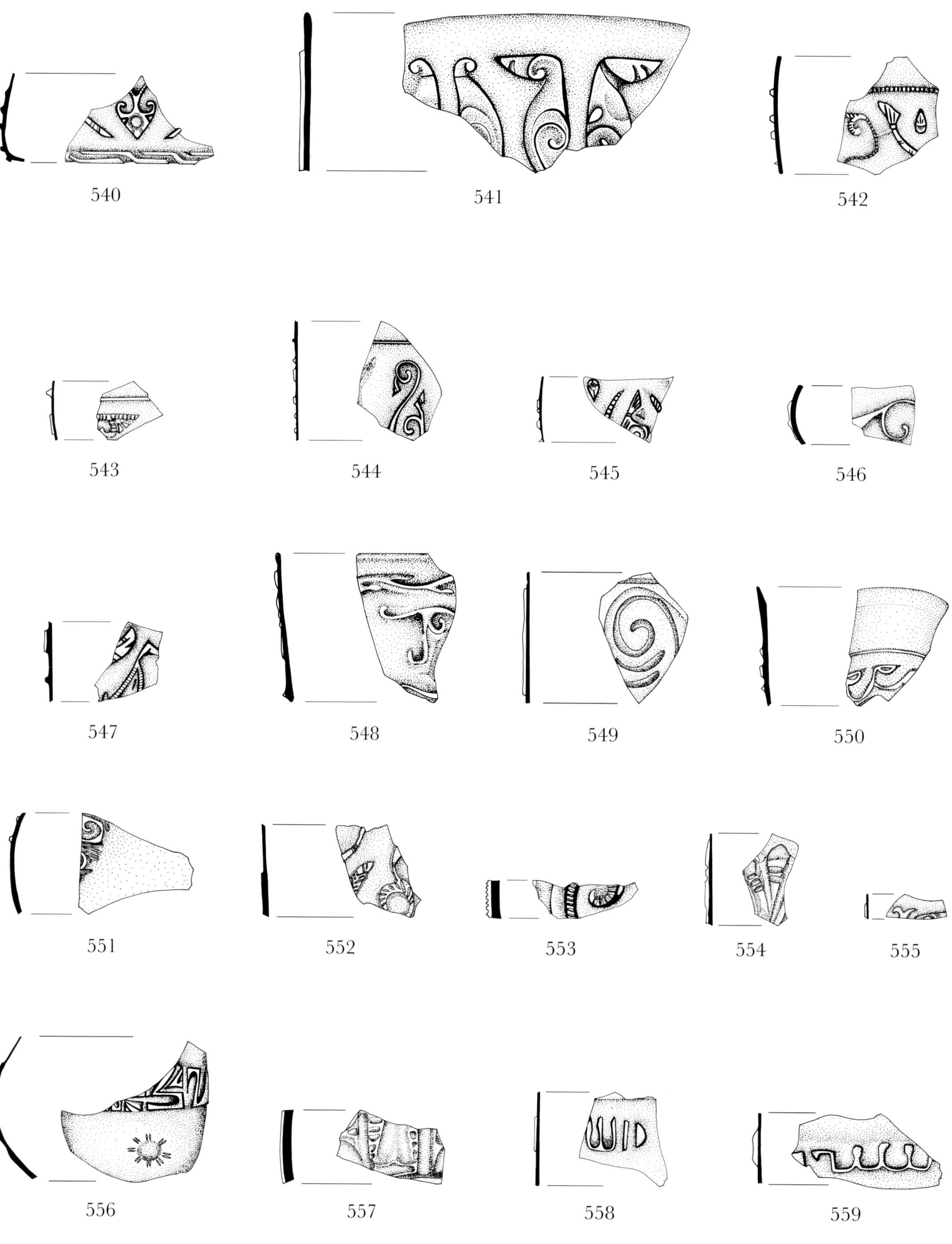

Cameo glass (1:2).

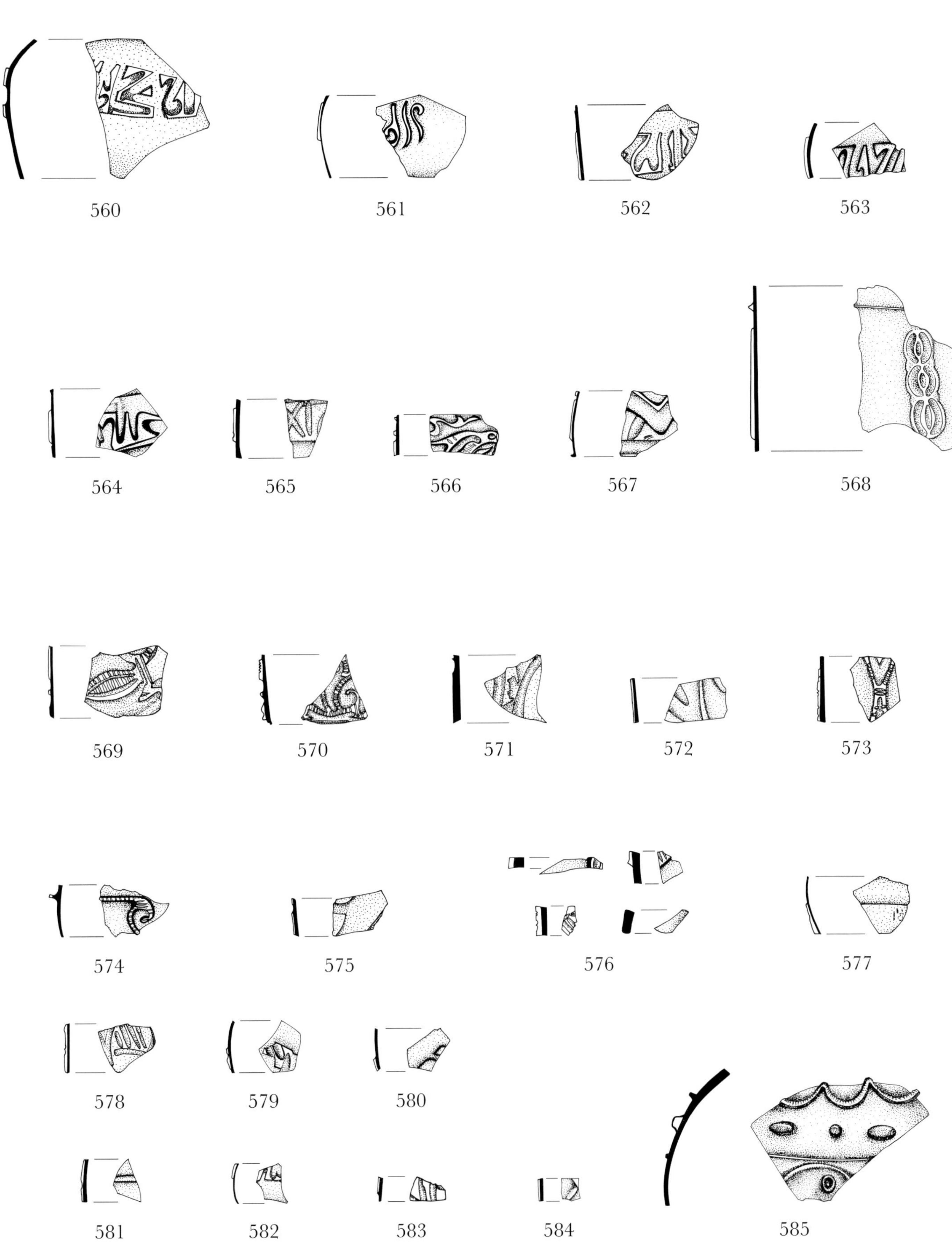

Cameo glass (1:2).

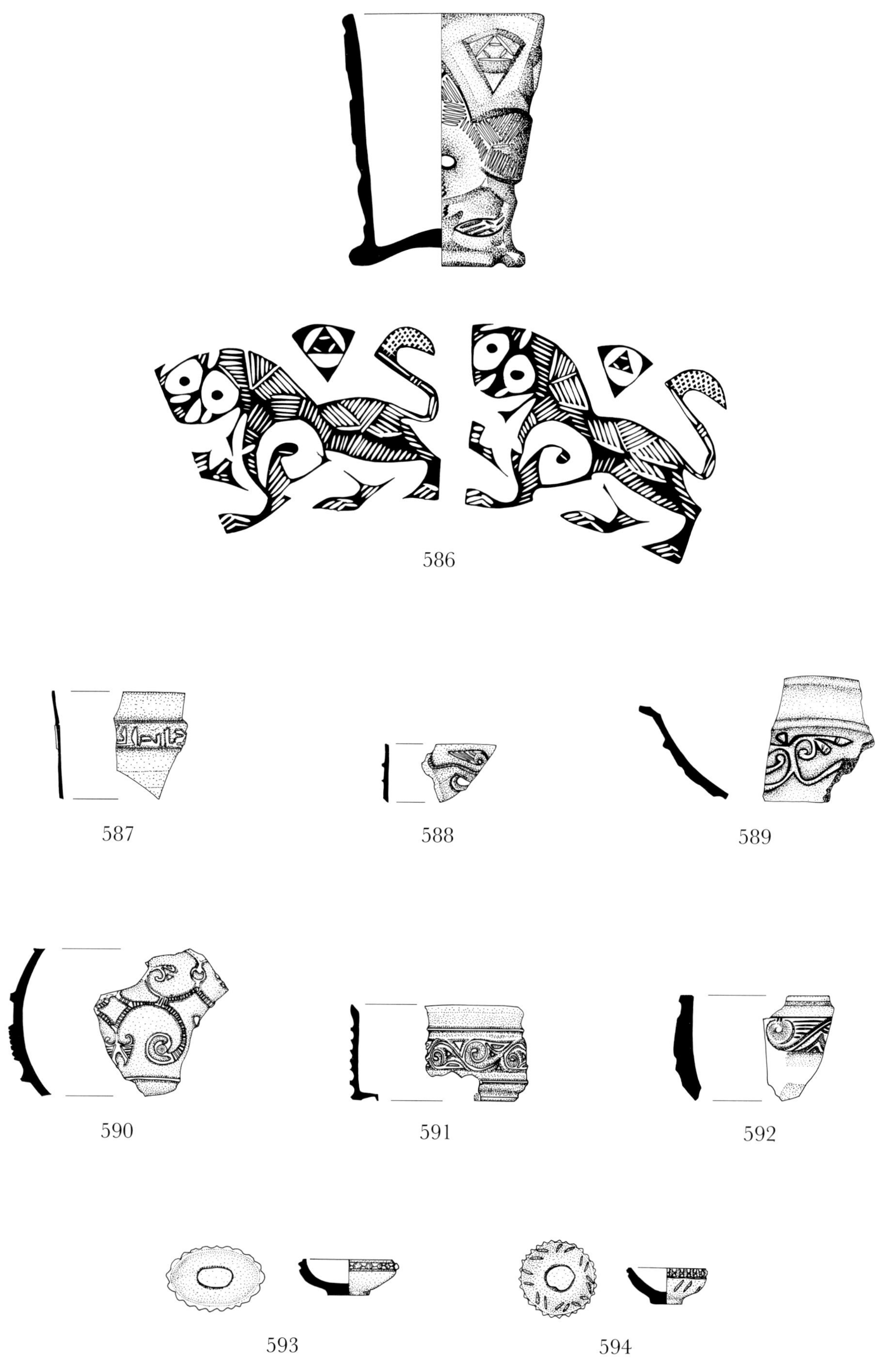

The Corning Hedwig Beaker, a polychrome fragment, and fragments of rock crystal objects (1:2). ***595*** *is not illustrated.*